beginner's guide to
creating portraits

3dtotalPublishing

3dtotal Publishing

Correspondence: publishing@3dtotal.com
Website: www.3dtotal.com

Beginner's Guide to Creating Portraits

First published in the United Kingdom, 2021, by 3dtotal Publishing.

Address: 3dtotal.com Ltd, 29 Foregate Street, Worcester, WR1 1DS, United Kingdom.

Soft cover ISBN: 978-1-912843-39-8
Printing & binding: Gutenberg Press Ltd (Malta) www.gutenberg.com.mt

Visit www.3dtotalpublishing.com for a complete list of available book titles.

Managing Director: Tom Greenway
Studio Manager: Simon Morse
Lead Designer: Fiona Tarbet
Lead Editor: Samantha Rigby
Editor: Philippa Barker
Designer: Joseph Cartwright

Cover images by individual artists as credited throughout the book.

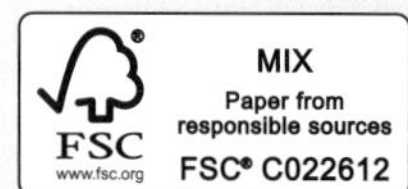

One tree planted for every book sold

From 2020, 3dtotal Publishing pledged to plant one tree for every book sold by partnering with and donating the appropriate amounts to reforesting charities. This is one of the first steps in our ambition to become a carbon-neutral company with carbon-neutral publications, giving our customers the knowledge that by buying from 3dtotal Publishing, they are working with us to balance the environmental damage caused by the publishing, shipping, and retail industries.

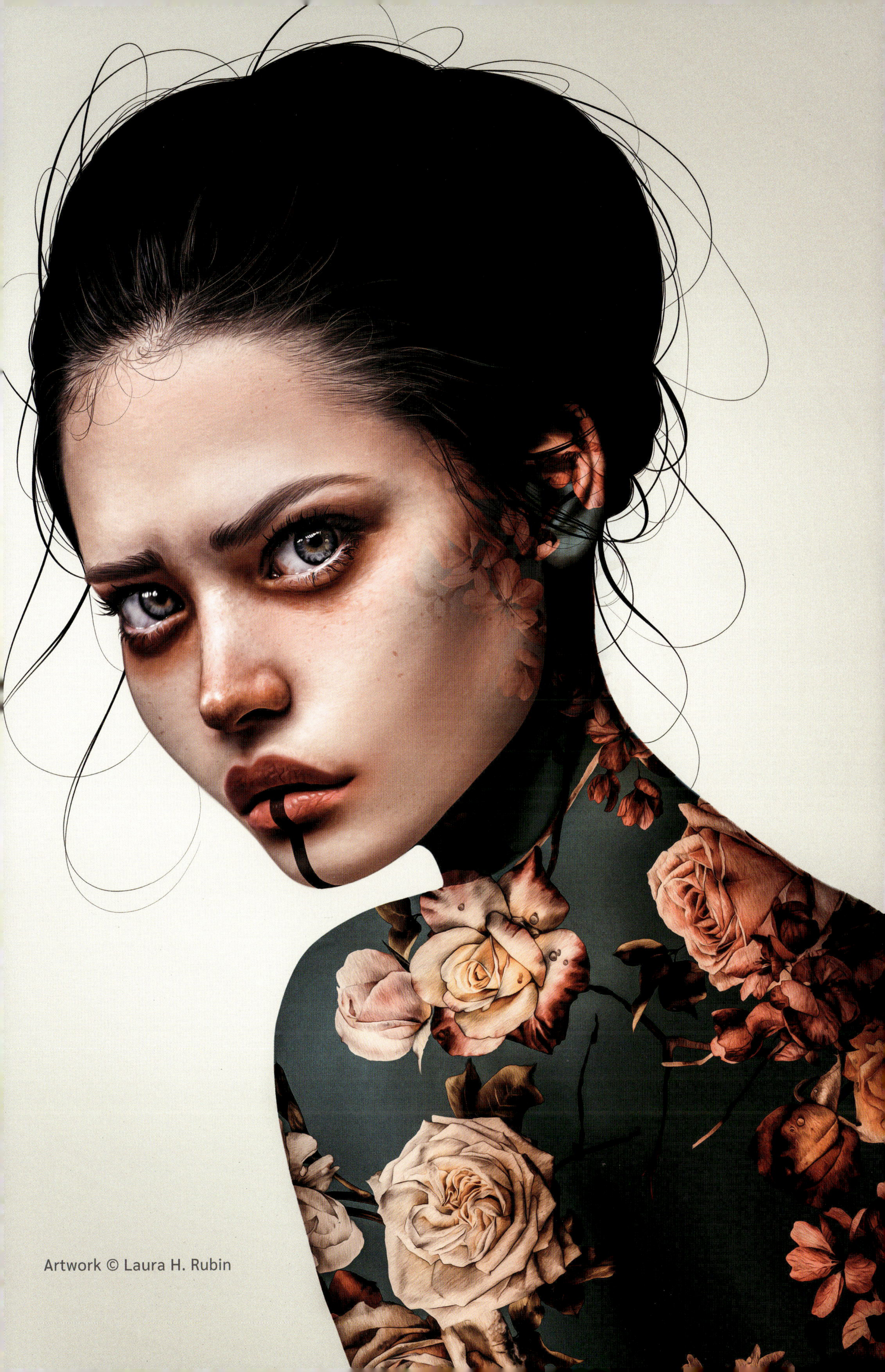

CONTENTS

FOREWORD By Cesar Santos 6

GETTING STARTED 8

Steve Forster
- Introduction 10
- Perceptual portraiture 11
- Reference imagery considerations 12
- Conceptual portraiture 14
- Setting up the reference image relationship to the canvas 16
- Two major proportional measuring approaches 17
- Finding a working rhythm 18
- The creation cycle 19

CREATION CYCLES 22

Steve Forster

Creation Cycle: Drawing
- Proportion 24
- Shape or line? 28
- Drawing: shape 30
- Drawing: line 38

Creation Cycle: Color Values
- Simplifying color to see the big relationships 50
- Color diversity 51
- Two approaches to developing values 56
- Understanding light, form, and color 58
- The color of light and shadow 64

Creation Cycle: Edges
- Four types of edges 68
- A spectrum of sharp to lost 74
- Complex edges 76
- Brushstrokes, edges, and style 77
- Creating movement with edges 78
- Ways of creating various edges 80

OTHER CONSIDERATIONS 82

Steve Forster
- Perfect likeness vs. artistic freedom 84
- Finishing a painting 85
- Lighting and color mood 86
- Background motifs 87

PRO TIPS: Features & Details 90

Robyn Leora Lowe
- Eyes 92
- Nose 95
- Mouth: lips & teeth 98
- Ears 104
- Hair: straight & curly 107
- Skin: young & old 112
- Skin: freckles & scars 117
- Skin: Tattoos 120
- Jewelry & piercings 123
- Glasses 126

TUTORIALS 130
- Nick Runge 132
- Astri Lohne 156
- Justine S. Florentino 178
- Sara Tepes 204
- Gennadiy Kim 226
- Aveline Stokart 250

PORTRAIT GALLERY 270

Laura H. Rubin • Tran Nguyen
Gennadiy Kim • Maria Dimova
Justine S. Florentino • Aveline Stokart
Nick Runge • Valentina Remenar
Astri Lohne • Sara Tepes

GLOSSARY 312

CONTRIBUTORS 316

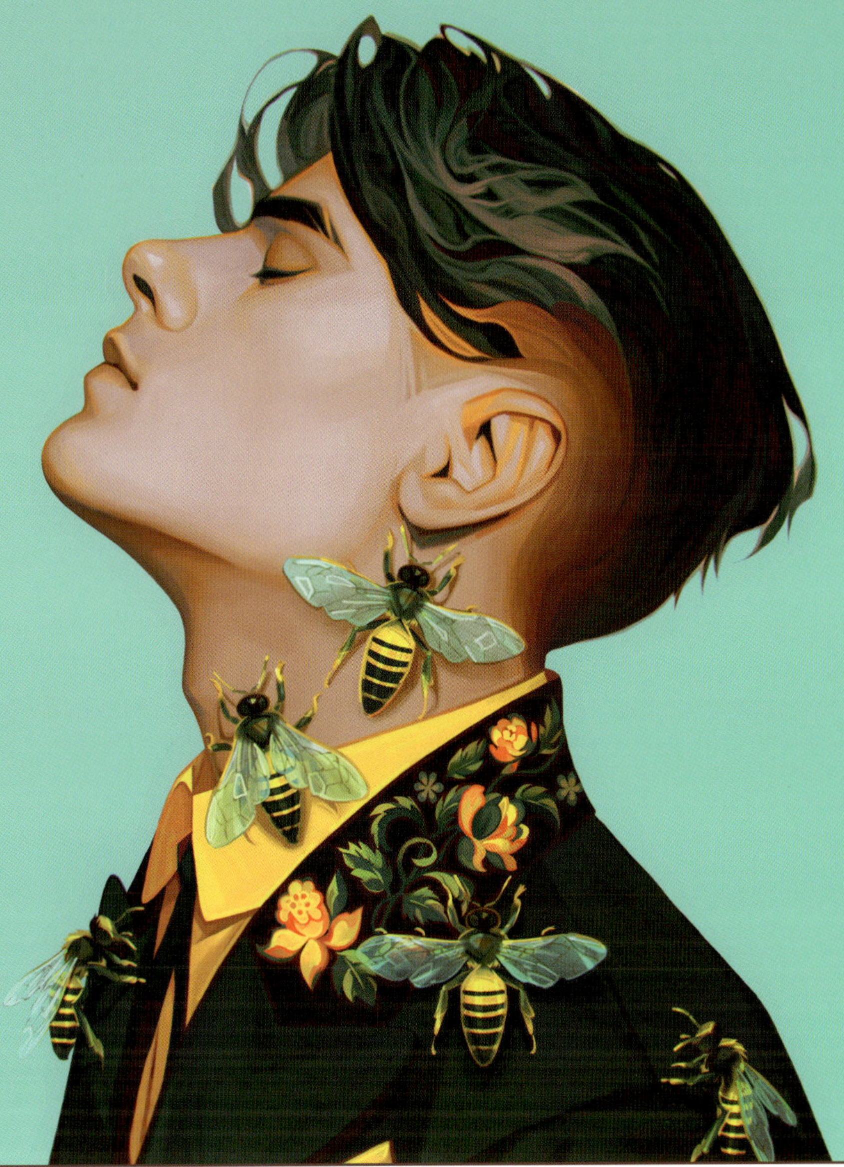

How to use this book

Begin with **Getting Started** and **Creation Cycles**. Whether you already have some experience, or are a complete beginner, these sections detail the basics of portraiture to provide you with the solid foundation needed. Insightful topics are covered, from capturing a likeness to finding a working rhythm.

Once you have a good understanding of the basics, move on to **Pro Tips: Features & Details**. These demonstrate how to construct and paint the different aspects of the face. Experiment as you go, learning how to map out and recreate each element before progressing on to a whole portrait.

When you feel ready, move on to the **Tutorials**. Guiding you step-by-step through how to create a portrait from a reference photo, the tutorials range from semi-realistic to stylized, and can be followed using traditional media or digital software. Look out for the Artist Tip boxes that share nuggets of expert advice to help you on your way.

For extra inspiration, visit the **Portrait Gallery**, where further styles and subjects can be found, created by both the tutorial artists, and other experts in the field. Finally, there is a useful **Glossary** of portraiture terms at the end of the book to refer to, as needed.

FOREWORD

CESAR SANTOS, artist & portrait painter

Written by visionaries often known as artists, this book uncovers the secrets of how to capture people's most exposed yet mysterious feature: the face. The mystery of portraiture is something I live with every day. It is beyond me to understand why I've dedicated so much of my life to the possibility of creating a portrait that carries with it the living spirit of a natural person. Portraiture is present in our daily lives; we all unconsciously know the importance of the physical face as it is the façade of every individual. The significance of any relationship we have with others is influenced by the ability to see ourselves as the main reference as we project ourselves onto the world around us. It is from this point of view that we can interpret the different elements that have been taught to us.

Whether you are a beginner or an experienced portrait artist, your role is to express yourself with the knowledge and ability you have available to you in the moment. Technical ability results from previous experiences, which can then be applied to how the subject makes you feel. History has proven this is all you need to create memorable artwork. The difficulty comes when connecting the vision with the method; we are exposed to a myriad of artists and teachers from the past and present, which can sometimes prevent us from finding ourselves. Yet by studying the work of other artists, we learn principles that have become universal due to their usefulness and relationship with natural rhythms.

In the following chapters, the ocean of information available to artists today has been condensed into smaller springs from which drinking brings true refreshment. Each artist shares their portraiture knowledge in a comprehensive way, taking different perspectives with a common end. The complex visual world has been organized into simpler steps and objectives, helping the reader to build a portrait by applying elements such as lines, shapes, edges, values, color, and texture to create the illusion of form and life. In certain situations, people need a special skill before attempting an activity; you can't skydive alone without knowledge of how to control the parachute and first developing landing skills. Yet artists intuitively represent a human face before acquiring any skills on the subject; we select our tools, make marks on a surface, and leave a trace of the impression the subject had on us.

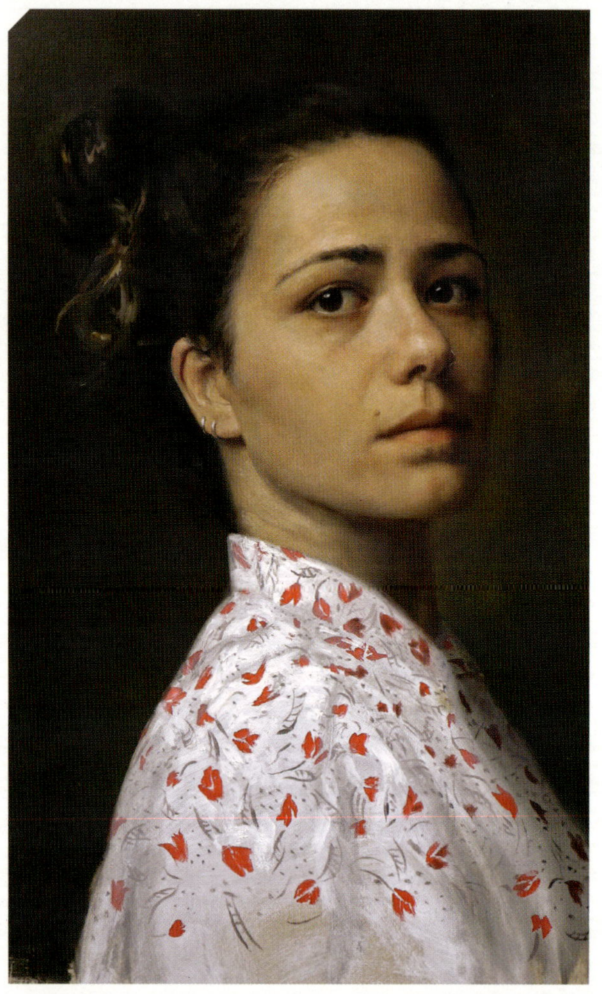

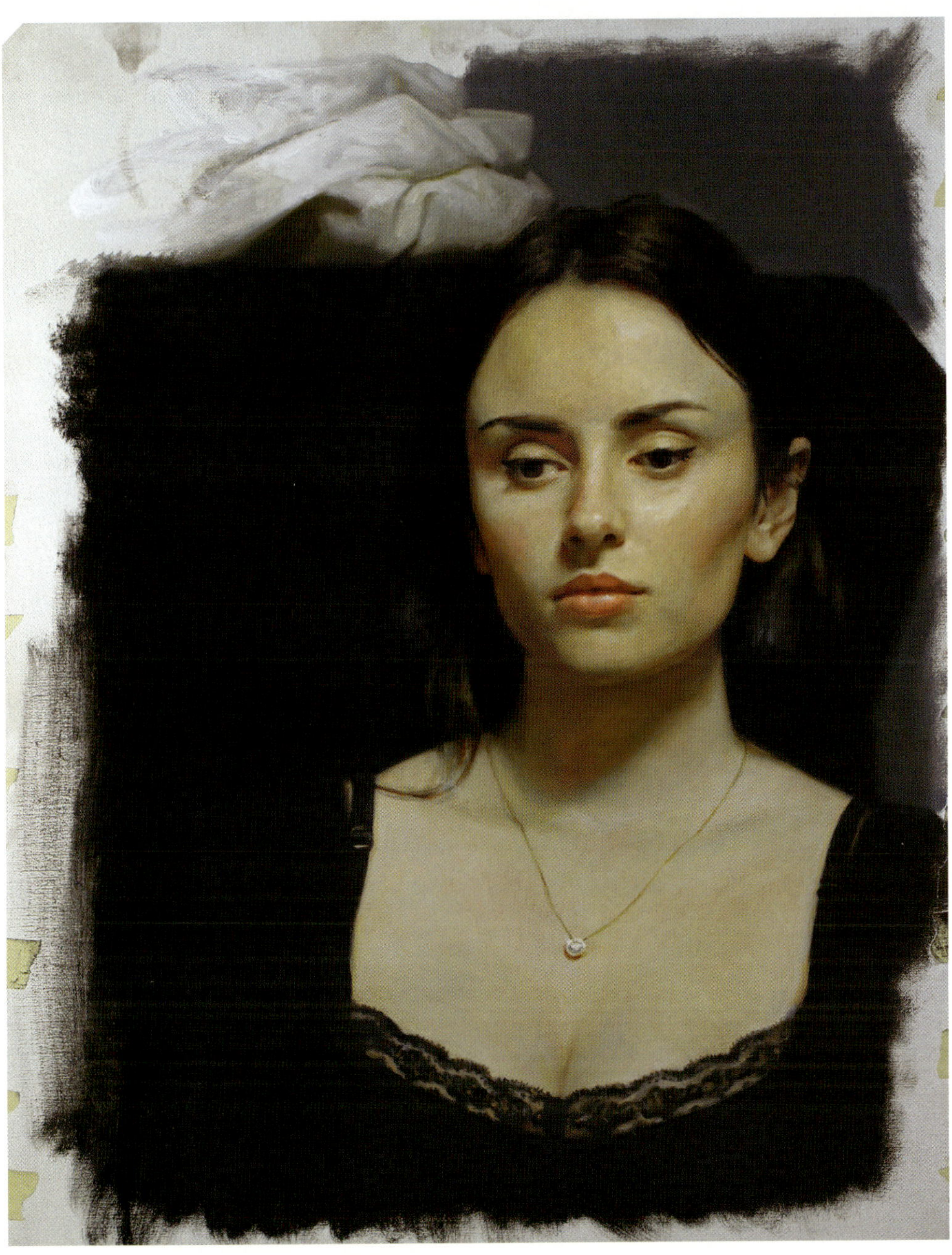

The importance of intuition and willingness to progress toward an envisioned end comes naturally to us. This freedom should be held on to, while also developing more complex artistic skills that will communicate to others at a deeper level. The acquisition of expertise and an ordered workflow only adds to the development of that process. A portrait is the result of a personal experience through a series of steps that add up to a final image.

This book approaches portraiture from a rich variety of points of views. Each chapter condenses the knowledge into an orderly format to communicate a specific vision and process. Just like nature has its limits and follows a certain order, one occurrence at a time – such as the cycle of the seasons – this book purposely unpacks one aspect at a time, following a comprehensive structure. In this way you can build consistency in your development, even though in the end all of these portions coexist with one another. While the different approaches covered in this book are the result of each artist's experience, don't be overwhelmed. There is only one path to follow: your own. It's ok to be unique. Uniqueness and originality combined with highly developed skills, practice, and persistence will develop into inspiring and timeless artwork.

Artwork © Cesar Santos
santocesar.com

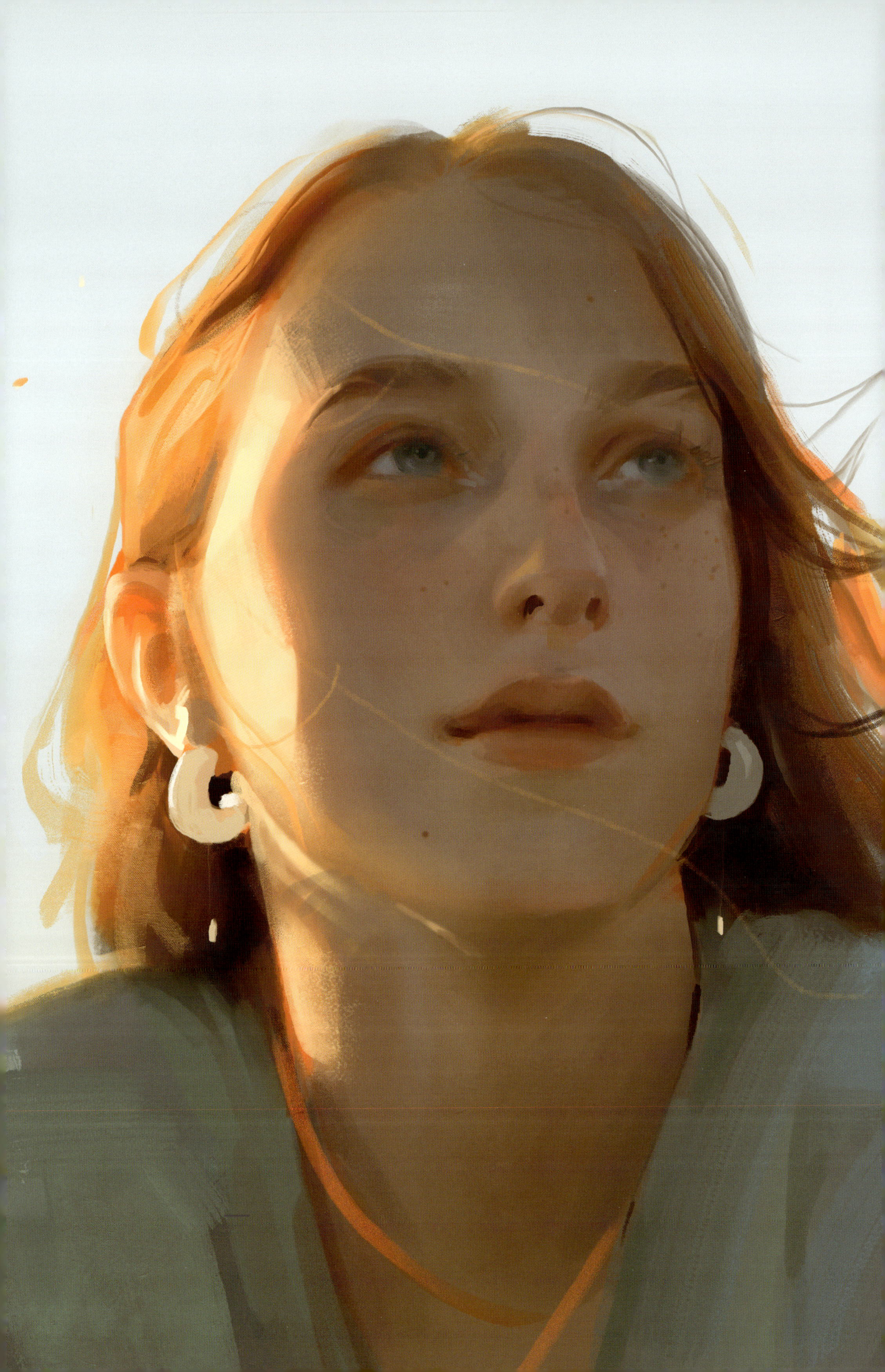

GETTING STARTED

Steve Forster

- INTRODUCTION
- PERCEPTUAL PORTRAITURE
- REFERENCE IMAGERY CONSIDERATIONS
- CONCEPTUAL PORTRAITURE
- SETTING UP THE REFERENCE IMAGE RELATIONSHIP TO THE CANVAS
- TWO MAJOR PROPORTIONAL MEASURING APPROACHES
- FINDING A WORKING RHYTHM
- THE CREATION CYCLE

INTRODUCTION

The portrait is perhaps the most psychologically engaging subject an artist can depict. It attempts to understand who we are by looking at how we are made (external), while also conveying some sense of our emotional capacity (internal). How these two forces interact is a great mystery. To depict that interaction is a lofty goal, especially for a beginner, but it is truly captivating and rewarding, while also testing your imagination and skill. Many artists are engaged and drawn in by the challenges these two ideas present.

As with many things, portraiture appears easier than it is in reality. To develop good, sound portrait practice, you should have a rough idea of the entire process. Studying progression demonstrations will help with understanding the framework of this process, which are detailed in abundance throughout this book.

In general, a portrait can encompass many different spheres of understanding, such as proportion, anatomy, color values, textures, mood, and more. All of these separate skills are important to learn to be aware of and eventually master, but it is best to try to master only one or two of these at a time. Don't try to learn everything perfectly all at once; this will prove overwhelming and discouraging, as you may not develop a clear understanding of any single drawing or painting concept. Beginners will achieve much more success by focusing on learning one core skill at a time – blocking-in, for example – and practicing that, rather than trying to master all of the portraiture skills at once.

The following chapters contain a wealth of concepts and techniques shared by a host of top artists working in the portraiture field. See this book as a compendium of the teachings of many excellent voices in contemporary portraiture, and use it best by focusing on one or two ideas at a time as you grow in your own understanding of drawing and painting a portrait.

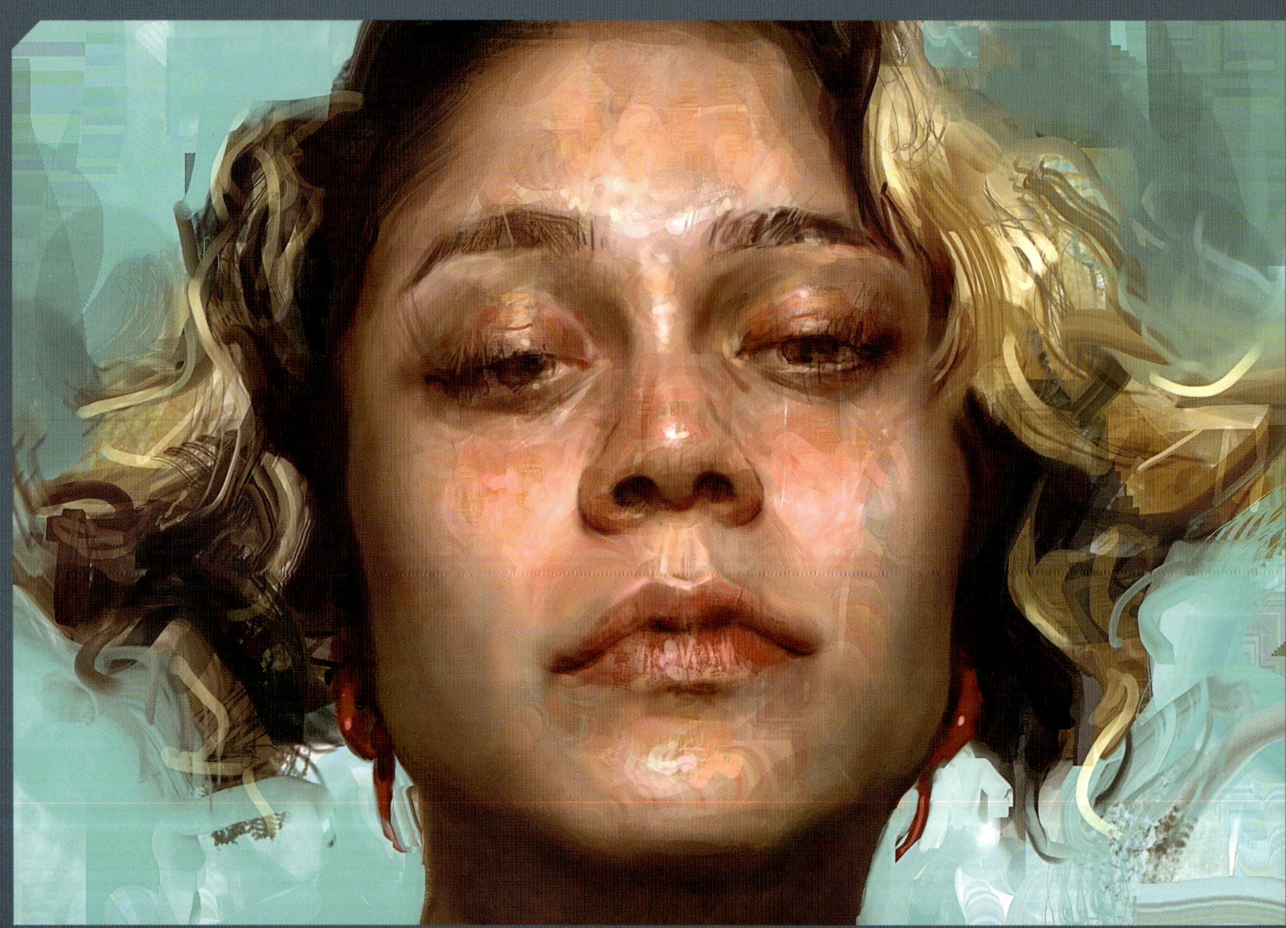

Perceptual portraiture

Perceptual, or naturalistic, portraiture is trying to render what you see from real life or nature. Within this genre there are two camps: working from life or rendering from high-quality photography. Both are valid, but working from life does offer a true and direct experience with your subject. It has its problems and is not easy, but there is no filter between you and your subject and many artists believe this to be the richer experience. Drawing from life is usually the most traditional route of learning how to draw.

Most arts schools highly prize drawings from life. Here are several reasons why:

1. You can't cheat when drawing from life.

2. Drawing an object from a three-dimensional format is more difficult. It teaches you more about the 3D world than a 2D reproduction that is fixed and therefore more quickly rendered.

3. When working from life, elements change over time. The light may change. The model may move. You may forget where your easel was set up. The model may come in with a slightly different look, or simply feel different from pose to pose. These challenges can make you a more confident draftsperson, but they can sometimes prove too difficult for the beginner and may hinder you from establishing basic principles. In this case, working from photography can be helpful.

4. Drawing from life can be artistically freeing. You are not competing with a photograph and can therefore create more unique results.

5. The values, colors, and sense of form are true. When you work from a photograph, the true nature of the subject has already passed through a filter, which translates your subject before you get to it. This can lead to a stilted understanding of form and limits you to what the camera can perceive. It often creates an overly contrasted image, simplifies the color, and shows much more detail than the eye can see. That said, beginners can use this to their advantage and accept that the result will have a different aesthetic than created when drawing from life.

All of these points are true, but working from a photograph has its benefits as well, especially when it's not possible to find a live model. The advantages of working from photography include:

1. Difficult lighting situations become manageable.

2. Photographs can capture fleeting expressions.

3. Photographs allow you to zoom in and study detail more closely to understand the minute forms in a different way.

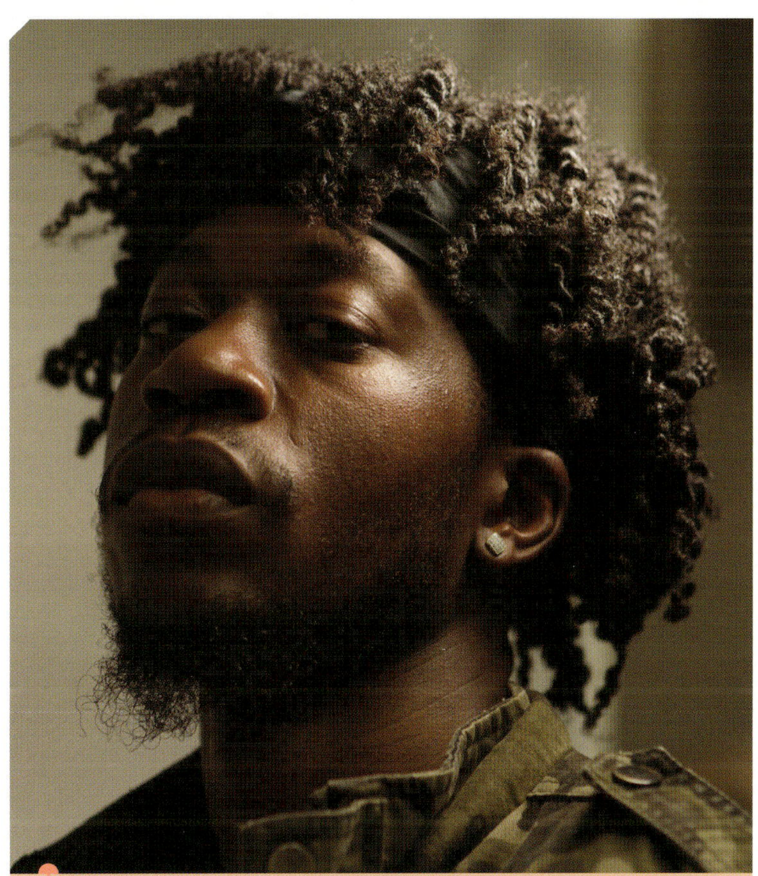

A perceptual portrait involves painting or drawing in a way that tries to be faithful to what is seen, whether from life or a photograph

Reference imagery considerations

When not working from your imagination or conceptually, it's important to keep certain considerations of your reference material in mind. These considerations include:

- Are you working from a photo or from life?
- What are the lighting conditions?
- How close or far away are you from the model?

The answers to these questions, and others, will dictate your working methods.

2D: Screen or reproduction

If you are only just beginning your journey into portraiture, you may find it easier to work from a 2D reproduction, such as a photograph or a screen, at first. Starting off working from life is often too difficult for the beginner, and it's important to develop an amount of confidence and experience in working from a simple image that won't move or change position like a live model. This was even done in the French Academy in the nineteenth century. The standard progression of the student was to copy other drawings before working up to drawing a live model. In the present day, working from a screen is also desirable, especially if you have a larger screen you can position next to your easel. A large digital tablet is ideal.

3D: From life

Working from life or 3D is much more challenging, which is why having a basic foundation of working from the two-dimensional is invaluable. When you draw from the three-dimensional, you are faced with a moving target; you are moving and so is the model. You will soon realize that you must have a fixed reference point that allows you to make clear decisions. This could be a plumb line, or bony landmarks on the face, which allow you to understand the correct distance from the cheek to the nose, for example, as a point of orientation.

Good images

If you're working from photographs, how do you know if your chosen images make good reference material? This is somewhat subjective. As you start out, opt for images with higher contrast that have significantly less detail, rather than a sharp, bright picture. As you become more familiar with the structure of the head, move on to more flattering lighting that emphasizes the linear qualities of the face. This will be necessary in order to grow your understanding of the relationship between line and shape (which will be covered in more detail on page 28).

Beginners should choose reference photos that are dramatically lit. This will produce clear shapes on your portrait by consolidating the information down to a manageable amount. This technique is nothing new; simplifying an image using dramatic lighting was the approach Charles Bargue took when teaching beginners in the nineteenth century French ateliers, and it is still taught in many schools today.

Sharp detail vs. soft & painterly

When choosing a photo for reference material, should the photo be razor-sharp or slightly blurry? A little blurriness can be a good thing, as it allows you to see how forms are connected. For example, John Singer Sargent painted portraits using soft, connected forms that generally allow the eye to travel through his paintings.

However, beware of areas that appear very sharp, where you are not exactly sure how they are supposed to be because of the lack of clear information in the image. A little experience painting from life can help you to understand how an exterior edge of a form will be sharper than an interior edge of a form (as explained on page 34).

Likewise, the same concept applies when working from life. It is helpful to have a little distance between yourself and the model to ensure you don't get caught up in the details before first viewing the big picture. Only once your painting or drawing is blocked in is it necessary to focus in closer on the details and intricacies of the face. This balance between the soft connected forms and sharp details, where needed, is a constant struggle for any artist.

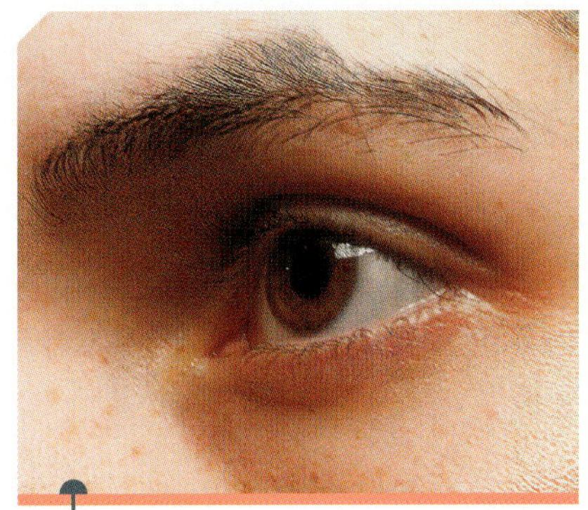

Razor sharp detail

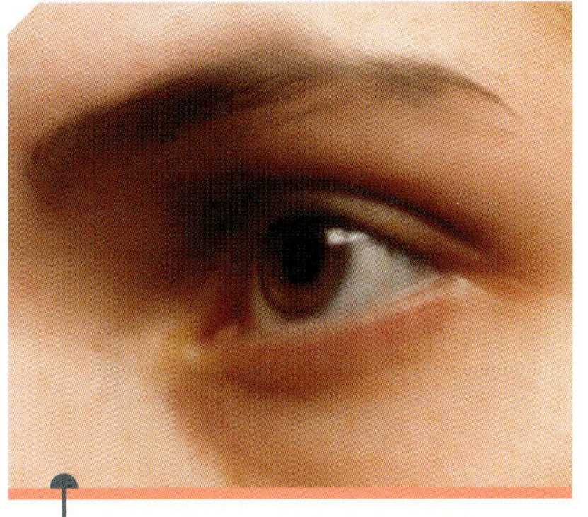

The same image, but softer

Hard light vs. soft light

Consider the quality of the lighting. Is it a spotlight, or a frosted floodlight? This is the difference between hard light and soft light. Hard light produces shadow and light shapes, which are more easily drawn and seen, as shown on the female model. This helps to abstract the face into manageable pieces.

Conversely, frosted floodlight produces more lines and an abundance of detail, as seen on the male model. Typically, most people would rather be photographed in soft light, as it enhances the personality of the sitter and pulls you into a more intimate situation. However, it is much easier to paint a hard light, shape-driven picture.

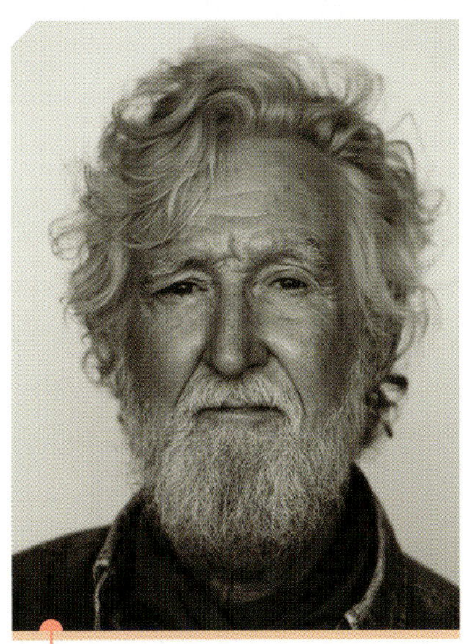

Soft lighting

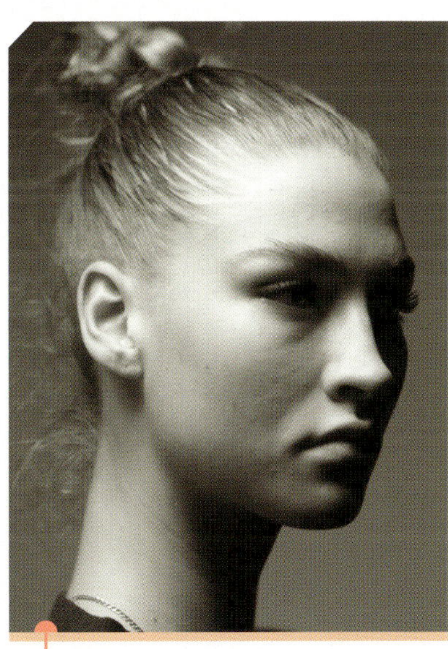

Hard lighting

Conceptual portraiture

Conceptually driven portraiture often involves straddling two different worlds. You have one foot in the perceptual world, drawing what you see, to a point. But you also have a foot in a conceptual world, which sometimes supersedes what you see in order to convey a concept. Understanding and having confidence and balance between these ways of seeing is the key to understanding your artistic voice or style.

What does conceptual mean? A concept could be a certain color combination. It could be the idea that the brush is the author of the mark, creating its own interpretation instead of naturalistic illusion. The concept could be the subject breaking apart, versus coming back into focus. Or it could be more intellectual, drawing upon life experience and personal story. There is no limit to what ideas or concepts can be applied to the portrait, and in some ways this is truly what art is about.

Artists love a good story or concept that drives a painting or drawing. Here are a few reasons why:

1. A concept gives you something to talk about. It is the thing that reveals a story in a unique way. What would *Starry Night* by Van Gogh be like without swirly brushstrokes?

2. A concept can help you to engage with the larger world of ideas around you. When you have a concept, your work becomes more than a portrait; it starts to associate with other experiences and feelings that people viewing the portrait can relate to.

3. A concept can help you to realize when a painting is finished, which is a great struggle for many artists! It is often difficult to know when a piece is complete, but when you have a concept or idea that you are working toward, and then you achieve and execute that idea, it can be easier to tell when it's time to put down your paintbrush. This, more than anything, can provide clarity about how your work is progressing. Of course, there will still be the usual challenges related to drawing, values, and edges, but if you are working toward a predetermined concept, often it proves more important than these other technical considerations. There are many masterpieces in museums in which the drawing is imperfect, but the concept has been achieved, and those artists are celebrated for it.

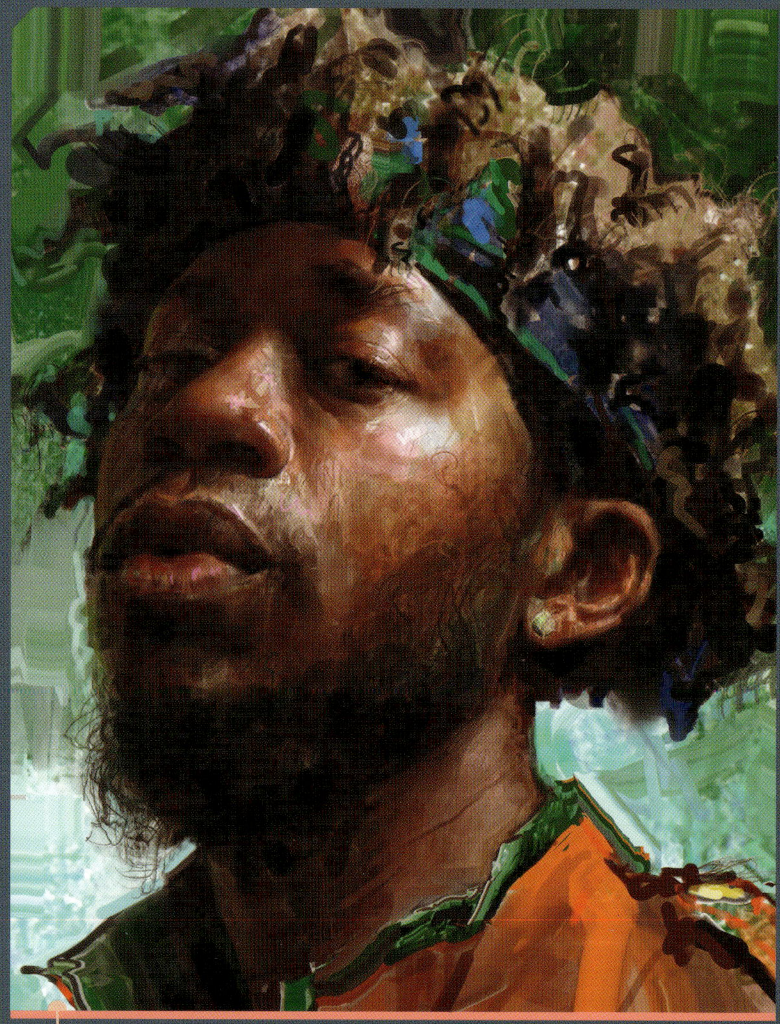

A conceptual portrait involves interpreting your subject through the lens of a specific concept

Reference imagery: concept mood board

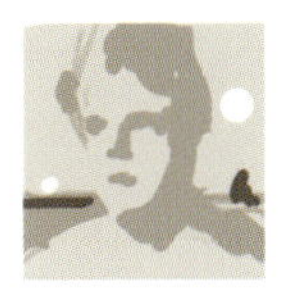

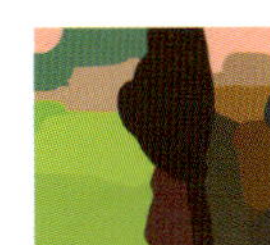

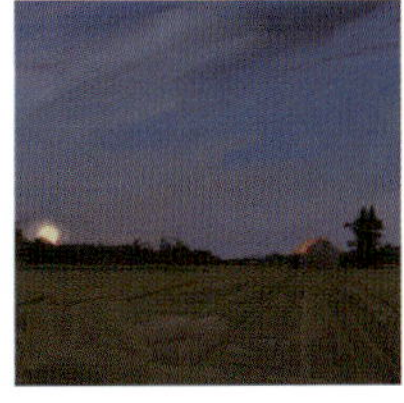

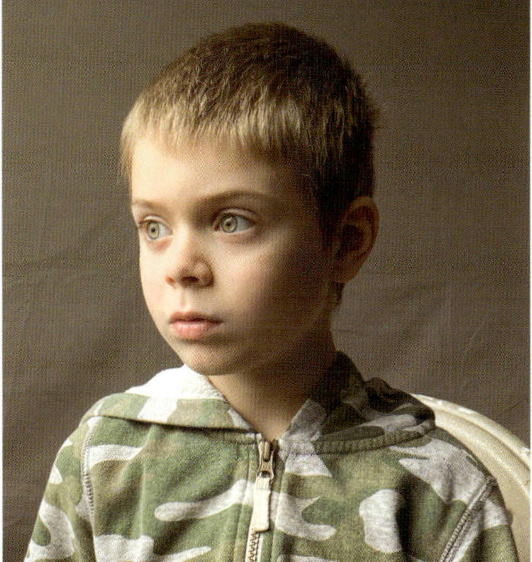

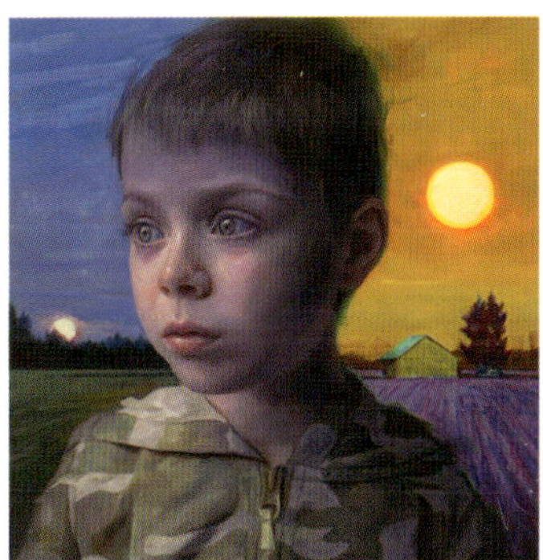

A concept mood board can be used to gather color palettes, thumbnail sketches, background compositional aids, and other ideas to help inspire a conceptual portrait

Concept reference library

Not all artists wish to work perceptually (rendering what they see). In fact, most look forward to translating the face into an artistic concept or creative idea of some kind, such as an Impressionistic style or personal story. As discussed before, the concept can be deep or superficial. Some artists need no help translating the head into an idea and creative ideas flow quite easily for them, while others may struggle with breaking free from what they see in the natural world. If the latter is you, consider creating a mood board to gather together concept references next to your portrait. It's helpful to see your target next to your work, and then you can modify and push it even further beyond your reference imagery if you choose.

Your concept reference imagery can include thumbnail sketches, desired colored palettes, background, compositional aids; anything that encapsulates the ideas you wish to convey in your work, but isn't found in the original portrait image. This is particularly helpful in bridging the gap between what you can see and what you want to see in your painting. If you are confident using digitial software, you can redesign your reference portrait to incorporate your creative ideas so that translating it onto canvas is that much more direct.

Practice

To put this into practice, take a photo and then paint over it to modify your reference material toward a more visionary place. You can do this digitally, using a software like Photoshop or Procreate, or you can print out an image, seal it with a clear acrylic medium, and then paint over it with whatever medium you choose. The idea is to experiment and modify your reference material to include the style, colors, values, and background you would like it to have.

Setting up the reference image relationship to the canvas

Frame of reference

Creating a frame of reference requires setting your resource image at exactly the same ratio as your canvas. This doesn't necessarily mean they are exactly the same size. It could mean your reference image is 8 x 10 inches and your canvas is a 16 x 20 inches, for example. This creates a relationship in which the shapes and proportions can be seen more easily without the visual confusion of your reference and canvas shapes being mismatched.

As seen below, **Fig. 1** is not the same ratio as **Fig. 2**, but **Fig. 3** is the same ratio as **Fig. 2**, only bigger. Having the same ratio, even if it is a different size, helps with the internal spacing of the shapes and proportions, as your overall drawing/painting surface is already in proportion.

Using a frame of reference is a valuable tool, because:

- It can help you to more accurately visualize how your resource image will be translated onto your canvas.
- It allows you to use the negative spaces around your subject as a way of judging your drawing.

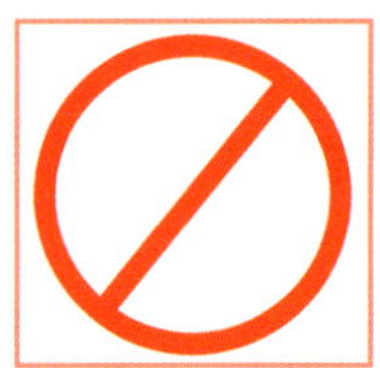

Fig. 1

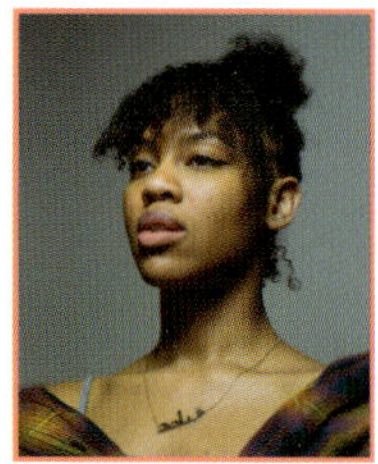

Fig. 2

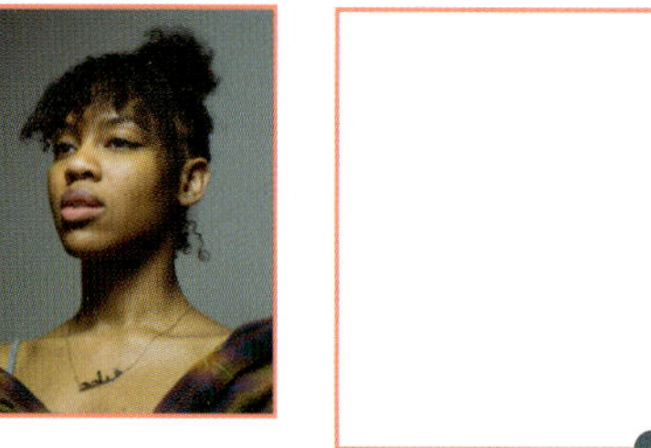

Fig. 3

Choosing a canvas size with the same ratio as your reference image will help as you recreate spacing and proportions

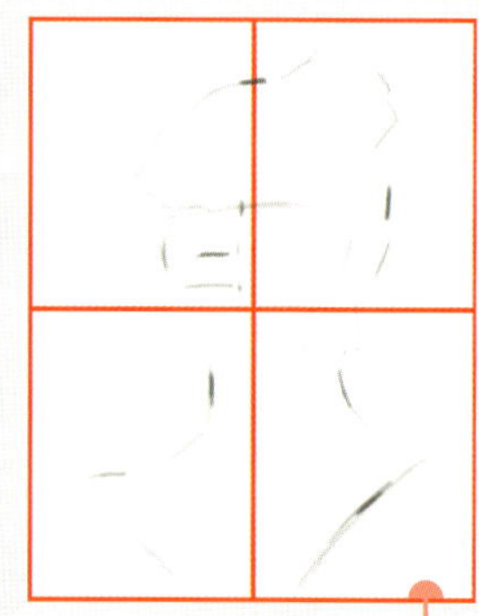

A grid is an efficient way of capturing proportions accurately, or scaling the image up or down

Grid

Using a frame of reference when setting up your canvas will allow you to use a grid system to start placing your drawing. A grid involves drawing horizontal and vertical lines on your resource image, then replicating the exact same lines and proportions of those lines on your canvas. This creates quarter-page modules that allow you to see the placement of lines in a more efficient way.

Using a grid can be a helpful tool as:

- It takes away some of the difficulty of proportion when sketching out your drawing.
- It can be used for scaling the image up or down with accuracy.

Tracing and projecting

A lot of artists will trace out their drawing using either a projector, a light table, or using a transparent layer in digital software such as Photoshop. This is an easy way to produce very accurate results. However, in order to gain true confidence and grow as an interpreter of the natural world, the slow process of learning how to draw without this type of guide is an important one. It may not yield the quickest results, but it produces integrity in your work and a solid foundation for your growth as an artist.

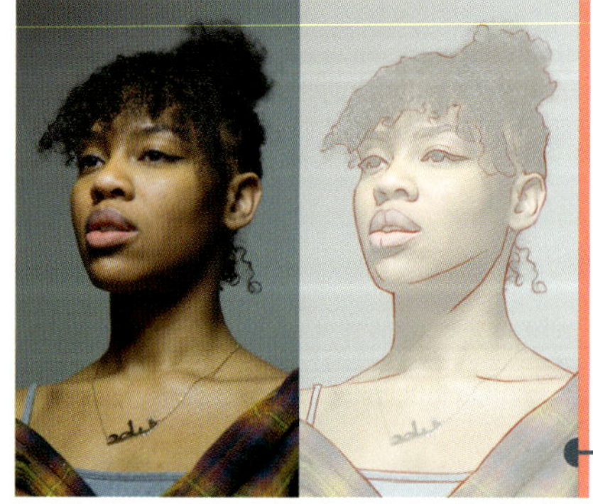

Tracing your reference photo onto the canvas is quick and easy but won't progress your structural drawing skills

Two major proportional measuring approaches

Comparative measurement

Comparative measurement is, in some ways, the essence of proportion. It involves taking one shorter measurement, or span, and seeing how many times it fits into a longer span to create a ratio. This ratio can then be used to scale a face up or down to whatever size you like. Many artists use this technique when they are working from life and cannot sight-size.

A simple example of how you could utilize this technique is to measure the width of a head, then see how many times it fits into the height of a head, creating an imaginary box. Once you understand the ratio of this box, you can translate this to your drawing with confidence. The measuring can be done with your finger, the tip of a paintbrush, or a pencil.

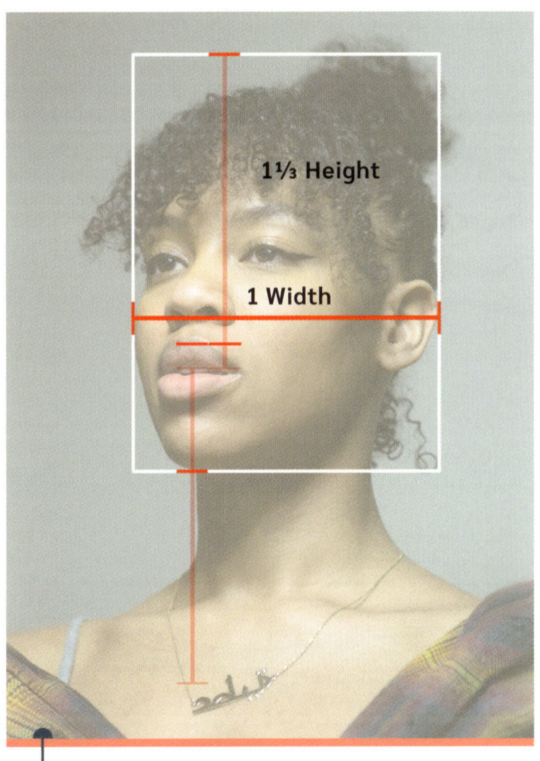

Comparative measurement involves creating a ratio by measurement

Sight-size

The sight-size method is the preferred choice of classical portrait painters when rendering to an absolute likeness. There is no better technique for attaining drawing accuracy. In sight-size, your subject is always on a one-to-one ratio with your drawing; in other words, they are exactly the same size. The smallest inaccuracies become apparent when you don't have the extra work of scaling up or down, as you do when using the comparative measurement method. In **Fig. 1**, notice that the canvas is bigger than the reference image, whereas in **Fig. 2** they are the same size. Sight-size does not have to be dictated by the frame of reference.

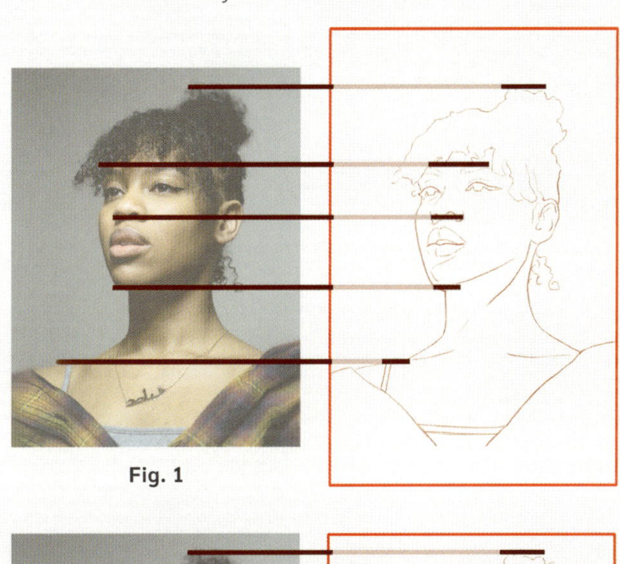

Fig. 1

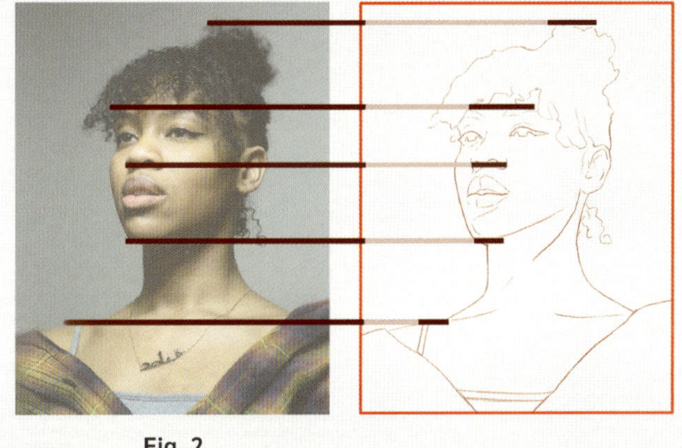

Fig. 2

The sight-size method requires drawing your subject on a one-to-one ratio

Finding a working rhythm

When attempting to accomplish something as difficult as drawing a human portrait, it's helpful to establish a working rhythm to act as a guide as you work through the drawing or painting process. Your creation cycle is the way you rhythmically work through several different ideas in a cycle. It is your overall working method and pattern.

Why does working in a rhythm or cycle matter? Portraits usually possess some level of sophistication and it's very difficult to get there in a straight line. As in sailing, you have to change from one direction to another to reach your destination (**Fig. 1**). You proceed a little bit to the left, a little bit to the right, a little bit to the left, a little bit to the right, and so on... But always forward. A cycle (**Fig. 2**) is slightly more complicated, but still involves rhythmically working by spiraling upward toward your finish, slowly tightening up with every turn.

It's important to avoid aimlessly wandering (**Fig. 3**) through your painting, which is quite easy to do. Getting distracted or not quite knowing where you are going can turn a seventy percent finished painting back into a fifty percent finished painting. Working rhythmically will help to implement a track for your mind to roll on. Your working method can be as simple as sailing: drawing lines and softening, drawing lines and softening, back and forth until the drawing is finished (**Fig. 4**). Or it could be more complex, like rotating between drawing lines, applying color values, and considering edges, before returning back to drawing lines, color values, edges, and so on.

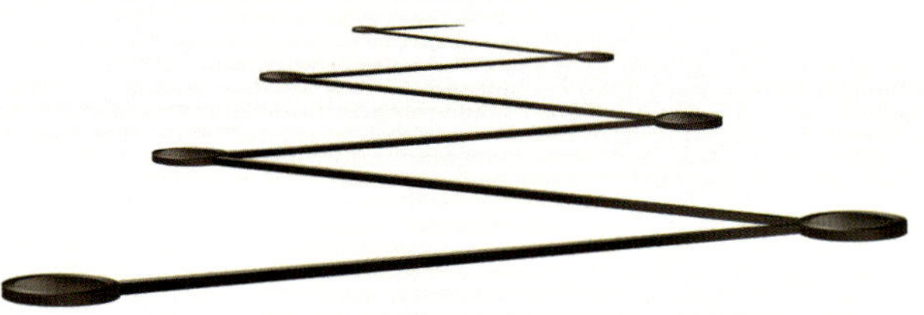

Fig. 1. Sailing

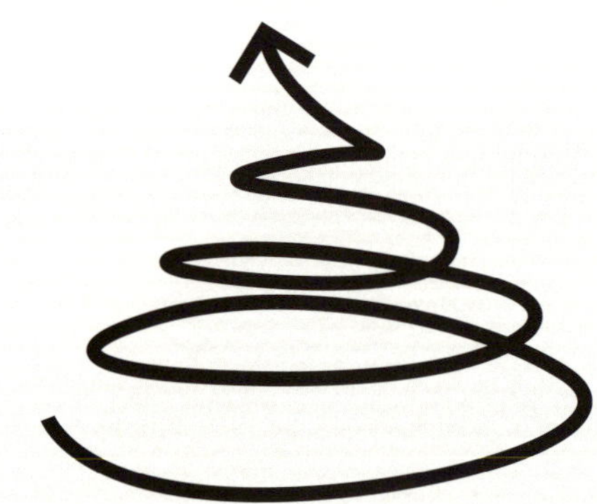

Fig. 2. Cycling

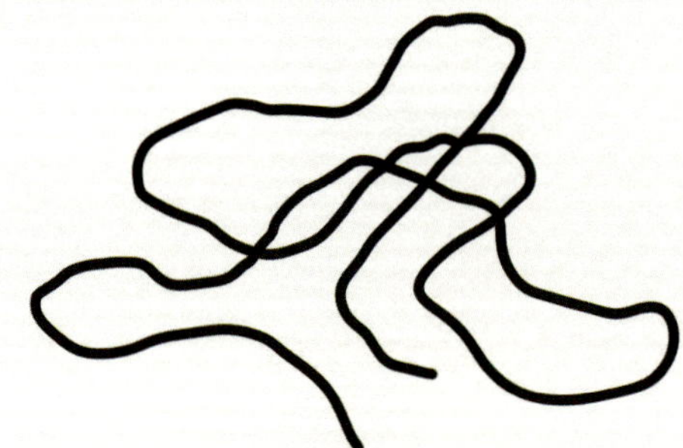

Fig. 3. Wandering

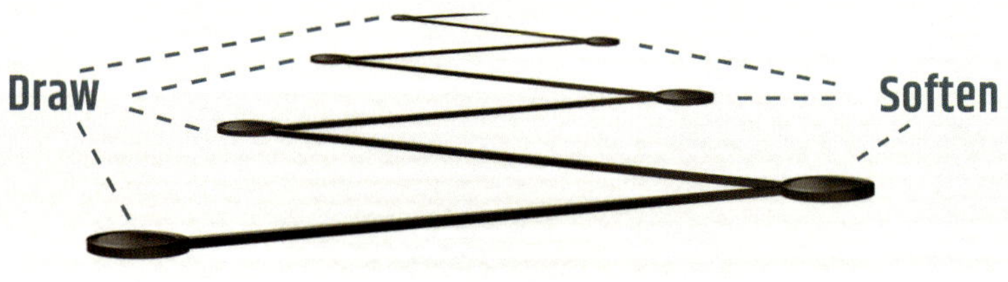

Fig. 4. Drawing and softening

The creation cycle

Each creation cycle phase contains several concept layers to explore. For example, within the drawing category, you may work through layers of concepts, such as the envelope shape, triangulation, and rhythm angles. The following chapters will explore this three-phase painting cycle (see page 22).

The three categories to be explored are drawing, then building colors and values, and finally edges. Not every artist works this way and not every concept layer fits neatly into just one of the phases, but as you learn it is best to understand and practice these particular phases and their concept layers one by one, as they make up almost every important decision in painting and drawing the head.

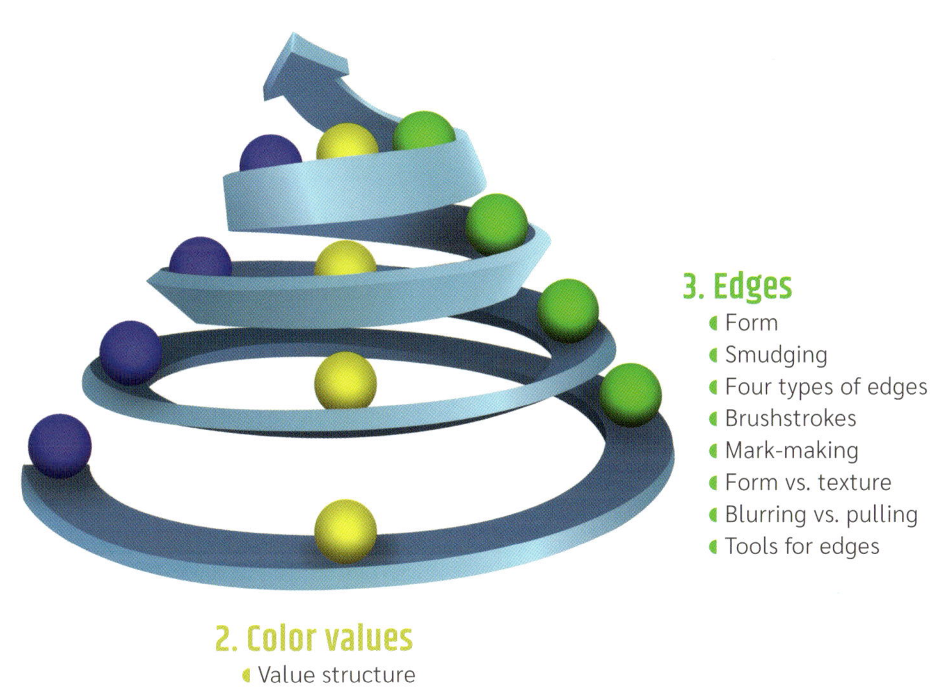

1. Drawing

- Proportion
- Envelope
- Facial armature
- Structural symmetry
- Alignment
- Plumb lines
- Line structure
- Shape design
- Gesture

2. Color values

- Value structure
- Color key
- Window-shading
- Color diversity
- Color of the light

3. Edges

- Form
- Smudging
- Four types of edges
- Brushstrokes
- Mark-making
- Form vs. texture
- Blurring vs. pulling
- Tools for edges

Establishing this working rhythm is one of the most important things an artist can do, no matter what medium you are using. Start by drawing, then add the colors and values where you have mapped out the drawing, then move on to the edges. Each phase has many different types of considerations and they don't all have to be completed at once; if you get distracted, or even bored, move onto another phase so your mind becomes active again.

Each time you add something to a painting, work through a few turns of the cycle. You can spend five minutes in a phase, or an hour and a half, before moving onto the next phase of color values and edges. This provides plenty of flexibility, depending on your attention span. There will be times when you are losing interest and need to work quickly to move onto the next phase or concept layer to help manage your boredom. At other times your attention span may be longer, allowing you to spend more time on a certain phase or concept layer while your focus is sharper.

Another benefit of the creation cycle is that it is not constrained to any one specific technique. You can use this creation cycle while trying to paint a baroque, alla prima, or digital portrait. It transcends the history of techniques and styles, and in this versatile way creates clarity of purpose for the beginner and advanced artist alike.

The creation cycle can be applied to many different types of media. The example below shows **Cycle 1**: a rough outline, followed by blocked-in colors and values, and then a softening or smudging that brings it together in a slightly more naturalistic, out-of-focus look. That is one spin on the cycle, which is followed by **Cycle 2** (another spin), **Cycle 3**, and so on. You don't have to be one hundred percent accurate when using this approach. Sometimes your aim with **Cycle 1** is to be fifty percent correct. Then, when you work through the next cycle, your goal is to be seventy percent correct, and so on.

One of the most important practices is the idea of redrawing and resetting your boundaries after you have softened or smudged your edges at the end of a cycle. This is especially true when painting in oil. Hard edges are not often found in an overly blended oil painting.

For digital painters, there is often not enough softness or play in the edges, and often smudging the paint a little further allows for edges to breathe a little, so they are not too hard.

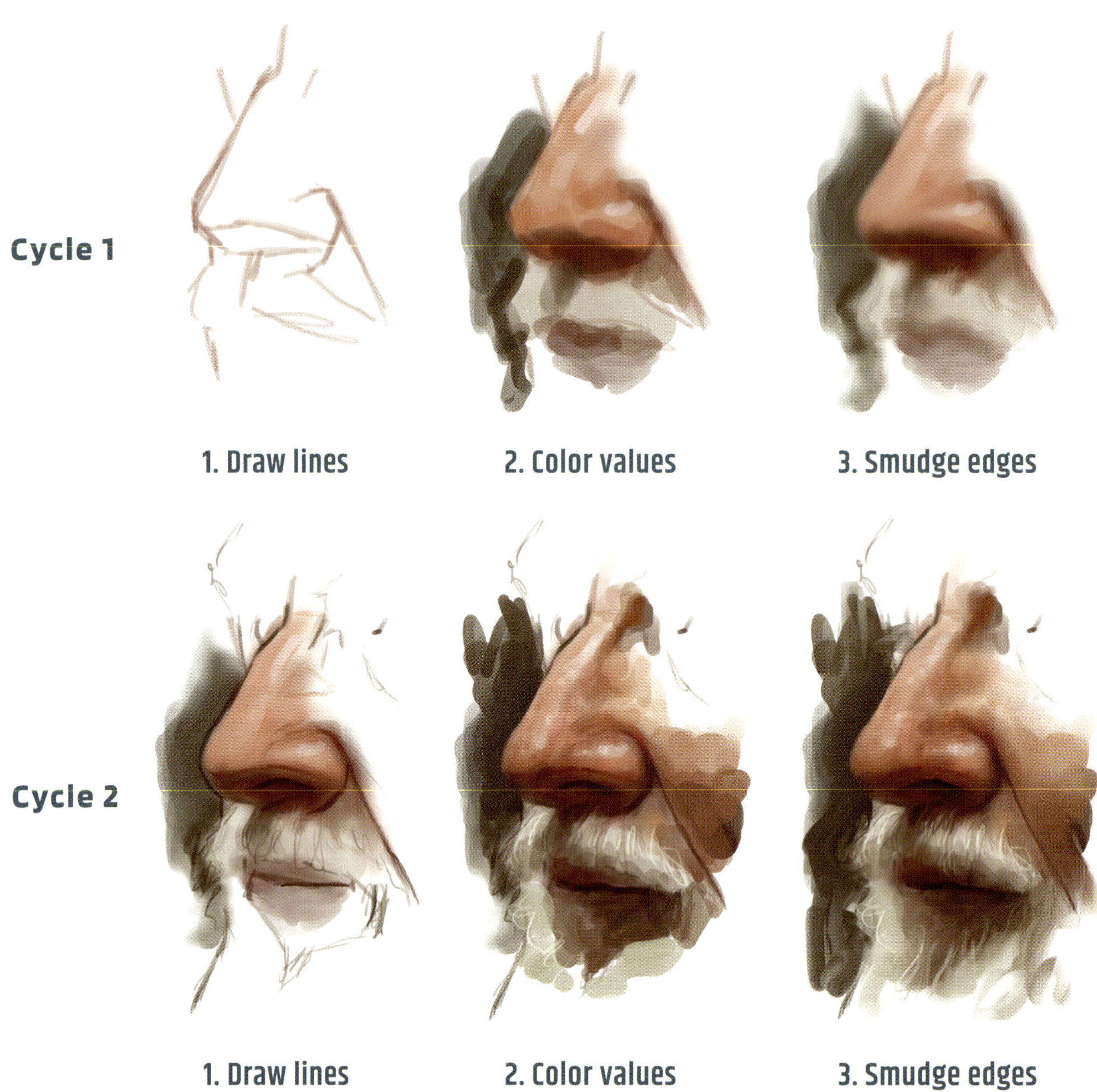

Layers of concepts within each phase

Inside of each phase of the creation cycle are endless concepts and ideas to help you see a unique attribute of the portrait. Though these layers of concepts are your targets and are important to hit, they are not themselves the end goal. They are layers that add depth and understanding to your knowledge of the portrait, and together build sophistication in your work.

If artwork only has one layer, it typically does not have much depth, nuance, or three-dimensionality. The more layers of concepts and understanding you can attain and project onto your portrait, the more depth it will have. Of course, this is not going to happen all at once and an artist must learn these individual concepts over time. This is what makes learning and painting the portrait so endlessly fascinating. It has no end.

The three main categories mentioned previously – drawing, color values, and edges – are ways to classify these layers of concepts. But in drawing there are hundreds, if not thousands, of target concepts to explore. For example, if drawing is a main category, then proportion and shape design are layers to address inside of it. Similarly, if edges are a main category, then mark-making and smudging are layers inside of it. Not everything fits neatly into this philosophy, but for the most part it is a working method that acknowledges how these layers work together.

As you advance, you will begin to see how some layers coincide. For example, sometimes you may need to draw with the right color value so there is a crossover. At other times, drawing involves using a soft edge, so there is a crossover there as well. As you are starting out, it is helpful at first to simplify and keep these layers in neater mental categories to provide a track for understanding your trajectory and system for working.

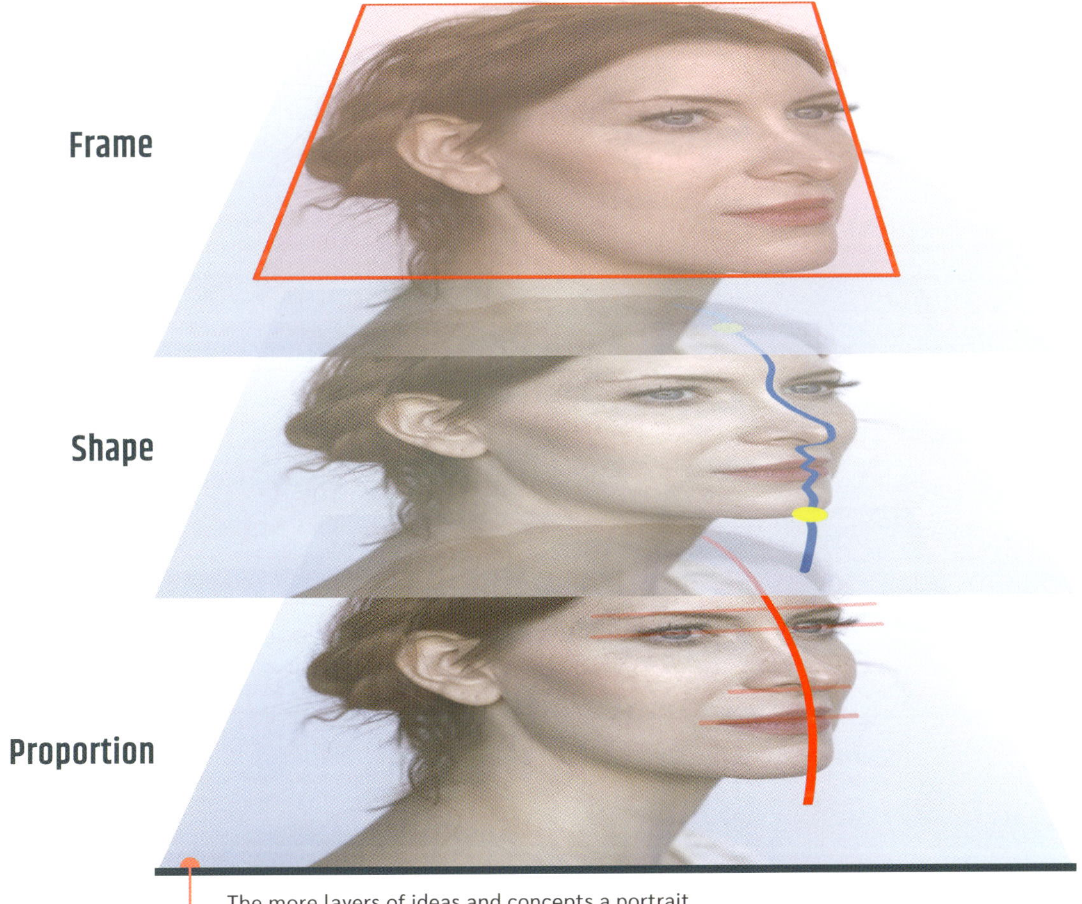

The more layers of ideas and concepts a portrait has, the more depth and interest it will possess

CREATION CYCLES

Steve Forster

- CREATION CYCLE: DRAWING
- CREATION CYCLE: COLOR VALUES
- CREATION CYCLE: EDGES

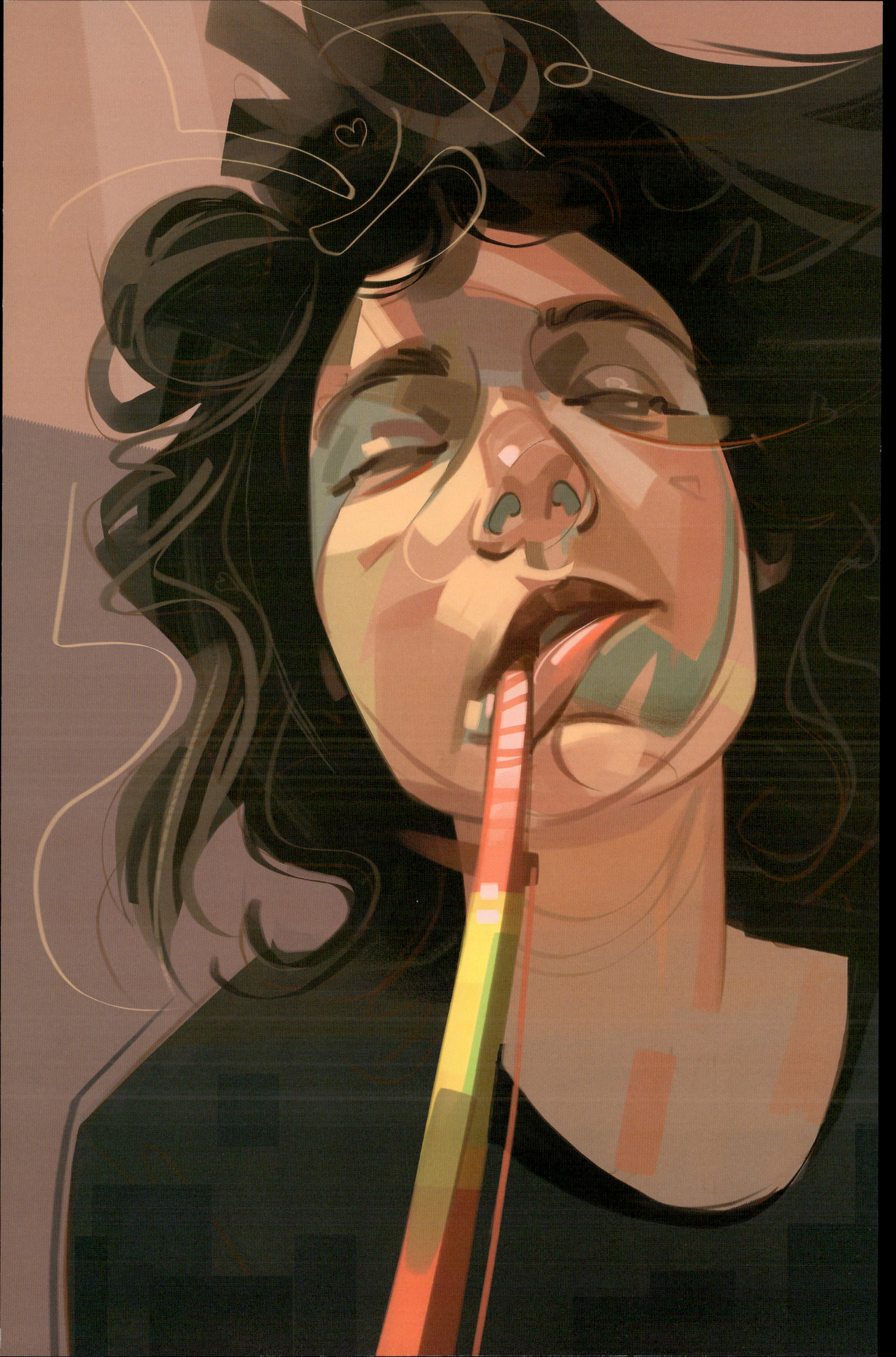

CREATION CYCLE: DRAWING

Photography and artwork © Steve Forster

This chapter will cover:

- Proportion
- Shape or line?
- Drawing: shape
- Drawing: line

Proportion

Comparative measurement

Comparative measurement is the essence of proportion. It is, generally speaking, the relationship between two "spans" or measurements. For example, a square's comparative measurement is a one-to-one ratio, or the rectangle seen in **Fig. 4** is a one-to-one-and-a-third ratio. Understanding this simple idea is often misunderstood and causes great frustration for beginners, but once you understand it, it is an invaluable tool that should be referenced constantly. It is well worth the trouble.

The following pages will discuss different techniques for comparative measurement.

Span proportion

The simplest type of proportion is span proportion. Here there is an overall distance, as seen in **Fig. 1**.

Somewhere along that distance there is a point that subdivides the span, creating a shorter space and a longer space, as seen in **Fig. 2**.

The easiest way to understand the proportion of the shorter space to the longer space is to take the shorter space and see how many times it fits into the longer space, thus creating a proportion, as seen in **Fig. 3**. The proportion in this scenario is 1:2.

With portraiture you will often need to subdivide a long space like this to ensure the relationship between features is correct, such as the relationship from the top of the head to brow, brow to chin, nose to sideburn, and sideburn to the back of the head.

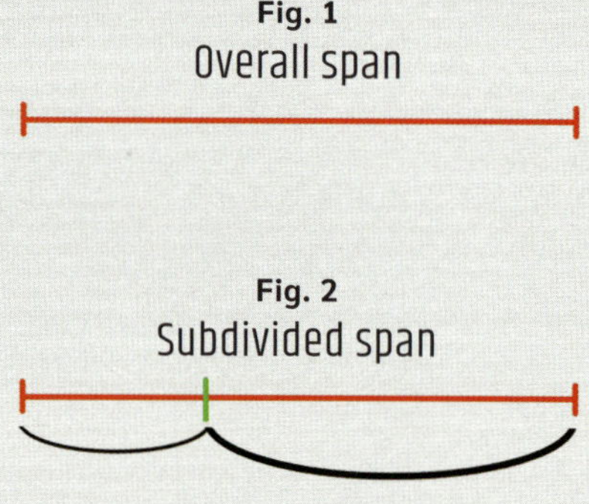

Fig. 1
Overall span

Fig. 2
Subdivided span

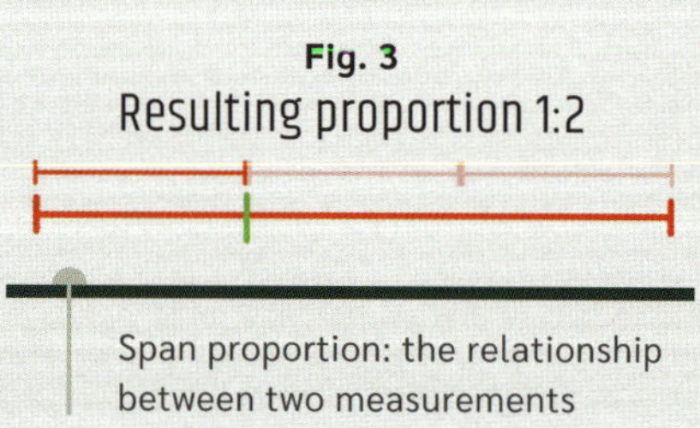

Fig. 3
Resulting proportion 1:2

Span proportion: the relationship between two measurements

Box proportion

Box proportion, as shown in **Fig. 4**, is similar. It involves taking the shorter end (A) and rotating 90° to see how many times A fits into the longer end (B). In this case, the proportional ratio is one-to-one-and-a-third height to width.

Fig. 5 shows box proportion applied to portraiture. This is perhaps the most important proportion to use to accurately calculate the overall head shape. However, the specific ratio of one-to-one-and-a-third of this head will change based on the situation.

Measuring with your eyes

Measuring is typically carried out using either a stick/pencil and your thumb, or calipers. By sliding your thumb to the appropriate point on the stick, you can take a measurement and use this to create a proportion, as seen in **Fig. 6**. However, some artists just don't connect with measuring mechanically. Or sometimes, as you advance and grow in experience, measuring with your eyes comes a little more naturally. This is not a reason to dismiss measuring mechanically. Learn to measure; it is important. However, if you don't connect with measuring, or would like to use a slightly more intuitive approach, measuring with your eyes is also an option.

For example, in **Fig. 7**, study the distance from the brow to nose, and nose to chin. Ask yourself which is longer, and by how much? Is it 4060, 50:50, 55:45? It's useful to ask these sorts of questions for features that are too difficult to measure manually.

In **Fig. 8**, consider whether the model's head shape is a tall rectangle or short rectangle? By simply asking the question, your eyes can often tell if something is inaccurate. This technique doesn't work for everyone, but give it a try. If you ask the question, you are more likely to find the answer.

Fig. 4

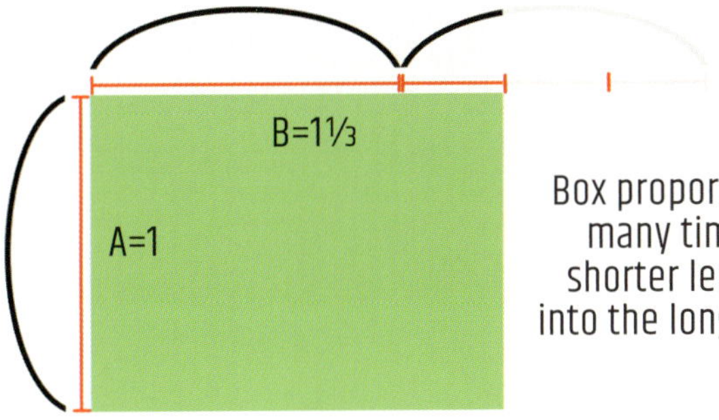

B=1⅓

A=1

Box proportion: how many times the shorter length fits into the longer length

Fig. 5

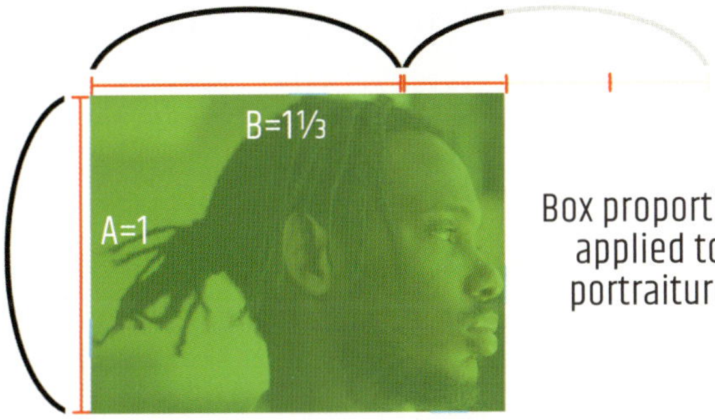

B=1⅓

A=1

Box proportion applied to portraiture

Fig. 6

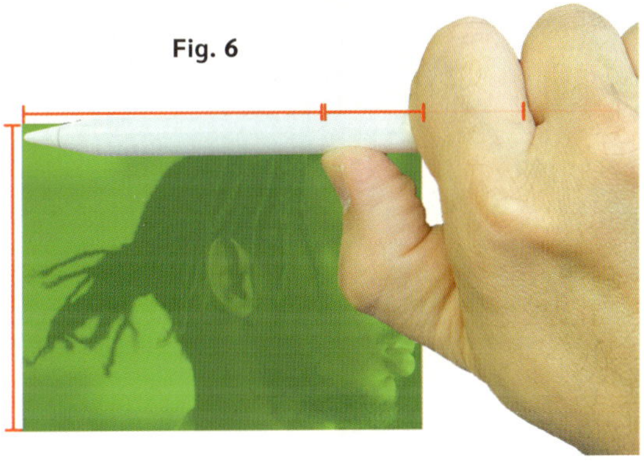

Measuring using a pencil and your thumb

Fig. 7

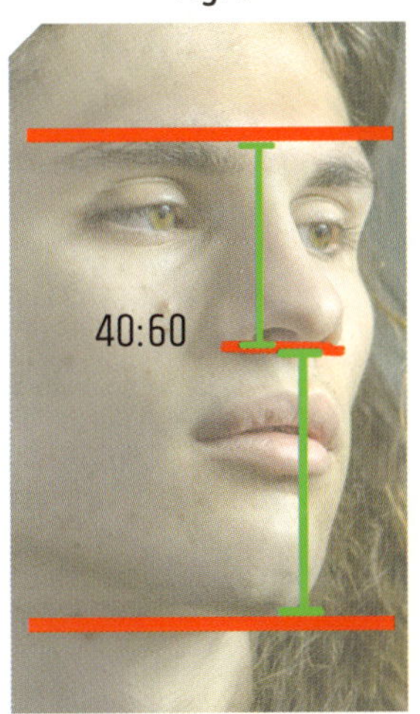

Observe the distance between facial features

Fig. 8

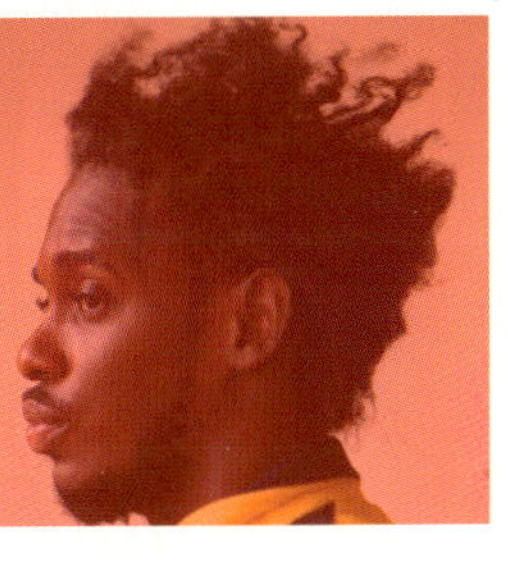

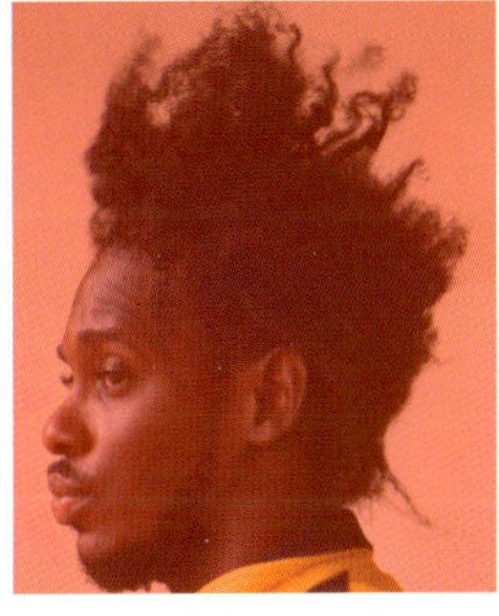

Measuring the subject's head shape with your eyes

The four most important proportions of framing the head

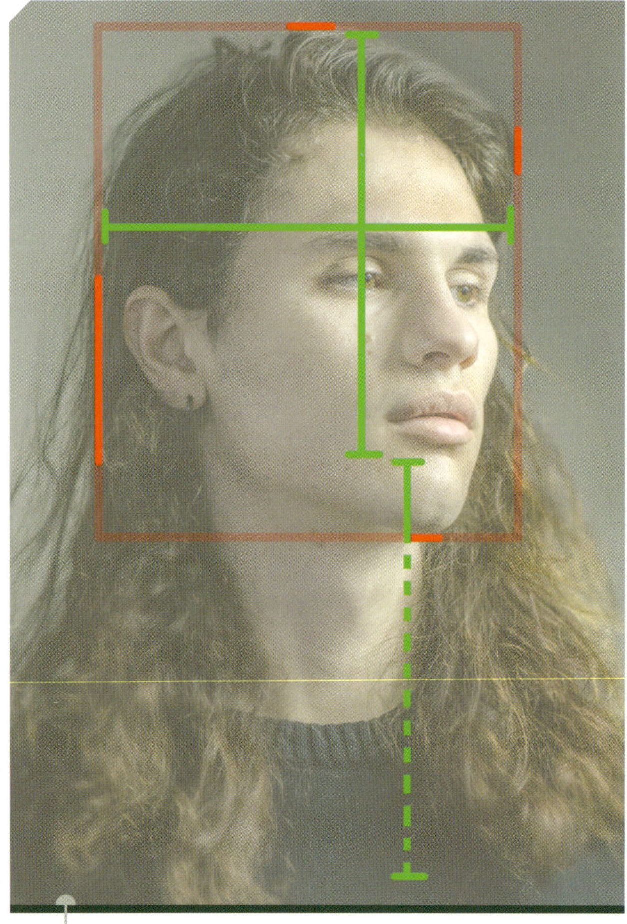

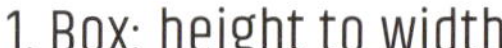

Height to width proportion

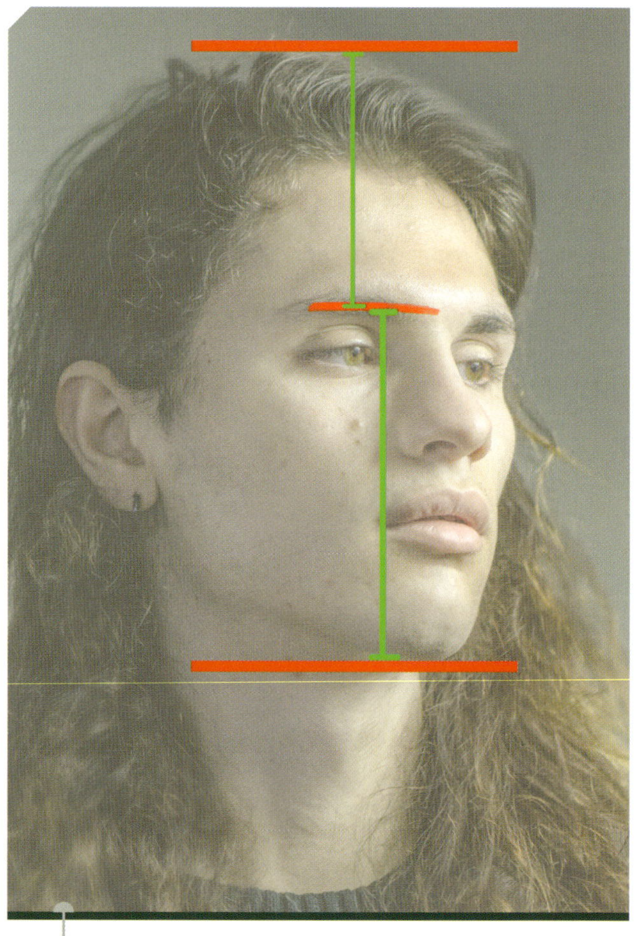

Top/brow/bottom proportion

1. Box: height to width

What defines the box? Typically it is the chin, the top of the hair, and the furthest points on the sides that create the box's edges. This is the general proportion and shape of the head, and is your absolute foundational measurement for starting to frame out the portrait. It's easy for this measurement to change over time while you're working, so it's important to check it continually to make sure it's correct.

2. Top/brow/bottom

After the box has been established, subdivide the height of the head at the brow. It's better to use the brow instead of the eyes as it's typically clearer to see than the eyes, especially if the eyes are in shadow. The brow is always a clear landmark to judge its proportion to the top and bottom. Universal proportions are untrustworthy, but typically this relationship is 40/60. However, this can change depending on whether you are viewing the head from above or below, or if the model has a lot of hair on top of their head.

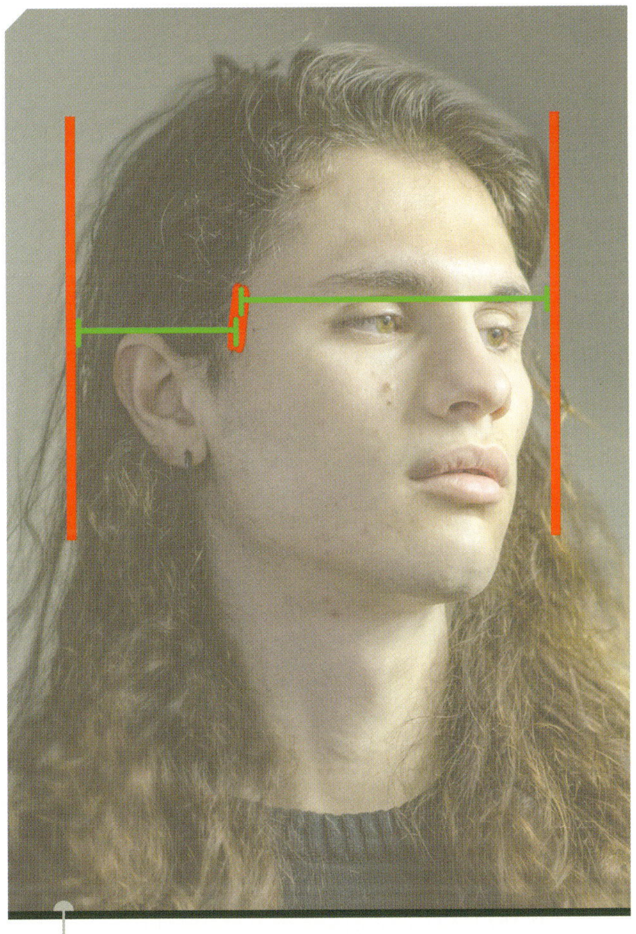

Back/side/front proportion

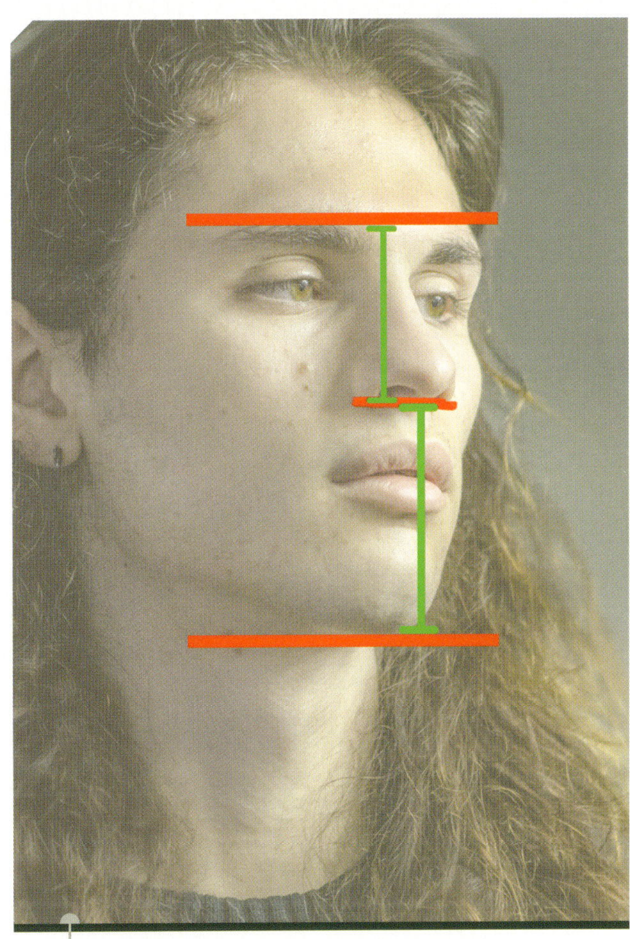

Brow/nose/chin proportion

3. Back/side/front

The third big measurement is finding a clear landmark that defines the side of the head from the front of the head. This can be elusive, as it may be easier to see a sideburn than a boney landmark such as the zygomatic arch, which defines the side plane of the head.

Whichever landmark you pick on the side of the head, make sure it has the correct proportional relationship to the front plane of the head. Too often this measurement is incorrectly proportioned and leads to a wide front plane and a squished back plane, or vice versa.

4. Brow/nose/chin

The next proportion of the head is setting the base of the nose, guided by the position of the brow and chin. You should do this last, as you need to double-check the other three proportions again before setting this one. This proportion is arguably the most important in defining the likeness and character of the features, even more so than the others. If you draw the nose too long, for example, the mouth and chin will appear squashed and you won't have enough room to describe everything. If you draw the nose too short, you will end up with a long chin and a big mouth. It's very easy to get this wrong, so ensure you check it regularly throughout your painting or drawing session.

Shape or line?

Emphasizing the right scheme for the situation

This next section will explore two primary subcategories of drawing: shape and line. These are the lenses through which artists look and vacillate when constructing a head. Ask yourself: are you crafting or designing the shapes? Or, are you thinking more structurally by drawing with lines? These two tools are intrinsically intertwined and very helpful conceptually when drawing the head.

Though it's tempting, it's a mistake to start by drawing eyes, eyelashes, and pupils. A wiser approach is to abstract and simplify the head, applying layers of concepts in order to effectively map it out. However, different light qualities will often help you to pick the best scheme for your situation.

When starting a portrait, begin by establishing the lighting situation to choose the best scheme or technique. There are two major types of light quality: hard light (spotlight) and soft light (overcast). Everything else exists on a spectrum in between.

Hard light emphasizes shapes

It's best to choose a hard light situation when beginning a new portrait, as this makes it slightly easier to see and design shapes, and is rewarding to render the full value spectrum.

Hard light tends to unify intricate detail into an envelope of shape. For example, in the photograph below you can't see the pupil and the iris of the left eye, and can barely see the right eye at all. This is a gift when first learning how to draw the head, as when you don't have to draw these details, you only need to draw the shape, value, and edge, and the viewer's brain will fill in the rest. For this situation, the shape and pull technique (explored on page 36) is the most helpful.

Some areas on this head are fairly easy to simplify down to shape, while other areas, such as the jawline and hair, are more difficult. When painting using the shape method, you need to work out how to describe these areas using only shapes and edges to avoid getting caught up in lines and detail that will only confuse the process.

Sometimes the painting and design of these shapes can be the beginning and end of a beautiful, simple painting. Of course, many artists want to proceed further than this, but there is so much more to learn and understand about this painterly way of blocking in the head that it bears some amount of study.

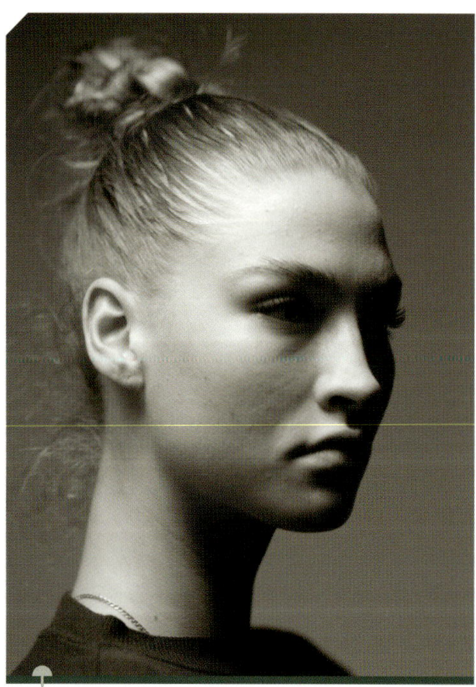

Original photograph

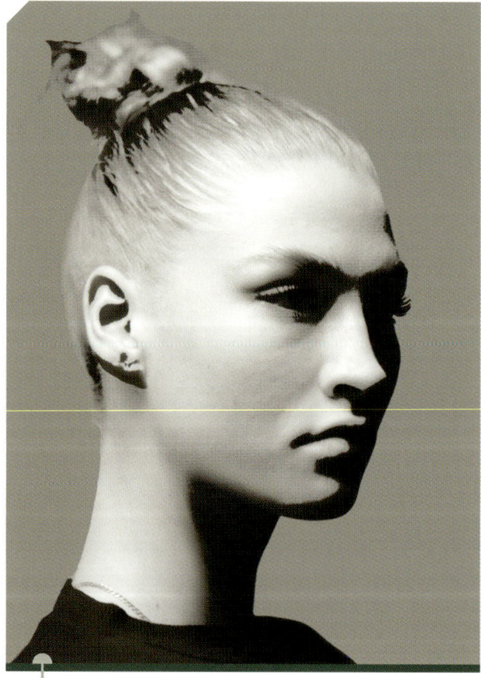

Hard lighting can help with simplifying the photograph into shapes

Soft light emphasizes lines

As you progress and want more of a challenge, the soft light situation is an important phase in your growth as an artist. Soft light emphasizes structure and draftsmanship, especially in the features, and enhances intimacy with the viewer. You can hide in a shadow shape, but you can't hide in the light. Since not every lighting situation has strong shadows, soft light demands more of a linear structure approach.

Soft light tends to reveal intricate detail and the specificity of every line and form that makes up the subject's face. For instance, in the photograph below you can see almost every strand of hair and every line in the model's face. You may also notice the soft gradation that gently rolls away from these lines. This kind of light requires extreme sensitivity with the placement and rendering of these details. It's very easy to draw something in the wrong place, or make a detail too important by emphasizing it with marks that are too harsh and cartoon-like. It's crucial to formulate a plan and technique to meet the demands of this lighting situation before you put pencil to paper.

The sketch and ghost technique (detailed on page 44) is the most helpful technique when dealing with this lighting situation. It allows you to draw and make mistakes as you progress, without the mistakes becoming a detriment to the final product. By drawing lines and softly ghosting them out, you can change your mind about where your lines should go based on a first draft. The second draft enables you to make another pass, further correcting your work, and so on. This ghosting allows for new linear decisions to be made, while softly building up tone.

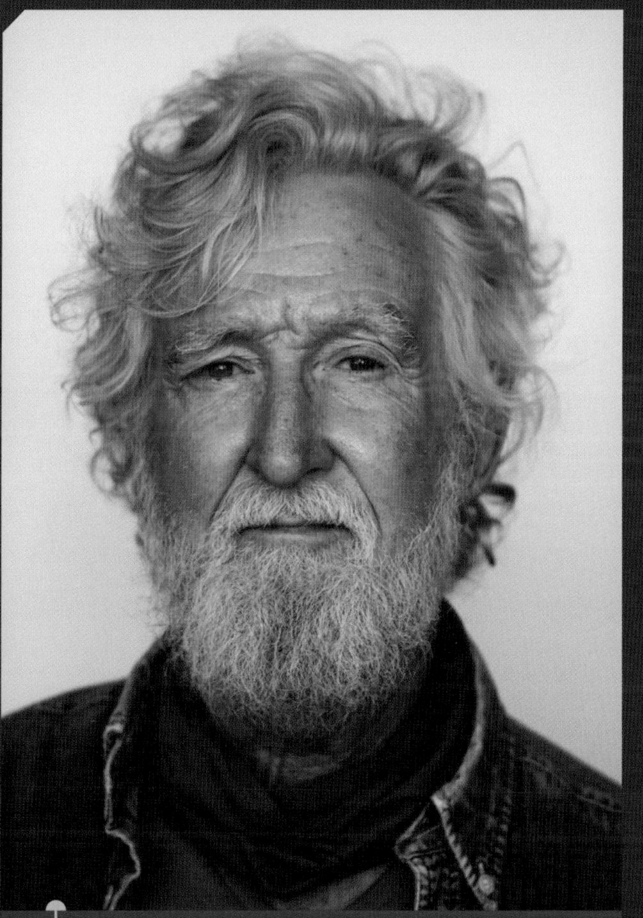

Original photograph

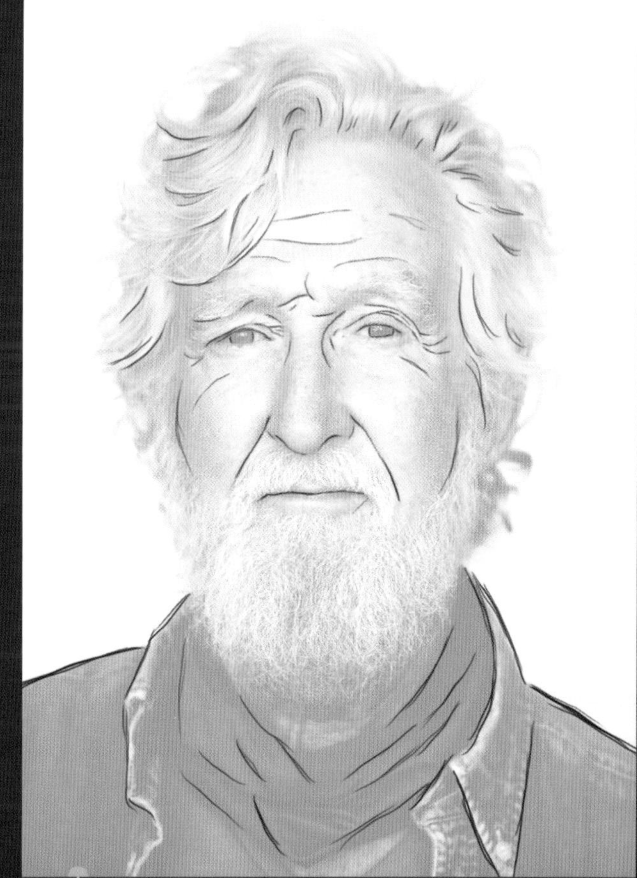

Soft lighting is more complex and requires the precise placement of detail and lines

Drawing: shape

Shape design

Seeing and drawing shapes is one of the most important tools an artist can possess. When looking at something as complicated as the human head, it's extremely beneficial to be able to simplify it into big shapes, or "continents."

When you lose these major shapes, or don't acknowledge them, the solidity and structure of the portrait suffers. If a portrait has become too smudgy or lacks clarity, checking the major shapes and going back to redesign these fundamental building blocks will usually set you back on the right track. An easy way to conceptualize this is to think of the bigger shapes as continents (**Fig. 1**) that set into motion every other smaller decision of shapes, or islands (**Fig. 2**).

To create a continent, imagine that you don't see any details inside or around the edges, simplifying the shape into its most basic essence. This is usually envisioned with straight angles and flat tones. If these big shapes are not right, all of the smaller shapes in the world won't make them right. It's also worth checking these continents again toward the end of your portrait creation to make sure they haven't suffered from continental drift or erosion. Once the big shapes are established and understood, you can then add more intricacy and detail to them, including the smaller shapes, or islands, that provide specificity and character to your subject, as seen in **Fig. 2**.

In addition to thinking about continents and islands, there are shapes that set the foundation of the other shapes around them (see **Fig. 3** & **Fig. 4**), carrying a greater amount of weight than the others. These are called keystone shapes and are arguably the most important. In this example, the macro keystone shape is formed of the hair and shadow of the neck and jaw. The nose shadow is the micro keystone of the face. The micro keystone is in the middle of the face and acts as the relational hub of all of the features. When placing this micro keystone shape, you need to consider its relationship to the macro keystone shape and the proportional placement top to bottom and left to right.

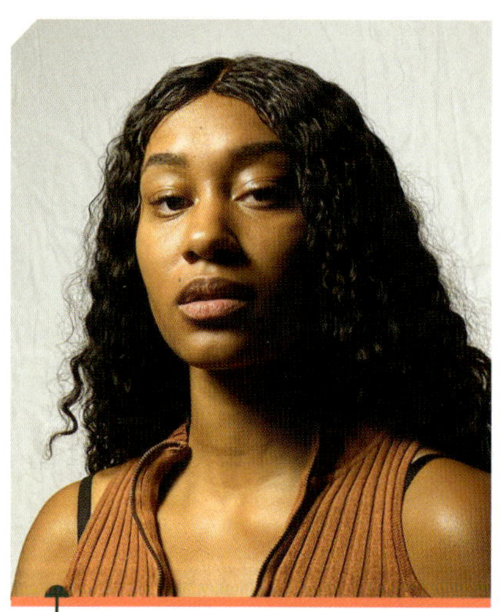

Original photograph

Fig. 1. Big shapes: continents

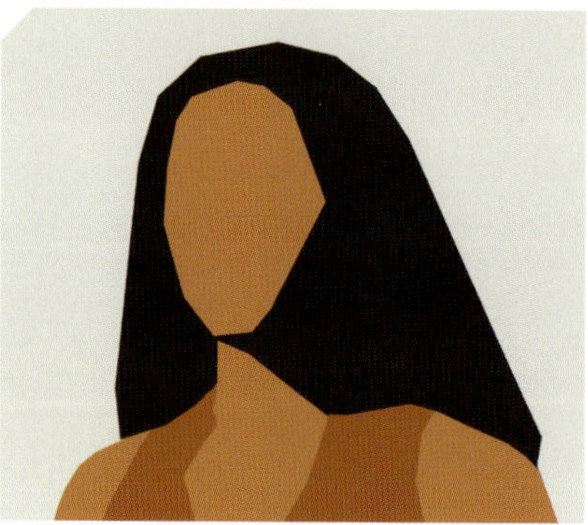

Fig. 2. Small shapes: islands

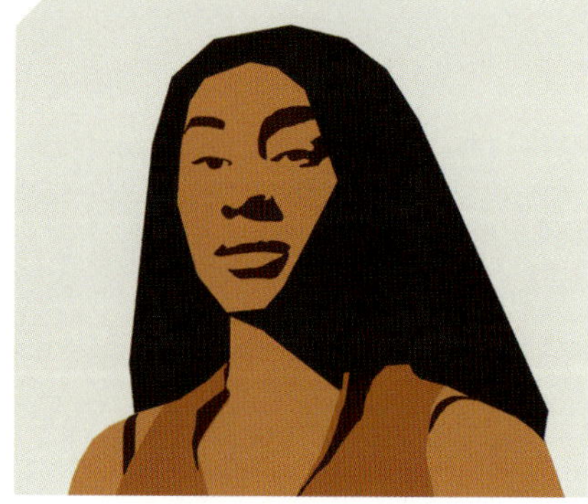

Fig. 3. Macro keystone

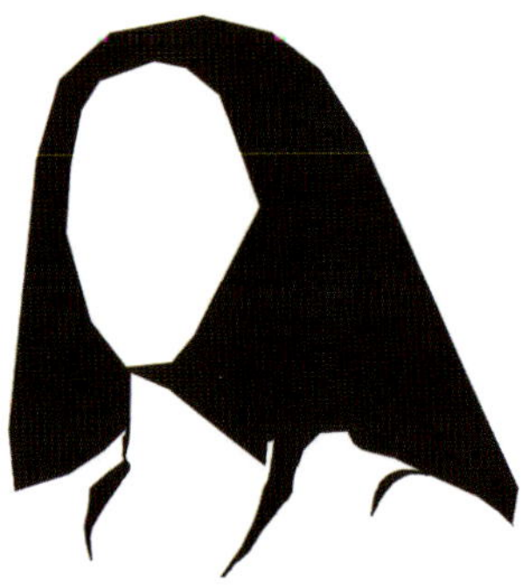

Fig. 4. Micro keystone

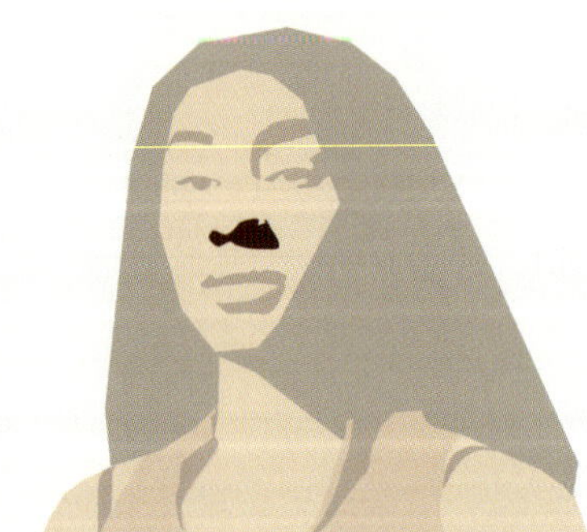

Developing a shape: Simple to complex

Observing the simplicity in a complex shape can be quite difficult if you don't have a plan. No matter how confusing or intricate a shape may be, it's important to first see it in its simplest angles. This is done by creating a blocky representation of the overall spirit of the shape. The creative decisions used to simplify shapes can be quite challenging, but in general you should seek simple angles that don't oversimplify the form beyond recognition (**Fig. 1**). The example below shows the difference between filling in a solid mass of shape (**Fig. 1**) and drawing outlines to express the edges of a shape **(Fig. 4**). Both methods work.

However how you express the shape, simplicity is important for recognizing its general slope and proportion before adding detail. When detail is added too soon, the mind is no longer sensitive to these things. It's easy to become attached to what you have drawn, meaning it's no longer as malleable.

After blocking in a big shape, you can take steps to give it more character and likeness to your subject. Instead of just using ten straight lines to describe the shape, add ten more so you have twenty descriptive lines (**Fig. 2** & **5**). This transitional step continues to give your shape structure, while allowing you to develop it in a simplified yet accurate way.

Depending upon your personal aesthetic, you may choose to leave the shapes with this intermediate look, or you may prefer to progress to a more intricate expression of shape (**Fig. 3** & **6**). If you do choose to advance to a more complex level of shape, a more curvilinear or detailed edge is typically required. The first two versions are a mere means to an end. Progressing on from straight edge and simple curves, you come to the details you likely wanted to add at the start. Now with the foundation of a blocky structural shape, you will have a base to attach your detail to.

SOLID EXPRESSION OF SHAPE

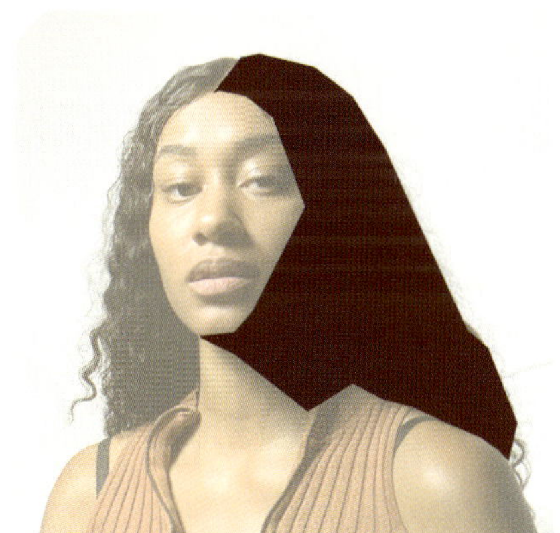

Fig. 1. Simple

Fig. 2. Intermediate

Fig. 3. Complex

LINEAR EXPRESSION OF SHAPE

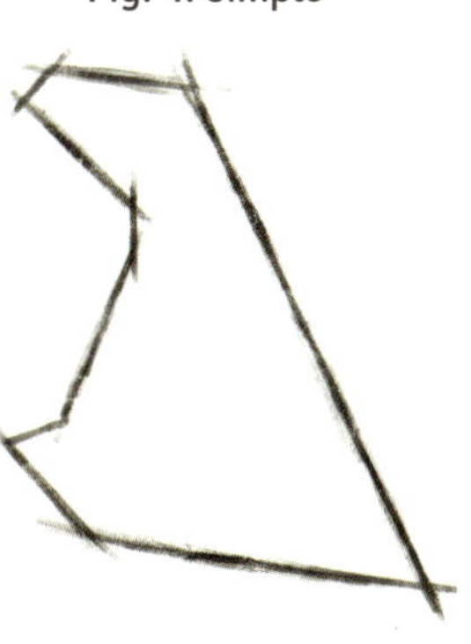

Fig. 4. Simple

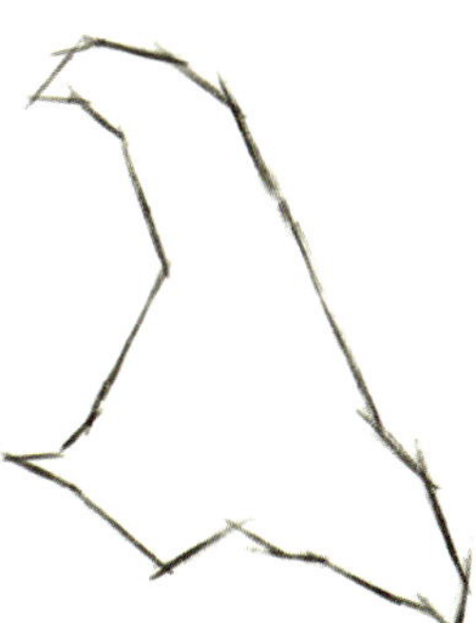

Fig. 5. Intermediate

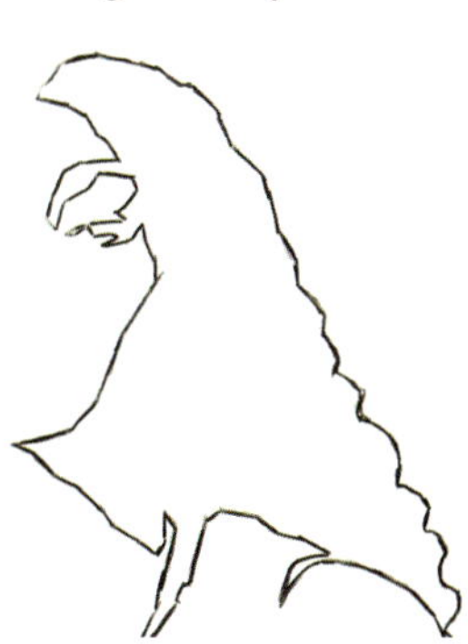

Fig. 6. Complex

Two ways of crafting shapes:

1. Outline, fill in, modify edges

Outline

Start by drawing an envelope shape, using the minimum amount of straight lines to create the overall boundaries (envelope) that the shape should have. It's important not to rush onto the next step, but to take the time to understand the basic proportions to see if this overall big abstract shape feels right.

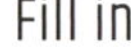

Fill in

From your simple reductive straight line block-in, add more complexity by doubling the amount of straight lines. Try to capture the true character of the shape without using curved lines. Notice how the overall envelope shape influences the trajectory of those more nuanced decisions. Fill in this shape with a flat, even tone that helps you to understand the impact of your decisions so far.

Modify edges

Continue to modify the edges of the shape, emphasizing hard edge versus soft edge and finding the true beauty of the curves that you have been itching to add from the start. In academic traditions, the edge of the shadow shape is often kept slightly darker than the inside of the shadow shape, creating a sense of control and purposefulness about exactly where the shadow ends and begins.

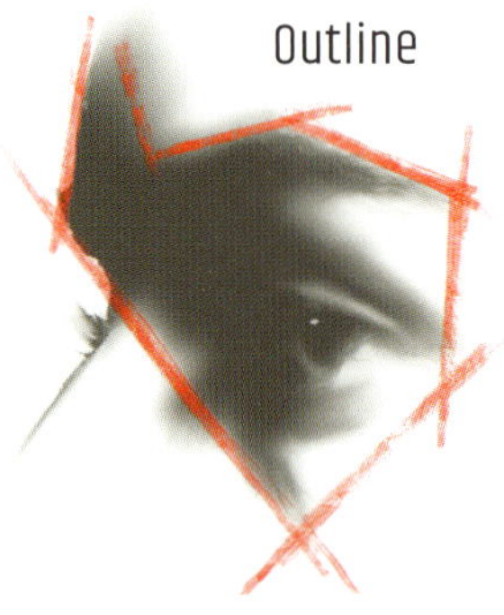

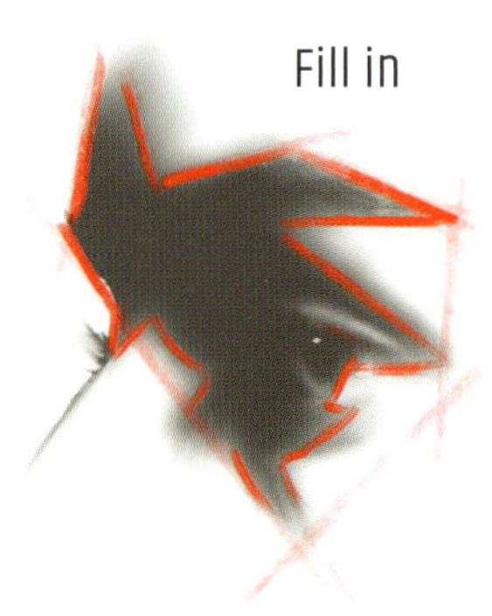

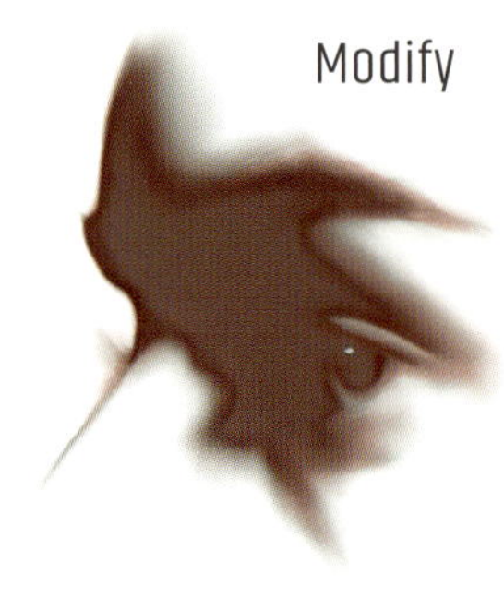

2. Mass in, nibble away, pull edges

Mass in

Mass in the overall shape without the use of lines. The emphasis should be on simplicity and the big overall shape. This is achieved particularly well by using an additive and subtractive process such as can be created when using charcoal and an eraser to build the shape. This can be messy, but it is a very direct experience and will help you to understand the give-and-take of shape design.

Nibble away

Continue to add more complexity by adding and taking away with increasing specificity. At this point the shape should look more unique, with borders resembling that of a country – something that is hard fought over and whose edges have changed over time.

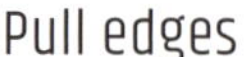

Pull edges

Finally, after this shape has been designed in a flat two-dimensional way, pull the edges of the shape in the direction of softness (described in detail in the Features section on page 48). This often means pulling from the shadow shape toward the light source, but it can also mean smudging the darker areas wherever the edges need to be softened, creating a sense of roundness and three dimensions.

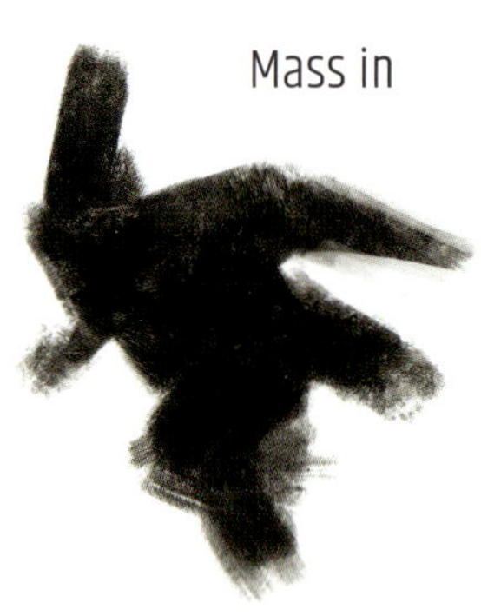

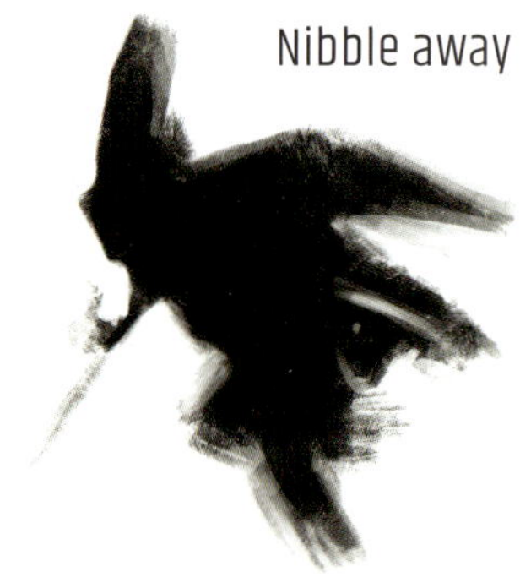

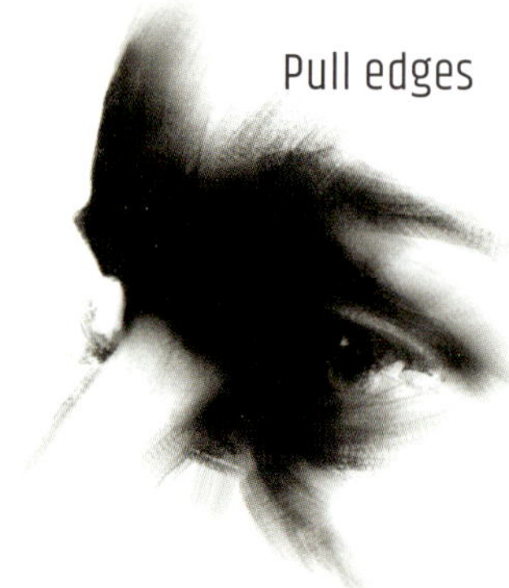

Proportion of shapes

Just because a shape has been defined and established, this doesn't mean its proportion is correct. It's very easy to simply draw a shape because it's a clear shape; however, the height and width really do matter, as these can change the character of a face, as demonstrated below. You can generally judge these shapes much more objectively than is possible when you fill the face with detailed parts, as this obscures your vision of the shapes, but you still need to take care with proportions.

After finding the simplified shapes and their proportions, you can go back in to find the details present inside of them. The overall simplicity of placing the major shapes correctly at the start should save you the frustration of realizing the details are in the wrong place later.

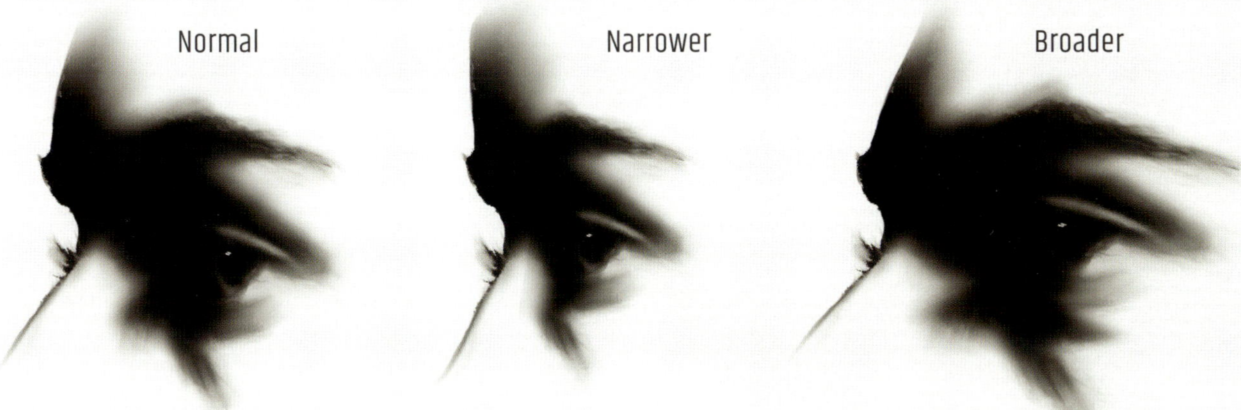

Spacing of shapes

Once a keystone shape (such as the eye socket) has been established, consider the spacing between that shape and another shape, such as the nostril. The overall proportion of the eye socket (red line) in relation to the negative space between it and the next shape (orange, green, and blue lines) is critical in order to develop a successful likeness of the nose.

It's very important to measure the spatial proportion between these shapes, as it's all too easy to create a nose that is too long or too short if you don't consider this space. This is also helpful when spacing out the nose shadow to the lips, and so on. You don't need to use equipment like calipers to measure this distance. Repeatedly studying the subject along with a lot of practice will allow you to measure with your eyes.

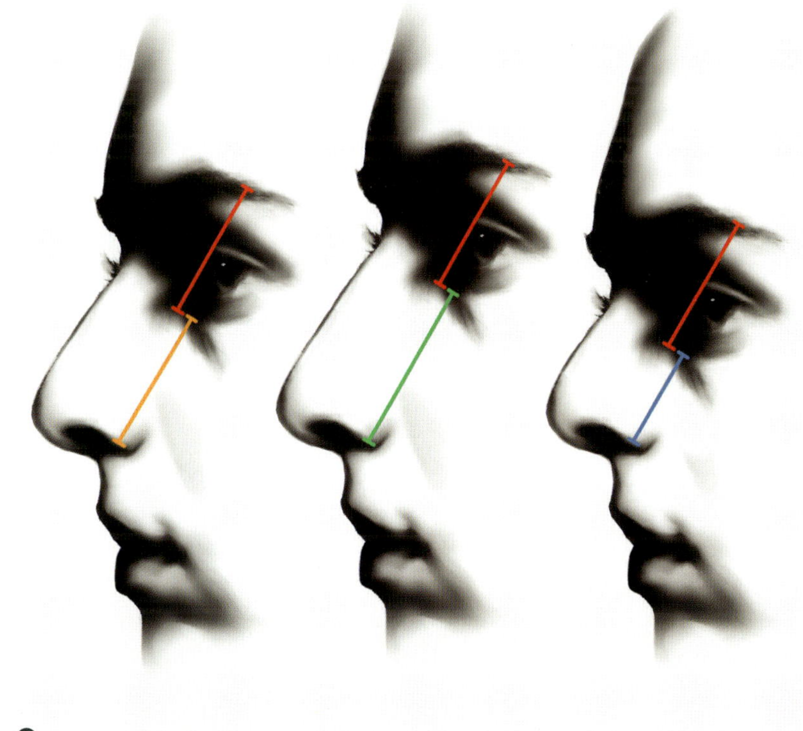

Establish the keystone shape of the eye socket, then consider the space between it and the other facial features

Edges of shapes

Creating roundness

The easiest way to turn a two-dimensional shape into a three-dimensional form is to consistently pull the interior edge of the shadow shape toward the light. Artists will know this is easier said than done, but softening this edge creates the illusion of light traveling over an object as long as there is a consistent flow from shadow to light. There is a struggle between defining the shape and softening its edge when drawing. Though it's perhaps one of the most frustrating techniques to learn, it's a necessary skill to acquire.

Interior / exterior edge

Edges are a vast topic and there is an entire chapter on them starting on page 68, but this is a good time to introduce one of the most important nuances of shape: most shapes have a soft edge to them somewhere.

A simple way to approach edges on a form is to understand that the interior edge of the shadow shape is generally softer than the exterior edge of the form. This is a rule of thumb that can help you to comprehend where soft and hard edges should be on a shape, and how that is decided by the direction of the light.

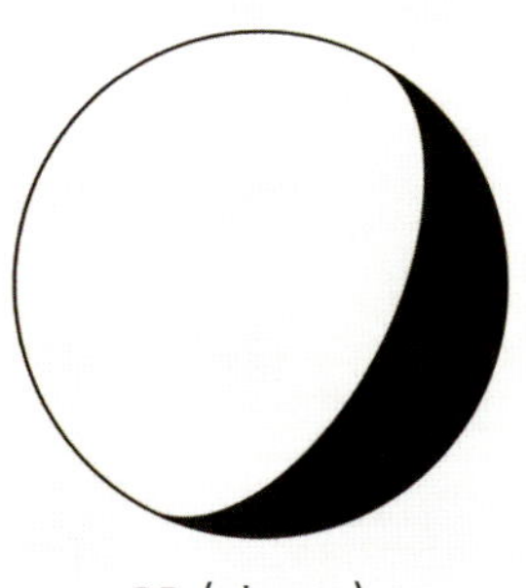

2D (shape)

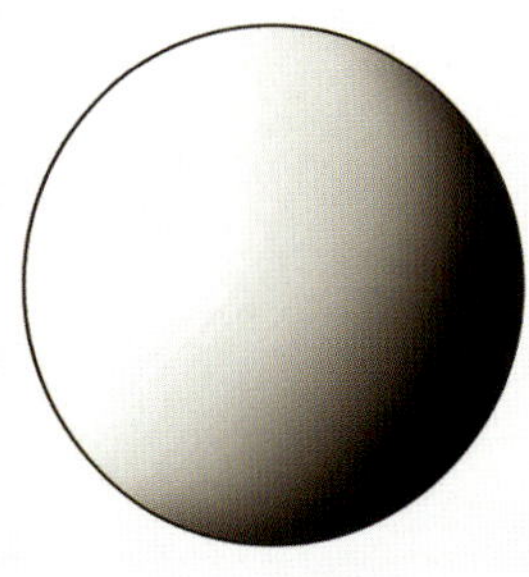

3D (form)

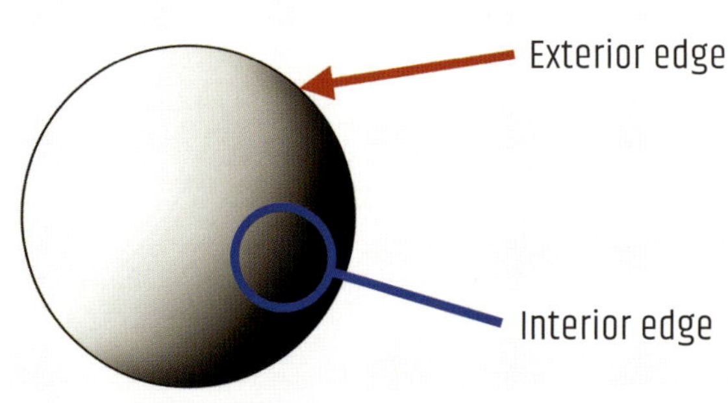

Shape, form, detail

What do you do with shapes after they have been established? This simple demonstration shows how they fit into a basic workflow from start to finish. In **Fig. 1**, details such as the nostrils have been ignored so that proportion and character of the shape can be established first. **Fig. 2** shows how form is rendered out from this base sketch, followed by **Fig. 3**, which shows how the details can fit into a solid foundation that has character and three dimensions.

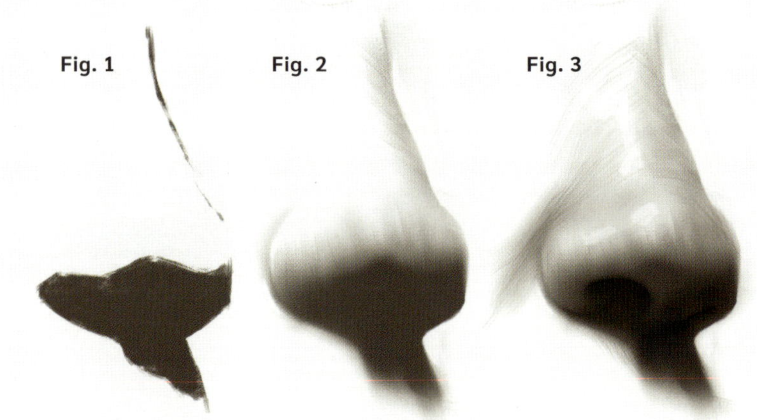

Sharp and soft boundaries

A significant portion of drawing is about the placement of sharp and soft boundaries. In portraiture, soft boundaries include the hairline, jawline, and the information surrounding the clavicles. These are difficult areas to define and it's easy to make them too hard or over-modeled with sharpness. Conversely, soft boundaries are much harder to develop with character than sharp boundaries.

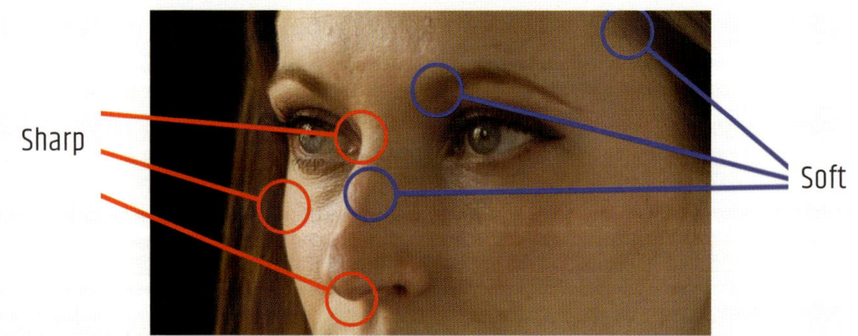

Seeing shapes when there is no strong shadow

It's easy to see shapes when the lighting situation is dramatic, as in a Rembrandt or Caravaggio painting; however, you will also encounter soft light situations in which the shapes are not so apparent (**Fig. 1**). It's still important to be able to discern the big shapes, even when there aren't many of them or when they don't appear obvious. Considering the big shapes first will help with blocking in and understanding the continents, which can make a difficult drawing situation a little easier.

This involves visually taking away the detail that seems so very important initially (**Fig. 2** & **3**). Plugging up the holes and the details of the features to observe the foundation of values and shapes they sit upon will help with the rendering and the placement of these details when you reach that stage. In this way, you place the details into a better designed shape, which takes some frustration out of rendering them.

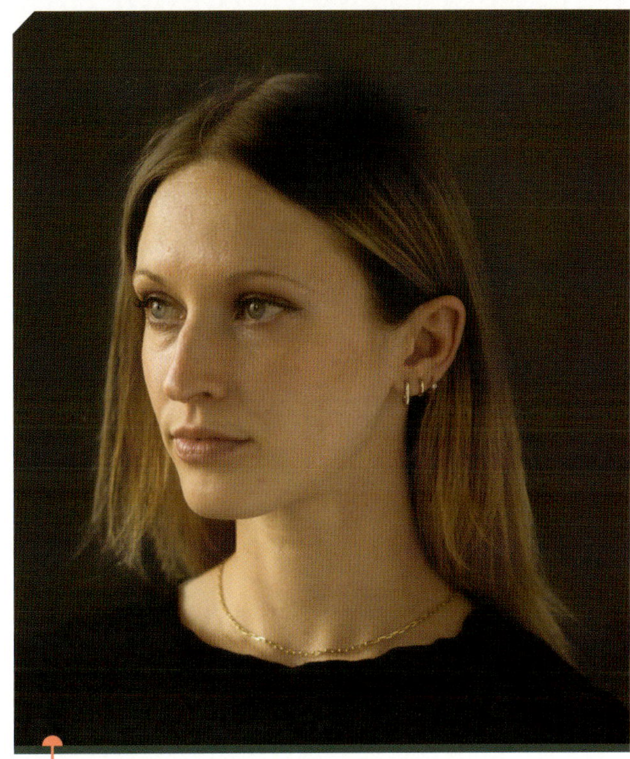

Original photograph

Fig. 1. Soft lighting can make it trickier to observe the shapes in a face

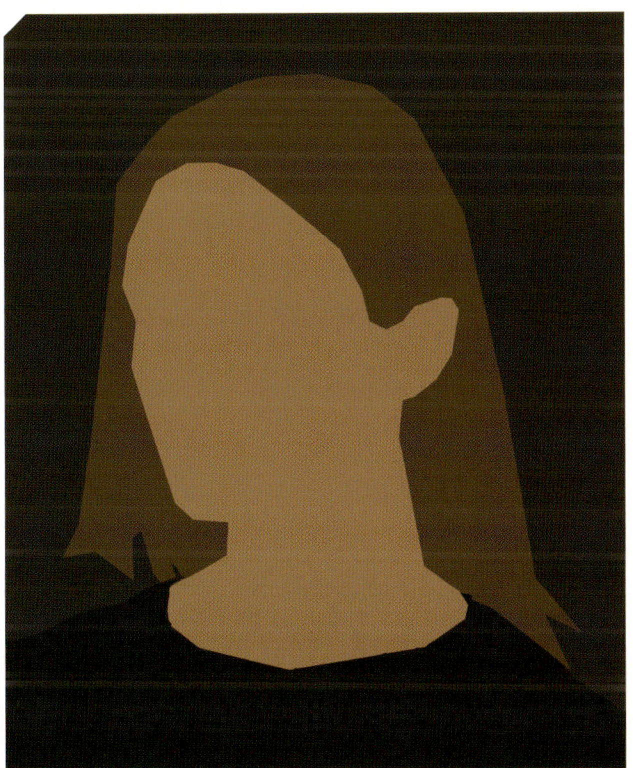

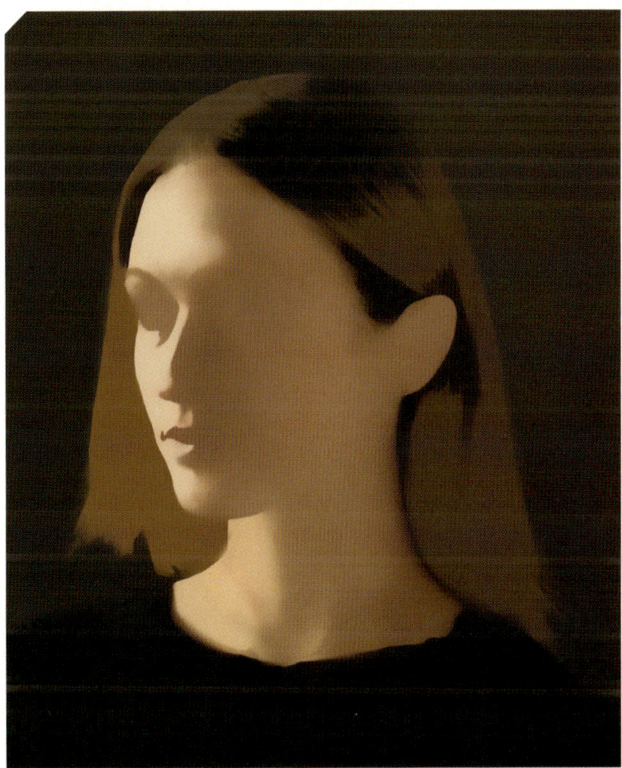

Fig. 2 & 3. Start by removing the detail to discern the big shapes, or continents

Putting it together:

Shape start demo – shape and pull

The following demonstration will cover a shape start block-in. "Blocking in" is simply roughing in the portrait using straight lines. This technique works best with charcoal, oil paint, and digital media. While it can also work with other media, such as graphite or watercolor, these don't move as well on the page, meaning it could be more tedious.

The main concept of this demo is to establish relationships in the core part of the face, working out to the periphery, using a technique called "directional softness" or "pulling." This is an especially helpful way of learning how to block in a portrait, as it can help you to overcome the fear of starting by forcing you to attack the features and deal with them right away. Slowly you fade out into the surrounding areas, measuring and basing your decisions off of this central core.

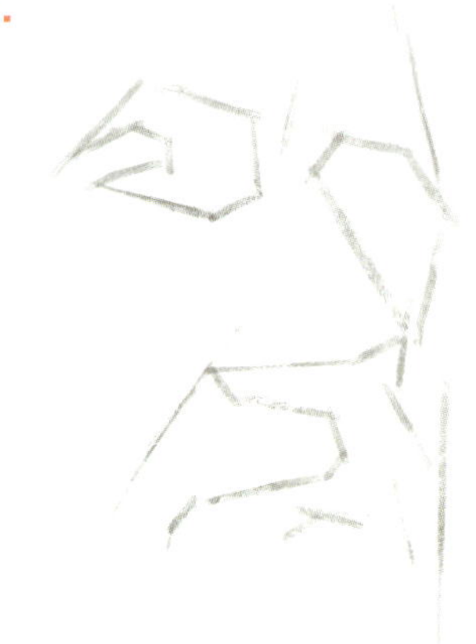

1. Linear expression of shape

Even though this is a shape start technique, it's still helpful to map out where the strong shadow shapes will be using lines. Use straight lines and try to simplify the shapes into basic, blocky angles.

2.

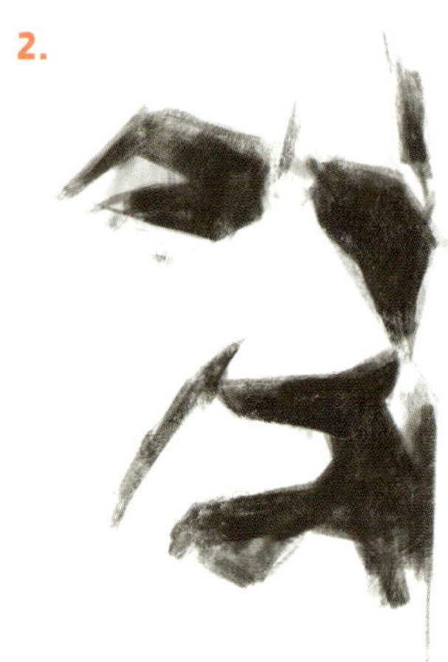

2. Massing in

Next, mass in the shape with solid tone, trying to make clear binary decisions between light and shadow. It's either in the light or it's in shadow; there is no in between at this stage. This will help you to draw with graphic 2D clarity and create a strong statement before you begin softening and adding nuance. Don't be shy about these binary decisions. Later on in the process, when the drawing gets softer, it will be helpful to reestablish this graphic shape.

3.

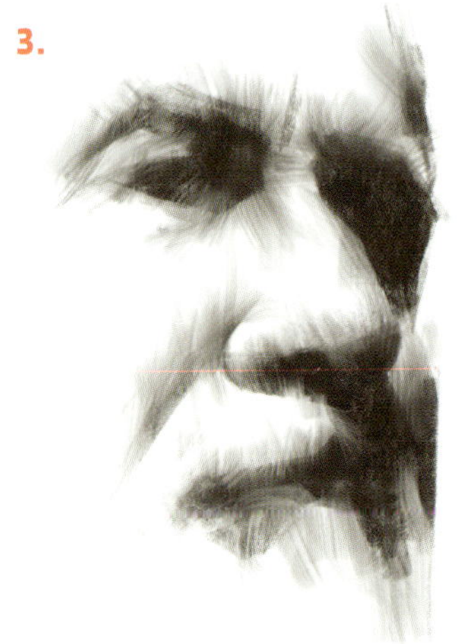

3. Pulling edges of shapes

Begin to pull from the edges of the shape in the direction of the light, but also wherever the edges soften on the subject. You may find it helpful to pull from the light into the shadow to lighten up shadows that were too dark.

4.

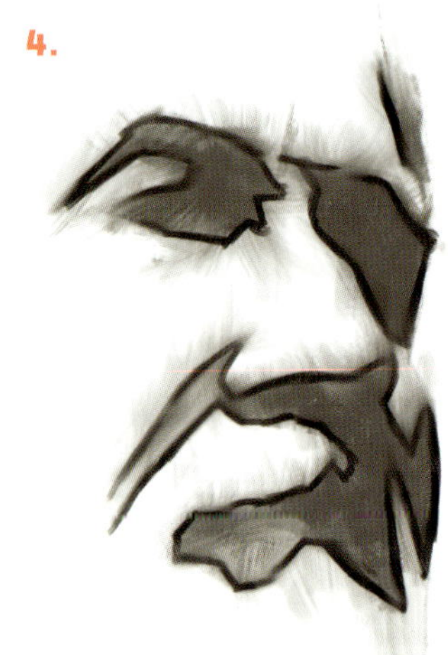

4. Reestablishing edges of shape

Start reestablishing the shapes by sketching in details, expanding into the peripheral area. This will create a soft bloom from that central core area, which by now you should feel confident about.

5. Soft bloom

Once you feel the core structure is sound, start blooming out to the peripheral edges and building out the portrait. This can sometimes be left a little vague in case you decide to vignette the portrait and not fully render the background. There is still a focus on shapes in their proportions, but it is a little less bold than at the start.

6. Texture and mark-making

After the intense focus of drawing out the core features and mapping out the major forms, create a little texture and mark-making in the background to loosen it up again and clear your mind.

7. Finishing

Numerous steps go into finishing a portrait, more than could ever be fully conveyed here. However, one of your main goals should be trying to balance out the rendering of detail without sacrificing the major shapes and their visual impact. It's very easy to lose the overall visual impact of the shapes by adding too many details that reduce their power.

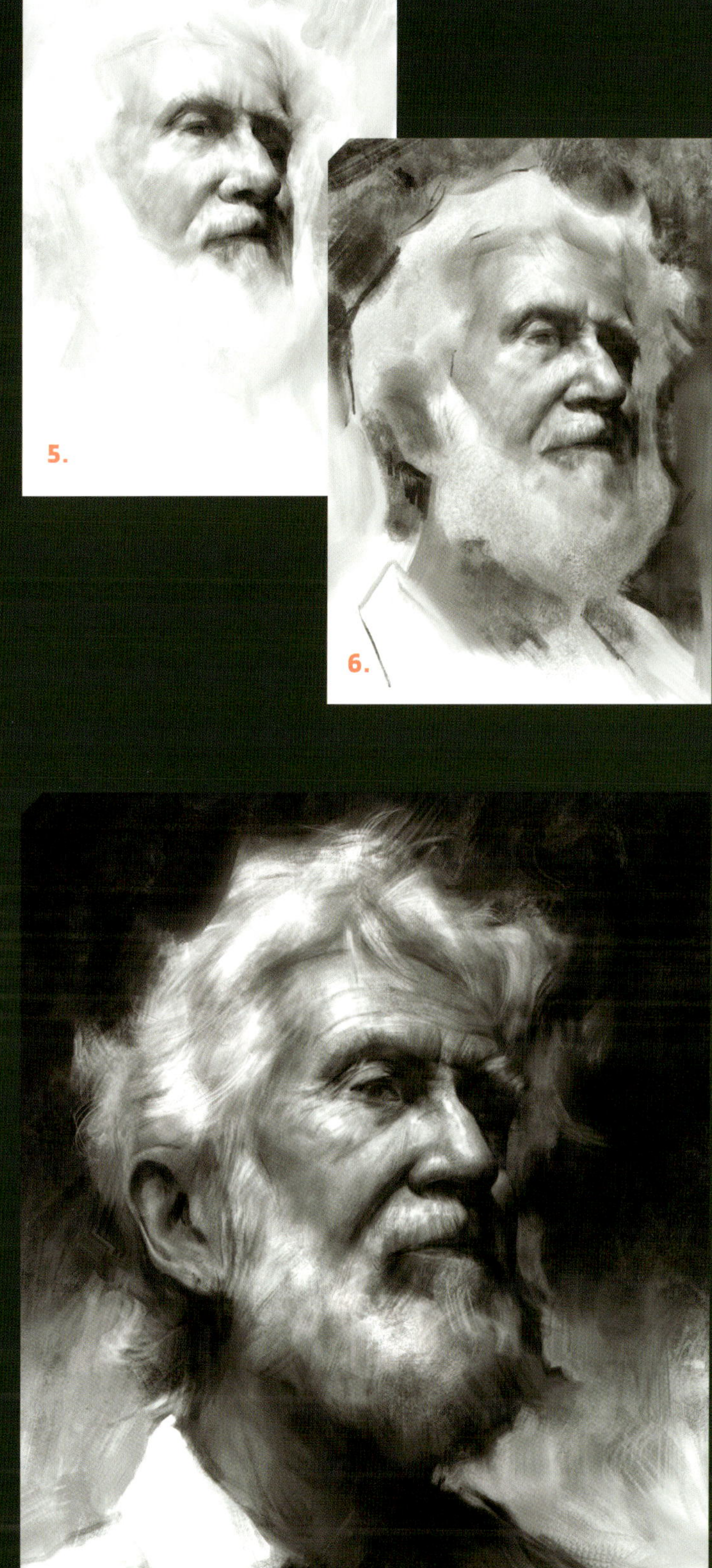

Final portrait

Practice

1. Create a portrait by blocking in the major shapes of the head in a two-dimensional way. This means not softening or modeling any aspects, but instead designing the shapes in an additive and subtractive manner. Do this for as long as possible, creating a strong foundation and simple statement of the head.

2. Next, pull or soften the edges of the shapes where necessary, considering where the light source is coming from.

3. Repeat step 1 to restate the character of the edges of your shapes in a 2D way.

4. Finally, pull or soften the edges again, creating even more range between the hard and soft edges. Continue to modify and make your shape stronger and more specific, ensuring your edges having increasingly more variety.

Drawing: Line

Linear structure concepts for drawing the head

It's now time to focus on how to construct a face using line. While most painters respond to shape concepts, many draftspeople prefer a linear approach to drawing. The linear aspects of drawing are often regarded as the more difficult concepts to grasp, master, and integrate into your process. They offer more of a constructivist approach, rather than a perceptual approach, requiring you to think like an architect as you build a face, instead of looking at a face then copying its shapes. This understanding of line in a constructivist approach leads to a more confident and sound structure of the head.

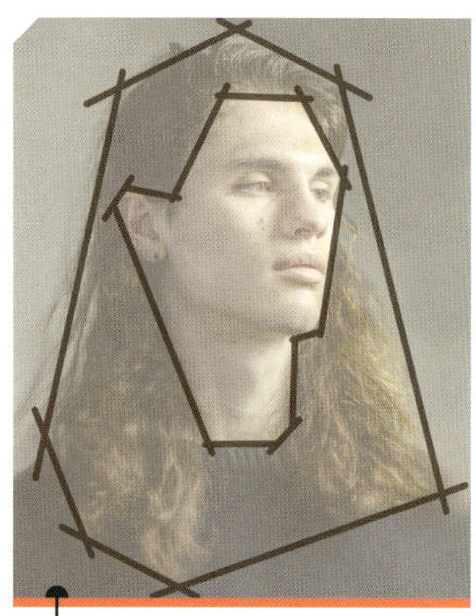

Use straight lines to roughly outline the main form of the head to create the envelope shape

Envelope shape(s)

Perhaps no other way of drawing feels as simultaneously loose and structured as finding the big linear "envelope" shape of a complex form. You can start by measuring, however, some artists struggle under the stress of measuring too much, too soon, and it can leave your drawing feeling rather stiff. Starting with an envelope shape can solve this problem.

The envelope shape is the simplest outlining of the major forms that creates an envelope (or container) that encloses them in a series of straight lines. You may choose to sketch in the envelope before measuring, so there is something there to start comparing and judging.

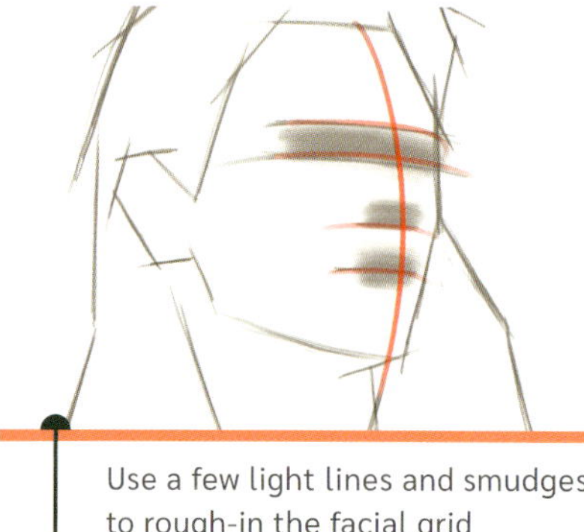

Use a few light lines and smudges to rough-in the facial grid

Rough-in with grid

After framing the main envelope shape, rough in the facial grid with a few light lines and soft smudges at the eye sockets, base of the nose, and muzzle. This will establish a working armature to hang your drawing on. You can always modify this slightly later, but a good rough-in will set your drawing on the right course. It's easy to rush past this stage to get onto the "fun" parts, but it pays to practice how to do it right, as it will give you more confidence in building a head.

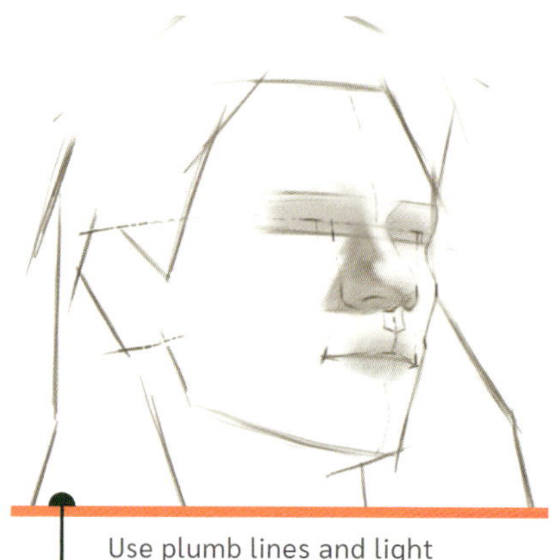

Use plumb lines and light sketching to build visual connections between the nose and other facial features

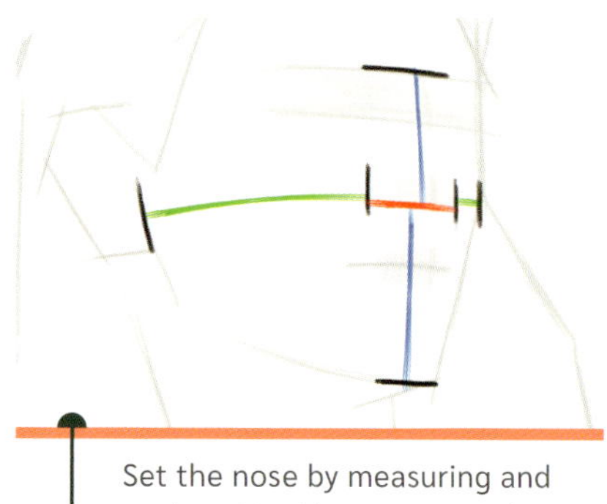

Set the nose by measuring and paying attention to proportion

Setting the nose

After the armature has been lightly roughed in, it's important to set the nose. Setting it too high will result in an oversized muzzle and chin, while setting it too far to the left will make the face appear "frontalized." It's therefore crucial to understand span proportion for this step (see page 24). Learning how to measure may at first seem painful and frustrating, but with time it will become second nature and eventually you will start to measure with your eyes.

Building out

The nose is the keystone of the face. Once it has been set, it makes sense to build relationships to the other features using plumb lines and sketching light angles to make visual connections between important spots. For example, it's easy to create a relationship between the lateral edge of the nose and a point in the eye above, like a tear duct, or the lateral edge of the nose with the corner of the mouth. All of these points and their connections start to form a network of lines that establish structural harmony between the features.

Cross-checking your spots

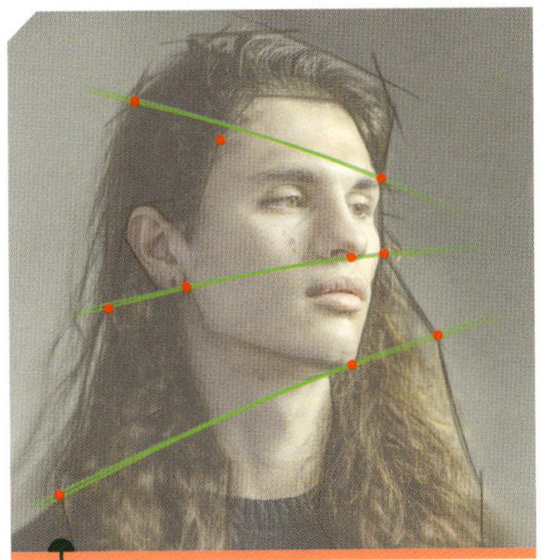

Rhythm angles help to ensure your envelope shape is structurally sound, forming connections and alignments between points across the head

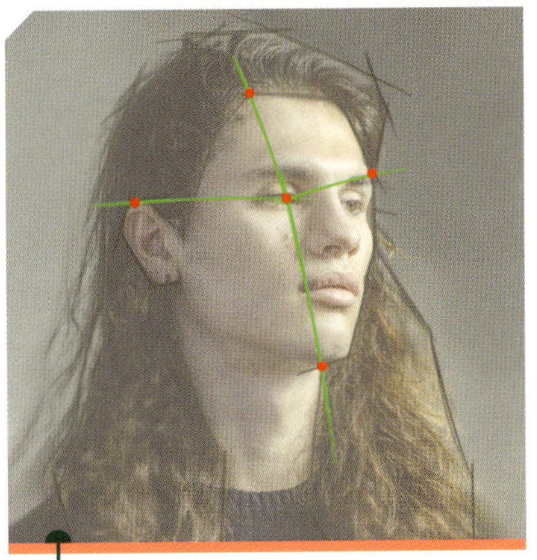

Triangulation is an intuitive way of measuring a structurally sound head

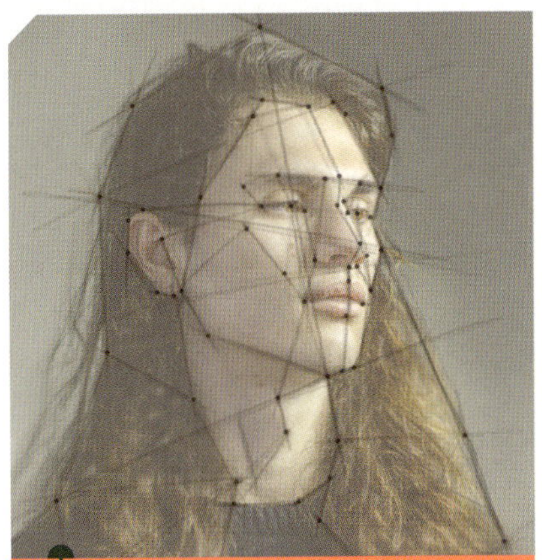

A triangulation web creates a network of relationships to lock in the location of different points around the head

Rhythm angles

This diagram illustrates how seemingly disconnected points of the envelope shape can create associations that help points to align. It's easy to draw the silhouette or contour of a form and never think about how it relates to another point on the head. Rhythm angles are a great cross-check to ensure you're not just drawing the silhouette, but are making sure it's structurally sound in relation to the other points across the head.

Starting from a point in the left contour, observe then draw across to a point on the right contour, and check if there are any other points that can be found along that line. Sometimes you will find two or three spots, while at other times it may be a little off, as seen with the line across the forehead. At the very least it provides you with a reference point.

Triangulation

Triangulation is one of the most effective tools for creating a structurally sound head that isn't as mechanical as using the span proportion technique of measuring. It's quite fluid and helps you to associate multiple points, or "triangulate," to find a point's location. In this diagram, study how green lines are drawn out from the eye to other points, and notice their angles.

The more points you can draw a line to, the more accurate the placement and relationship between them will be. This may be the poor man's measuring tool, but it is a more intuitive way of measuring.

Triangulation web

Triangulation taken to the extreme can create a web, or network, of relationships that force you to lock in the location of the various points. As long as the angle and the distance is somewhat correct at first, as you add more points with adjoining angles you will begin to self-correct any mistakes you may have started with. You can draw this in, or you may prefer to mentally visualize these points before you put pencil to paper. This will help you to ensure all of the features and points interlock and create a structural integrity that is hard to achieve in any other mechanical way.

Practice drawing this way by drawing points on a photo then connecting the dots. Eventually it will become part of your base of knowledge and you will be able to draw traditionally without making these marks on the page.

Practice triangulation

Try drawing a head by focusing on these spots, or landmarks, exploring how they connect with lines rather than concentrating on drawing the features. This will cause you to think about their alignment and relationship, rather than simply letting them land somewhere. Let go of your notion of what a portrait drawing should start out as and focus instead on creating this web of interconnecting spots. Draw with an ease and a flow from your arm, rather than your wrist.

Structural symmetry

Facial grid plumb lines

Drawing with a focus on structural symmetry involves drawing in an abstract way where the focus is on making marks in the right places, in alignment with each other. This is achieved through a series of concepts, which will be discussed in this section, each providing a unique lens through which to view the face. These concepts initially act as structural ways to sketch the head, and later as diagnostic tests to ensure the portrait is working correctly. You may choose not to use every one of them all of the time, but it can be helpful to use them all at some point in the process, as the drawing situation calls for it.

These are strange and difficult concepts for the beginner to accept and utilize, as they require you to ignore rendering the features in a recognizable way in order to first place them correctly, which can initially feel counter-intuitive. It's actually a hindrance to draw in the features from the beginning, as there is a ninety-nine percent chance you will draw them in the wrong places. These abstract concepts are designed to save you the trouble and heartache of later needing to move a beautifully rendered feature on finding you have misplaced it.

There are three key points to keep in mind when implementing these ideas in your work:

1. You must have a light enough touch to ensure you aren't creating marks that you won't be able to be erase or integrate later.

2. It requires a mental shift from what is recognizable about a face, to an architect's blueprint of a face, and where those features will go before they are developed.

3. It requires you to consider the head as a three-dimensional object on which you are mapping out the forms to align symmetrically in a structural way that acknowledges a center line and/or plumb lines.

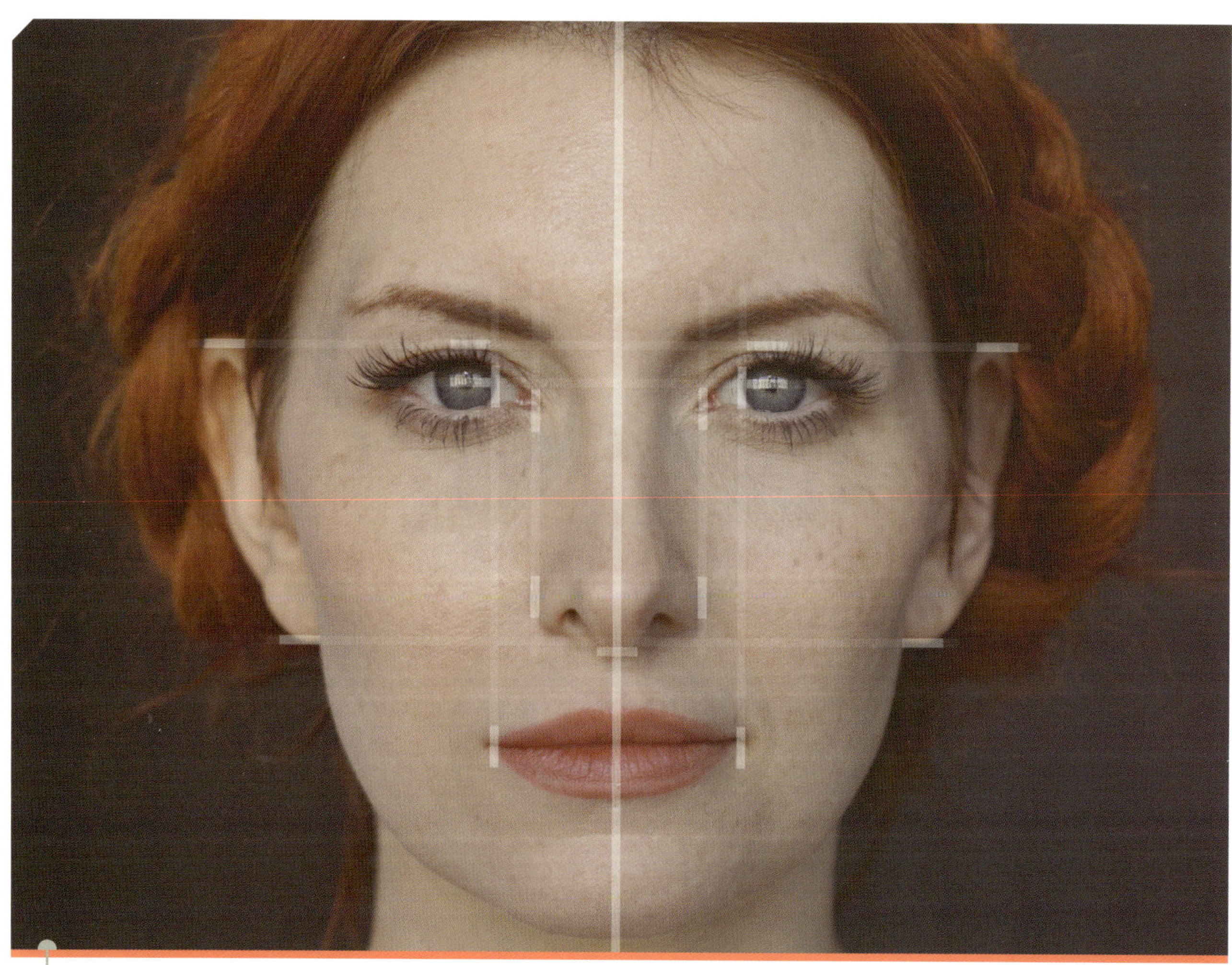

Structural symmetry allows you to make accurate aligned marks to map out the face

Simple linear structure

Spirit of the center

The spirit of the center is defined as a gentle curved line, starting at the anatomical center of where the forehead meets the hairline and reaching all the way down to pass through the center of the chin. It is a line that helps to define the y-axis of the head, providing a general idea of bisecting the sphere of the head. This line does not necessarily start at the hair parting, and the gentle curve that emanates from these two points can change slightly, depending on the model's features. For example, is the nose flatter, or does it protrude more from the skull? Every face is different. Also, it is worth noting that this concept is different to the center ribbon described on the next page.

Facial armature

The facial armature continues to build upon this idea, but with the addition of horizontal lines that generally intersect this center line perpendicularly. Even though you may not see perfect symmetry in the head, it's helpful to establish this armature as a way of relating the features and ensuring they fall along a structure. Drawing these in the right location matters less at the start of a drawing, but you should aim to establish a good general angle to them and make sure they are all parallel. Sometimes you may wish to capture a head in extreme perspective and these lines can start to converge, but generally this is overthinking things and can lead to a distorted face.

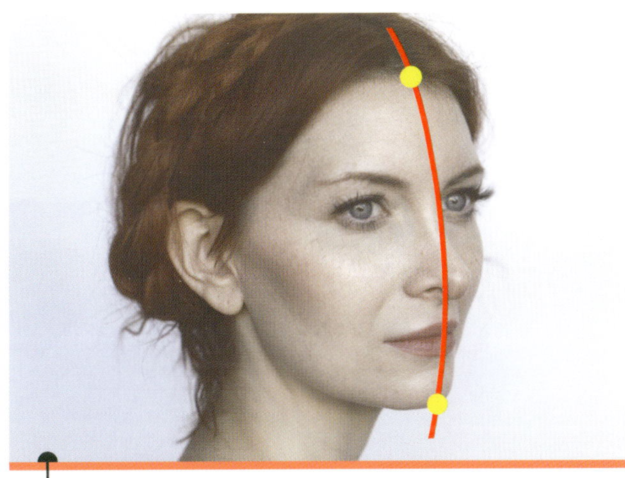

The spirit of the center is a gently curved line that passes from the anatomical center of the forehead to the center of the chin

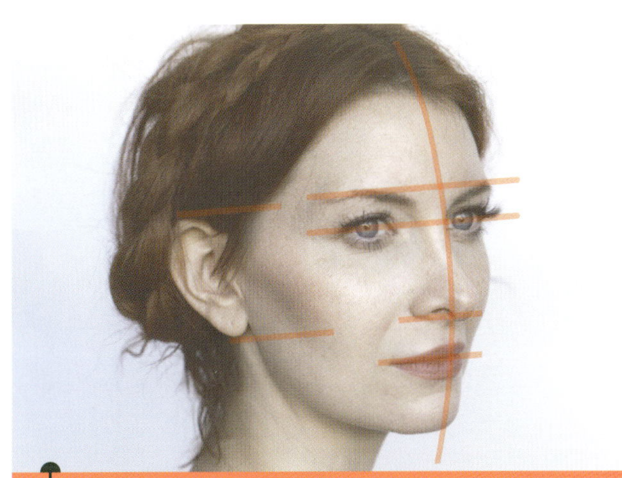

Establish the armature, ensuring the lines have a good angle and run parallel to one another

Plumb lines

A plumb line is a perfectly vertical or horizontal line, and is one of the best alignment tools at your disposal. Relating the points of the features to points of other features with the use of plumb lines is one of the easiest structural concepts to understand and implement in your portraits. There is always something wrong, structurally speaking, with any drawing, and the simple use of this concept can be illuminating as an abstract principle to help improve it.

The more abstract concepts you can use to draw a portrait, the more likely you will be to capture the likeness of your subject. If you distance yourself from the personality of the model and block in the head using the abstract principles discussed on these pages, you will find yourself able to achieve a much closer likeness than if you only focus in on the details of your subject's face.

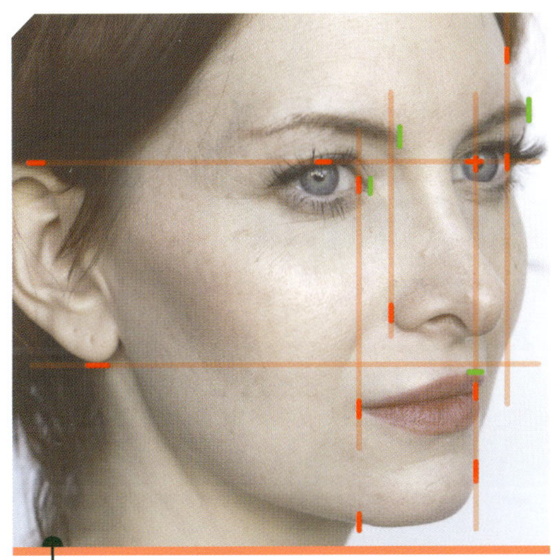

Plumb lines are straight vertical or horizontal lines that can be used to help structurally align your portrait

3/4 structural symmetry

Architectonic structure

2D artists can sometimes struggle with understanding 3D structure. This becomes especially apparent when drawing a three-quarter view of the head. You observe the features, measure the proportions, and find the shapes, but sometimes it still may not look right. This is often because it's a structural problem.

The head needs a center line from which two symmetrical halves are born, and architectonic structuring is an excellent way to figure this out. The definition of architectonic means "having structure." This image illustrates this idea applied on a face. Using architectonic lines and shapes in order to understand the structural symmetry of the head brings order and understanding to the difficult task of thinking about the head in a three-dimensional way. Of course, most people are not perfectly symmetrical, but if you construct the head symmetrically and then bring out the model's character and uniqueness on that symmetrical armature, you will stand a much better chance of success.

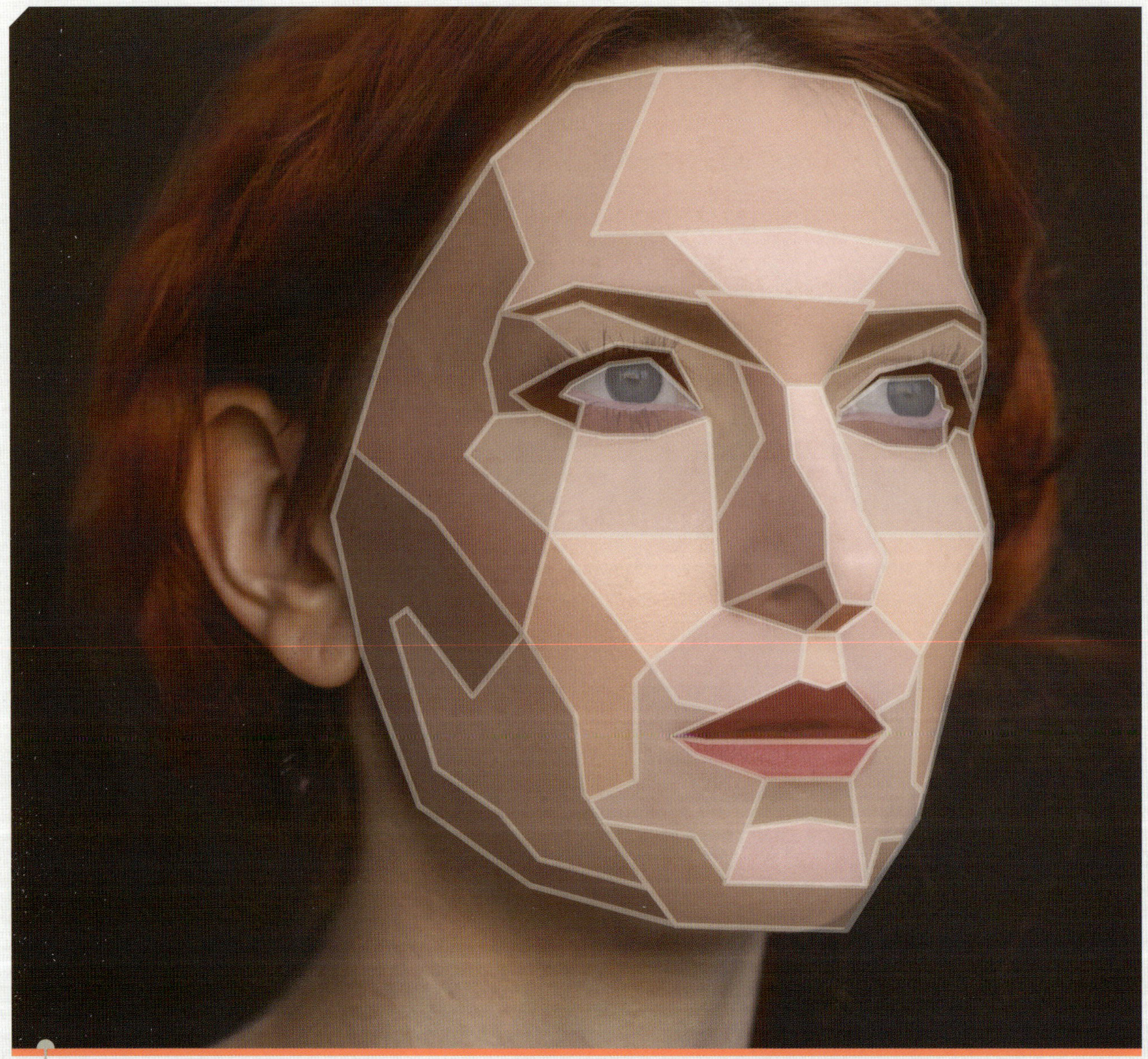

Architectonic structure applied to the face to aid understanding the face as a three-dimensional form

Architectonic linear structure

Center ribbon with landmarks

The center ribbon idea encourages you to think structurally from the center out. It's easy to simply draw a nose, two eyes, and a mouth, and hope they will line up, but most of the time they won't unless you consider the points along the center line that create a strong sense of structure and relationship between the core features. You don't always need to draw this line in if you embed the concept in your brain as you draw the features, or check your drawing for errors. A good way to understand this is to draw on top of a photo to see if you can find these hidden structural lines. It can seem foolish to draw something in that is invisible, but it will help grow your understanding of the three-dimensional head.

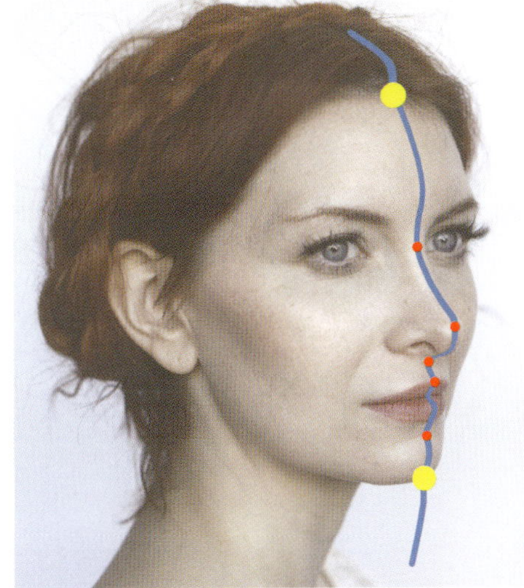

Drawing a center ribbon with landmarks marked as points along it can help to establish the structure

Symmetry with the front plane

This center image shows the relationship between the center ribbon and structural symmetry between the two halves of the front plane of the face. This helps you to conceive of the symmetry of the face in a three-quarter view, which is the hardest view to draw. It's easy to simply draw in the right side contour and hope it works, but it's a much better plan to understand its relationship to the other side of the face. It can be difficult to ascertain the exact points in which all of this aligns on the face, but if you are at least asking the question, or using this as a drawing check, you are much more likely to end up with a solid and correct structure.

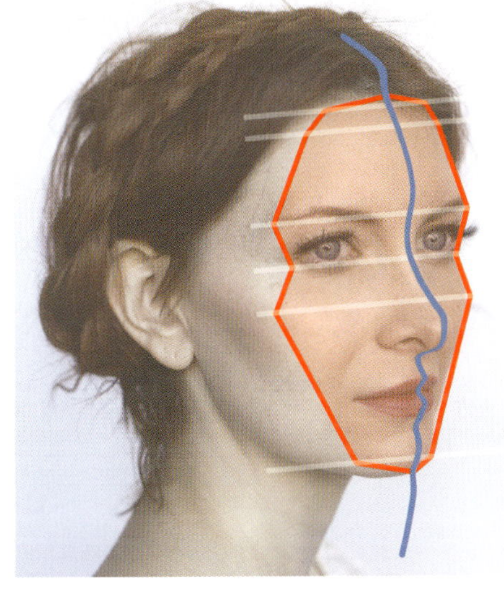

Drawing the center ribbon, along with structural symmetry between the two halves of the front plane of the face, can help with accurately capturing a portrait in three-quarter view

Symmetry with the central core

This image shows how the center ribbon sets into motion the idea of structural symmetry from the center out, in an architectonic way. Notice how these points of symmetry (red dots) line up on the grid of the face (white lines).

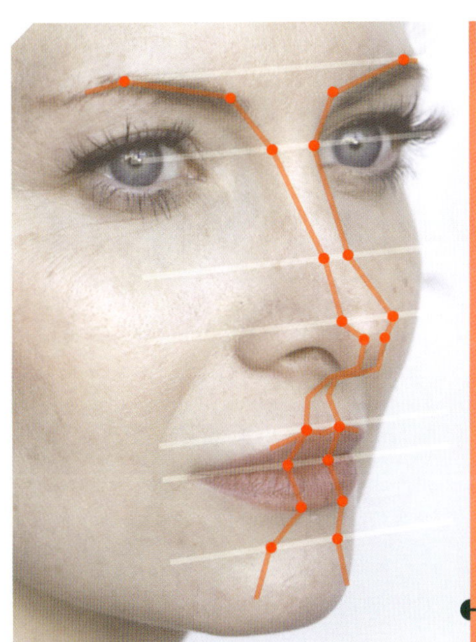

The center ribbon can be used to create structural symmetry outward from the center

Putting it together

Linear start demo: line and brush

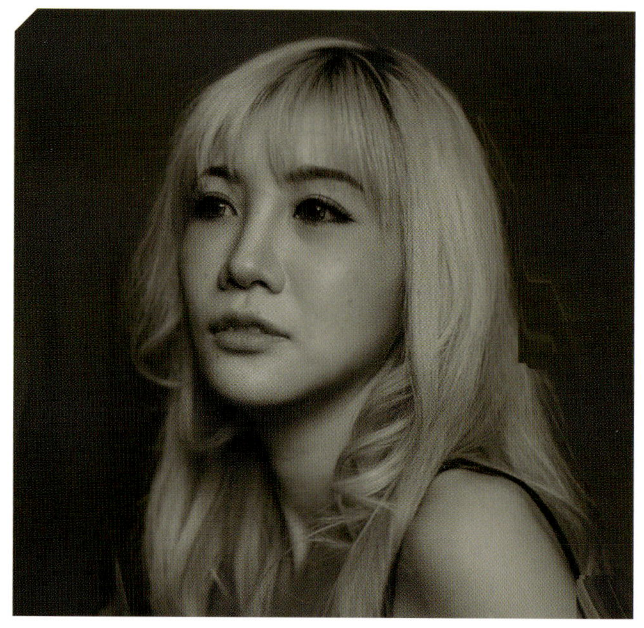

Original photograph

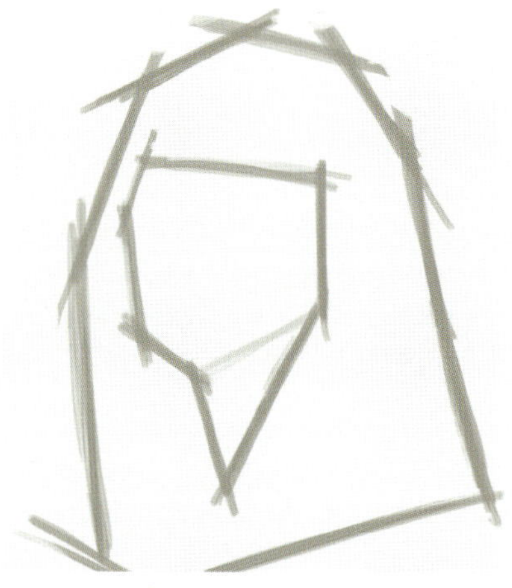

1. Envelope shape

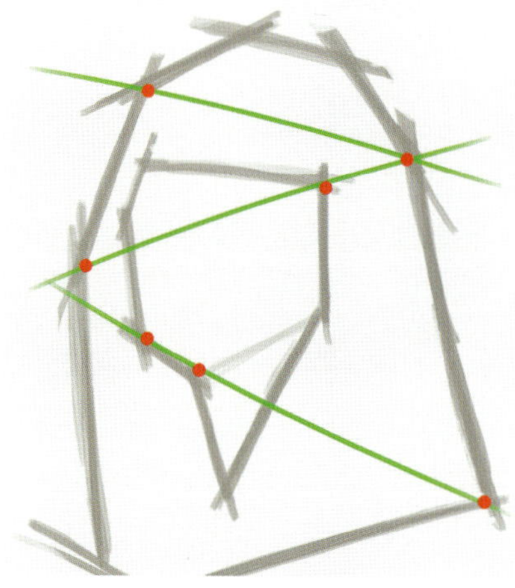

2. Rhythm angles

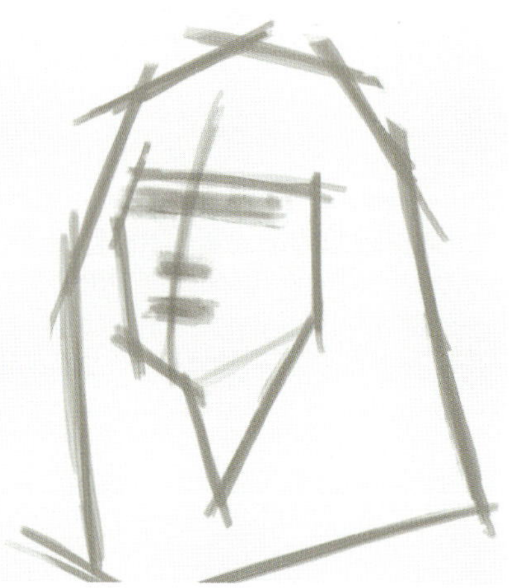

3. Facial armature

1. Envelope shape

Start by using simple lines to frame the big outer shapes. Try to limit the amount of lines used to ensure you are only capturing the biggest forms. Challenge yourself to use around fifteen lines in total to describe the envelope shapes, otherwise you risk moving onto another more detailed phase. It will serve you well to start simply, working on the accuracy of the inclination of the angles and the overall spacing of the big forms. It may be helpful to sketch first and then measure your proportions later, as too much measuring too soon can lead to a stiff drawing.

2. Rhythm angles

Check the accuracy of your envelope shapes by sketching the cross-checks of rhythm angles. See if you can visually connect a few dots along one of these lines on your reference material to help you, then find these same lines on your drawing. You only need a couple of these lines, so choose them wisely to ensure you strike through multiple landmarks in one stroke.

3. Facial armature

Lay out the beginnings of the facial armature. No matter where you are in a portrait, you can refer back to this as it becomes more complicated. Understand where the center line is and indicate the brow, nose, mouth, and the side plane as important touchstones to hit. Remember that you're not drawing in the features right now, but rather placing lines that will offer structure for where they begin and end, maintaining continuity.

throughout the face.

4 & 5. Setting the nose

The next step is to set the nose, which first involves understanding the relationship of the nose to the box of the face. The box is the height and width of the extreme edges of the face. Check the proportion of the box, then measure two points on the nose (x- and y-axis) so you can place the nose correctly in the box.

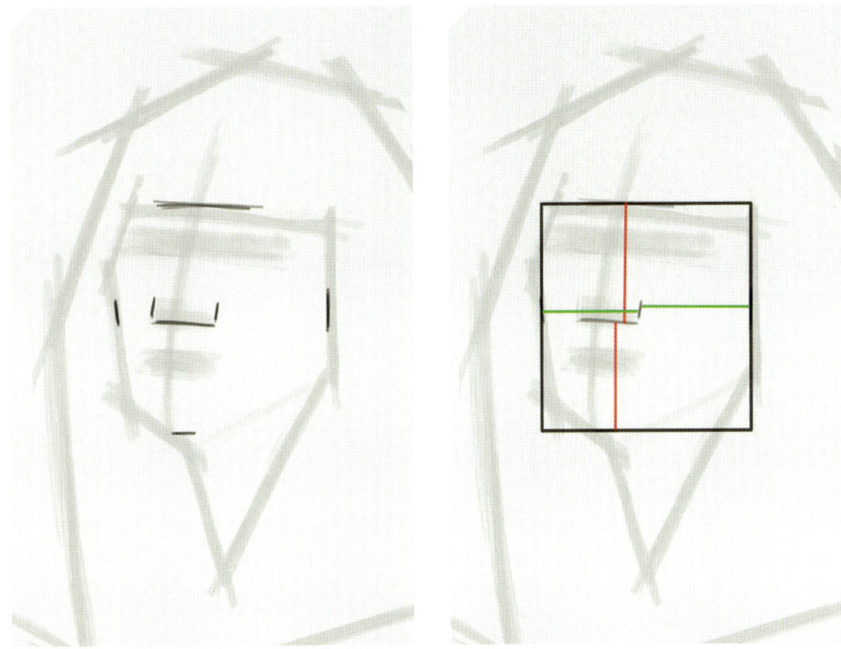

4 & 5. Setting the nose

6. Triangulation

Once the width of the nose is set, start building relationships with triangulation lines to the other features surrounding the nose. The nose is the keystone of the face, and as at this stage in the process you can start committing, the nose is the natural choice that allows you to easily build the face from the inside out.

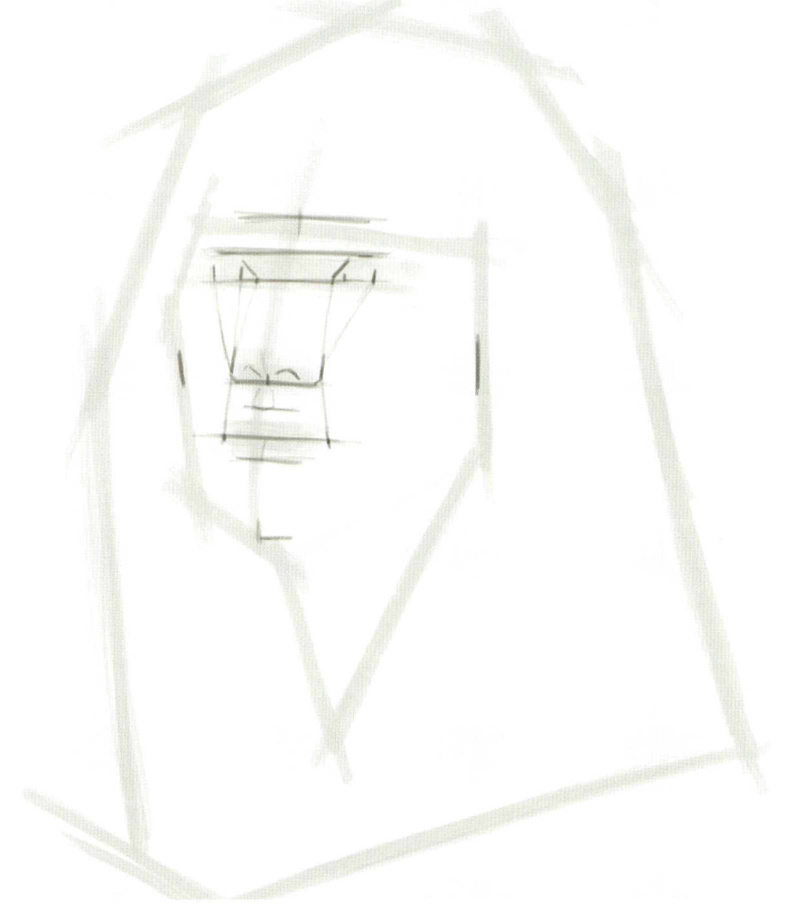

6. Triangulation

7. Building the core

After this technical start, begin to use a brush or stump to softly lay in the first pass of shadow, starting to make it more solid and recognizable.

8. Ghosting/brushing

Ghost out the initial decisions you have made using a rag or another blurring tool. This will fade your linear start a little, before you refine it again. This overall softening leads to a much more poetic expression of the face, but with your facial armature and technical start, you should have much more confidence about where these features will be. Explore different softening tools such as a brush, stump, paper towel, or your finger. Whatever your choice of tool, you should aim to become as adept with it as you are with the pencil. Learning how to soften and erase in the right way will become as important as drawing.

9. Triangulation with highlights

When tone has been built up by ghosting out and redefining the drawing in a repeated cycle, it's time to use an eraser to create highlights. Try to use the concept of triangulation in order to conduct another cross-check of your drawing process. The more concepts you can apply to your drawing, the more likely it is to be accurate.

10 & 11. Brushing in tone/ relining edges

This stage onward is largely focused on brushing in tone, softly building up the form and definition of your subject while balancing it out by continuing to restate the edges of your forms by relining them. This cycle continues until you are satisfied with the portrait. This is the working rhythm detailed earlier in the creation cycle section (see page 19): drawing in the lines, adding in the tones, and polishing the edges.

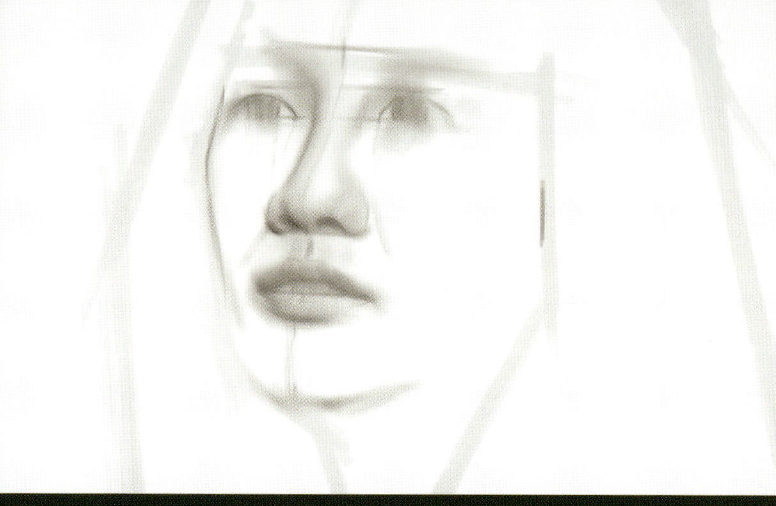

7. Building the core

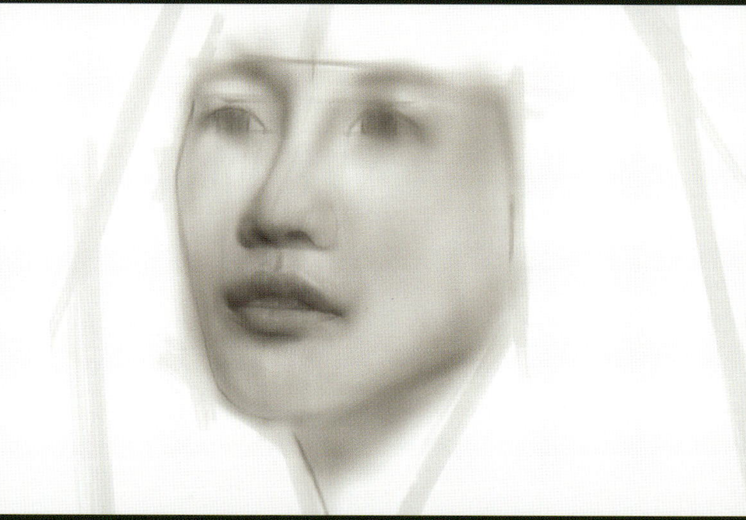

8. Ghosting/brushing

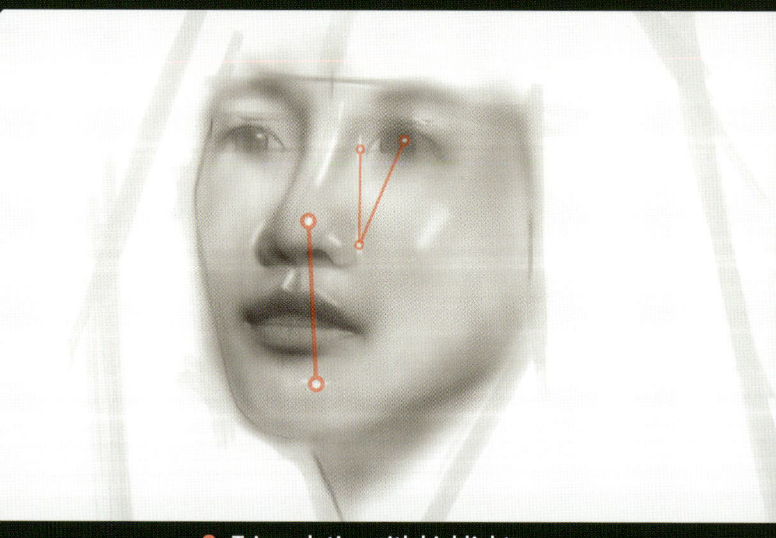

9. Triangulation with highlights

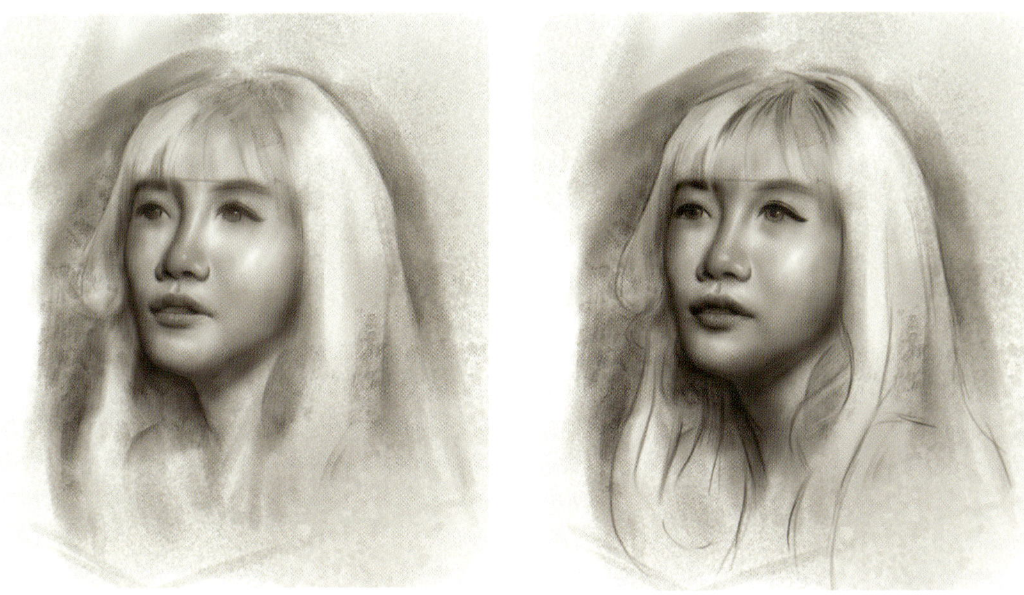

10 & 11. Brushing in tone/ relining edges

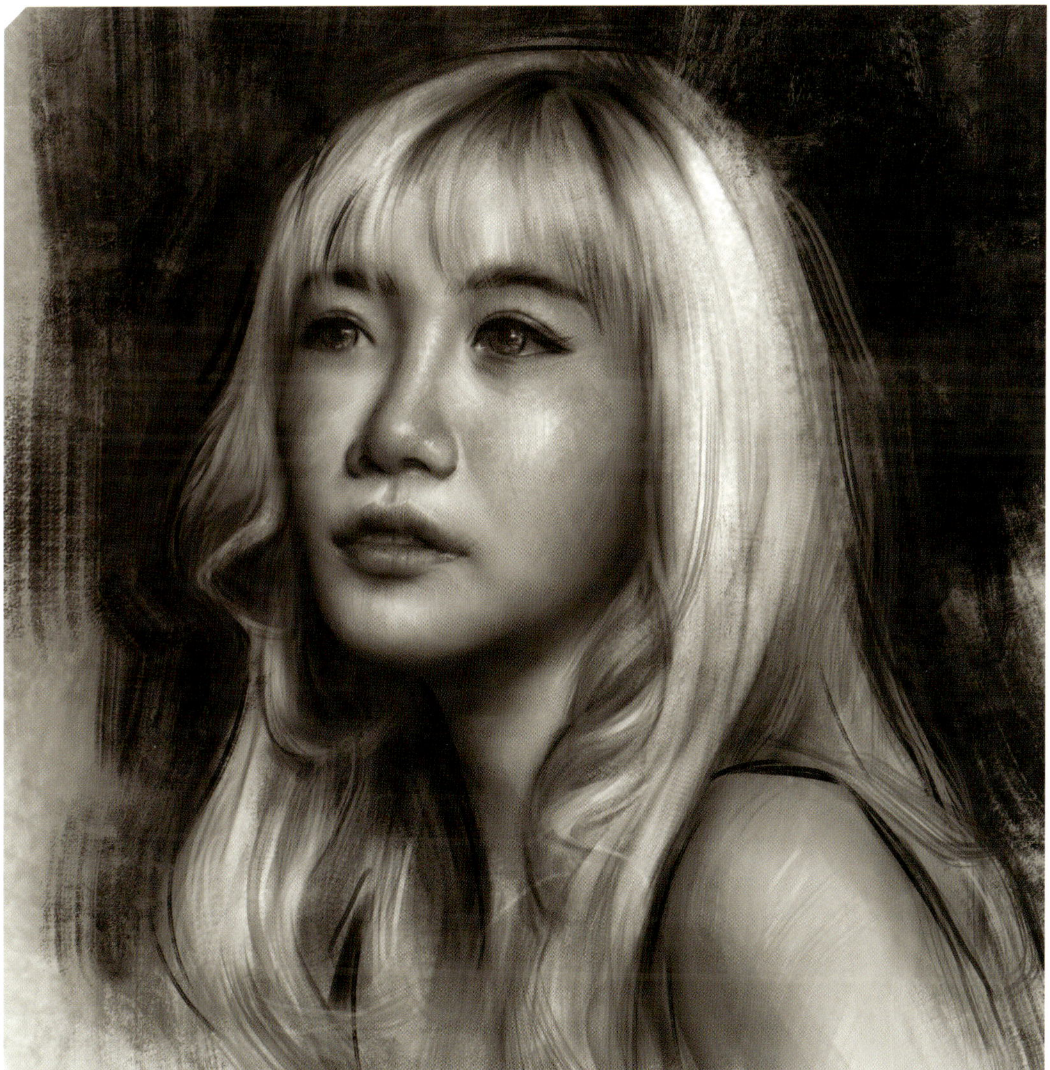

Final portrait

Features

Lines of the features

Shapes are the preferred way of blocking in any feature, but if they are not present, or if they have already been established, look for the lines of the features instead. Looking at **Fig. 1**, you may not initially see the lines, but they are highlighted on **Fig. 2**. These lines are also called occlusion shadows and typically have a sharp, dark edge from which a soft gradation emerges. They should be drawn in very clearly (**Fig. 3**), after which you can create a gradation in the direction it needs to soften the most (**Fig. 4 & 5**).

As you move on and there is more subtlety to your understanding of the form, you will realize there are many directions to pull gradations from this line (**Fig. 6**). However, there is usually one side of the line that is softer than the other.

Lines of the features are often drawn in and then softened, drawn in and then softened, and so on. Sometimes, after drawing them in, you may discover that they are completely wrong. When this happens, try softening them before erasing, and then restate them. Learn how to be flexible and manipulate these lines to where you want them to be by softening and restating them until they find the correct position. These lines are hard fought over, but add an immense amount of particularity to any features. John Singer Sargent once said: *"A portrait is a painting with something wrong with the mouth."* The lines of the features and where they are placed will change the expression of a mouth. This is critical to creating the likeness and feel of a portrait, so they must be mastered.

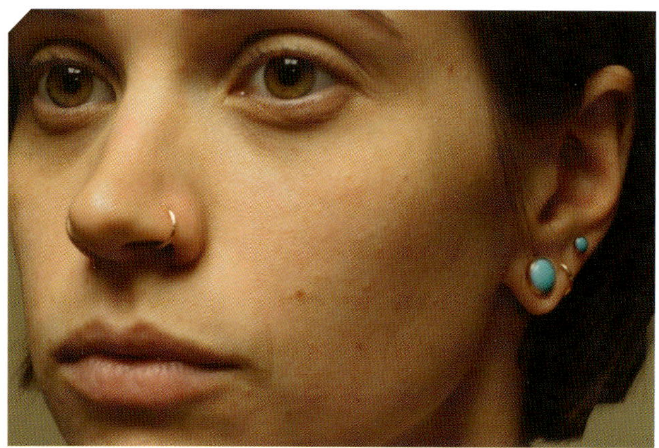

Fig. 1. Original photograph

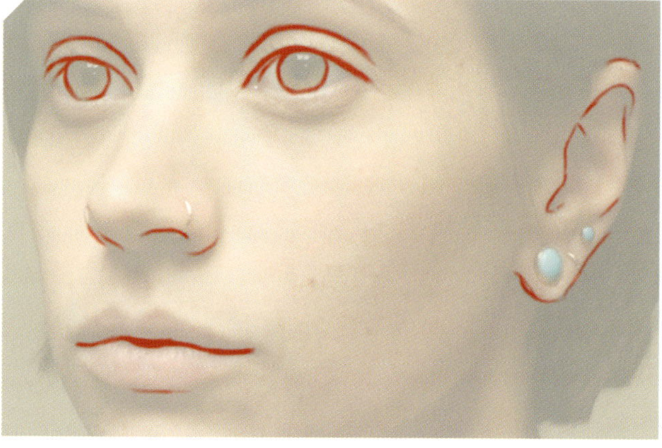

Fig. 2. Photograph with occlusion shadows drawn on top

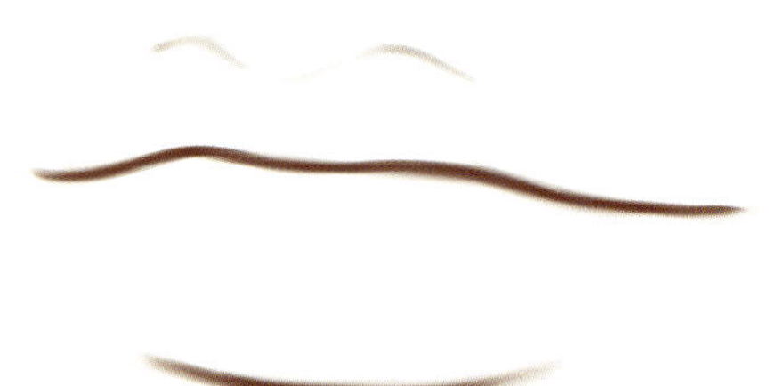

Fig. 3. Occlusion shadows clearly drawn in

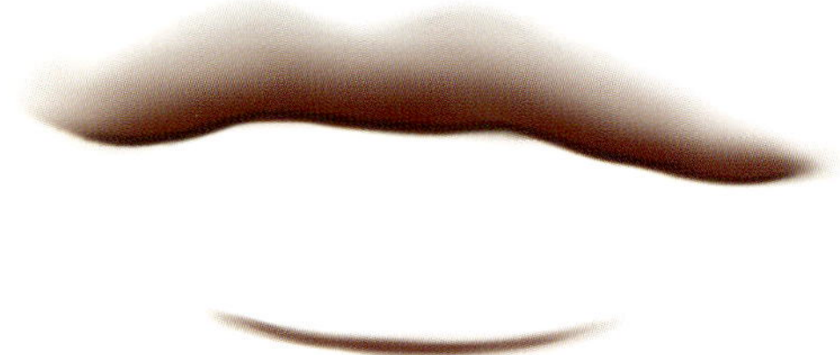

Fig. 4. Occlusion shadows with added gradation

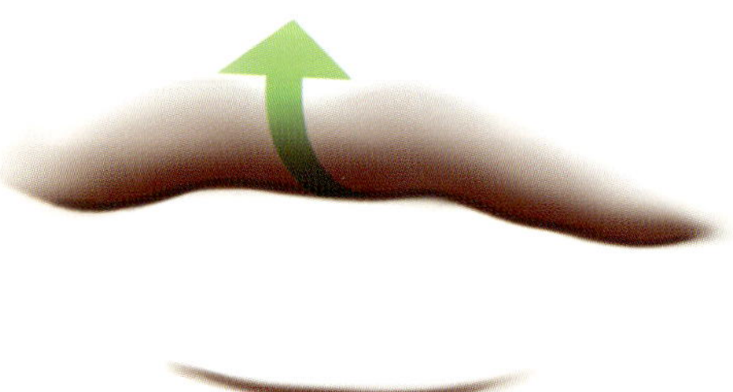

Fig. 5. Gradation pulled in the direction it needs to soften

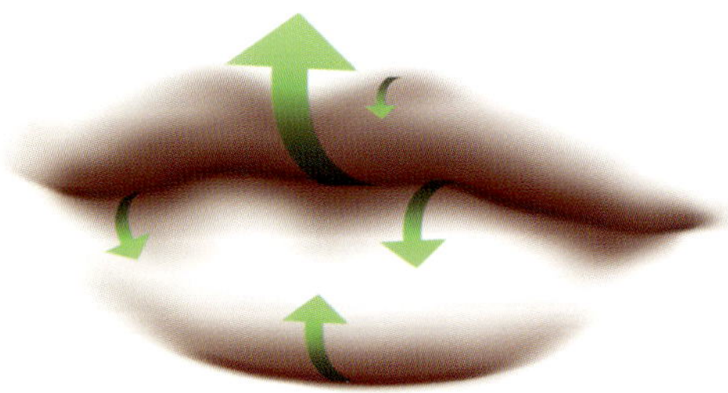

Fig. 6. Gradation pulled in multiple directions

Directional softening, or pulling

The quickest way to turn a 2D line drawing into a 3D form is to soften the edge of the line, creating a gradation. Though lines must be used when drawing, they can often flatten and create harshness, especially if they're drawn in the wrong place. It's crucial to learn how to create form and softness by creating gradations away from these lines. This is called directional softening, or pulling. Pulling can happen in several ways:

Fig. 1 shows a line. When a gradation is pulled downward from it (**Fig. 2**), it is not a line anymore. In **Fig. 3**, the line is softened on both sides.

In some cases, it will soften downward, then change its mind and soften upward (**Fig. 4**). These gradations can be quite elusive, especially on a form such as an ear or mouth. You must keep your eye on them and make sure you're being sensitive to which way the softening is going.

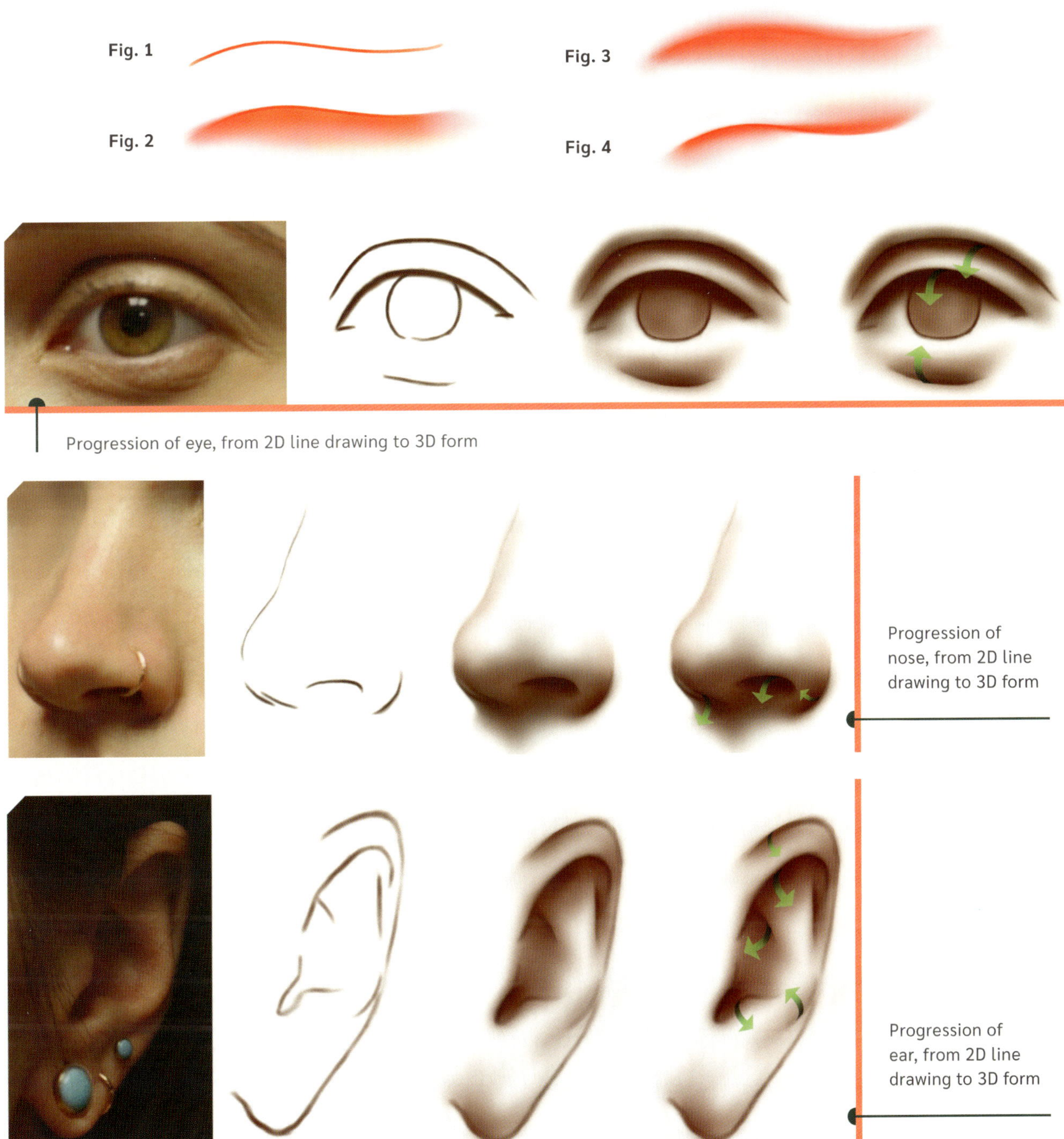

Progression of eye, from 2D line drawing to 3D form

Progression of nose, from 2D line drawing to 3D form

Progression of ear, from 2D line drawing to 3D form

CREATION CYCLE: COLOR VALUES

Photography and artwork © Steve Forster

This chapter will cover:

- Simplifying color to see the big relationships
- Color diversity
- Two approaches to developing values
- Understanding light, form, and color
- The color of light and shadow

Simplifying color to see the big relationships

When you block in a portrait, it's much more important to consider the big color value relationships than the smaller ones. Though the small color decisions with all of their interesting variations are important, and they are the qualities that get all of the glory, you must first lay a foundation that is solid and well-considered before investing the time it takes to create all of the other nuanced color decisions. When drawing a portrait, you consider the facial armature and where those features will go before you start rendering out each feature. The same is true with color. Start by considering the big value relationships. Only by first paying attention to these will all of the other smaller decisions find their right place (**Fig. 1**).

When blocking in an image, select six to ten of the major color values and stick to them, unifying all of the many color decisions into these simple colors. This simple set of colors will act as the color, or value, key of your picture (**Fig. 2**). This is incredibly valuable, as it helps you to focus more on drawing and the big value shapes, rather than getting distracted by other decisions. When transitioning from drawing to painting, it can help to set yourself a limited color palette to simplify the incredible amount of information you're looking at. For example, try setting yourself two values in the light zone of the face, one value for the shadow, two values for the light and shadow of the hair, one or two values for the background, and one for the subject's clothing.

When a simple, solid drawing meets a simple, solid block-in of the colors and values, and is lightly softened, this is what John Singer Sargent called the "wigmaker's block" (**Fig. 3**). He believed that starting a painting with this mannequin-head approach was the foundation of any good portrait, especially in oil.

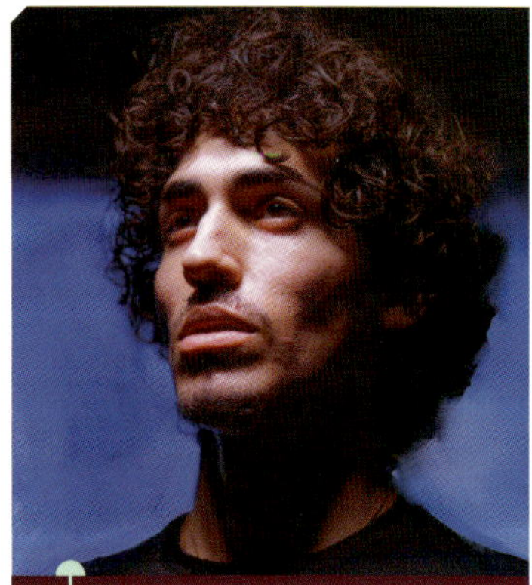

Original photograph

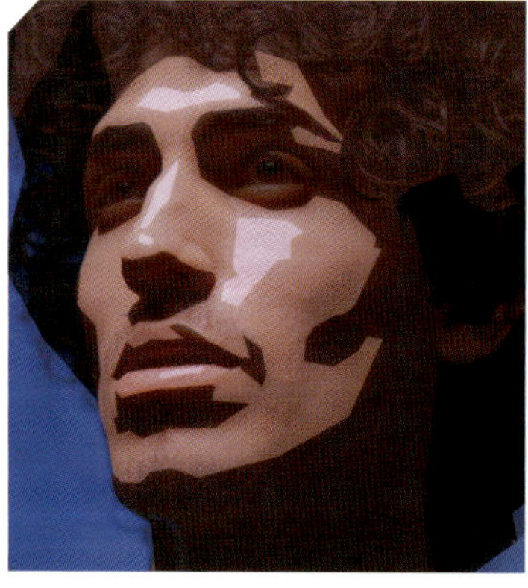

Fig. 1. Study the colors in the reference photo, then begin to block in color and build a foundation

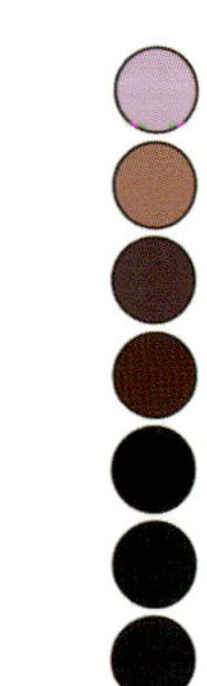

Fig. 2

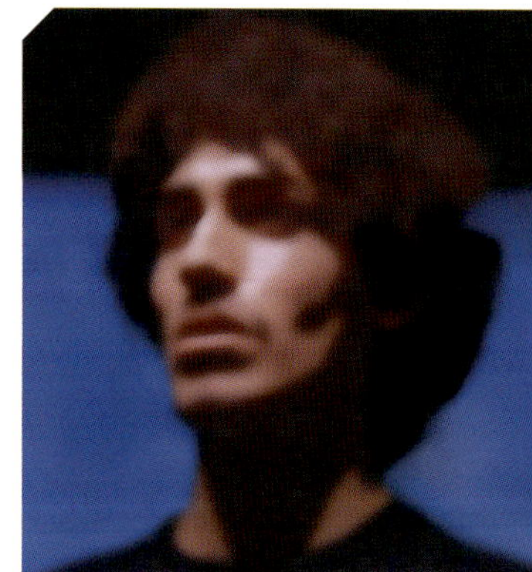

Fig. 3. The wigmaker's block

Color diversity

Once the foundation of the basic color values is established, opening your painting up to color diversity is one of the most fun and engaging aspects of painting flesh. It's the skill that most artists want to learn when it comes to painting skin. However, as mentioned earlier, this is laid on a foundation that allows for that diversity to thrive.

Fig. 4 shows a standard palette after the foundation has been laid. The middle string (A) shows the average flesh tone, ranging from light to dark, then lightening into the background tone. The wings (B and C) show a slight departure from these mother tones for the sake of color diversity. This is a useful way to set up a color palette, whether using a traditional medium like oil paints or painting digitally using software.

This color diversity palette is a basic way of understanding how flesh color can start to diverge from the major tones. The next page will explore messy diversity, where this is pushed even further. Each artist likes a slightly different kind of color diversity in painting. Some artists may prefer monochrome or a very limited palette, while others love strong colors with maximum diversity. There is no one correct way of choosing a color palette.

Photography can limit color diversity. Squeeze your hand to make a fist and you will see the many different colors your own flesh tone possesses. However, if you take a photograph of that fist, or put it under dramatic light, the camera will often compress these colors and completely change the colors and values you see. A major benefit of painting from life is that there is no simplification of the color. If you are working from a photograph, it can be helpful to modify it digitally to ensure it possesses the right kind of color diversity before you use it as reference.

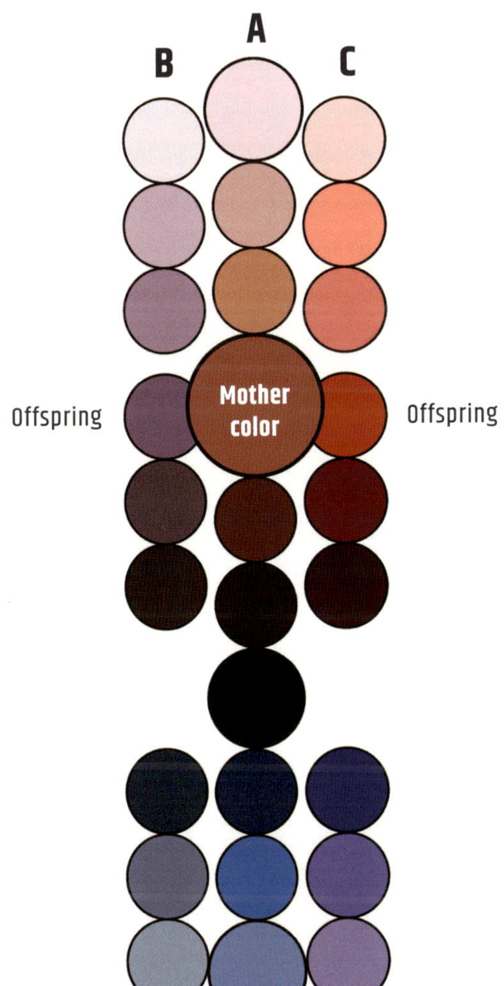

Fig. 4

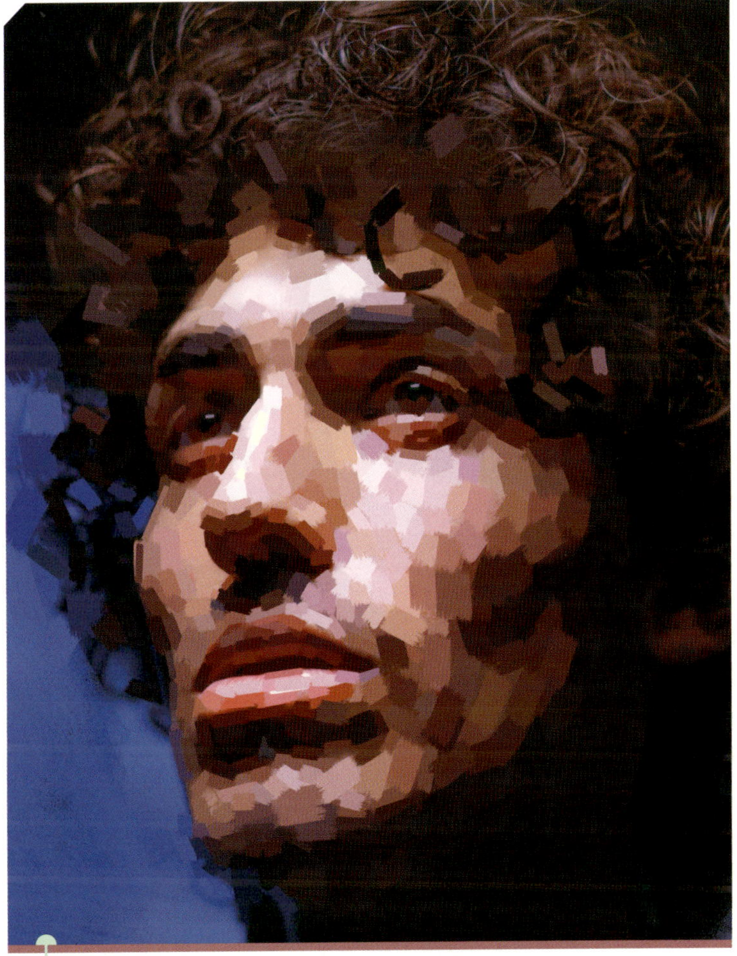

Fig. 5. Colors are added to the foundation from the mother color palette and offspring color palettes

Messy color diversity

When considering flesh tones in relation to color theory, it's all about the values. You can use any color you like, but staying true to the values is most important. The value has to do with the relative lightness or darkness of a color, and nothing to do with the hue or saturation of the color. This can be a profound mystery and can be a steep learning curve for many artists. However, once you understand it, it can open up a world of iridescence and sophisticated color that will make your portraits shine.

Portraits don't always have to make sense or be perfectly realistic. It can sometimes be fun to experiment and push the color beyond what is natural. You may want to paint a yellow-green highlight, or a shade of blue-violet that sneaks into the flesh tone. This is color diversity pushed to its limits, and while it can be pushed even further, avoid going too far by remembering to aim for the right value.

A messy color diversity palette, as seen in **Fig. 1**, may not be consciously set up as a palette. Rather, it is often derived from the mother and offspring color palettes, as seen on the previous page, created by working and pushing color diversity further out from that main structure. The main structure is helpful for instilling organization in the chaos of creating beautiful color.

Fig. 1. Messy color diversity palette

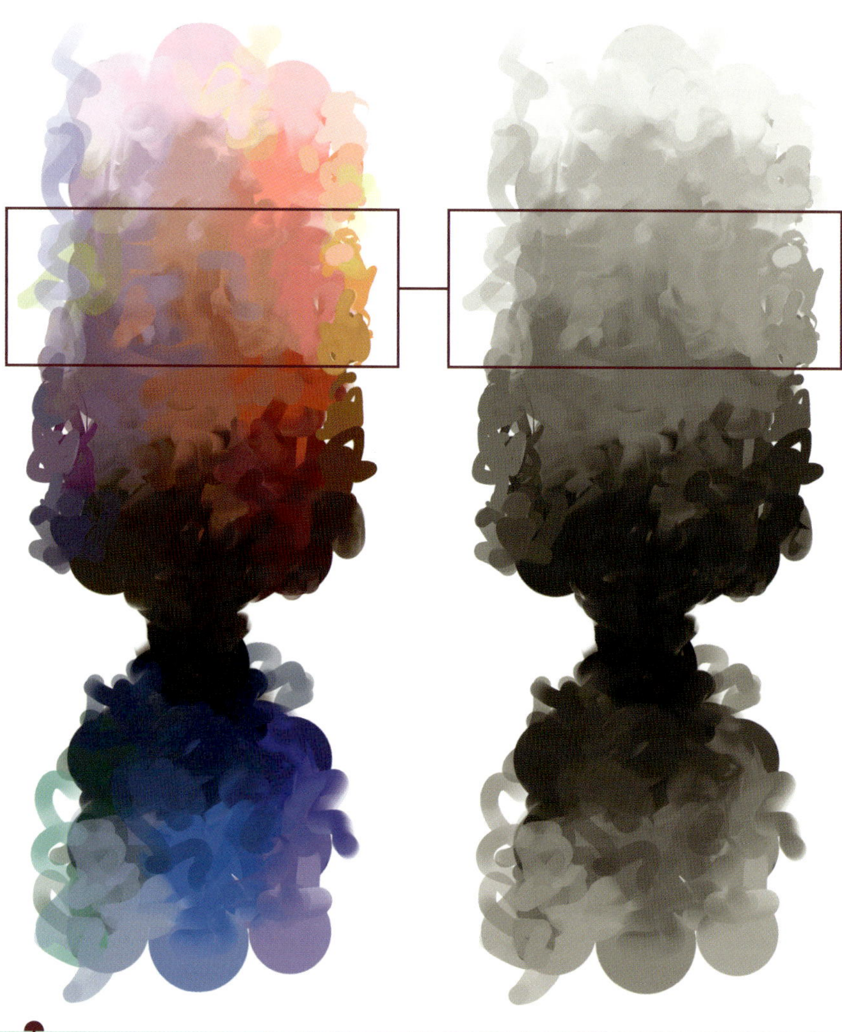

Notice how in these areas there can be color diversity (hue and saturation shifts) but minimal value shifts; this is color diversity within value unity

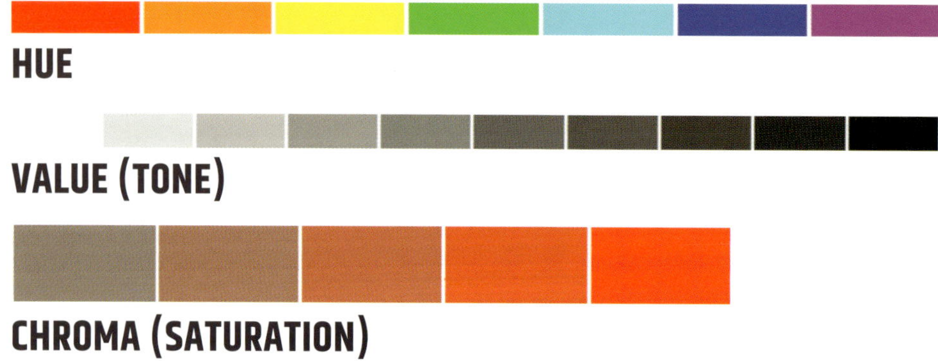

Mother color, local color, and color diversity

Color diversity can progress your color knowledge into a greater understanding and sensitivity to shimmering, beautiful color. However, it also risks becoming a little random and can lead you down some strange paths if you don't have a few trusted guides to keep you on track. As explored on the previous page, value is the most important concept when it comes to color diversity. The second most important concept is understanding the mother color, or local color, of the area you are working on. No matter how diverse the colors become, there needs to be a local color into which all colors unify.

The mother color is the general hue of the skin that most people would identify as the model's complexion within the given lighting situation. Typically the mother color is not the lightest value, nor is it the darkest value on the skin. It usually resides somewhere between light and shadow. It is incredibly important to identify this color before creating diversity. It's very easy to create diversity in skin tone and then suddenly notice that the painting is too green or too red. However, if you find and establish the mother color first, all of the shimmering pinks and purples and greens will not subdue the underlying tone of the mother color. If painting traditionally, the mother color should be the first color you mix up. You want to make sure you get it as close to perfect as possible, as it will inform the majority of your other color and light decisions.

The local color of a shadow or highlight area is different from the mother color, as it changes color based on the zone of light it sits in. For example, there can be a different local flesh color in the shadow than there is in the highlight area. Both of these areas can have color diversity, yet unify into the average tone of the given area.

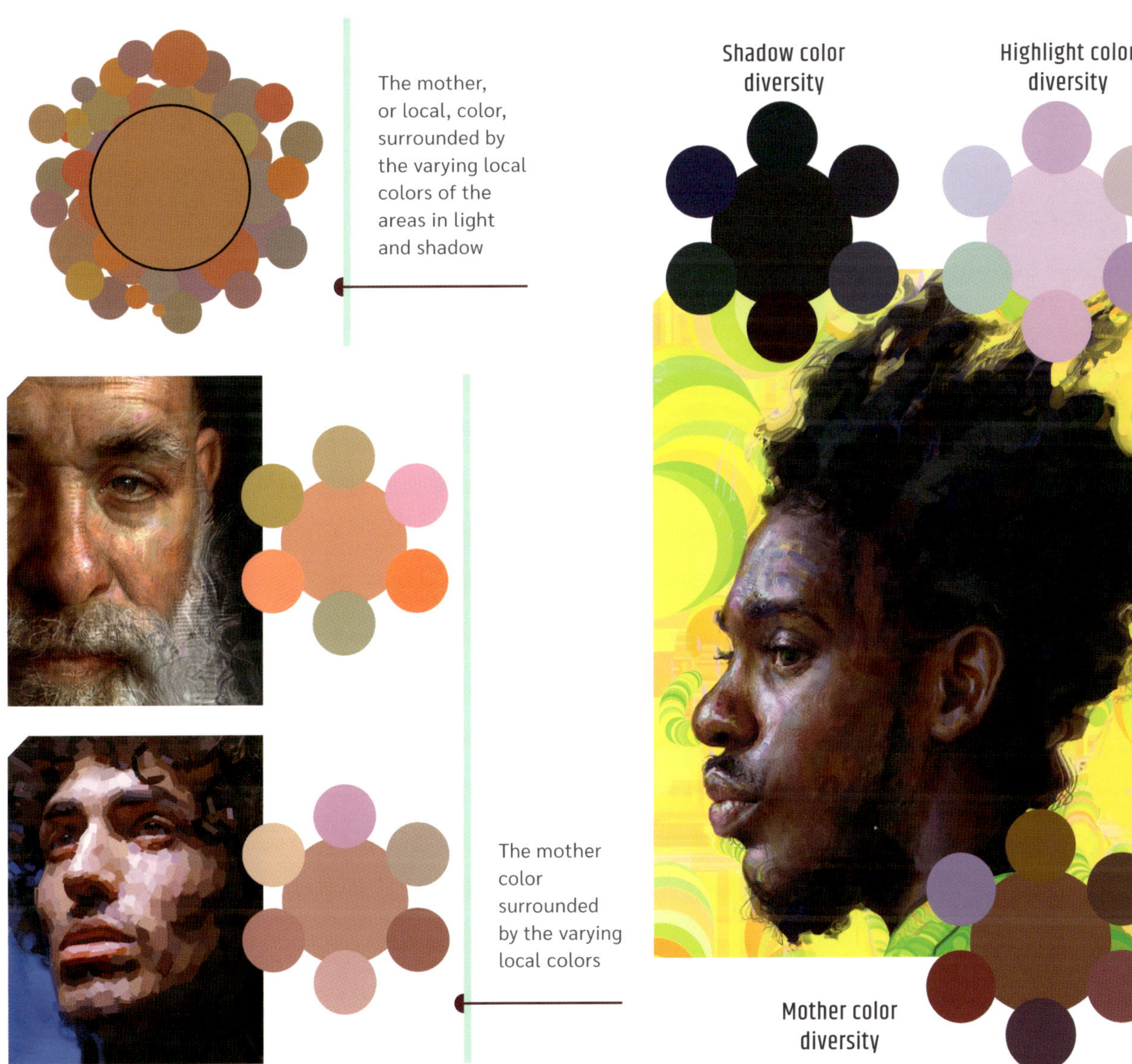

The mother, or local, color, surrounded by the varying local colors of the areas in light and shadow

The mother color surrounded by the varying local colors

Setting up a palette progression

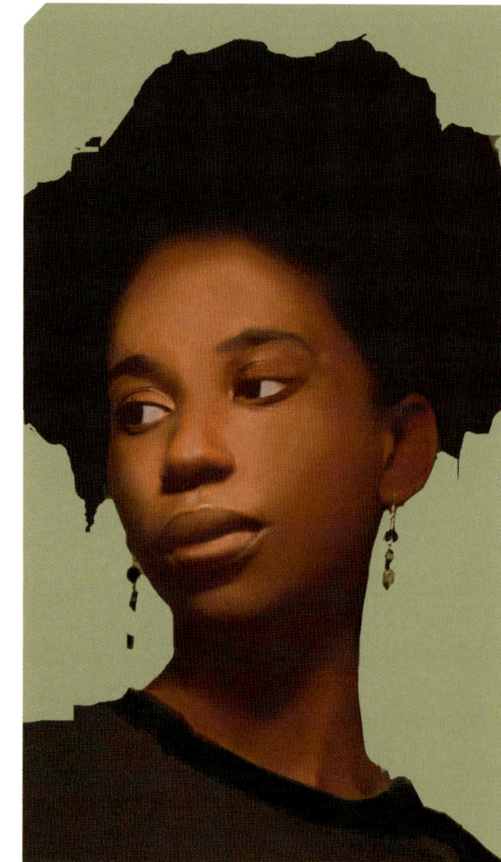

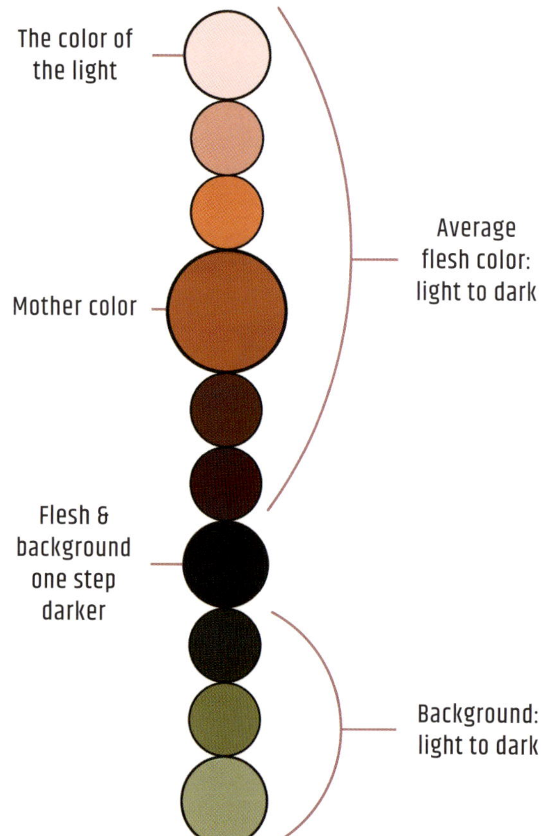

Setting up a palette

When painting a portrait, it's important to set up a palette well. This can be created in a variety of ways and calls for careful thought in how you lay out the colors to ensure there is an organized approach to how you use the colors on the canvas. How you lay out your colors is similar to how the keys of a piano are laid out in a progression of notes. If you hit the wrong note, you move either up or down one note in order to find the right one.

When blocking in a portrait from scratch, start with a basic color palette of no more than eight colors. It will be a waste of time to mix additional more nuanced colors too early, as it's better to see the bigger, most important relationships first before progressing to exploring nuance and color diversity.

Mother color

If mixing colors to work traditionally, start with the mother color. You will need to mix a fair amount of it, as it is the most important color and a lot of other colors and values will be born from it. It can be difficult to discern what this color is, but it's usually the color you would use to describe the model's complexion in the particular lighting situation. It's the color you would choose if you were to make a custom band-aid color for your model, again in the specific lighting situation you are capturing them in. The mother color is also the average skin color in this light. So much emphasis is put on the mother color because it sets into motion so many other color decisions, so it's important to get it right from the start.

The color of the light

After you have mixed a decent amount of the mother color, you can start progressing toward the light. Don't just add white, but consider the color of the light and how that may shift the mother color to a different hue.

The color of the flesh and background

After establishing the lighter colors, clean off the brush and mix the darker tones of the skin and hair. It's very easy to make these too black and gray, or too colorful. Instead, try to find colors somewhere in the middle; delicately balance this spectrum by creating dark enough tones, while also keeping them colorful.

The eventual aim is to reach the maximum darkness for the image, though this does not necessarily have to be black. This darkness should be made up of the flesh tone and the background tone combined, then progressing one step darker. Often this area seems colorless; the darkest tone for the value key of the image.

Background tone

The final stage is to begin building out the background tone on the other end, creating a bridge from the flesh tone to the atmosphere, or background tone. It would be easy to switch to a lighter tone if your background is light, but it is worth building the tones in between, even if it's difficult to find them. These are often found in places you may not suspect, such as the hair or where the background color bounces onto the subject.

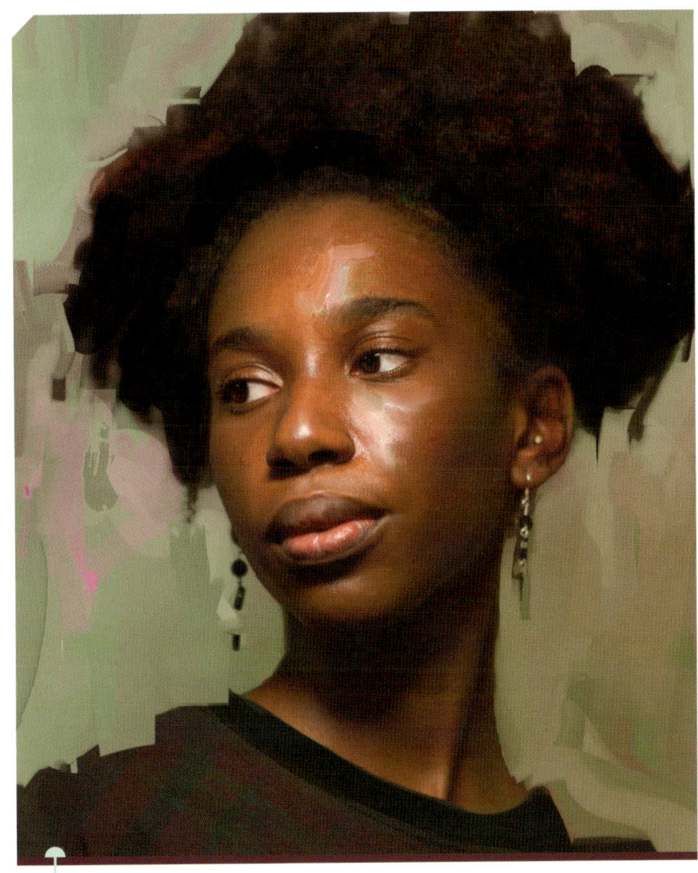

The darkest areas of the image should be a combination of the flesh tone and background tone, progressed one shade darker

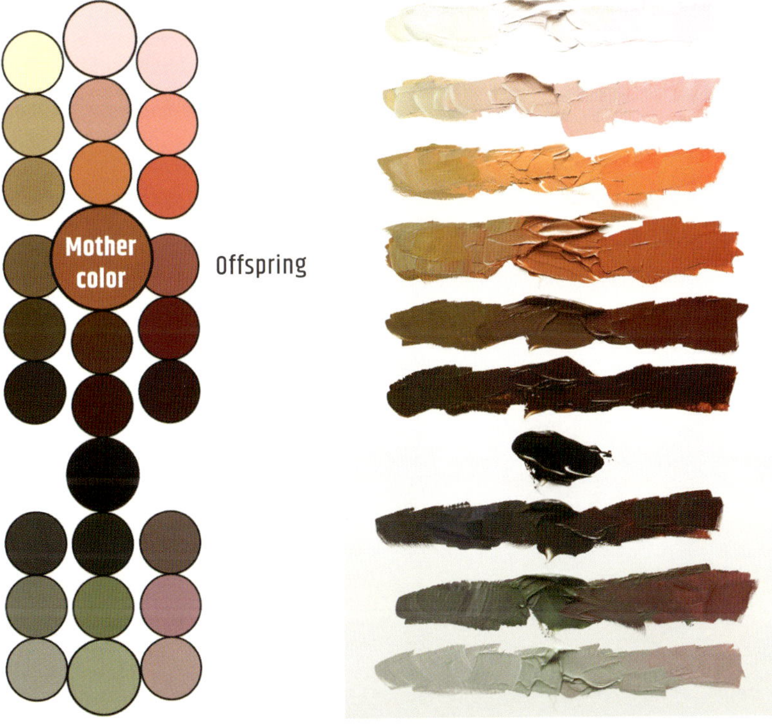

Advanced palette for the above portrait, with diversity

Two approaches to developing values

Soft mirage of increasing intensity

The advantage of this first approach to developing values is that it's cohesive and is much more likely to represent the way light passes over an object. The disadvantage, however, is that an artist can easily become too shy and not hit the right note because they think it will interrupt the cohesion. In other words, the portrait risks becoming wimpy and tentative.

To create a soft mirage of increasing intensity:

1. Start with a rough outline, emphasizing straight lines. Softly build up the value, taking care not to make it too harsh.
2. Continue to softly block in colors and values in the appropriate places, maintaining edges as needed.
3. Be increasingly specific with your colors and edges, picking up the intensity and not allowing it to become too soft.
4. Introduce accents of dark, light, and color. Don't be too timid, but consider adding a little flair to your brushstrokes and textures.

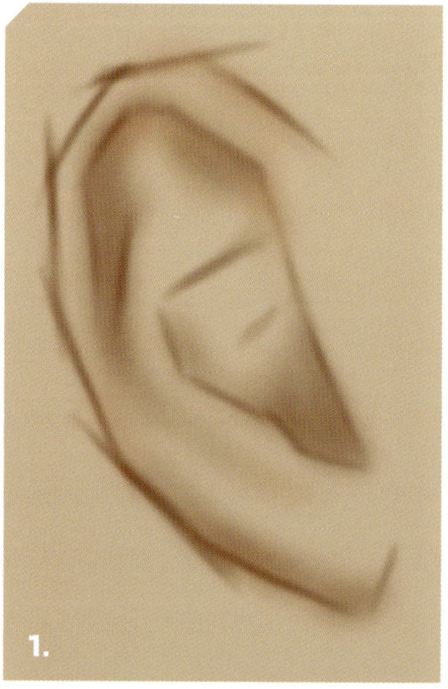

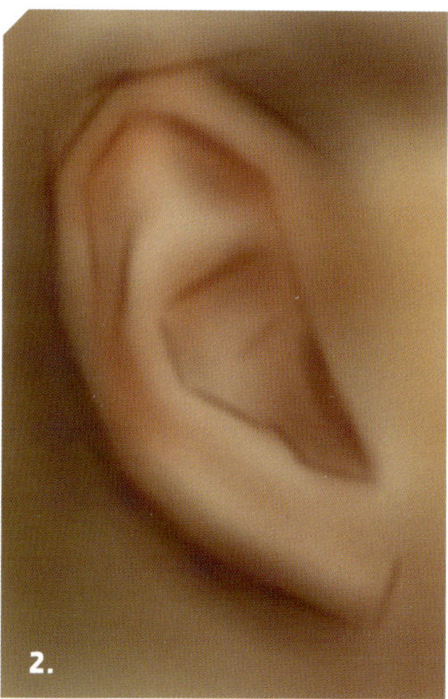

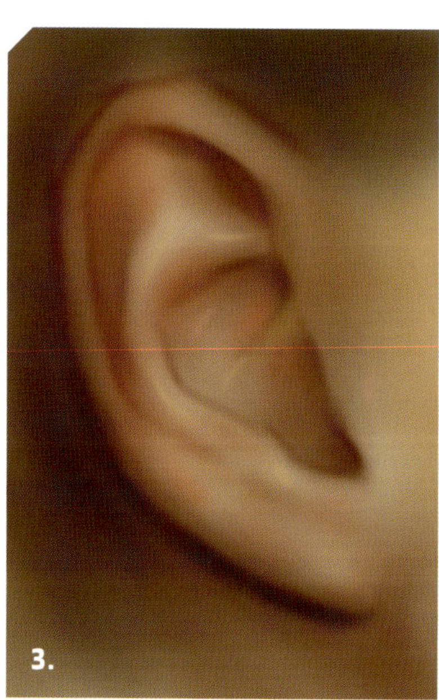

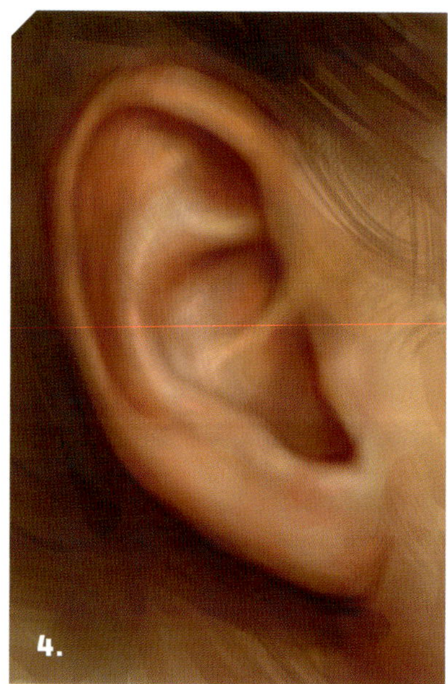

Hard messy notes of increasing subtly

The advantage of this second approach to developing value is that it forces the artist to consider the relationships between color and value immediately, which can feel a little more direct in its response to your subject. The problem with this approach is that it can often lead to abrupt, disconnected parts that lack cohesion. It also risks becoming overly busy and intense.

To create hard messy notes of increasing subtly:

1. Start the painting with an outline. Many artists find it helpful to know where the different colors are supposed to go, and in this way the outline functions much like a coloring book.
2. Paint in the color note for each individual area aggressively. Pay no attention to softness and prettiness, but focus only on accuracy in color and value.
3. You may choose to soften it a little, or you may prefer to simply paint more subtle notes. As shown here, the cycle of a portrait often involves painting the right notes, then softening, then painting the right notes, then softening.
4. Focus on painting in accents, creating sharp, soft, and broken edges. Try not to lose the spirit of the wild, painterly quality you started with.

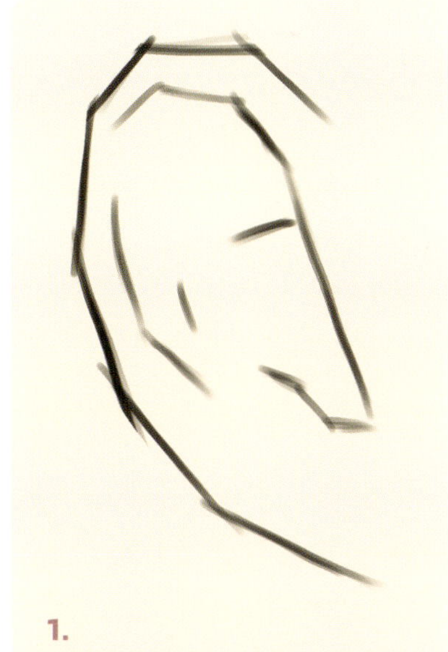

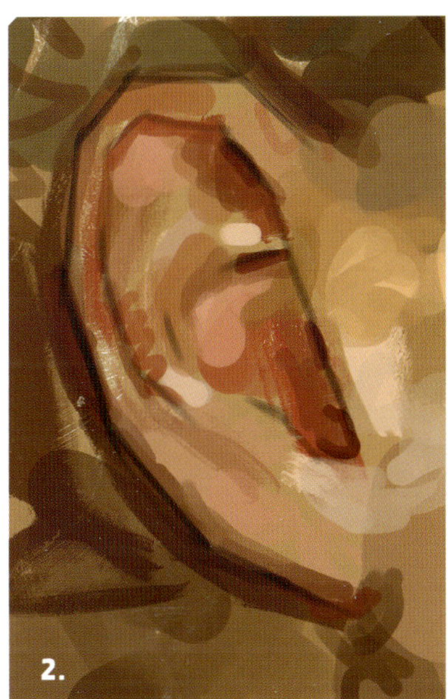

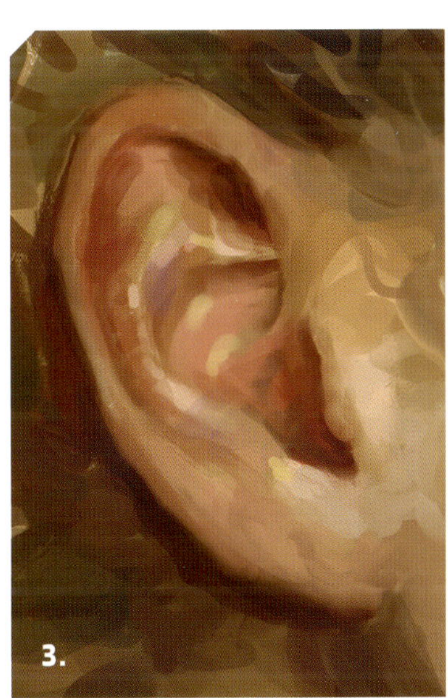

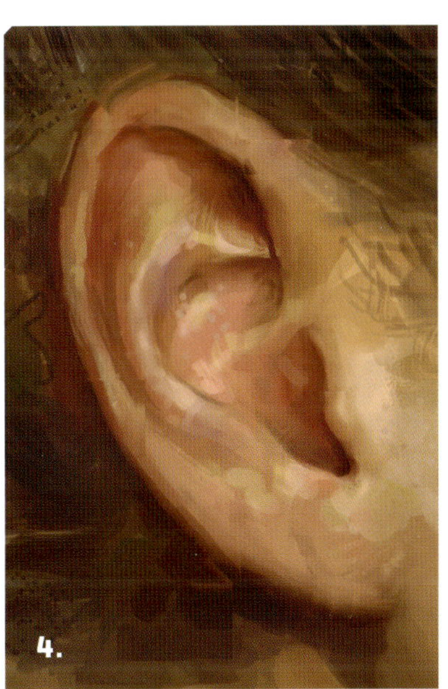

Understanding light, form, and color

The anatomy of light

One of the most difficult skills to acquire is the proper rendering of form; that is, to take something two-dimensional and make it three-dimensional in an illusionistic way. This is the alchemy of painting or drawing. In order to master this skill, artists must start by considering a basic concept: what is light and what is shadow? No matter how basic of an understanding you may have, it's extraordinarily beneficial to gain clarity about where light ends and shadow begins. As you add more and more layers of information that fill out the light and shadow spaces, this will bring you to the anatomy of light and shadow.

Simplified shadow and light

Fig. 1 is an oversimplification of how to separate shadow from light. This is helpful in understanding how to draw your shapes and create a separation between what is seen in the light and what is seen in the shadow.

The form principal

One of the primary rules in creating form is not to break the form principle. This is when the halftone, or turning, is not as dark as the reflected light in the shadow, as seen in **Fig. 2A**. This can sometimes be true when this principle is broken, as seen in **Fig. 2B**, but usually only of transparent or translucent objects such as a droplet of water, glass marble, or grape. The moment the reflected light appears brighter than the turning, you have broken the form principle and it ceases to be a solid object.

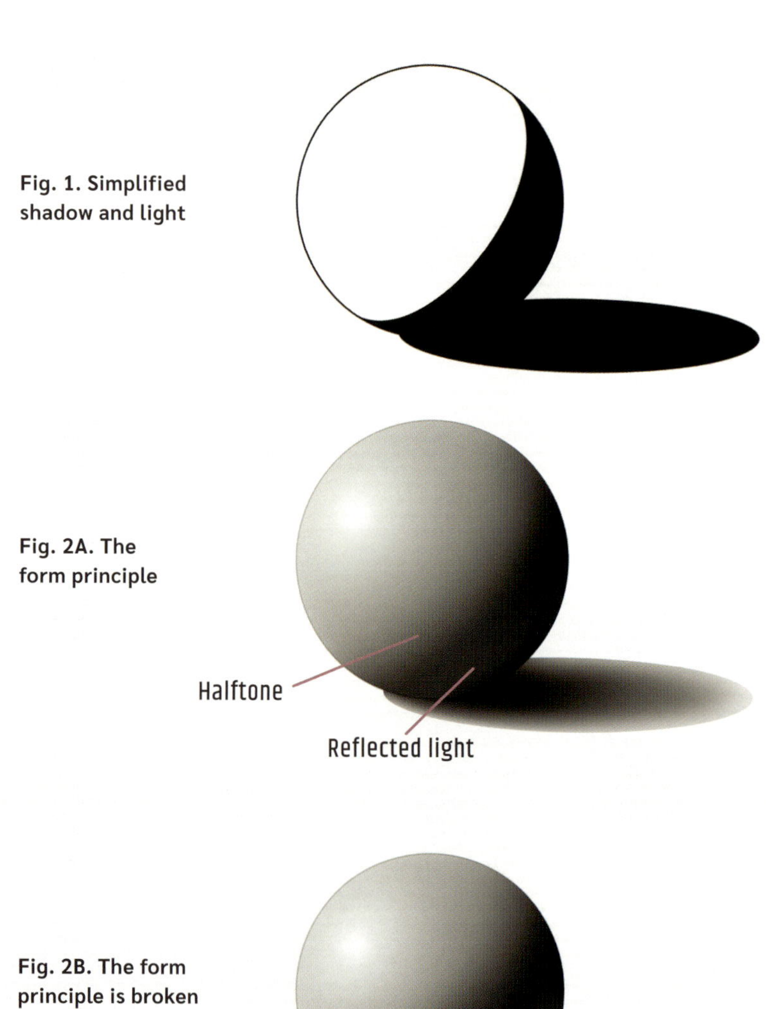

Fig. 1. Simplified shadow and light

Fig. 2A. The form principle

Fig. 2B. The form principle is broken

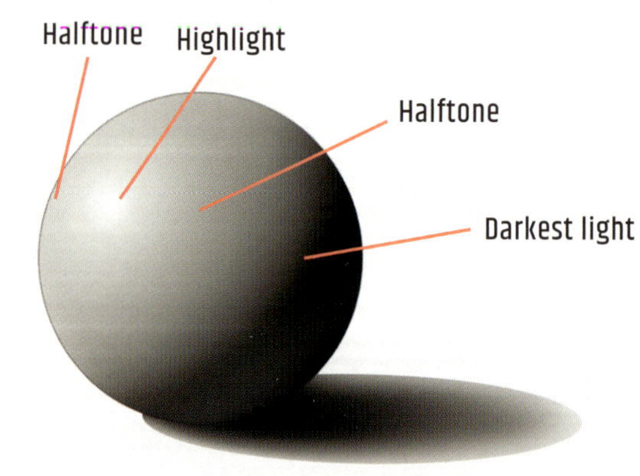

Fig. 3. The highlight, surrounded by halftones

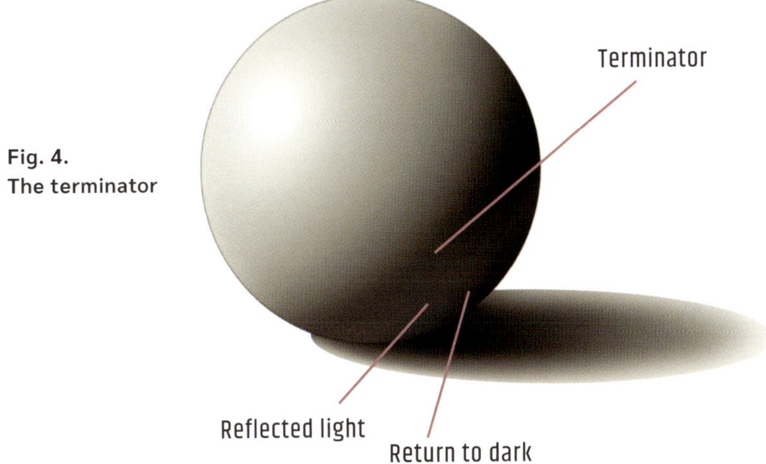

Fig. 4.
The terminator

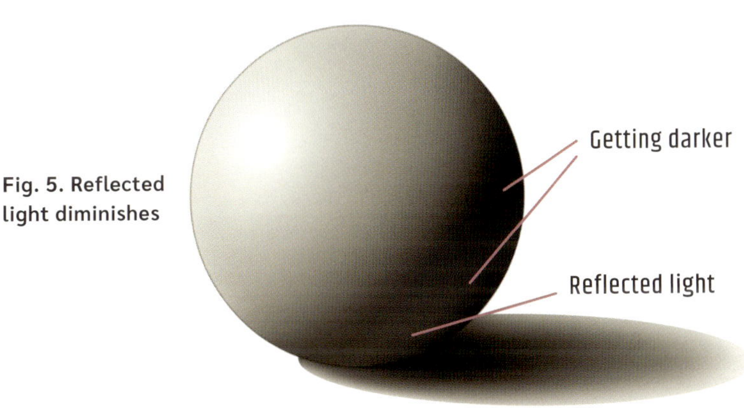

Fig. 5. Reflected light diminishes

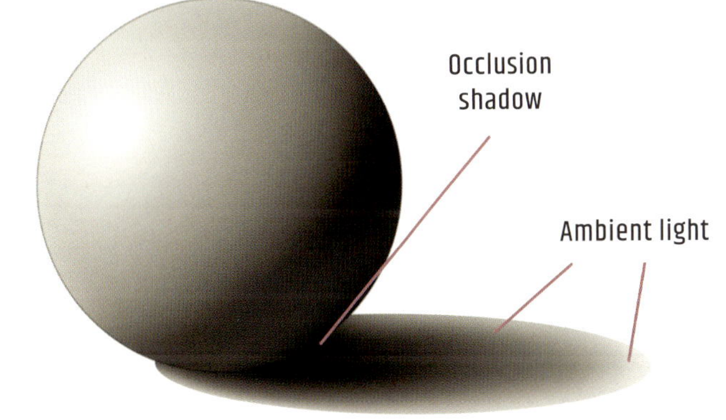

Fig. 6.
Cast shadows

Fig. 3, **4**, **5** & **6** show specific qualities inside the anatomy of light that are very important to render.

The highlight

Fig. 3 shows how the brightest light is often not at the edge of the form, but somewhere inside of it. This is known as the highlight. Halftones sit all around this highlight and it becomes increasingly darker (the darkest light) as it approaches the terminator.

The terminator

Fig. 4 illustrates how the terminator remains darker than the reflected light. The shadow is then lightened with reflected light, but then returns back to darkness as the sphere turns away from the reflected light. This produces a round and brilliant shadow.

Reflected light

Fig. 5 shows how the reflected light will diminish as it moves up the side of the sphere. This is because it moves further away from the ground plane and that light fades.

Cast shadows

Fig. 6 demonstrates how cast shadows have a range of values too. The occlusion shadow, which is typically the darkest of all shadows, because no light reaches it, helps to anchor a form to appear as if it is sitting on a plane. Further out in the cast shadow, ambient light starts to create a smooth gradation out from the occlusion shadow's darkness. In the execution of all of the features that make up the anatomy of light and shadow, keep in mind **Fig. 1**. In creating all of these shadows and highlights, artists can sometimes lose the big picture and break the form principal.

The anatomy of light with color

All of the principles that make up the anatomy of light and shadow become much more interesting when they include color. Not only does the artist have to deal with the challenges of creating form, but also bending color and changing its hue or saturation, along with its lightness or darkness. Typically artists like to change the color of the light and make it a slightly different hue to the object it hits.

As seen in **Fig. 1**, the light has a bluish cast and it bends the skin tone toward itself. This effect can be quite beautiful, as it not only indicates a highlight, but also a contrasting color that activates the skin tone. This can be seen in the portrait, shown in **Fig. 2**, with a little more color diversity of that tone.

Fig. 3, **4**, **5** & **6** show how some of these color qualities affect form. **Fig. 3** demonstrates how the color of the light morphs the local color of the object toward itself. **Fig. 4** illustrates how the ground plane color bounces into the reflected light, producing a greener shadow. **Fig. 5** shows how this greenish quality diminishes as it crawls up the side of the sphere. **Fig. 6** demonstrates how the yellow ambient background color filters into the cast shadow and bends the green shadow toward yellow.

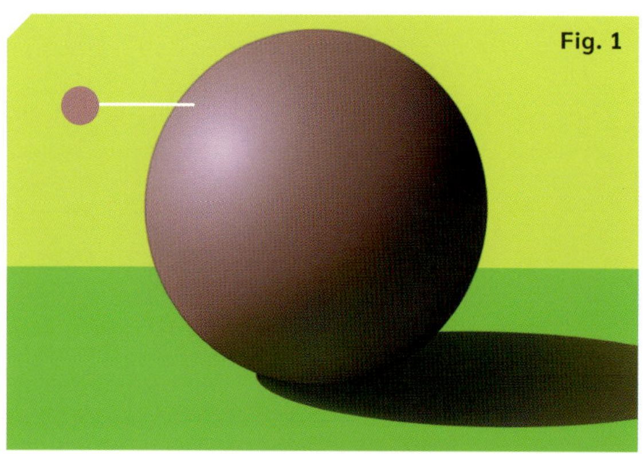

Fig. 1

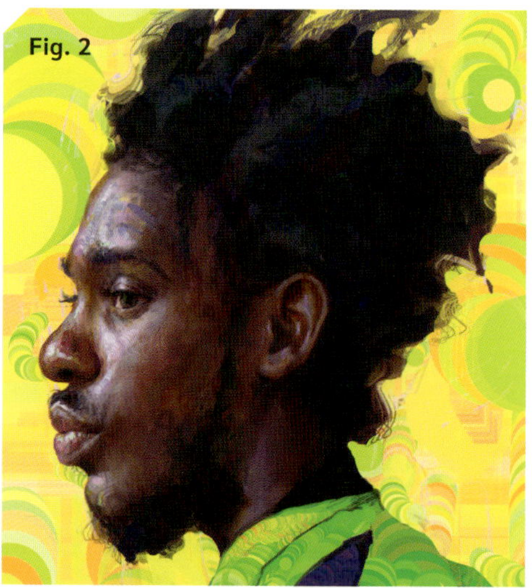

Fig. 2

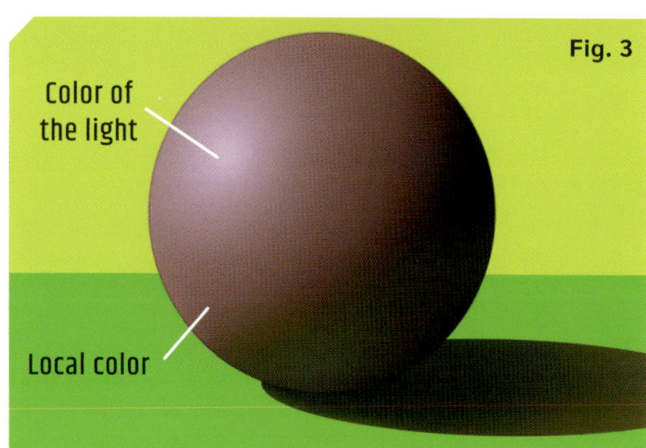

Fig. 3

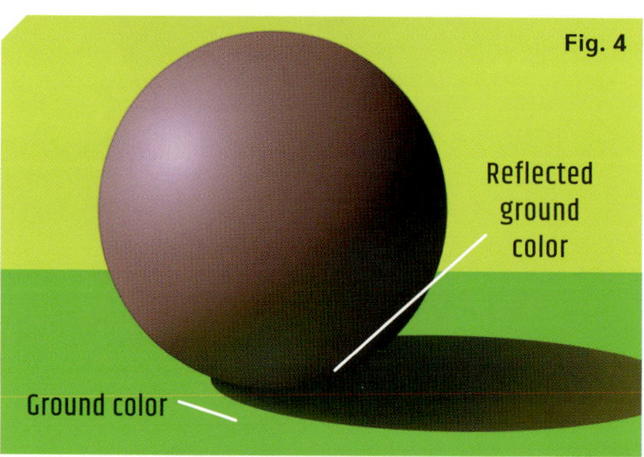

Fig. 4

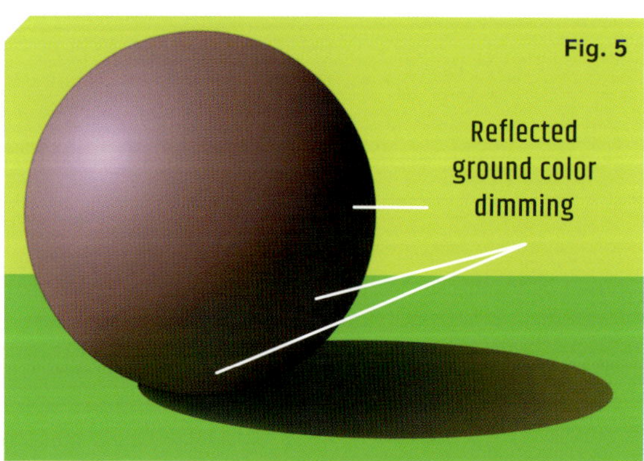

Fig. 5

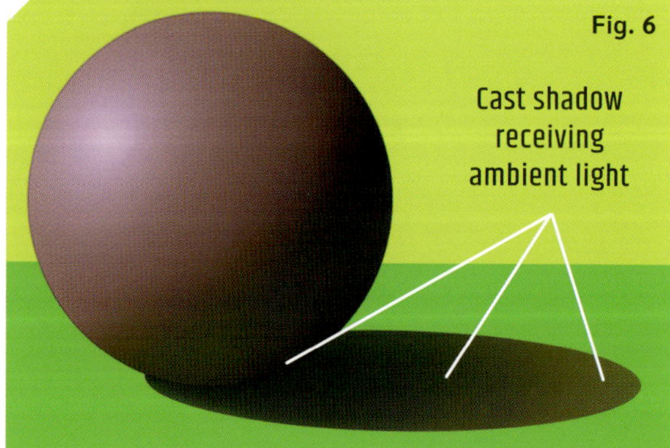

Fig. 6

How light flows from A to B

The simplest way to understand how light flows is by observing how the highlight (point A) rolls to a darker area (point B), or vice versa. If you are looking for these highlights, thinking in terms of moving from point A to point B will make it easier to understand how the light diminishes as it rolls away, thereby creating form.

After you have blocked in a subject's head and grouped the major lights and darks, add this dimension of form on the smaller scale. As you work from form to form, follow the simple formula of working from point A to point B, establishing landmarks of where the light is strongest and where it decreases to a darker tone.

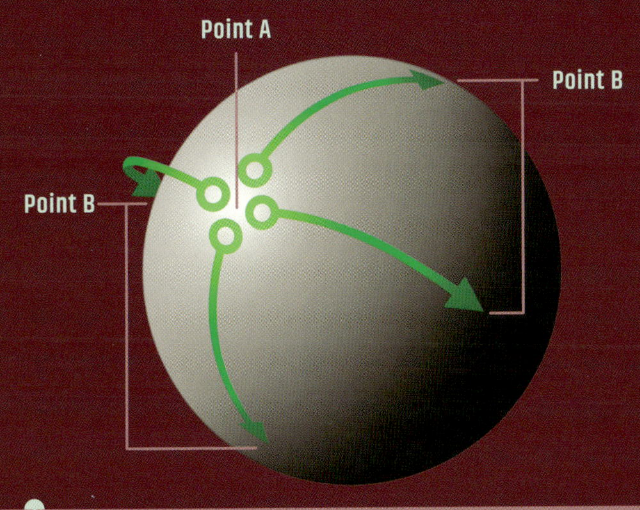

Observe how light flows, from highlight to shadow

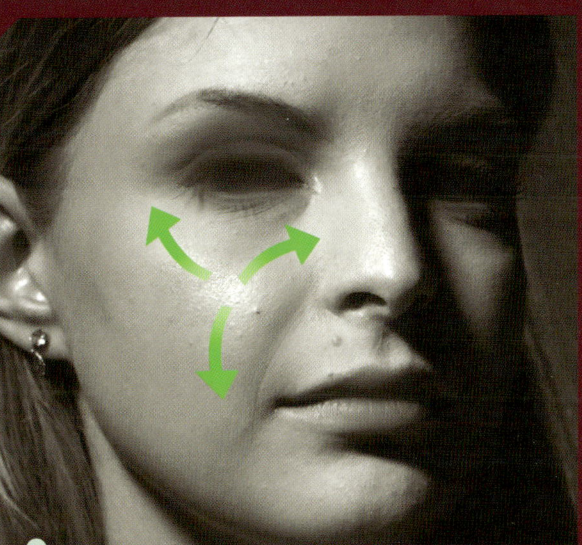

Think of each facial feature, such as the cheek, like a small sphere to understand how the light flows across it

Simple form and interruptions

It can be helpful to imagine the head as a sphere and the features as interruptions on that simple form. This will help to remind you that a highlight on the chin should not be as bright as a highlight on the cheek or nose, as the head turns in the same way a sphere does. Also, as shown here, the dark side of the face with the little triangle of light on the left cheek should be dimmer than the right cheek.

It's nearly impossible to render the form in a consistent manner without thinking about the head in a spherical way. The cheeks, nose, and lips are merely interruptions of the light flowing consistently across the sphere of the head, and furthermore they are like little tiny spheres in and of themselves, creating this spherical notion on a smaller scale many times over.

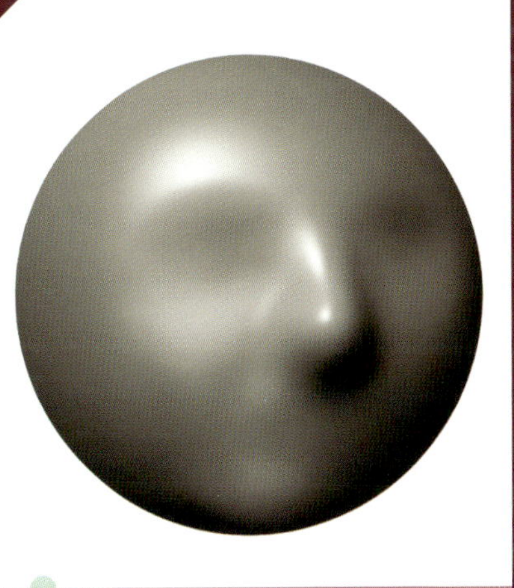

Think of the head as a sphere and the facial features as interruptions on its form

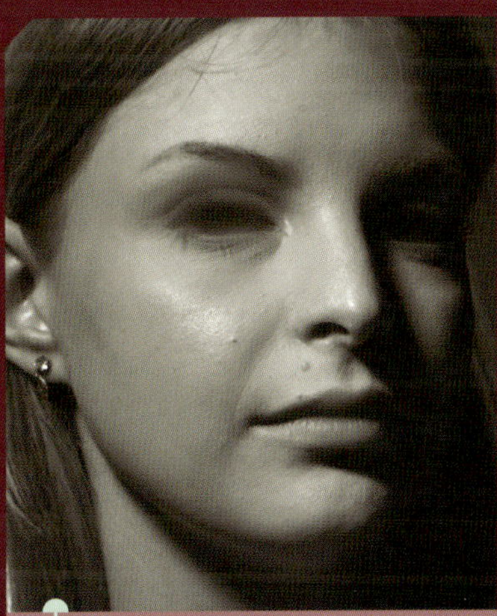

The shadow side of the subject's face with the smaller triangle of light on her cheek should be dimmer than her right cheek

Form vs. texture

Form and texture are two elements that don't pair very easily. Creating texture will often flatten the surface of a painting. This happens when a random texture that develops is not connected to the consistent changing of light. To create form you need to have a consistency with the turning of the light toward the shadow, but this can often lead to a softness that is devoid of texture. The unique pairing of both is a challenge that, if you can bring them together, will create a very dynamic surface that feels full of life.

Some artists will create a form and then stipple or paint texture on top of it. Others will start with texture and visible brushstrokes, then glaze those textures into harmony by creating a sense of form by adding a transparent color on top.

Whether texture is added first or last, with most paintings you will typically need to go back and forth between creating texture and adding form on top, repeating this process until you strike the fine balance between enough texture and enough form. It's important to remember that shadows tend to be quieter than light, as texture often evaporates and unifies in the shadows.

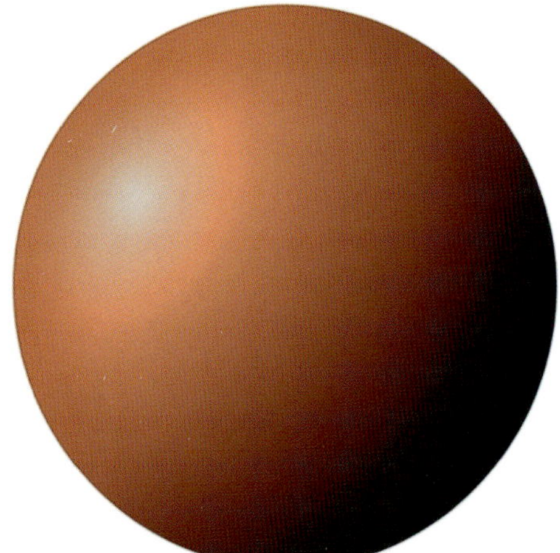

Form

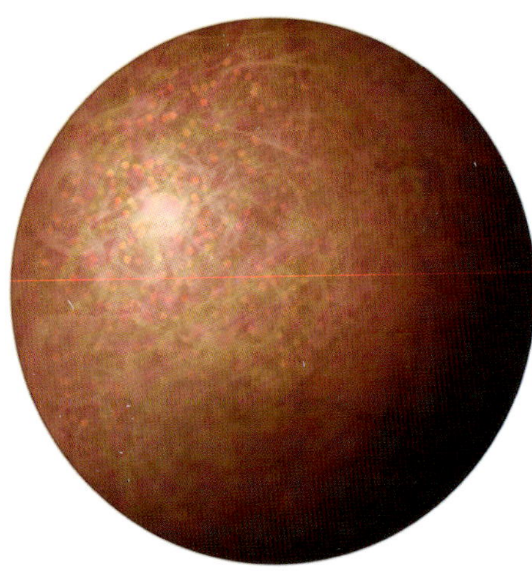

Form and texture

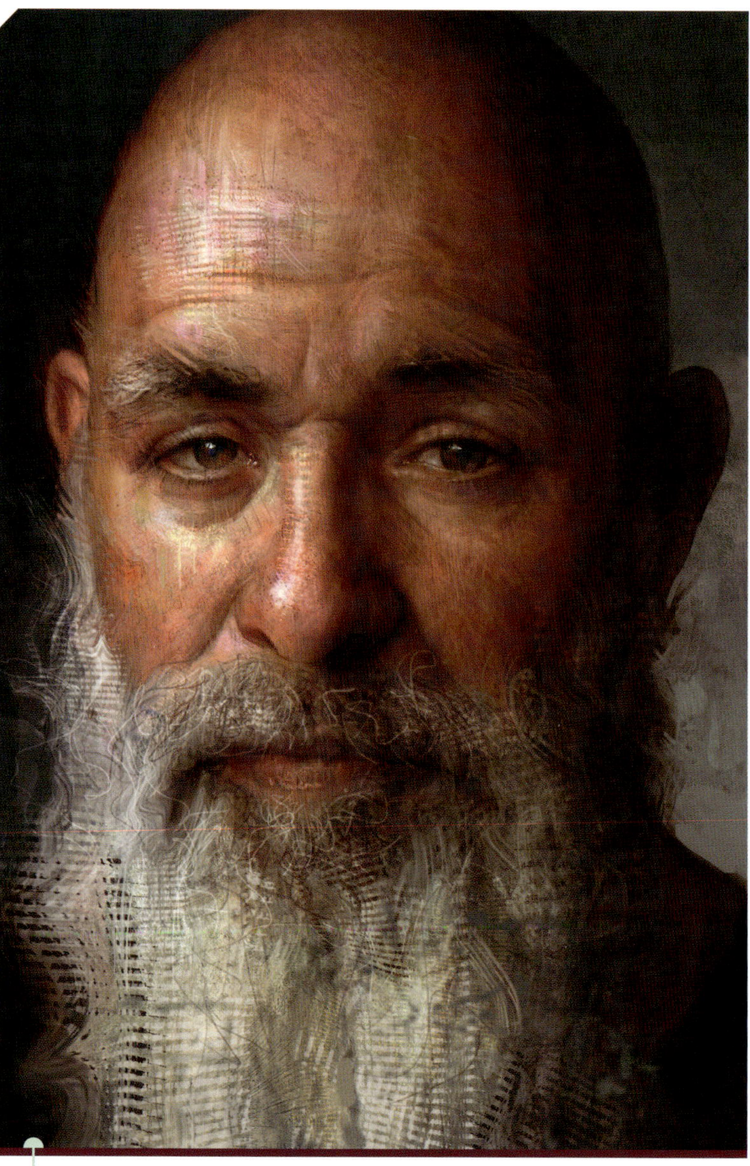

This portrait has both form and texture

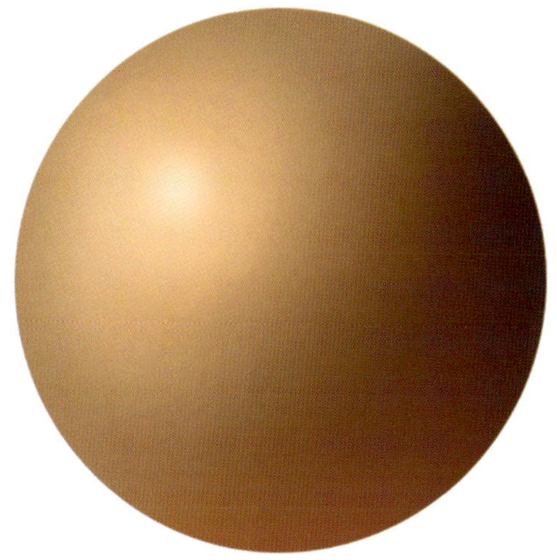

Apollonion model

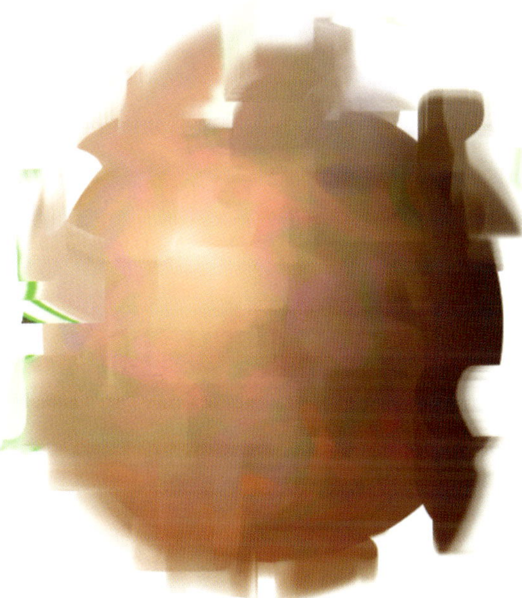

Dionsyian model

"Confused"

Different aesthetic conceptions of form

There are many conceptions of form and style in the world today. This can lead to confusion when deciding which road to go down when it comes to developing your own sense of form. The Apollonian sense is perhaps the most solid and introductory way of understanding light and form. Though at first it may look simple and easy, it's far from it. Artists have studied for years to perfect their understanding of light and form across many different surfaces in the truest sense that nature has to offer. Likewise, in the Dionysian model, there can be many different and wild interpretations of forms that are unique and fun.

In fact, there are limitless ways to interpret form in an artistic way. To a great degree, this is what style truly is. Van Gogh had his own unique conception of form, as did Monet. John Singer Sargent, Rembrandt; all great stylistic artists have their own unique conceptions of form. It is the melding between the Apollonian sense and this Dionysian sense of form that best grounds an artist when interpreting light.

It's easy to become confused when trying to create a stylistic interpretation. Artists often paint random color notes and marks where they don't belong. This is especially true for those trying to create a unique sense of style in their work, but have no foundation. The Apollonian sense is the foundation you should always start with, then interpret away from. Some artists may disagree with this, and there is plenty of room for unique "confused" interpretations in the world; but when you are trying to render a portrait, it helps to have a real conception of how to interpret what you see in a way that makes sense and is also stylistically unique.

The color of light and shadow

Compressed rainbow

The compressed rainbow is one of the most beautiful color concepts found in nature and is often a staple of landscape painting. This is because what is found in landscape painting is often a primary light source; the sun, which is warm, and the sky, which is an ambient light source and is cold. This produces an interesting array of colors on your subject, and it's therefore important to understand this effect and phenomenon when you are painting a subject with multiple light sources.

There are many different ways that this can happen, but typically when using a primary warm light source and a secondary cool light source, the general flow of the skin tones and values progresses through the tones of the rainbow. The flow of skin tones goes from yellow to orange to red to violet to blue, and sometimes even green. Of course, these colors are not as bright as a bag of sweets; they are usually compressed, meaning they have a slight amount of gray in them that creates a subtle and natural color harmony. Sometimes they are so subtle it can be hard to see or understand them, in which case it's especially important to keep this idea in mind to ensure you have an organizing principle to how you are painting. In the beginning, however, it's more helpful to practice this in exaggeration, so you can more easily observe how the progression naturally occurs.

One of the difficulties in practicing the compressed rainbow in skin tones is that it requires you to mix every transitional color. You cannot mix yellow and blue to produce the transitional color of red. So where the warm side of the face intersects with the cold side of the face, you must mix up a transitional tone that can bridge the gap between these two color worlds as you go back and forth between them.

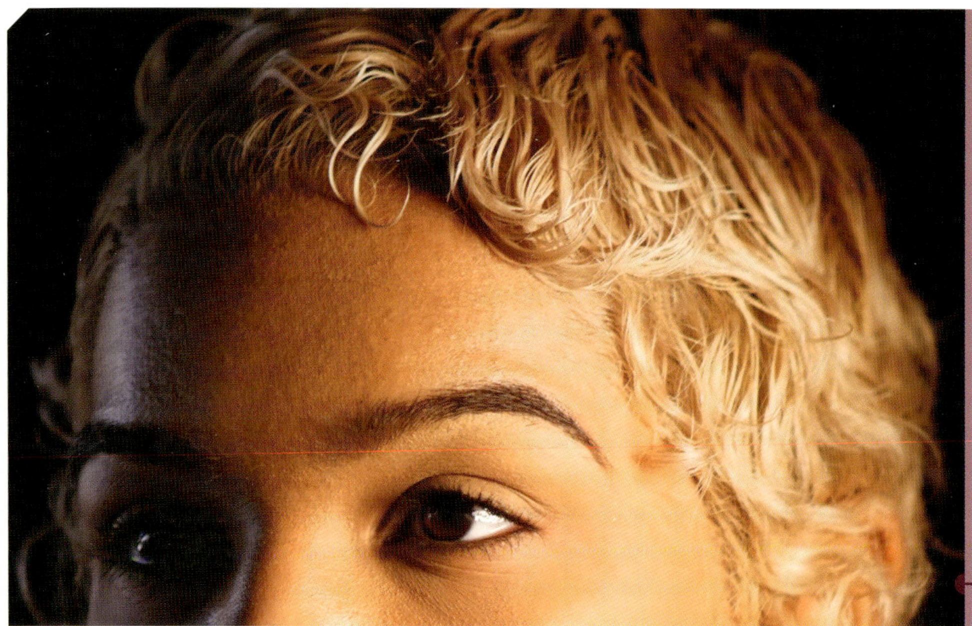

Observe the compressed rainbow effect across the subject's face

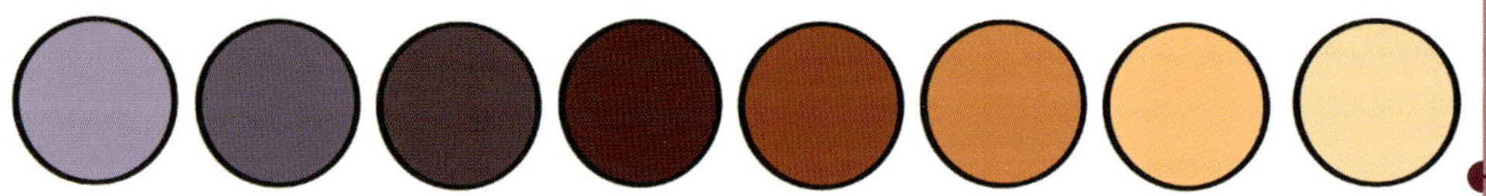

The flow of skin tones moves from yellow to orange to red to violet to blue

Color in the shadows

Split-toning

In the early days of Instagram, models and photographers would very often overuse the split-toning effect. At its best, it's a great way of turning a photo that lacks color into one that shows the light as being a different color to the shadow, improving its overall colorfulness and sense of atmosphere and light. With the numerous apps and editing features that are so easily accessible now, it's helpful to occasionally create a greater sense of depth by altering the color of the general light tones to make them different from the general tone of the shadows.

In painting, however, sometimes you may need to improve this overall generic quality and add a little of the shadow color into the highlight of the light area, and also add a little color from the light into the shadow. Warm lights don't have to be monolithically warm; they can contain a little bit of cool. Likewise, cold shadows don't have to be monolithically cold; they must contain some warmth if you want them to be more dimensional and engaging.

Bounce light

Color in the shadows can be quite a mystery. Shadows don't often have any color in photography; they are only perceived as black as the camera cannot render the shadows properly. This is one of the reasons why many artists prefer to work from life. In life, shadows often take on the color of their surroundings. They are easily swayed by the atmosphere in the room or by color and light bouncing into them. The light side of the face is a little less prone to influence by its surroundings than the shadow.

The photograph of the marble head (below) shows how bounce light can affect the shadows in a strong and significant way. It's much more easily seen on a white cast than on skin tone, but the same effect can happen to a lesser degree on skin. When your camera cannot capture some of the subtle color effects that you know are there, your conceptual knowledge can help you to activate the shadow, keeping it from being a big, dark, empty mass and instead giving it personality and tying it to its surroundings.

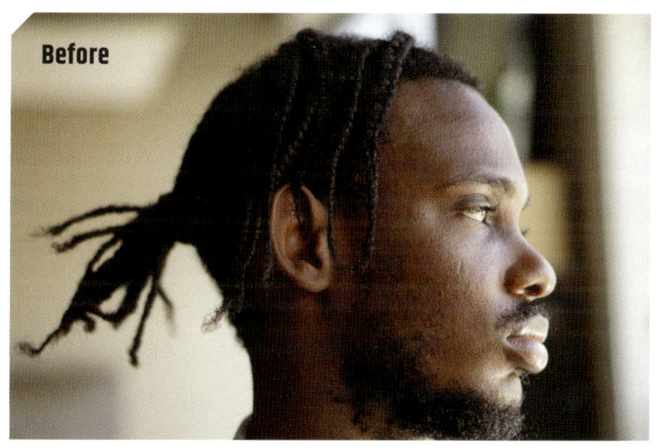

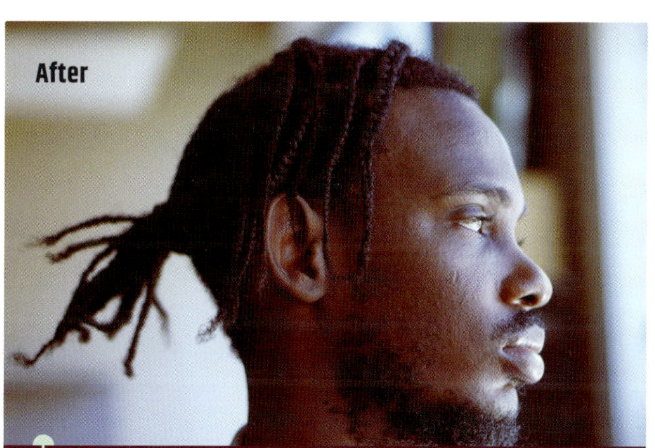

Split-toning can be used to make the light appear a different color to the shadow, enhancing the vibrancy and light of the photo you are painting from

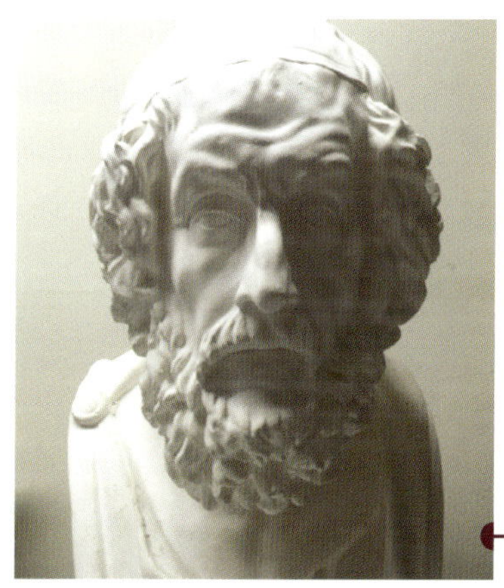

Shadows can be simple and dull when there isn't the presence of other forces acting upon them

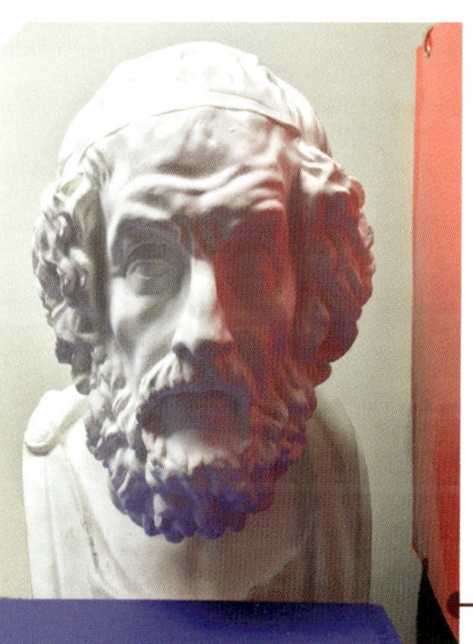

The light bounces off the red and blue screens to reflect in the shadows, showing how shadows can take on the color of their surroundings

Color zones of the face: problems with photos

Interspersed throughout these introductory chapters is a steady conversation about photography's shortcomings when it comes to portraiture. The rendering of color is perhaps one of the most frustrating aspects of working from photographs. Sometimes, under perfect conditions, taking a photograph and working from it is a dream and everything goes perfectly, whereas at other times, the rendering of the color is quite poor and stilted. In **Fig. 1,** the rendering of the color on the model is overall warm and lacks specific color zones. If you are shooting under very warm lighting conditions and your camera is not properly set, you will experience this loss of color.

To compensate for this tendency, either in the rendering of your paintings or in the modification of your photographs, you must understand color zones. This is not only true for photography in general, but understanding color zones on the face will also improve your skills.

For example, in **Fig. 2** there is a purple-ish color around the eyes and a slightly more yellow-orange color on the forehead. You may also see a spike of red in the nose, lips, and ears. There is usually less color in the skin directly around the lips, as the lips draw more blood than the surrounding skin. As illustrated, the face is not monochromatically orange as seen in **Fig. 1**, yet sometimes photography does not show this. To develop your colors, it's important to understand how different zones should activate the overall presence of color in your portraits.

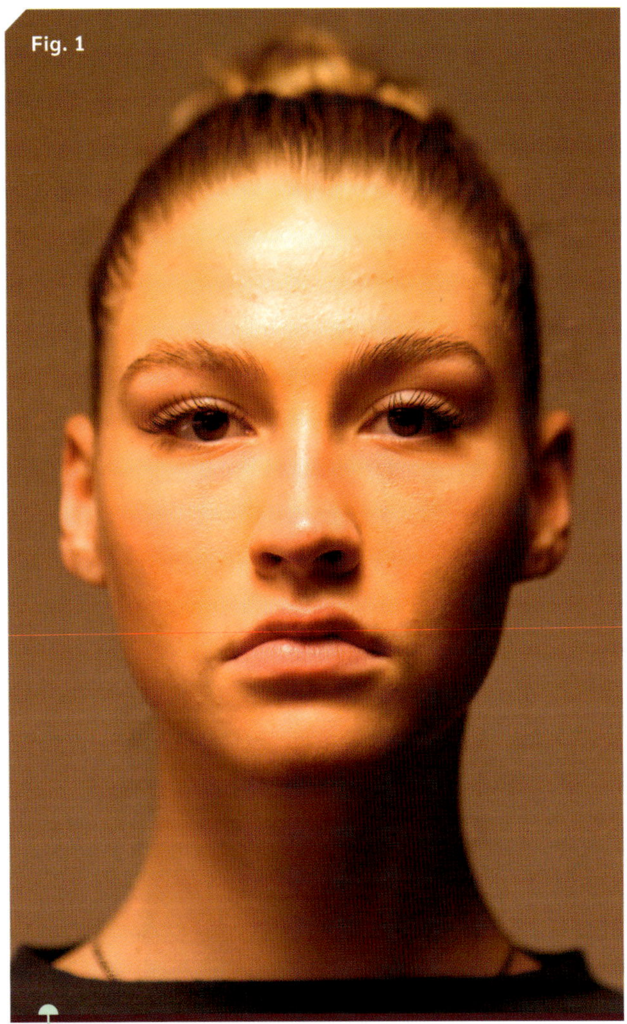

Fig. 1

The same photo, but with an overly warm tone, which makes the color zones less visible

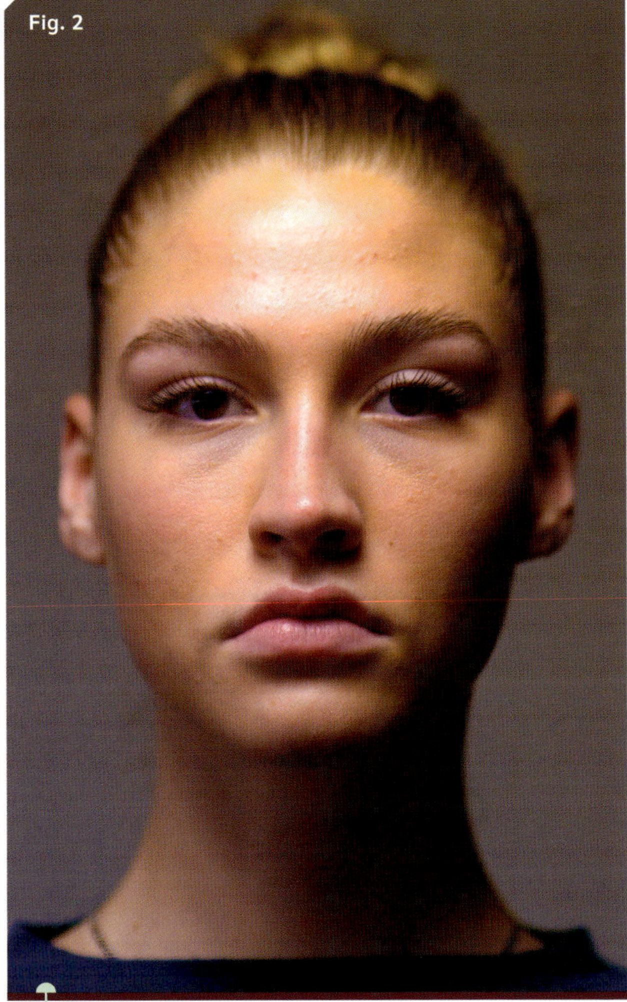

Fig. 2

Observe the different color zones on the model's face, including the purple tones around the eyes, the orange-yellow forehead, and the pale area around the lips

Unity and diversity

The elusive yet ever-interesting idea of flesh color comes down to creating unity with diversity. Unity with diversity is difficult to achieve in painting, but it must be sought in order to create a sense of order to your work. In simple terms, unity is less contrast, whereas diversity is more contrast. These alternating patterns and how they weave their way through a given subject are what add interest, while also giving your eyes a rest. You want the eye to be stimulated, but also to find quieter areas in which to rest.

The question is how much unity you want, versus how much diversity. This is a decision every artist needs to make for themselves. Generally speaking, too much unity can create a simplicity to the color that can appear boring, while too much diversity can create a randomness or chaos that does not unify the colors into a flesh tone. Shadows are typically more unified and contain less contrast in color and in value. They are also perceived as softer, while the light has more contrast, diversity of color, texture, and detail.

Both diversity and unity can be found in the detail of this oil painting. There is a shimmering sense of color diversity throughout the skin, but it's most pronounced in the light. There are greens, grays, yellows, and pinks, but they all unify into the mother color. You can also see a little diversity in the shadow, but it is mostly quiet and more unified. Likewise, because there is so much diversity in the light, the background has been unified into a much simpler tone.

There is also a sense of variety with the brushstrokes. The brushstrokes used to describe the eyebrows and hair are different from the ones used to describe the flesh. They are also much less pronounced in the shadows. However, overall the brushstrokes are unified in the way they appear to transition in and out of those differences seamlessly, therefore creating a sense of unity even in the brushstrokes.

This concept of unity with diversity can be extended from ideas of color into those of edges and even notions of drawing. It is a driving rhythm behind creating harmonious and interesting work.

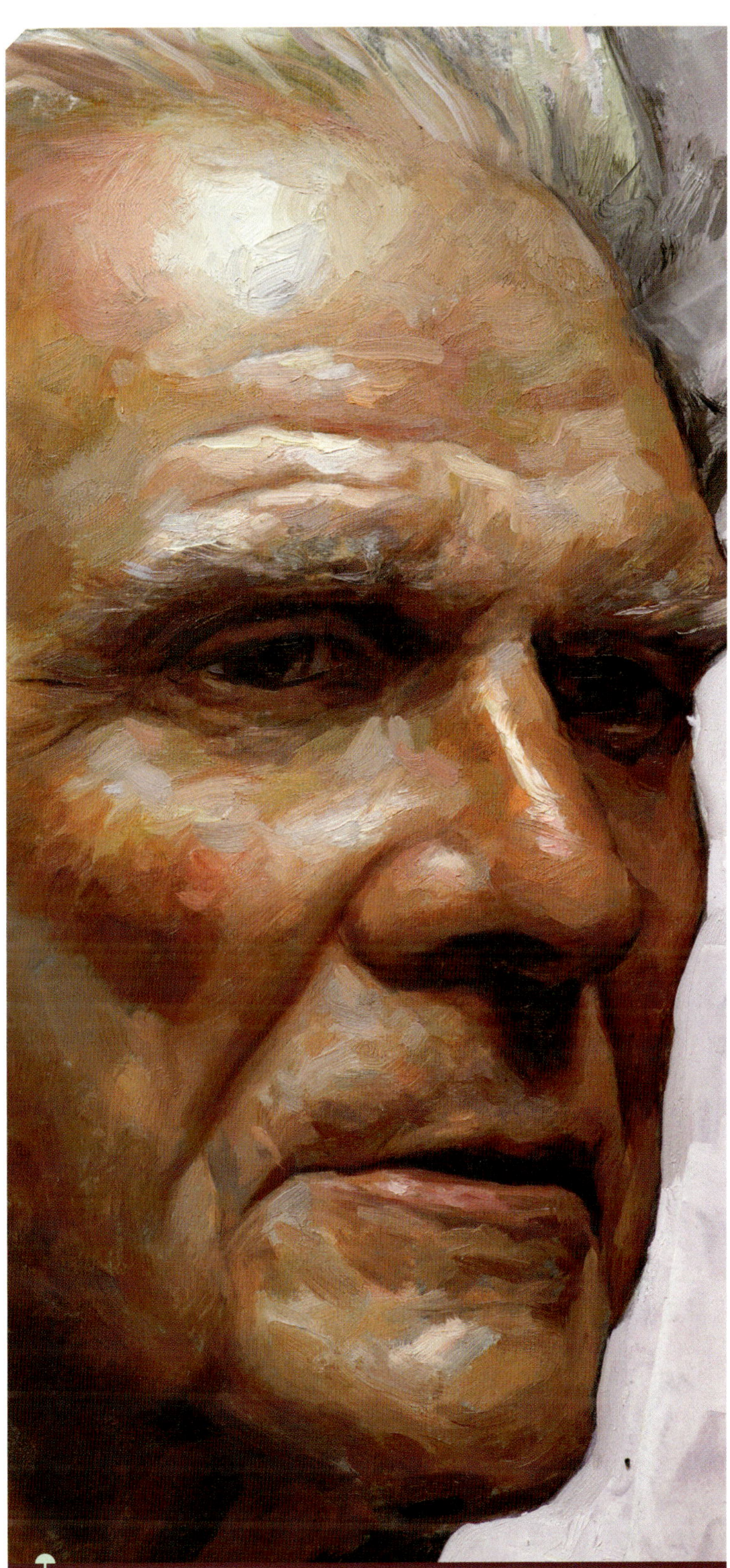

Color diversity is present throughout the skin tone, most notably in the lighter areas

CREATION CYCLE: EDGES

Photography and artwork © Steve Forster

This chapter will cover:

- Four types of edges
- A spectrum of sharp to lost
- Complex edges
- Brushstrokes, edges, and style
- Creating movement with edges
- Ways of creating various edges

Four types of edges

As the great David Leffel said: "edges are the soul of a painting." In the creation cycle detailed in these chapters, you may think they would be the easiest of the components. However, even dealing with edges is a difficult and mysterious task for the artist.

As a simple introduction, edges can be simplified into four categories: sharp (hard), soft, lost, and broken. This is an oversimplification and will be addressed later in the chapter when discussing complex edges (see page 76), but it's a helpful way of classifying the quality of most simple edges. There can be different kinds of sharp edges and different kinds of soft edges, but for introductory purposes this chapter will keep it simple.

In some ways, the two most important edges are hard edges and lost edges. These are the beginning of creating a spectrum of form, but it is difficult to maintain a spectrum of them in your work. Most artists are usually either too hard-edged or too soft-edged, but rarely do they achieve an effective balance of both.

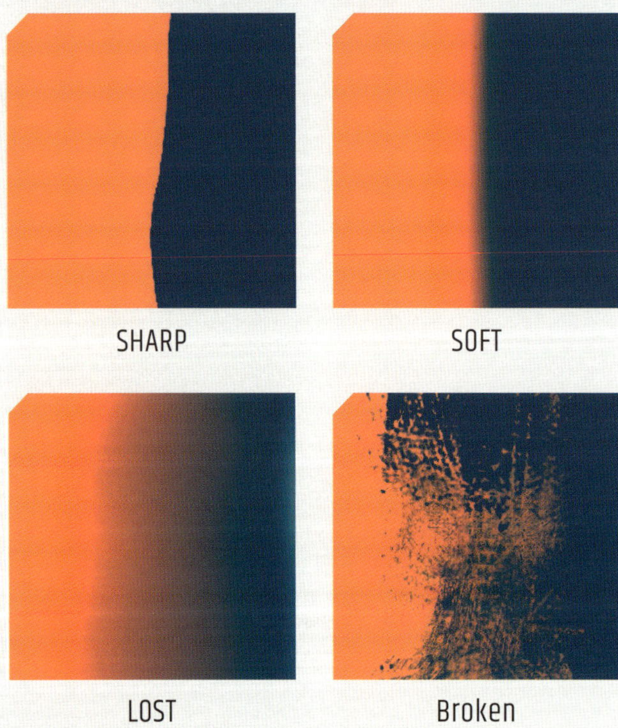

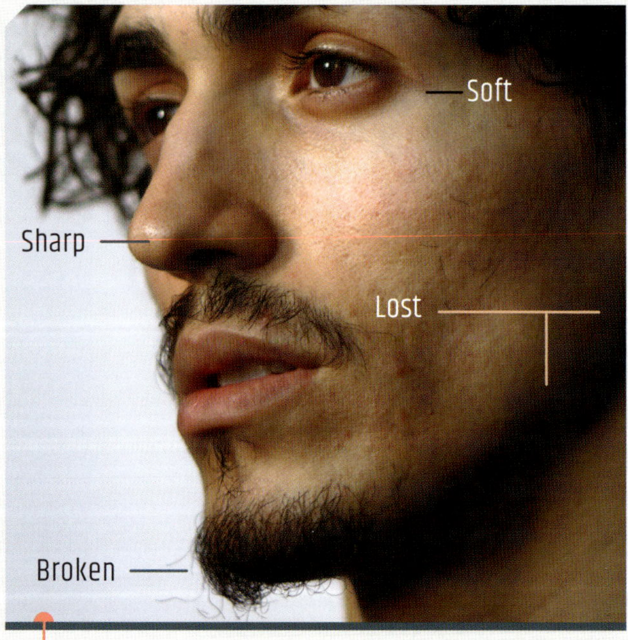

The face contains many different types of edges, which can be simplified into four main types

A healthy balance of all four types of edges

It's healthy to create a balance of all four types of edges in your portraits. If your subject does not contain one of the types of edges, you may wish to add it in anyway. It's pleasing to the eye to view a variety of different edges, preventing you from becoming bored. It also provides a greater sense of sophistication in understanding the unique qualities of your subject.

A portrait painted with oil paints can very often become overly soft and smudgy. This can also be true in digital painting, especially if you are trying to render form and create the sense of light rolling over your subject. Textures and variation are often lost when smudging to create form. If this is true for you, then it's important to focus on sharp edges and broken edges in order to provide a greater sense of depth and visual interest. Conversely, in pastel work the drawing can sometimes become too broken and rough, as this medium produces broken edges more easily. The antidote to that problem would be to create sharpness with a pastel pencil, as well as softness and lost edges with brushes or a finger. No matter the medium or what your personal proclivities and biases are to the types of edges you prefer, there will be more depth to your work when there is the presence of, or at least a nod to, the other types of edges.

Of course, not every painting has to subscribe to this philosophy, but the eye craves unity with variety. It's helpful to maintain a healthy balance of all four kinds of edges. Now, within this variety of edges, certain styles dictate that perhaps one edge is privileged over another; there doesn't always have to be an equal balance between all four types of edges. But even so, it's good to show contrasting edges to prevent the eye from getting tired of looking at the same type of edge everywhere.

Naturalistically speaking, there are places where specific types of edges usually occur. Hair, for example, always contains broken and soft edges, but may not have hard edges. Or when the edge of the nose meets a background, this will typically have a hard edge. When light is cast from above the jawline, the edge where it meets the shadow will likely be very soft, or even lost.

With careful observation and study, you will learn to recognize patterns and places where the four types of edges typically occur. Even when they don't occur in your subject, such as if you are working from a blurry reference photograph, you may want to enhance the spectrum of edges by introducing hard edges or broken edges where they would typically be found. This will add visual interest and keep your painting from becoming boring by being too soft.

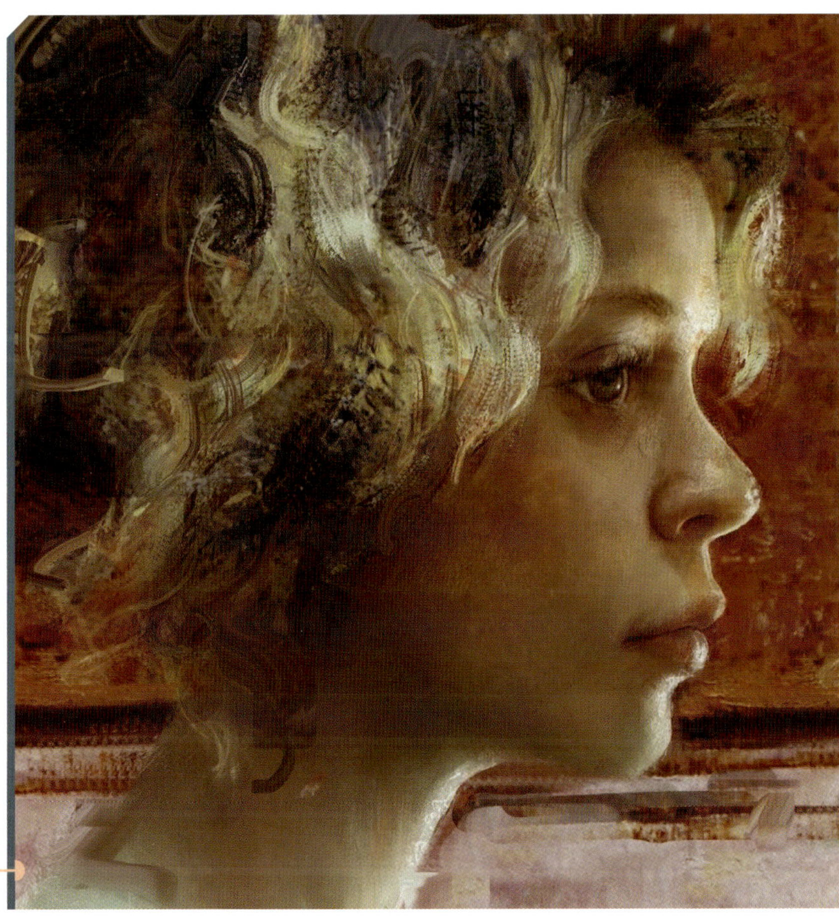

Contrasting edges will create visual interest and a feast for the eyes

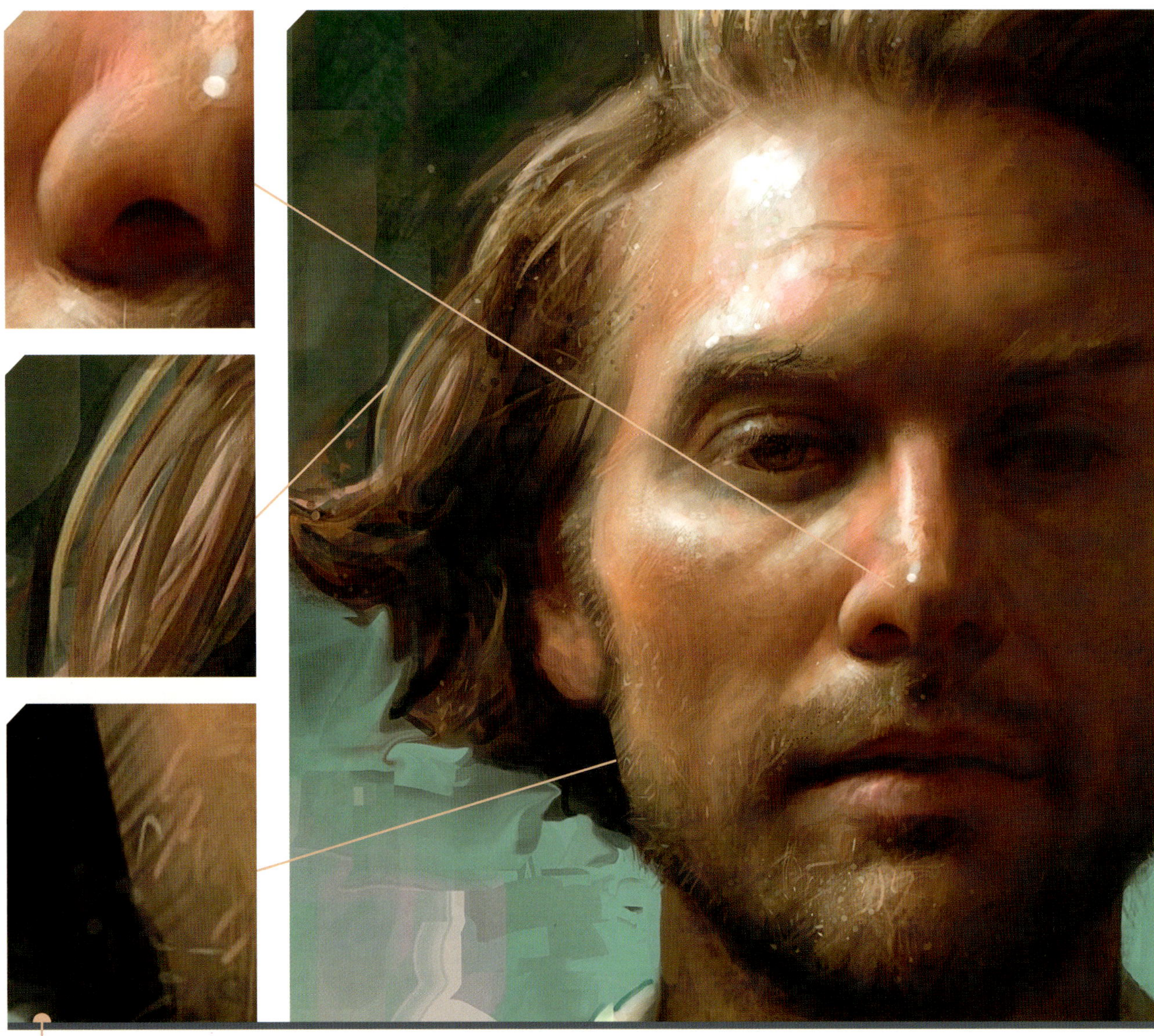

A small number of carefully placed sharp edges can guide the viewer's focus and enhance the overall portrait

Sharp edges

Sharp, or hard, edges probably command the most attention of all of the types of edges – the exception would be a very busy, broken edge – as hard edges with contrast are typically a lightning rod for the eyes. Your eyes will always be drawn to hard edges, whereas they will tend to travel over a soft or a lost edge. Keeping this in mind, you want to create hard edges not only where they naturally occur, but also where you want to command the most attention. If there's an area where you want the viewer to look and there happens to be a soft edge there, consider making it a hard edge instead.

Some digital painters only paint with hard edges, making their shapes very strong, graphic, and easily read from a distance. Within the hard edges of the shapes they will then create gradations of color and value. This is one way they keep that balance between sharp and soft. They are not actually showing soft edges, but within their sharp shapes there are soft gradations.

Typically, you should aim to keep your hard contrasting edges to a minimum and be mindful of where you place them. They are like highlights; a small amount of highlight is attractive, whereas too many highlights become confusing and difficult to look at. Similarly, a few well-placed sharp edges in the right areas will illuminate the subject and create a sense of focus about where the viewer should look.

Soft edges

Soft edges are a transitional edge from sharp to lost and are the basis of being able to control your medium. To have control over your medium, you need to be able to create sharp graphic edges along with smooth transitions that melt away from those sharp decisions into soft or lost areas. The middle language between this lost quality and this sharp quality is soft edges.

As they are transitional, soft edges can be frustrating to create. They are neither sharp, nor perfectly lost. This is especially true in oil paint.

Often what you think is a hard edge is actually a soft edge. When drawing the mouth, most people will make the upper lip a hard edge because they see a white rim of light above the lip. However, upon further examination, what you will see is that the lip softly rolls and dissipates into the flesh tone above it, with a soft highlight above that. Also, in pictures that possess a strong sense of depth of field, soft edges are almost everywhere, and therefore must be controlled and observed. Even a hard edge like the front edge of the face in this image is slightly soft due to this effect.

Soft edges and transitions are what show whether or not you have control over your medium as you turn form. They are worth your time and practice.

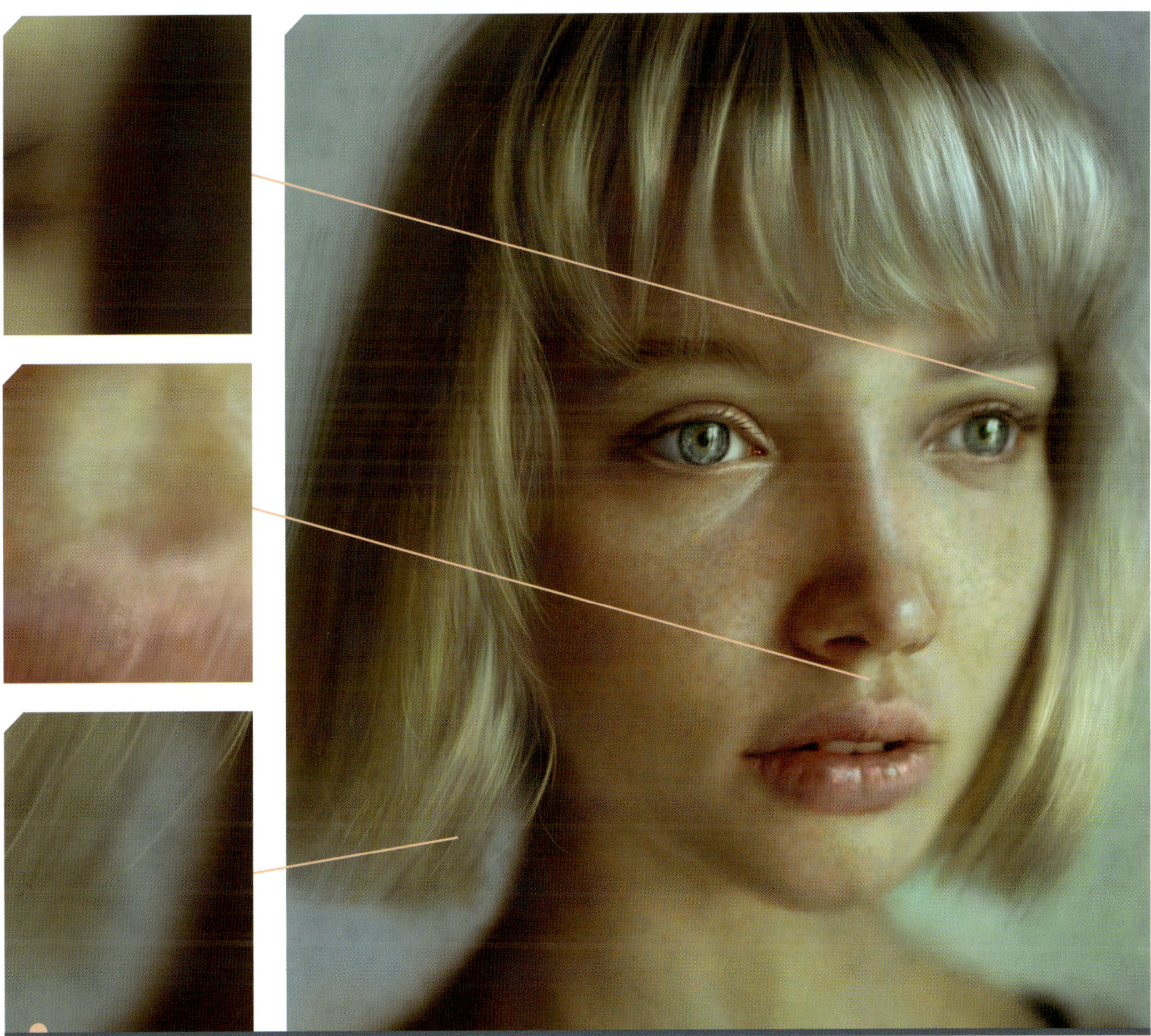

The face contains many soft edges, transitioning from a hard edge to a lost edge

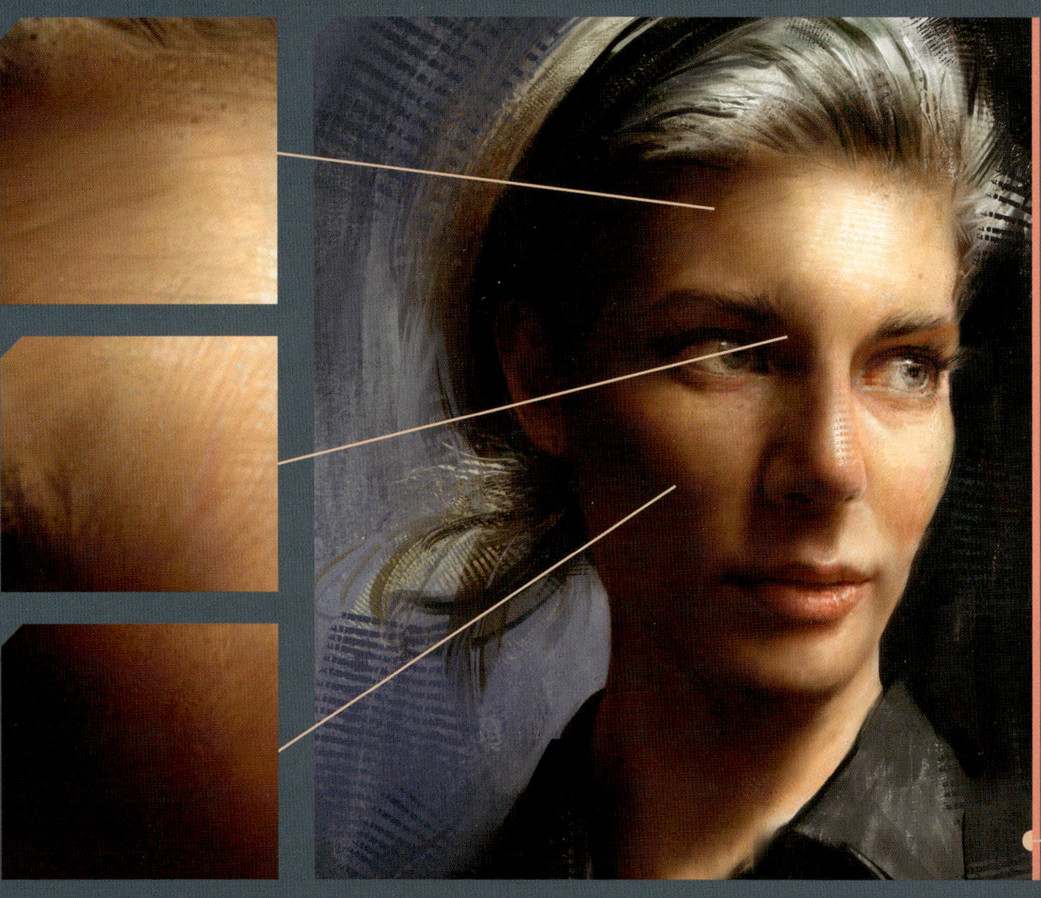

Using lost edges, or slow soft gradations, in a portrait will create variety and balance with the other types of edges

Lost edges

Lost edges could be classified as gradients, or very slow gradations, or super-soft edges. Though they are typically areas people don't pay much attention to, they amplify the presence of hard and broken edges. Lost edges are the unsung heroes that create variety and harmony with the other edges. They are often found in the jawline, hairline, and where the hair meets the background, but they can also be found where the darkest light meets the edge of the shadow. Many classically trained artists make a big deal about the shadow edge, outlining this terminator and making it strong when blocking in a portrait. However, this area where the terminator and the darkest light are touching is usually quite soft, or lost.

As seen in the portrait above, there are many examples of lost edges. They are visible where the light meets the shadow in the forehead, in the edges of the beard, and in the slow turning of light on the nose. A lost edge can also be classified as when the value of the subject is exactly the same as the value of the background, making it unnecessary to outline that edge. You can see this where the top right of the subject's head gets lost into the background.

Sometimes lost edges aren't even considered edges at all. Some artists simply refer to them as a gradation, or say that the lost edge is simply a very soft touch. However, for the intents and purposes of this book you can consider these slow gradations as lost edges and an important part of the vocabulary of using edges purposefully.

It is also worth making the distinction of lost edges as something that is separate from a soft edge. The moment a soft edge becomes a super-smoky lost edge, the image gains a greater sense of atmosphere and "bigness" needed to set off the sharp, detailed edges. Remember, the goal is to show a full, well-rounded spectrum of edges.

Lost edges can sometimes get artists into trouble, as in the effort to make them, there is the risk of spoiling other details in the process. It's therefore helpful to set your foundation using only hard and very soft edges, so the details you work hard to create later – including textures and hatch marks – don't get wiped away as you try to create a lost edge at the end of the process. If you build them into your work right from the start, the detail can sit on top and won't be washed away.

Broken edges

Broken edges are perhaps the most fun and expressive of all the edges. It's likely they contain the most variety as well. You can create broken edges using the side of a piece of charcoal or by dragging your paintbrush, or using any tool that causes a little interference and is not a totally solid mark-maker. Pastels also mimic this effect on a rougher type of paper, as does dragging paint over a canvas in a dry manner.

These examples can suggest a fake or simulated amount of detail very easily. For example, you could treat eyelashes as a broken edge, along with stubble on a beard. You could also treat the highlight on the nose as a broken light. In this way, broken edges are very useful for creating the appearance of detail without the effort of drawing each individual strand of hair or pore on the skin.

As mentioned earlier, it's advisable to maintain a balance between all four types of edges, but if you look closely at this painting, you will notice that most of its edges are broken. Within that spectrum of brokenness, there are areas that are a little sharper and other areas that are a little more broken and scattered. A painting can sometimes have a general proclivity toward a certain type of edge, but it's important to somehow acknowledge the idea of the spectrum of all four types of edges with a general pull toward brokenness. For example, there are sharp broken edges, lost broken edges, and so on.

Some painting styles need to include this type of edge more than others, however it's an important edge to be aware of and use in your painterly vocabulary.

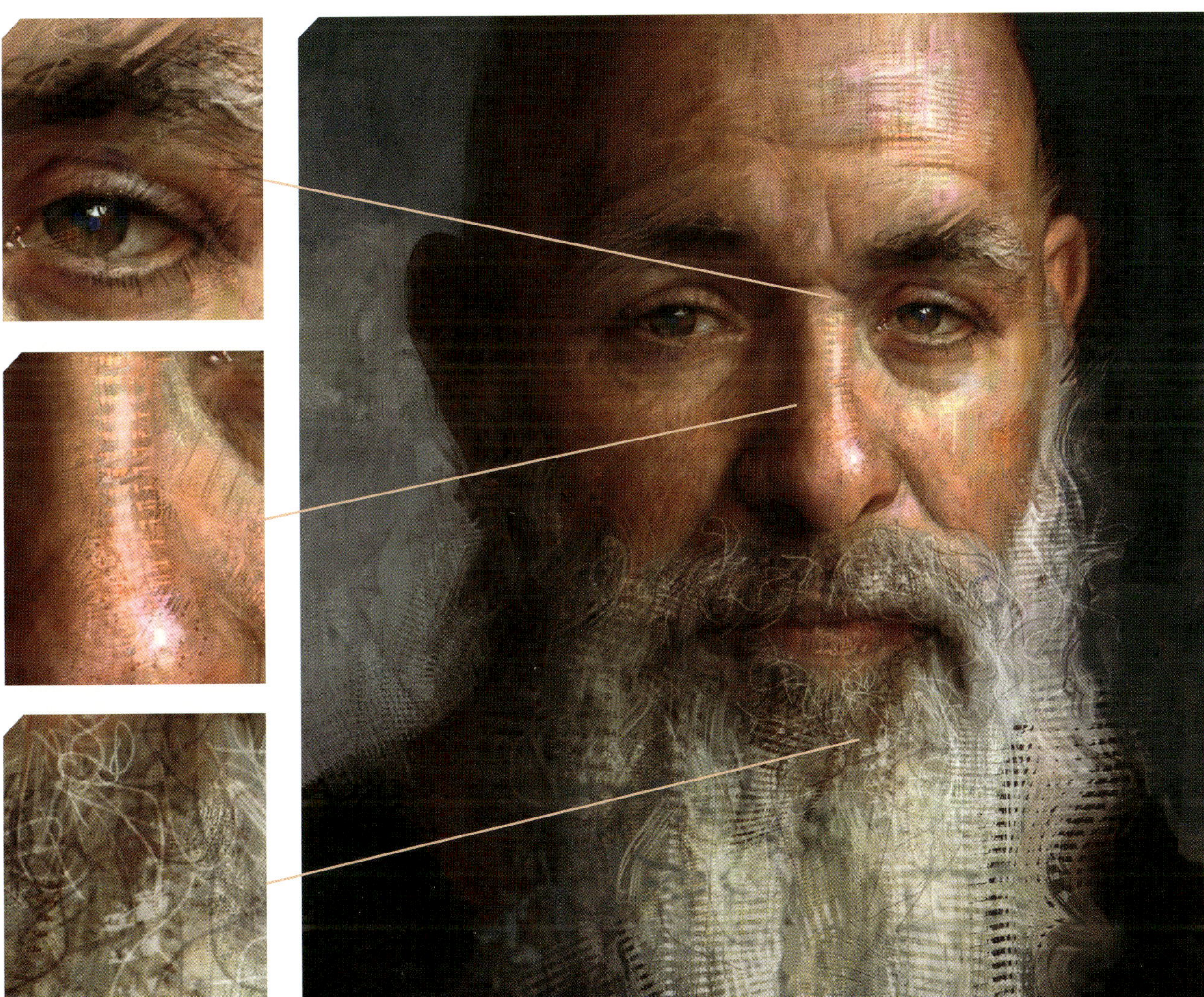

Broken edges can be used to suggest detail, such as eyelashes and facial hair

A spectrum of sharp to lost

The first major distinction in edges is to understand that there are sharp and lost edges, plus a spectrum in between. If this was your only understanding of edges, it would be useful in describing the natural world. As detailed earlier when exploring form, it's critical to maintain control of your edges; for example, creating sharp exterior edges and soft interior edges, as seen in **Fig. 1**. This section will progress your understanding of edges, exploring the idea of a spectrum from sharp to lost.

To establish this spectrum in your portraits, locate the sharpest edges and replicate them in your work, then find the lost edges and make them smoky. This will establish the brackets of your spectrum, allowing you to then fill in the variation in between (**Fig. 2**). However, if you don't make your sharp edges sharp enough or your lost edges truly lost, you risk getting stuck in the middle ground where nothing is distinct. To avoid this when building the foundation, build your painting up with this simple spectrum of edges, then progress to add more visual variety with broken and complex edges (complex edges will be explored on page 76). Building this variety of edges from the simple foundation of sharp and lost edges will create a more beautiful effect.

As seen in the simulated start of a painting (**Fig. 3**), underneath all of the textures in the background, the hair, and even the nose in the finished painting (Fig. 4), there is a simple foundation of soft and sharp edges that creates gentle gradations of light and shadow. This simple foundation allows the textures painted on top to act as a way of finishing the piece with greater intensity. Sometimes a painting can be started with texture and the soft, gentle gradations appear later. There is no right or wrong answer here, but it is often more efficient to start soft and sharp, before finishing with textures.

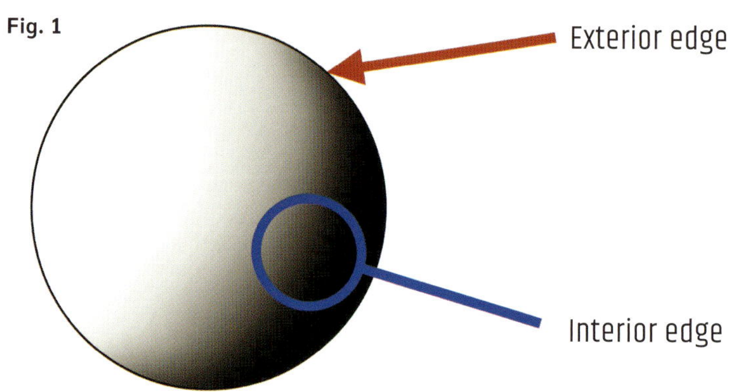

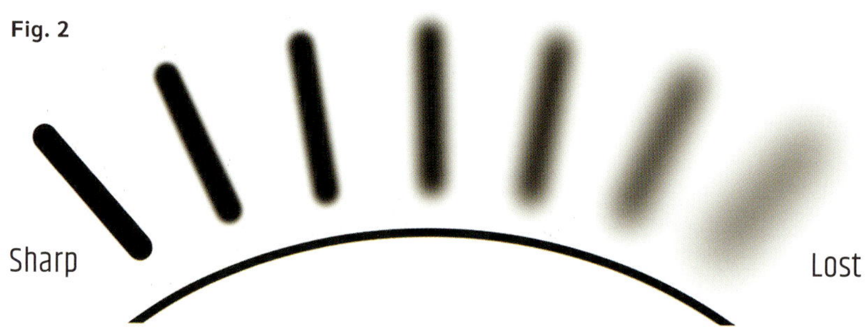

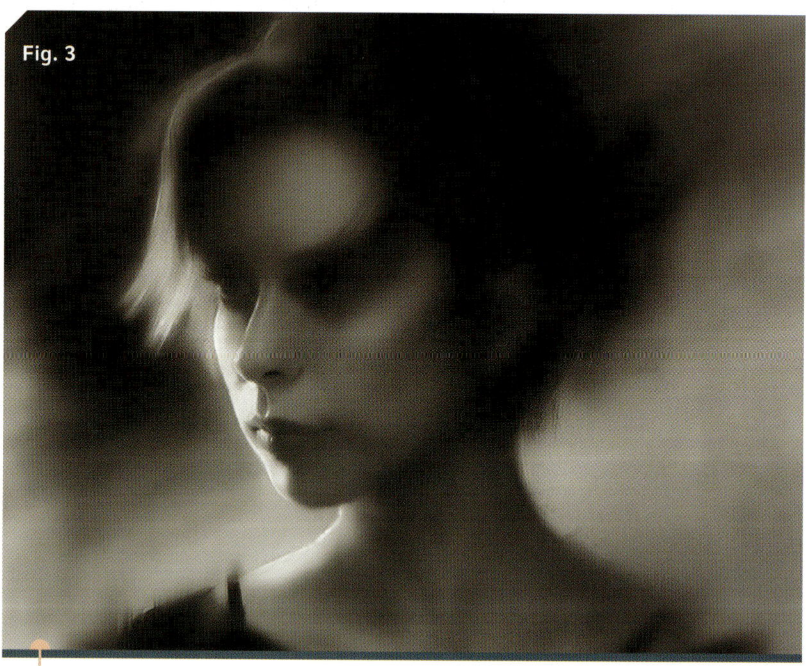

A foundation is built up using sharp and soft edges, creating smooth transitions of light to shadow

Studying **Fig. 5**, you can see the spectrum of sharp or soft contrast within broken edges. Broken edges can have a soft appearance, but may not actually be soft or blurry. They can look soft because of low contrast. For example, there is a soft look to the nose, but it is actually made up of broken edges, which adds to the intensity of its surface. This is also true of the section of the background that touches the back of the neck and trapezius. The contrast is sharper, or higher, with broken edges on the front section of the hair, the back section of the hair, and as the hair grazes across the forehead. The area of the background as it approaches the mouth is somewhere in between sharp and low contrast. Overall, this painting has a spectrum of broken edges that suggest the look of sharpness or softness, but provide a little more intensity than just making them blurry.

This is not the only method of creating such edges. You may question whether you should add the texture first and then soften, or conversely, lay a soft foundation first and add the textures on top afterward. The reality is that if you are experienced enough, you can choose either approach. Sometimes taking different paths can lead to a greater sense of uniqueness. However, early on in your portraiture journey it would be wise to lay the soft foundation first and then work detail and texture into it. You can also do this more than once throughout the painting cycle.

When you first begin painting, it's likely that you will want to start off with these exciting textures and details, as they are the first thing you see. However, it's better to begin with a soft underlayer that will make adding detail on top easier. If you paint on the detail first, you risk destroying it by softening later, as there was no foundation of soft and lost edges underneath.

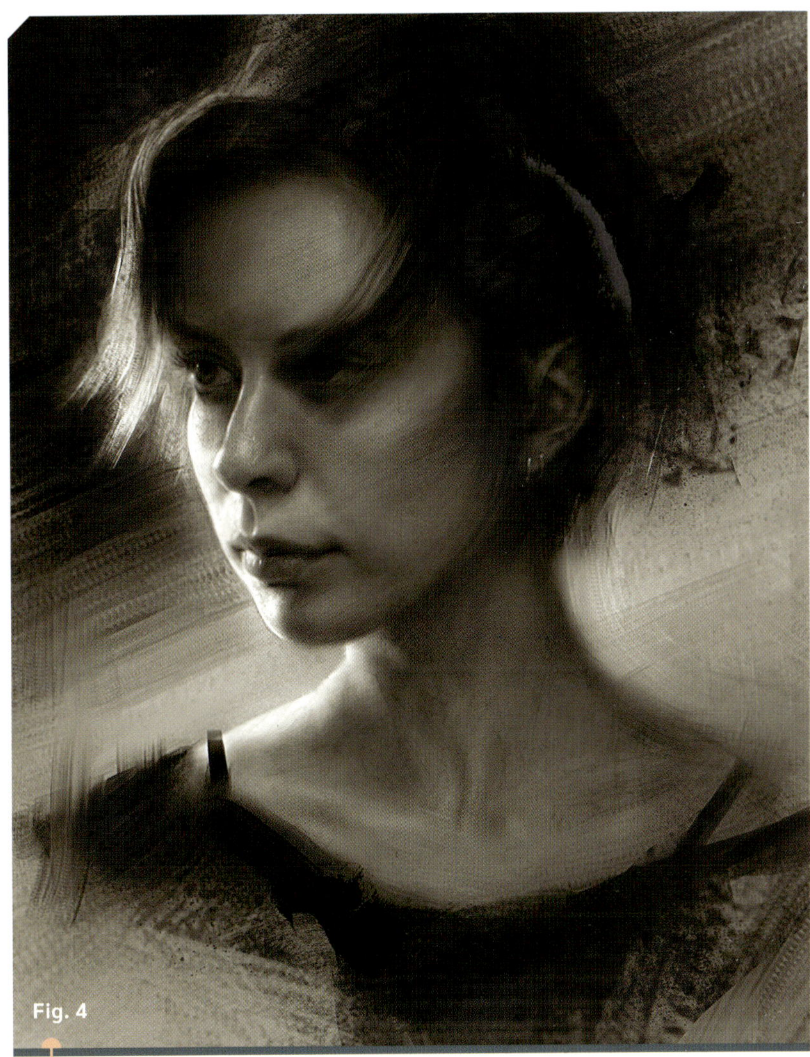

Fig. 4

This finished portrait contains a spectrum of broken edges that provides an intensity to the image

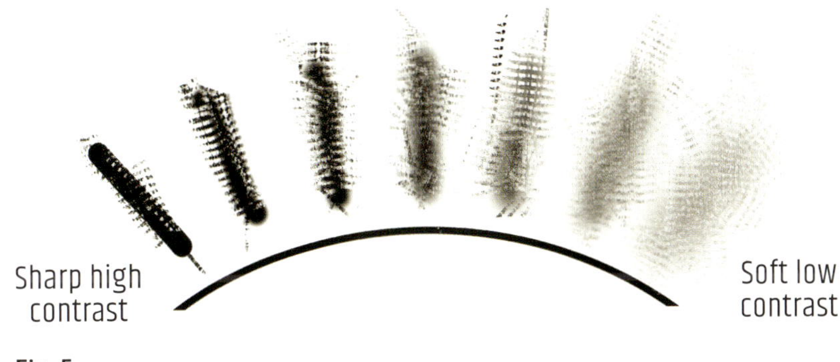

Fig. 5

Complex edges

Complex edges are hybrid edges in which there is a combination of two, three, or four different types of edge in a compact space. For example, there can be an edge that is both broken and soft, or there could be an edge that is sharp yet lost. Johannes Vermeer was the master of this. He was able to create hard edges that appeared soft through gradations that led up to them.

Complex edges are typically the most beautiful because they are a combination of ideas and create a dynamic look. Most edges found in nature are complex to some degree, but it's still best practice to introduce edges in a simple manner using the four basic types of edges outlined earlier. Once you have mastered and gained an understanding of the vocabulary of these four types of edges, you can move on to creating a more complicated and sophisticated look by creating complex edges.

Studying the details in the images below, you will observe the presence of sharp, soft, lost, and broken edges together in close proximity. This creates a layered look; layers of texture and edges, almost like a brushstroke soup. A soup is typically made of many different ingredients, yet the ingredients maintain their distinct individual flavors. So it is with complex edges. In a small area there can be the presence of soft, broken, sharp, and lost edges working together in harmony to produce a complex and bold flavor to the painting.

It's easy to miss the presence of lost edges when looking at complex edges, but sneaking that lost quality into these complicated areas is essential to keeping them from getting too busy. Too much softness in a painting leads to a boring quality, but if there's too much intensity, it can appear chaotic and stressful. Finding a balance between the lost edges and the intense edges is key to harmony.

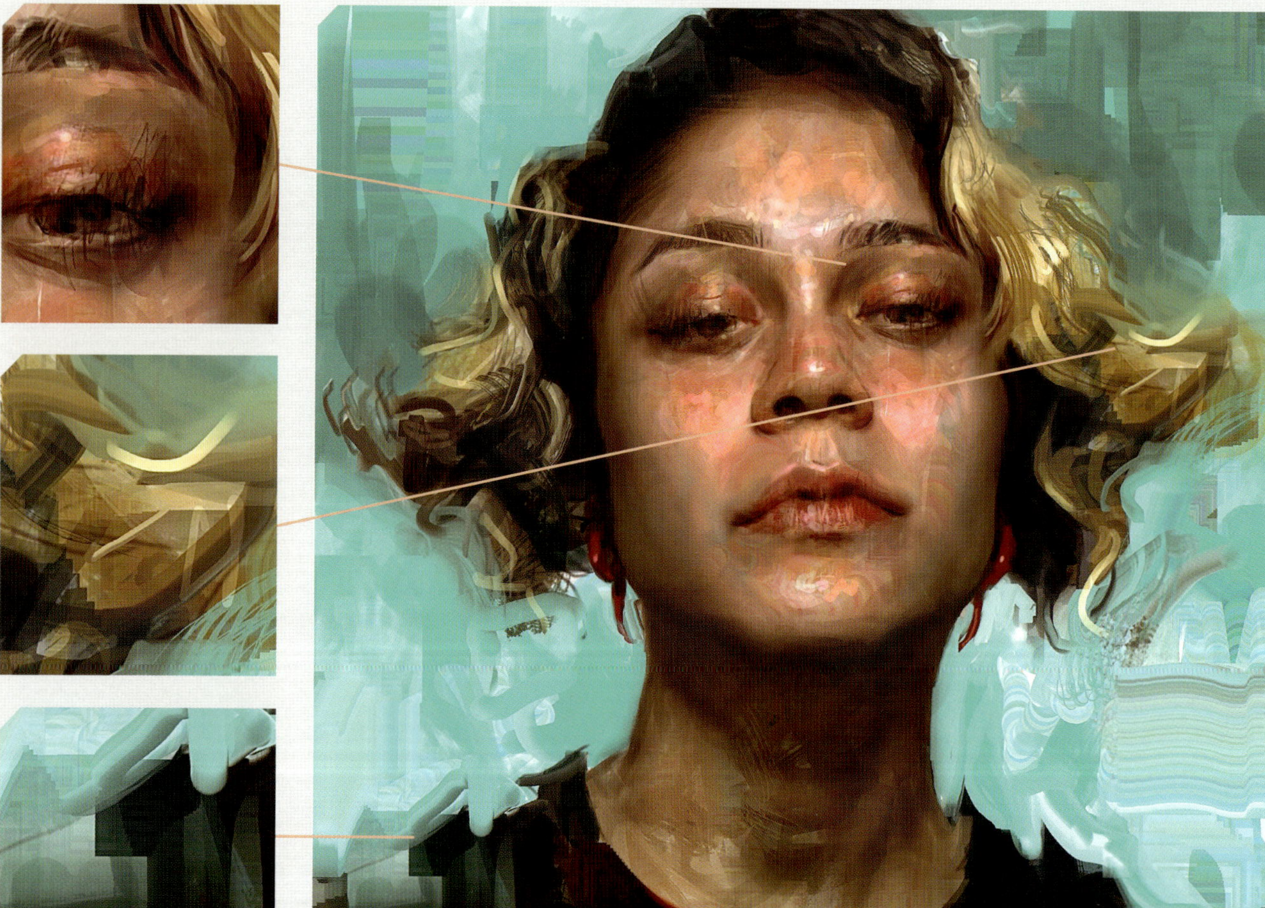

This portrait includes sharp, soft, lost, and broken edges in close proximity, which work together to create a complex, bold look

Brushstrokes, edges, and style

Brushstrokes are not as easily defined as you may think, and style is often defined by how brushstrokes are used in a painting. A brushstroke is a unique synthesis between drawing, color values, and edges, but for the purposes of this book, you can equate brushstrokes to the way edges are used in style.

This portrait of the female subject (right) has a more photographic effect, or style. It is realistic, has depth of field, and there is an overall lack of creativity with the edges. Some artists like this style because it's impressive and has an absolute fidelity to nature. It shows a care and a love for every nuance present. The study and appreciation of that can be a beautiful thing and can inform your understanding of nature and the human form.

In the portrait of the male subject (below), a creative style has been introduced into the surface of the work. The brushstrokes (or marks and edges) create the look of a digital interruption, such as you would see on a frozen TV screen. The textures and little details of squiggles and slashes create an overall sense of artistic creativity.

Both paintings demonstrate good drawing, values, and edges. What is interesting about the comparison is that one displays a sense of creativity and freedom, while the other is tied to the subject and the faithful depiction of exactly what is seen. One is not better than the other, but you can observe how the creative interpretation of edges can lead to an overall sense of style that doesn't necessarily depart from good-quality observation.

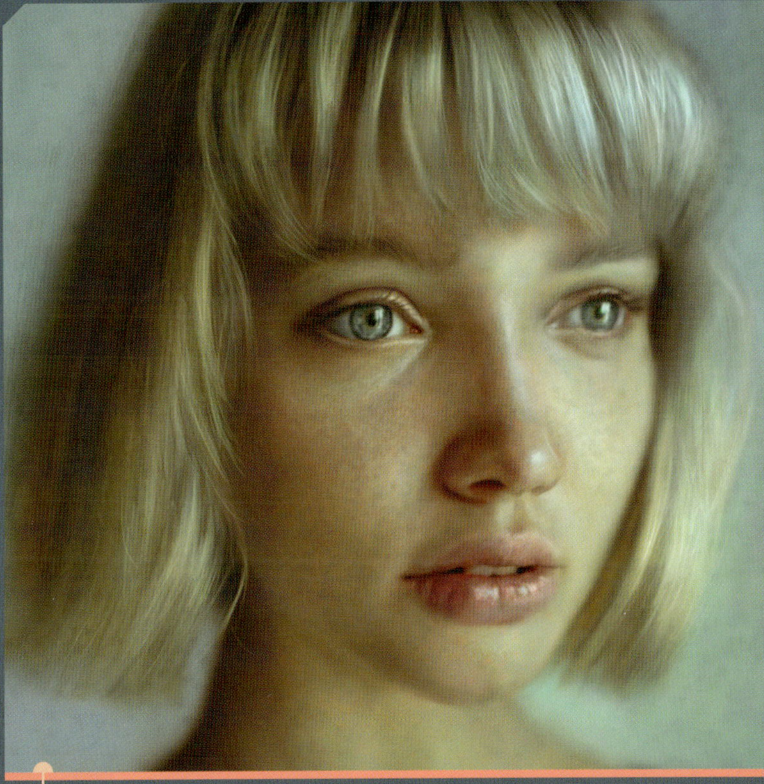

This portrait has a photographic, realistic style that captures every detail true to life

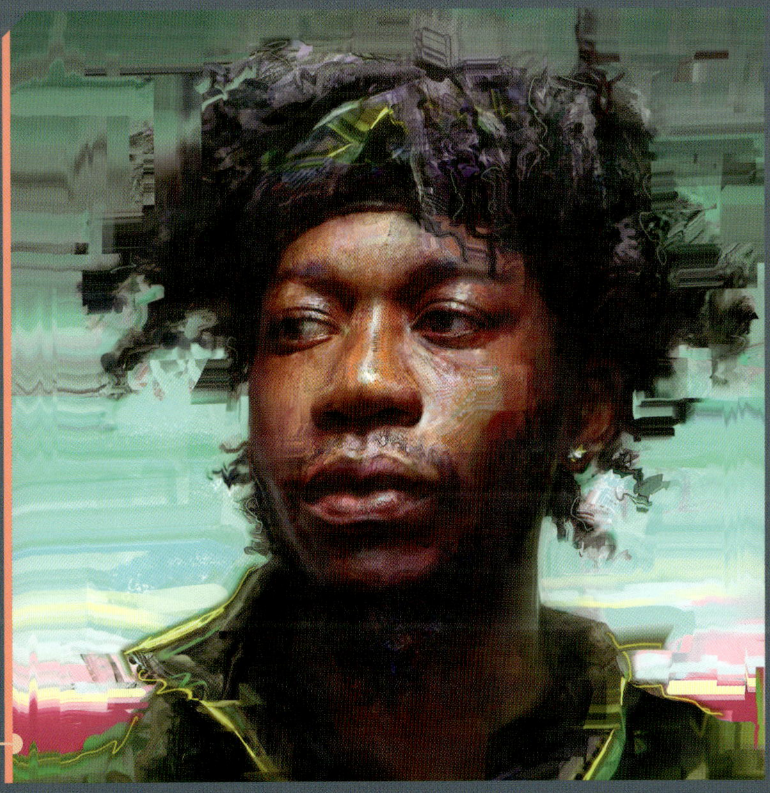

This portrait includes bold brushstrokes and edges that demonstrate artistic creativity and freedom

Creating movement with edges

Directional brushstrokes and fall-off

The premise of these introductory chapters is to condense the main ideas of portraiture into three separate categories: drawing, color values, and edges. Often these ideas overlap and are not so separate, creating a dynamic quality. This is true of creating movement with edges, or in other words, creating directional brushstrokes that have fall-off.

As seen in **Fig. 1**, a brushstroke can become more opaque with more pressure and less opaque with less pressure, creating a beautiful tension between the edge and the value. This is called fall-off. It's very difficult to separate value gradation from brushstroke as it falls off and changes value due to pressure, but this effect can be very dynamic and an attractive way of creating form that is expressive and full of life.

In the natural world, everything is in a constant state of change. An object is either moving into the light or moving into the dark, growing sharper or growing softer, becoming grayer or becoming more colorful. Fall-off and brush pressure can create these movements with a simple brushstroke. This is not an easy skill to develop. It requires you to have a little drawing in your background and for you to be willing to take some risks. Understanding the directionality and the movement of these transitions, and trying to abbreviate them through the use of the brushstroke, is something that is quite brilliant and pleasing to look at. It doesn't always work out, and sometimes you make a mistake in attempting these risky moves, but practicing will make you a stronger painter. It will pay off in the end.

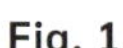
Fig. 1

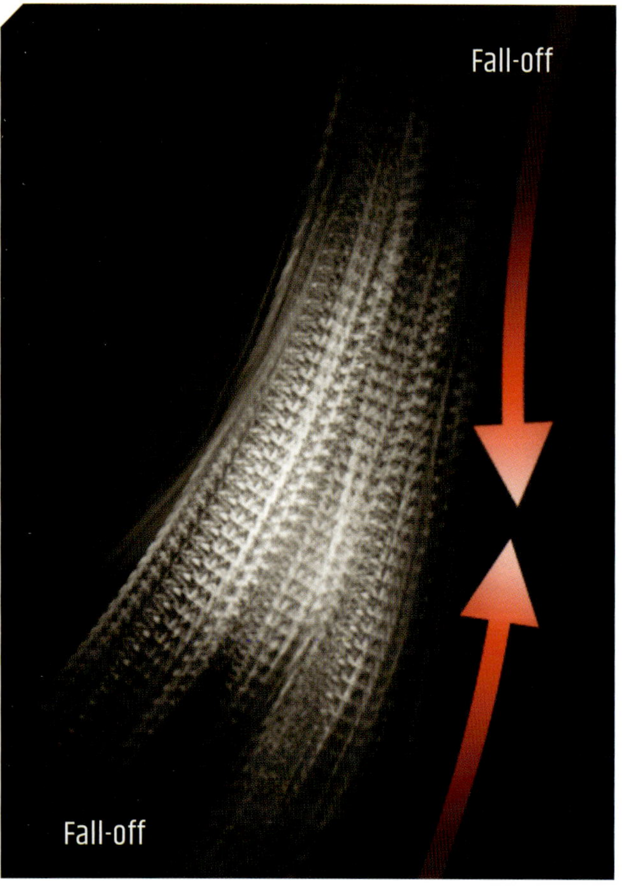

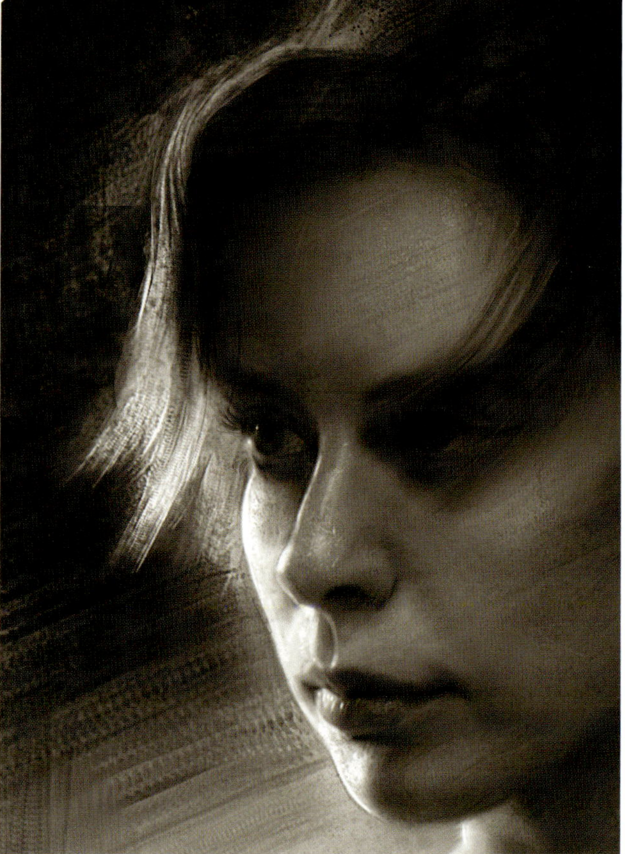

The direction of the light: pushing paint and form

The direction of light affects how you can push paint directionally to create gradations. You start by hitting a spot with the brush, then push paint in the direction of form. For example, in **Fig. 2** there is a dark spot at the origin of each arrow, then it lightens through fall-off, toward the light. If your brush hits a dark spot, and then through fall-off and brush pressure you pull away in the direction of the light, you will create shadow form with a stroke. Generally, all of these shadow strokes move toward the light source.

Likewise in **Fig. 3**, the origin of each arrow illustrates hitting a light value and pushing the paint directionally toward a darker value; another way of creating light form with a stroke. All of these strokes typically move in this downward direction away from the light source.

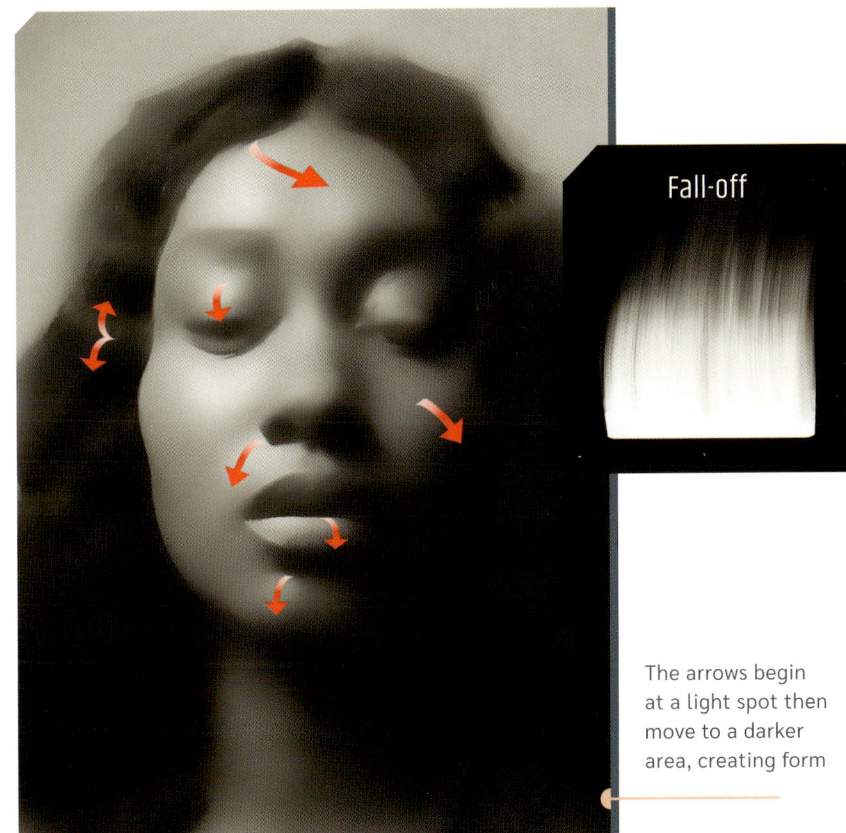

The arrows begin at a light spot then move to a darker area, creating form

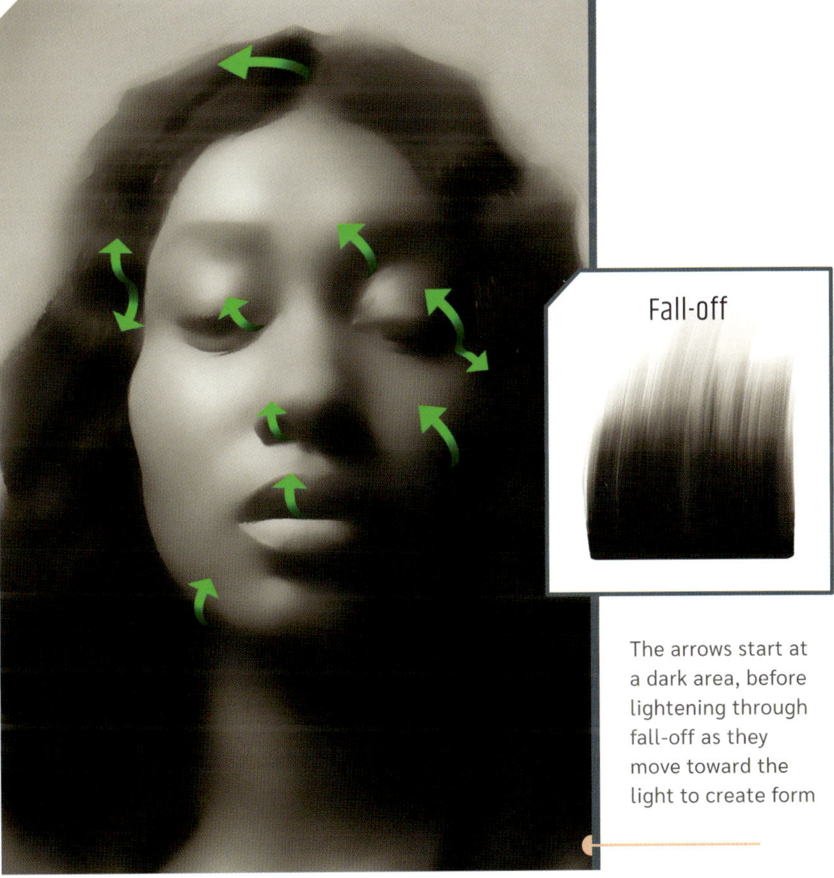

The arrows start at a dark area, before lightening through fall-off as they move toward the light to create form

Ways of creating various edges

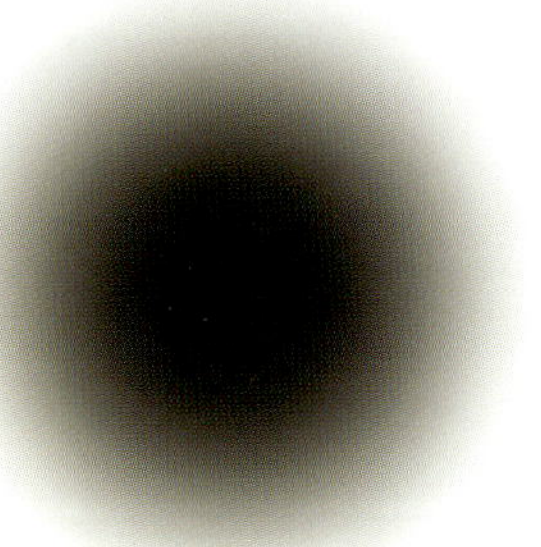

Digital soft brush

Soft brush, soft edge

To achieve different types of edges, it's important to consider different types of brushes and how you use them. Whether using a digital medium or traditional paint, it will come as no surprise that you need to use a soft brush to create soft edges. If traditional, this brush should be soft to the touch, almost like a makeup brush.

Whether you are working digitally or traditionally, it's essential to use a light touch and a sensitivity for creating soft edges. A heavy hand will produce a heavier, sharper edge, but with a light enough touch, you can use almost any brush to create a soft edge. However, for lost edges you will need the softest of brushes in order to produce such an even, slow gradation.

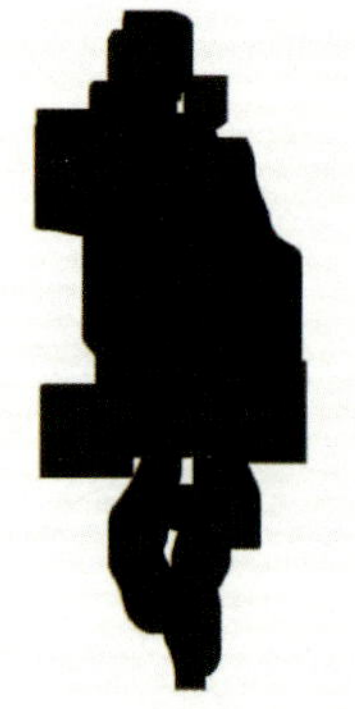

Digital sharp brush

Sharp brush, sharp edge

With traditional media, creating a sharp edge is often dictated by how you load the brush, rather than what kind of brush it is. Thoroughly loading the brush so the paint fills its entirety, or even thoroughly loading it at only the tip, will make its bristles pull together and produce a very sharp edge. Synthetic flats will also help to produce a very graphic hard edge.

There are numerous brushes to choose from when it comes to digital media, including those that will create a hard graphic edge. Sometimes these brushes will also contain texture, but it's still helpful to classify them as sharper brushes with more graphic edges.

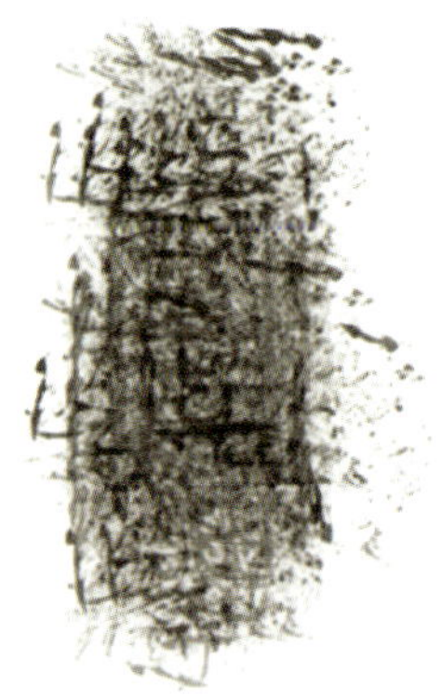

Digital broken brush

Broken brush, broken edge

How you load a paintbrush will create different textural effects. The brushstrokes to the left are produced by a very dry brush that has been pounced so it splays out like a rake, then the tip has been loaded with paint to create this broken, random stroke. The goal with traditional brushes is to create a little bit of air, or a little less of a solid line, so that it can comb through the surface like a rake. You can use other tools to produce the same effect with variation, but the idea is to avoid a solid mass of brush.

With digital software, there is no shortage of broken brushes. Most of them have this effect built into them, however it can be difficult to draw with them if you are not using them in combination with the previous two types of brushes.

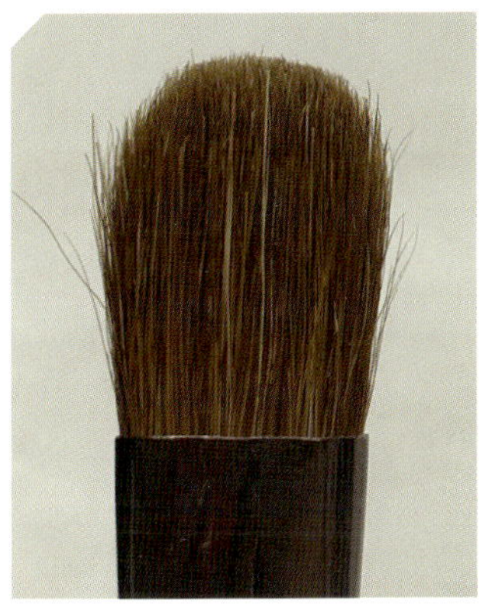

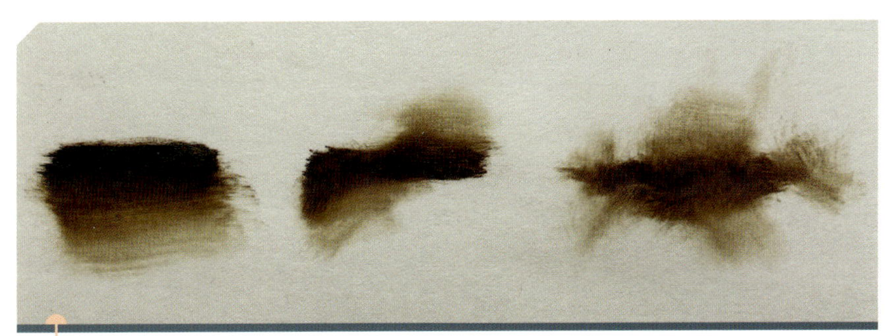

Use a soft brush with a light, sensitive touch to create soft edges

Traditional soft brush

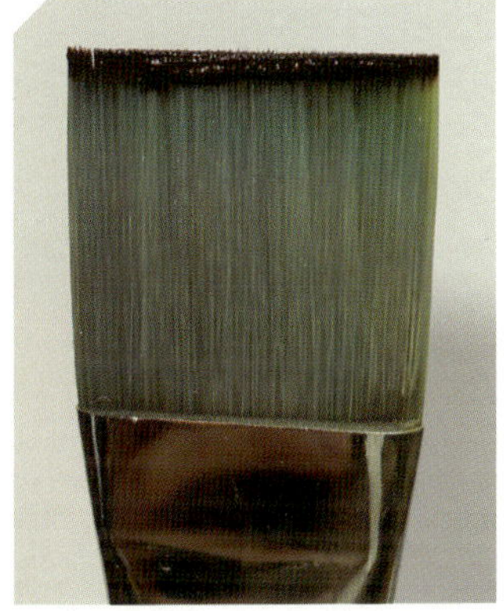

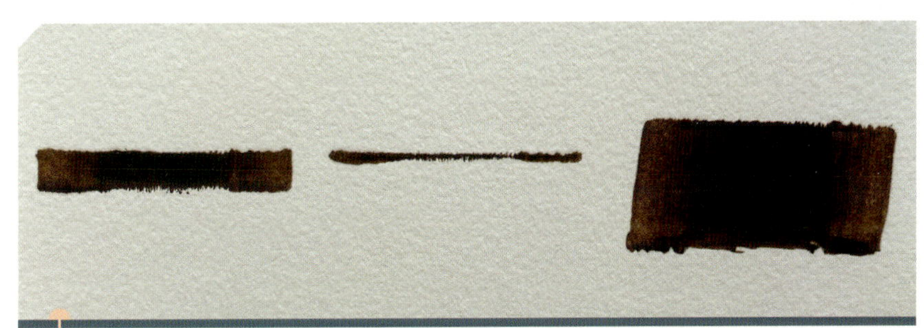

Fully load the brush with paint to pull the bristles together to create sharp edges

Traditional sharp brush, the tip loaded with paint

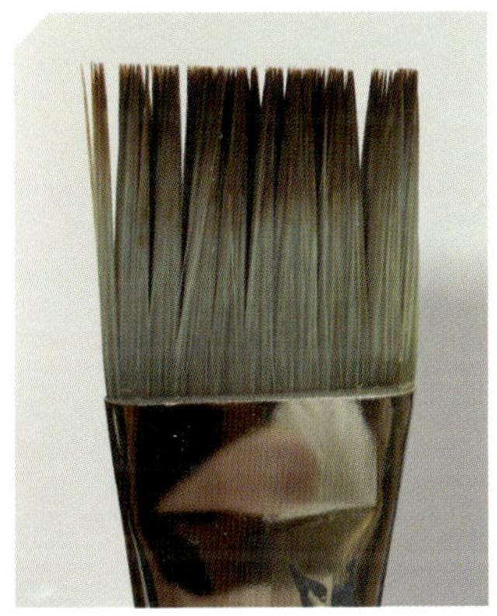

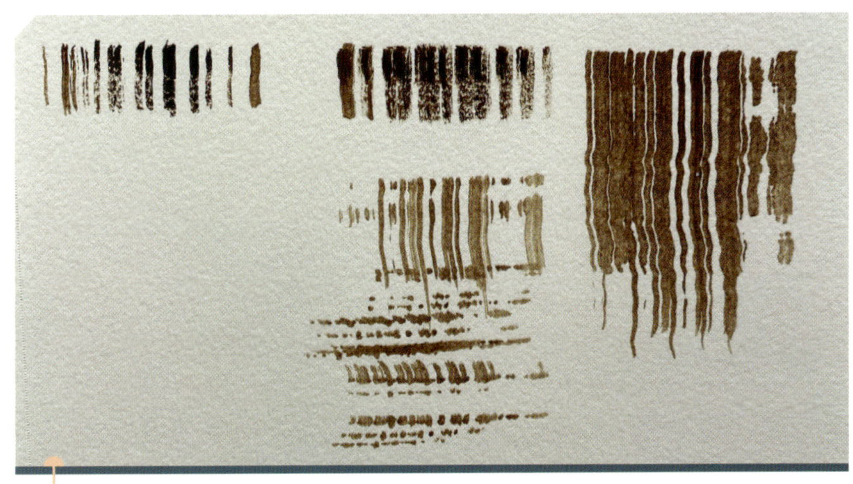

Traditional broken brush that has been pounced to splay the bristles

Use a dry brush that has been pounced to create broken, random brushstrokes

OTHER CONSIDERATIONS

Steve Forster

- PERFECT LIKENESS VS. ARTISTIC FREEDOM
- FINISHING A PAINTING
- LIGHTING AND COLOR MOOD
- BACKGROUND MOTIFS

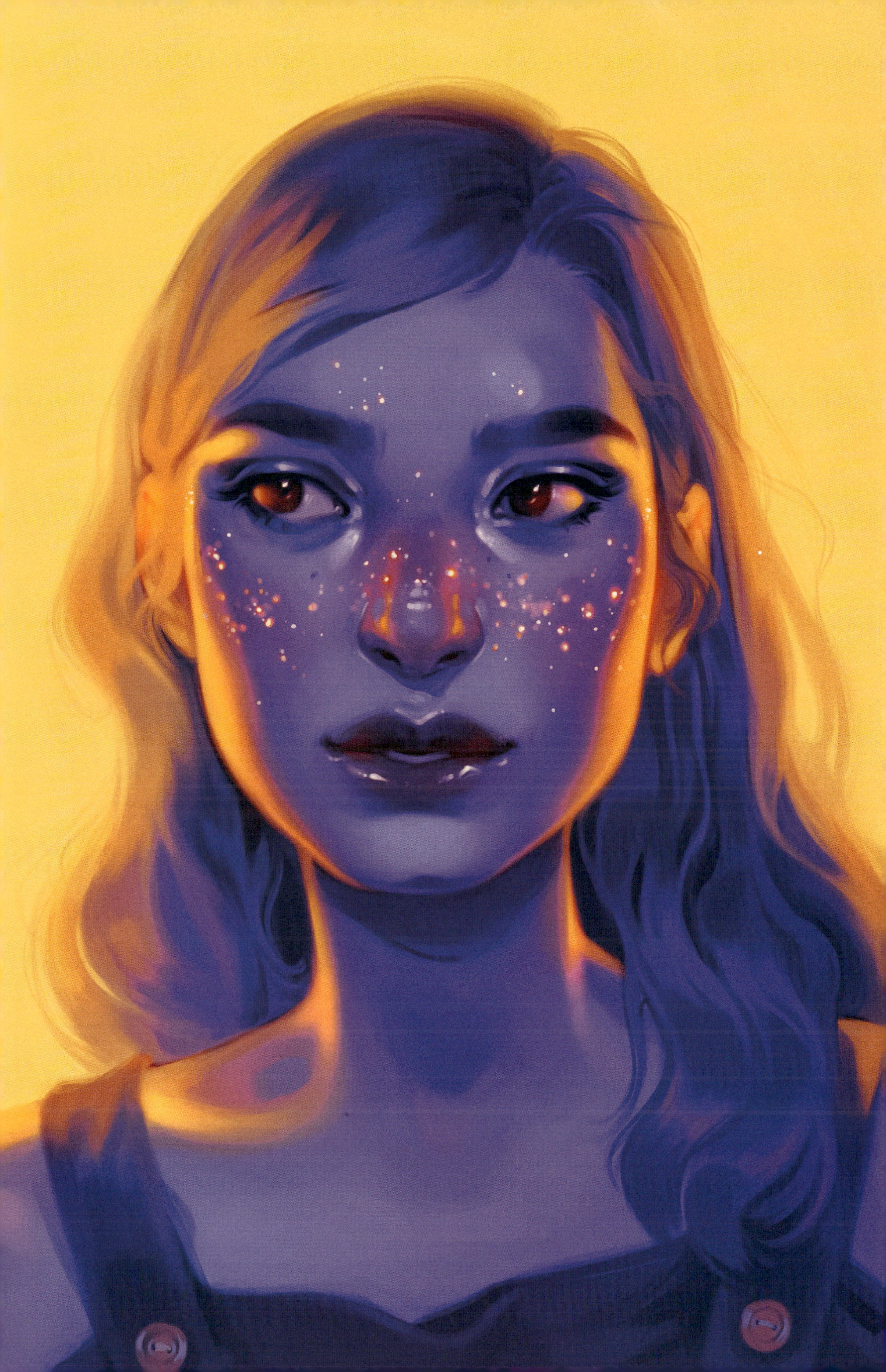

Perfect likeness vs. artistic freedom

Most artists come to portraiture with the expectation that one day they will be able to capture a likeness and the essence of their subject, yet the road of an artist somewhat diverges from this idea. With the passage of time and the more skills and experience acquired, many artists find they become much more interested in style and artistic freedom of expression than attaining a perfect likeness. This pursuit often evolves and plays out, with some level of likeness beginning to naturally occur out of this freedom as a by-product, but not always.

When you first start out, it's not unusual to experience some stress and frustration when trying to capture a likeness and the specific features of your subject. First, try to relax. Next, learn how to draw a head, exploring its structure and the colors present. Understand the medium you are using to create the different types of edges and permit yourself a little artistic freedom. Try not to put so much stress on yourself that you forget to enjoy the process.

The portrait below does not look exactly like the model in the photograph, yet the artistic freedom gives it new life, is enjoyable to create, and perhaps capturing a more accurate likeness would have lost the spirit of the painting.

There is always a delicate balance between artistic freedom and accuracy. Introducing a little artistic freedom is a good thing. If you want a flawless likeness, take a photograph, trace it out perfectly, and copy every pixel. But once you get tired of that, delve into the role of creative interpreter and grow as an artist.

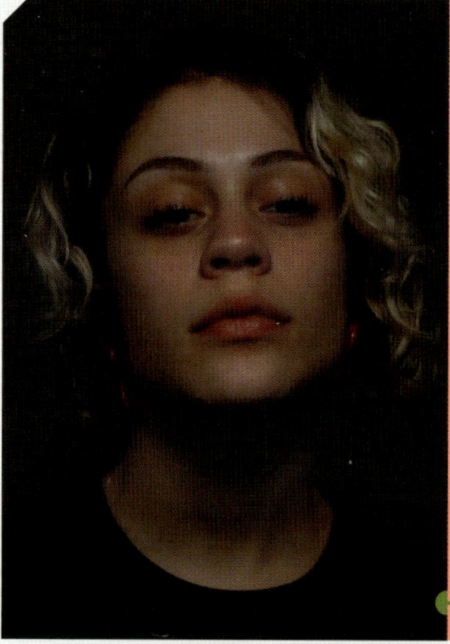

Original photograph

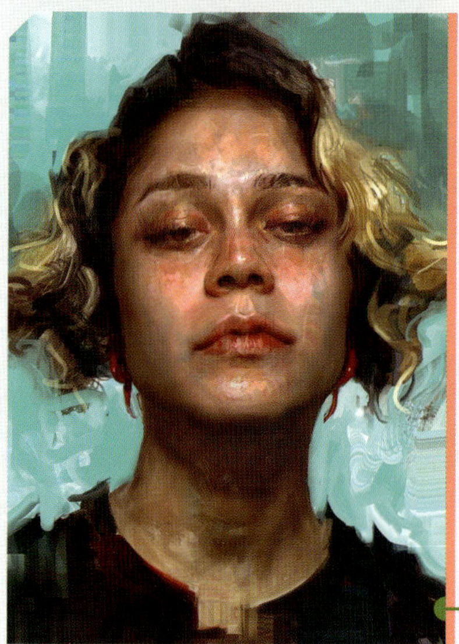

Rather than aspiring to a perfect likeness, artistic freedom has been used to capture this subject, creating a unique portrait with character and depth

Finishing a painting

Transparent and wimpy vs. opaque and bold

Finishing a painting can be the most difficult stage in portraiture. A useful technique for pushing an eighty percent finished painting to ninety or ninety-five percent is to start with transparent or "wimpy" brushstrokes, find your bearings, and then progress to bold, opaque brushstrokes.

If you have a studio session in which you wish to finish painting, that last session is very much a balancing act between these two steps. The first step involves unifying and making small adjustments by painting transparently, or wimpily, which prevents you from messing up what you already have. The second step is then to paint boldly, which increases the larger effect you are trying to achieve and prevents your painting from becoming inconsistent or aimless. This usually means playing it safe by painting transparently, before taking some risks by painting opaquely at the end.

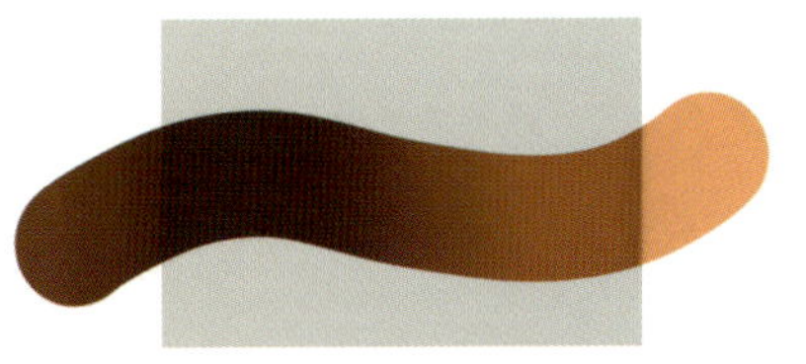

Glaze: a dark color used transparently over a lighter color – this has a warming effect in traditional media

Scumble, velatura, glaze

Within this idea it can be useful to understand transparency disambiguation, especially for artists in the traditional painting field. When nearing the end of a painting, but it's not completely finished and you find you constantly need to make value changes and slight modifications to what is otherwise a fairly solid painting, this is where glazing or working transparently comes into play. You don't want to mess up what's already there, but you still need to be able to tweak it slightly.

That could mean lightening through the use of a scumble or velatura (lead white works best), or it could involve darkening by glazing, which is painting a darker color over a lighter color. Sometimes artists use glazes and velaturas synonymously as they're both transparent, but with traditional media it's important to understand the difference. In traditional media, a scumble has a cooling effect as it becomes transparent, while a glaze has a warming effect as it becomes more transparent. These things may not be true in the digital platform.

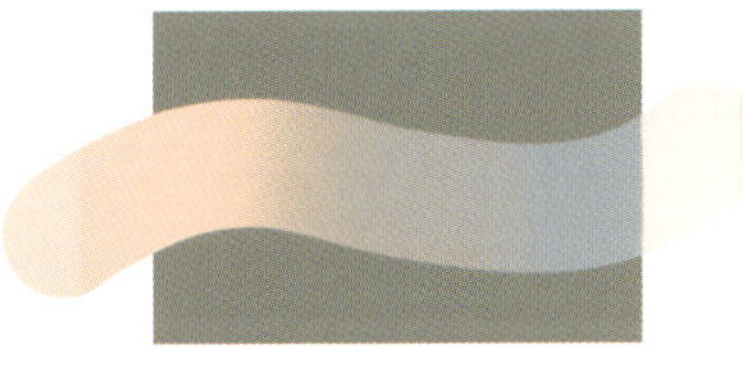

Scumble, velatura: a light color used transparently over a darker color – this has a cooling effect in traditional media

Ebauche

Another technique is the ebauche. One approach is to create an underpainting on which to try to hit the values perfectly, before transparently painting the correct color over the top of it, without trying to change the value. Technically this is not a glaze or a velatura, as it's trying to perfectly match the value of what is below it. This is applicable to both digital and traditional media.

In digital media, you can create a monochrome underpainting, then paint a layer on top that changes the color using a color blending mode. In oil painting, if you make an underpainting and are happy with the values, you then need to transparently glaze using the correct color, almost like a watercolorist with oil paint, gracefully transitioning from an underpainting to a full color palette.

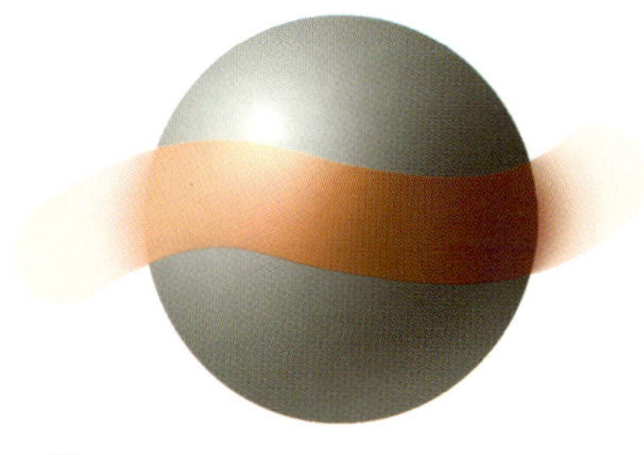

Ebauche: changing color used transparently to create the right final color over values that are correct

Lighting and color mood

Every artist has a natural pull toward a certain lighting or color mood in their work. Some favor a bright, high-contrast color palette, while others prefer a more subdued, harmonious, and subtle color palette. Some don't care about color and are happy working in black and white alone. Whatever your preference, how you express value and color in the final image will affect the overall mood and look of your portrait.

Throughout history there have been many different lighting and color motifs that have been used as standard practice for that era. In Rembrandt's Baroque era, for example, they favored a dramatic use of light and dark, as seen in the portrait below. The sculptural, high-contrast look is dramatic and eye-catching.

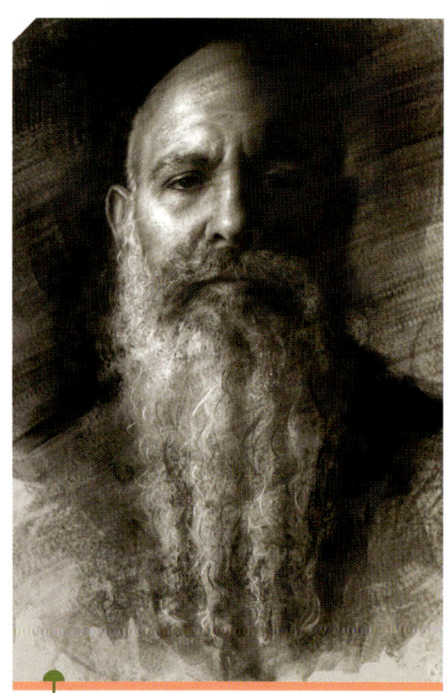

Art in the Baroque era used dramatic, high-contrast lights and darks

In the nineteenth century, when William Bouguereau was working, there was an overall lighter feeling with fewer strong shadows. This typically led to more colorful artwork that used a dynamic range of warms and cools. You can also observe this in Impressionist work, which favors a higher key in which, on a value scale from one to ten, the shadows rarely go below a value of six. This can often lead to an intimate experience with the viewer, as it replicates the light you live in.

The modern era has welcomed more intense experimentation with color. This is especially true on digital platforms, where there is an abundance of color that can be used in ways that traditional pigments typically cannot, especially when these pigments are blended in oil paint and the intensity of the color is lost.

If the subject requires a little drama, you can evoke a bolder sense of contrast using light, perhaps eliminating color completely. At other times you may wish to capture an intimacy with the subject and deeply study all of the particular features of their face. Sometimes you might want to introduce a little extra color and experiment with how to make that bold, dynamic statement work.

Study the numerous motifs of how color and light are used throughout art history as you discover your own preferences and interests, and be willing to try out different moods and motifs in your work. Your willingness to explore and push beyond what is comfortable and familiar will have a positive impact on your work as you problem-solve and hone your skill.

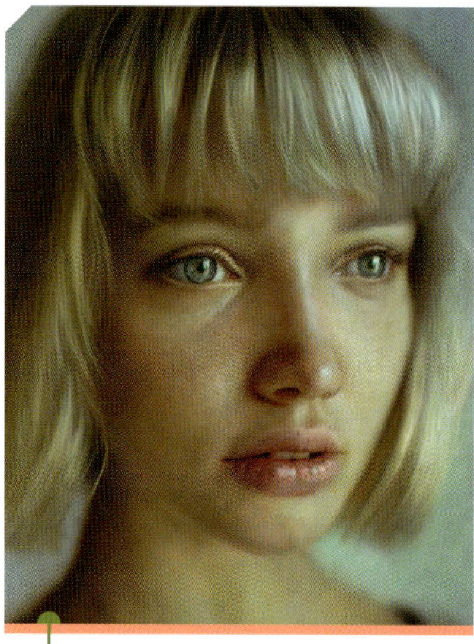

Nineteenth-century portraiture had less dramatic shadows and an overall lighter feeling

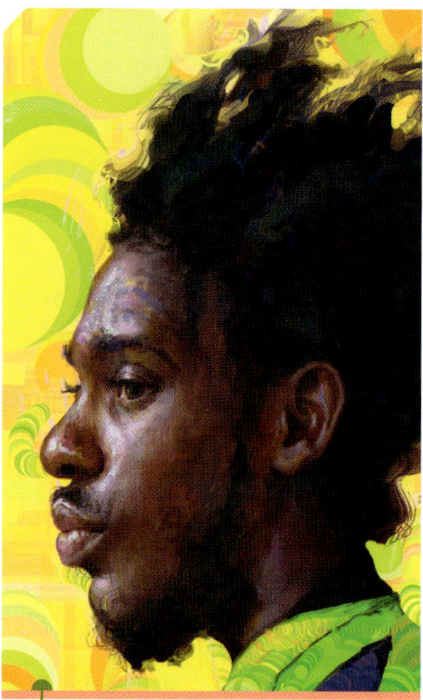

Digital software of the modern era has introduced a greater vibrancy and experimentation with color

Background motifs

Sometimes the overall look of a painting is dictated by the concept or motif used in revealing your subject. These are visual ideas that help to conceal or reveal your subject. Here are three useful motifs, however there are many more.

Light dark, dark light

Perhaps the most classic way of revealing your subject, this motif involves the interchange of light and dark. Imagine if the light side of the face had a light background and the dark side of the face had a dark background. The edges of the face would become lost and lose their sense of definition. Therefore, if you want to control where the viewer looks, reveal the light side of the face against a dark background, and the shadow side of the face against a light background. This simple idea can make drawing much more visually engaging and can provide added clarity for your edges.

This motif may not always be in your resource material, but if you can adjust your resources accordingly, not only will the contrast make drawing easier, but it will also help your portrait to stand out and have more of an impact.

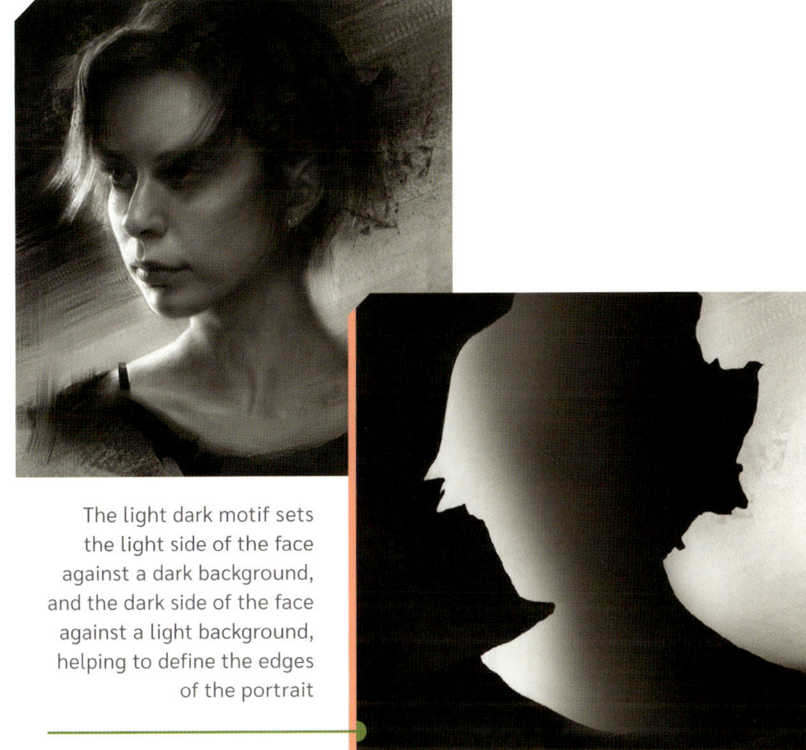

The light dark motif sets the light side of the face against a dark background, and the dark side of the face against a light background, helping to define the edges of the portrait

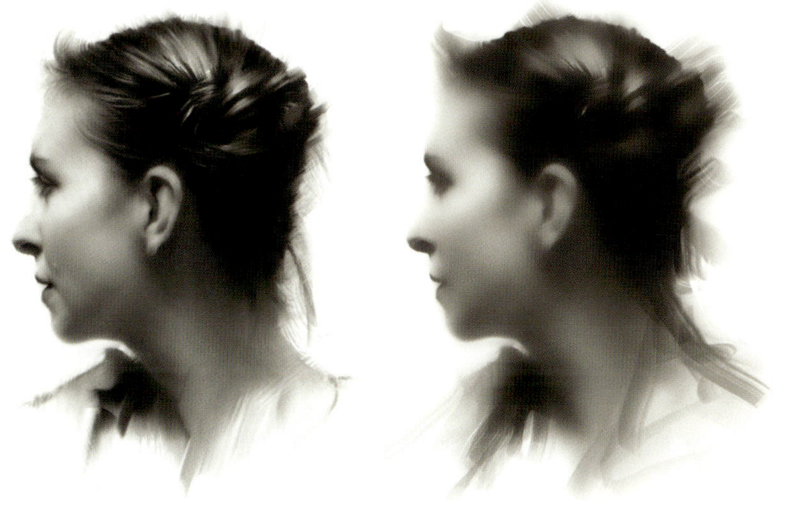

A vignette motif can be used to direct the viewer's attention to the subject by softening the edges and blurring the background

The vignette painterly blur

The vignette motif is ideal if you don't wish to consider the background. It directs all of the focus onto the subject, while letting the edges fade away. The question becomes, how soft do you want the edges to be, or how loose do you want to make them to create the effect of fading into a sense of abstraction?

Using a vignette motif is useful when painting a portrait from life, as it will prevent you from getting caught up in the background and all of the ways it interacts with the subject so you run out of time without truly investing in painting the actual subject. It also forces you to focus on what should get the majority of your attention and energy.

Opposite color pop

This motif helps to create contrast with the background when the light dark, dark light arrangement is not appropriate. The color pop interaction can be subtle or extreme. Your subject will have a general hue or color that it leans toward, and therefore you want to introduce the opposite color into the background to enhance your subject.

For example, when you paint a red-haired person, choosing a greenish background will often create a striking effect. Similarly, if your subject has a red-orange tint to their skin, then pairing it against a blue-green background will look attractive. Sometimes these background colors can be quite gray so as not to stand out too much, but this motif is a classic technique and very helpful if you want to create vibrant, colorful portraits.

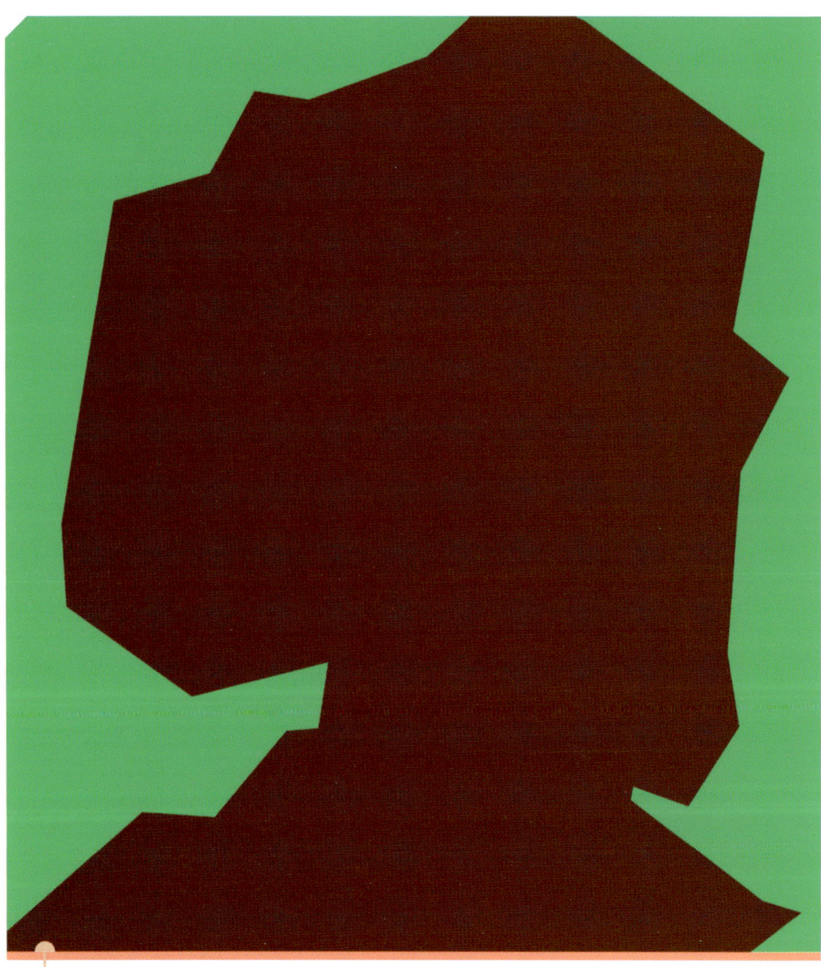

The opposite color pop motif sets the portrait against a background of the opposite color to the general hue of the portrait, creating a vibrant visual impact

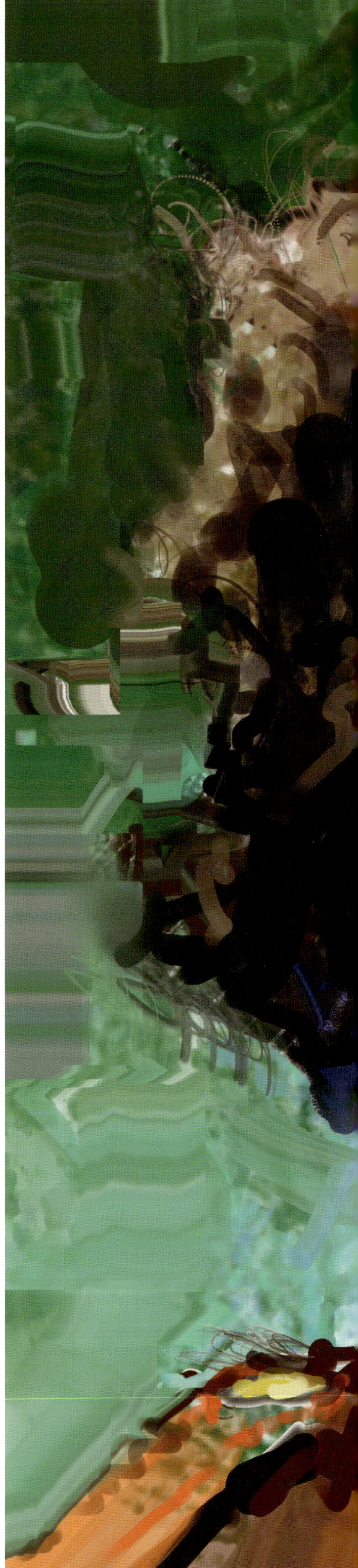

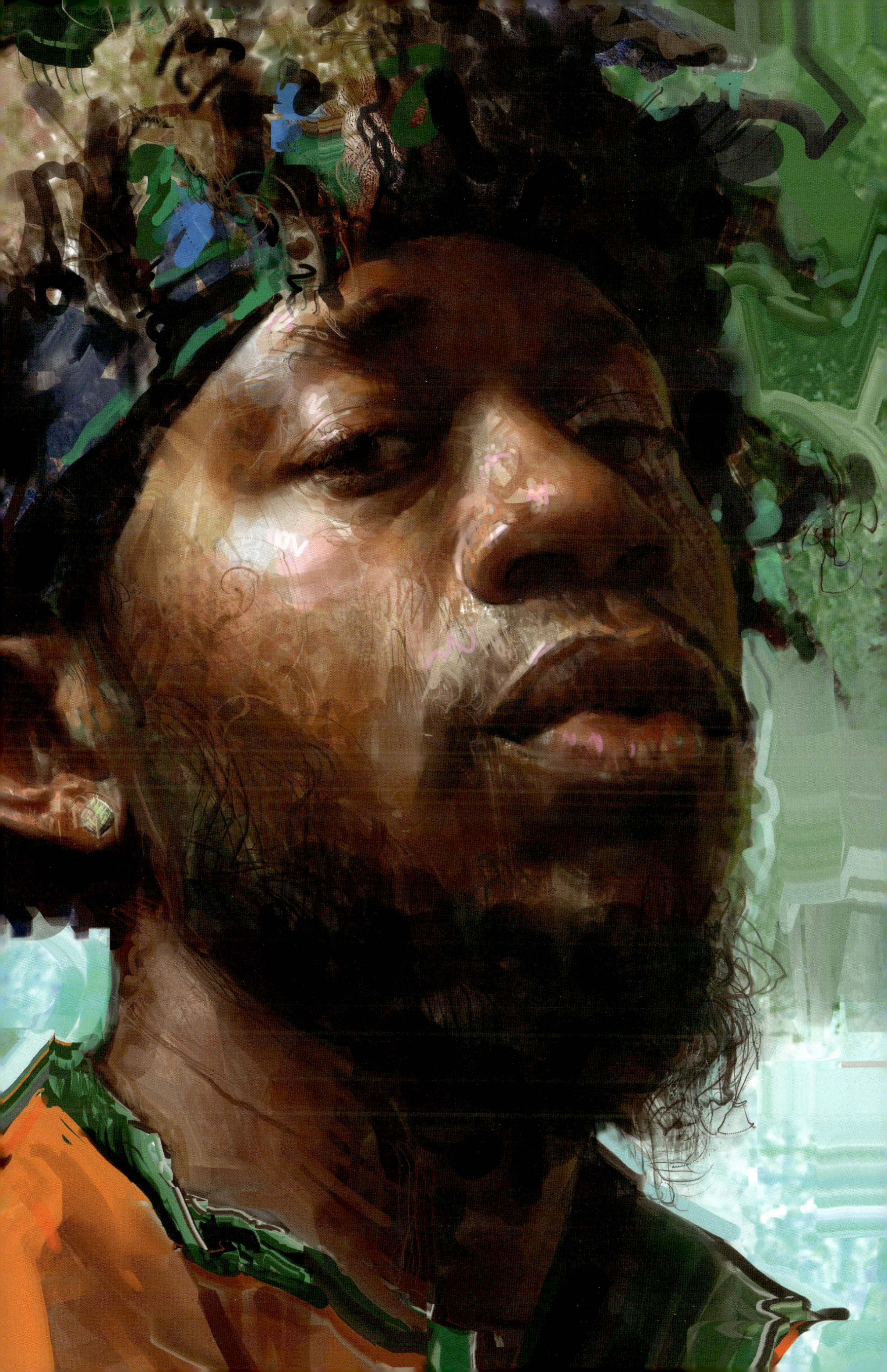

PRO TIPS: FEATURES & DETAILS

Robyn Leora Lowe

EYES ◦ NOSE ◦ MOUTH: LIPS & TEETH ◦ EAR

HAIR: STRAIGHT & CURLY ◦ SKIN: YOUNG & OLD

SKIN: FRECKLES & SCARS ◦ SKIN: TATTOOS

JEWELRY & PIERCINGS ◦ GLASSES

The facial features and materials covered in the following Pro Tips chapters have been painted using digital software. However, working through the step-by-step instructions and techniques described will allow you to recreate each subject matter in any software or medium.

While you will need to work from a reference photo or with a live model, you can decide how much you wish to stylize each feature. You may wish to take a perceptual approach and seek to capture each feature as you see it. Alternatively, you may prefer to take a more conceptual route, creating a stylized interpretation of each feature through the use of exaggeration and simplification. Take your portraiture skills to the next level by experimenting with the different styles and finishes you can create!

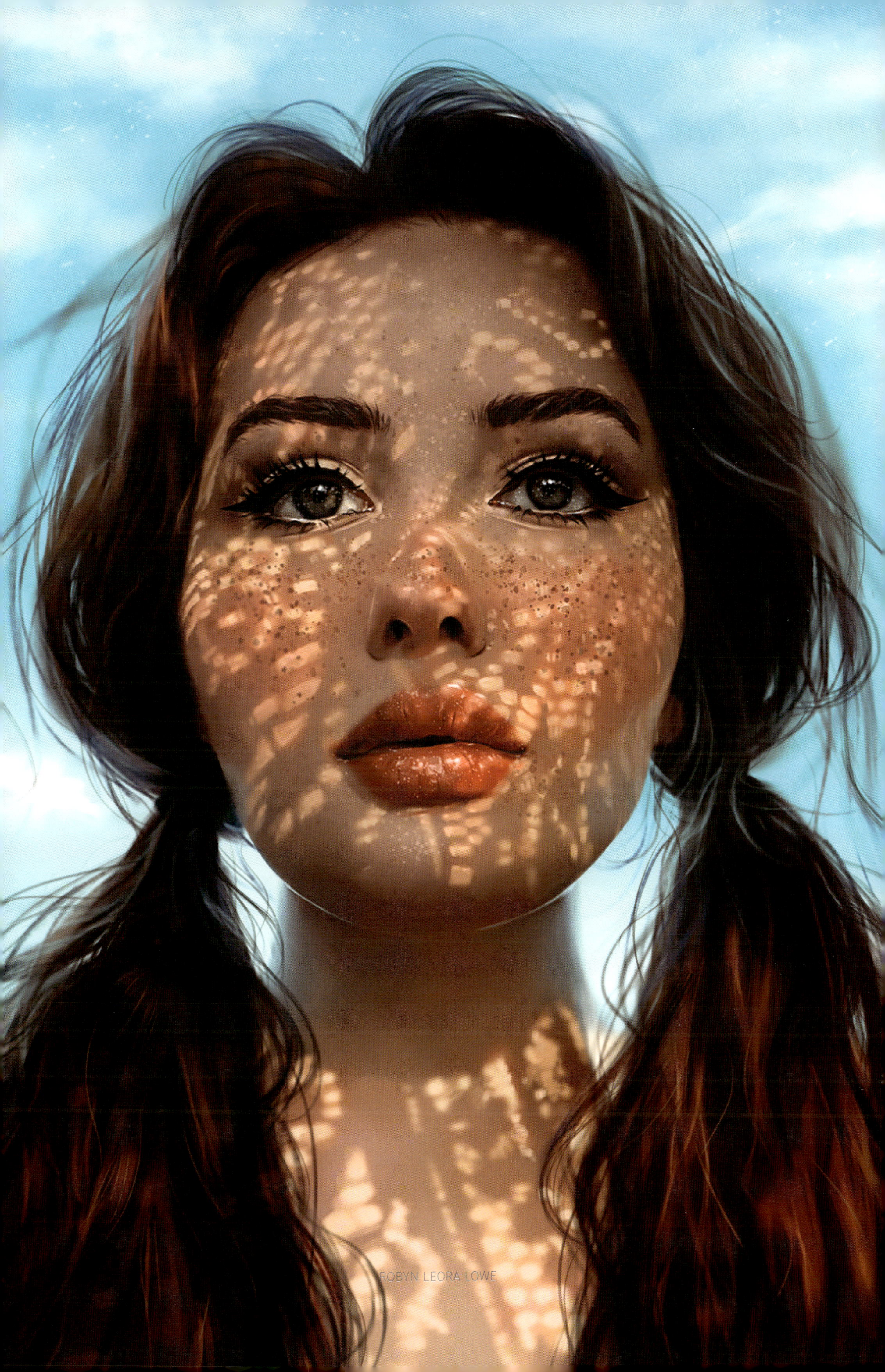
ROBYN LEORA LOWE

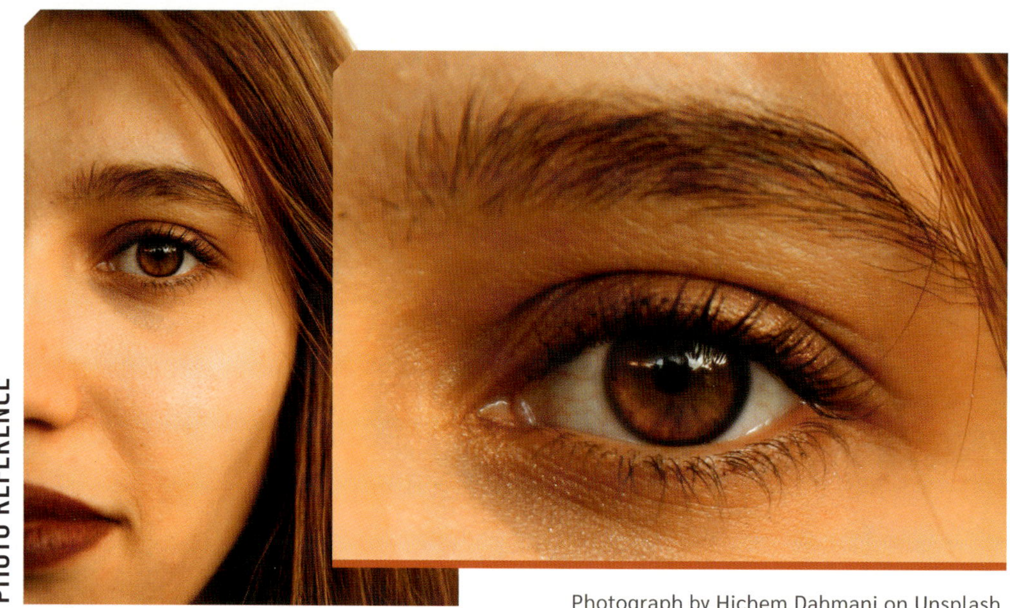

Photograph by Hichem Dahmani on Unsplash

Eyes

01 Line work

(a) Take some time to carefully study your model or reference photo, observing the size, shape, and proportion of your subject's eyes. Consider whether you wish to depict them realistically or stylize them by simplifying and enlarging their shape. It's also important to familiarize yourself with the basic anatomy of the eye before you begin. Knowing the main shapes that make up an eye will help you to accurately capture and simplify each element.

(b) Start by drawing basic shapes for the eye. Focus on the largest shapes: the horizontally pinched oval eyeball shape, the curved line of the eyelid crease, and the circle of the iris. If you are drawing eyes in a portrait that shows the entire face, keep in mind that the corners of the eyes usually line up vertically with the outer nostrils. You will also need to tilt and scale the eyes to ensure they match the perspective of the face.

(c) Lightly erase or lower the opacity of the rough line work, depending on the medium you are using.

(d) Using your rough line work as a guide, draw refined line work on top. Use a small tool for this to ensure it is as precise as possible, with minimal sketchiness. This refined line work should contain smaller shapes, including the circular pupil, elongated curved lower and upper eyelash lines, and the curved vertical line indicating the corner of the eye. It's not necessary to include details like the individual eyelashes in the line work – these will be added later.

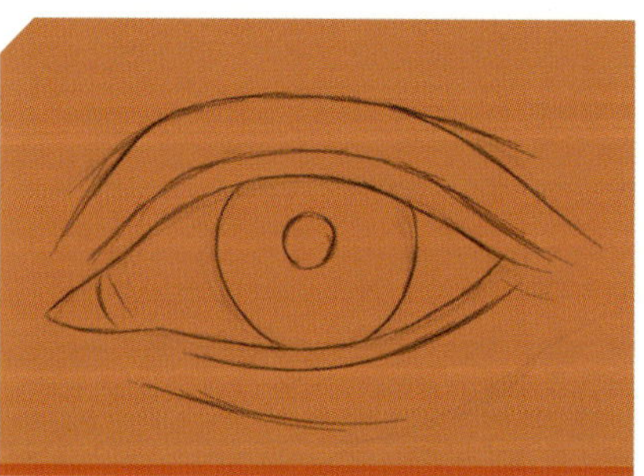
Sketch refined, clean line work for the eye, using main shapes with little detail

02 Base shapes

(a) Use your line work as a guide to establish your three base shapes: the eyeball, iris, and pupil. Ensure the eyeball shape is true to the line work by keeping its pinched corners on both ends of the oval. The iris and pupil will be perfectly circular, but often cut off by the eyelid on the top or base, depending on the expression of the subject. The placement of the iris and pupil within the eye can create very different moods. These shapes need to be completely opaque with no patchiness, and the edges should be smooth and clean.

(b) Make sure the iris and pupil shapes stay perfectly within the eyeball shapes.

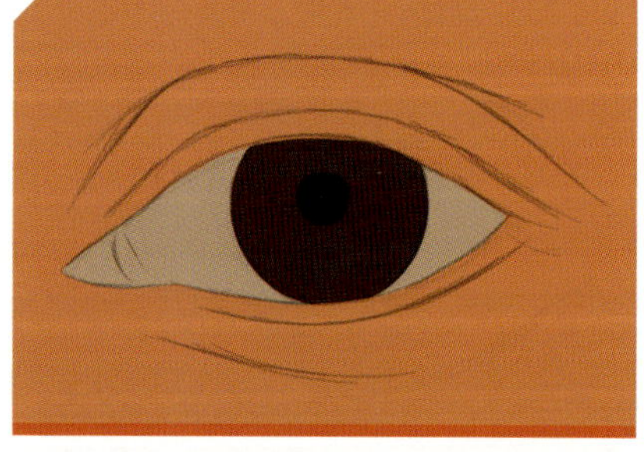
Block in the main shapes, including the eyeball, iris, and pupil

03 Hard-edged shading

(a) Study the colors present in your subject's eye, as well as the surrounding skin tones, shadows, and highlights. Keeping the light source in mind, establish the general tones in each area of the drawing. Understanding your light source is essential for this step.

(b) Starting with the skin, use a relatively large brush to paint the broadest skin tones and values surrounding the eye. It is important to keep your tool quite large at this stage to avoid getting caught up in the details too soon.

(c) Paint the basic tones for the eyeball, staying within the eyeball shape. Note that the white of the eye rarely includes actual white – opt for an off-white or dull cream color instead, depending on the light source and colors present in your reference. Keep in mind that usually the tones of the eyeball will get slightly darker as they curve toward the inner and outer corners of the eye.

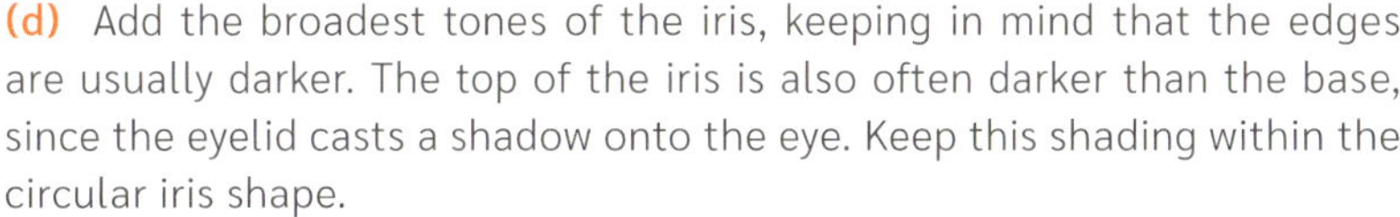

(d) Add the broadest tones of the iris, keeping in mind that the edges are usually darker. The top of the iris is also often darker than the base, since the eyelid casts a shadow onto the eye. Keep this shading within the circular iris shape.

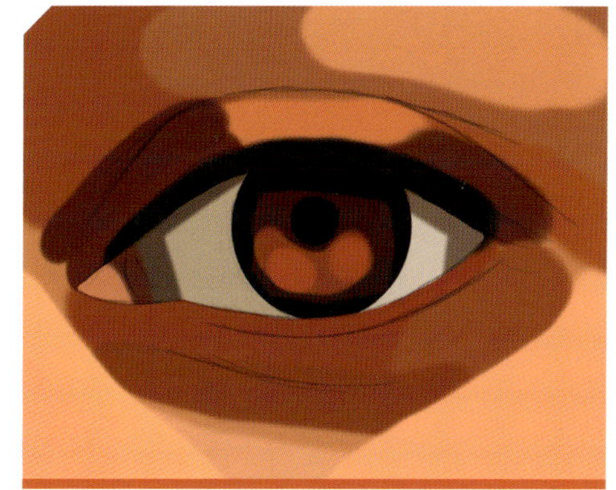

Use broad, rough, hard-edged shading for the eye and surrounding skin – don't worry about form or detail yet

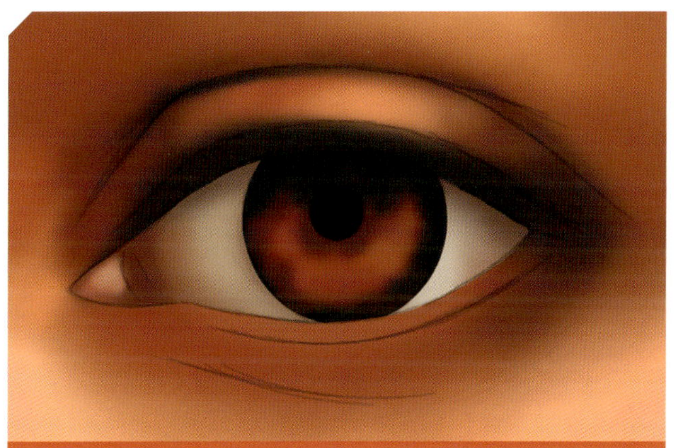

Blend the hard edges to create a smoother look with subtle form and the main values established

04 Blending and initial refining

(a) Blend each section of hard-edged shading, starting with the skin, then the eyeball, and then the iris, using your preferred blending tool. Keep the shading close to its original placement to avoid any loss in clarity.

(b) Use your line work as a guide as you begin to establish the different forms of the eye and create volume. The main forms to start to establish here are the eyelid and curve of the eyeball. On the skin, there will typically be soft, saturated highlights on the center of the eyelid, on the brow bone, and near the corner of the eye. There will also be deeper shadows within the actual crease and outer edges of the eyelid. As discussed in step 03, the center of the eyeball is usually brighter than the corners, since the edges recede into the head.

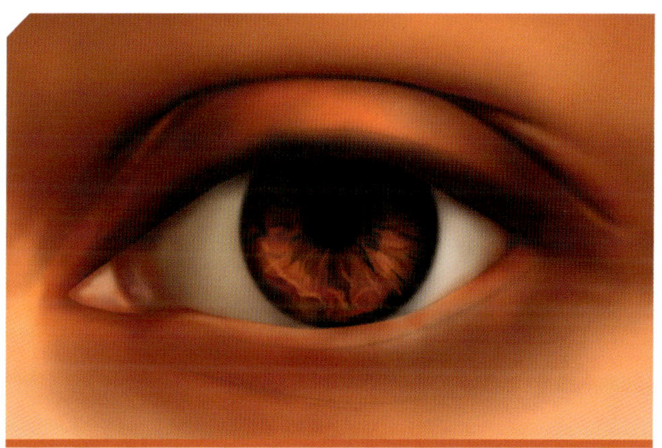

Refine the forms of the eye, adding subtle detail

05 Form refinement

(a) Frequently referring back to your reference, define the small forms, values, and color subtleties of each section of the eye. Think of this stage as painting everything that is underneath the main textures and details. This includes forms like the edge of the eyelid crease, the main textured details in the iris, and the forms of the eyeball. At this stage, you should be starting to use a smaller tool.

(b) For added realism, feather out the harsh outer edges of the base shapes, including the eyeball, iris, and pupil layers; but only blur these slightly to avoid losing their definition.

06 Final details

(a) Use a smaller brush to finish defining the forms of the eyelid and under-eye creases. The line work should now be hidden, as all of the forms are now completely defined.

(b) Closely observing your subject, paint saturated speckles for the skin highlights and freckles using a round or speckled brush. For skin highlights, choose a color brighter than the base skin tone that reflects the color of the light source. For freckles, choose a slightly deeper tone of a similar hue to the base skin tone. Soften any harshness of this skin texture by erasing or lightly going back over the speckles with the base skin color shade, depending on your medium.

(c) Use a small, round brush to paint the eyelashes and eyebrow hairs using short, precise strokes. When painting eyelashes, keep in mind that they rarely point straight up. Upper eyelashes curve down at first and then point upward at the ends. Both eyelashes and eyebrow hairs will often clump together and have a certain amount of randomness.

(d) Add any smaller details to the eyeball shading, such as blood vessels, highlights on the corner of the eye, and lower eyelash lines.

(e) Use a small tool and a bright color to paint the harshest highlight on the eyeball. This highlight will reflect the main light source as well as reflections from the subject's immediate surroundings, such as their eyelashes or a nearby window. Paint these reflections within that highlight using a smaller brush and a dark color taken from the iris, carving out little shapes to indicate those reflections.

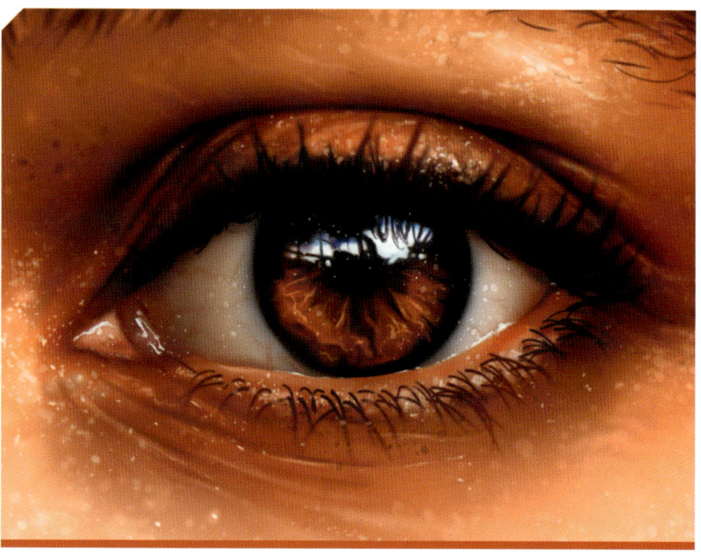

Finish by defining the forms and painting highlights and details, as well as the eyelashes and eyebrow hairs

ARTIST TIP

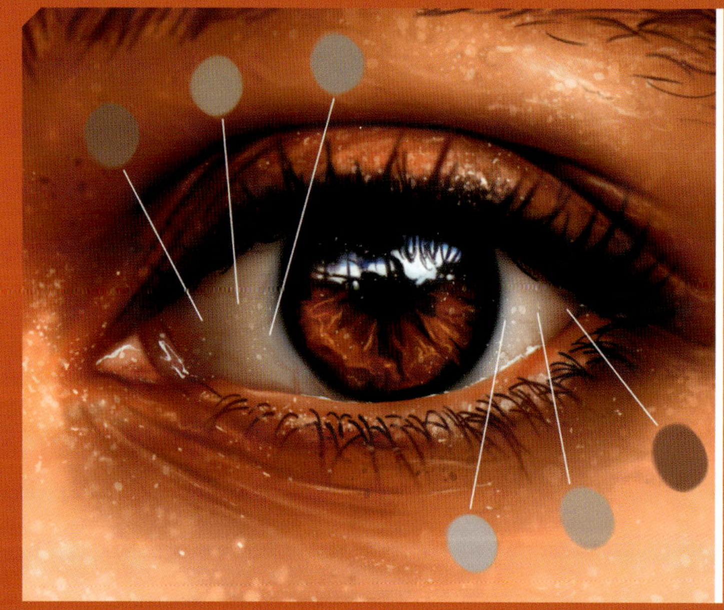

When painting in a realistic style, let go of what you think certain features should look like, or what color you think they should be. For example, when a child draws a picture of an eye, they draw the eyeball pure white. But in reality, you will very rarely use pure white when painting realistically. Eyeballs reflect their surroundings, plus shadows and other discolorations prevent them from being pure white. Try to break down preconceived ideas of what objects should look like and instead paint what you actually observe.

NOTE HOW THE EYEBALL IS NOT PURE WHITE – IT IS MADE UP OF VARYING SHADES THAT REFLECT ITS ENVIRONMENT

Nose

01 Rough line work

(a) To paint a nose, you must first establish its general shape and direction. Study your model or reference photo and observe the largest shapes of the subject's nose, as well as the angle of the face. When placing a nose on a face, keep these shapes centered on the face in relation to the direction in which the face is pointing. You will also need to observe where the subject's nose is placed on the face vertically. Measure out in your mind the distance from the base of the eyes to the top of the nose, and the top of the lips to the base of the nose.

(b) Draw one large circle, favoring the direction in which the nose will point.

(c) Draw two smaller circles on either side of the large circle to indicate the nostrils. In this case, the small circle on the right will be slightly smaller and closer to the main circle, since that nostril is pointing away from the viewer. The small circle on the left will be larger and further from the main circle, as it is more exposed. These same principles will apply to any size or direction of nose.

(d) You should also decide at this stage whether you wish to stylize the nose, exaggerating or simplifying its shape and size, or create a more realistic representation. If you choose to stylize, these circles will be more exaggerated in scale.

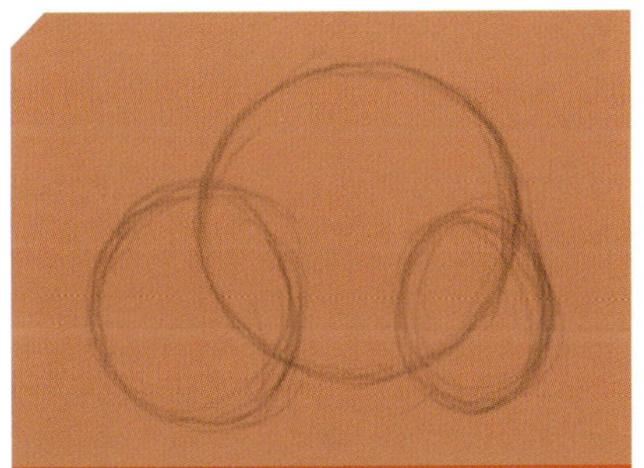

Sketch rough line work for the main circular forms of the nose

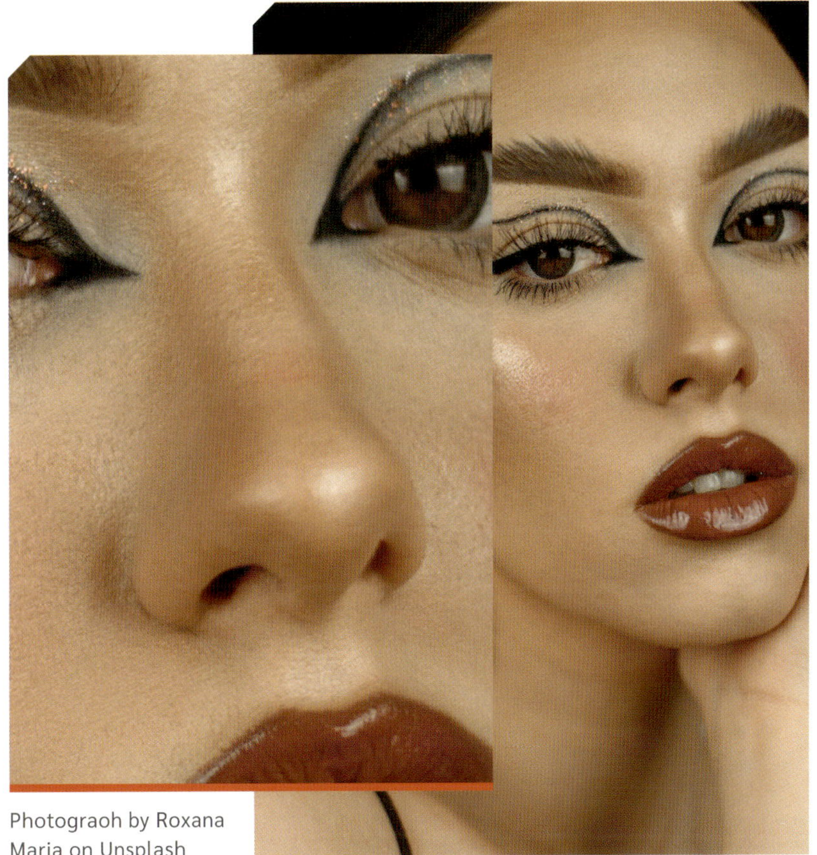

PHOTO REFERENCE

Photograoh by Roxana Maria on Unsplash

02 Refined line work

(a) On top of the circles drawn in step 01, sketch a minimal amount of thin lines to clearly define the nostrils and bridge of the nose. The outside of the small circles will serve as a guide for the curved line of the nostrils, while the base of the large circle will act as a guide for the line of the cartilage between the nostrils. The line for the bridge of the nose will be determined by vertically connecting the outer edges of the small and large circle.

(b) Erase any sketchiness to ensure the final line work is as thin as possible. Your mark-making at this point should be clean and refined.

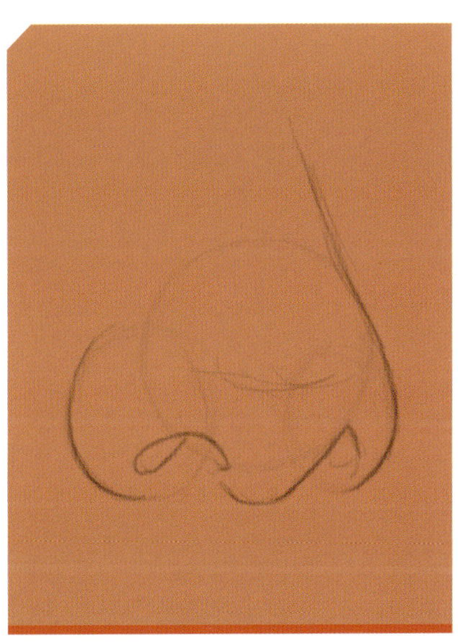

Draw more refined line work over the top, using the rough, circular shapes as a guide

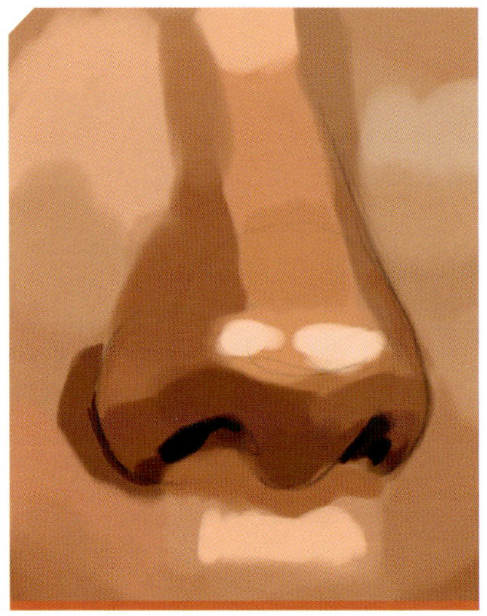
Paint rough, hard-edged shading, defining the broadest colors and values

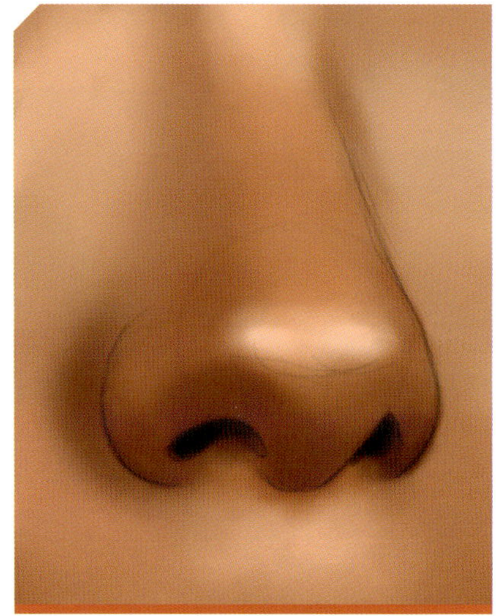
Add blended and smooth shading, without defined form or details

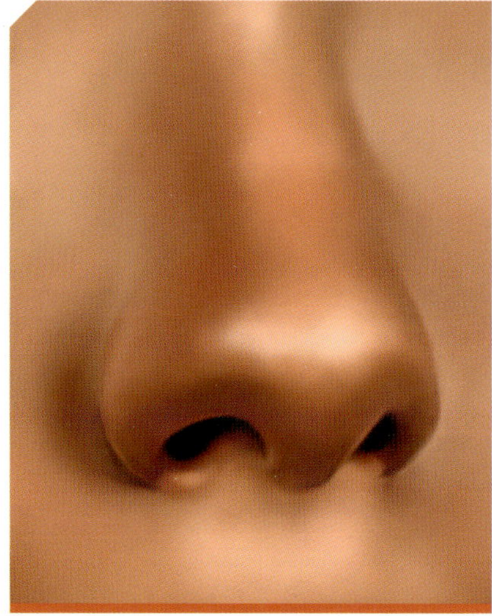
Define the nose, covering any remaining line work

03 Hard-edged shading

(a) Study the color of your subject's skin tone, noticing where the light hits the nose and how that light creates shadows.

(b) With these observations in mind, use a large brush to establish the main values and colors of the nose. Keep the shadows and highlights equally saturated to the base skin color, with subtle hue variations.

(c) Ensure you are painting the colors in roughly the correct places. The underside of the nose will be the darkest area in most lighting conditions, as it is usually in shadow. The tip of the nose is often the brightest, since the light source typically hits that area the most. Establish the general shape of the nose bridge with a slightly deeper midtone and large vertical strokes. More dramatic lighting conditions will change these rules.

04 Initial blending

(a) Blend out the hard-edged shading using your preferred blending tool. Try to keep the shading in its original area, despite the blending.

(b) Once all of the hard edges are fully blended, paint additional smoothness to the skin using large brushstrokes and various transition shades.

(c) As the nose sits in the center of the face, it is vital that the skin on and surrounding the nose is as equally blended and smooth as the rest of the face. Take the time to ensure this blending is done carefully.

05 Form definition

(a) Referring to your model or reference photo, continue to refine the nose's structure using various brush sizes. Use a larger, soft brush on the bridge of the nose and surrounding areas, and a smaller brush in more condensed areas, such as the nostrils.

(b) Paint hard edges around the nostrils, as they require adequate definition to indicate the presence of cartilage.

(c) At this stage, the line work should no longer be present.

06 Final details

(a) Refine specific areas where the forms need further definition, such as the bridge of the nose and nostrils.

(b) Paint any textures you wish to include on the skin, such as pores, highlighted bumps, pimples, moles, or freckles. This will usually only require various subtle darker and highlighted specks. You can paint each mark individually, or use special texture brushes.

(c) Soften any areas where the texture is too harsh by lightly erasing or using a subtle wash of skin-colored paint. Texture should generally stay within a few shades lighter or darker than the skin it sits on.

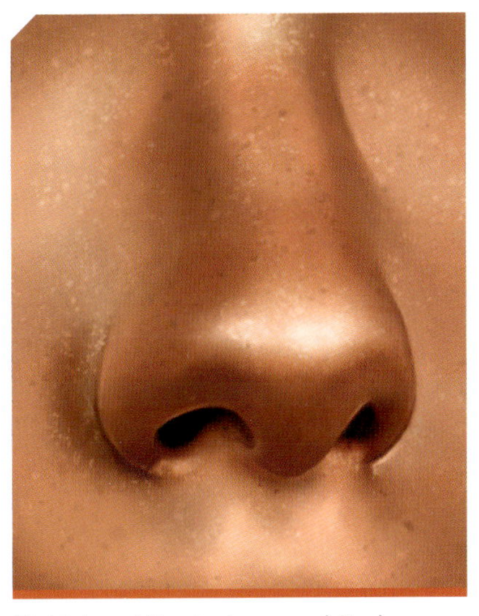

Finish by adding textures and final details, including freckles and highlights

ARTIST TIP

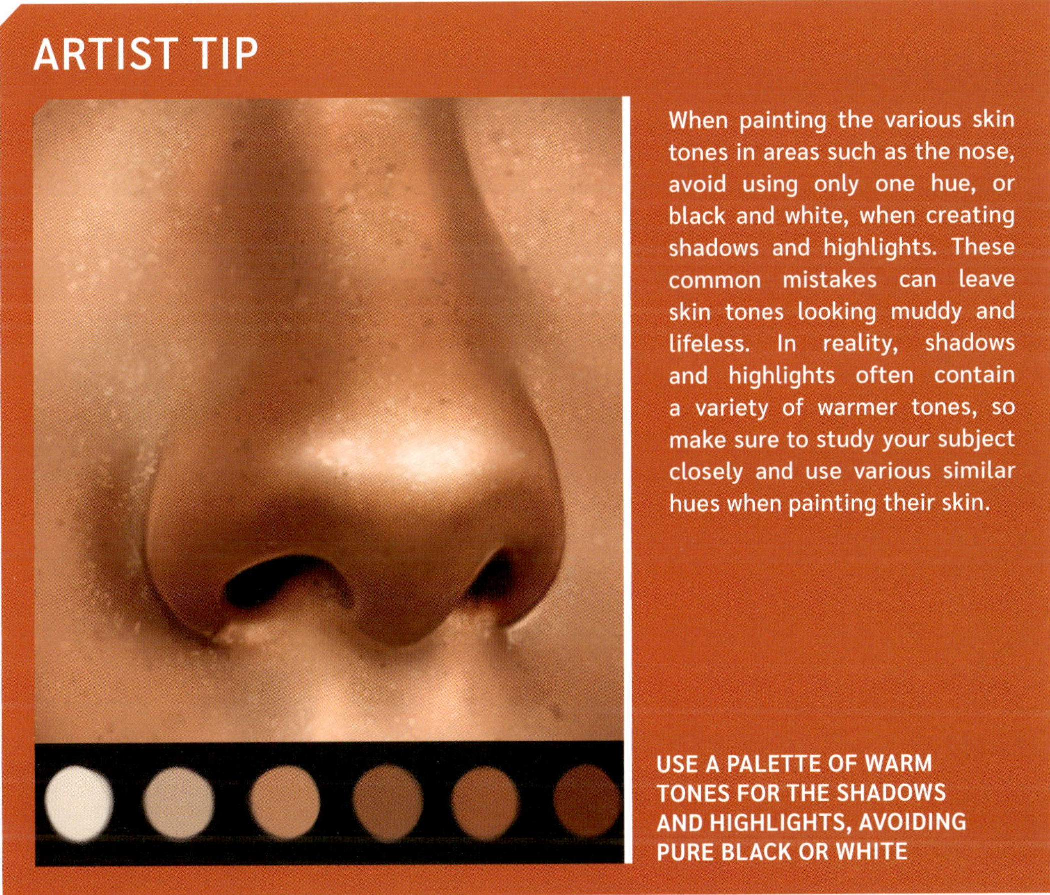

When painting the various skin tones in areas such as the nose, avoid using only one hue, or black and white, when creating shadows and highlights. These common mistakes can leave skin tones looking muddy and lifeless. In reality, shadows and highlights often contain a variety of warmer tones, so make sure to study your subject closely and use various similar hues when painting their skin.

USE A PALETTE OF WARM TONES FOR THE SHADOWS AND HIGHLIGHTS, AVOIDING PURE BLACK OR WHITE

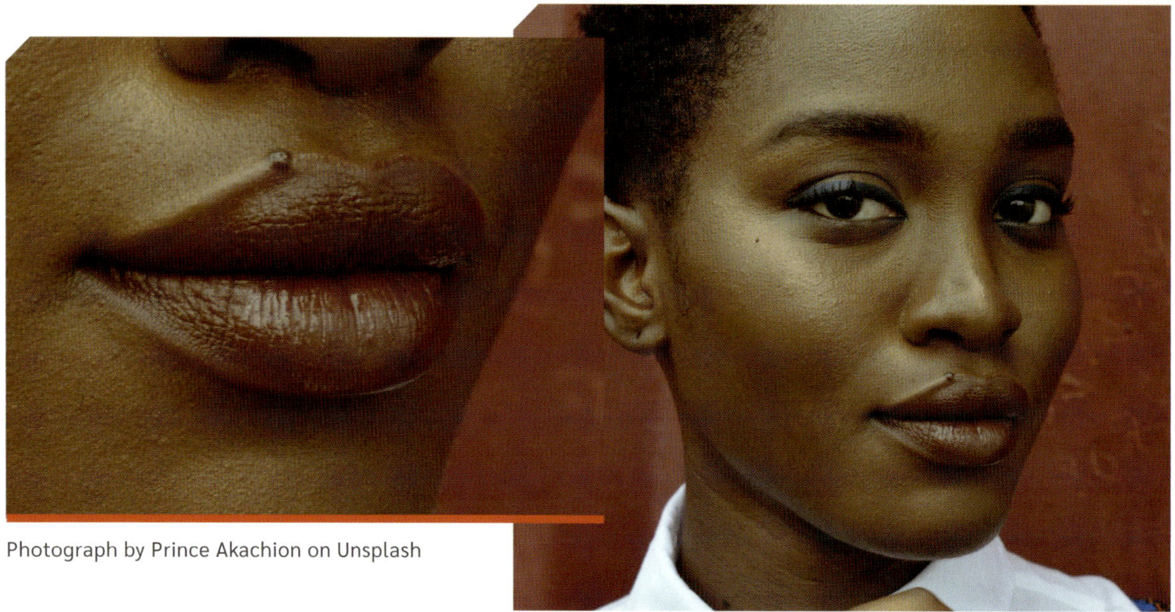

Photograph by Prince Akachion on Unsplash

PHOTO REFERENCE

Mouth: lips & teeth

LIPS

01 Line work

(a) Study your model or reference photograph, observing the shape and size of the mouth and lips, and if the subject is at an angle. Consider whether you wish to stylize the lips, exaggerating or simplifying their proportions and shape, or to paint a more realistic depiction. In addition, observe the placement of the lips on the subject's face in relation to the nose and base of the chin.

(b) Consider how the lips compare to each other. Observe whether the top lip is larger, smaller, or equal to the bottom lip. Next, sketch rough line work for the mouth using three circles and a horizontal line between them. The two upper circles represent the volume of the top lip. Where they converge at the top represents the Cupid's bow. The lower circle determines the volume of the lower lip, then the horizontal line in the middle separates the upper and lower lips.

(c) The placement of these circles is directly related to the perspective of the mouth. The circles shown here are concentrated on the right, as that is the direction in which the subject's face, and therefore mouth, are pointing in the reference photo.

(d) Draw more defined structural lines for the lips on top, using your rough line work as a guide. Sketch faint dots to mark the corners of the lips, then draw a curved line from corner to corner for the top lip, followed by the same for the lower lip, connecting all of the shapes. Sketch in the dipped shape of the Cupid's bow on the top lip. The exact angle of these lines will be determined by the unique shape of the subject's mouth. For example, some lips are much more voluminous at the center, while on others the volume is more equally distributed.

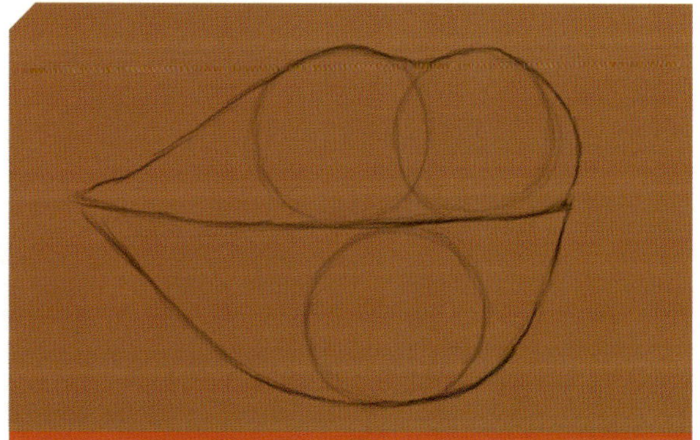

Sketch rough line work followed by more refined lines over a base skin tone

02 Base shape

(a) Opaquely fill in the base shape of the lips using a medium-toned color. The specific hue is up to you and can be significantly altered if the subject is wearing lipstick. Make sure the shape has clean edges, minimal patchiness, and keeps within the line work.

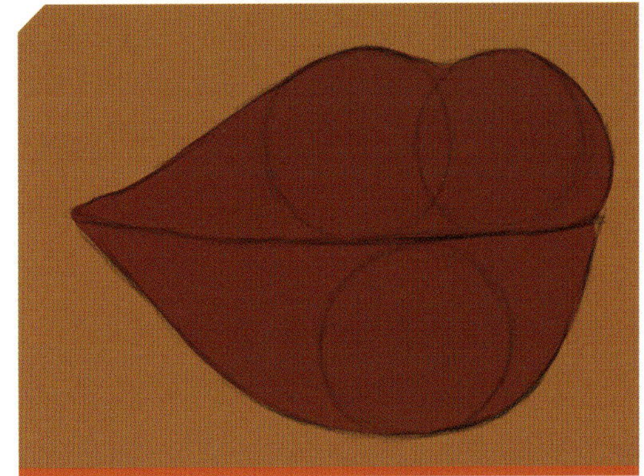

Fill the lips with a deep pink shade

03 Hard-edged shading

(a) Study your model or reference photo, noting the color of their skin tone and what areas on and surrounding the mouth are in shadow or well lit.

(b) Establish the vague, hard-edged shading for the skin surrounding the mouth, depicting the largest shadows and highlights.

(c) Paint the basic colors and values of the lips, staying within a few shades and hues of the main lip shade you established for the base shape.

(d) As the lips curve under, in most cases the values should be darker to indicate the form. Here the light is shining from the left, so the left side of the mouth is highlighted, while the right side is in shadow. Adding these highlights and shadows will create contrast and volume, making the lips begin to appear more three-dimensional, rather than flat. Taking the time to do this step carefully will help the lips to appear as though they belong to the rest of the face.

04 Initial blending and definition

(a) Blend out the edges of the hard-edged shading using your preferred blending method.

(b) Use a large, soft brush with various transition shades to smooth out the shading even more.

(c) Once everything is blended to your satisfaction, use a slightly smaller brush to establish basic form. Use this stage to introduce more color and shading subtleties to the lips and skin, increasing the appearance of volume. This includes basic highlights and shadows in areas such as the highlighted center of the lips and darker corners of the mouth.

(d) Soften the outer edge of the base lips shape so it appears to seamlessly blend into the surrounding skin.

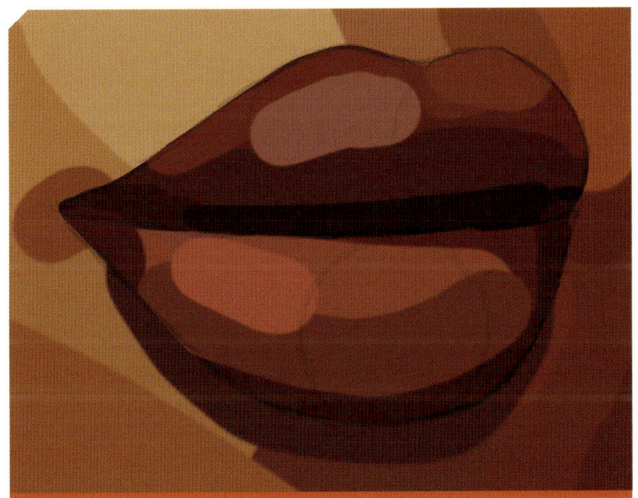

Paint broad, hard-edged shading onto the lips and skin, defining the main colors and values

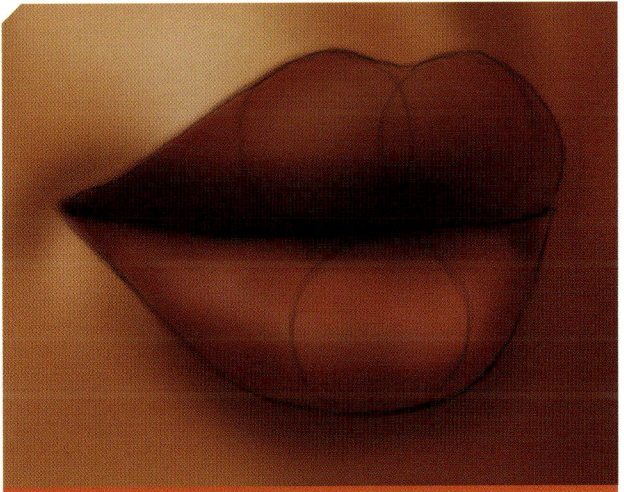

Blend and smooth the shading to create the appearance of volume

05 Form refinement

(a) Referring back to your model or reference photo at frequent intervals, continue to add more form and details to the mouth. Paint in details like curved lip creases using a smaller brush. These creases should be curved in relation to the perspective of the lips and painted with both highlight and shadow colors. Other details include ridges around the Cupid's bow and subtle texture.

(b) Add the same level of form refinement to the skin. Paint in details like highlighted ridges and indented shadows around the corners of the mouth.

(c) Use a speckled brush to create skin texture, or individually paint various highlights and freckles.

06 Final details

(a) Use a small brush to paint final form refinements, such as creases and highlights to the skin and lips.

(b) Select a bright color and a small, round brush with which to paint highlights, placing these strategically between the darker lip creases.

(c) Carry small speckles of the highlight color subtly through the lips to create the appearance of moisture.

(d) Study your model or reference photograph closely, then paint on any final highlights, freckles, or moles to help create a sense of realism. Here there is a small mole just above the top lip.

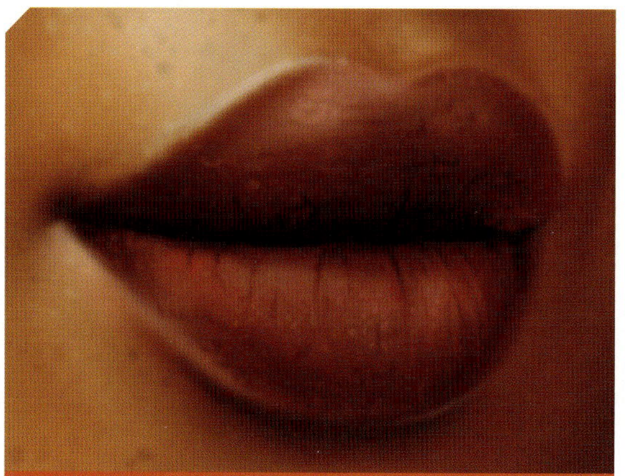

Establish basic details and texture

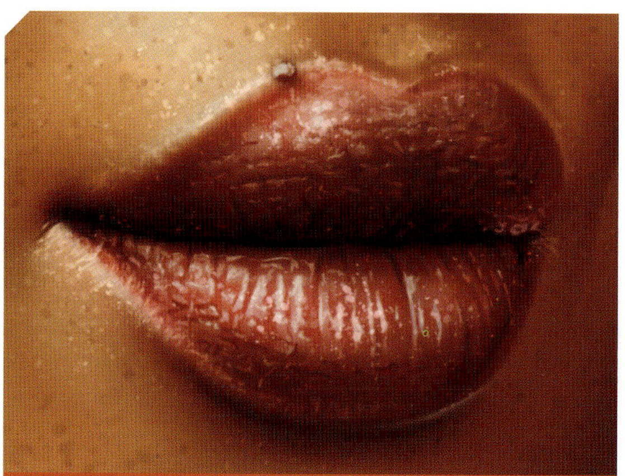

Finish by painting darker lip creases and brighter highlights, plus any final details

ARTIST TIP

Keep in mind the ways in which the lips can affect the surrounding skin. Subtle shading can help to indicate where they protrude outward slightly. Here you can see indentation shadows at the corners of the mouth, a shadow under the lower lip, and a subtle highlight above the upper lip. These form indicators help to ground the mouth as part of the face, rather than something separate that looks as if it's floating above the skin.

NOTICE HOW THE LIP CASTS SHADOWS ON THE SURROUNDING SKIN

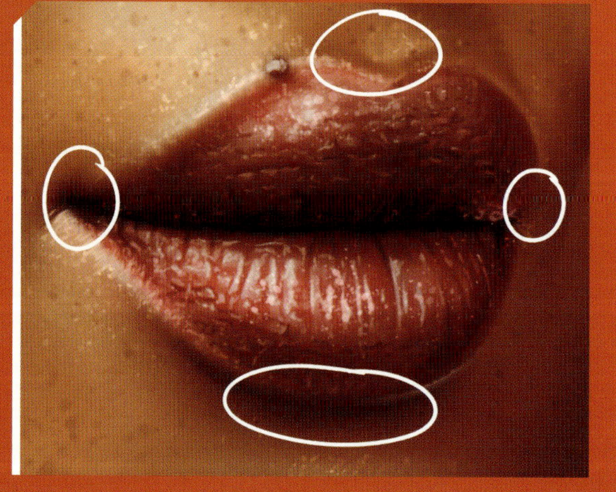

PHOTO REFERENCE

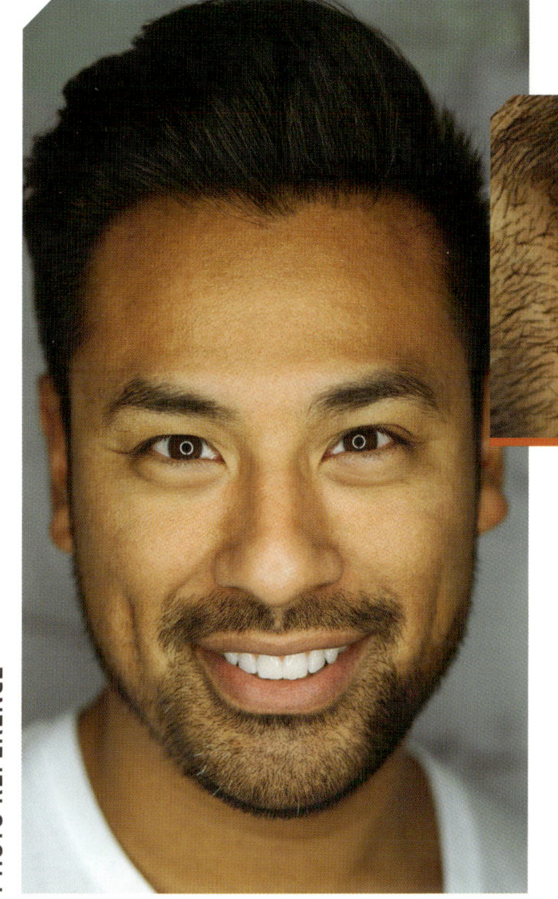

Photograph by Joseph Gonzalez on Unsplash

TEETH

01 Base shape

(a) Select a painting you already have of a mouth with slightly parted lips, then start by opaquely blocking in the shape of the inside of the mouth with a medium-toned color.

02 Line work

(a) Take a close look at your model or reference photo, then use vertical lines to carefully map out the spacing between each tooth, starting with the first line in the perfect center of the mouth. Keep in mind that the two top front teeth will be the largest, with the teeth becoming smaller as they recede back into the mouth. As a result, draw the lines slightly closer together as they get closer to the corners of the mouth.

(b) Using the previous vertical line work as a guide, draw the shape of each individual tooth within those lines. These more refined lines should include any shape imperfections within the teeth.

(c) Next, draw the curved triangular lines between each tooth for the gums. Their size will depend on how much of the gums are showing in the reference photo.

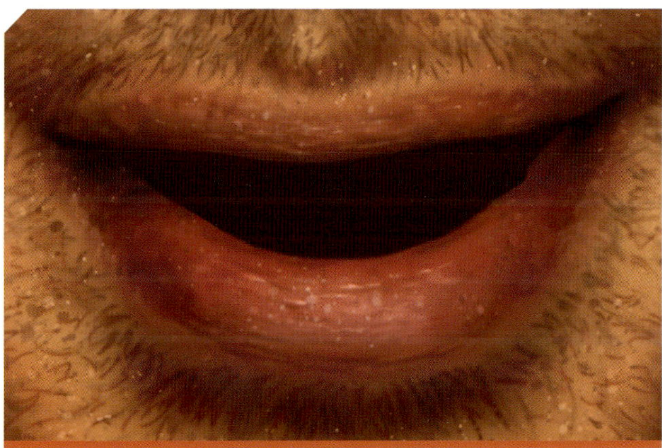

On a painting of a slightly open mouth, block in the base shape of the mouth interior

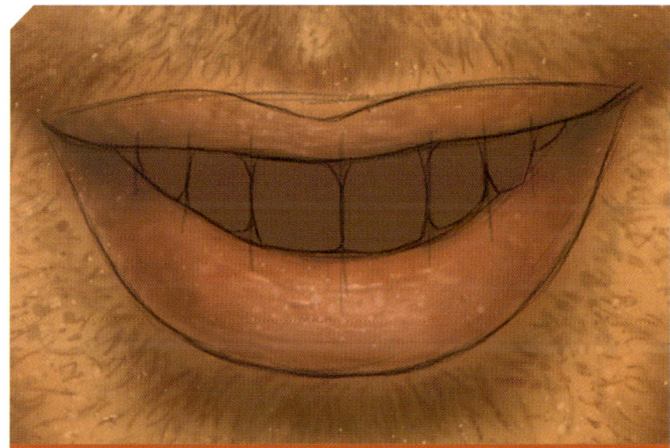

Sketch in rough line work for the teeth, followed by more detailed line work

03 Filling in with color

(a) Using your line work as a guide, opaquely fill in the shape of each tooth using an off-white color. Next, opaquely paint in the small, pinkish triangular shapes between the teeth that will become the gums.

(b) Ensure these shapes don't go outside of the base shape for the inside of the mouth.

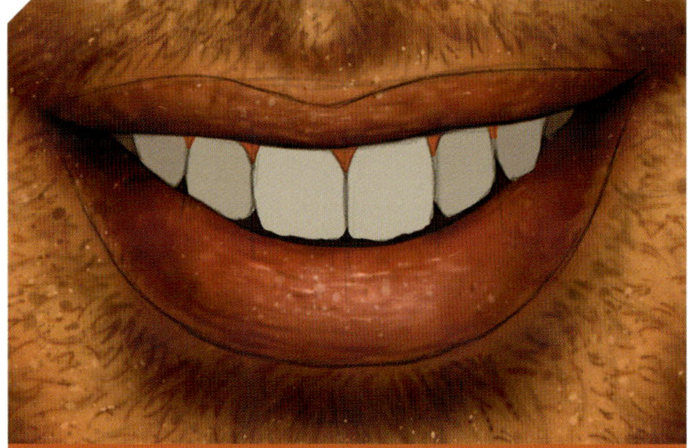

Block in the lower teeth, upper teeth, and gums

04 Hard-edged shading

(a) Study your model or reference photo and observe the direction of the light source, then paint in the basic shading using a hard-edged, round brush. Ensure the highlight color reflects the color of the light source.

(b) The shading should get slightly darker as the teeth get closer to the corners of the mouth. With a centered light source like this, the soft highlights of each tooth will be on the side closest to the center of the mouth. The division between each tooth should also have a very subtle shadow to indicate depth.

(c) Repeat the general shading process for the gums.

(d) Paint in subtle shading to indicate the lower teeth beneath the main top teeth. Your subject's smile will determine how much of the lower teeth you need to include.

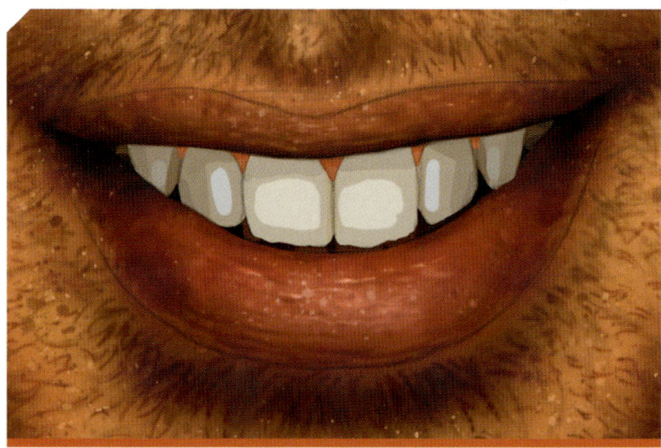

Paint hard-edged shading for the teeth, including basic colors and values

05 Blending and form refinement

(a) Completely blend out the edges of the hard-edged shading of the teeth and gums using your preferred blending method. Softly paint transition shades within the teeth and gums to create a smooth finish.

(b) Use subtle highlights and shadows to add form, definition, and color variations to the teeth. Using the existing colors as a starting point, begin to define the shape of each individual tooth. Continue to make each tooth slightly darker as it recedes into the corners of the mouth. Take care not to make the edges between each tooth too dark, as this can look unrealistic.

(c) At this stage the line work should be almost gone.

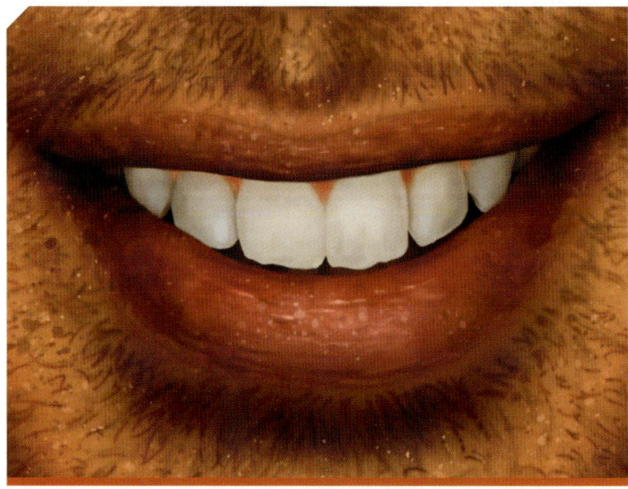

Blend the hard-edged shading, then use subtle highlights and shadows to help define the forms

06 Final details

(a) Use a small brush to paint in final form refinements, such as sharpening the edges of individual teeth, defining the gums, adding ridges, deepening shadows, and adding any last secondary highlights.

(b) Select a very small, round brush and a bright color that is the same hue as the light source. Use this to paint in the harshest highlights on each tooth that is exposed to the light source. The highlights should be organic in shape, have subtle ridges, and follow the general form of each tooth.

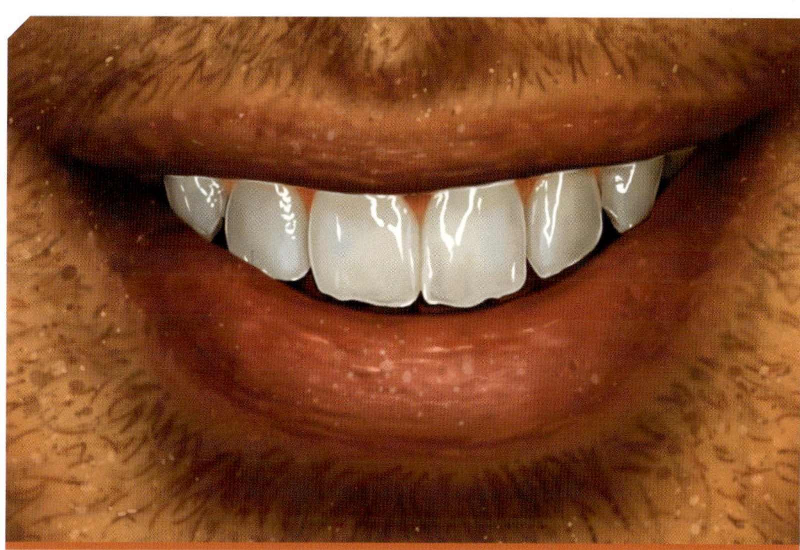

Finish by defining the forms, deepening shadows, and painting highlights

ARTIST TIP

By following these steps, you will have seen the importance of subtlety beneath the harshest highlights. Much like when painting eyes, you will very rarely use true white when painting teeth. Teeth reflect many subtle colors from their immediate surroundings, including the light source, shadows, and even the color of the lips. The only time you might use true white is when painting in the final harsh highlights. Overall, the main word to keep in mind when painting teeth is "subtlety."

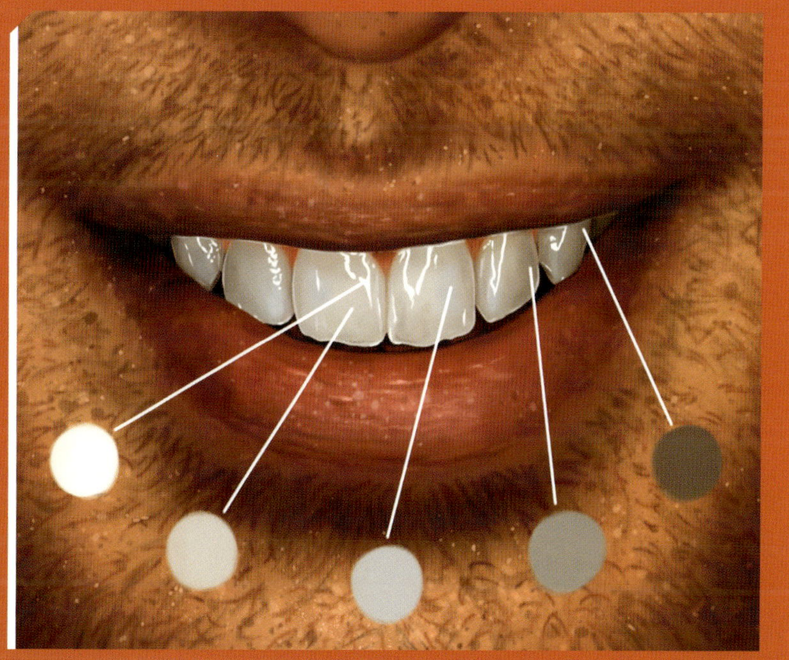

THE VARIOUS COLOR SWATCHES USED FOR PAINTING TEETH

Ears

PHOTO REFERENCE

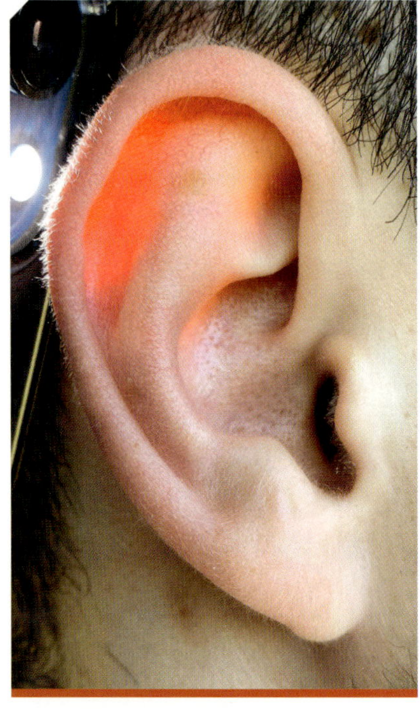

Photograph by Robyn Leora Lowe

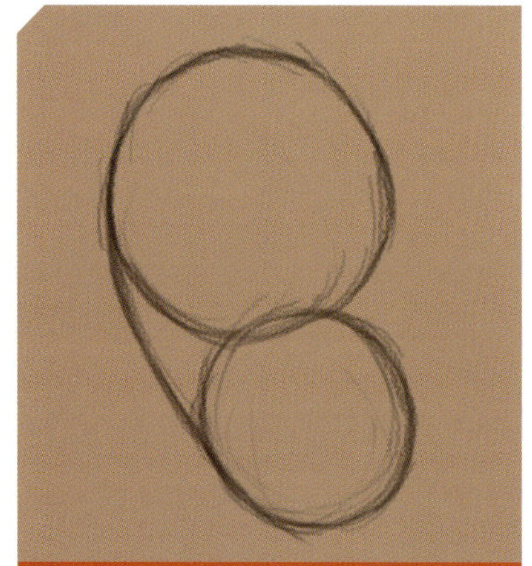

Sketch the basic shapes of the ear

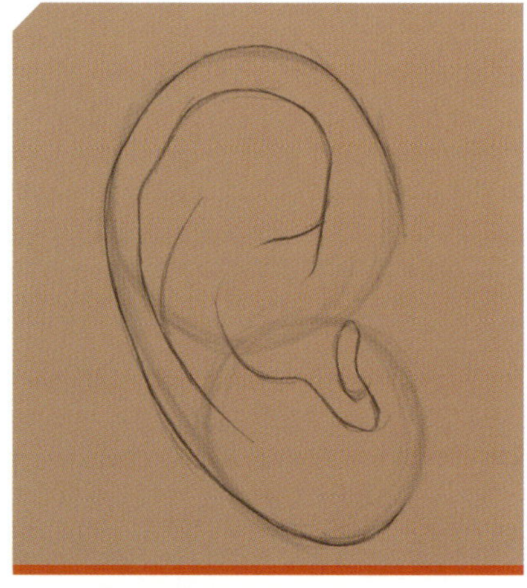

Draw more refined line work for the ear cartilage on top of the rough line work

01 Rough line work

(a) Look closely at your reference, observing the size, shape, and proportions of the ear. The exact placement, size, and angle of the ear on a portrait will be completely dependent on the angle of the head. Generally, however, the ears usually sit somewhere between the eyebrows and the base of the nose if there were horizontal lines connecting them.

(b) Two circles and a connecting line make up the initial basic shapes for an ear. Start by drawing one larger circle for the top of the ear, followed by a smaller circle below it at about half the size to represent the lobe area. The smaller circle should overlap the larger circle slightly and be positioned at an angle.

(c) Connect the outside of these two circles with a curved line.

02 Refined line work

(a) Using your rough line work as a guide, study your model or reference photo, then draw refined lines for the main areas of cartilage. Familiarize yourself with the anatomy of the outer ear, including the helix, tragus, and antitragus. Consider whether you wish to create a realistic painting or a more stylized representation by simplifying or exaggerating these shapes.

(b) Refine the drawing by erasing any sketchiness. Your line work should now be thin and precise.

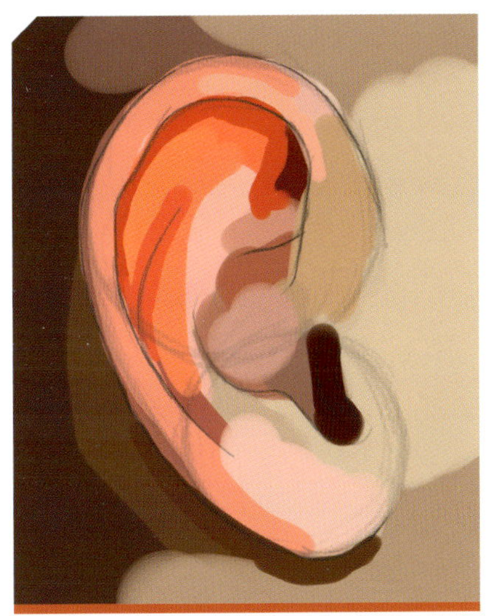

Paint rough, hard-edged shading, guided by the colors in the reference photo

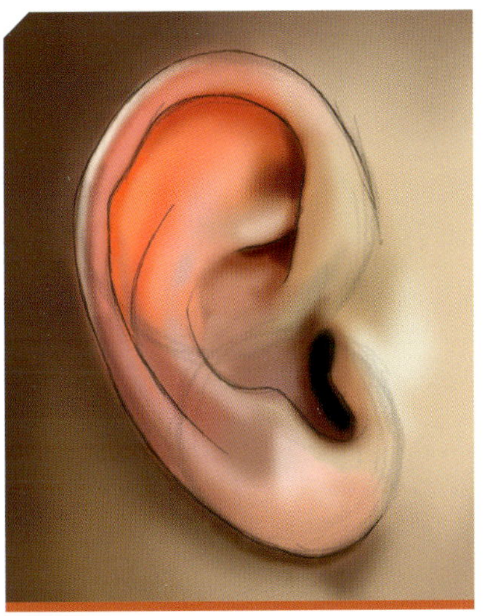

Blend out the hard-edged shading, then begin to add shadows and highlights

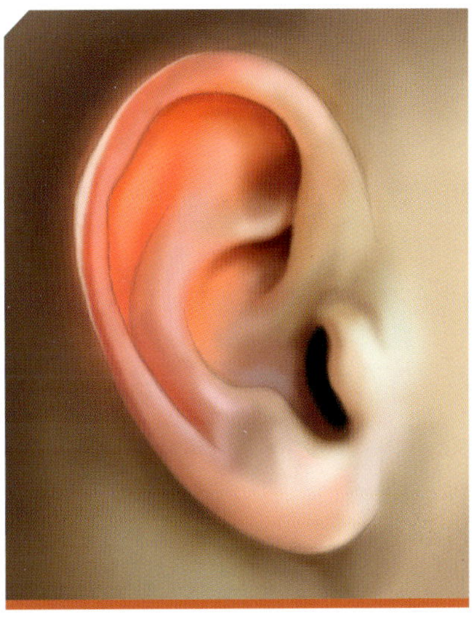

Define the line work, then paint warm, glowing tones on the areas nearest to the light source

03 Hard-edged shading

(a) Study your subject's skin tone and the variety of colors present in the ear. Use a large, hard-edged brush to paint the broadest values and hues using your line work as a basic guide. This can be rough, as it will be blended out in the next step. Do not include any details at this stage.

(b) When laying down the colors, keep your light source in mind and consider how it will affect the skin tone, shadows, and highlights. For example, this painting has a central light source, as well as the harsher light source shining from the left. With the light source so close on the left, it will bring out warmer red tones of the ear on that side.

04 Blending and initial refining

(a) Blend out the edges of your hard-edged shading using your preferred blending method. You may also paint using a large brush and transition shades to smooth the shading further.

(b) Once your painting is completely smooth, use a slightly smaller brush to start defining the main values of the cartilage, as well as highlights and shadows created by the light source. This will help to create volume and contrast. Your reference should be relied on heavily for maximum accuracy. Don't worry about details or refined edge control at this stage; focus instead on painting the general colors and values in the correct places.

05 Form definition

(a) Define the outer and inner edges of the ear using a smaller brush. The ear contains a combination of both hard and soft edges, depending on the area of cartilage. There will generally be a hard edge where your line work is, which requires a smaller brush. For soft edges, opt for a larger soft brush.

(b) If your subject's ear is backlit by a harsh light source, as in this example, you need to create a soft glowing effect to convey this. Paint harsher orange-red tones throughout the ear, focusing especially on the most translucent areas on the edge of the ear, closest to the light source. Roughly paint a small amount of this orange color outside of the ear to show how the light subtly bounces off its surface.

(c) By this stage your line work should almost be completely hidden.

06 Final details

(a) Finish adding more color subtleties, glowing effects, and edge refinements within the ear. By now the line work should no longer be visible.

(b) Studying your reference photo, paint on skin textures manually or by using special texture brushes.

(c) Use an eraser to soften any areas of textures that are too harsh, or lightly paint back over them using a base skin shade, depending on your medium.

(d) Paint on final details, such as small veins, freckles, or tiny hairs that you notice in your reference photo.

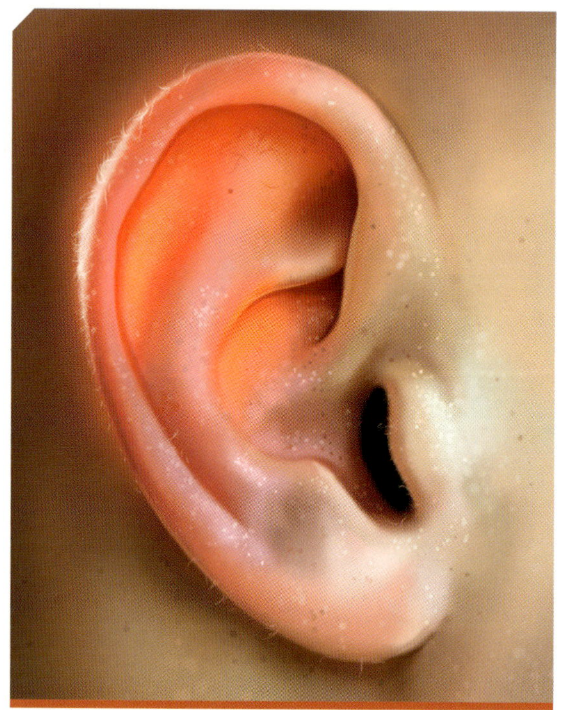

Finish by refining the edges and painting color subtleties, textures, and small details such as tiny hairs

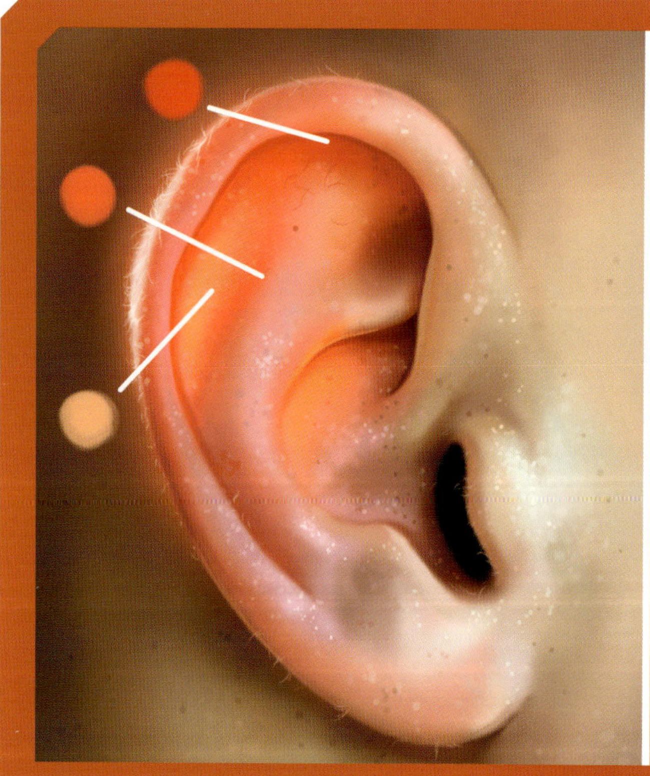

ARTIST TIP

Following this process, you will have learned the importance of edge control and form definition when painting a feature as structural as the ear. Once you have defined the forms, you can take your work to the next level by adding a subsurface scattering effect. This is when a strong light source interacts and scatters within a semi-translucent object, exposing the colors within, such as blood just below the surface of the skin. For example, the left side of this ear has bright red and orange tones due to the strength of light source behind it.

SUBSURFACE SCATTERING IS PRESENT WHEN LIGHT PASSES THROUGH THE EAR

Hair: straight & curly

STRAIGHT HAIR

01 Base

(a) Study your model or reference photo, observing the variety and depth of colors within the subject's hair, as well as the lighting conditions and direction of the light source.

(b) Lay down a medium or dark shade for the base, depending on how light or dark your subject's hair is.

(c) Even though this subject has straight hair, there will still be a fair amount of movement and volume. Use a large brush to map out this movement, painting sweeping motions with a slightly deeper color than the base. This will determine the direction of future hair strokes, as well as preventing it from looking too uniform and unnatural.

PHOTO REFERENCE

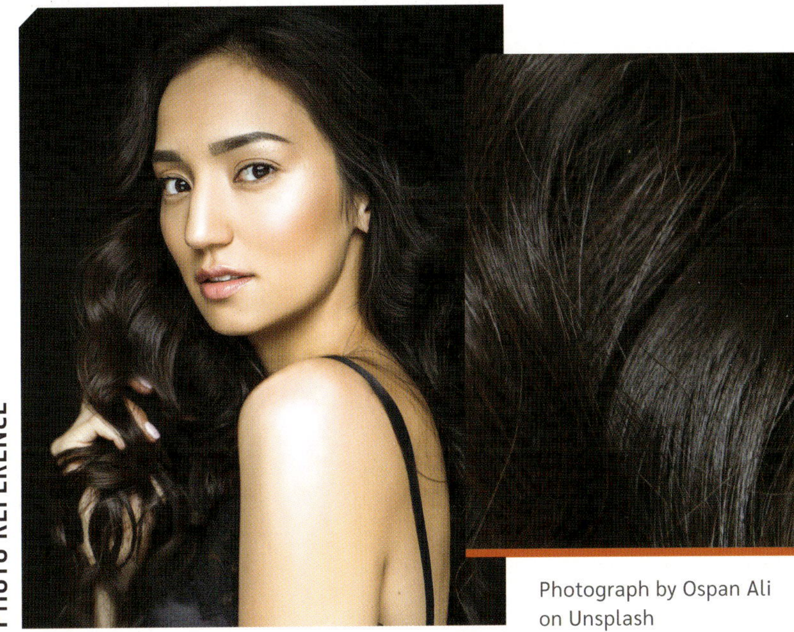

Photograph by Ospan Ali on Unsplash

Paint a dark brown base, with subtle shadow definition

02 Soft highlights

(a) Select a color that is slightly lighter than the base shade to establish the basic, soft highlights. This color tone will be determined by the type of lighting conditions. In this reference photo the lighting has a cool tone, and therefore the highlights will also have a cool tone.

(b) Using the directional shading from the last step as a guide, use a large brush to paint in soft highlights on top of the previous shading.

(c) Soften the abrupt ends of the highlighted strokes by erasing or blending to create the illusion that everything is blending seamlessly.

Create soft, cool-toned highlights on top of base directional shading

ARTIST TIP

Whatever type of hair you are painting, it's important to work from large to small shapes. Not only does starting with the large shapes save time, but it also creates a much more natural look. Individual strands of hair should be left until the very end, with the larger shapes underneath helping everything to blend seamlessly and create volume. Applying this principle will save you time, as well as achieving a more believable result.

03 Main definition

(a) Use a smaller brush to paint darker-toned hair strokes. These hair strokes should not be too fine, as you don't want to paint individual strands of hair yet.

(b) Repeat this step for the highlights, using the highlight color. At this stage you should still be following the original established direction of the hair with little variation.

Continue to define the hair, introducing the main shadows and highlighted strands

04 Volume

(a) With a light-medium tone, paint larger hair strokes in any areas that appear too sparse, taking care not to cover too many of the smaller strands of hair you have already established. This step keeps the hair from looking stringy and creates the appearance of volume.

(b) Use a small brush to add more individual highlighted strands. These should start to stray from the originally defined direction, becoming slightly random.

Create more volume, then start to paint highlighted strands of hair

05 Individual hair strands

(a) Using a very small, hard, round brush, paint individual highlighted hair strands throughout the hair. Use large, sweeping motions to replicate the way straight hair flows.

(b) These strands should begin to break from the directional shading established at the beginning of this process.

Paint individual highlighted strands throughout the body of hair

06 Final details

(a) Erase or paint over any highlights that hide too much of the shadow areas and overly distract from the forms.

(b) Study your reference closely, then use a very small tool to carefully paint the thinnest individual strands of hair. These strands should be extremely fine and completely random in direction, adding interest and movement, while also breaking up any areas that look too uniform. But don't overdo it; too much random detail will overwhelm the image, while strands painted all in the same direction will make it look fake.

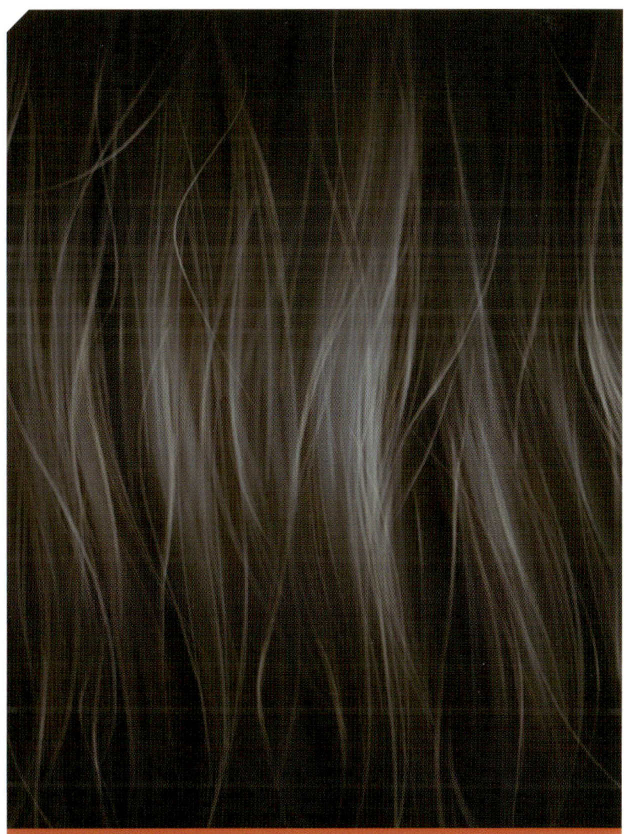

Finish by painting thin strands of hair, taking care to add a natural randomness to any areas that appear too uniform

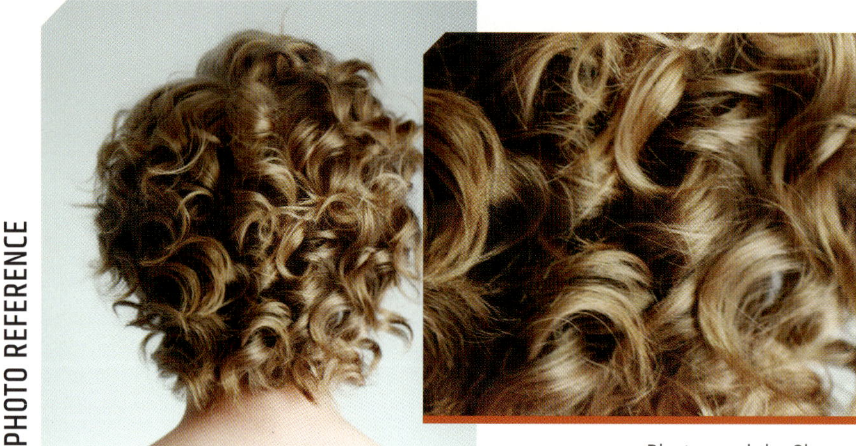

Photograph by Sharon McCutcheon on Unsplash

CURLY HAIR

01 Initial curl shapes

(a) Take some time to study your subject's hair, observing the variety of colors and shapes, and the volume of their curls. Start by laying down a medium-dark shade, relative to your subject's hair color.

(b) Begin with larger shapes, saving the finer details and individuals strands until the end. Map out the main shapes of the curls using a semi-hard brush and a light-to-medium shade. This should look like lots of "C" shapes that vary in size and direction.

(c) Remove the harsh ends of each curl shape using an eraser, or paint back over the ends with the base shade, depending on your medium. This will help the ends of the curls to appear to fade into the shadows of the rest of the hair, creating a more natural-looking result.

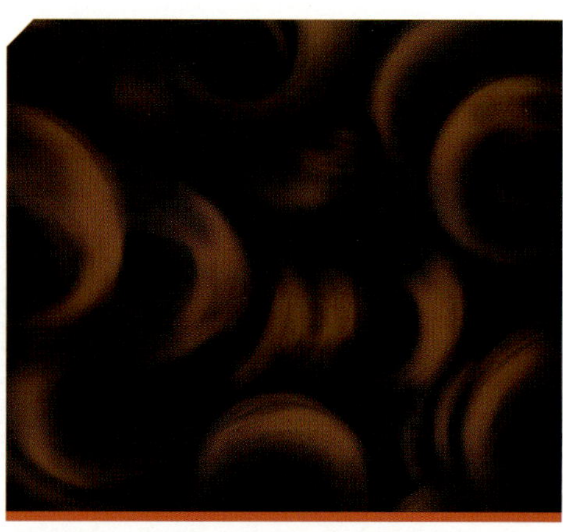

Paint the main, larger shapes of the curls, varying their direction and size

02 Secondary hair strokes

(a) Use a semi-hard brush to paint smaller hair strokes. These should be lighter than the base shade and darker than the main curl shapes, which will start to create volume.

(b) You don't want to paint individual strands of hair yet, so make sure your brush is not too small. These strokes should also follow the general direction of the main curls, with subtle directional variation.

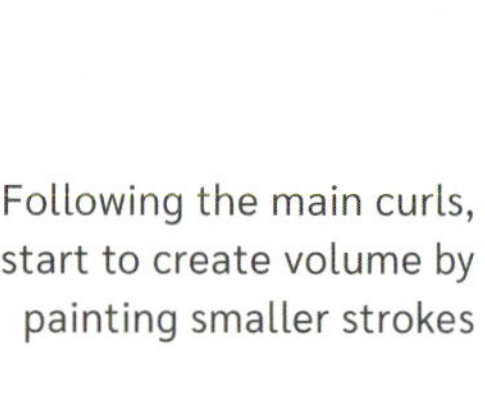

Following the main curls, start to create volume by painting smaller strokes

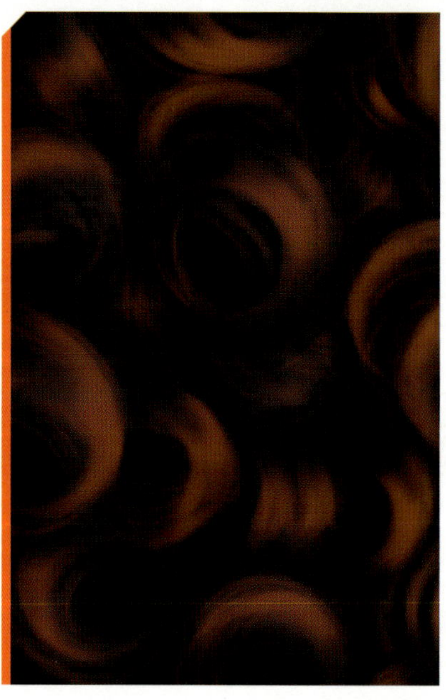

ARTIST TIP

Painting curls may at first seem complicated and artists are often apprehensive about it. However, if you work from large to small shapes and use highlights to do most of the defining, it can be a relatively easy process that yields impressive results. Curly hair is defined by its highlights, due to how shadowy and dense it can be. Remember that the rounded center of the curl is the brightest part, as that is where the light source hits the most.

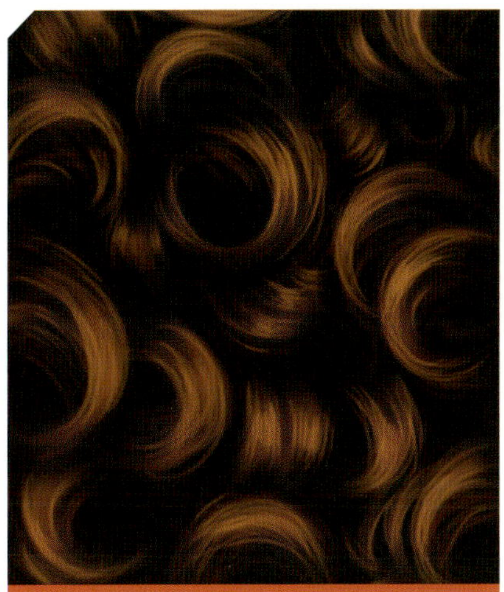

Paint small, soft highlights on top of the basic curl shapes

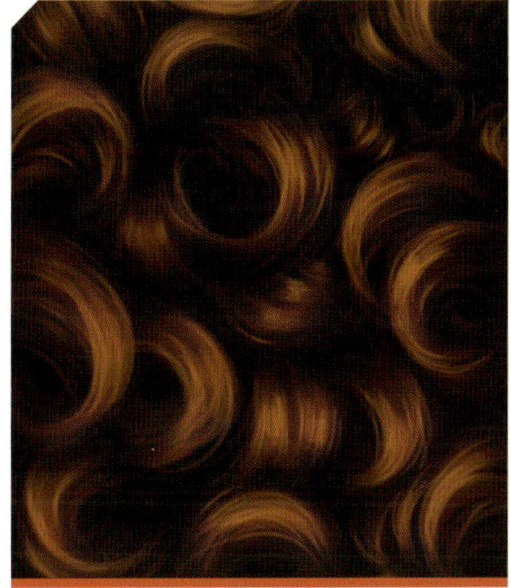

Add darker strands of hair in the shadows to create volume and form

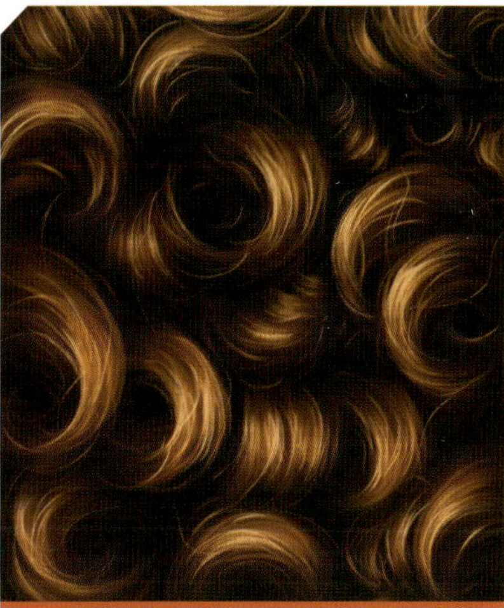

Paint individual strands of hair in a bright highlight color, while also avoiding uniformity

03 Soft highlights

(a) Paint in the smaller, softer highlight strokes using a color that is brighter than the main curl color, and a hue that reflects the type of light source. The light source in this reference photograph is warm-toned, so the highlights should also be warm-toned.

(b) Depending on your medium, erase any harsh edges or paint over them with your base shade. Keep in mind that the highlights should still follow the "c" directions of the main curls and focus on the center of each individual curl.

04 Volume

(a) Use a medium-toned color and a medium-sized brush to very lightly paint volume, focusing on the center of each curl. This will add volume, while also helping the hair strokes to blend seamlessly.

(b) Using a small brush, add darker individual strands of hair in the shadows of the curls, again creating volume and form.

05 Individual hair strands

(a) Select a very small, round brush and your brightest highlight color, then paint individual strands throughout the hair, focusing on the center of the curls. This will contribute to the illusion of texture and roundness, so the curls appear to emerge from the shadows.

(b) Add a few random strands that stray from the direction of the main curls to ensure the hair doesn't look too uniform and unnatural.

06 Final details

(a) Take some time to paint in any more color subtleties, contrast, saturation, fading, and definition to each curl.

(b) Using the brightest highlight color, paint stray highlighted strands throughout the hair. Adding fine hairs that don't follow the direction of the curls will help to create realism and movement.

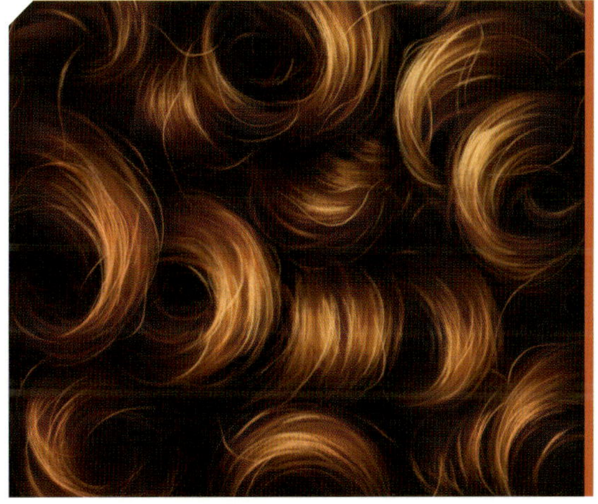

Finish by deepening the shadows, enhancing the highlights, and painting fine stray hairs

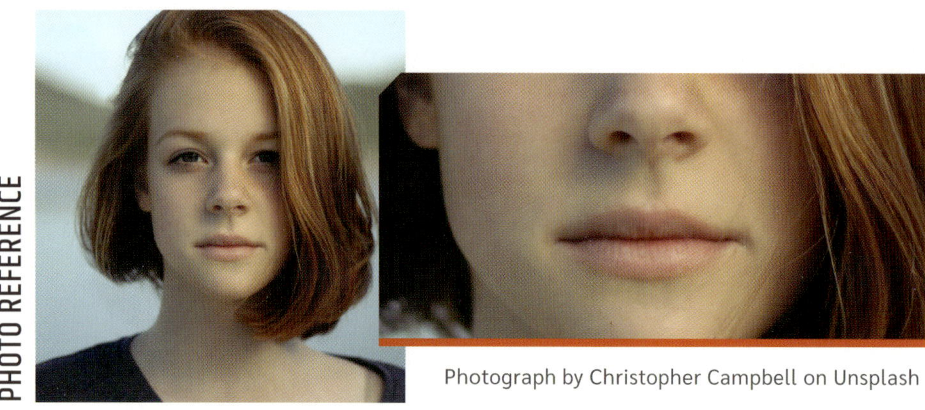

Photograph by Christopher Campbell on Unsplash

Skin: young & old

YOUNG SKIN

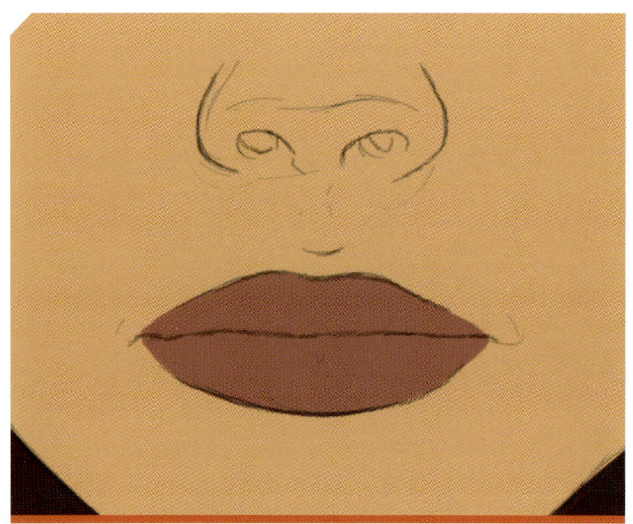

Sketch base flat shapes onto the face

01 Base shapes

(a) The skin of an elderly person has a different appearance and texture to the skin of a younger person. It's important that you know how to paint each type to ensure you accurately represent the age of your subject. Take some time to observe your model or reference photo, paying careful attention to the texture and feel of their skin.

(b) All skin shading begins with establishing basic shapes and line work. Your line work can be fairly rough to begin with, before you refine it into clearer, more precise lines.

(c) Paint opaque shapes for each area, such as the skin and lips. These shapes should be a medium tone with the general hue of that area.

(d) Once you have created thin, precise line work and clean base shapes, you are ready to start establishing your shading.

Paint rough, hard-edged shading on the lower face, containing the largest values and colors

02 Hard-edged shading

(a) Take a large brush and paint in the broadest tones for the skin and, in this case, the lips and nose. This step is the same regardless of the person's age.

(b) Study your reference photo and identify the direction of the light source, then consider how the tone and position of the light source will affect the skin. Here the lower part of the face is in shadow, while the top part receives more of the light. Reflect the most general lighting condition of your reference with large swatches of color on the skin, avoiding adding any detail at this stage.

03 Initial blending and shading

(a) Blend out your hard-edged shading using your preferred blending tool and large, soft brushstrokes. This will help to establish the general form of the skin and give it a soft and youthful appearance.

(b) Unless working in condensed areas, such as around the nostrils, use a large, soft brush when painting young skin to avoid indicating small forms, such as wrinkles and creases. Generally, the larger and softer the brush used, the younger the skin will appear.

(c) Use a slightly smaller brush to begin establishing very basic forms, such as around the nostrils and mouth.

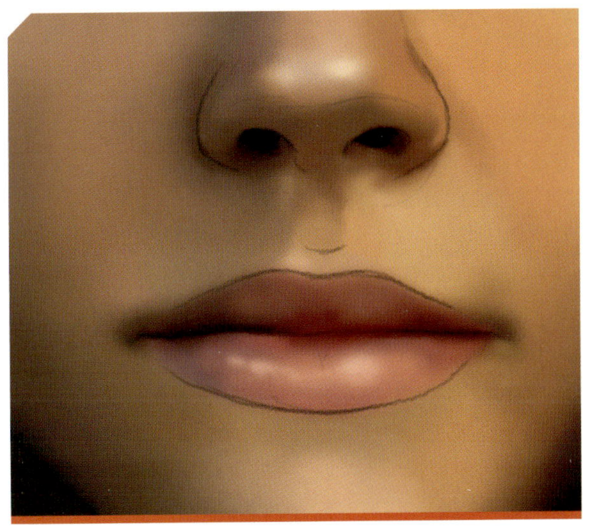

Blend out the hard-edged shading, using a large, soft brush to create a youthful appearance

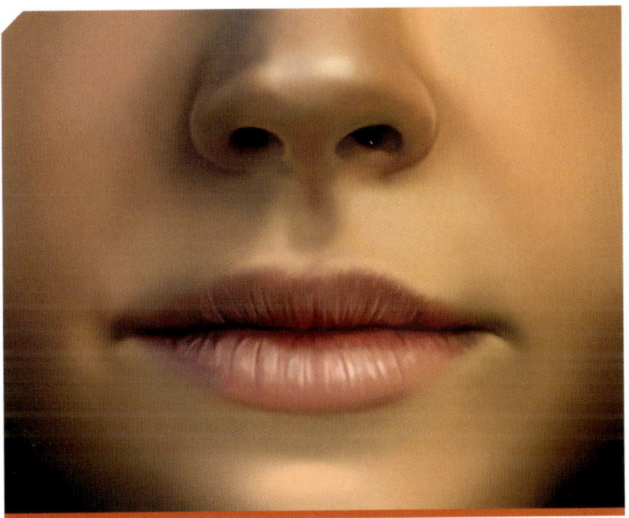

Refine both subtle and defined forms of the skin

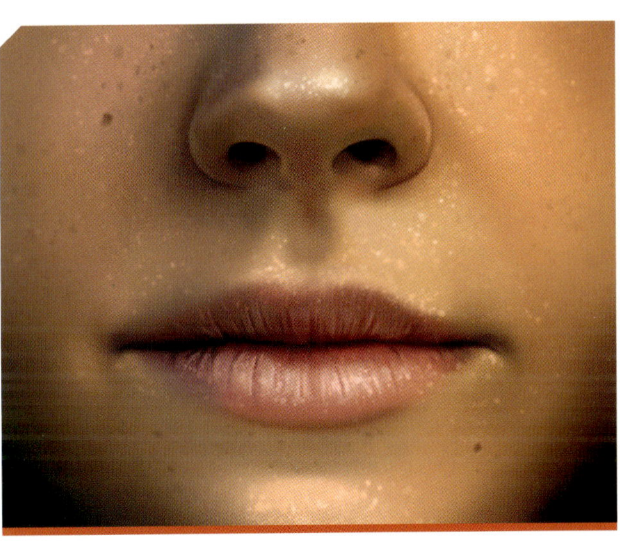

Paint on details and texture to make the skin appear more lifelike, such as freckles and pores

04 Form definition

(a) Continually referring to your model or reference photo, establish all subtle and defined forms of the skin. By the end of this step, you should have a balanced and intentional combination of hard and soft edges. Hard edges will be reserved for areas like the edge of the nostrils.

(b) Paint all values, such as the forms of the mouth indentation, the highlights on the nose, and the lips.

(c) Your line work should be completely hidden by this stage. If you have defined your forms enough, the piece will hold up without it.

05 Texture

(a) All skin has texture, including young skin. This texture can either be visually subtle or more obvious. Focus first on the more subtle quality.

(b) After carefully studying your reference, paint various dots of highlights, freckles, and discoloration over the skin's surface.

(c) Erase or paint over any places in which the highlights or detailing is too harsh. One way to convey youthful skin is by keeping texture to a minimum.

(d) Add a few final freckles, moles, or highlighted pores on top of the subtle texture, which will remain more obvious.

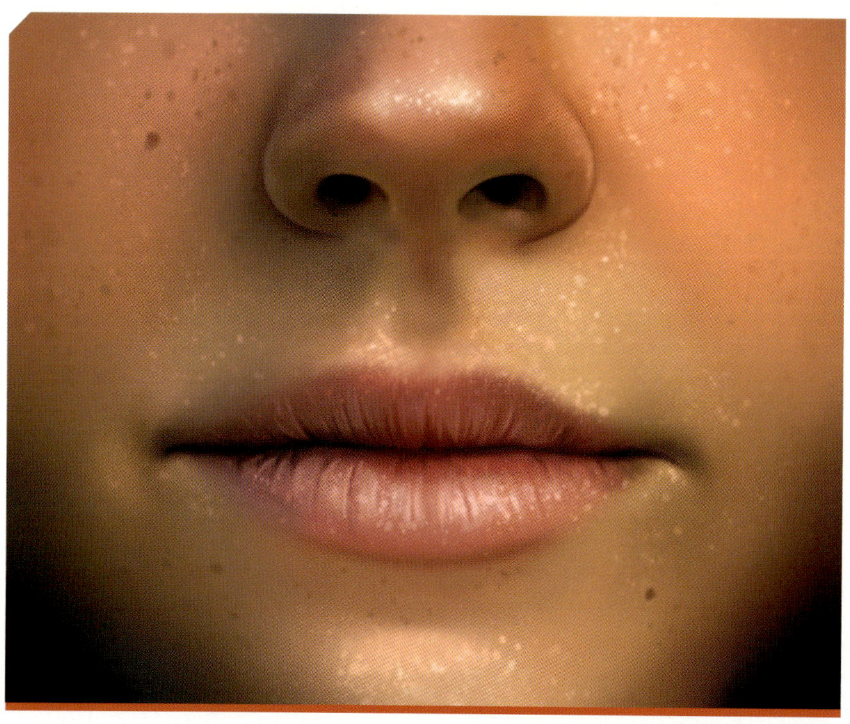

Finish by painting vibrant blush tones on the skin to convey youthful vibrancy

06 Vibrancy

(a) Young skin will often have a youthful, vibrant glow to it, which some artists choose to exaggerate when stylizing their work. Create this youthful vibrancy by adding blush-like hues to the skin; large washes of red, orange, or pink tones.

(b) Use a very large, soft brush to lightly add blush tones throughout the face, focusing on the cheeks and sometimes the nose too. Do not add too much at once. Instead, focus on lightly building it up to your desired level of vibrancy.

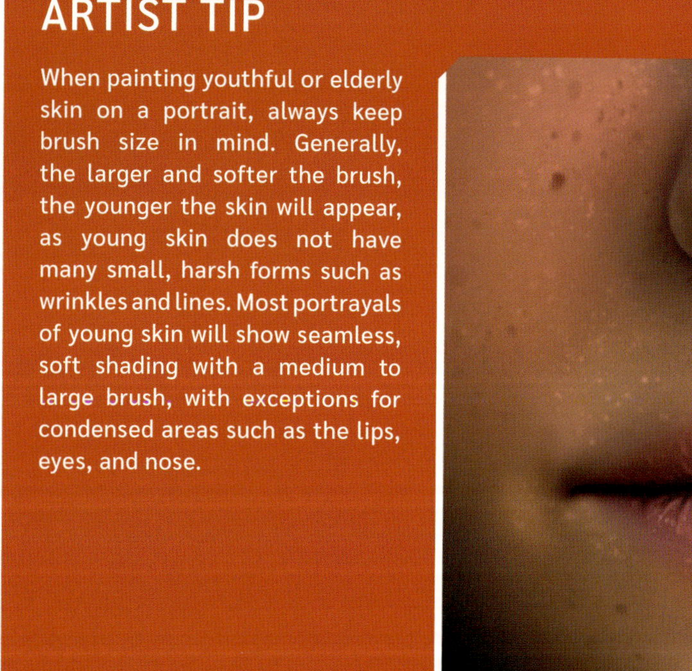

ARTIST TIP

When painting youthful or elderly skin on a portrait, always keep brush size in mind. Generally, the larger and softer the brush, the younger the skin will appear, as young skin does not have many small, harsh forms such as wrinkles and lines. Most portrayals of young skin will show seamless, soft shading with a medium to large brush, with exceptions for condensed areas such as the lips, eyes, and nose.

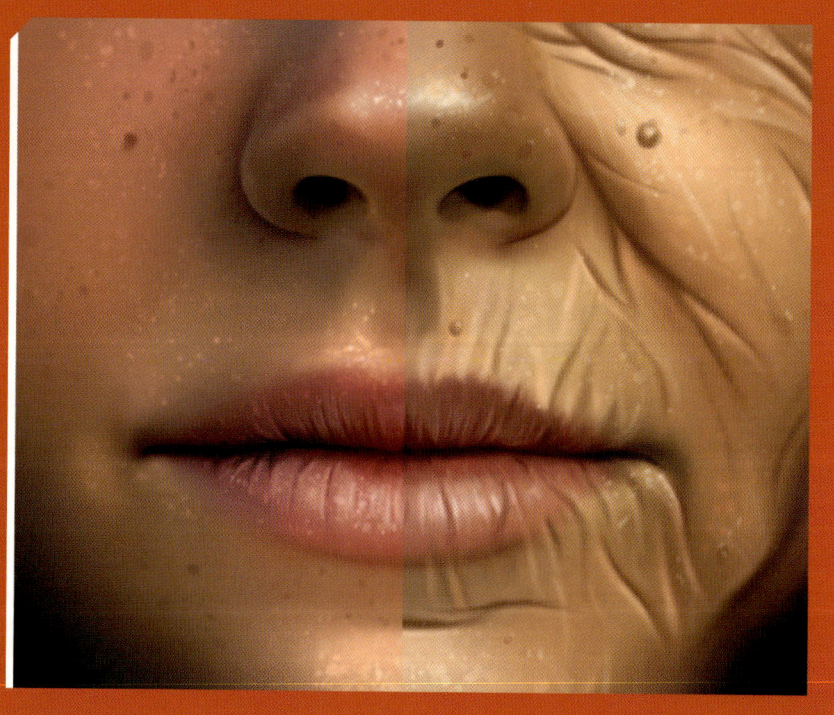

COMPARISON OF YOUNG AND OLD SKIN

OLD SKIN

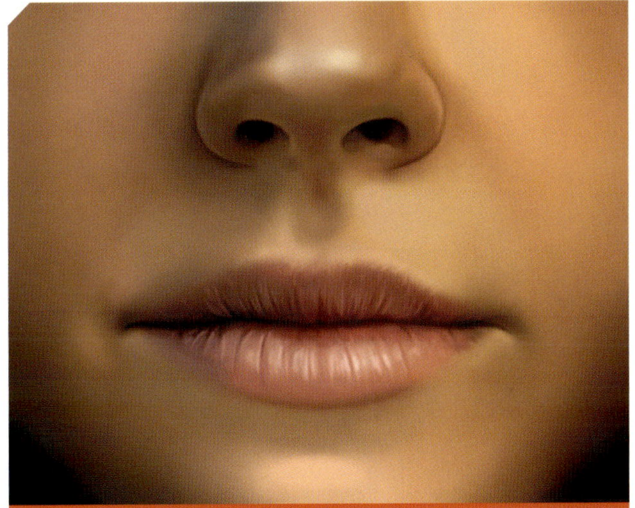

Start by following steps 01-04 for painting young skin

01 The base

(a) The essence of painting older skin is all in the details. During the early steps, the process does not differ too much from the process of painting young skin (see page 112). Follow steps 01 to 04 for painting young skin, which will form the base on which to begin painting textured older skin.

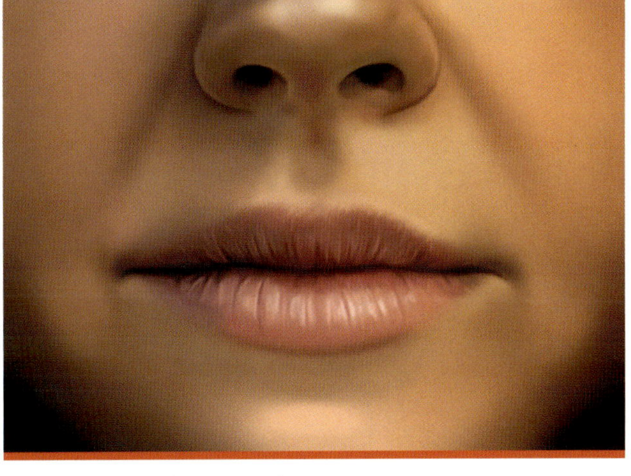

Paint broad, simple forms to begin to establish the basic direction of the wrinkles

02 Initial wrinkle mapping

(a) Study your subject or look at reference photos of older skin, then map out the general shapes of the main wrinkles using a light shading color on top of the base. This will determine the direction, placement, degree, and type of wrinkles and lines.

(b) It's important to understand how gravity and loss of elasticity affects the skin, particularly on the face. In this example, the main wrinkles are located around the sides of the mouth and jawline where the skin can sag slightly as it loses elasticity.

03 Wrinkle definition

(a) Using the general wrinkle shapes from the previous step, establish more defined wrinkles using a smaller brush and darker shade. The darker shade is because wrinkles and creases in the skin will cause shadows, so consider your light source when determining which lines and areas of the face will be the darkest.

(b) Study your subject, as well as familiarizing yourself with the types of wrinkles that typically affect older skin. For example, there can often be vertical wrinkles along the lips, long wrinkles along the sides of the mouth, and curved wrinkles beneath the eyes.

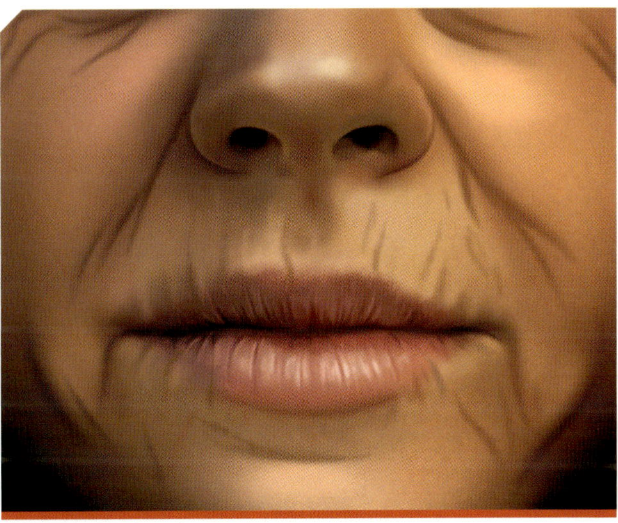

Use a darker shade to paint thin wrinkles on top of the broader shading

04 Highlights

(a) As wrinkles are indented into the skin, a light source will usually highlight their ridged edges. Paint these highlights, using a small brush and a color a few shades brighter than the base skin tone. They should not be too harsh and require equal saturation to the original skin tone.

ARTIST TIP

When beginners paint wrinkles, they will often make them too "airbrushy," meaning they are soft-edged and without structure. Even though you may think of skin as soft, wrinkles actually have plenty of structure to them and can even have hard edges. While it's tempting to use a medium-sized airbrush to paint wrinkles, this will ensure they have no structure and will ultimately result in an unrealistic final portrait.

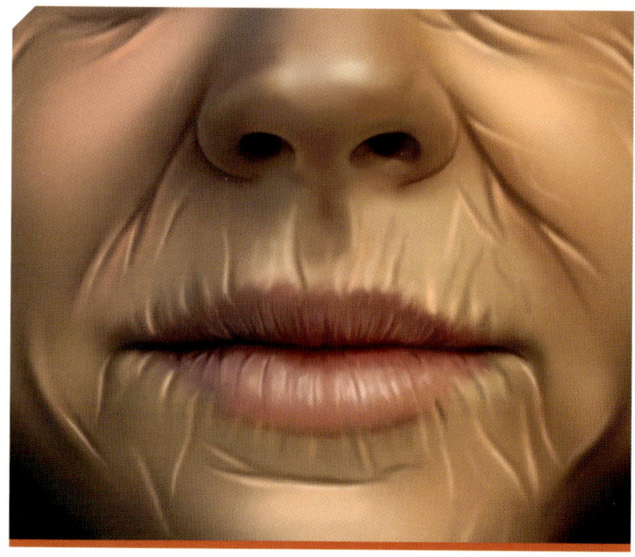

Paint highlights onto the wrinkles in a lighter shade

05 Smallest wrinkles

(a) Using a smaller brush and the deepest wrinkle color, carefully paint in the finest wrinkles. These small wrinkles should still be based on the main wrinkle shapes, but they should stray slightly to create an organic randomness.

(b) Give these finer wrinkles subtle highlighted ridges for added realism.

(c) Determine if your wrinkles are too harsh in their values. If any appear too harsh, softly erase them or lightly paint back over them using your base skin shade, depending on your medium.

06 Texture

(a) The process of painting texture onto elderly skin is similar to that of younger skin, in that it includes adding details such as highlighted pores and skin imperfections. In older skin, however, the darker textures should be slightly less saturated, and it should be less vibrant overall. You may also choose to include other imperfections to make the skin look even more aged.

(b) Study your model or reference photo, observing any moles, scars, or age spots. Age spots are often larger in scale than other types of spots or freckles. Adding such details can add realism and character, though an excessive amount will stylize, or could even overwhelm, the portrait.

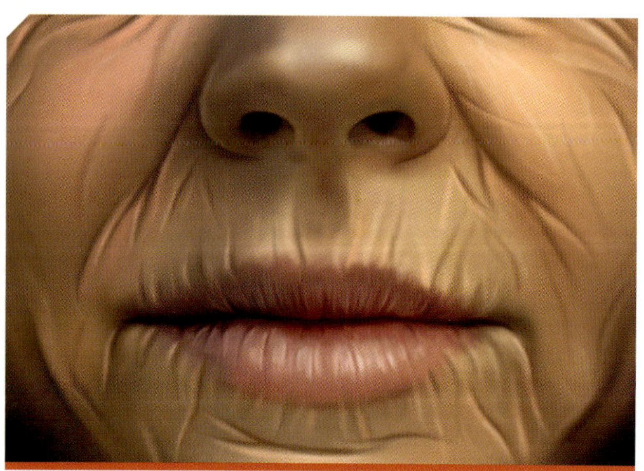

Paint the finest wrinkles, straying slightly from the main wrinkle shapes to make them appear more natural

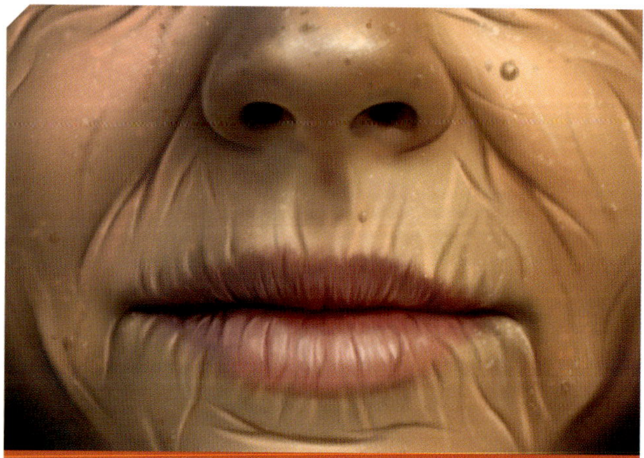

Finish by adding texture and details, such as age spots, for added realism

PHOTO REFERENCE

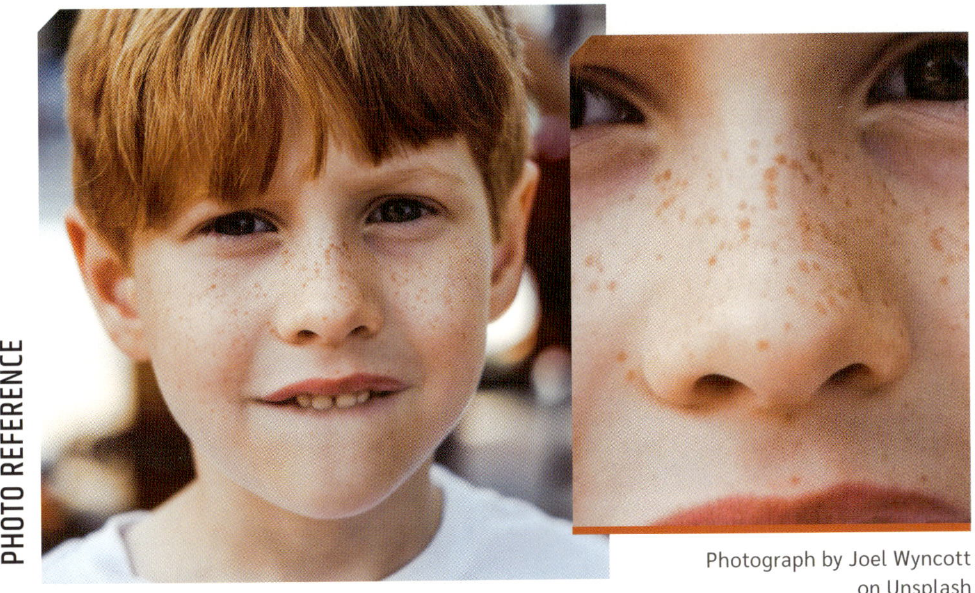

Photograph by Joel Wyncott on Unsplash

Skin: freckles & scars

01 Base and initial freckles

(a) Before painting on freckles and scars, you will need to have already established a fully defined base image for them to sit on, as has been created in the earlier chapters. This base should include finalized forms, edges, colors, values, and textures.

(b) Scars sit on top of freckles, so if your subject has freckles, you will need to paint these first.

(c) Study your model or reference photo, observing the freckles and whether they are spread fairly evenly or cluster in certain areas, such as across the nose and upper cheeks.

(d) Start by painting lots of rough freckles that lack nuance and perspective. Use a deep, saturated color for this. These will be small, slightly bumpy circular shapes.

02 Refining

(a) Soften the appearance of the majority of the harsh freckles. To do this digitally, simply erase them using a soft, round eraser, leaving behind only a subtle trace. If using traditional media, lightly paint over these freckles with the base skin color.

(b) Studying your model or reference photo, you will notice that your subject's freckles are not all the same shade, shape, or size. Paint on deeper toned freckles, varying the size and shape. This will imply a variance in freckle value.

(c) Paint on the freckles that are in perspective. In this case, the freckles on the side of the nose are not perfectly circular, as they are viewed at an angle.

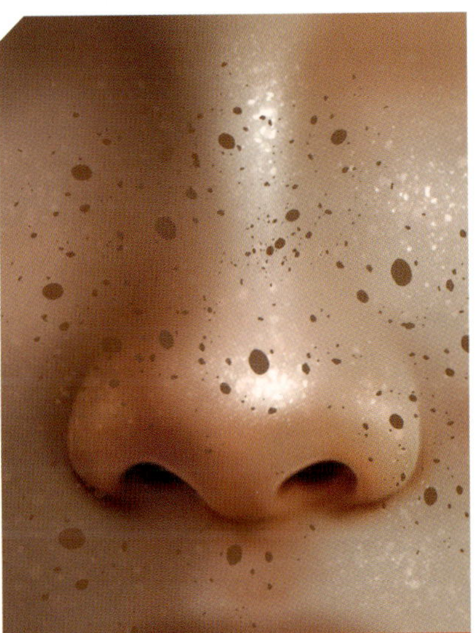

Paint on rough freckles using a deep, saturated color

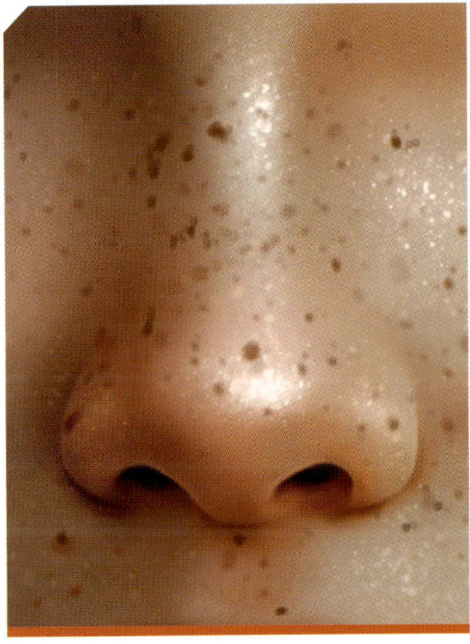

Soften any harsher freckles, plus paint on any freckles that are at an angle

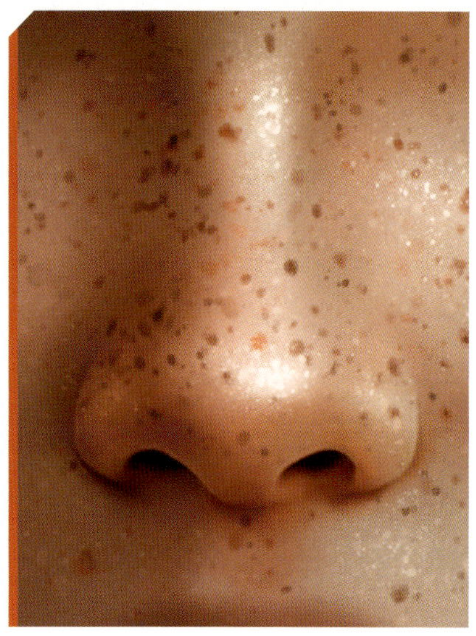

Ensure the freckles vary in pattern, color, value, scale, and focus level for believability

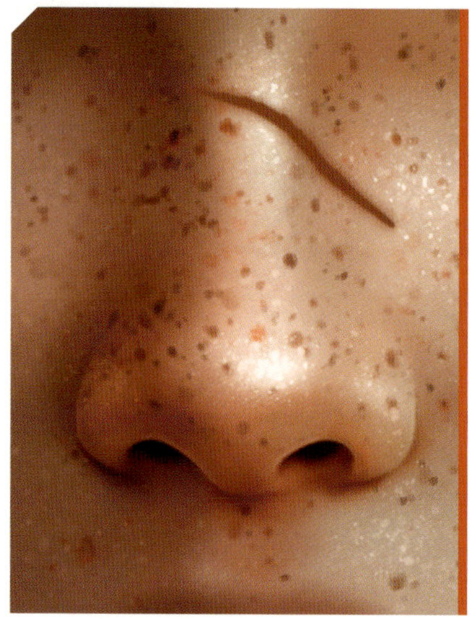

Paint a basic scar using a deep flesh color, ensuring it thins at either end of the line

03 Final freckle details

(a) Refer back to your subject as you add extra freckles, keeping in mind perspective and value. Make sure the freckles are not too uniform in pattern, color, value, or scale. You want them to appear random and natural. Any uniformity will conflict with the realism of the piece.

(b) On the brightest areas of skin, add saturated and brighter freckles that appear to be in the light.

(c) It is also important to consider the focus levels of the freckles, depending on where they sit on the face. Much like photography, some art styles include areas that are in focus and others that are out of focus and blurred to imply depth and realism. For example, freckles on a cheek that is closer to the viewer may be perfectly sharp, but on the other cheek, facing away from the viewer, they might be slightly blurred to bring depth and unity to the whole portrait.

04 Initial scar shape

(a) Your subject may have scars or marks on their skin; it's important to be able to paint these to add realism and believability to your portraits. On top of the freckles, use a small, hard-edged brush and a deep, saturated flesh color to paint an elongated line with thin ends for the basic shape of the scar. This shape should also follow the perspective of the area of skin it is sitting on for maximum believability.

(b) Use the same color and a larger soft brush to paint a diffused gradient effect to the outside edges of the scar shape. This is the first step in making the scar appear to be infused into the skin.

ARTIST TIP

When painting freckles or scars, they should always make sense with the rest of the portrait. If you have a freckle or scar in the brightest part of the face that is the same value as a freckle or scar in the darkest part of the face, this will immediately flatten the whole image. Similarly, if a freckle or scar is in an area that is out of focus or at an angle, it must reflect the same focus level and perspective to ensure it becomes a natural part of the face.

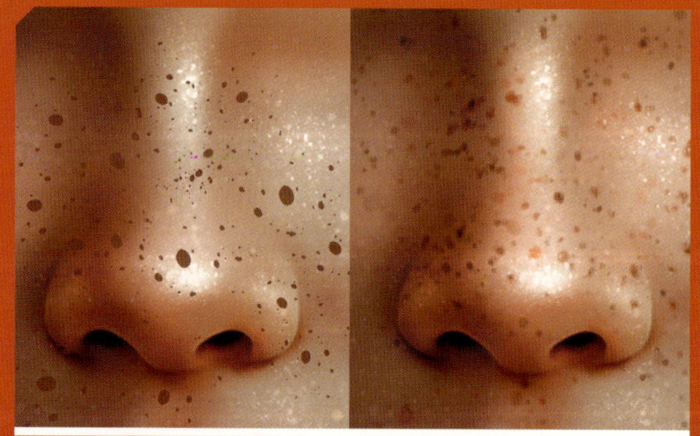

COMPARISON BETWEEN QUICKLY PAINTED FRECKLES (LEFT) AND CAREFULLY PAINTED FRECKLES (RIGHT)

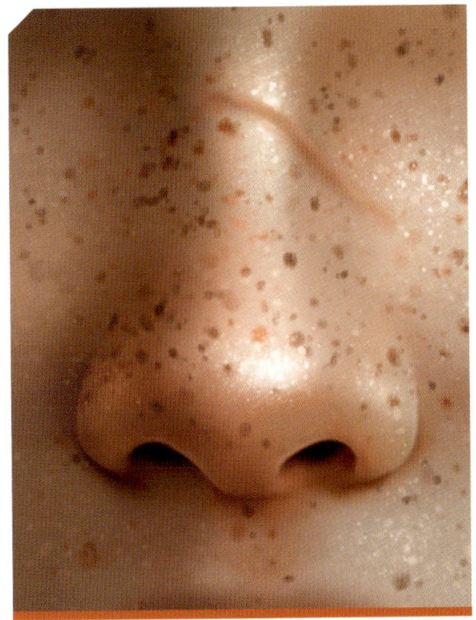

Establish the basic colors and values of the scar, fading or blurring it slightly to show its healing

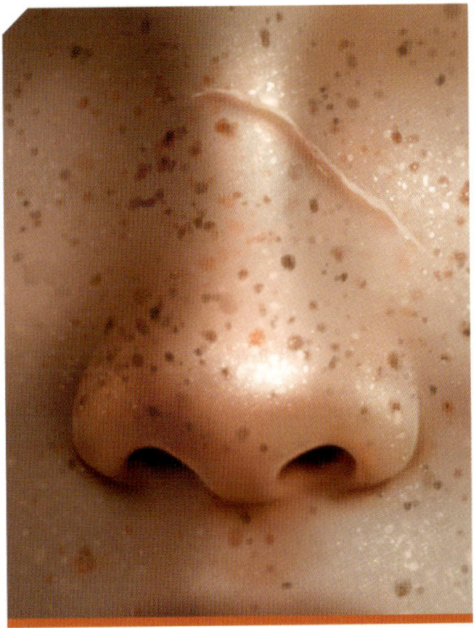

Establish the type of scar and direction of the light source, then paint rough highlights onto the scar

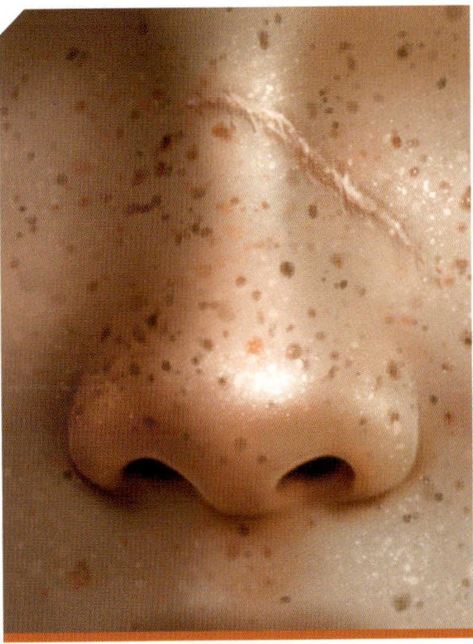

Finish by painting shiny, imperfect, textured lines over the scar, before diffusing the edges to fuse it with the surrounding skin

05 Values and colors

(a) Blur out the harsh edges of the base scar shape. You can do this using a soft brush to manually feather out the edges of the shape, or a blurring tool if painting in digital software.

(b) Study your subject to determine the age and type of scar. Is it fresh and inflamed, or older and faded? New scars will often appear bigger and redder, while older scars will tend to fade and appear slightly paler over time. In this case, the scar is in the healing process, so it is fairly light in value and has a combination of red tones and normal skin tones within it.

(c) Paint these basic values and colors inside of your base scar shape.

06 Initial highlights

(a) Before painting highlights onto the scar, study your subject closely to establish if the scar is atrophic (sunken) or hypertrophic (raised). You should also note the direction of the light source. In this case, the scar is hypertrophic, meaning it is raised slightly above the rest of the skin's surface. As the light source is above, the top of the scar will pick up the main highlights.

(b) Paint the highlight using a very small brush and a bright flesh color. It should be slightly rough to ensure it does not look too perfect or artificial.

07 Final details

(a) As they heal, scars can sometimes form shiny, vertical lines. Observe the intricate detail and textures of your subject's scar, then paint these lines using the same bright flesh color from the previous step. This shiny texture should face in the same general direction throughout the entire length of the scar and include various imperfections to prevent it from looking too uniform and fake. These bright lines and textures can slightly emerge from the base scar shape for more of an organic appearance.

(b) Use a soft brush and the deeper color used in step 04 to paint a more diffused gradient onto the outside of the scar. This will give the scar the appearance of being fused with the skin, making it look more realistic and less like it is stuck on.

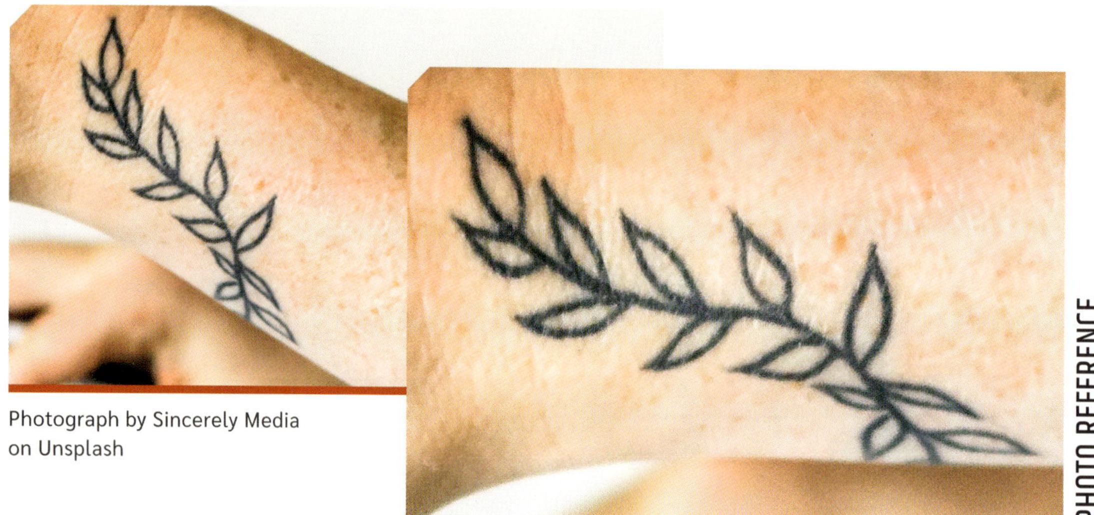

Photograph by Sincerely Media on Unsplash

Skin: tattoos

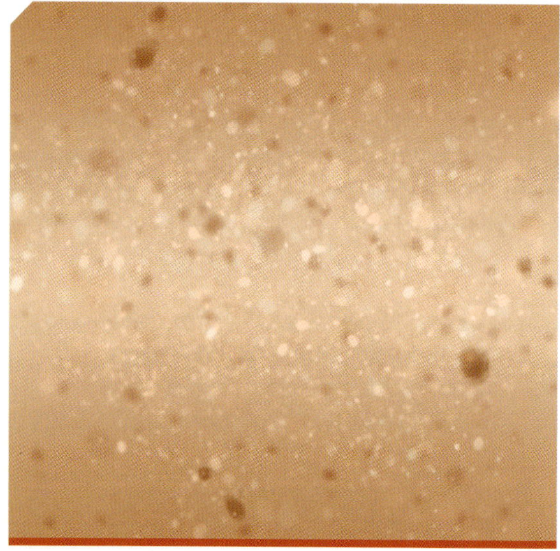

Begin with a fully detailed swatch of skin

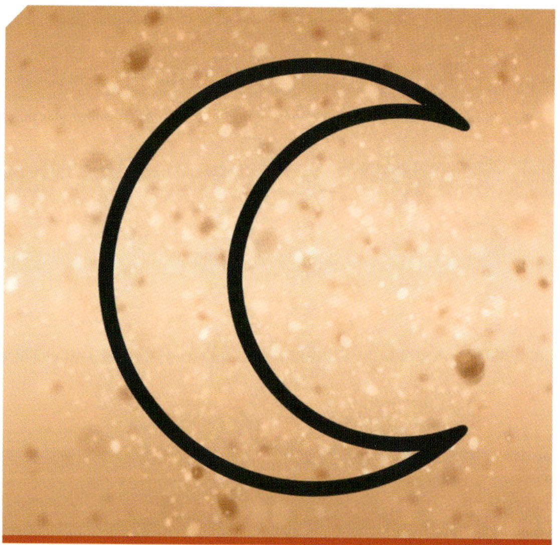

Paint a basic, smooth line for the tattoo

01 Finished skin

(a) Before you can paint a tattoo, you need an image of skin to use as a base. This base image should include all of the colors, values, forms, details, and textures of the skin. (See page 112 for how to paint young or old skin.) This is especially important when working traditionally, as it's difficult to go back and fix an area of the skin after you have painted a tattoo over the top.

02 Base shape

(a) Study your model or reference photo to observe your subject's tattoo, paying close attention to its size, shape, coloring, age, and how it is wrapped around the skin. This chapter will demonstrate how to paint a very simple crescent moon line tattoo, using the above photo as a reference for the style and color of the ink.

(b) Use a small, hard-edged brush, the chosen ink color, and a steady hand to paint the basic shape of the tattoo.

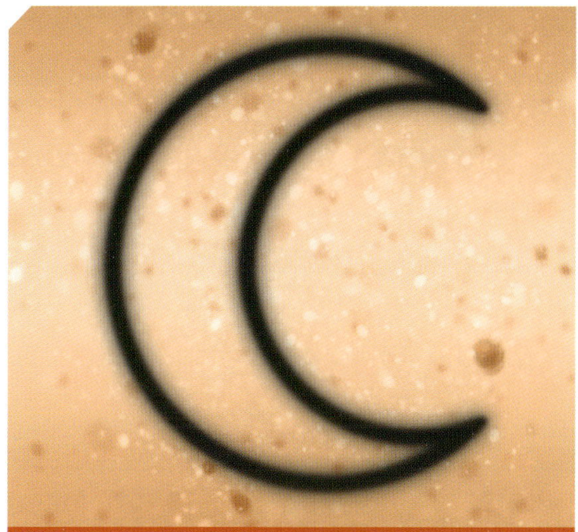

Feather or blur the tattoo shape to make it appear integrated with the skin

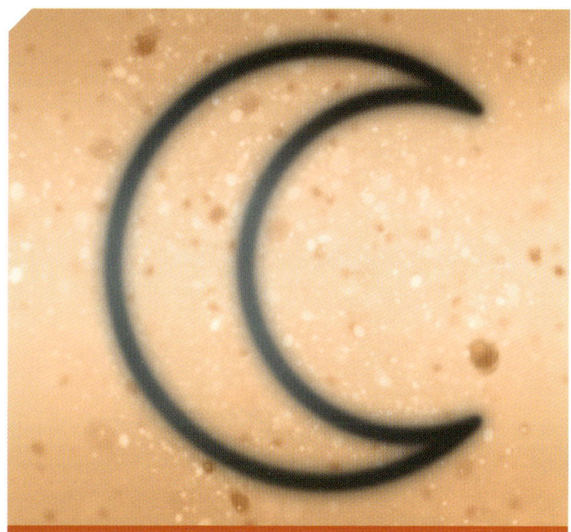

Paint initial shading and color variance to show faded areas within the tattoo

03 Edge softening

(a) It's important that the tattoo appears integrated with the skin, rather than stuck on top like a sticker. To create this impression, softly feather out or blur the edges of the base tattoo shape, depending on your chosen medium. Take care not to soften the shape too much, however, as you don't want to lose the definition of the tattoo.

04 Ink values

(a) When the black ink of a tattoo fades, the body begins to break down the ink and it can take on slightly blue or green tones in certain lighting conditions. This hue is especially apparent in areas of the tattoo that are most exposed to sunlight. A tattoo that is regularly exposed to sunlight on areas such as the face, neck, or arm will likely be more faded than a tattoo on the hip, thigh, or torso, which is usually hidden by clothing.

(b) If your subject's tattoo is old or starting to fade, add a brighter blueish shade to the highlighted areas of the design.

05 Initial skin texture

(a) A tattoo is a part of the skin and will therefore have skin texture, including small circular highlights and shadows. The highlights should be focused around the area of the tattoo that is most exposed to the light, so study your model or reference photo to determine where the light source is. The size of the texture is in direct relation to how large or small the tattoo is.

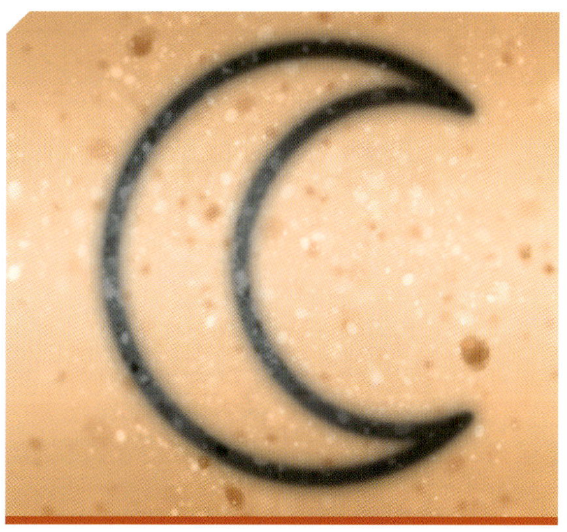

Use highlights and shadows to form basic skin texture

06 Final details

(a) Paint tiny dots of ink around the tattoo shape. This will create the impression that it is bleeding into the skin for added realism.

(b) Add any shading or further ink diffusion by using the main base ink color and a large, soft brush to subtly paint softness on the interior and exterior of the tattoo shape.

(c) As this is a close-up image, you need to work texture from the skin into the tattoo. Pay close attention to your subject's skin, observing details such as freckles and tiny hairs. Paint subtle streaks of highlight over the tattoo using a bright flesh color to depict skin highlights or fine hair.

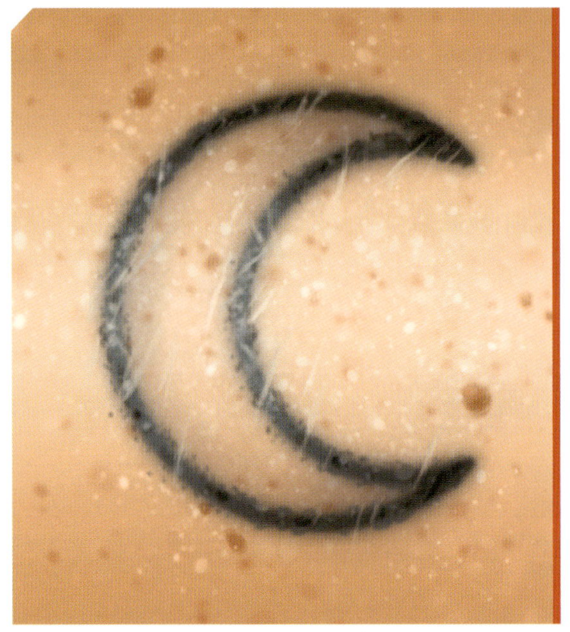

Finish by painting final details and texture, such as minute spots of ink and fine hair for believability

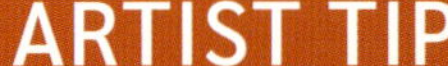

ARTIST TIP

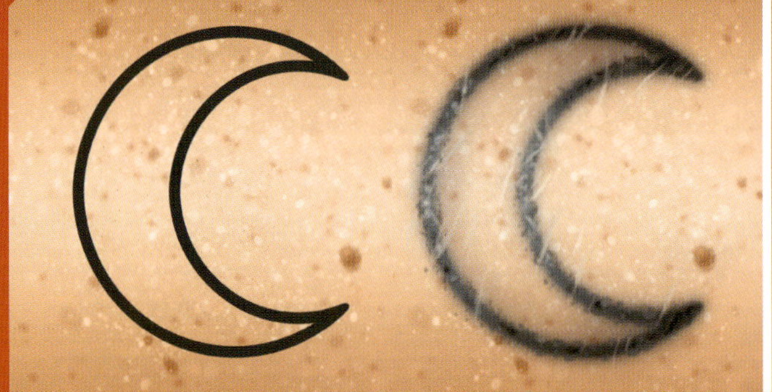

SIDE-BY-SIDE COMPARISON OF A TATTOO THAT IS NOT INFUSED INTO THE SKIN VS. A TATTOO THAT IS INFUSED INTO THE SKIN USING THE STEPS DESCRIBED ABOVE

Taking the time to properly infuse the tattoo into the skin will create a much more believable result. Beginners often stop at step 02, with only hard-edged lines and no diffusion, values, or textures, resulting in tattoos that merely float on top of the skin. Putting in the extra work to properly integrate your subject's tattoo will elevate your portrait to a whole new level. However, it's also important to keep in mind that you may not be painting a tattoo this close up, and therefore won't need to continue to the fine details of step 06. If you the tattoo you are painting is not close-up, painting until step 05 could be enough to create a realistic image.

PHOTO REFERENCE

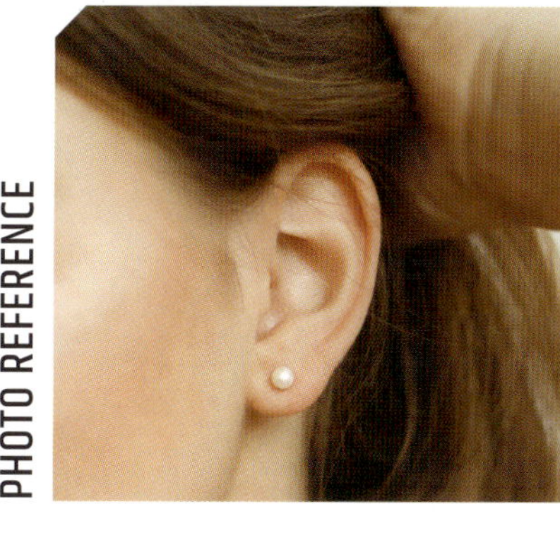

Jewelry & piercings

Photograph by Joeyy Lee on Unsplash

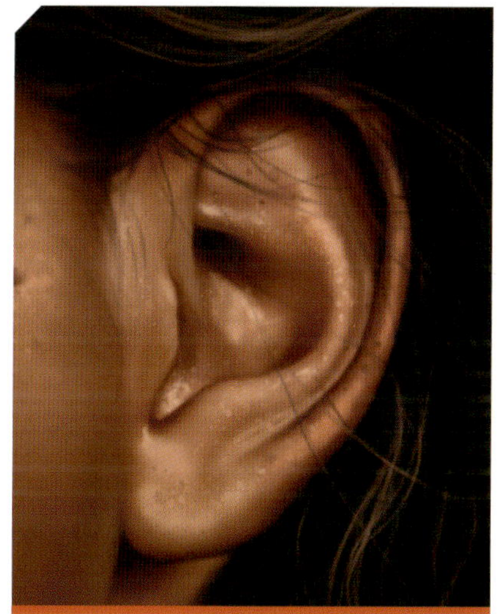

Ensure the area you wish to paint jewelry on top of – such the ear – is as finalized as possible

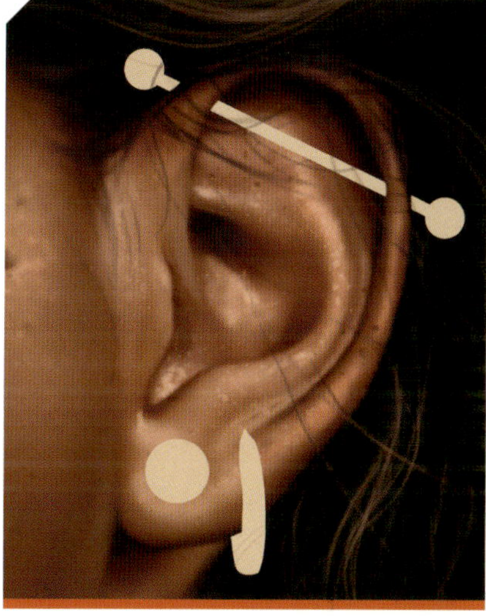

Paint the earrings onto the ear using flat, opaque shapes, leaving gaps for where the earring passes through the lobe or cartilage

01 Finalized base

(a) Before you can paint jewelry onto a portrait, the area should be as complete as possible. This base image should include finalized forms, colors, textures, details, and values.

(b) This tutorial will guide you through how to paint earrings, so you will first need to paint an ear. This is covered in the Ears chapter on page 104.

02 Base shapes

(a) Study your model or reference photo to see what kind of jewelry or piercings your subject has. Pay attention to the size, shape, angle, and detailing of each item, as well as how it sits on or passes through the skin. This reference photo has a single stud, but you may decide to add more piercings if your portrait has a conceptual focus or a certain motif.

This tutorial will demonstrate how to paint a stud earring in the earlobe, a hoop earring through the upper earlobe, and an industrial bar piercing through the cartilage.

(b) Create a new layer or paint directly on top of the base image, depending on whether you are working digitally or with traditional media.

(c) Fill in the shape of each piercing opaquely using a light color, hard-edged brush, and a steady hand. Paint a simple circle shape for the stud earring. Next, paint by a thick, curved line with an extra shape to the side, implying a ring that moves behind the ear, for the hoop earring. For the industrial piercing, paint a thick line with a sphere on each end, with two breaks in the line to indicate where the piercing passes through the cartilage.

ARTIST TIP

Familiarize yourself with the qualities of each material you need to paint. Pearls can be bright, shiny, and sometimes iridescent. They have harsh highlights, limited shadows, and pick up subtle hues from their surroundings. Gold is usually yellow in hue and very reflective. Gold jewelry often has harsh highlights, deep shadows, and will reflect colors and shapes from its immediate surroundings. Similar to gold, silver is also very reflective and will have harsh highlights and deep shadows. Unlike gold, however, silver does not have a particular hue to it.

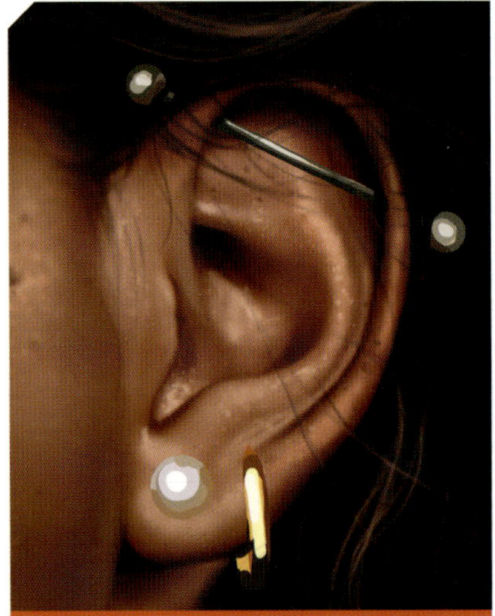

Ascertain what your subject's jewelry is made of, study the properties of each material, then use rough, hard-edged shading to depict this on each shape

03 Hard-edged shading

(a) Study your subject closely to establish the material each item of jewelry is made of and how it is affected by the light source. In this case, the stud piercing is pearl, the hoop is gold, and the industrial piercing is silver.

(b) Use a hard-edged brush to vaguely reflect these qualities within each earring shape, roughly shading in light and shadow.

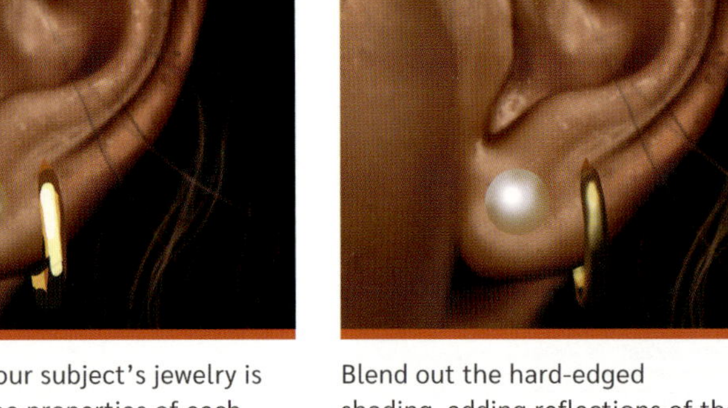

Blend out the hard-edged shading, adding reflections of the skin tone on any items of jewelry that have a reflective surface

04 Blending

(a) Blend out the hard-edged shading on each item of jewelry using your preferred blending method for your medium. Try to keep the shading in its original location.

(b) Continually referring back to your model or reference photo, start to establish initial color and shading subtleties within each earring using a small, soft brush. Include reflections of the skin tone in reflective areas of the earring that are closest to the ear. For example, in the industrial piercing, there are reflections of the skin color on the side of each sphere that faces the ear.

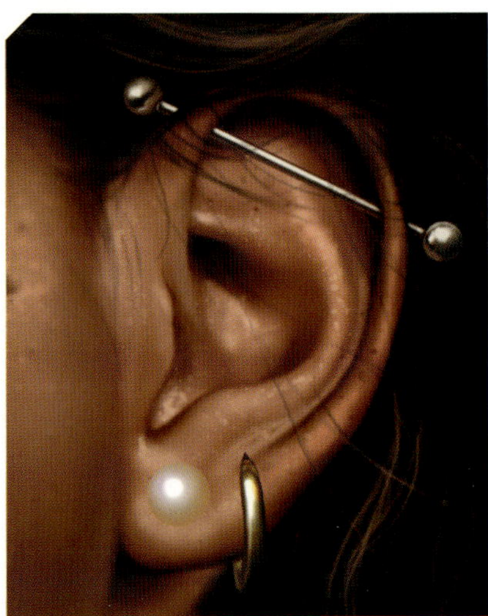

Refine the form of each item, adding any smooth shading or harsh highlights

05 Form refinement

(a) Studying your subject closely, make any final refinements to the form of their jewelry. This includes sharper details in the reflections, defined highlights and shadows, and any other color subtleties.

(b) Add details like sparkles, scratches, imperfections, or dents. You can imply scratches to reflective jewelry by adding subtle lines using a bright color and a very small brush.

(c) Ground the jewelry by using a deep, saturated skin color to add shadows to the skin around each earring, ensuring it looks part of the image and not stuck on top like a sticker. The shadows should be less diffused in the areas where the jewelry is directly touching the skin.

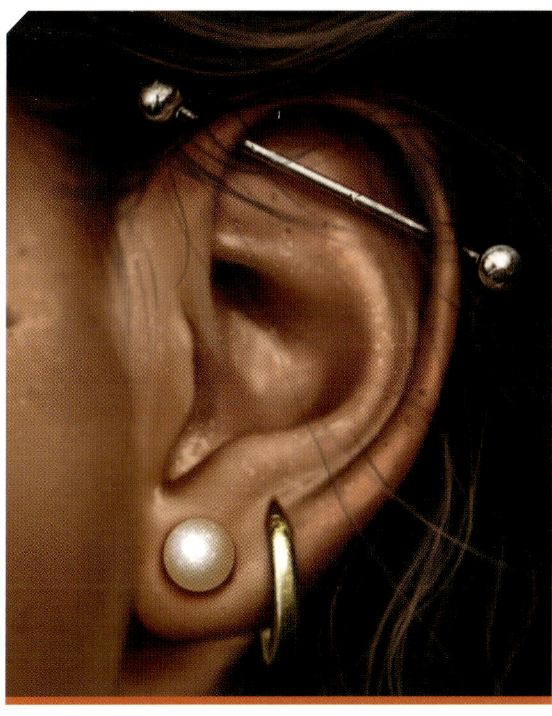

Finish by adding final details, such as sparkles and imperfections, before using shadow to ground each item into the skin

06 Final details

(a) Studying your subject closely, make any final refinements to the form of their jewelry. This includes sharper details in the reflections, defined highlights and shadows, and any other color subtleties.

(b) Add details like sparkles, scratches, imperfections, or dents. You can imply scratches to reflective jewelry by adding subtle lines using a bright color and a very small brush.

(c) Ground the jewelry by using a deep skin color to add shadows to the skin around each earring, ensuring it looks part of the image and not stuck on top like a sticker. The shadows should be less diffused in the areas where the jewelry is directly touching the skin.

ARTIST TIP

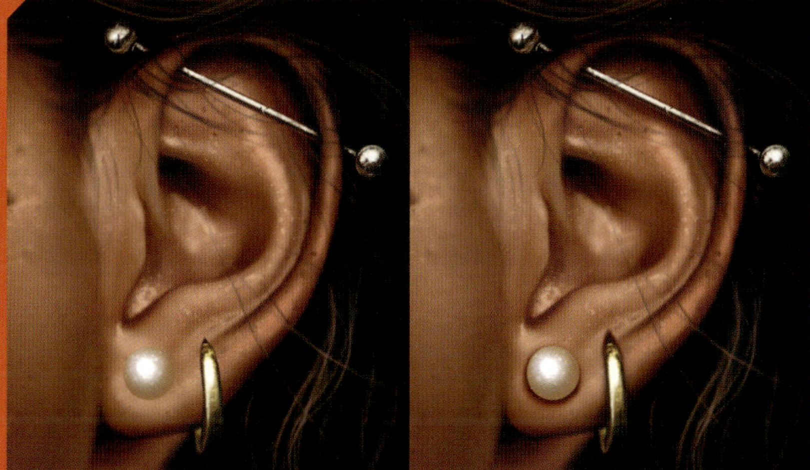

THESE EARRINGS HAVE NOT BEEN GROUNDED AND SO FLOAT ABOVE THE SKIN IN AN UNNATURAL WAY

THESE EARRINGS HAVE BEEN GROUNDED INTO THE IMAGE THROUGH THE USE OF SHADOW ON THE SKIN SURROUNDING EACH EARRING

You could be very thorough and paint incredibly realistic jewelry on your portrait, but if it's not grounded it will always appear to be missing something. The key lies in accurately portraying the relationship between the jewelry and your subject's skin. Without introducing shadows, there will be no such relationship and the jewelry will merely float above the skin in an artificial way. The severity of these shadows will vary depending on the light source and the amount of contact the jewelry has with the skin.

PHOTO REFERENCE

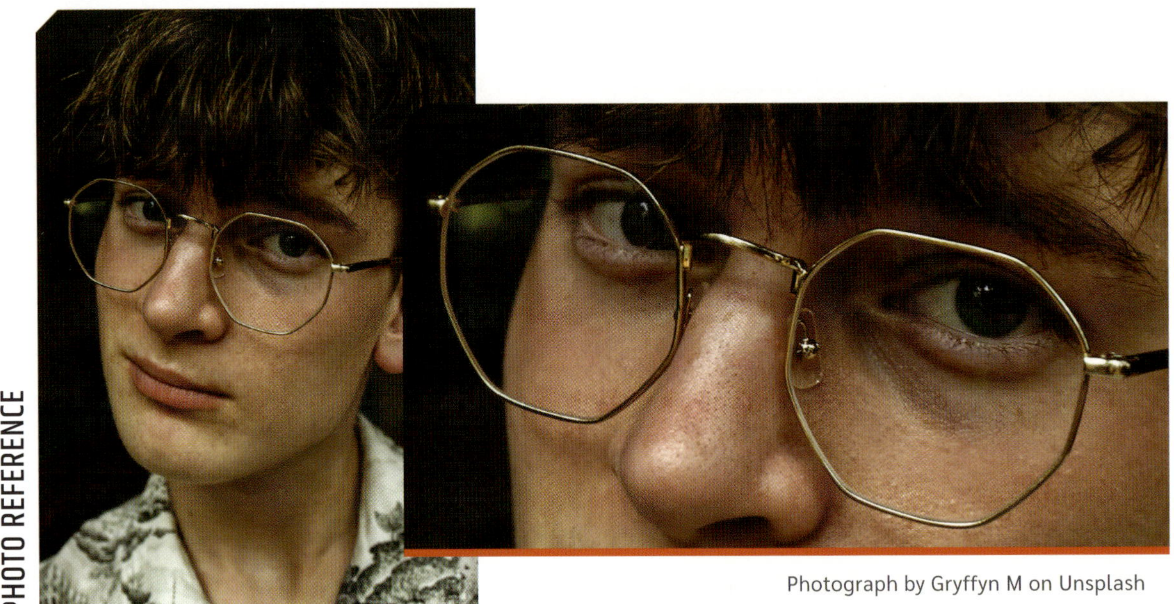

Photograph by Gryffyn M on Unsplash

Glasses

01 Perspective

(a) As with jewelry, before you can paint glasses onto a portrait, you must first finalize the base image underneath. If working digitally, all line work for glasses should be on a new layer above the face. If using traditional media, use a very light touch to paint the line work directly over the finalized face.

(b) The perspective must be correct for a painting of glasses to be visually believable. Study your model or reference photo, paying attention to the angle of your subject's face and their glasses. Establish the rough perspective lines, starting with a vertical line running down the center of the face.

(c) Indicate the eye level with a tilted horizontal line. This line will differ in height and tilt depending on the direction in which your subject's face is turned.

(d) Observe the size and height of your subject's glasses, marking the upper edge with a tilted horizontal line above the eyeline, and the lower edge below the eyeline.

(e) Establish the width of the glasses by sketching vertical lines on either side of the face.

(f) Study the shape of your subject's glasses and decide whether you wish to capture them as they are, or stylize them for visual interest. Draw the rough outline of the frames, using your subtle perspective lines as a guide. This should include the lens shape, the bridge that connects the two lenses, and the temples that start at the eyeline then extend either side of the face to rest behind the ear.

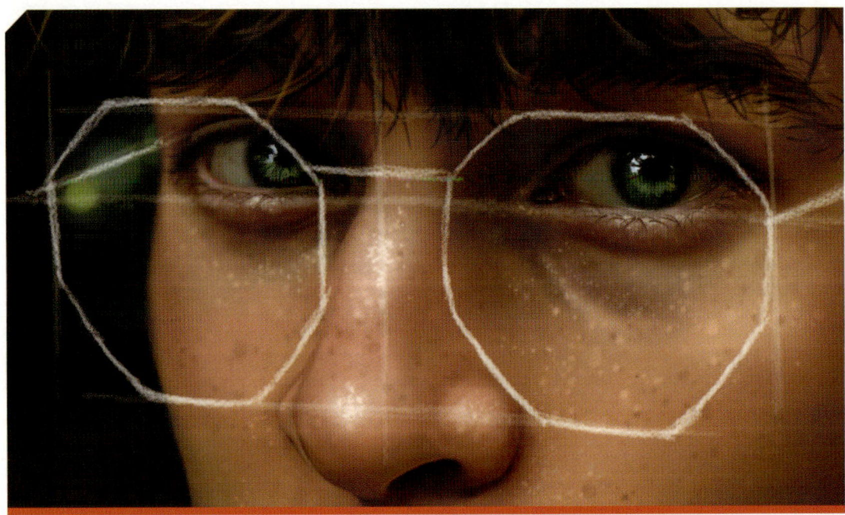

Sketch the rough perspective lines that will eventually form your subject's glasses, paying attention to size and shape

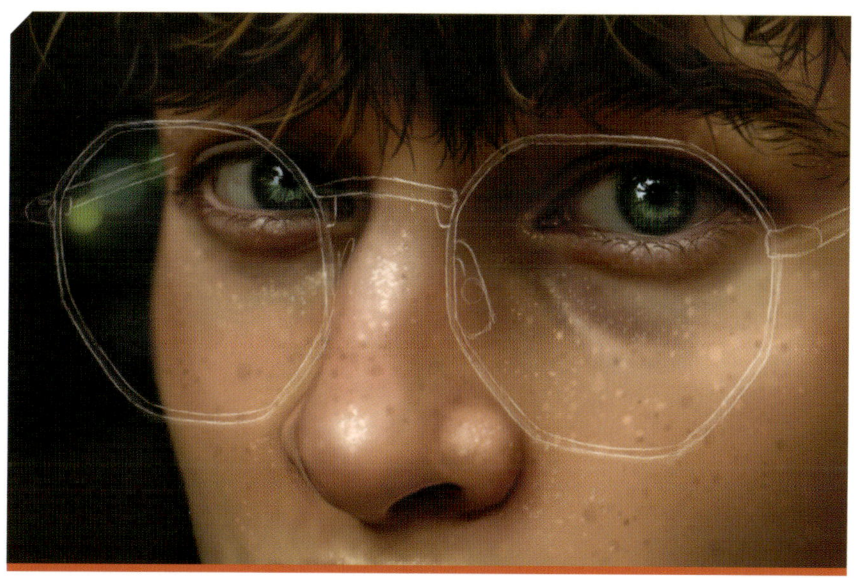

Draw detailed, refined line work for the frames

02 Final line work

(a) With the rough outline of the frames as a guide, use a small brush to draw more detailed line work on top. Referring back to your reference, add details such as the nose pads, end pieces, bridge shape, and rims.

(b) By the end of this step, the line work should be clean and precise, with minimal sketchiness.

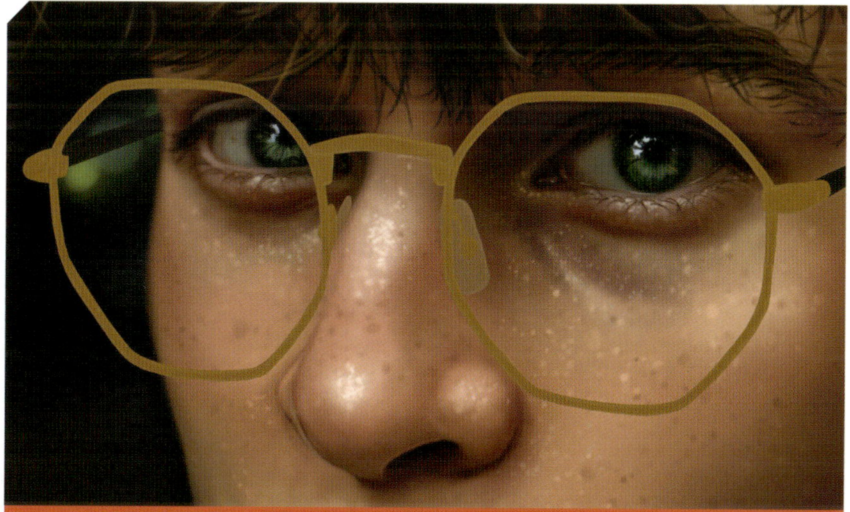

Paint flat, base shapes for the frames

03 Base shapes

(a) The next step is to lock in the base shapes for the frames. Select a medium-toned color and carefully outline the shape of the frames, using your refined line work as a guide. Ensure all of the edges are extremely smooth.

(b) Use different colors for areas like the nose pads and temples to help differentiate the different parts.

04 Hard-edged shading

(a) Observe what material your subject's glasses frames are made from and consider the qualities of that material. In this example the frames are made from a smooth, gold-colored metal. Gold is very reflective, bringing out harsh highlights and shadows, and has a yellow hue.

(b) Keeping the qualities of your frame material in mind, establish the rough, hard-edged shading within your base shapes. This can be very rough, since it will be blended.

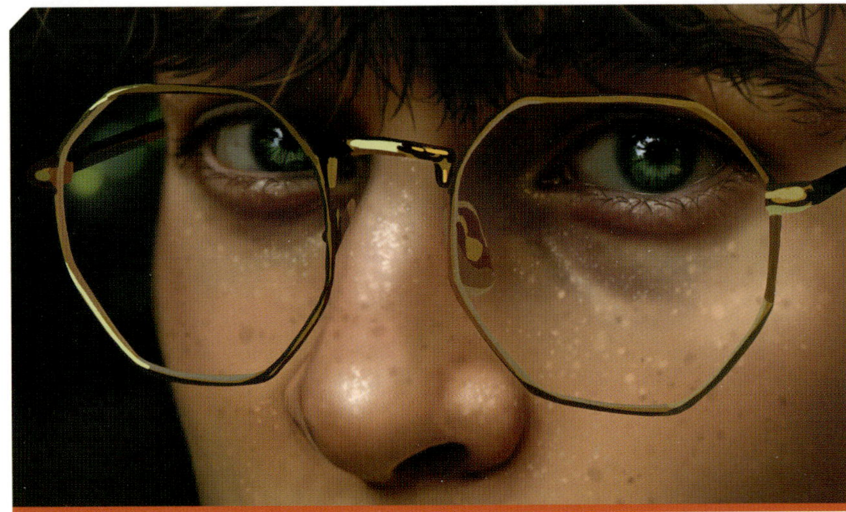

Determine the material of the frames, considering the light source as you establish the hard-edged shading

05 Form refinement

(a) Blend out the hard-edged shading using your preferred blending method for your medium.

(b) Use a small, soft brush to establish the forms of the glasses. When working with elongated reflective materials like metal frames, the shading will mainly consist of long stripes of highlights, values, and midtones.

(c) Observing the direction of the light source, paint the brightest highlights on the areas of the frames that receive the most light. The light is shining from the top right in this example, so there are bright highlights on the top of each part of the frames.

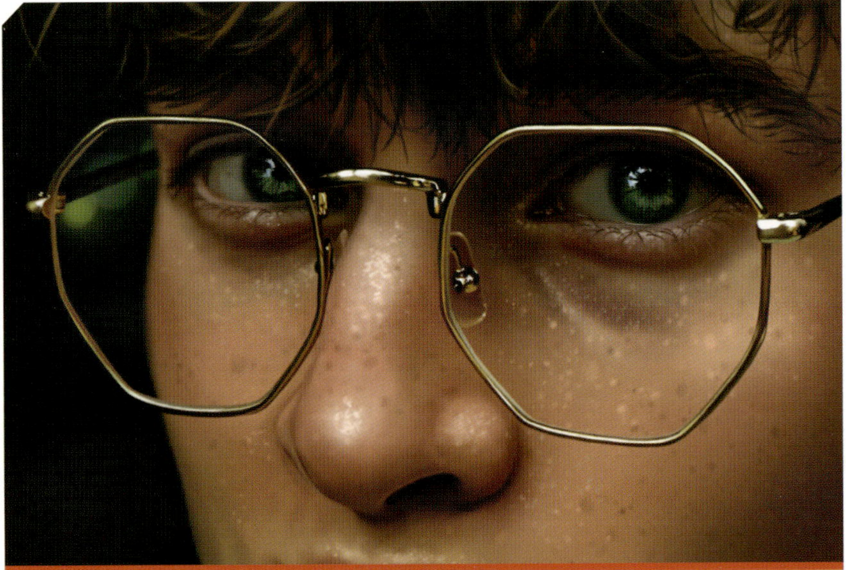

Blend out the hard-edged shading, then use a soft, small brush to define forms, colors, and values

06 Details

(a) Once you have finalized the frames, begin to add details to make the glasses look even more realistic.

(b) Observe the angle at which you are painting your subject's glasses, then paint a thin, grayish line along the interior of the frames to show the thickness of the lens. This is visible on the left and lower part of the frames in this image due to its angle.

(c) Paint grounding shadows on the face where the frames cast a shadow onto the skin. This will ground the glasses into the image, preventing them from looking stuck on top of the face like a sticker.

(d) Study your subject to determine whether their lenses are farsighted or nearsighted. The glasses in this example are nearsighted, so the left edge of the face behind the lens appears slightly indented. If the subject was farsighted instead, this edge of the face would be slightly protruded. The degree of this effect will depend on the intensity of the prescription. Paint this indentation or protrusion, depending on your particular subject.

(e) Lenses will often make the background behind them appear slightly distorted. This often appears as though the background is swirling behind the glass. You can create this effect by painting a subtle distorted effect in the background area within the lens.

(f) Studying your subject's glasses closely, paint subtle reflections onto the lenses to show they are made of glass and not just empty frames. Paint subtle, bright stripes of a transparent color that is reflective of the light source across the eye area.

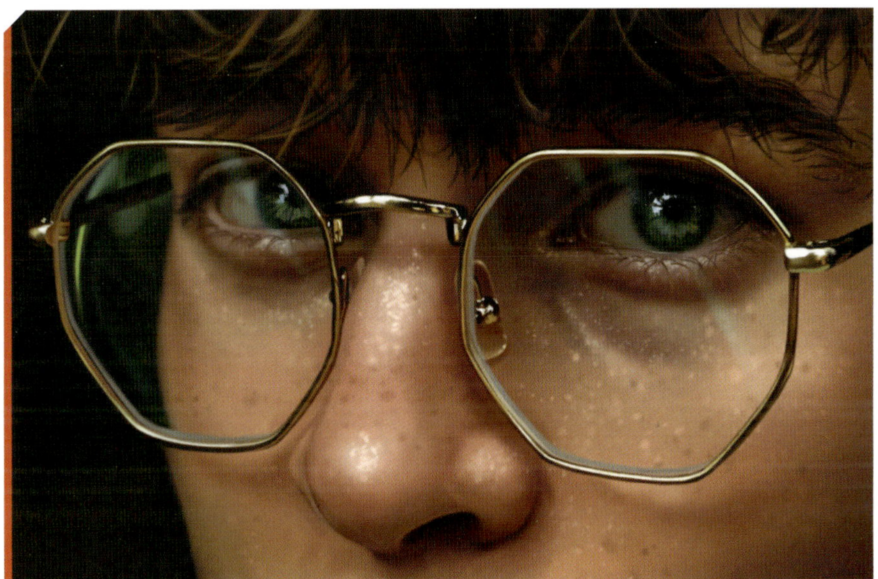

Finish by painting on details, grounding shadows, and lighting effects for added realism

ARTIST TIP

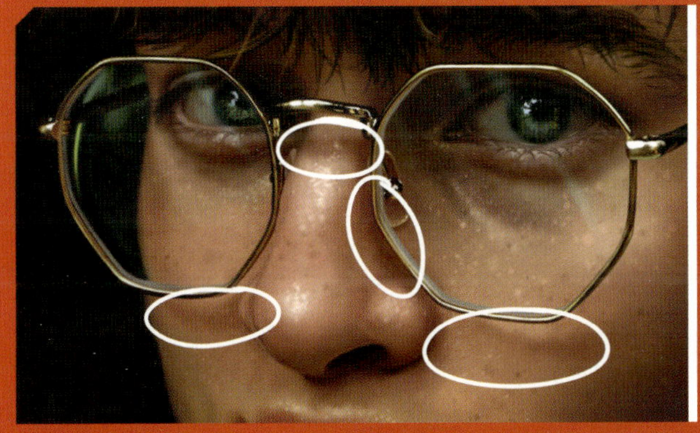

As with jewelry, it's important the glasses are grounded onto the face. A pair of glasses could be beautifully painted and incredibly detailed, but if there are no grounding shadows they will appear to merely float over the face. If a certain part of the frame is touching the skin, there should be a small shadow with little diffusion. If the frame is close to the skin but not touching it, it will cast a broader, more diffused shadow.

ADD GROUNDING SHADOWS TO TAKE YOUR PORTRAIT TO THE NEXT LEVEL

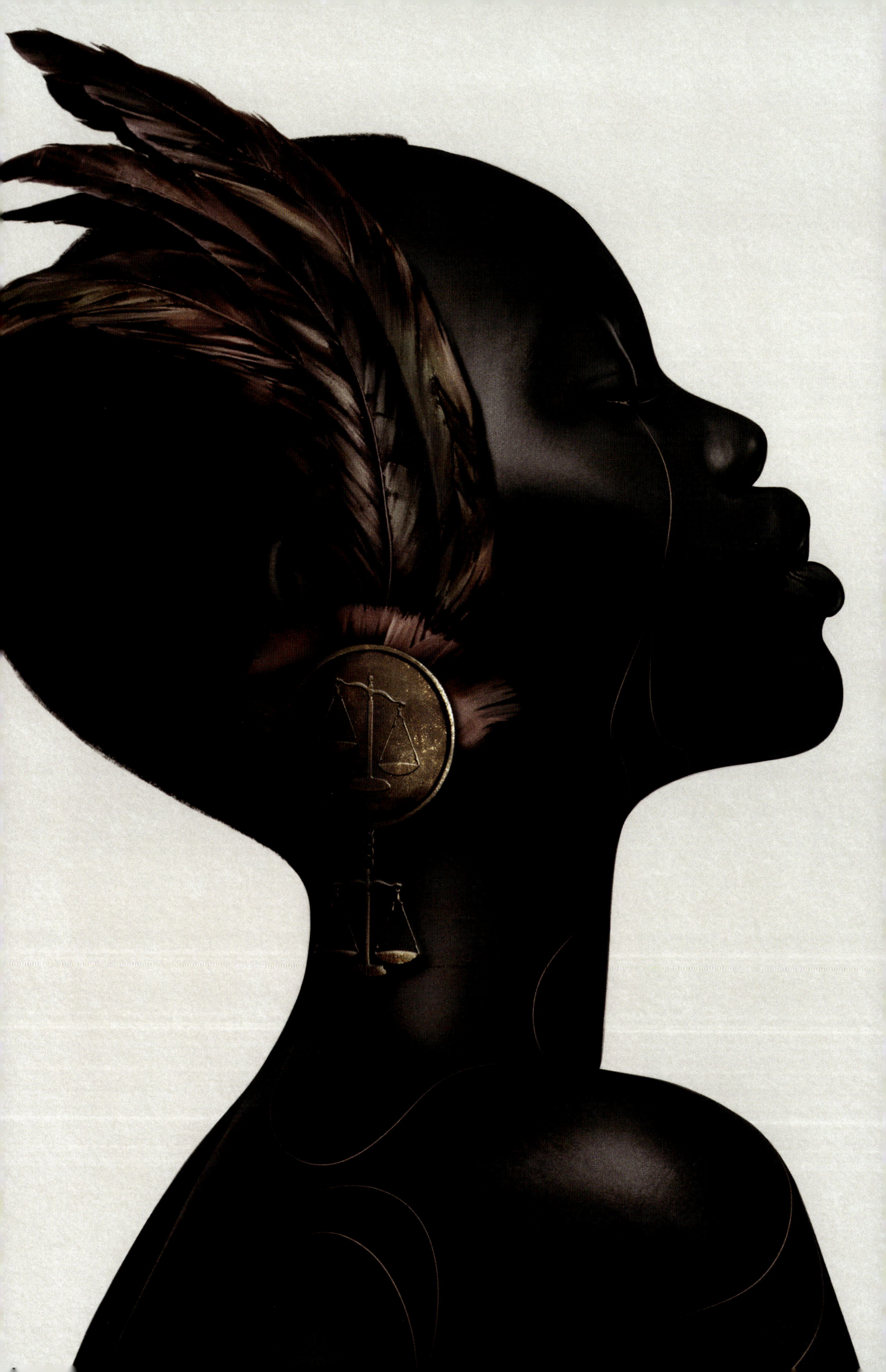

TUTORIALS

- NICK RUNGE
- ASTRI LOHNE
- JUSTINE S. FLORENTINO
- SARA TEPES
- GENNADIY KIM
- AVELINE STOKART

NICK RUNGE

Introduction

This tutorial will walk you through the process of creating a striking portrait using the traditional medium of watercolor. The step-by-step approach will guide you from the first construction lines and forms to the final details and brushstrokes. You will create a full color painting of a human face in three-quarter view, learning how to break down a reference subject into abstract shapes and values of light and shadow. It will also show you how to make specific color choices to affect the mood as well as the believability of the artwork, allowing you to construct an intriguing image. By starting with a pencil drawing and moving through each transparent layer of paint, you will create a lifelike face using both principals of realism and abstraction together.

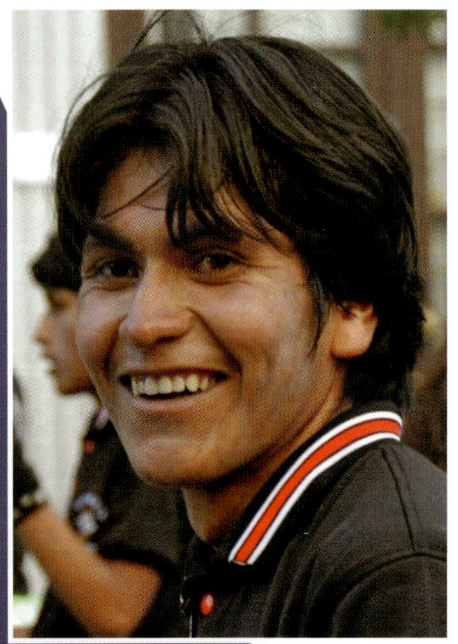

Photograph by
Vladgalenko on Dreamstime

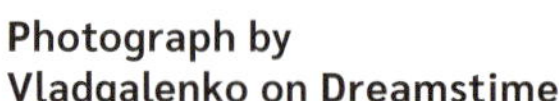

01

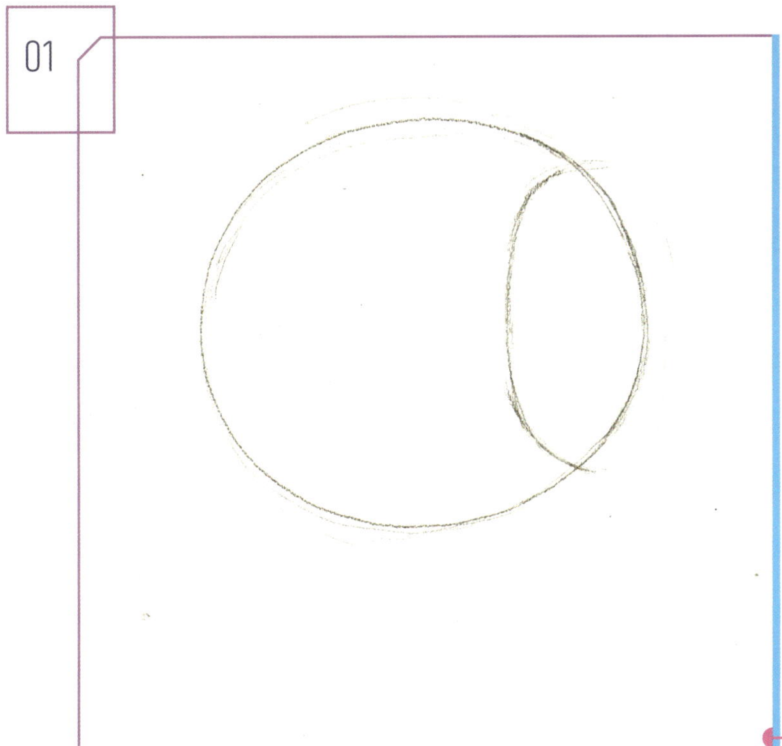

Study your reference photo and the shape of your subject's face, then begin by using a 2H graphite pencil to draw a horizontal oval shape in the upper half of your paper. Avoid making the graphite too dark. After drawing the oval, you need to construct the face at an angle, as shown in the reference photo. Think of the face as inside of a box. In perspective, draw a vertical oval at the right-hand edge of the skull. Think of this as cutting a side off of a sphere. You will then see the flat side of the head that's facing you, which will help you to keep the facial features pointed in the correct direction.

Sketch the rough shape of the human skull using an oval

02

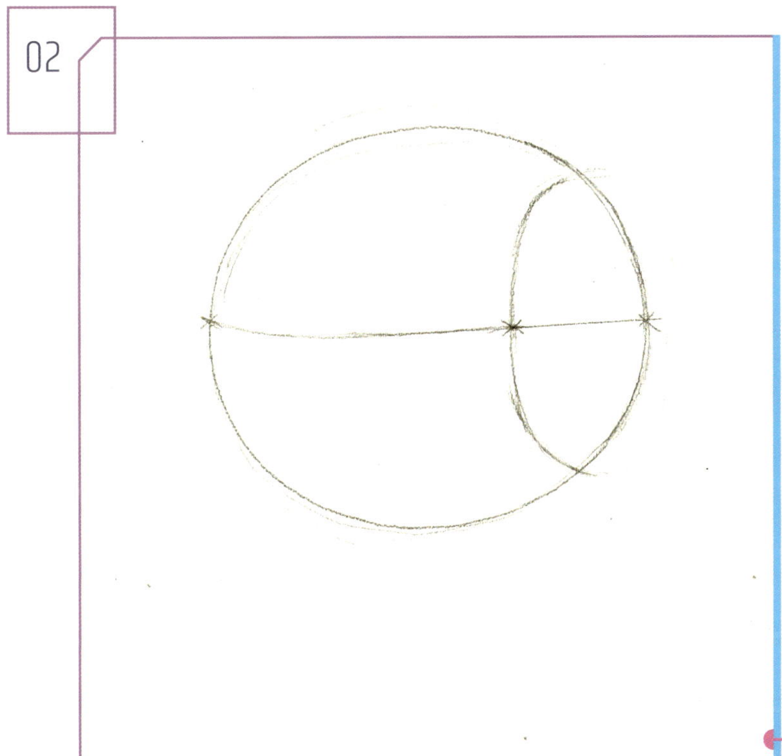

Draw a horizontal line through the center of the vertical oval. This line will show you the direction in which the eyes are facing. Continue this horizontal line across the front of the sphere with a slight curve. This will provide the top of the eyeline or eye socket, while also acting as the first measurement in breaking the head into three sections. Establishing the top eyeline this early in the process will allow you to place the eyeball more accurately.

Establish the angle of the face by dividing the oval skull shape in two

03

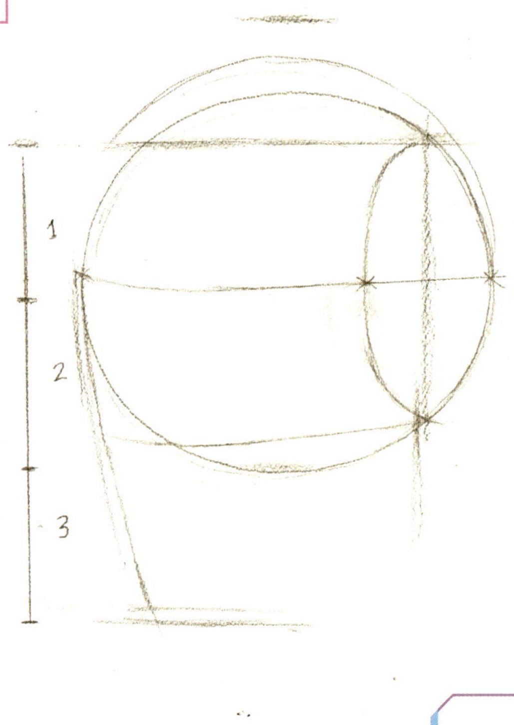

Draw a horizontal line from the top of the vertical oval across the sphere. This is the hairline. The distance from here to the eyeline is the top third of the head. Next, sketch a curved horizontal line from the bottom of the vertical oval across the sphere. This line will be where the lower part of the nose meets the face. Repeating the distance, draw a horizontal line to establish the bottom jawline below this. Next, draw an angled vertical line down from the eyeline to the bottom of the jawline to mark the edge of the face. Divide the vertical oval in two.

Divide the face into three sections: the forehead, nose, and mouth

04

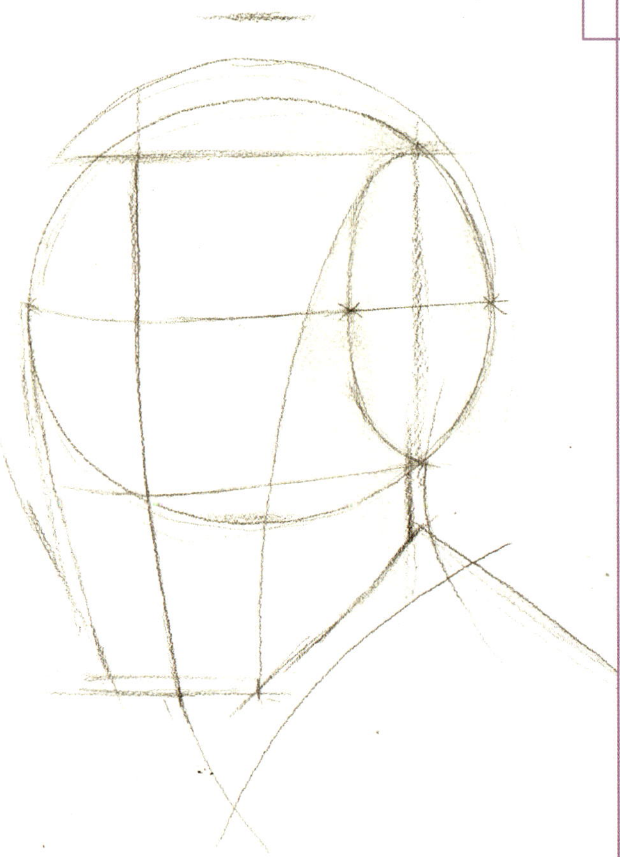

Think of the first oval skull shape as two pieces. Locate the center of it, then move downward until you hit the bottom jawline. This marks the corner of the jaw. Lightly draw a curved line up from here, to the top of the vertical oval. This establishes roughly where the side of the cheek will be. Find the center point between the jaw corner and edge of the face, then draw a slightly vertical line up to the hairline. This will be the center line of the face. From the jaw corner, sketch in the side jawline.

Establish the center line of the face by dividing the head vertically

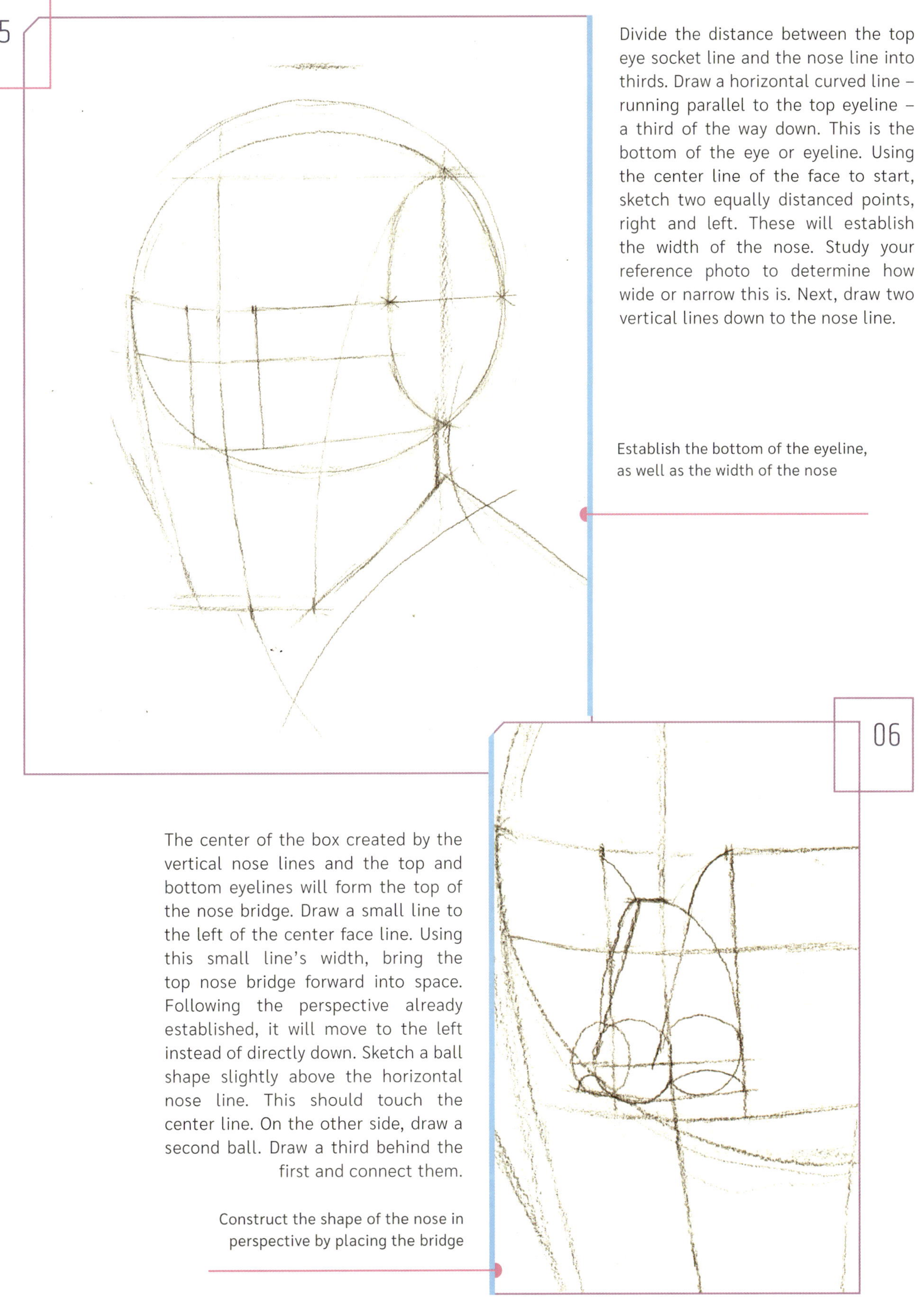

Divide the distance between the top eye socket line and the nose line into thirds. Draw a horizontal curved line – running parallel to the top eyeline – a third of the way down. This is the bottom of the eye or eyeline. Using the center line of the face to start, sketch two equally distanced points, right and left. These will establish the width of the nose. Study your reference photo to determine how wide or narrow this is. Next, draw two vertical lines down to the nose line.

Establish the bottom of the eyeline, as well as the width of the nose

The center of the box created by the vertical nose lines and the top and bottom eyelines will form the top of the nose bridge. Draw a small line to the left of the center face line. Using this small line's width, bring the top nose bridge forward into space. Following the perspective already established, it will move to the left instead of directly down. Sketch a ball shape slightly above the horizontal nose line. This should touch the center line. On the other side, draw a second ball. Draw a third behind the first and connect them.

Construct the shape of the nose in perspective by placing the bridge

07

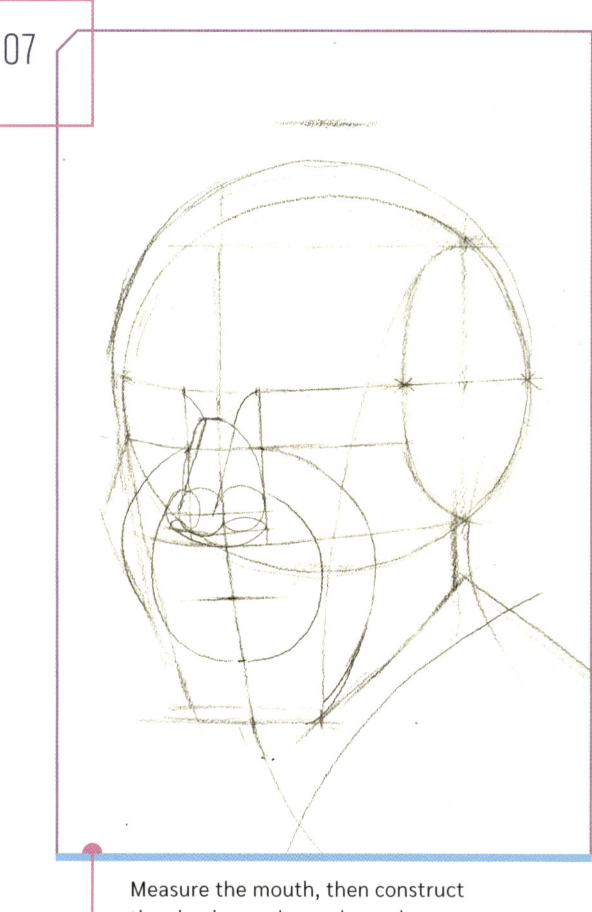

Measure the mouth, then construct the cheek muscles and muzzle

After you have divided the nose's height into thirds, do the same with the distance between the bottom nose line and the bottom chin line. The top third of that distance is where the mouth line will sit. The bottom third will be the lower lip. Sketch an oval shape to connect this point to the top of the nostrils (ball of the nose and two spheres). This shape is the mouth or muzzle. For the cheeks, draw lines from the bottom chin line (corner points of the chin) up to the bottom eyeline, where it will intersect with the nose width lines.

08

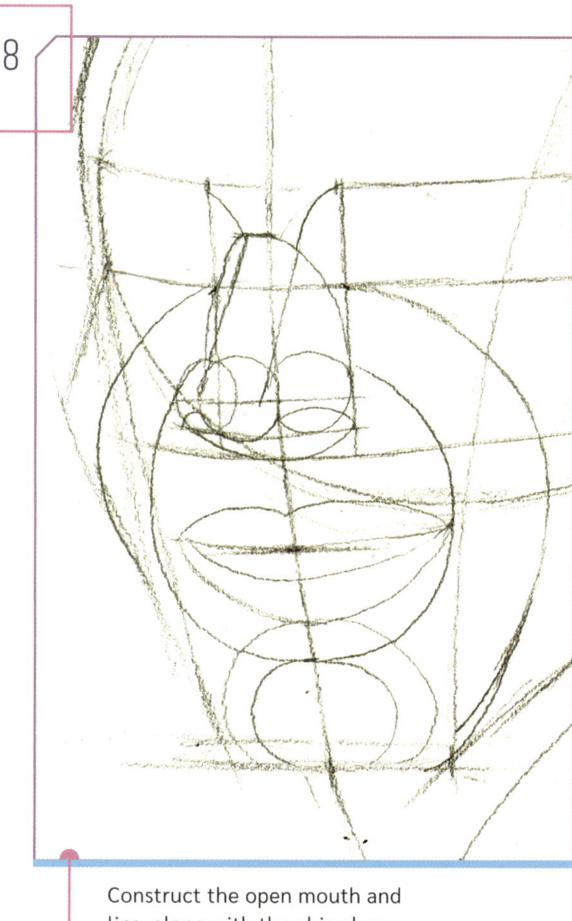

Construct the open mouth and lips, along with the chin shape

Draw a small oval between the bottom chin line and the line of the lower lip area. This area is actually slightly under the lip, but is often used at first as a distance guide for drawing the lower lip before refining. Next, draw a slightly larger oval around the first. This oval shape should overlap the lower lip line. The actual lower lip is slightly higher and this overlap will create the shadow overhang of the lower lip. The width of the mouth is created by the oval between the nostrils and lower lip area.

Artist tip

At this point you may be wondering, why so much construction if you're using a reference photo? It's really important to not only draw what you see, but what you understand. Building the forms and rhythms of the human head is very effective in creating a face from your imagination, but it's also a great way of finding these points and lines when you're looking at the photo. That way, when you begin to construct a face, you can base the proportions on your practiced imagination, but also adjust them as you examine the reference.

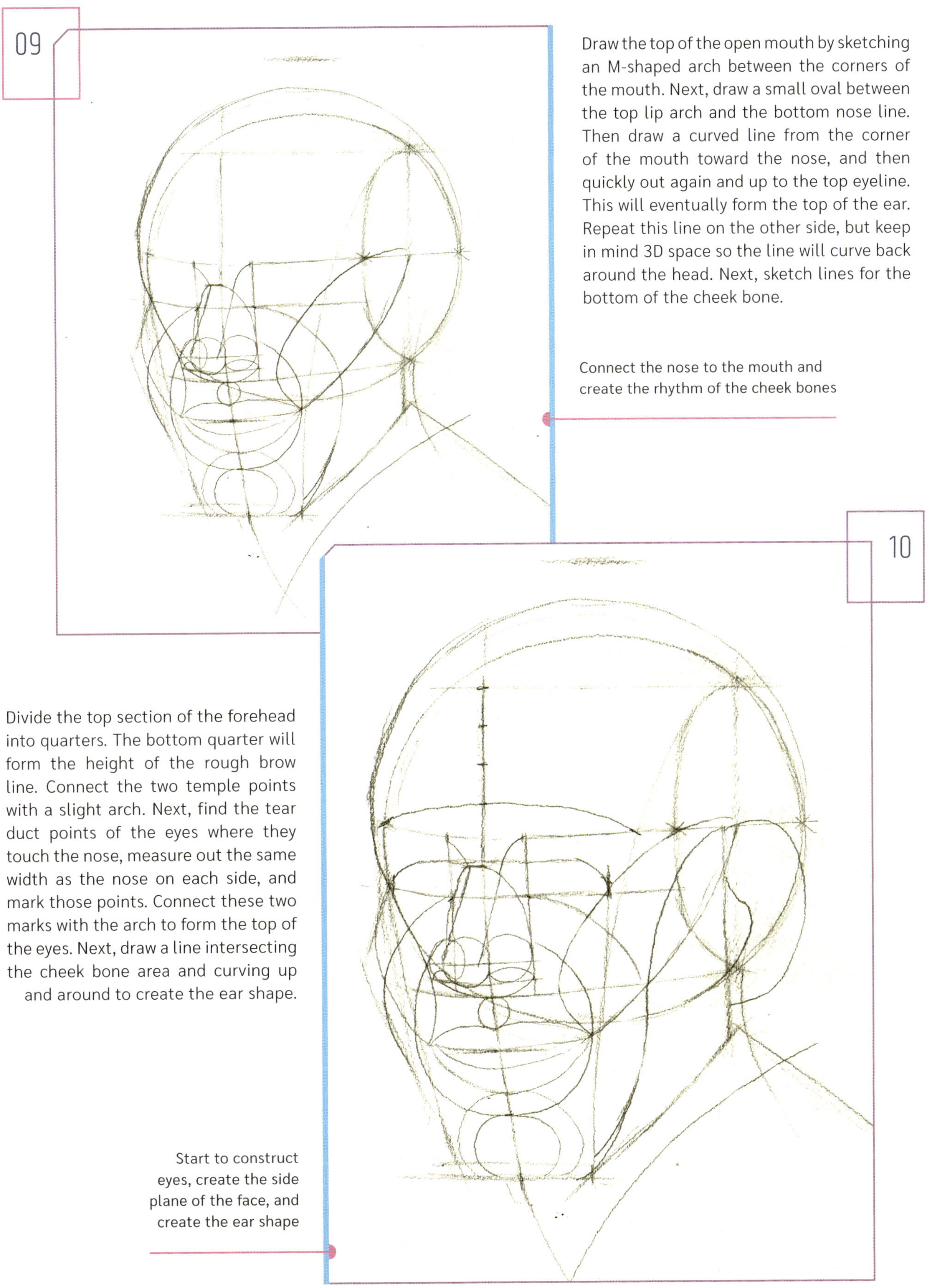

Draw the top of the open mouth by sketching an M-shaped arch between the corners of the mouth. Next, draw a small oval between the top lip arch and the bottom nose line. Then draw a curved line from the corner of the mouth toward the nose, and then quickly out again and up to the top eyeline. This will eventually form the top of the ear. Repeat this line on the other side, but keep in mind 3D space so the line will curve back around the head. Next, sketch lines for the bottom of the cheek bone.

Connect the nose to the mouth and create the rhythm of the cheek bones

Divide the top section of the forehead into quarters. The bottom quarter will form the height of the rough brow line. Connect the two temple points with a slight arch. Next, find the tear duct points of the eyes where they touch the nose, measure out the same width as the nose on each side, and mark those points. Connect these two marks with the arch to form the top of the eyes. Next, draw a line intersecting the cheek bone area and curving up and around to create the ear shape.

Start to construct eyes, create the side plane of the face, and create the ear shape

11

Draw a curved line from the top of the vertical oval shape (the cut-out chunk of the main skull sphere) down to the corner of the top eyeline. This will establish the side plane of the temple. Next, start at the tear duct points, where the bottom eyeline meets the width of the nose, and sketch a tilted line upward to finish the eye shape. You can then add the iris and pupils, if desired. Next, draw an oval between the bottom eyeline (the middle of the nose bridge) and the hairline. This is will form the forehead.

Build the temple of the head and finish the basic eye construction

12

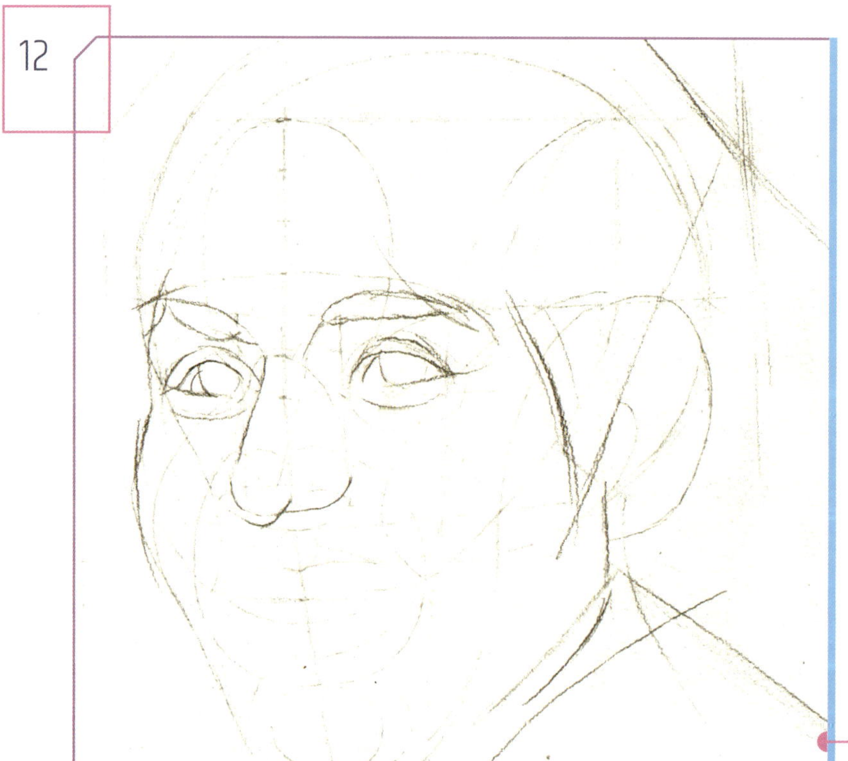

Now that you have constructed the face, it's time to refine it and focus on creating a good likeness. Erase the lines with a kneaded eraser. This will erase most of the mess and leave the important lines very faint, which you can then use as a guide. Start by refining the bottom eyelids and finding the edge of the face. Clean up the nose and study the reference image to capture the accurate length of the nose, from the top of the bridge to the shadow under the nostrils.

Erase the dark construction lines and refine the start of the underdrawing

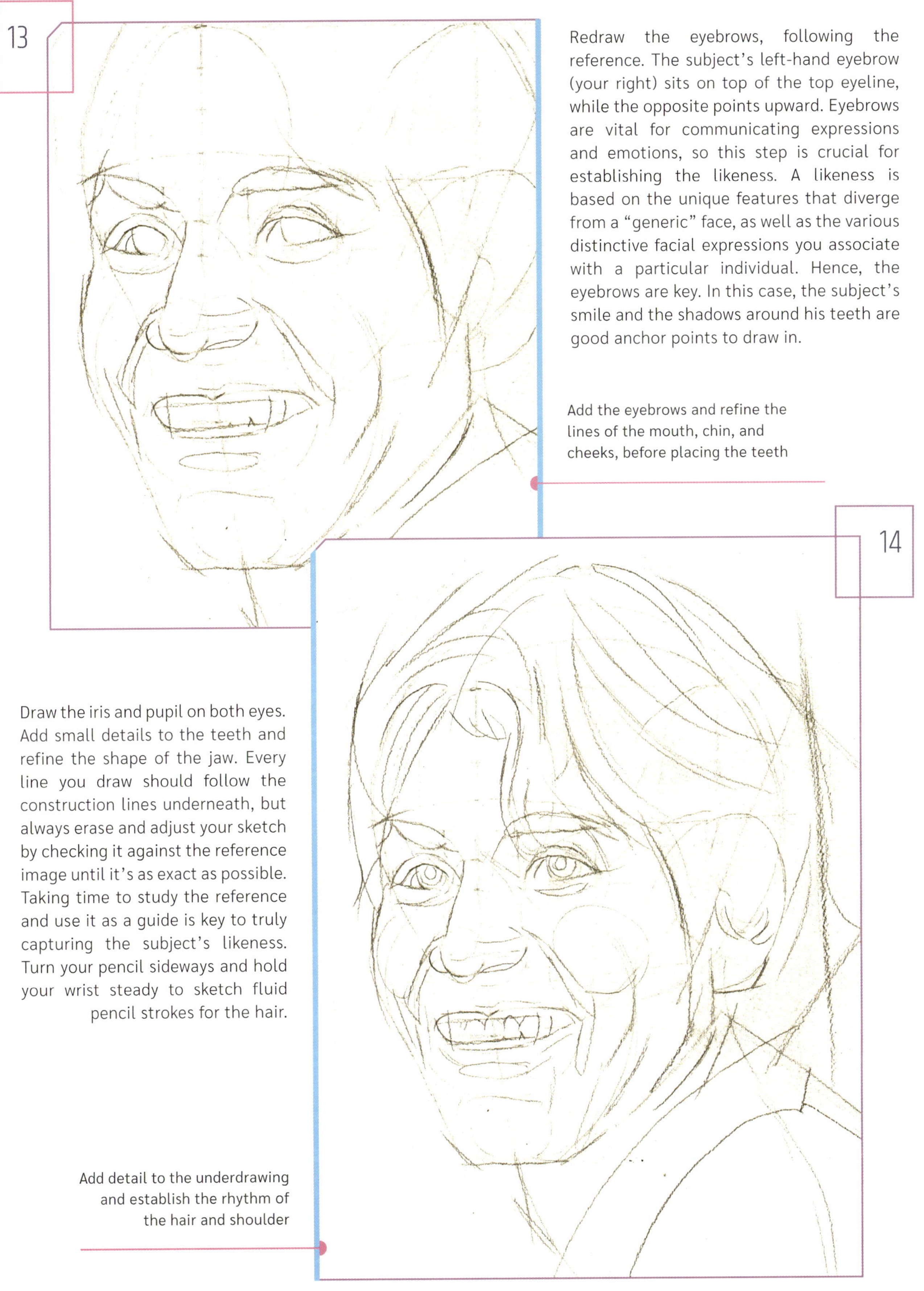

Redraw the eyebrows, following the reference. The subject's left-hand eyebrow (your right) sits on top of the top eyeline, while the opposite points upward. Eyebrows are vital for communicating expressions and emotions, so this step is crucial for establishing the likeness. A likeness is based on the unique features that diverge from a "generic" face, as well as the various distinctive facial expressions you associate with a particular individual. Hence, the eyebrows are key. In this case, the subject's smile and the shadows around his teeth are good anchor points to draw in.

Add the eyebrows and refine the lines of the mouth, chin, and cheeks, before placing the teeth

Draw the iris and pupil on both eyes. Add small details to the teeth and refine the shape of the jaw. Every line you draw should follow the construction lines underneath, but always erase and adjust your sketch by checking it against the reference image until it's as exact as possible. Taking time to study the reference and use it as a guide is key to truly capturing the subject's likeness. Turn your pencil sideways and hold your wrist steady to sketch fluid pencil strokes for the hair.

Add detail to the underdrawing and establish the rhythm of the hair and shoulder

15

Erase the lines of your drawing again and clean up any excess graphite. The refined lines will show through. Take a #4 round watercolor brush and get a good amount of water on it. Add some pyrrole red and burnt sienna, mixed with a little ivory black, to the dark lines of the eyelids and under the nose. These lines won't always stay, but they are good anchor points to help keep proportions in place. With this unique approach, you can later disrupt or soften these dark areas as they dry and lighten to more medium values.

Prepare your drawing for painting and begin adding the first layers of watercolor

16

Add a large amount of water to your brush (as much as you can), turn it sideways, and rub it across the paper so it glides on the water. Do this right up to the first lines created by the red-sienna mix. The water will reactivate the half-dry paint and pull it into the wet area. As this dries, apply a little more pure pyrrole red to your brush, so it's watered down, and add this medium value to the top and bottom of the nose. Paint it under the cheek muscles also.

Begin rendering and adding a secondary value to the nose and eye sockets

17

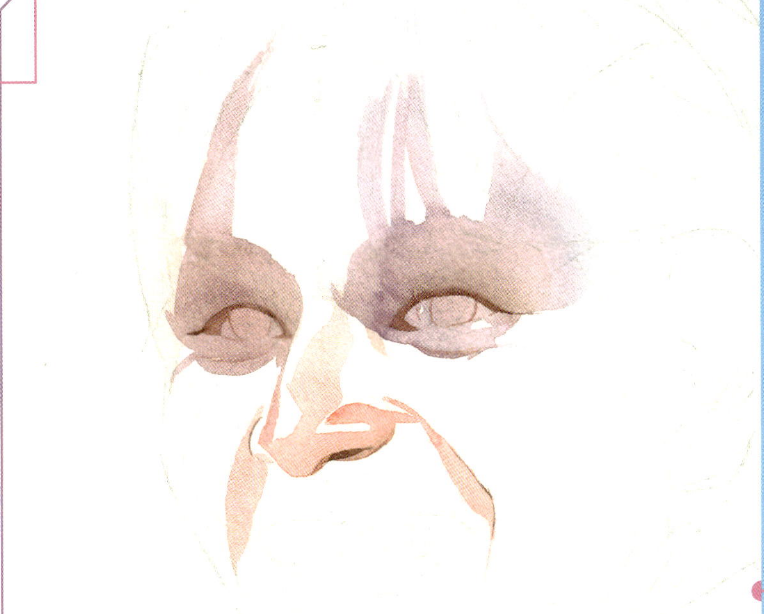

Take a mix of ultramarine blue and burnt sienna, then add a tiny amount of rose or opera pink to create a dark magenta tone. Add a large amount of water to your brush and get a saturated brush-full of the blue-sienna mix. Wash this mixture over the top, like a glaze, covering the eyes and whites of the eyes. A common mistake is to leave the whites of the eyes white because we know they are white in color, yet they are almost never white in the reference photo or in most situations. Lighting is everything.

Paint shadows under the eye sockets and begin to blend the warm and cool tones

18

Take a mixture of pyrrole red and permanent orange, then choose a large round brush (#16-20). Add a generous amount of water, until it drips, and wash the mixture across the top. Do this as quickly as possible, so there is minimal disruption underneath. The traditional approach to watercolor would require you to do this step first, but you want a little movement and softness to happen to the paint beneath to prepare it for the next step.

Unite the different areas of the face with a large warm wash

19

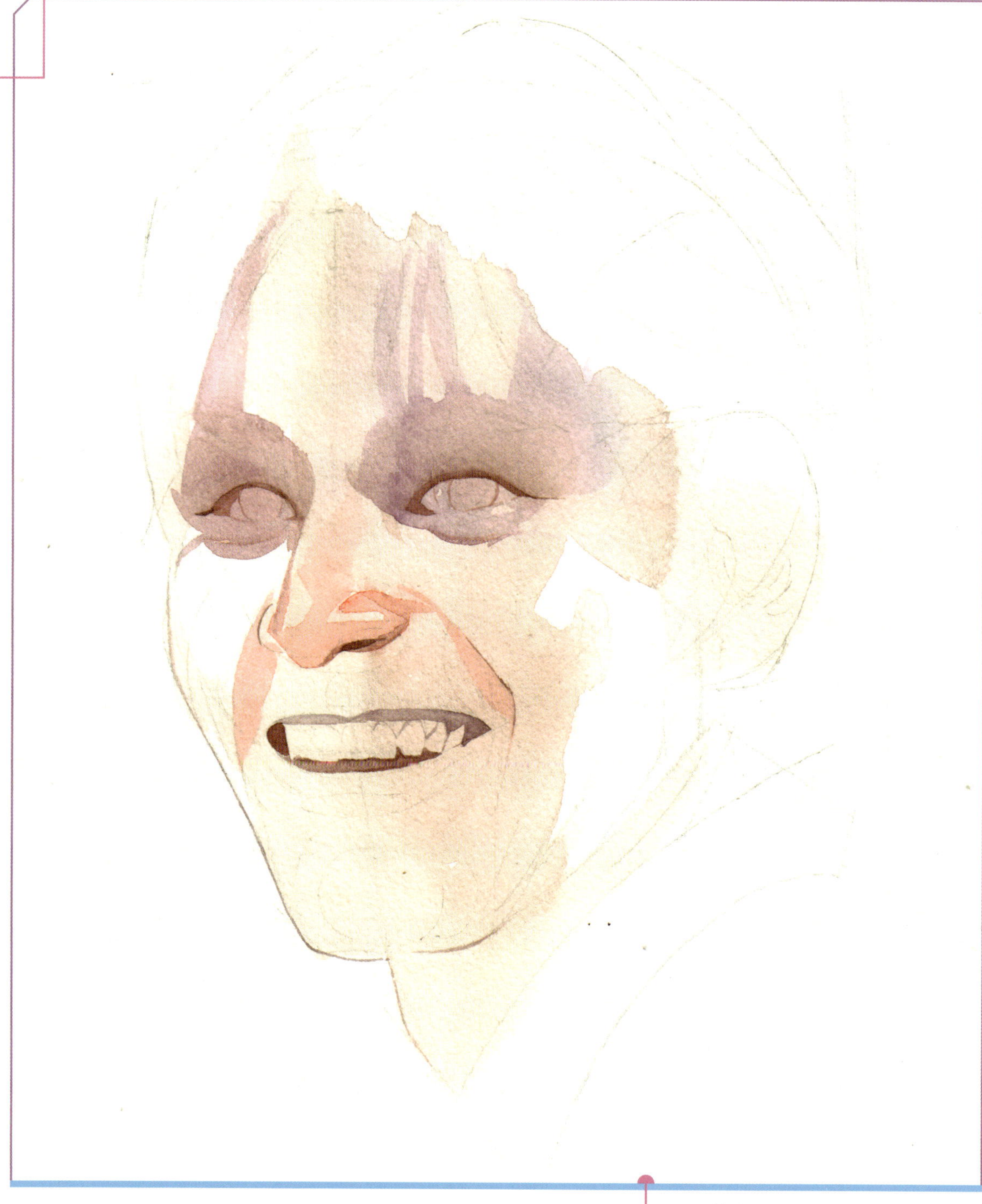

Establish the anchor points of the lips and open mouth, and add a partial outline

Before you begin this step, make sure the wash from the previous step is completely dry. If it's not yet dry, use a hairdryer to speed up the process. Take a mixture of ultramarine blue, burnt sienna, and opera pink, and fill the shape of the open mouth. Don't fill in all the lines of the teeth, as this will look too messy at this point. Instead you want to focus on a very gradual build up of color and shadows. The man may look a little scary at this point, but don't worry – it's all part of the plan.

20

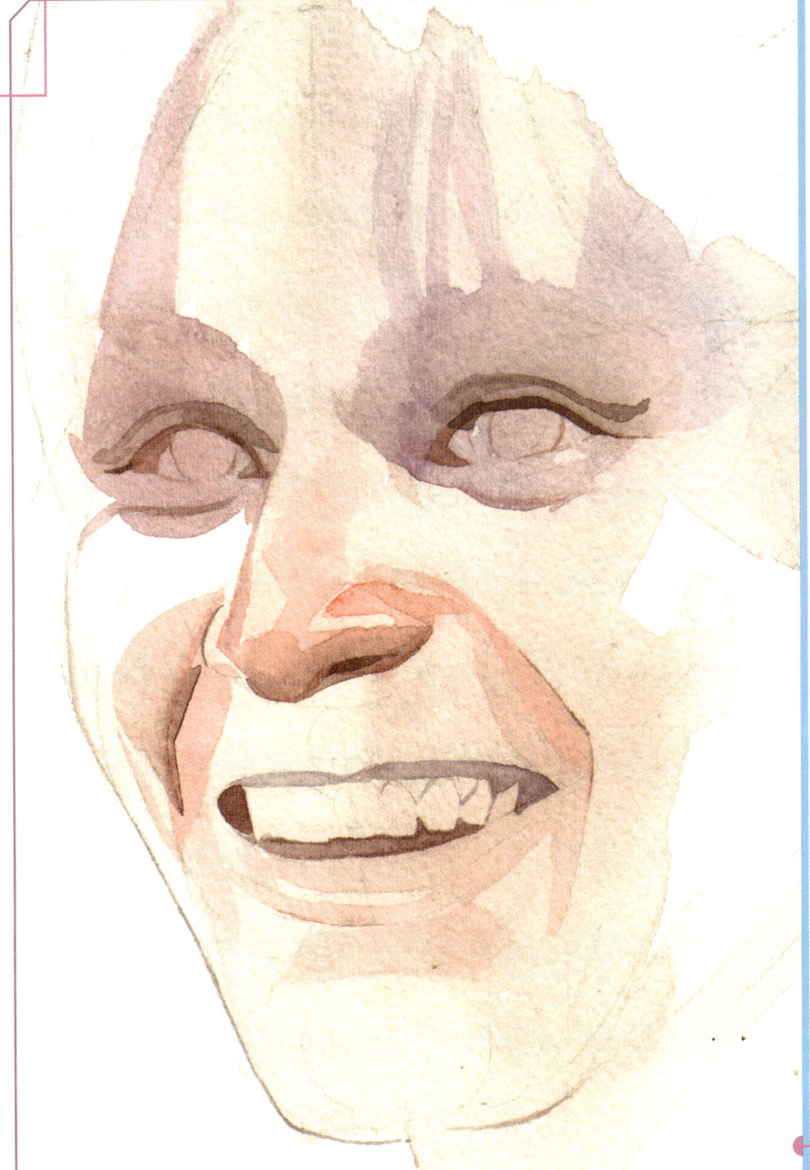

Take a mix of pyrrole red and ivory black and water it down. Begin to paint it in using a small #4 round brush. Let the water take the pigment until the shape you're adding across the bottom lip is very light and extremely transparent. Start to think about the round form of the cheeks and how you can begin to build the soft shadows by adding light, flat, transparent shapes that overlap each other.

Add shadows and form to the nose, cheeks, and lips, and continue to add depth

Artist tip

So far you have learned about creating color and value by painting colors separately in transparent washes. Much like a printer can create any color you need from combinations of cyan, yellow, magenta, and black inks, you are learning how to combine specific mixes of two or three colors and combine them on top of each other to create a brand new color in between. You should also be beginning to apply your observation skills to develop the constructed forms underneath the drawing into a lifelike painting.

21

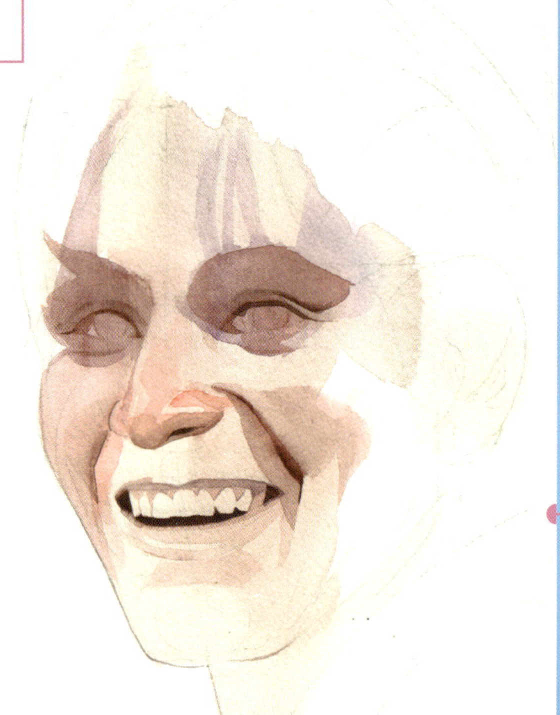

Start to think more about where the subtle light is coming from in the reference. To add shadows in slowly, without cooling the image down too much, start with a mix of pyrrole red and ultramarine blue. Add a large amount of water to your larger round brush and water down the red-blue mix so it's very light in pigment, but medium in value. The light in the reference is shining from the top right-hand side, so the shadows should be moving down and slightly to the left.

Begin to establish the direction of the lighting and start to build the cheeks

22

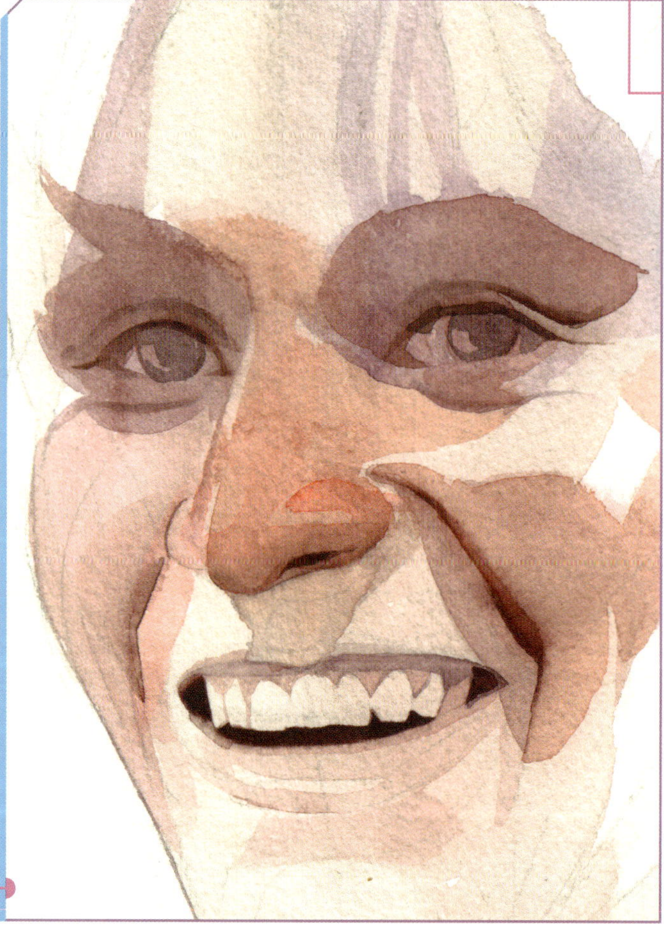

Fill in the iris and pupil of the eyes with a light mix of ultramarine blue and burnt sienna. Next, make a mixture of permanent orange and opera pink, with a small amount of burnt sienna added in. Leave a fair amount of pigment on the brush, while also making sure it contains enough water to ensure the pigment glides cleanly across the top of the nose. Paint a second large shape over the top of the right cheek with this same warm mix and watch it start to combine with the purple-red hues underneath.

Begin to bring the eyes to life and add warmth over the top of the nose

23

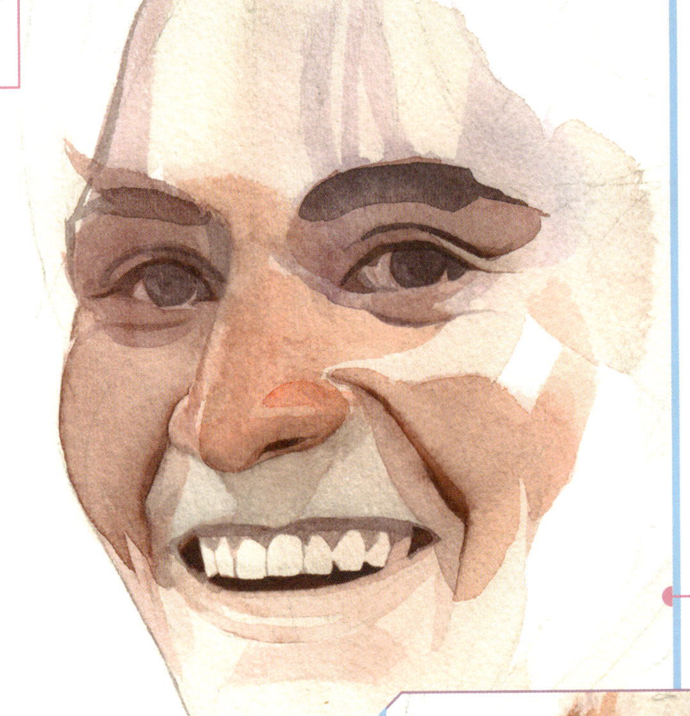

To continue building the form and depth of this portrait, you will need to repeatedly dry and re-dry the painting in between each layer. As you do this, you will be able to add more and more washes over the top without losing the clean look you want to create. Make another mix of permanent orange and opera pink, then add a little ultramarine blue into the mix. Paint this mix over the entire nose and the left side of the face. Mix a little blue, red, and black, and water it down, then paint another wash across the right cheek.

Darken the eyebrows, eyes, and mouth, then add a wash under the nose

24

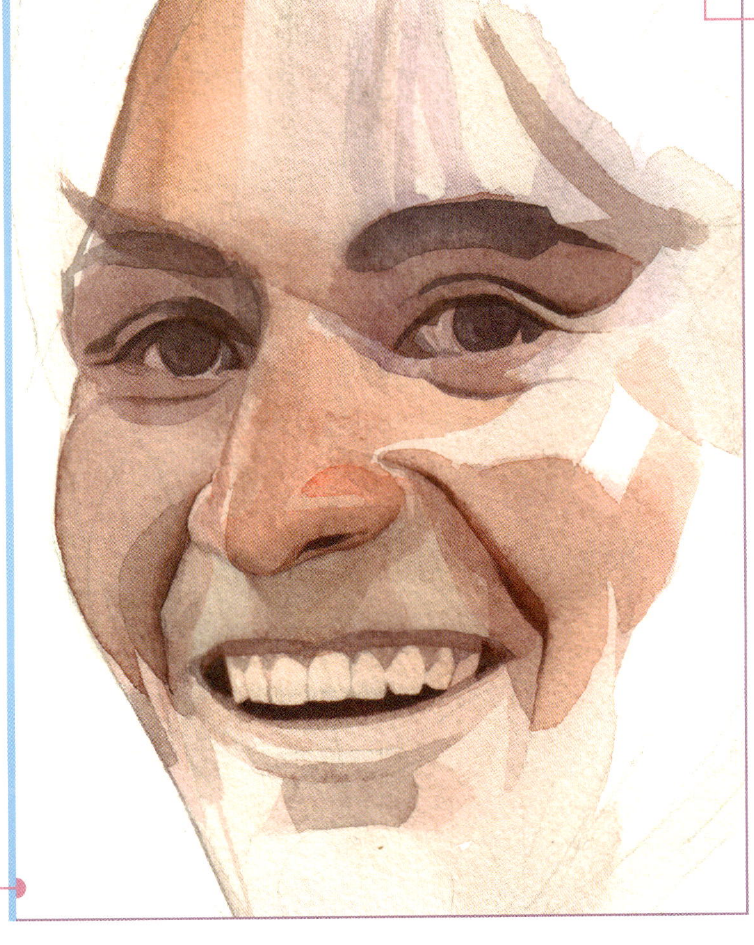

Create a gray-reddish mix and soak the large round brush in the water until it's saturated. Starting underneath the bottom lip, paint a rounded rectangular shape and cover the lips and teeth. Keep painting all the way up to the hairline, then use a hairdryer to quickly dry this section so it sets. Next, saturate your brush with water again and add some burnt sienna. Paint a vertical shape on the left side of his forehead, then paint a wash next to it to soften the shape.

Darken the teeth and build the form around the mouth and lower lip

25

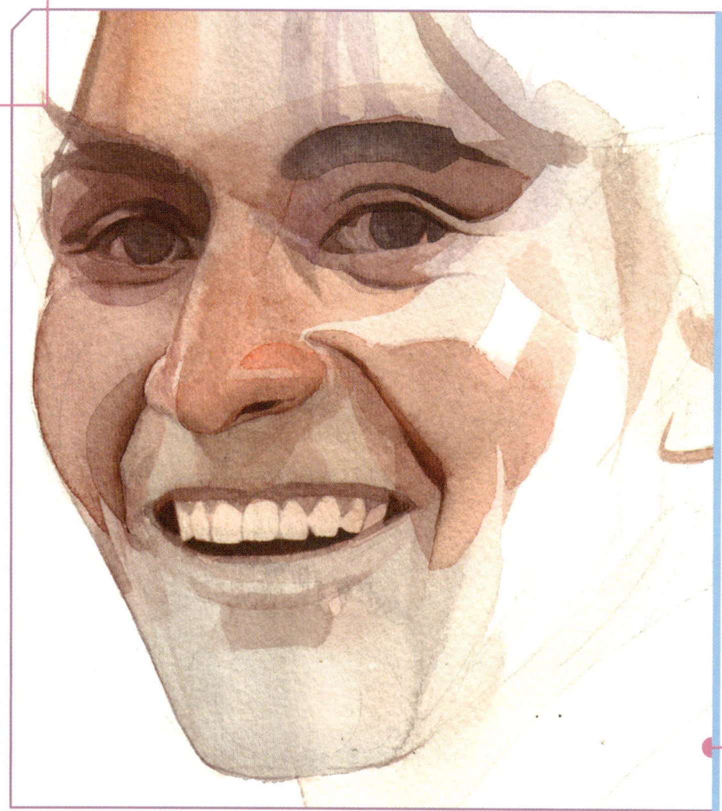

Darken the left eye with the mixture of red and blue, then dry it. Next it's time to balance the portrait by introducing more darkness to the bottom of the face. Make a gray mix of mostly ultramarine blue with a small amount of burnt sienna. With the larger round brush, paint a wash starting under the nostrils and move it down across the teeth, all the way to the chin. Use it to define the edge of the man's face and further ground the jaw.

Add darkness to the bottom of the portrait to balance it and add opacity

26

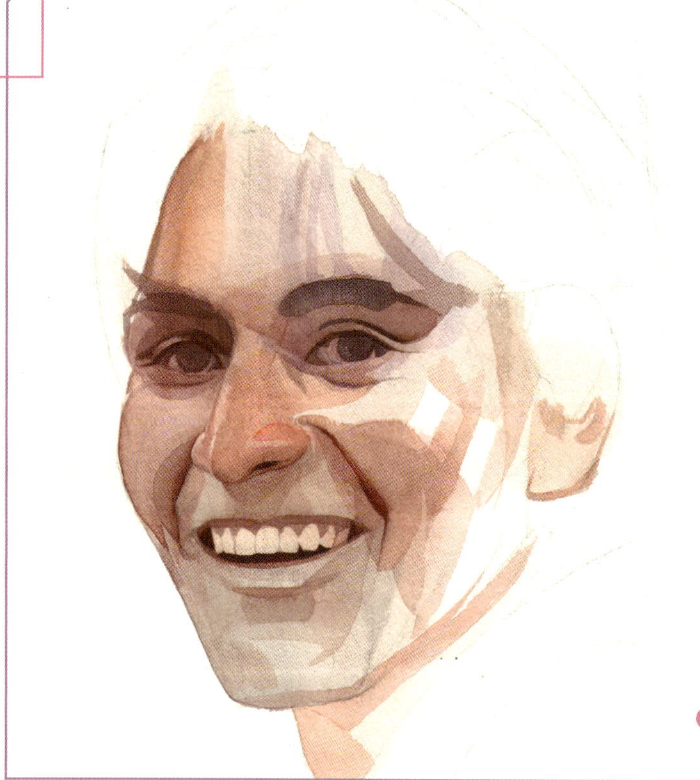

Using the small #4 round brush, paint a warm wash with pyrrole red and permanent orange underneath the bottom lip. Move it down to the left side of the chin, and then back over the front of the chin. Continue the wash along the bottom edge of the chin, down onto the neck, and use this shape to define the right side of the jaw. Next, start to paint a new wash of the same colors and move it up the left side, running along the left edge of the nose, crossing over the left eye, and ending on the eyebrow.

Add more details through warm washes to add saturation to the portrait

27

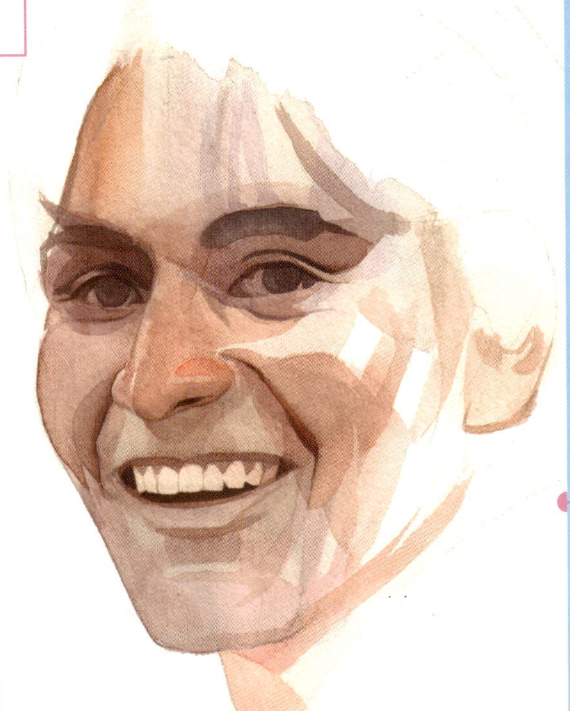

Starting above the right nostril, paint a large wash of purple (made from opera pink and ultramarine blue) down over the right cheek, darkening it ever so slightly. Keep painting the wash down along the stretch lines of his smile and cover the chin completely. Continue the wash to cover the shape under the chin and slightly darken it. Think of the bottom third of the face as containing more blue, the middle third as more red, and the top third as more yellow. This is a common color combination that can be found in most faces.

Add opacity to the bottom of the portrait by using a cold hue

28

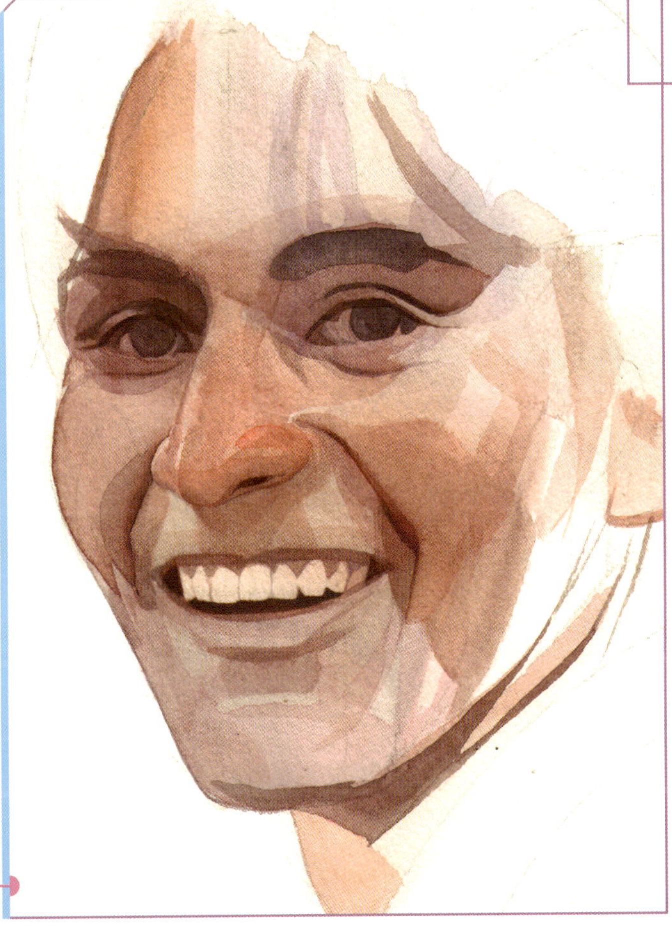

Paint a dark brown shape (made from pyrrole red and ivory black) under the chin to start establishing the shadows at the bottom of the face. The values are what ground this particular image, so the shadows and darkest areas can't only be toward the top. The hair will be dark when it's added, so it's important to build enough of a balance underneath the chin. Next, paint a larger wash of yellow, permanent orange, and burnt sienna over the top of his right cheek to soften the white paper and tie the colors together.

Harmonize the colors by tying them together with an additional warm wash

29

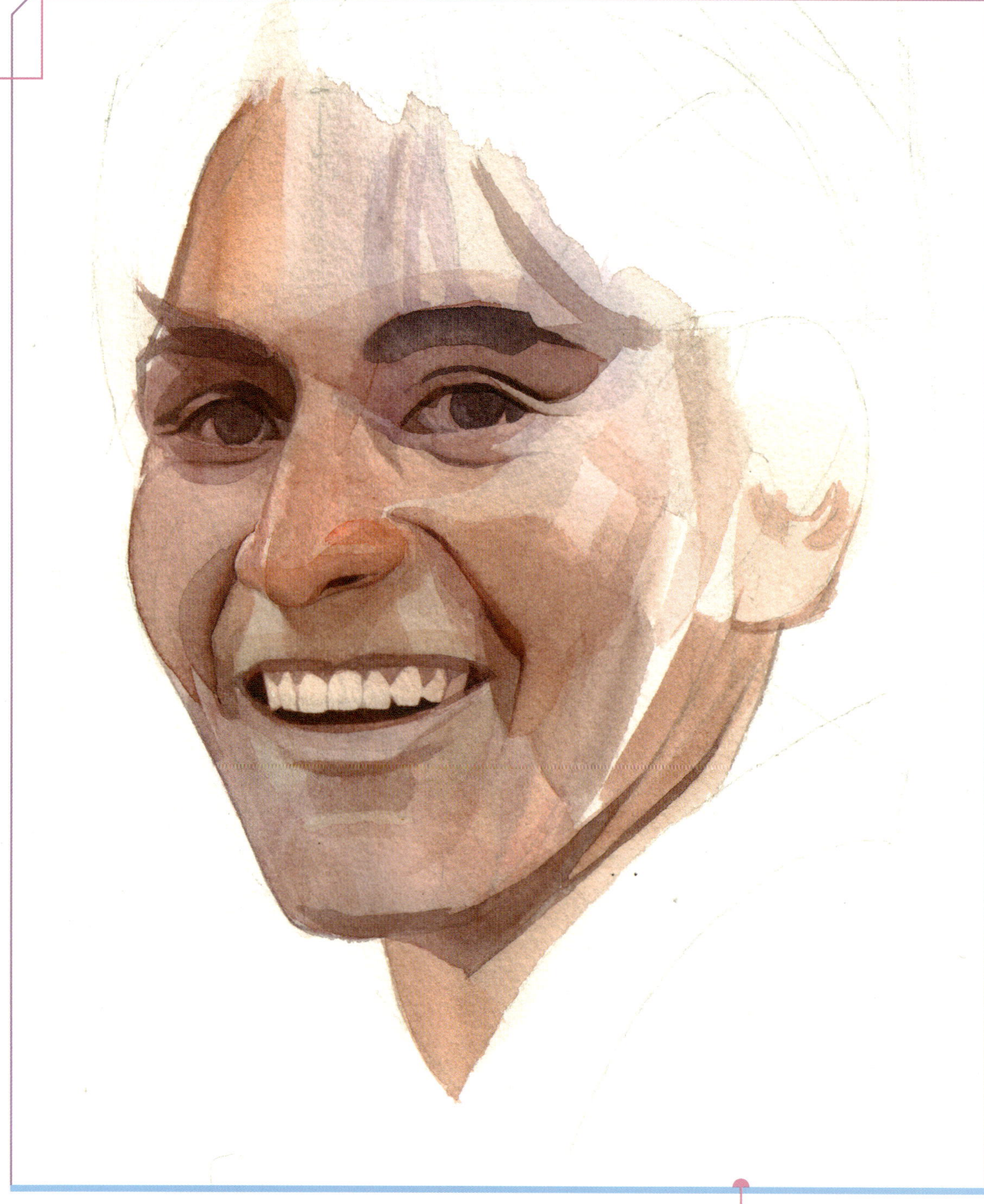

Using the larger round brush, mix another combination of pyrrole red and burnt sienna to cover the entire chin and lower lip. Bring the wash down so that it covers the neck. Instead of drying this area quickly with the hairdryer, let it sit. This will give you a chance to really examine the portrait and see if any areas need more saturation, or perhaps a darker value. Sometimes it's fun to bring in more color from your imagination, stylizing the portrait slightly. By examining the many subtle local colors in the reference image, you can add more saturation based on those hints, making colors more drastic.

Build more opacity and darkness to slowly darken the skin tone

30

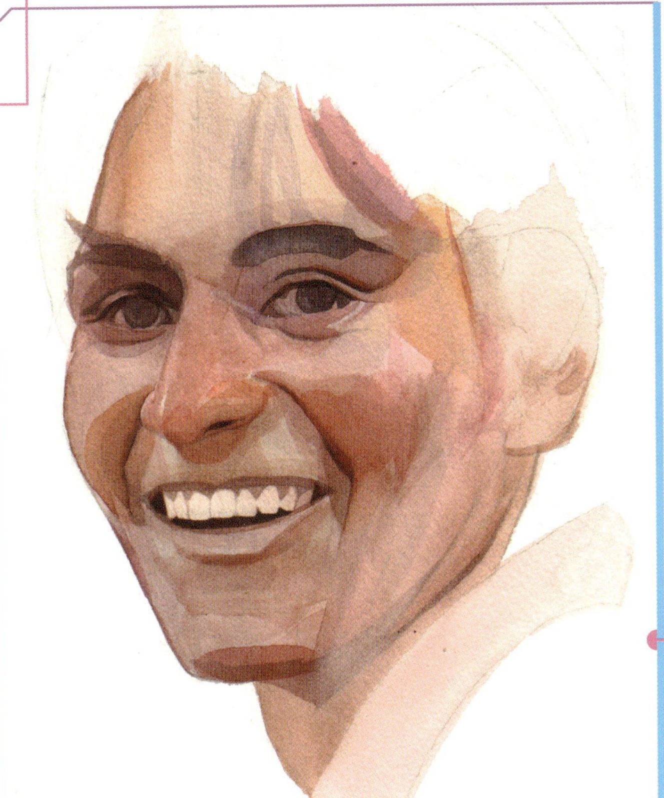

At this stage the portrait is looking good, but still lacks the three-dimensional quality it needs to be truly believable. Using the #4 round brush and red pigment, paint orange on both cheeks. Paint a rectangular shape to the chin using the same colors, then paint this pigment over the nose and under the nostrils. Next, take the larger round brush and soak it in water. Scrub it across the lower right side of the face to blend the pigment underneath. This will unify and simplify some of the mess that is starting to form.

Add more saturation and darkness, while blending pigments and simplifying

31

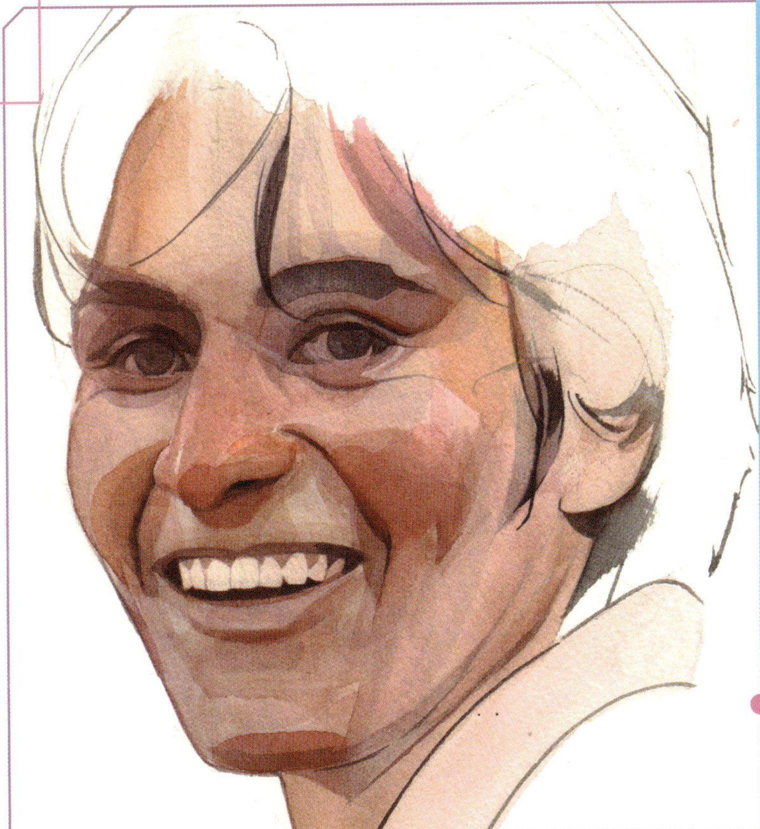

Using a blackish mixture made up of ultramarine blue, burnt sienna, and alizarin crimson, take the #4 round brush and paint a few lines to define the edges of the hair. Establish the sideburn to contrast with the soft tones underneath. The warm values may start to get a little muddy and busy, so applying a clean, dark edge over these will create a slight graphic feeling that will start to shift the planes toward the final range of values. These darkest areas and lines are very close to their final intensity.

Reestablish the lost planes of light and define the edges of the hair

32

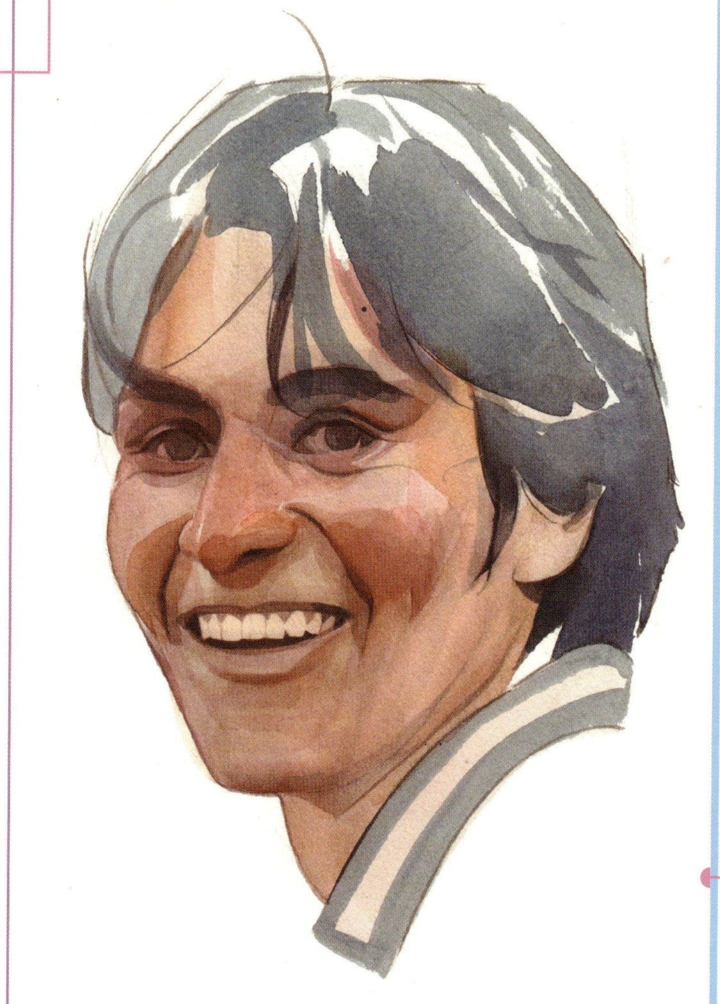

Before you start work on the hair, use the larger round brush and some clean water to blend and soften the red shape on the front of the chin. This will provide a more realistic illusion to the face. Next, saturate the large brush with a mix of ultramarine blue and burnt sienna, ensuring the blue is dominant. Following the construction lines, though not too strictly, paint spontaneous, fairly abstract brushstrokes. Only the outline really matters for starting the hair. The eye sockets can be darkened a little too using the same mixture.

Paint the main underpainting for the hair and cool down the entire portrait

Artist tip

So far you have learned how to break a reference image down into shapes before constructing it, and now are in the process of rendering and working the values out with color. Many of those values are physically applied to the paper through transparent washes. A major problem when working on dry paper is running out of water while halfway through a wash. Water is then added in, but this creates blooms and bleeding pigment. To avoid this, add the water, but go back over the entire shape again and re-wet it. This will even out the drying area.

33

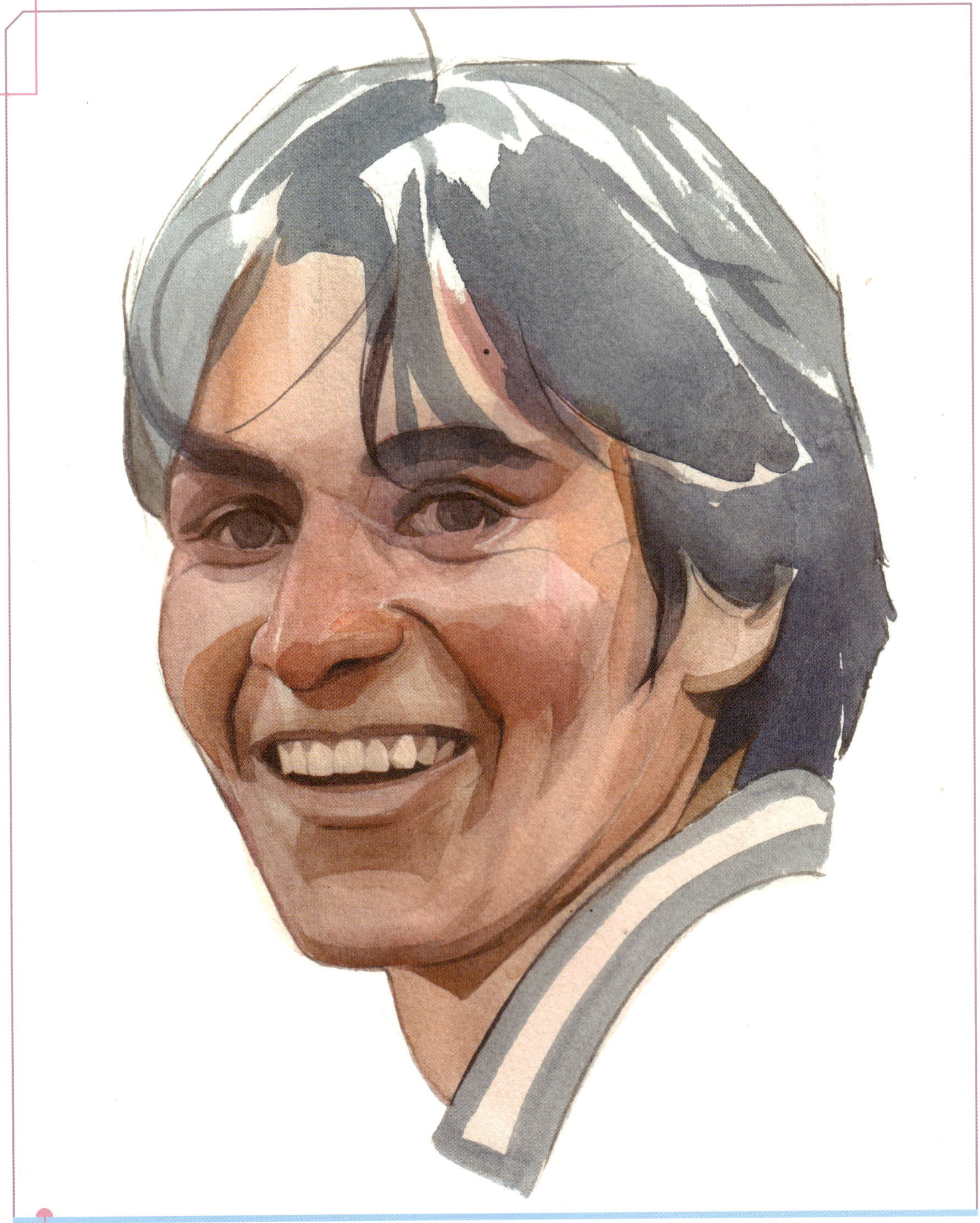

Add the middle values back into the bottom half of the portrait

While the hair is drying, use this opportunity to add more depth back into the lower section of the portrait. Take the #4 brush and a large amount of water (as much as the brush will hold without dripping) and add a mix of pyrrole red and ultramarine blue, with red being the dominant color. Use this to paint the shadow that turns the form of the chin. With this same wash, paint the sharp shape under the jaw. Paint a shadow to the bottom of the ear and begin to blend the left side of the face with the hair.

34

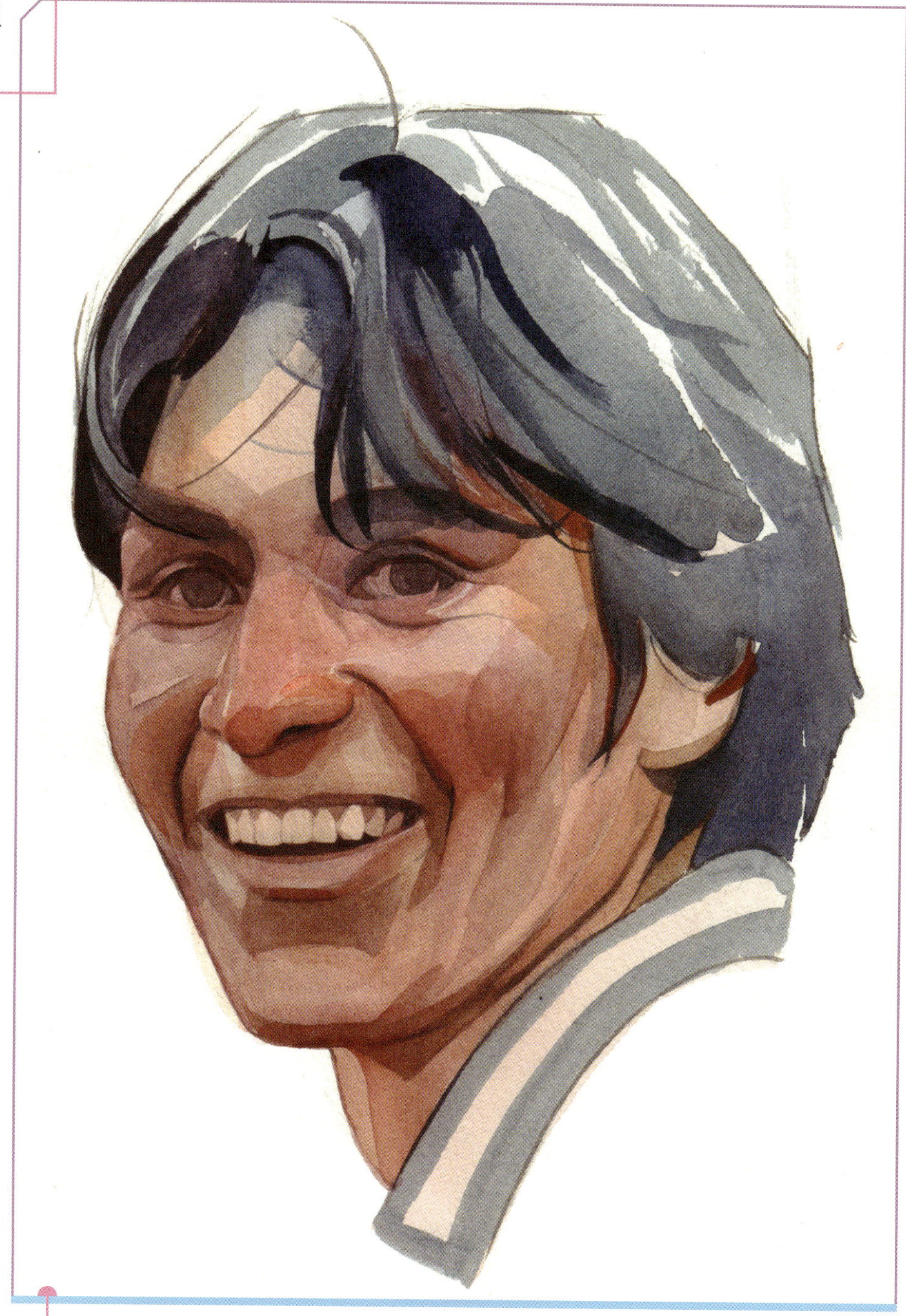

Start establishing the details of the hair and continue to add to the warm colors

Begin with a mixture of ivory black and ultramarine blue to paint the details of the hair. Follow the reference and enjoy the process. This stage will establish much of the subject's personality, but it should still be carried out fairly loosely and quickly. Try to feel the movement of the hair and mimic it with the small brush. Next, add a slight, light wash over the entire left half of the face with a very watered down blue. Leave some areas open to create a reflective feel.

35

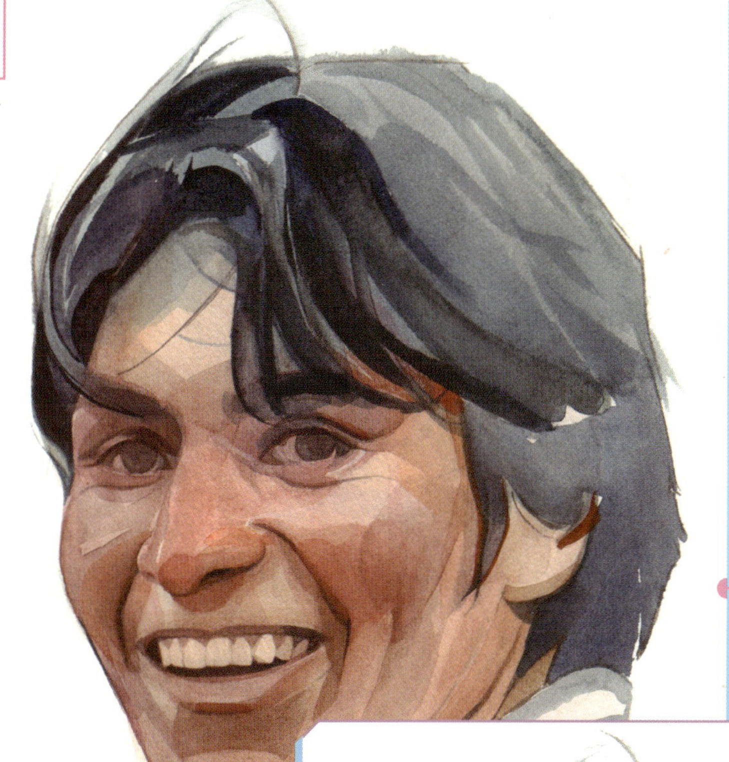

Using the same mixture of ivory black and ultramarine blue, continue to work out the details of the hair, always keeping in mind the light source, which in this instance shines from the top right side of the frame. Avoid adding too much detail to the hair; you don't need to follow the reference one hundred percent at this stage. You want the hair to be a balance between the detail of the shadows and the large flat washes created by the blue.

Add further details to the hair and prepare the image for the final touches

36

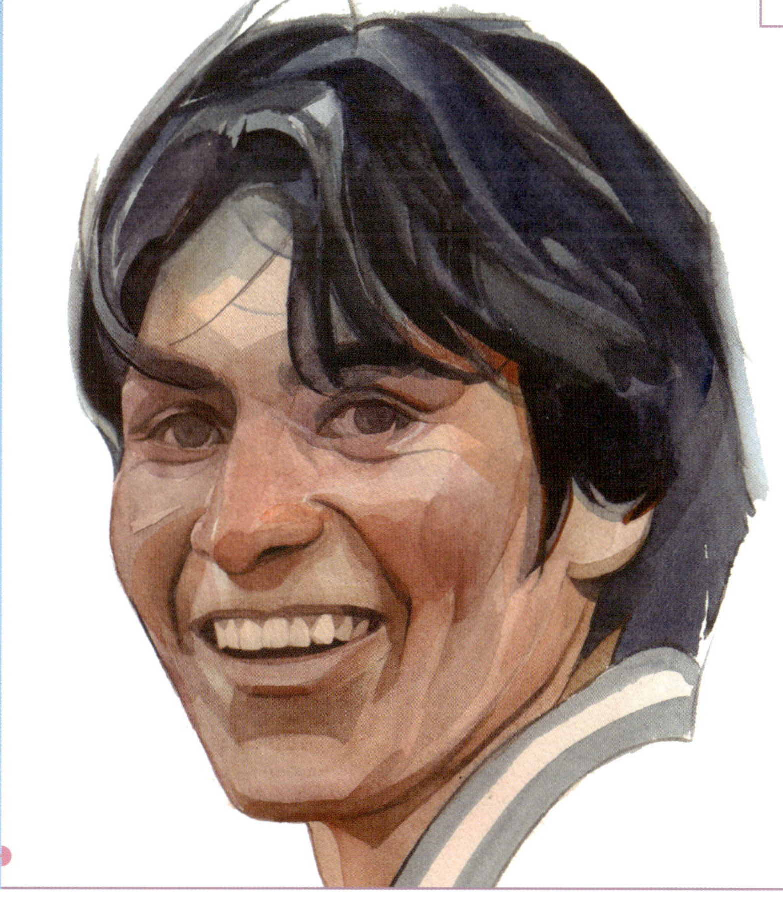

Start the final step from the top down. The darkest areas can finally be painted in. Saturate the blue and black mixture with more black, and then add some alizarin crimson. When the hair is complete and well balanced, begin to soften its edges against the white paper background. To do this, take the large brush and clean water, and rub the brush against the edge of the blue until it softens. Next, touch up and darken areas of red or black mixtures until you are happy with the result.

Finish by checking the balance of colors

Conclusion

Congratulations – you have successfully completed a stylized watercolor portrait! Take the knowledge and skills acquired through following this tutorial and apply them to your next portrait or painting experiments. You can now study a photo reference and recognize the underlying shapes and values needed to recreate and reinterpret it into art using the techniques of blocking, measuring, constructing, refining, and finally, rendering. You should also have a better understanding of value as the driving force behind believable lighting and color balance in your paintings. Enjoy being able to explore new faces and forms in a fresh light.

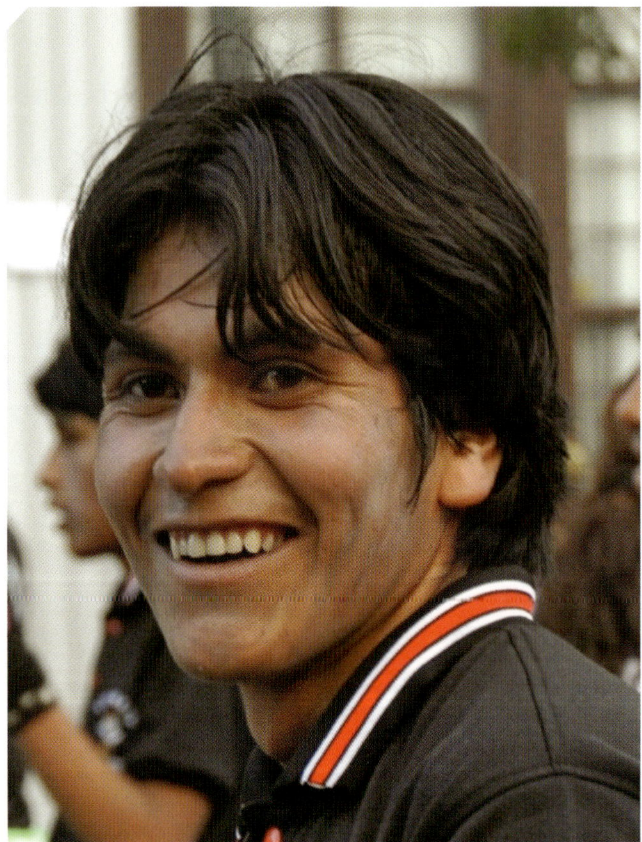

Photograph by Vladgalenko on Dreamstime

Final image © Nick Runge

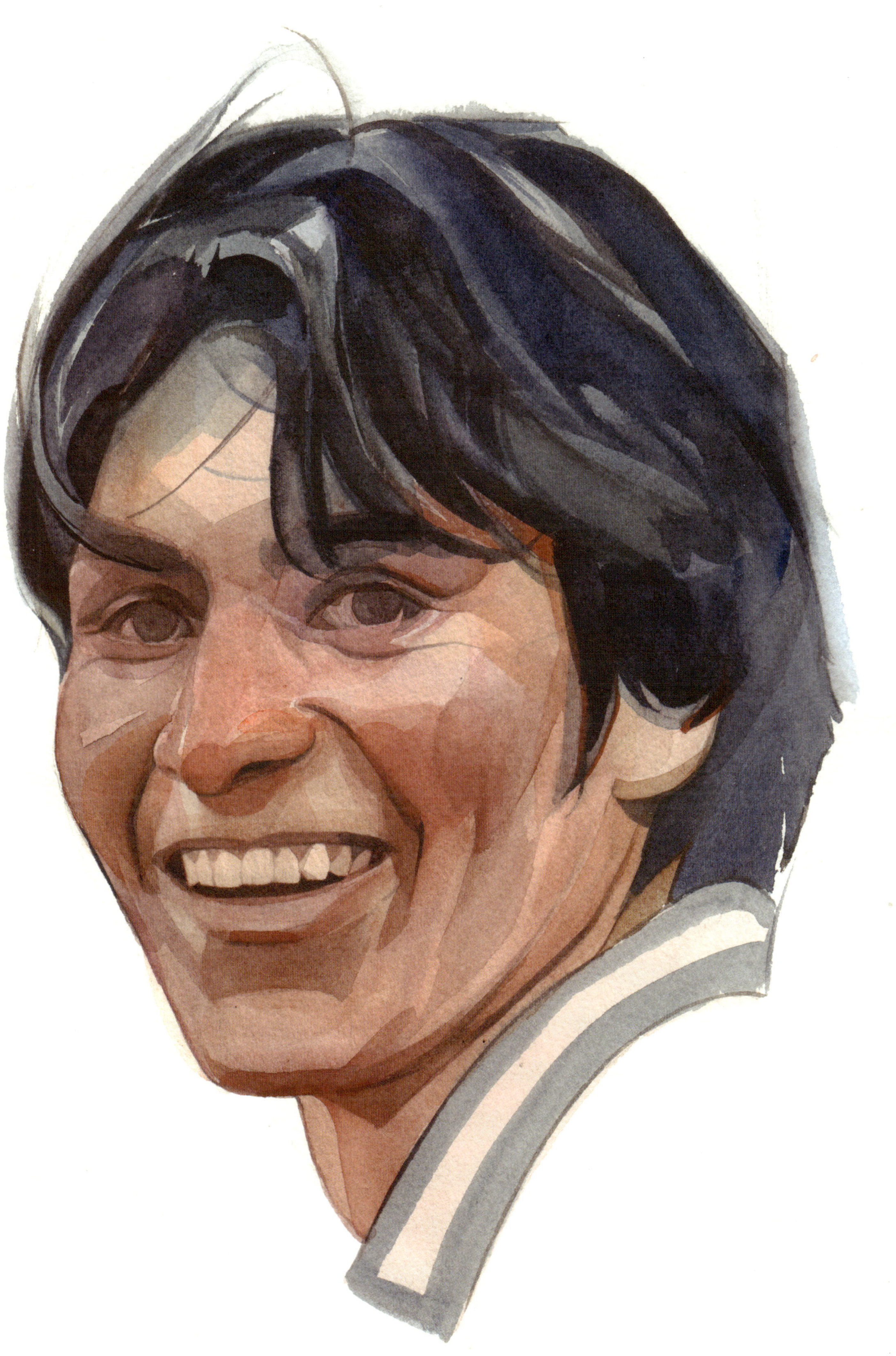

ASTRI LOHNE

Introduction

This tutorial will demonstrate how to create a vibrant yet soft portrait of a young man. You will learn how to implement an efficient, smart workflow, how to capture likeness, and how to make your subject come alive using color and light. It will break down how a face is constructed, as well as how you can paint any subject simply by starting with the base and slowly working up to the finer details. It's a slow and sometimes painstaking process, but once it all comes together, you will see that it's worth the time and effort.

While the process of creating a portrait isn't linear, these thirty-six steps will provide you with a solid foundation to start developing your own portrait workflow. Each artist is unique in their preferences and style of working, so experiment and shuffle steps around as you see fit, keeping the approach detailed in this tutorial as your guiding principle. This portrait has been created using digital software, but you can follow it along using the traditional or digital media of your choosing.

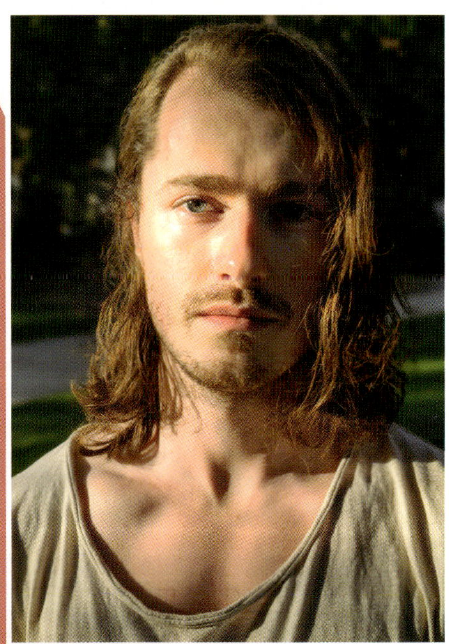

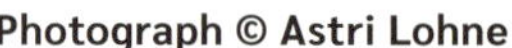

Photograph © Astri Lohne

01

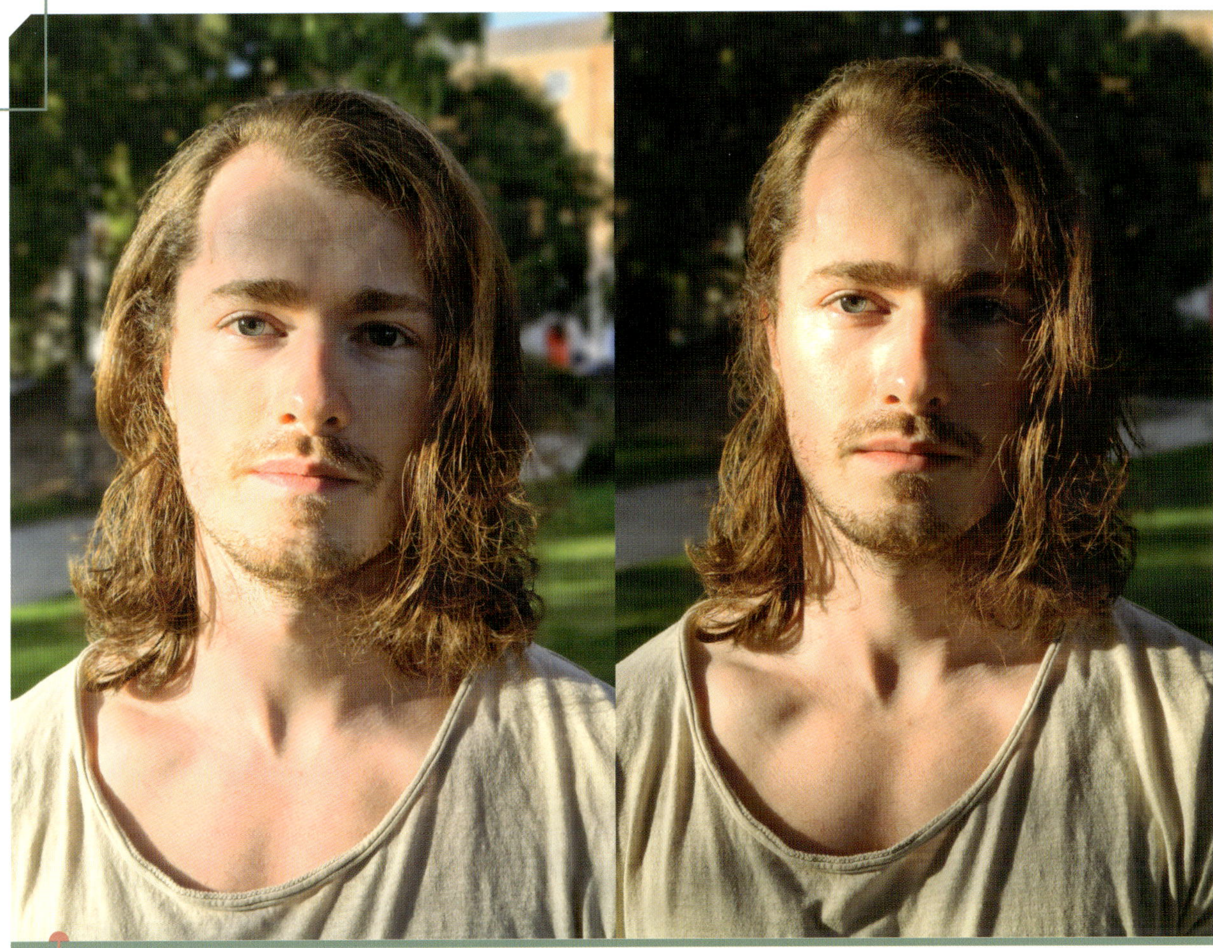

An example of a bad reference photo vs. a good reference photo

Bad reference photograph

✗ Overexposed lighting

✗ Off-center framing

✗ Unflattering hair shape

✗ Hard to see the planes of the face

Good reference photograph

✓ Full range of values

✓ Background makes the subject pop

✓ Easy to see the shapes

✓ Flattering angle

Unless you are painting from life, the first step to any portrait is finding a good reference photograph. It's important that it fulfills a few requirements, including: decent resolution, lighting that is both natural and flattering, a full range of values, and clear shapes. Working from a subpar reference will make the entire process more difficult, so take your time procuring a good reference photo. Look out for clarity of form; are the planes and shapes of the face easy to see, or is it muddy and blown out?

02

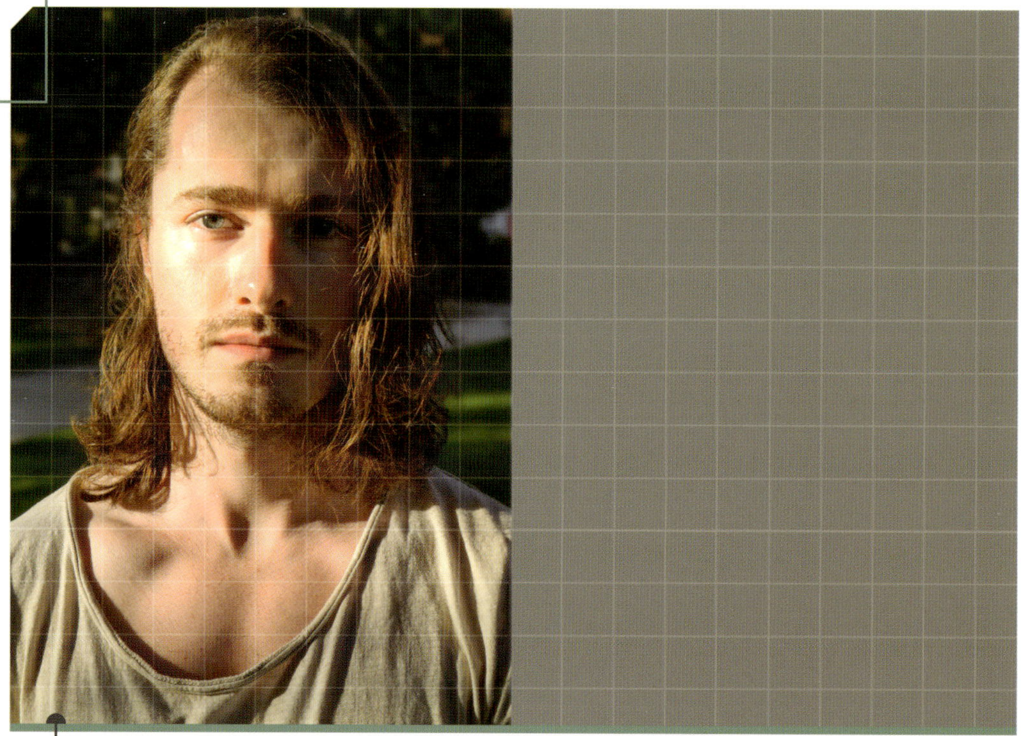

Position a grid over your reference photo using a clearly visible, but non-intrusive value

One of the biggest challenges of realistic portraiture is capturing an accurate likeness of your subject. To set yourself up for success, use a square grid to ensure your sketch lines up with your reference photo from the very beginning. This will act as a guide when drawing the shape of your subject's face, but don't worry about making everything line up perfectly. If using digital software, you can toggle this grid on and off throughout the process to make sure you are still on track, but don't get obsessive about it. If working traditionally, ensure the grid lines are faint so you can paint over or erase them.

03

Before you can start drawing, you need to first establish a background. Select a color that is not too vibrant or distracting, and will complement the overall color palette of the portrait. As the subject in this reference photo has a warm tone, selecting a cool, blue tone for the background will create some temperature contrast. While you want to find a value that will make your subject pop, avoid choosing a stark white or a true black. The background color can always be adjusted later if you are painting digitally, so don't overthink it and just fill the canvas with a suitable color.

Experiment with texture while laying down your background if you wish to create a more painterly look

04

Select a large, soft brush and start to sketch your first marks. Use a color that is not too harsh and will look good when incorporated with the rest of the painting. Brown or orange are good options here as they will blend well with the subject's skin tone. Start by drawing the silhouette and the biggest, most obvious geometric shapes. Try to imagine the shape of the skull, such as the placement of the eye sockets and where the jawbone sits. It's important to start at the base before moving on to surface-level features.

Sketch the big shapes to gradually build up the silhouette – you are not creating lines, but a soft block-in

05

At this early stage it's extremely important to stay zoomed out and view the canvas as a whole to allow you to get a sense of the big picture. Smaller details will come later. Beginners often fall into the trap of worrying about details such as the eyes, nostrils, and eyebrow hairs too early in the process. On the surface, it might seem like these features are the most important to creating a good portrait. It's the elements that connect these features, however, that form the foundation of the face. Getting these simple shapes down on the canvas will set you up for a smoother, more successful process.

Create the foundation using big, loose shapes before thinking about the smaller details

06

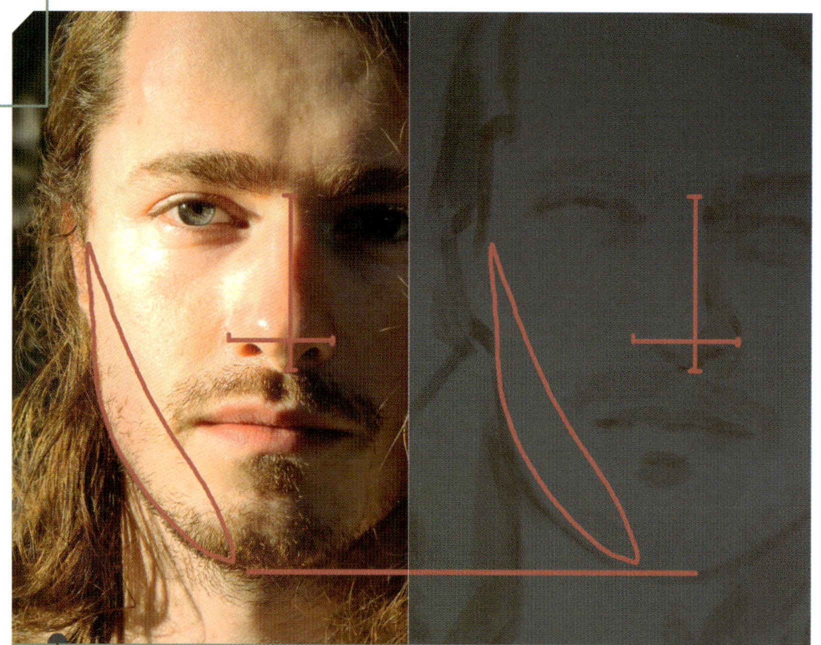

Keep measuring as you block in the shapes to ensure your sketch lines up with the reference photo. The grid will help with this, but you shouldn't follow it blindly. Look for patterns in the face. Are the eyes the same width as the nose? How wide is the chin compared to the eyebrows? Finding these patterns will help you to capture the shapes accurately, therefore obtaining likeness. Additionally, you should also be taking a critical look at the shapes that make up your subject's face. Try to distill how their features are unique to them.

Make sure the width and length of your shapes correspond with the reference photo

07

Once you have drawn the major landmarks of the face, the sketch is finished. This should not be a detailed sketch, but should provide you with the information you need to start sculpting the base of the face. Your sketch should have a strong focus on geometry, volume, and big shapes, not lines and fine detail. It might not look like much just yet, but this is just the first of the many building blocks.

Your sketch should be soft and void of detail, but still clear

08

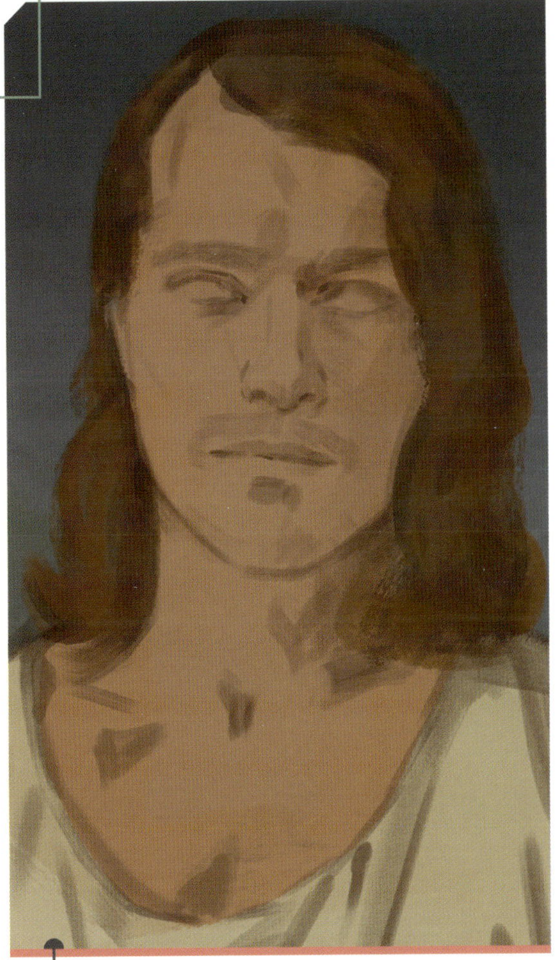

After studying the skin tone of your subject, choose a base skin color that is saturated and in the mid-levels

09

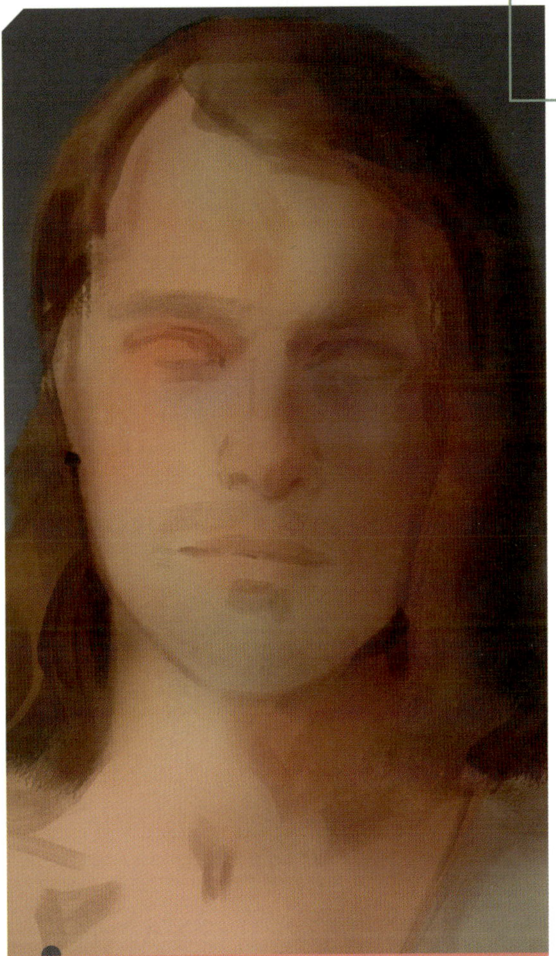

Look for hue shifts and soft gradients in the reference photo, then paint them on top of your base colors

Begin to paint in local colors for the skin, hair, and clothing. If working digitally, do this on new layers underneath your sketch. If using traditional media, paint on top of your sketch, taking care not to hide it. Study your reference photo closely to identify the true color of the skin. It's easy to think skin is lighter than it actually is, so make sure to pick a mid-value, saturated color, rather than one that is too drab or bright. Use a soft, textured brush, keep it loose, and don't think about lighting yet. These base colors don't need to be solid; let parts of the background bleed through if you want to create a painterly feel.

Use a soft brush to start painting some nuance into the local colors. Can you see any soft gradients or hue shifts in your reference photo? A good rule to remember is that the forehead will be often be yellow-toned, the under-eye area and the jawline will be cooler, and the cheeks, lips, and nose will be reddish. Don't forget about the hair either; look to see if there are any interesting tone shifts in its base color.

10

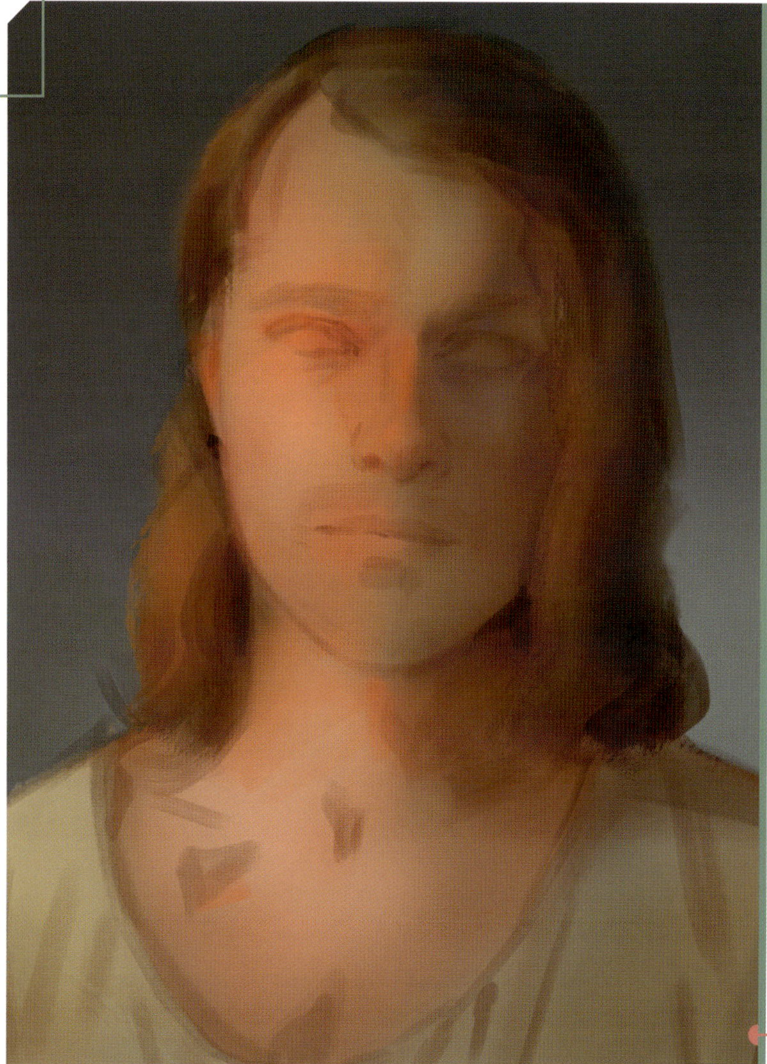

Now you have finished the base of the head, it's time to start building up the volume. The first step is to implement the lighting. Before you paint in the brightest parts, lay down the transition tones. Observe the direction, strength, and type of light source in your reference photo. In this photo, the subject is lit by sun, so there is a lot of subsurface scattering bleeding through under the light. This requires a bright red for the transition. Whatever light environment you are painting, subsurface scattering will be present somewhere on the skin. Study your reference to see what tones will work best.

Your transition tone should be soft, saturated, and not too bright

Artist tip

Often overlooked, subsurface scattering can be what distinguishes a vibrant and lively portrait from a gray and lifeless one. Skin is naturally a little translucent; when light shines on it, you can see the light traveling through the flesh where brightness meets shadow. To paint convincing skin, it therefore needs to look as though blood is flowing underneath it. Increase the reds and oranges at the transitions between light and shadow, especially on thinner parts of the skin or cartilage, such as the nose or ears.

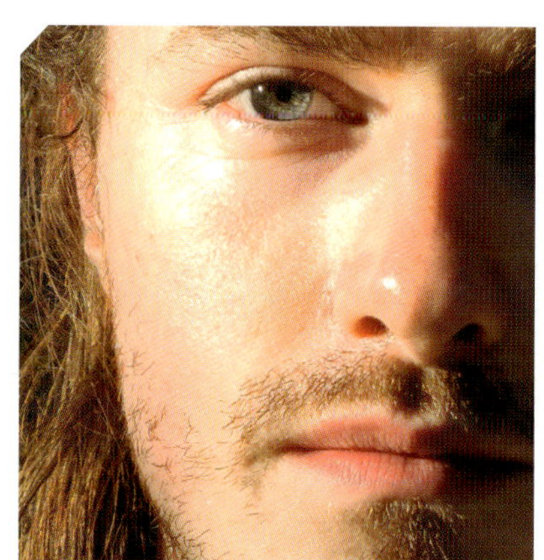

11

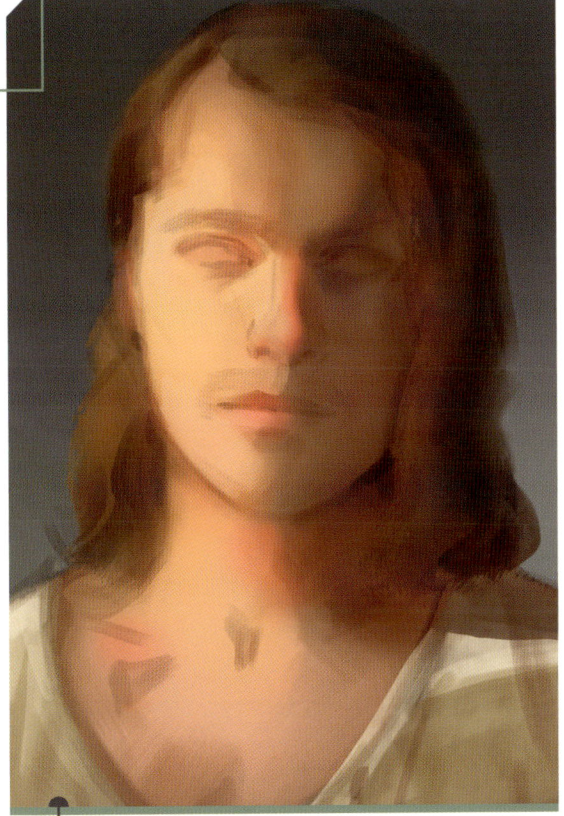

Build up the light, letting the transition tones bleed through at the edges

12

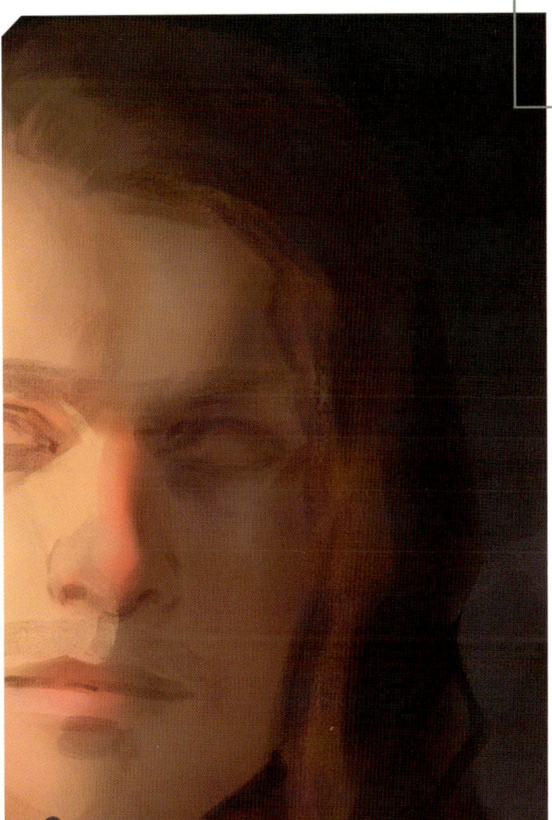

Though the portrait has a little more detail, you should still be zoomed out while painting over the sketch to view the image as a whole

Start to paint in the brighter areas on top of the transition color. You are still not painting in the very brightest parts; that will come later. Use a bright color and a soft brush to fill in the highlights. As the light source here is the sun, a muted yellow color works well. Pay attention to the shapes of the light and how it interacts with the form of your subject as you are painting.

The majority of the base is now complete and you can start to work a little more destructively. If painting digitally, up until this point you should have been working on separate layers underneath the sketch, but it's now time to change that. On a new layer above the sketch, use a soft brush to start deepening and tightening up the volumes of the face. If using traditional media, continue to paint on top of the image as before. Carefully paint over any remnants of the sketch to create a soft, 3D base for the rest of the painting. After seeing how the colors are progressing, you may decide to alter the background color. Here the background has been made a little darker.

13

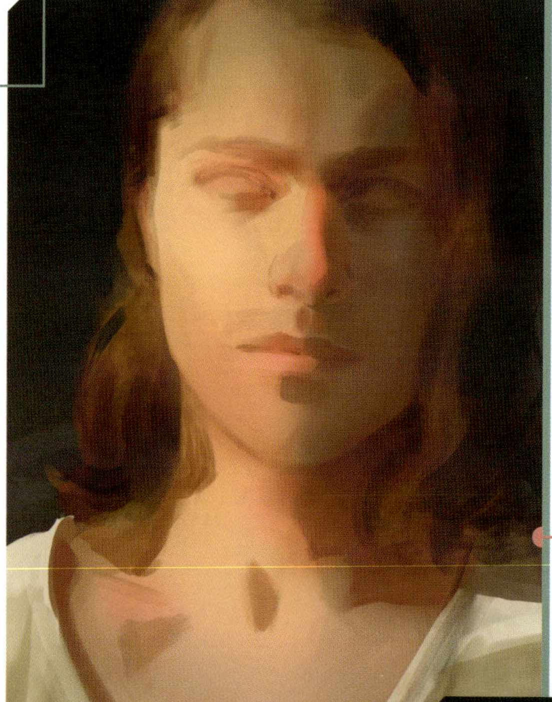

Now it is time to balance out the values and add some more depth to the portrait. Start to increase the shadows on the face and hair, using a saturated color rather than a gray. Dark reds that vary in saturation have been used here. As with the light, there are also transition tones in the shadows as they move from mid-level to darker. Their hue also changes depending on the ambient light. Study your reference photo closely and see what kind of saturation variation there is. If painting digitally, you can use the Color Picker to pick these colors from the reference photo.

Pay attention to the shapes and edges the shadows create

14

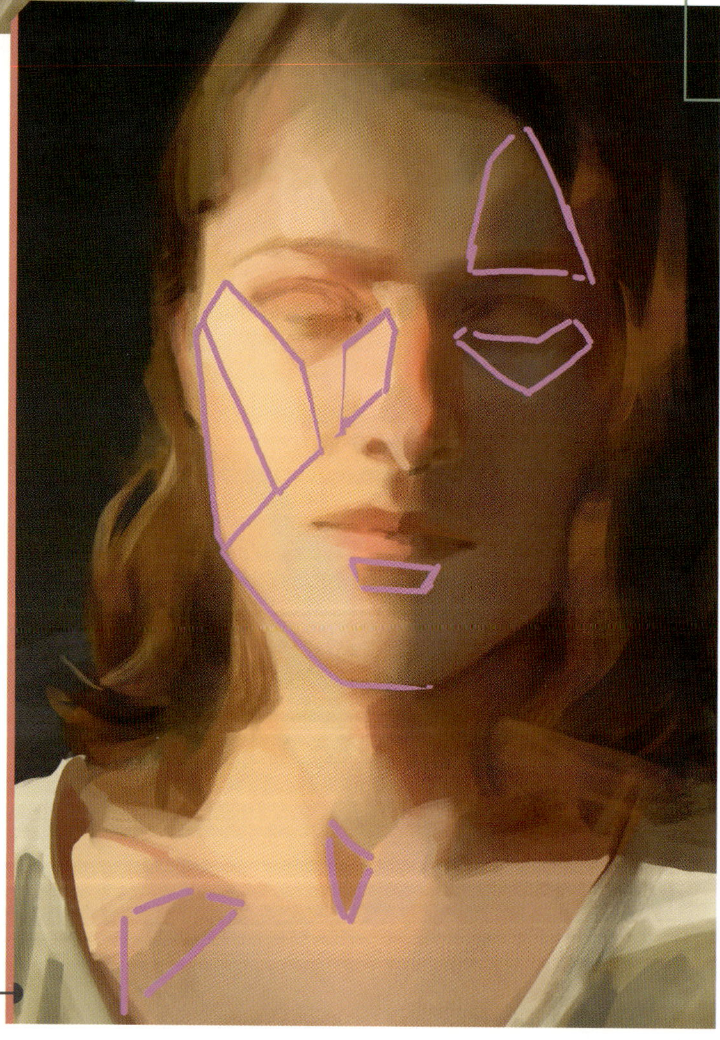

The next step is to identify and define the planes of the face. A plane refers to any distinct flat surfaces on your subject. Look for large, geometric blocks of value and paint in the shapes with a decisive but soft touch. These surfaces are often triangular (such as the under-eye area) or rectangular (such as the side of the nose). The most acute angles often sit around the nose and cheekbones. Identifying those planes can be challenging if you are new to portraiture. Practice by studying the Asaro head; this is a 3D model of the head that's broken into clear, identifiable planes.

Recognizing the size, shape, and placement of the planes is important to achieving both likeness and convincing forms

15

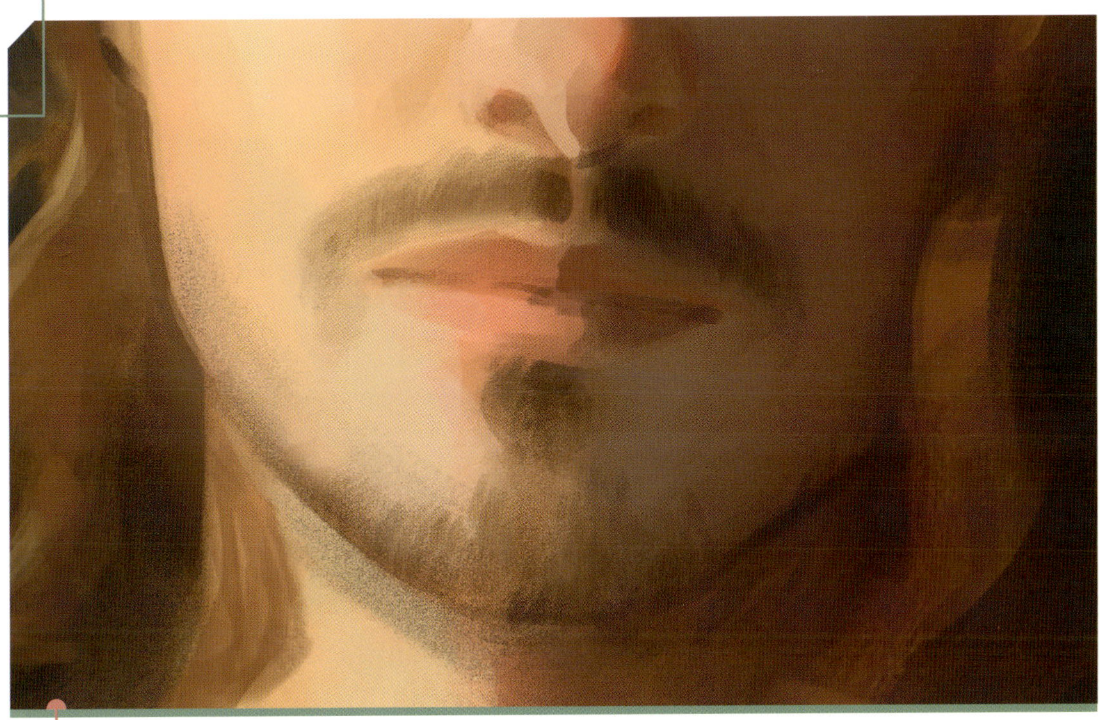

Use soft brushstrokes when painting in the facial hair – details will come later

Up until this point you have been building the groundwork for the face. This is to provide a vibrant, accurate, and voluminous base for the details. The portrait should now be in a good enough place that you can begin to consider the more surface-level elements, starting with the subject's facial hair. As before, keep the brushstrokes and shapes soft. Instead of painting in individual hairs, use a soft brush to gently define the area for the eyebrows, mustache, and beard. Pay attention to the placement of your subject's facial hair and how this is uniquely shaped to their face.

16

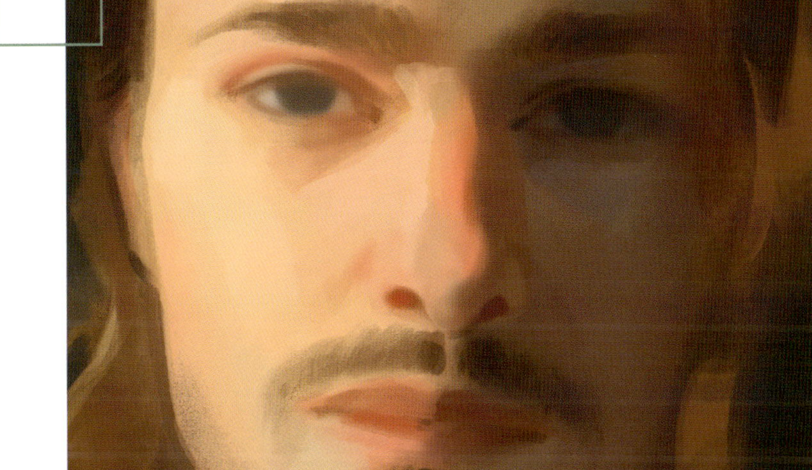

Once the facial hair has been added, the basic framework for the features is finally complete. The next step is to move on to laying down a base for the eyeballs, nose, and mouth. Continue to use a soft brush and be mindful of the values and color. Eyeballs are not true white, but are usually a slightly lighter and cooler version of the skin tone. Lips are often quite saturated, while the nostrils tend to be more red than black due to the translucency of the nose.

Study your reference photo closely to identify the color of the eyeballs, nose, and mouth

17

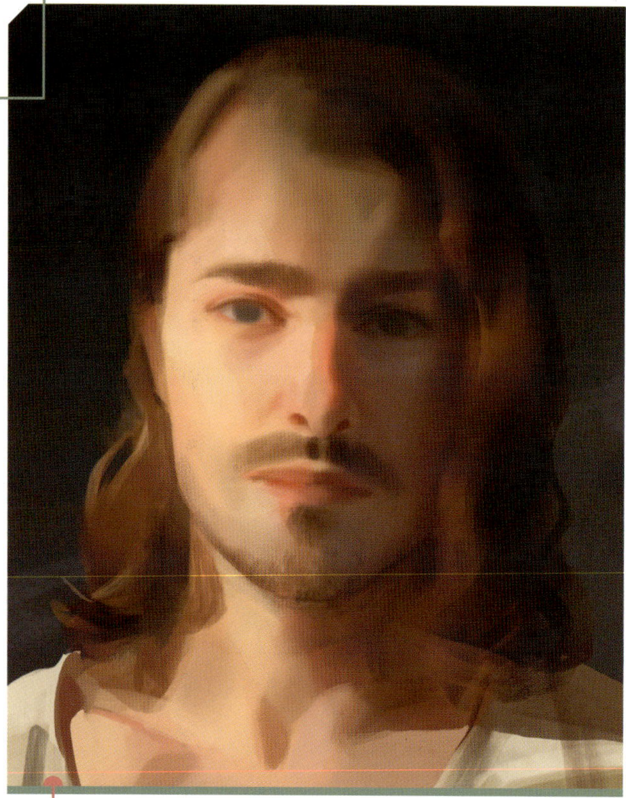

With a gentle touch, unify the face and deepen the occlusion shadows

It's still important to maintain a focus on the big picture. At each step, take some time to ensure that what you have just painted blends in with the rest of your painting. Define and soften the under-eye area and blend out the corners of the mouth. There should be no harsh edges between what you just painted in and the rest of the face. This is also a good stage to use occlusion shadows (see page 48) to blend in the hair a little and soften the edges around the hairline.

18

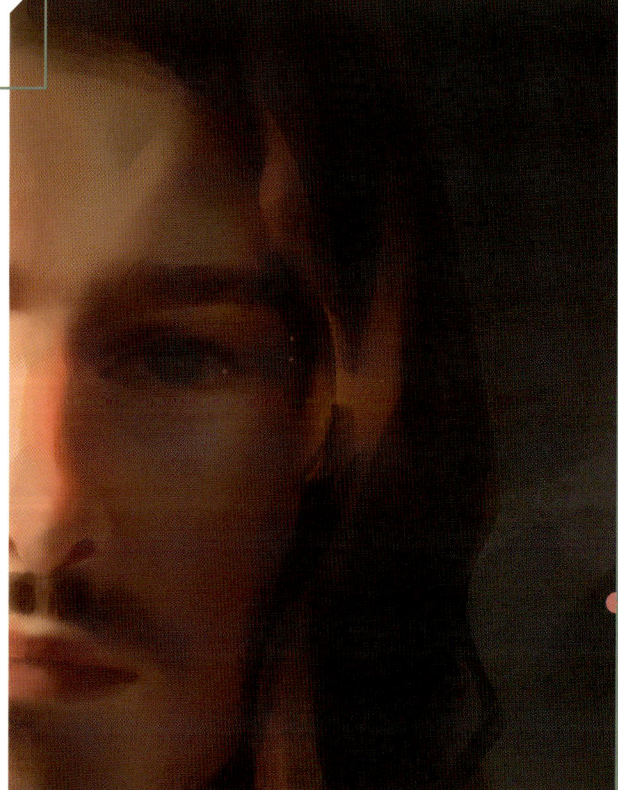

The next step is to add more depth to your portrait. Use deeper shadows to expand the value range, continuing to build up the volume. Once again, keep the hue in mind while painting. Shadows are rarely true black, but are often a saturated, dark color. Lots of warm browns and reds have been used for the deepest shadows here, focused most on the areas where the hair meets the face. Avoid going too overboard with the contrast on the face itself, as that can quickly end up looking too harsh.

As you add more dark values, your subject should begin to look more three-dimensional

19

As your aim is to expand the value range in both directions, add the brighter value next. Don't introduce specular highlights yet, as those can be added later with the more detailed elements. Through brightening the highest points on the forms and the plane surfaces that directly face the light source, you will start to achieve a full sense of depth. Brighten the cheekbones, forehead, and side of the nose, as well as adding to the hair, chest, and shirt.

Add the brightest highlights to the surfaces that directly face the light source – this will often be the high points of the face

20

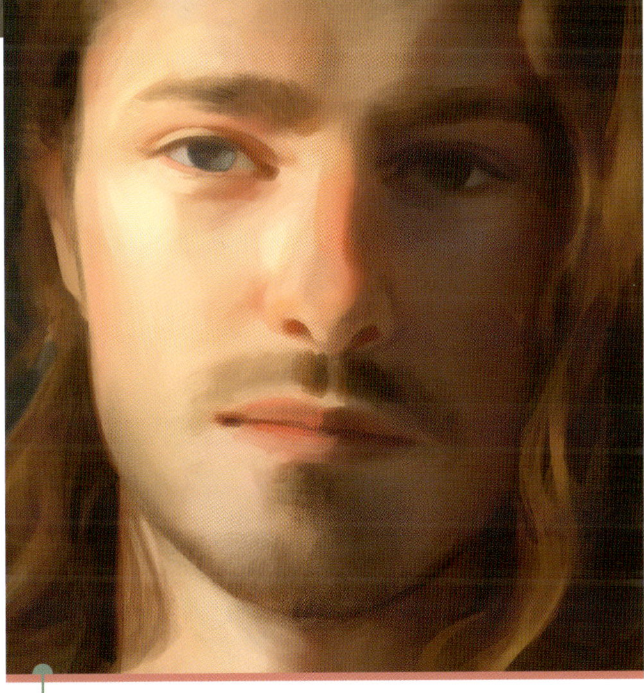

Start to bring the face into focus by tightening up some of the edges, while leaving others soft

Up until now you should have been working with the full canvas on view. Now it is time to zoom in slightly as you begin to tighten up the edges and add detail to the landmarks of the face. A common misconception about detail is that it's simply tightening things up, making the image sharper and clearer. In actual fact, detail encompasses numerous different elements. Texture, hue, value, and edgework all play their part in rendering a painting. While your priority here is to create a small amount of definition on the face base, which up until now has been very soft, don't forget to keep these other aspects in mind as well.

21

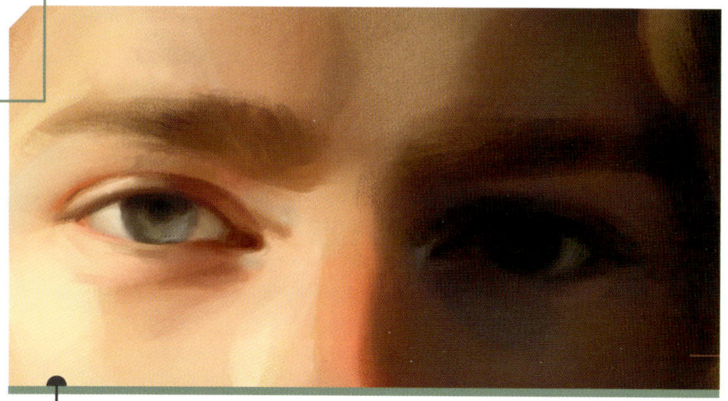

Don't be tempted to paint in any detail yet, but focus on creating a solid base for the facial features

Now that the entire base for the face is complete, you can move on to the focal points of the portrait: the facial features themselves. Starting with the eyes, begin by asking yourself what is special about the eyes of your model, then paint accordingly. Define the outline of the eye softly, then sharpen and darken the lower and upper eyelids so they match up with your reference photo. Make sure the top and bottom of the irises are slightly covered by the eyelids to create a relaxed, natural look.

Study your reference photo and consider if your subject's nose is sharp, round, or especially slim. Make sure you are paying attention to your reference and not simply painting what you think a nose should look like. The nose is the highest and sharpest point on the face, so take care to reflect that volume when value blocking. It can help to envision the bridge of the nose as the top half of a hexagon, with one plane as the flat of the nose bridge, then the two side planes connecting with the under-eye area at an angle.

22

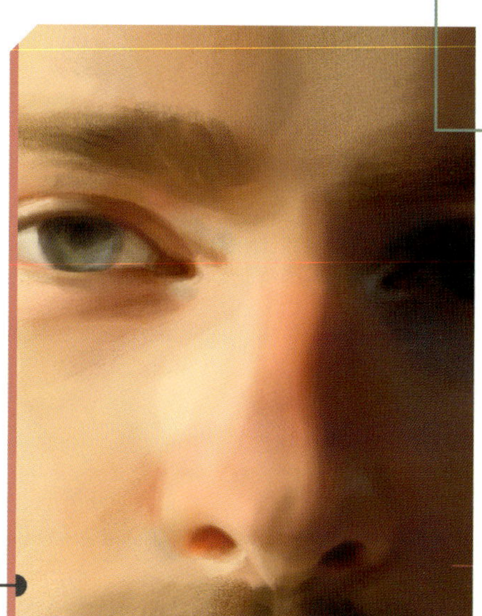

Imagining the nose as simple, geometric shapes will help you to capture it accurately

23

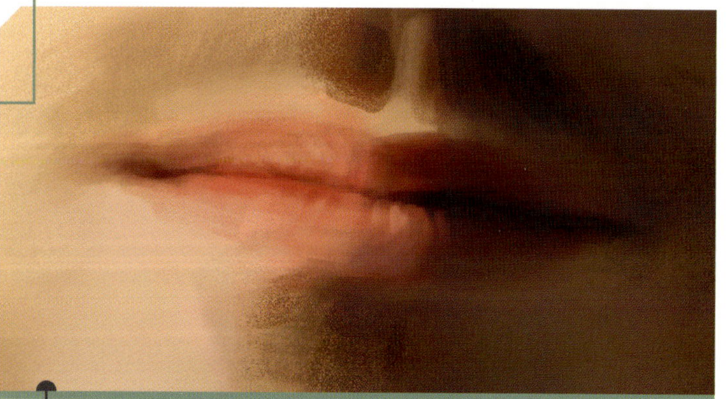

Use a saturated color for the mouth and don't be afraid to create strong contrast

When defining the mouth, it's again important to consider volume. The upper lip is often at an inward angle toward the mouth crease, while the lower lip protrudes outward. This means that, in most lighting setups, the upper lip will be dark, the lower lip will be brighter, and the mouth crease will be the darkest point due to occlusion shadows. Fade out the corners of the mouth and the edges of the lips, or it will end up looking like lipstick, or like the mouth is not a part of the face.

24

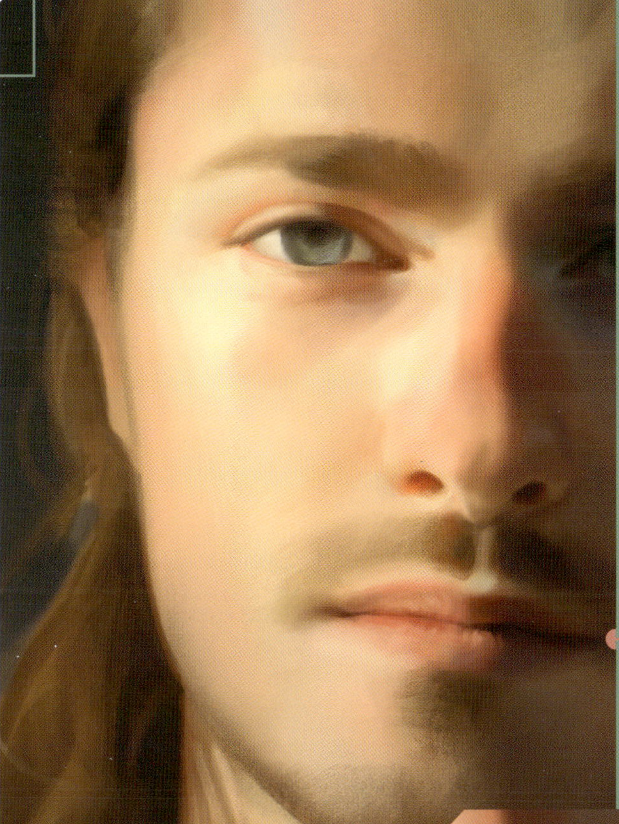

Take the time to blend in the features to ensure they don't look separate from the rest of the face. The transitions between the features are as important as the features themselves. It's all connected; the eye sits above the tear duct, which connects with the side of the nose, which ends where the nasolabial fold begins. This is another opportunity to go over the rest of the portrait, using a soft brush to focus on hues and values.

The facial features are not islands – make sure everything is blended together and connected

25

Although they are not the main focus of the portrait, don't forget about your subject's hair and clothing. This is a good stage to tighten them up to ensure they don't fall behind the progress of the rest of the portrait. When painting hair, think of it as ribbon-like sections, rather than fine, individual strands. It can be helpful to start by first painting in dark blocks where the sections separate, before building up the highlights on any sections on which the light source shines.

Hair is a key element of likeness, so make sure the hairline and outline match your reference photo

26

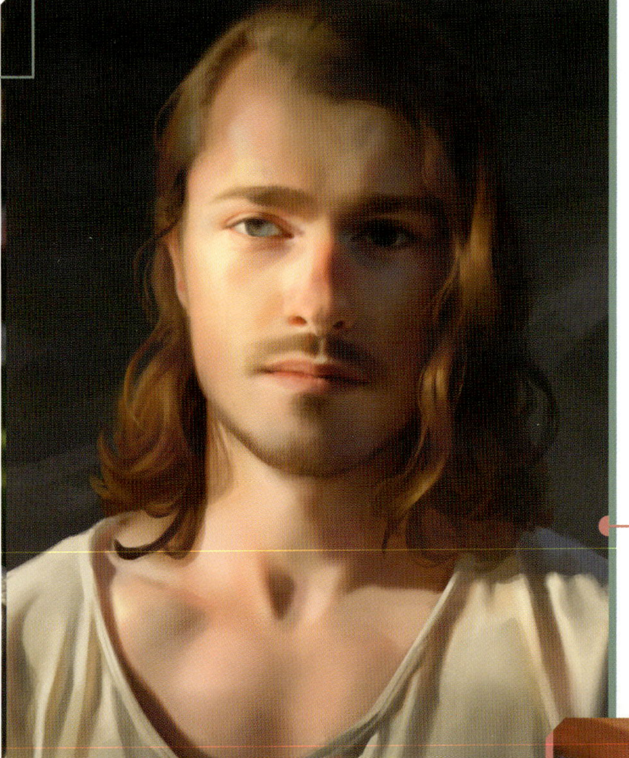

To add further nuance and realism to your portrait, consider the light environment of your reference photo. Paint in any light shining from the sun, sky, or your subject's surroundings. In addition, start to introduce any ambient light you can identify. In this case, this requires painting in ambient light from the blue sky, which consists of cooler highlights in the shadowed area on the face. At this stage you can also work on introducing further temperature contrast, experimenting with both cooler and warmer tones across the entire painting.

Adding subtle temperature shifts will create an extra level of depth to your portrait

27

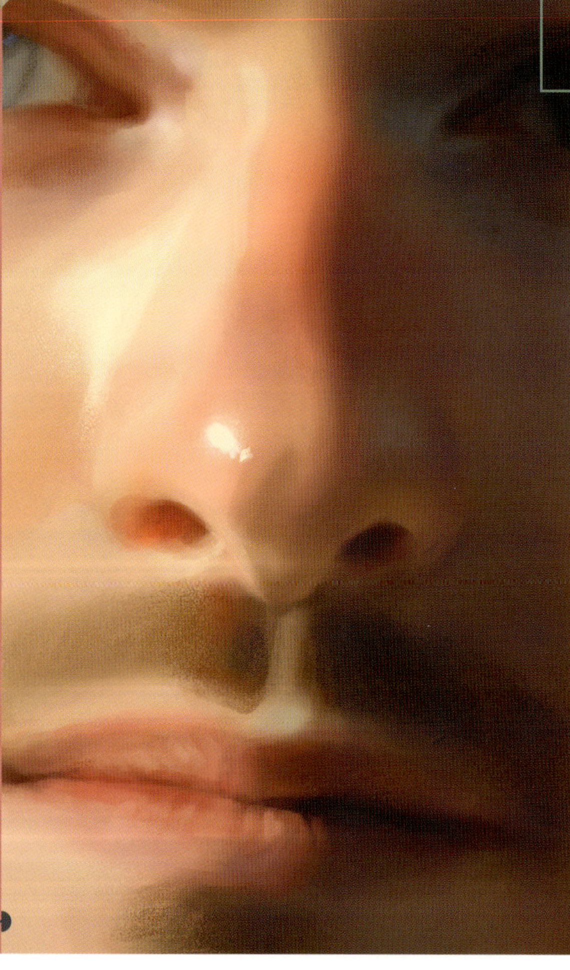

Another form of light to look out for is bounce light; bright spots created by light bouncing from a lit surface onto a shadowed surface. This typically features on any planes that are facing downward – such as the base of the nose, the upper lip, the jawline, and the neck – and is usually quite dark and saturated. In this reference photo, the yellow sunlight creates a golden, orange bounce light. You can also now add specular highlights; the smallest, brightest highlights. Observe how adding a tiny, bright highlight on the tip of the nose improves the sense of depth.

Add bounce light onto the jaw, nose, eyelid, and eye socket to bring volume to the shadows

28

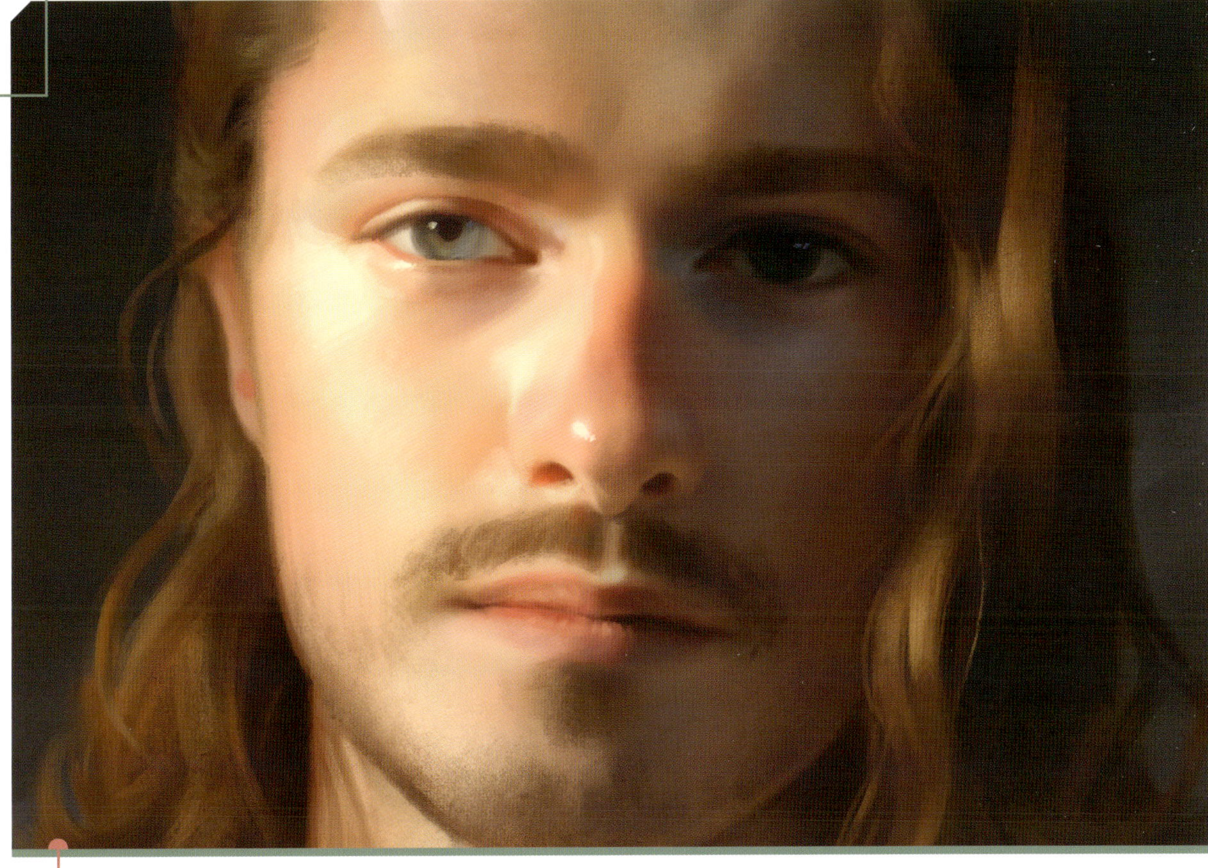

Focus the texture around high-density areas, such as the subject's facial hair, leaving the skin smoother

You will mostly have been using soft brushes up until this point. While soft brushes are perfect for building up form and creating a base to work on top of, the portrait is still lacking detail. Select a textured brush – one with a chalky or canvas-like finish – and start to paint over your portrait using sweeping brushstrokes that follow the form. This should create a more realistic finish, with lots of implied detail.

Artist tip

Rather than painting in every tiny detail, use the texture of your brush to do most of the work for you. The majority of people won't look at your portrait up close, so not every feature needs to be hyper-detailed and realistic on a small scale. Save yourself some time by using a textured brush to apply strategic brushstrokes instead. This may not look like much when you're zoomed in, but zoomed out, or viewing your portrait from a distance, all the noise and implied detail will look even better than stiff hyper-realism.

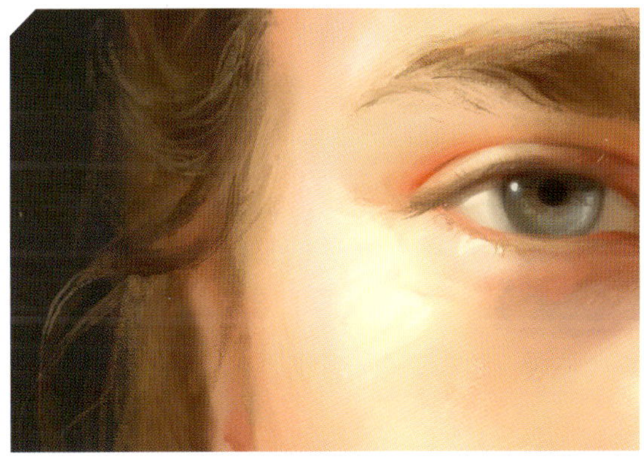

29

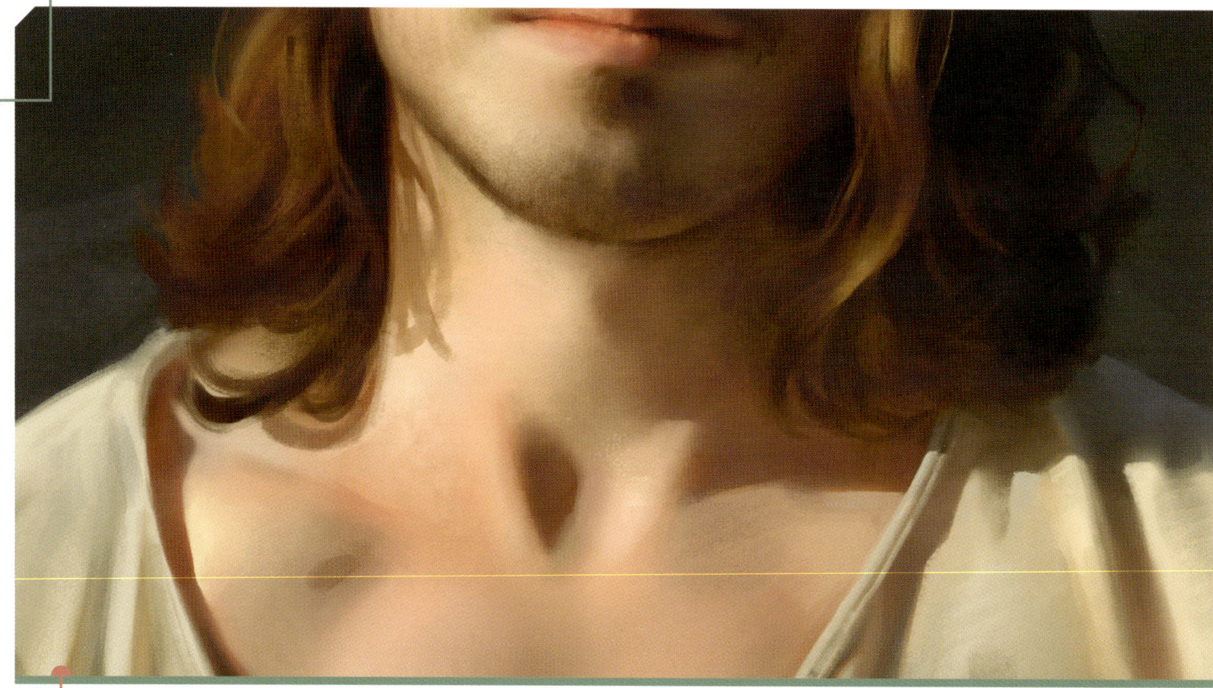

Create a variety of soft and sharp edges to guide the viewer's eyes to the focal points of the portrait

If every edge in your painting is the same, the image will look boring and static. The edges should all be fairly soft at this stage, so now is the time to sharpen some and further soften others. Select a slightly harder brush – this can be textured or smooth, whatever your preference – and chisel out edges where you feel your portrait needs more definition. One approach is to focus the hard edges around the focal points. To create an even more pronounced edge, paint a little brighter on one side of the portrait and a bit darker on the other.

30

Start to detail the facial hair. Study your reference photo, considering the direction and curvature in which the hairs are growing. Eyelashes, for example, grow at a sloping curve rather than straight out, meaning you need to paint them as curves. It's also important to group hairs together rather than painting them one by one. Think of hair as big shapes rather than separate strands. Use a textured brush instead to imply this detail. Fine, individual strands can be painted into a few focal areas later.

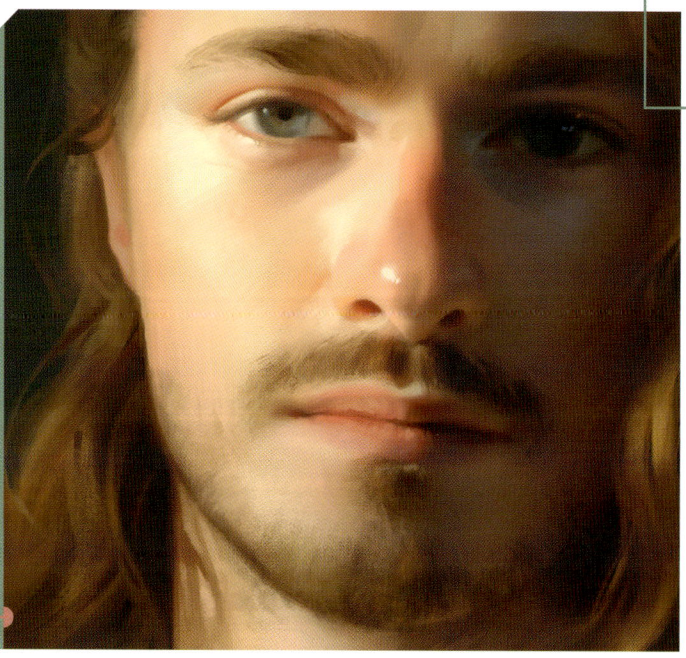

Group your subject's hair into key shapes, rather than painting each strand individually

31

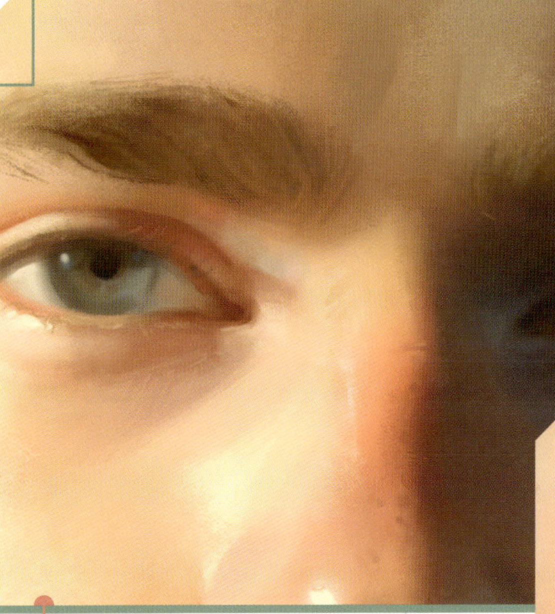

It's easy to end up with a fake, artificial-looking skin texture when using this soft, gradual approach to portraiture. This can be addressed in step 28 by going over the skin with a textured brush, but there are other tricks you can use as well to make the skin appear more real. Look for any freckles, wrinkles, or other marks on your subject, then – using a soft brush and a saturated color that isn't more than a couple of shades darker than the skin tone – gently paint on any freckles, moles, scars, or blemishes. Vary the shape, size, and value of these to make them appear natural rather than uniform. You can also imply pores using a large speckled brush.

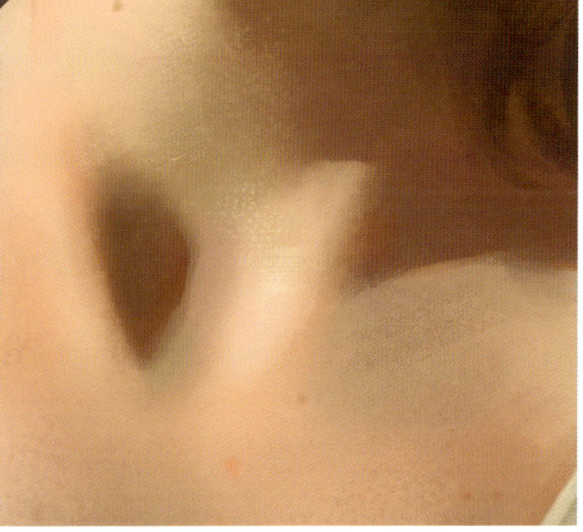

Paint freckles onto your subject softly and randomly, varying the size and shape

32

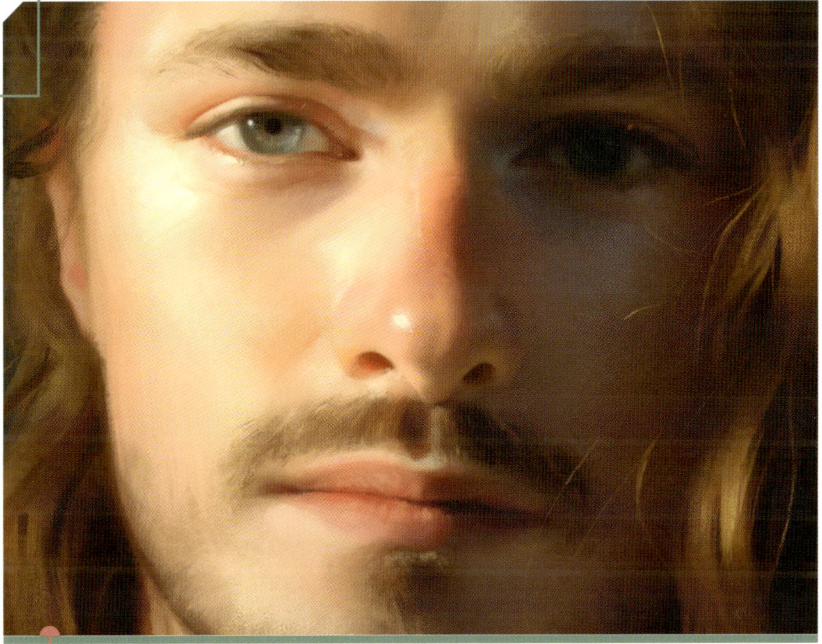

Pull the viewer's focus to the eye area by adding detail, while keeping the rest of the image softer and looser

Start to add fine detail, such as individual strands of hair and creases on the lips. Focus this in key areas, rather than detailing the entire image. If the whole portrait is tightly rendered, you will start to lose that painterly, lively feel. Fill the focal areas with detail, while keeping the rest of the painting looser. The eyes are a focal point of the image, so add detail such as eyelashes and highlights to this area. Conversely, soften the edges of the head and other areas you don't want the viewer to focus on. This technique is called quality contrast and will help create a dynamic look to your portrait.

33

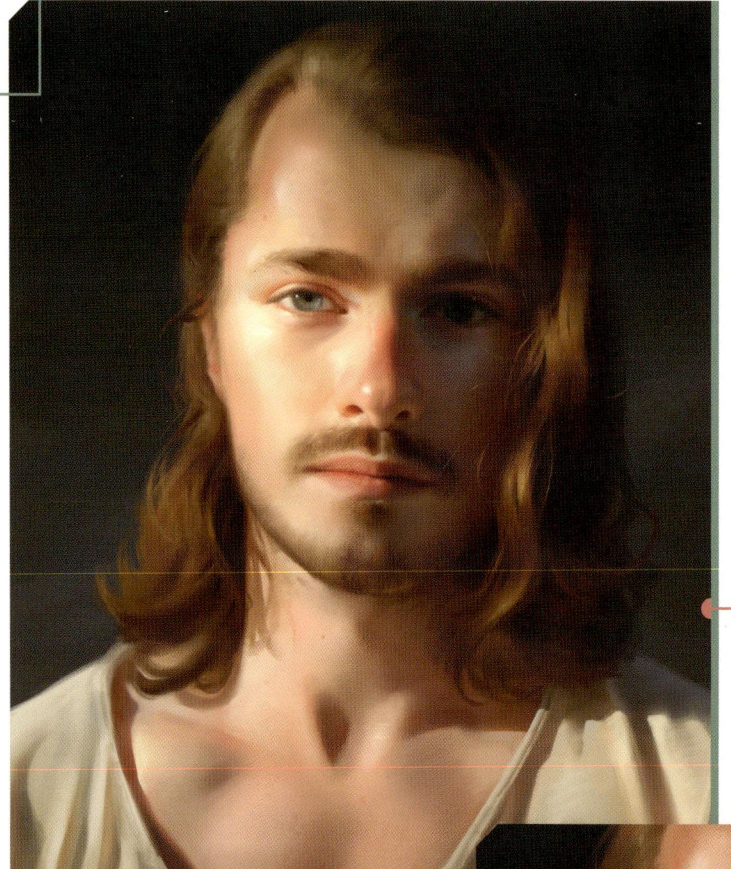

With all this detailing, it can be easy to lose track of the big picture. Zoom out or take a step back from the canvas to assess the state of your portrait. Adjust and soften values as needed, and blend or smudge anything that doesn't look quite right. This step may require a little back and forth between softening and tightening until it looks correct. Take your time and make sure all of the elements in the portrait appear unified.

Make sure the portrait is unified after the detail added in the previous step, softening and tightening as needed

34

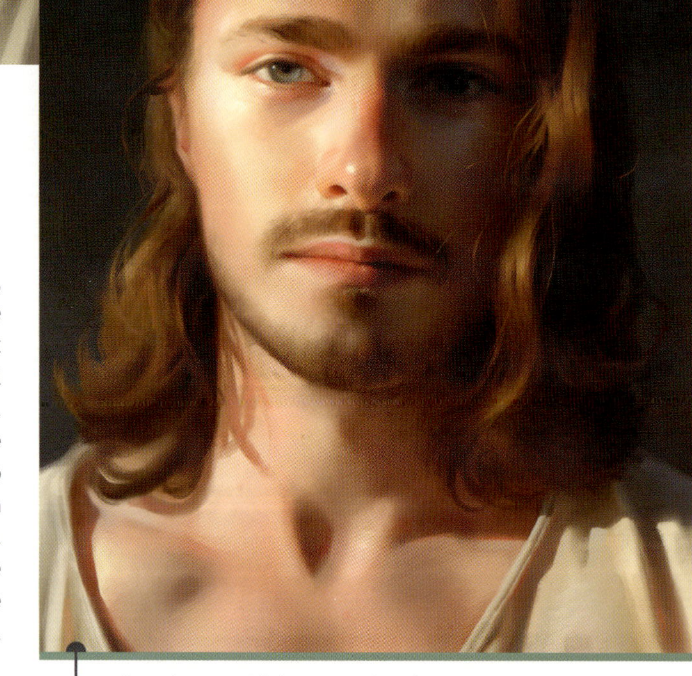

Your portrait should now be voluminous, detailed, and carry a recognizable resemblance to your reference photo. With the most challenging steps complete, it's time to instill your portrait with some more personality. One approach is to enhance the subsurface scattering, infusing the bright reds tones into other areas of the portrait. This can help to liven the image up, without being overpowering. Whatever your inclination or direction for the portrait, take some time to experiment and see what effects you can create.

Experiment with hue, or other factors, to make your portrait more interesting

35

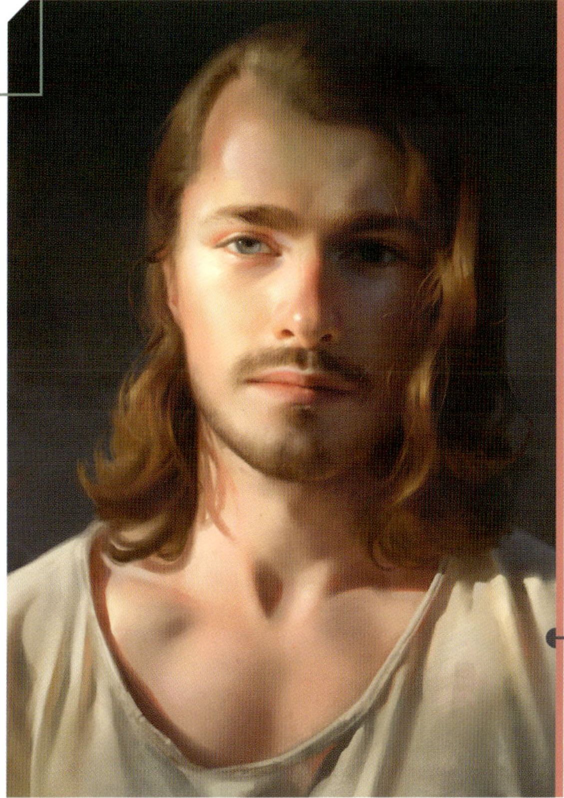

You may find at this stage that you have lost some of the saturation you introduced earlier on, or that your value range isn't quite right. Use this step to touch up and intensify areas that have lost their color, or soften areas that are too dark by lightly coloring over them with a brighter value. In this case, the contrast around the bottom edges has been reduced, the values of the background have been adjusted, and Photoshop's Smart Sharpen filter has been added for extra crispness. The color and value sliders in most painting software are invaluable for these last tweaks, whether you are working entirely digitally or cleaning up a scanned or photographed painting.

Whether it's a big change or a subtle detail, take some time to see if there are any elements of the portrait that need adjusting

36

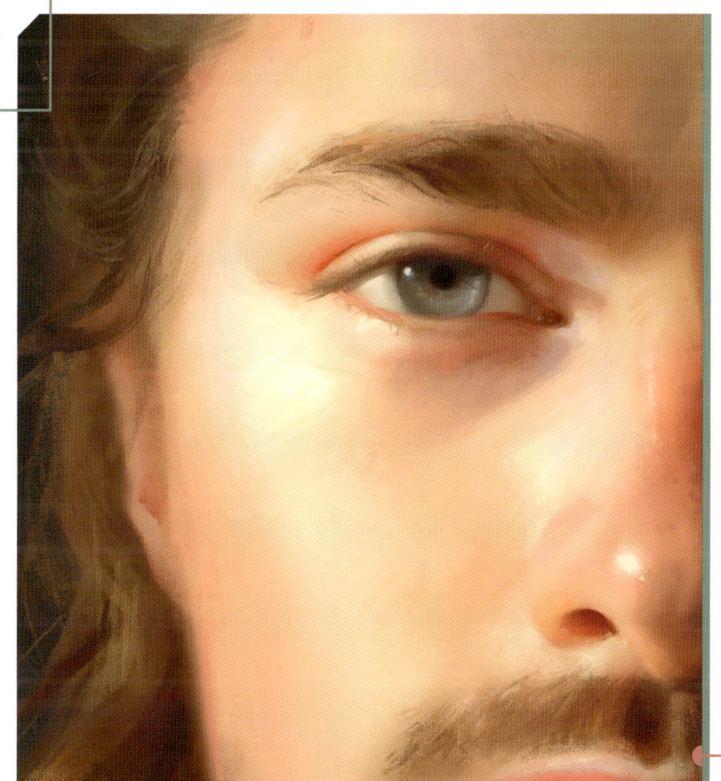

Take a final look at your portrait as a whole and tighten up anything that looks out of place. If you find that your portrait looks too stiff and lifeless, there is still time to loosen things up a little. Soften some more edges and add detail surrounding your focal points. In this case, the left eye has been tightened up and some more definition has been added to the hair close to it to help draw the focus of the viewer more successfully.

Do a final polish pass to make sure your portrait is achieving everything you want it to

Conclusion

And you're finished! Starting with a rough block in, you have learned how to build up the color and light of a portrait, before sculpting the planes, defining the features, and finally, unifying all of the elements with texture and fine detail. The overall result is a moody yet bright, realistic portrait. Painting a human face is not easy, but if you regularly practice steps 01-14 and study the Asaro head, you will soon be able to successfully draw any face. Take it one step at a time and remember that convincing form should always come before lines and detail.

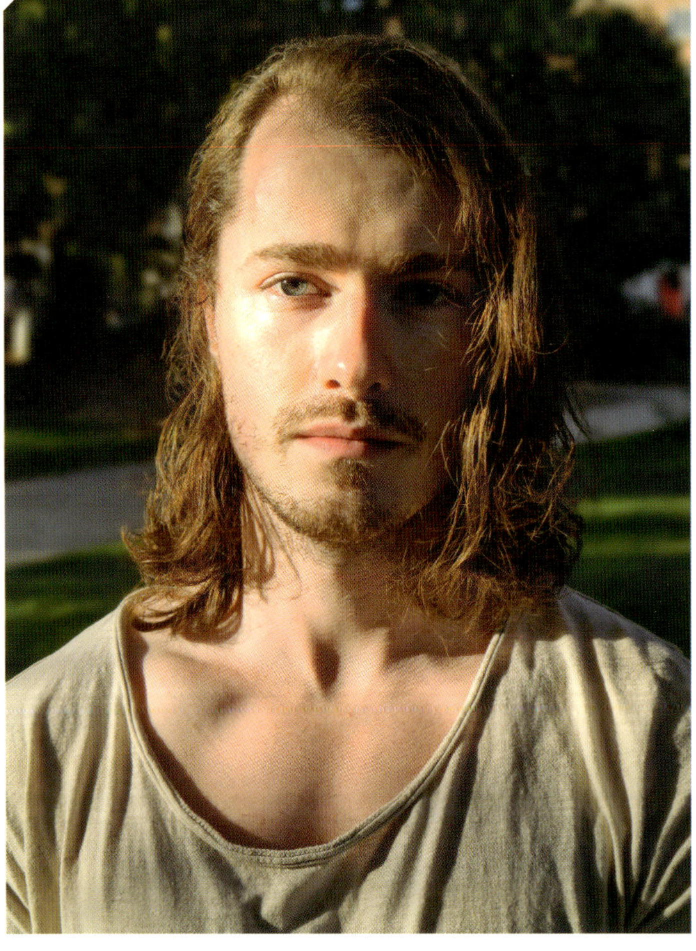

Photograph © Astri Lohne

Final image © Astri Lohne

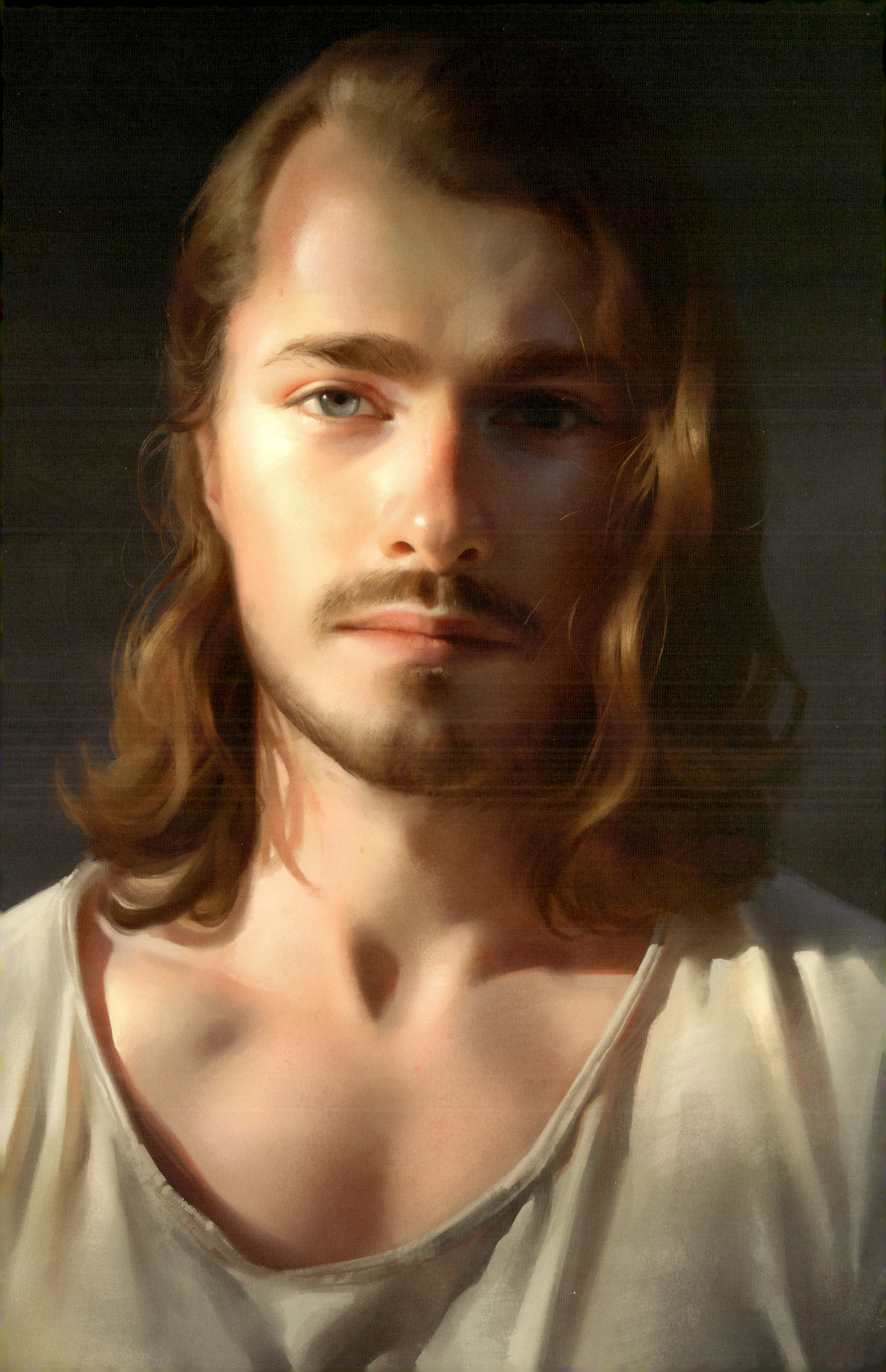

JUSTINE S. FLORENTINO

Introduction

This tutorial will guide you through how to paint a portrait from a photo reference. While this portrait has been created using Clip Studio Paint, you can follow along using any digital software or traditional media of your choosing. You will learn how to analyze a reference photo and translate it into a painting, "translate" being the keyword. You will not be matching it pixel by pixel. Instead this tutorial will explore techniques you can use to simplify and analyze your subject in order to better understand realism and portrait painting.

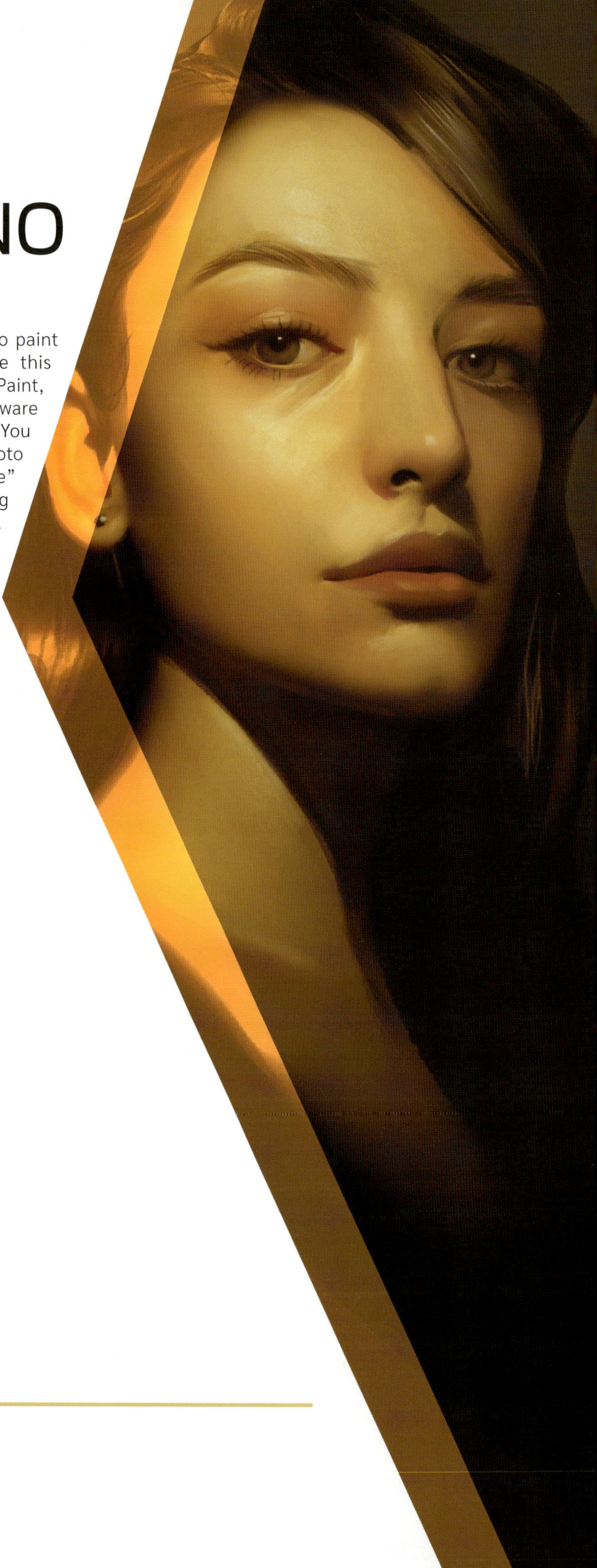

01

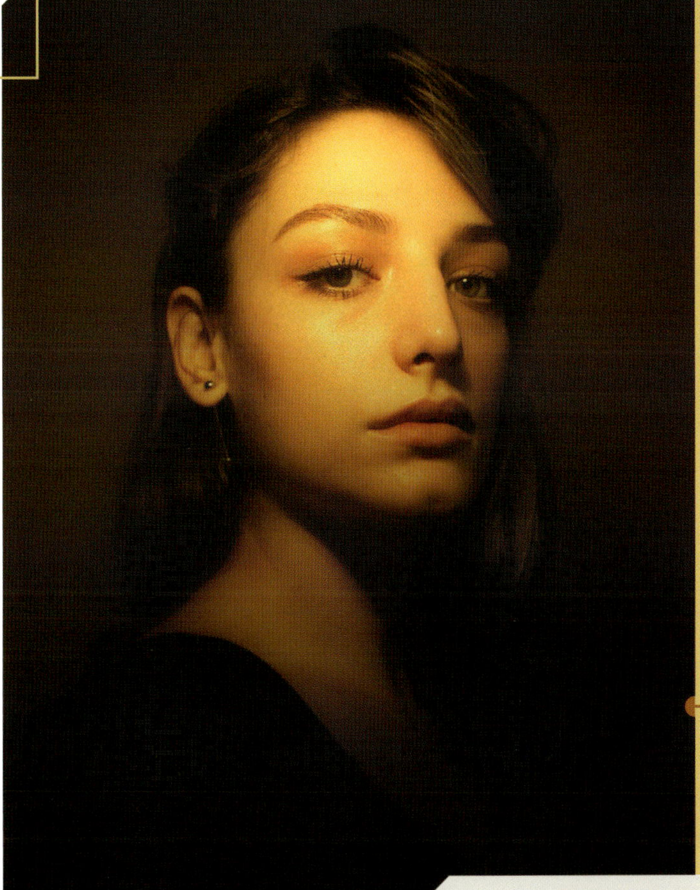

While there is no right or wrong photograph to use as a reference, there are a few key factors that will help in creating a more successful painting. The first element to look out for in a potential reference photo is a clear separation of light and shadow areas. Secondly, it's wise to choose a photo where the facial features are not overly blurry, as unclear areas can lead to a lot of guesswork. You should also consider the emotion of your potential subject, as well as the overall mood or theme of the image.

Start by choosing a clear reference photo with a good separation of shadow and light

Photograph © Natalia Jaclin Kareta

02

This tutorial will be completed digitally, using a drawing tablet plus a basic round brush, soft airbrush, and pencil brush. These simple brushes are available in most digital painting software, or you can choose similar brushes if using traditional media to create a similar brushstroke. Selecting a few simple tools will help to make your venture into portrait painting a little less daunting.

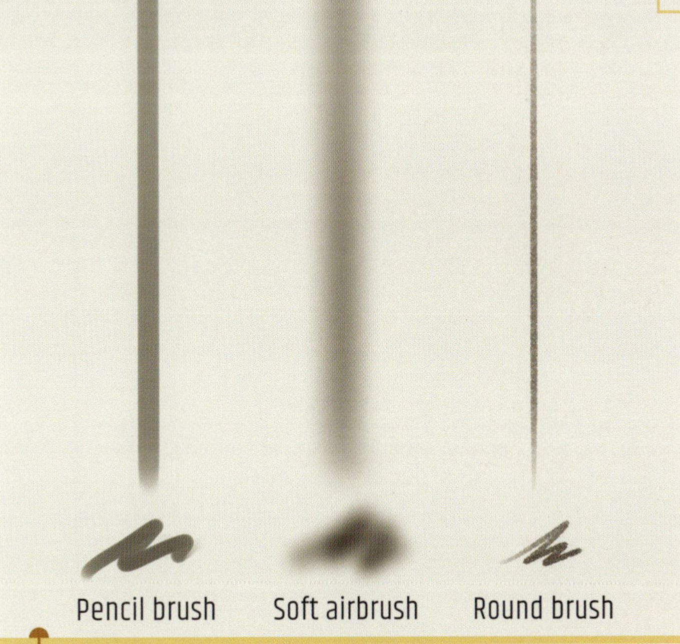

Beginners to portraiture should select a small number of simple brushes, whether digital or traditional

03

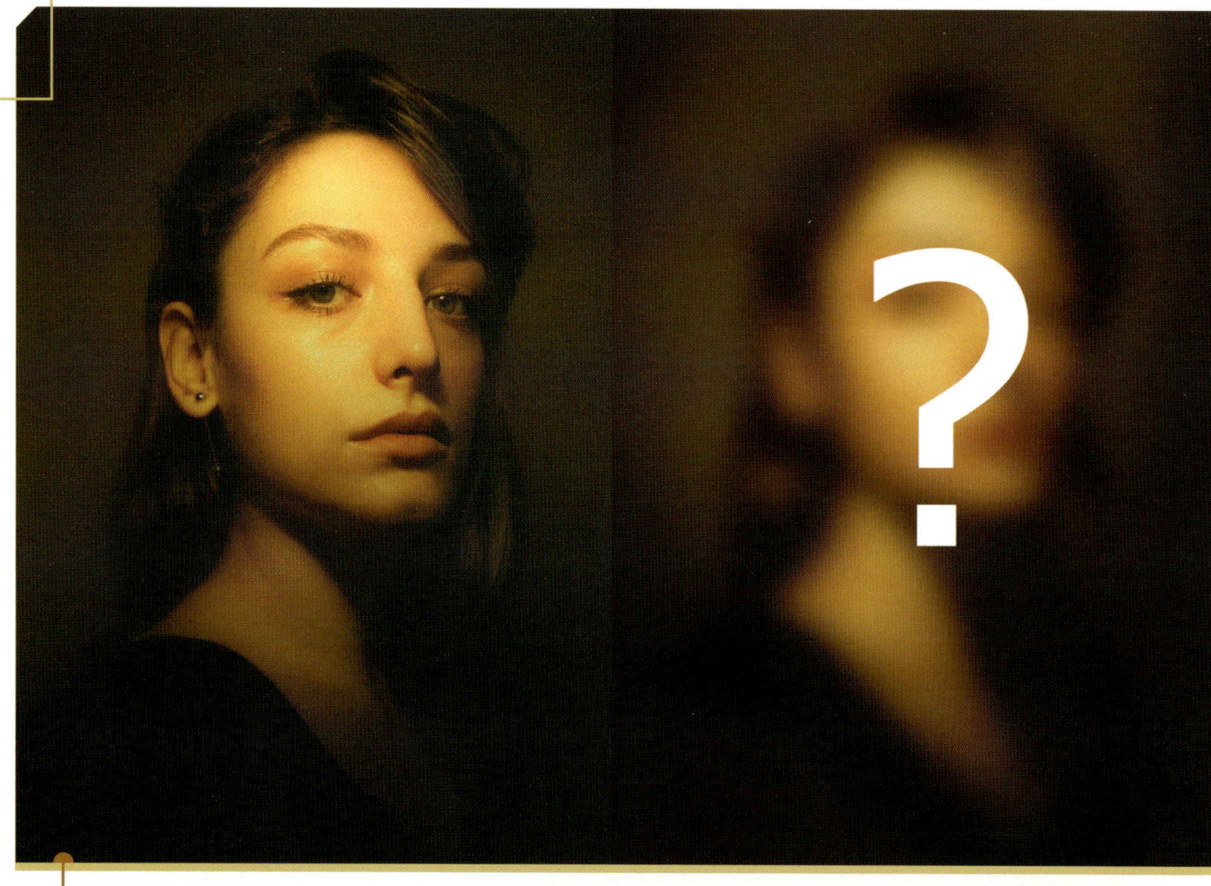

Consider what you are looking to achieve with your portrait

Before you put brush to canvas, ask yourself what you want to achieve through the portrait. Is it merely a learning exercise and way of improving? Or are you planning a grand masterpiece to show off your newly acquired portraiture skills? Do you want to play it safe or experiment with new ideas, techniques, or textures? It will help you to form a clear idea of want you want from the artwork before you begin.

Artist tip

Painting practice portrait studies is a great way to improve your skills and grow in confidence with painting faces from reference. The more faces you draw, the better you will become at capturing their likeness.

04

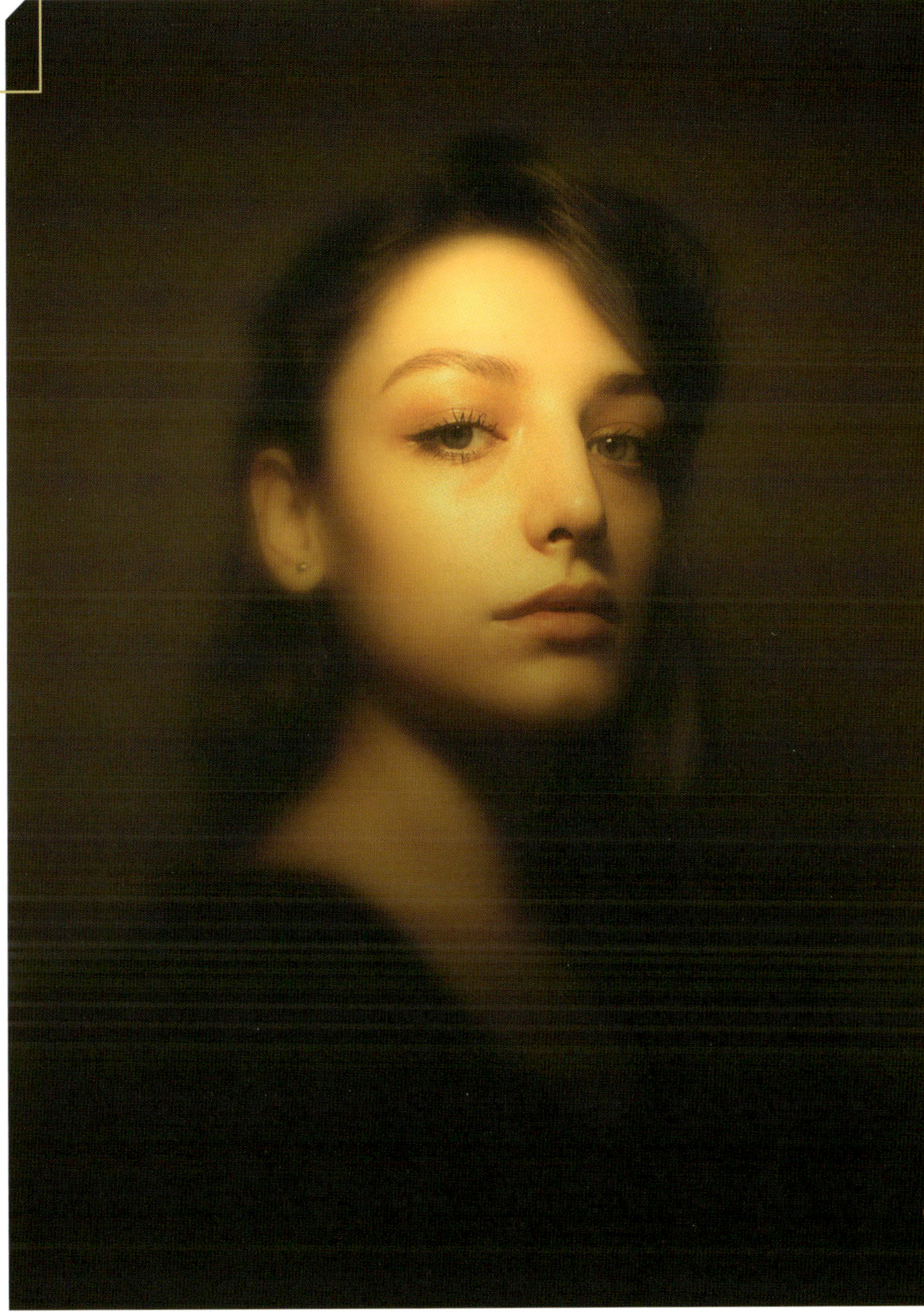

A representation of what the reference photo looks like when viewed through squinted eyes

Take some time to study the reference photo closely. Observe each facial feature in turn and the relationship they have to one another. Try to develop the simplest and most clear idea of the image in your head. One method for doing this is to look at the reference photo while squinting. Slightly closing your eyes in this way will allow you to view the photo with less detail and is an easy method for viewing the photo in its simplest form with a clear expression of light and shadow. Return to this whenever you feel overwhelmed by detail and need to take it back to basics.

05

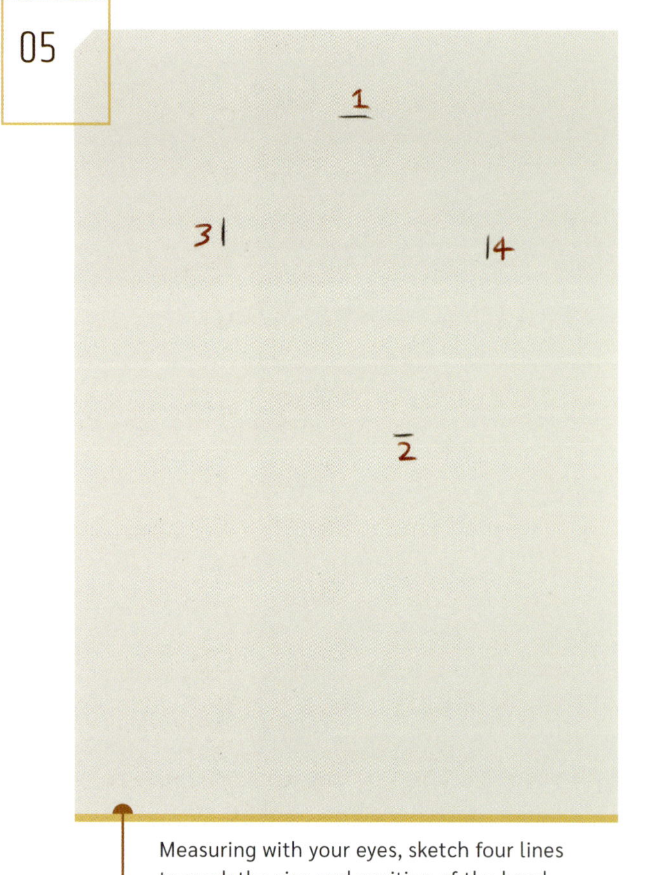

Measuring with your eyes, sketch four lines to mark the size and position of the head

Use a pencil brush, or traditional pencil, to establish the size and placement of the subject's head on the canvas. Start by making four marks. Don't guess at the distance of these, but study the reference photo and measure with your eyes. The first mark should note the highest point of the subject's hair. A few inches down from the top of the canvas, draw a second mark for the base of the chin. Sketch a third mark for the leftmost part of the hair, followed by a fourth mark for the rightmost part of the hair. These four marks will help you to place the subject on the canvas and act as a relative measuring point as needed.

06

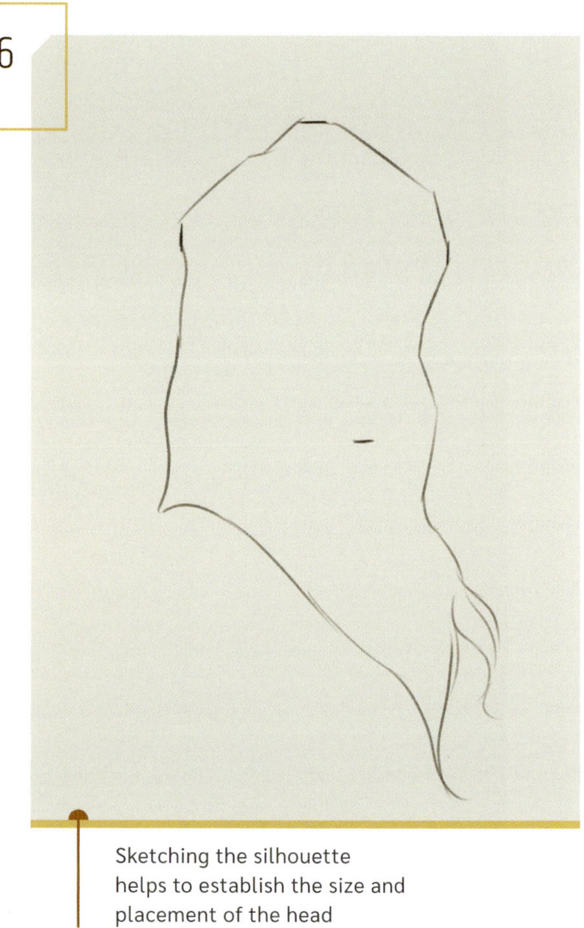

Sketching the silhouette helps to establish the size and placement of the head

To draw the silhouette of the subject's head, squint your eyes to view the reference photo in less detail and identify the biggest shapes. Sketch a diagonal line from the first mark to the fourth mark to connect them, then sketch a diagonal line left from the first mark to the third mark. Moving downward, sketch a curved line jutting outward slightly, simplifying the shape of the subject's hair from her ear. Going upward slightly, sketch a slightly curved line (like an "S" curve) for the clothing, though you can ignore the majority of the clothing for now. From the "S" curve of the neckline and clothing, sketch the shape of the hair in shadow on the right, then continue to create part of her shirt and hair. Continue drawing the line upwards to a bulging curve at the fourth mark to complete the silhouette.

07

Once you have established the silhouette, begin to sketch the face shape, starting with the jawline. Starting from the second mark, which indicated the chin, draw a line that curves upward to the left, but make sure not to pass the third mark. Check to see if you have drawn this in the correct position by looking at it in relation to the first four marks and comparing it with the reference photo. Next, return to the chin mark and sketch an upward curve to the right toward the fourth mark. Keep referring back to the reference photo to ensure you have captured the angle of the jawline, and where it ends, correctly.

Draw in the jawline

08

The next step is to draw the hairline. Squint your eyes and look at the reference photo again to identify the main shapes of the subject's hair, ignoring any smaller strands. Use a round brush to sketch out the main shape of the hairline. Locate where the face ends and the hair begins, deferring to the first four marks placed in step 05. Next, sketch the neck area and draw the silhouette of the ear, as these shapes meet the hairline and therefore need to be established as well.

Sketch in the hairline to separate the face from the hair

09

Locate the central point of the face by sketching a slightly curved line down the center. This is not the center of the reference photo, but the center of the actual face. It should run from the center of the forehead, down the center of the nose and lips, down to the chin. It can help to imagine this line as like the center seam or line on a ball, as the face and head are not flat, but three-dimensional.

Draw the center line of the face

10

The next step is to find the placement of the facial features. Imagine the face as split into thirds. The first third reaches from the top of the forehead down to the lowest point of the eyebrows. The second third covers the lowest point of the eyebrows to the base of the nose. And the final third extends from the base of the nose to the base of the chin. Keep this in mind every time you draw a face, especially when drawing from life or a reference photo. This will help to anchor your piece in realism.

Study the reference photo, then divide the face into thirds

11

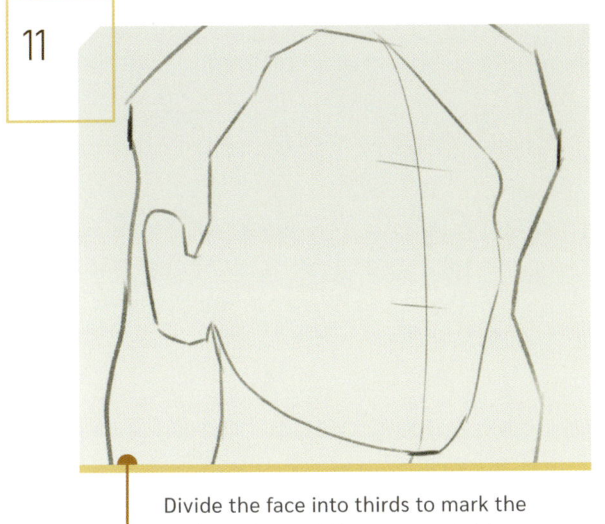

Divide the face into thirds to mark the eyebrow, base of the nose, and chin

Look at your sketch of the face and consider how to divide it into three almost equal parts. Use the marks made earlier as a guide; look at where they are positioned and use this information to locate the three sections. In this image, the fourth mark (made in step 05) sits just above the eyebrow, therefore the eyebrow line should sit just below it. Use the pencil brush to sketch a short horizontal line through the center line to note this. Next is the line to indicate the base of the nose. Measure the distance from the forehead to eyebrow line, then measure the same amount downward. Mark this spot to note the base of the nose, again using a short horizontal line through the center line. If you have placed these first two lines correctly, then the eyebrow, base of the nose, and chin should all be an equal distance apart.

12

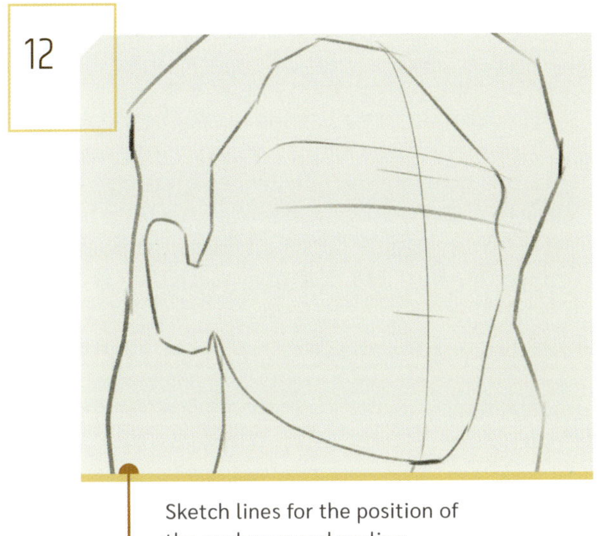

Sketch lines for the position of the eyebrows and eyeline

Use the mark you just made for the lowest point of the eyebrow as a reference point to find the angle of the eyebrow. In the reference photo, the left brow is slightly higher than the right, and therefore you need to draw this line at a slight tilt. Using the pencil brush, start from the left side and sketch to the right, passing through the center line. Ensure the line is confident and uninterrupted, ignoring any detail for the time being.

The placement of the brow line will make it much easier to draw the eyeline. Looking at the reference photo, you can see that the eye is positioned under the eyebrows, slightly higher than the ear. Sketch a small mark on the center line to indicate the point where you will place the eyeline, before sketching the full horizontal line from left to right. Take into account the height of both eyes and how they compare; the line should pass through the pupils of both eyes.

Artist tip

Be mindful of the lines you make and have confidence when making them. A good practice is to "ghost" the stroke first, acting the motion of the stroke just above the canvas before applying pressure and actually drawing it. This will familiarize your arm with the motion you are about to make. Familiarity plus actions develops confidence.

13

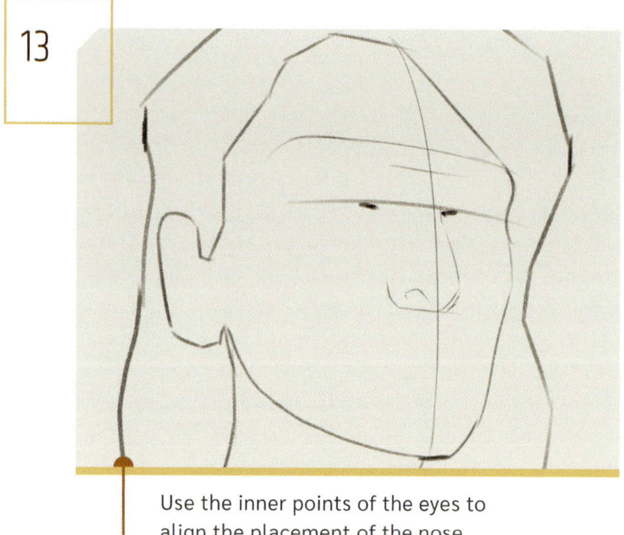

Use the inner points of the eyes to align the placement of the nose

Before you can locate the nose, you must first mark the inner corners of the eyes, also known as the tear ducts. Study the reference photo to see where they sit on the face, using the marks you have already placed on the canvas as a guide. Once you have sketched two small marks for the inner corners of the eyes, use small brushstrokes to align the sides of the nose. Taking note of the mark made in step 11 that indicated the base of the nose, sketch a small "V" shape, before marking where the nostrils will be.

14

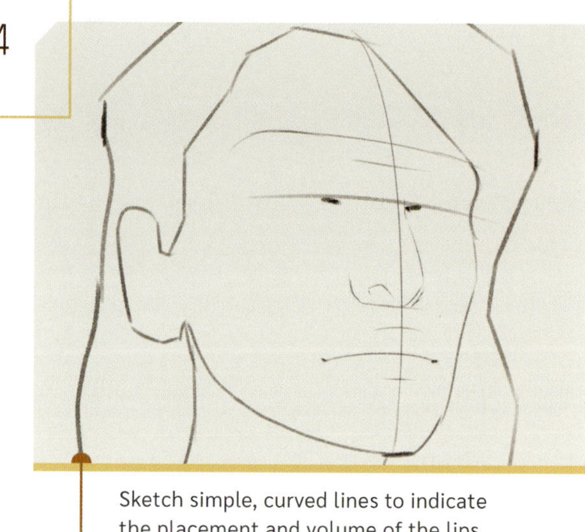

Sketch simple, curved lines to indicate the placement and volume of the lips

Use the pencil brush to mark the top of the upper lip and central horizontal line of the mouth. Looking at the reference photo, you can see how the middle line of the mouth sits almost perfectly in the center of the two marks noting the base of the nose and chin. When locating the corners of the mouth, look at the marks made for the corners of the eyes in step 13 and compare the alignment of these to achieve the best approximation of the relationships between the features. Next, sketch a line for the base of the lower lip, which will help to indicate their volume.

15

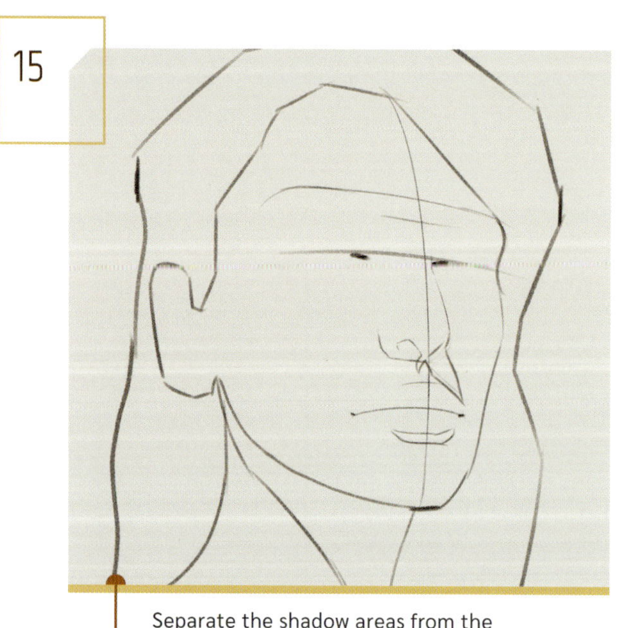

Separate the shadow areas from the light areas using simple lines and shapes

Now you have positioned the features, you can begin to identify and map out the shadow areas. Begin with the largest patch of shadow visible in the reference photo: the neck area, starting at the corner of the base of the ear. Using a round brush, draw a diagonal line to convey the shadow the chin casts on the neck. For the lower lip area, sketch a small semi-circle shape that echoes the curvature of the lower lip, before moving slightly to the right to create a curved line. The light shines from the upper left in the reference photo, so the shadows cast by the facial features will fall on the right side of the face. When sketching these shadow shapes, consider the forms casting them. For the nose area, sketch another diagonal starting from the base of the nose to create a triangular shape.

16

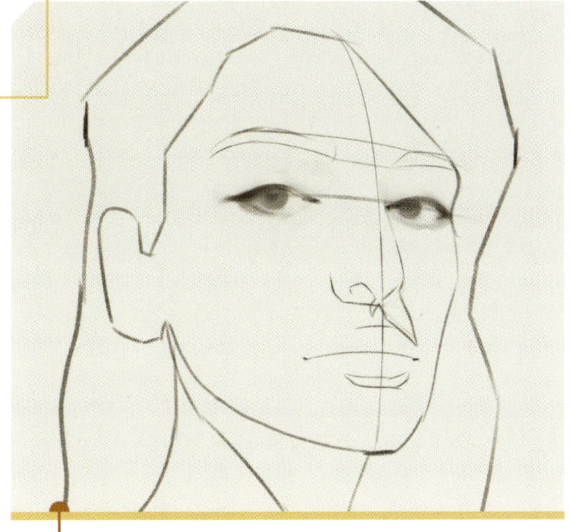

Mark the darkest parts of the eye, then sketch the eyebrows above them

Focus in on the eye area. Use the soft airbrush, or similar traditional tool, to mark the corners of the eyes. Note that the upper eyelids cast a shadow and, along with the eyelashes, create a darker area that you can count in the shadow family. This shading will help when you come to fully paint and detail the eyes. Although not a shadow shape, mark spots to indicate the darker parts of the eye, such as the iris and pupil. Next, sketch out the rough shape of the eyebrows. Studying the reference photo, you can see that the eyebrows sit at a certain angle, complementary to the shape of the eyes. Continually refer back to the reference when positioning features on the face to ensure you locate them correctly.

17

Move on to the hair. Starting from the top of the head, use the round brush to begin to form the shape, building up the form using multiple brushstrokes. Focus on laying down the big, dark shapes first, ignoring detail or smaller strands until later. Moving down toward the right of the face, fill in the negative space created by the outer silhouette and inner lines used to indicate the shadows. After creating this large shadow shape, turn to the left side of the face and locate the shadow on the section of hair beneath the left ear. Remember to squint your eyes to help you see the main shadow shapes more clearly. Moving upward, identify and mark the shadow shapes of the inner ear. The deeper into the ear, the deeper the shadows will be. You can add a darker tone to the side of the face here too.

Next, move down to the neck area and shade the shape of the subject's clothing. Using the round brush to cover a larger area, create a sharp angled shape from her upper neck down to the lower parts of her neck.

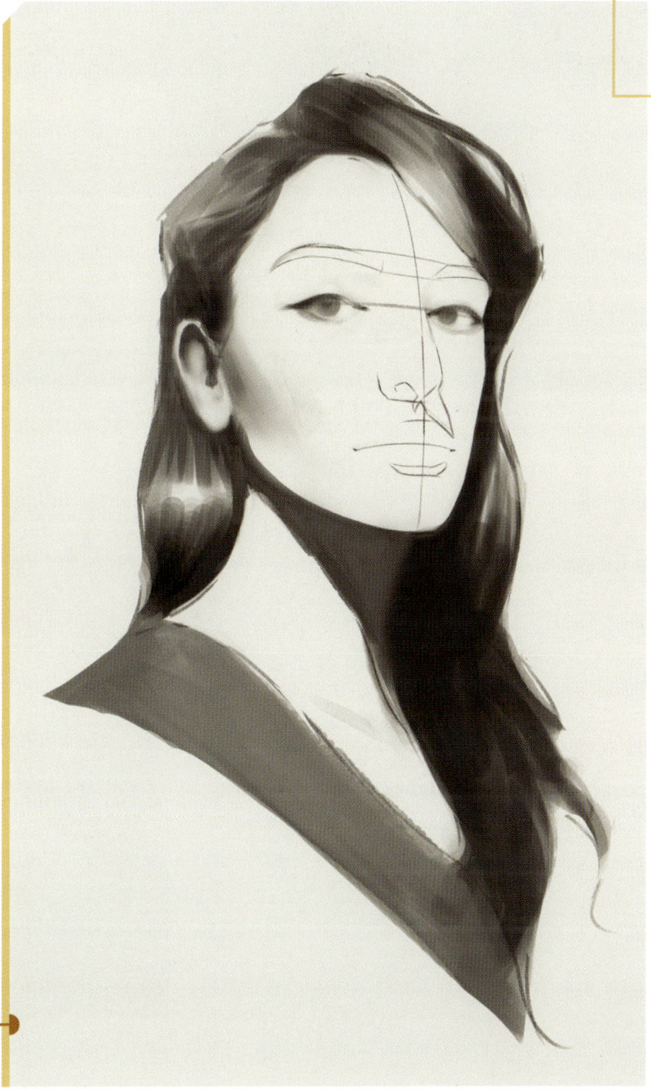

Block in the hair, shadows, and clothing

18

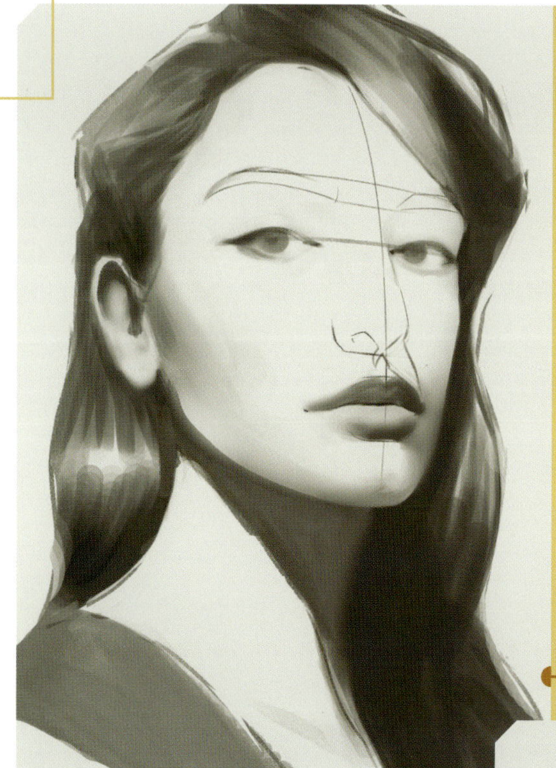

After filling in the shadows of the hair, it's time to create the shape and volume of the lips. Use the round brush to paint the darkest parts. The upper lip is in shadow, so shade this area with the value used for the shadow shapes. Ensure you follow the lines created in step 14 and remember to squint your eyes to help identify the main shadow areas. Don't forget the small "V" shape, or Cupid's bow, of the upper lip that echoes the shape of the philtrum (the central groove that runs from the upper lip to the base of the nose). Moving downward, find the mark you made earlier to indicate the shadow below the lower lip. As this is a cast shadow, it will create a hard edge. The shadow next to the lower lip will have a form shadow, which is a softer edge. A soft airbrush is perfect for these, as you can create the different shapes and edges by controlling the pressure with which you paint the tones.

Use shadow to create more volume on the lips

19

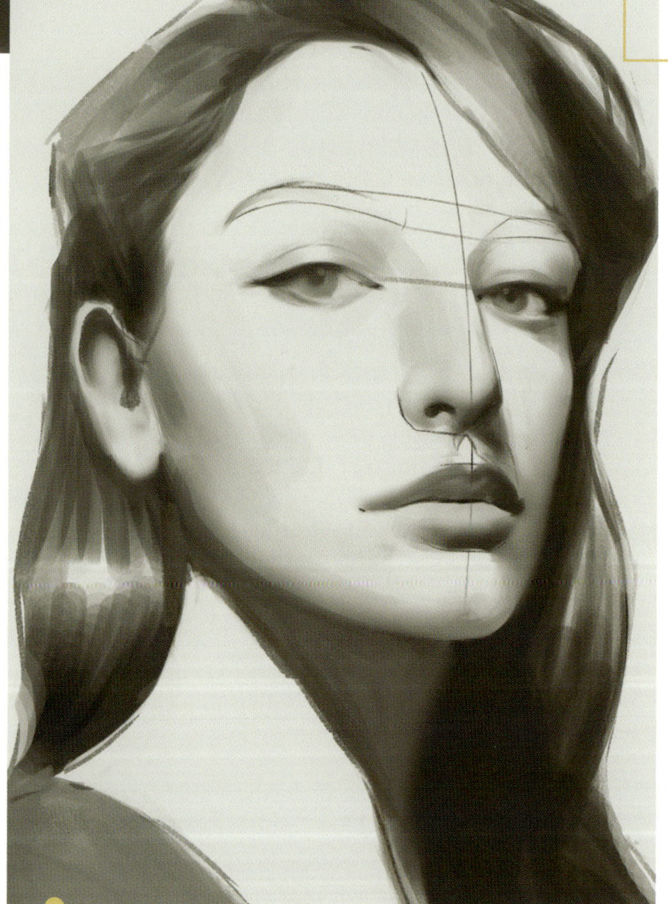

Paint in shadows and volume for the nose, as well as shadows at the jaw and eye socket

The next step is to develop the shape and volume of the nose. As you did for the lips in the previous step, use the lines made in step 13 as a guide to help you identify the areas where you need to softly paint in shadow. This will include the nostrils and the triangular shape on the right-hand side of the face. Observe the soft form shadow that sits on top of the nose, starting at the base, and use the round brush to achieve this soft transition. Next, paint a slightly darker tone at the bridge or the upper part of the nose.

Move on to the right-hand side of her face, which is mostly in shadow. Use a soft airbrush, or similar traditional tool, to darken the areas next to the shadows of the lips and nose, following the shadow shapes you observe on the reference. For the left-hand side of the jaw, paint a tone that creates a soft transition, as the transition between the jaw and base of the jaw is not a sharp turn. Next, paint the areas near the eyes a slightly darker value to create a sense of depth, as the eye sockets are concave, curving inward into the head.

20

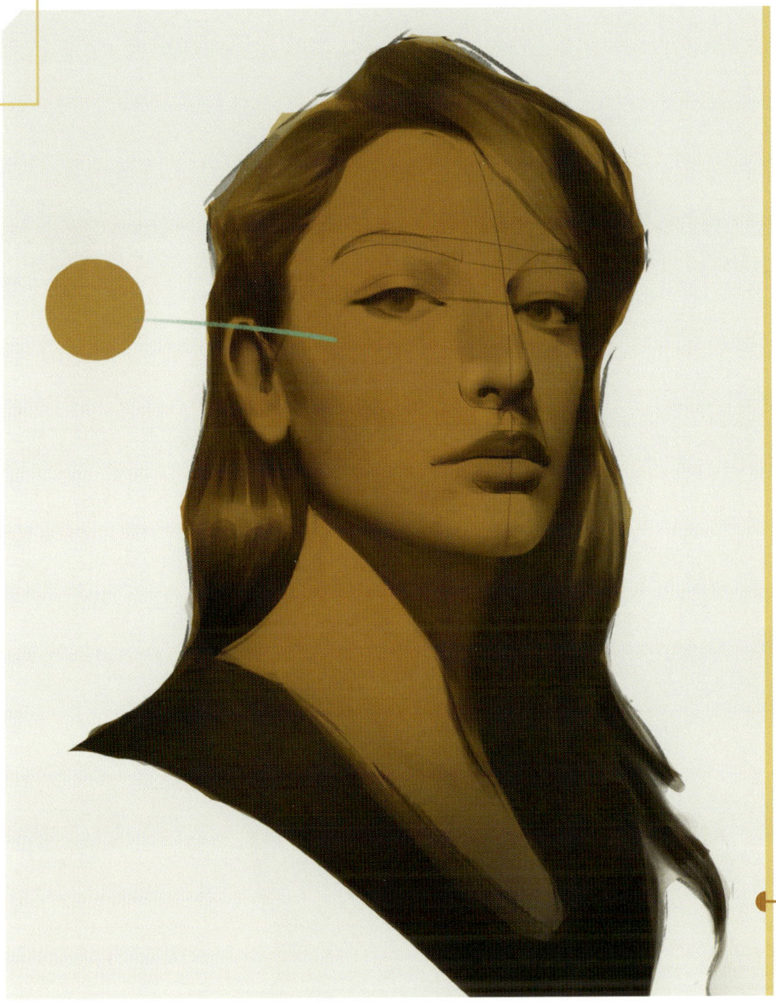

Lay down the base colors; this will help with the rendering process, as part of the halftone will already be done

Once you have defined the areas of shadow, start to lay down the base colors. If using digital software to create your portrait, use this to your advantage by selecting the Multiply layer blend mode on the drawing layer. Next, create a new layer beneath the drawing layer on which to paint the base tones. Here a warm ochre color has been chosen, reflecting the colors of the reference photo. If using traditional media instead, simply reverse the process and paint your base colors first, before drawing on top.

Artist tip

Value is the term used to describe how light or dark something is. Higher value means it is lighter, while lower value denotes it is darker. Finding the correct value for your portrait will anchor it in realism and make it appear more believable. If the values of your portrait are correct, you can use whatever colors you like. The color palette for this portrait is based on the colors present in the reference photo. Color can be interpreted in many ways to convey emotion, mood, and theme. It's open for experimentation and can drastically shift the overall look and mood of a portrait.

21

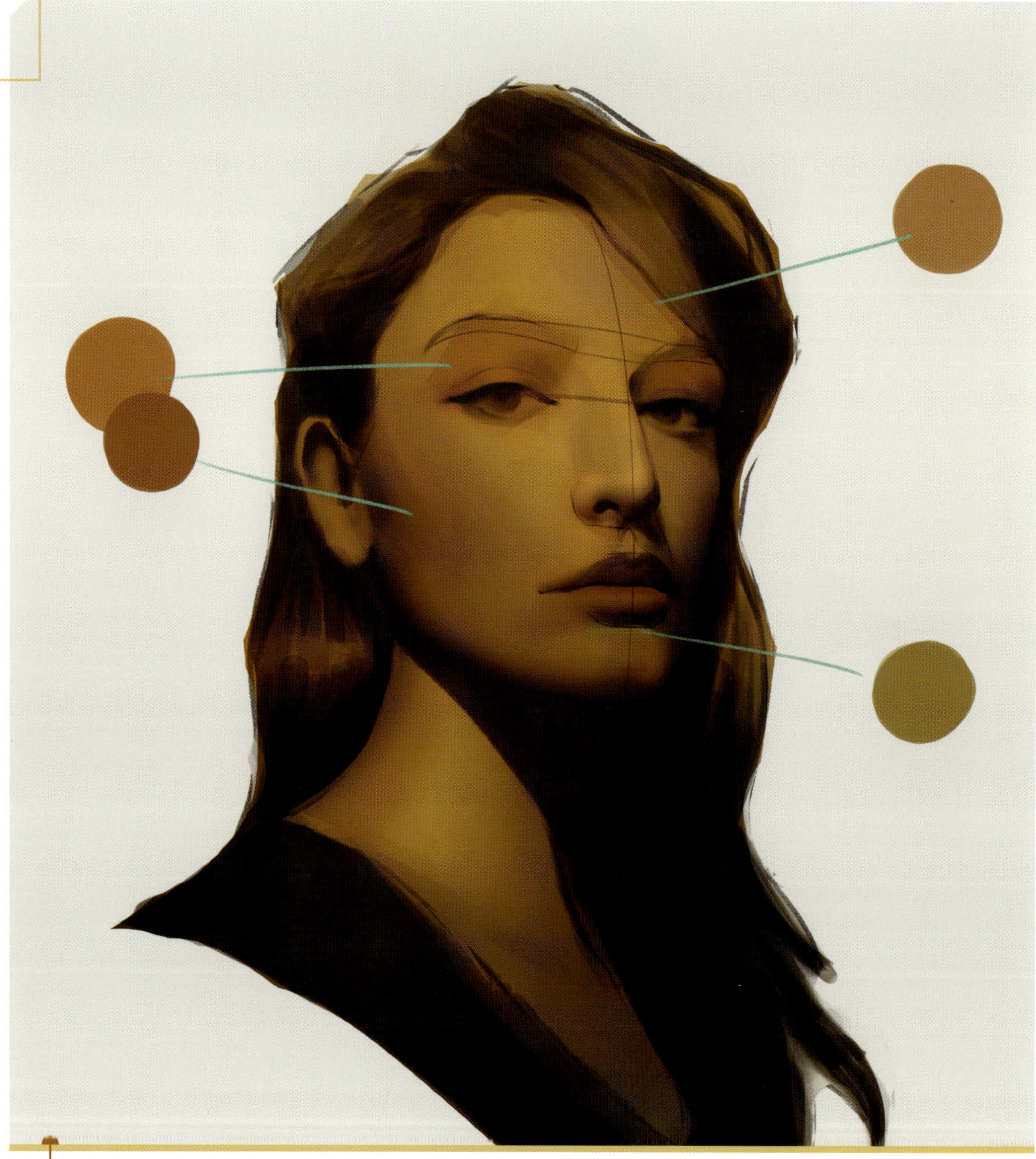

Paint the different color zones to convey shadow and variety in skin tone

Once you have painted the base tone, start to paint the different color zones. These convey the variety in the skin tone, as skin is never purely one color. There are many factors that can alter the way skin tone appears, from lighting to makeup. Use this small selection of ochre colors to define the halftones of the subject's face. Next, use a soft airbrush to paint reddish tones on the hair. Moving to the eye area, use a round brush to paint orange tones under the brow. Next, paint reddish tones along the jaw area, followed by a subtle green tone beneath the lower lip. This will help to make the red of the lips stand out, as green is the natural contrast to red. These are only the base colors, many of which will be painted over later in the process.

22

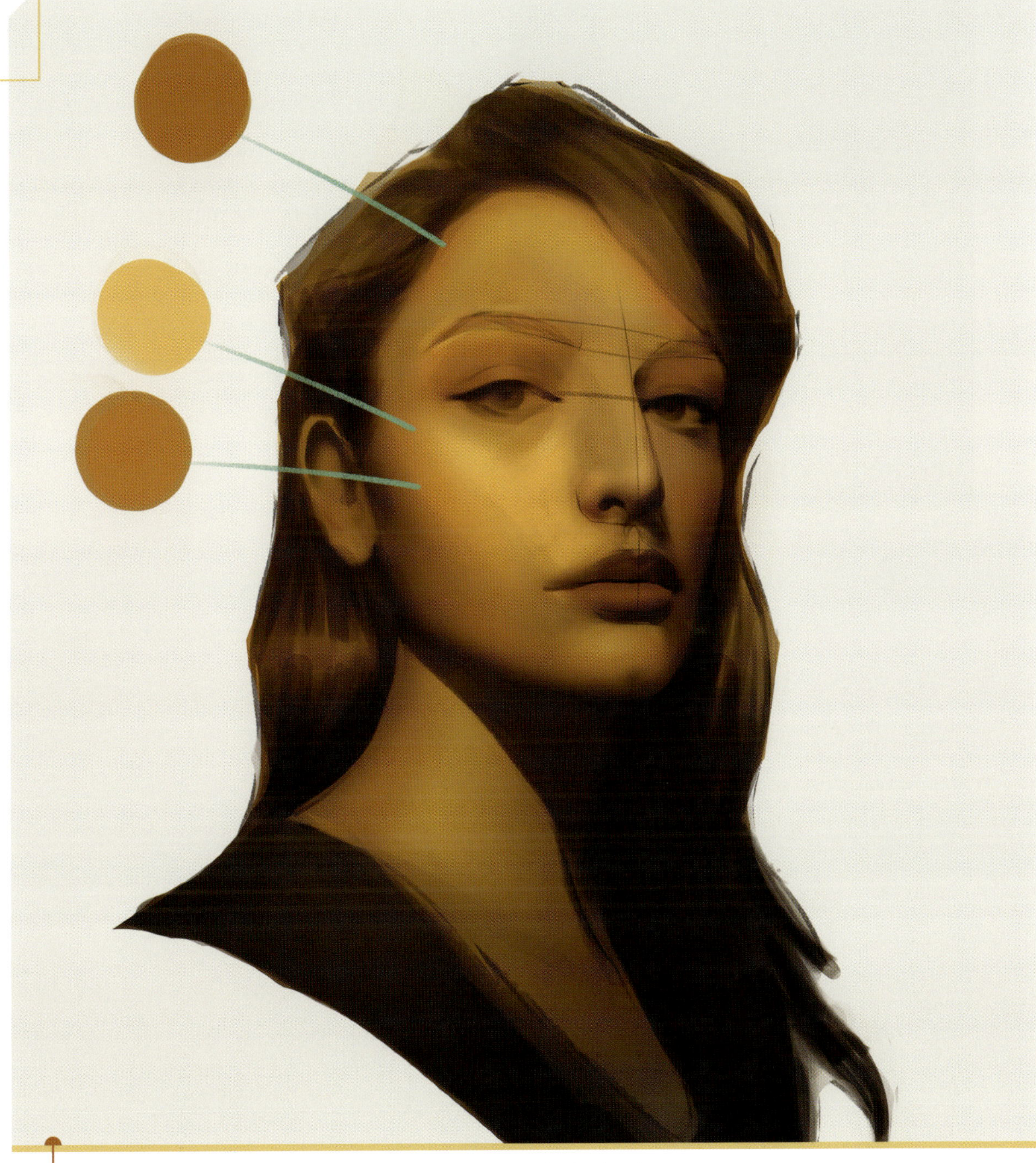

Increase the value of the painting by using colors with a higher brightness

Once the base colors and a few color zones have been painted, create a new layer above both the drawing and base color layer, if using digital software. If working traditionally, you can simply paint straight on top of them. This step involves contouring the face with colors found in the reference photo and is reminiscent of applying makeup. These are lighter halftones that add more volume to the face. Starting at the top of the hair, use a soft airbrush, or similar tool, to paint a tone near to where the hair and skin meet to convey the curve of the form and show it's not flat. Next, paint similar tones on the cheeks, adding a small amount of a lighter color toward the upper cheek area. These are very soft tones, so be mindful of the amount of pressure you apply on your brush.

23

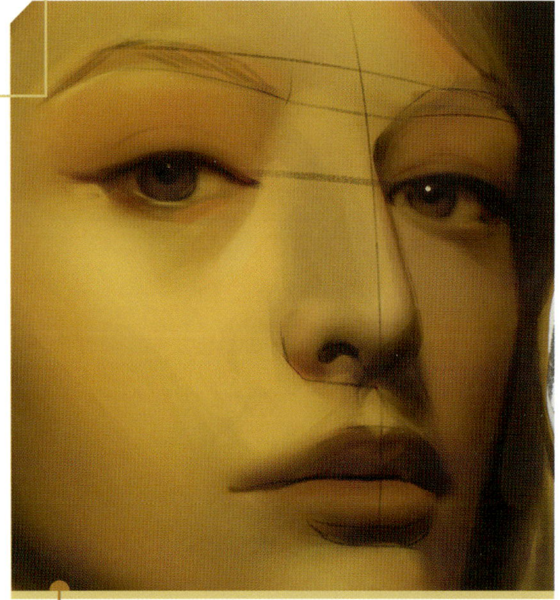

Begin to detail the eyes, adding color and a highlight

Using a round brush, paint a darker, more defined shape for the dark areas of the eyes. Create the colors of the eyes using circular brushstrokes, referring back to the color palette of the reference photo. When studying the subject's eyes, they appear to be as dark as shadows, but here is the importance of defining the values and identifying the darkest darks. As you have already established the shadows as the darkest value, you can use colors that are close to the value of black, but not pure black. Use your own artistic interpretation here, as some parts of the iris are indeed in shadow. You can either blend them together to create a lost edge (see page 72 for more on lost edges), or define them further to separate each part. This tutorial will utilize both approaches. Looking at the reference photo while squinting, you will see that parts of the left eye start to blend into shadow. You can therefore allow this eye to do just this, while keeping the right-hand eye as the focal point. Next, use a round brush to paint a small amount of white onto the eyeball for the highlight.

24

The nose is made up of varied shapes and planes. This tutorial will focus on the ones you can easily see and simplify. Starting at the base of the nose, use the round brush to create a soft diagonal toward the upper right section of the nose where the shadow meets the light. This shape will create the soft transition of shadow beneath the nose. Next, add more definition to the nostrils. The reference provides a clear view of the shape of the nostrils, which are not simply round holes. Observe how they are positioned underneath the subject's nose. To simplify it, think of each nostril as a sideways bean that has a tapering end toward the middle of the nose. Choose a dark shade of red to color them, as while the nostrils are in shadow, a hint of red will suggest a small amount of light seeping through from the skin.

Apply more color and detail to the nose and nostrils

25

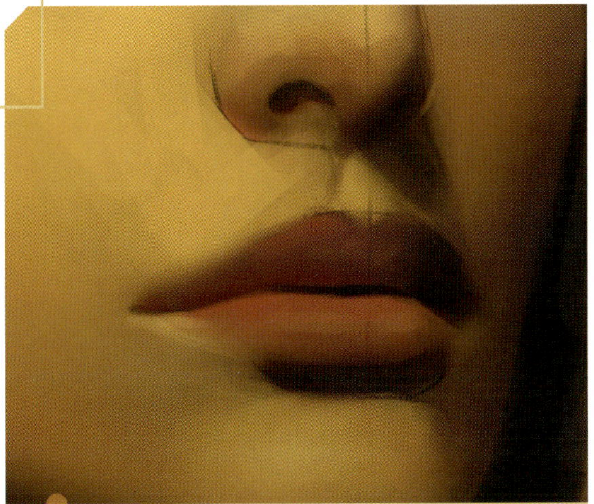

Paint the lips with color, making them appear soft

Moving down from the nose to the mouth, you find the philtrum. Paint a simple shadow shape for this, but avoid making it too dark or it will look a little off. Choose a color that is a slightly darker value than the halftones, with a hint of red once again. For the upper lip, paint a tone that is slightly darker than the base color used for the lips. Shape it to create a hard edge where the upper and lower lips meet, with a softer edge on top. Use the round brush to slowly build up a soft graduation on the sides of the mouth. Remember that these are not hard edges; make them soft and so they appear slightly curved. For the lower lips, use the round brush to create three shapes. Two should be slightly reddish, while the middle shape should be closer in value to the base skin tone. Study the shapes closely and observe how they interact with each other. The aim here is to make the lips look soft.

26

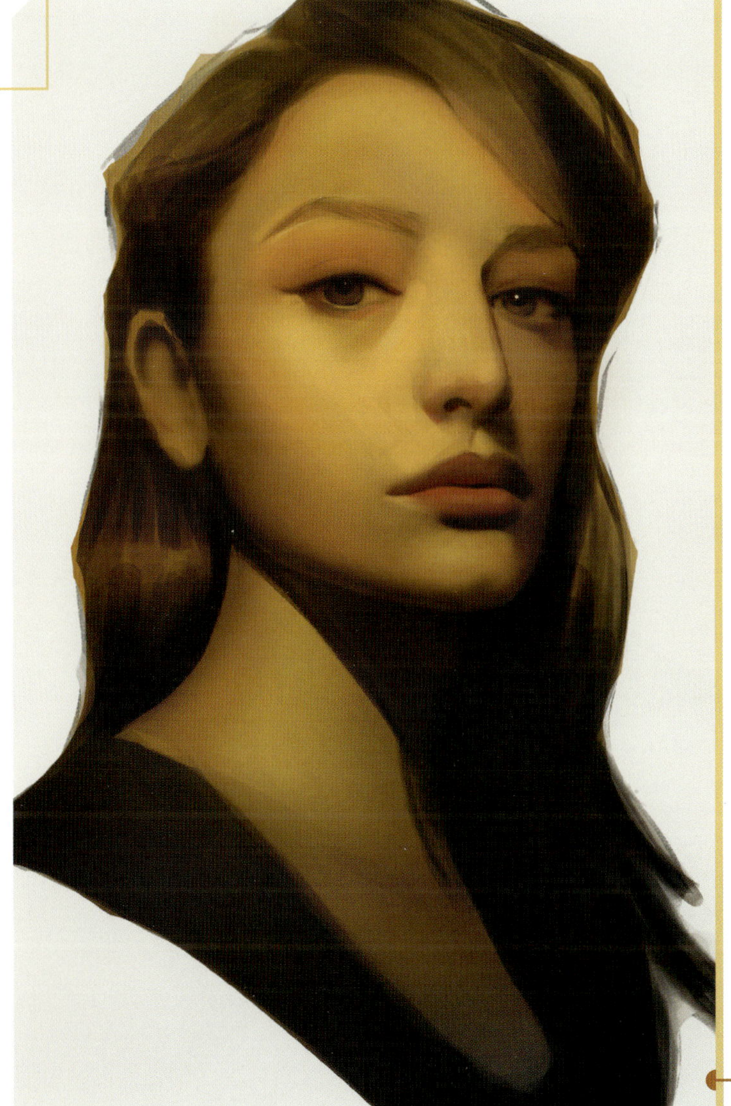

Studying the reference photo, you will see that the chin and jaw are mostly in shadow. You have already painted the shadow shapes for this area, so this step will focus on how to build the forms and the types of shadows that are present.

There are form shadows in the middle of the chin. These are identified by their softer edges, with no other object covering them to create a hard shadow. Looking at the reference photo, you can observe where the softness of the shadow starts from the light area. This is the terminator line; the end point of the light. Most of the time this is very dark; almost the darkest point of the shadow. Everything else past this will often contain bounce light. In the reference photo, you can observe how the jaw area has bounce light coming from the neck and upper parts of the torso. Use your round brush to paint a soft stroke on this area. Ensure it's not brighter than any of the tones in the light area, as this is the shadow area and should be darker. If working digitally, you can now hide your sketch layer, or simply erase the guidelines from the drawing phase. If using traditional media, you can erase these guidelines by hand.

Paint bounce light under the jaw, then remove the guide drawing

27

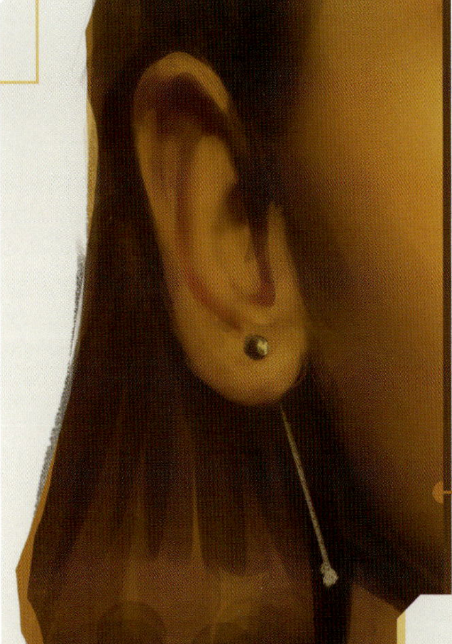

Use the round brush to paint the inner forms of the ear with halftones. Start from the inner ear, following the gentle curves observed on the subject's ear in the reference photo. Try to simplify it into basic "C" shapes within "C" shapes. Aim to create a variety of hard and soft edges within the overall shape of the ear. Switch to a smaller round brush to paint the smaller details. Next, use the round brush to paint a dark circle on the earlobe for the earring, approximately the same as in the reference photo. Paint a dot of white on top of this in the direction of the light source. Next, paint a thin line extending downward from the back of the earlobe, with a small dot at the end of it.

Detail the inner ear, then paint in the earring

28

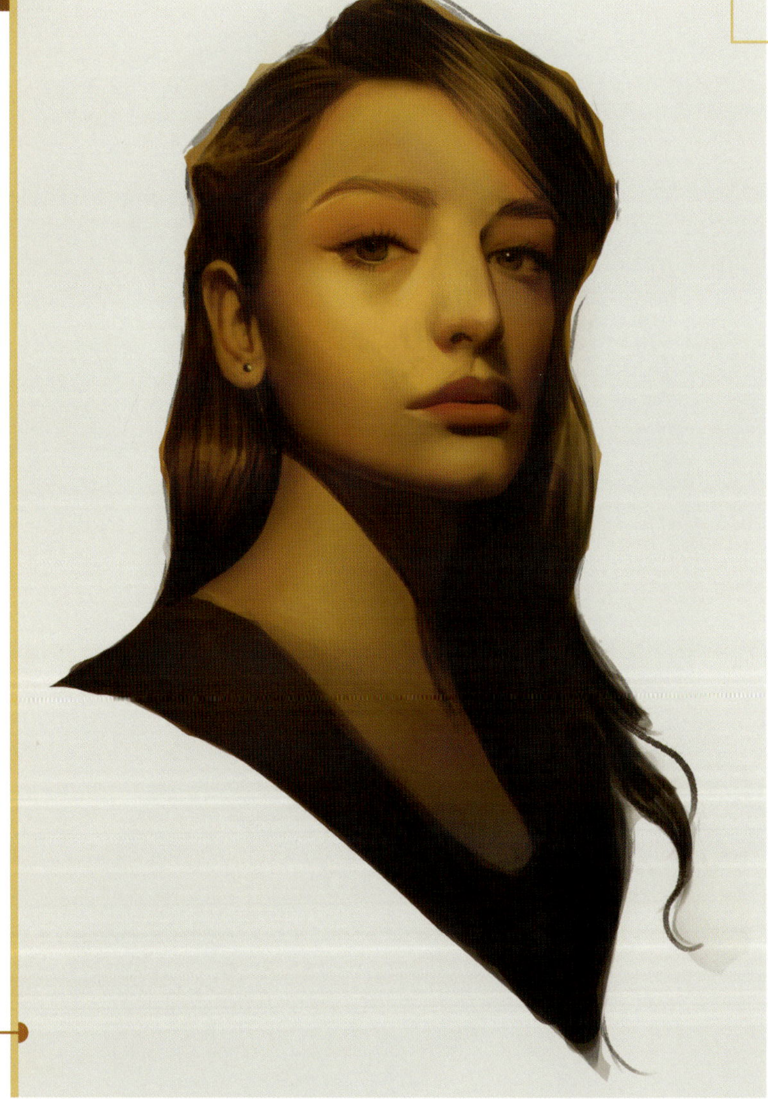

Use a round brush to block dark brown strands into the hair, referring back to the reference photo. While hair can look as dark as shadow on the reference, exaggerate these strands to a lighter value to ensure it reads well. Beginning from the top of the head, use the round brush and follow the shapes painted in the previous steps. As you have already created the silhouette and shadow shapes for the hair, this should be fairly straightforward. Follow the direction of the already established strands when painting your brushstrokes. Use multiple brushstrokes, rather than one giant stroke, to define the shapes with informed movement of the brush. A couple of stray strands will make it appear more believable.

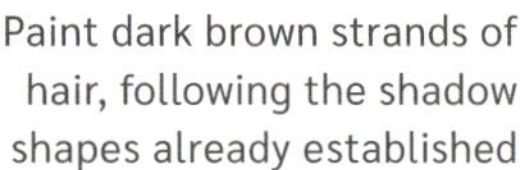

Paint dark brown strands of hair, following the shadow shapes already established

29

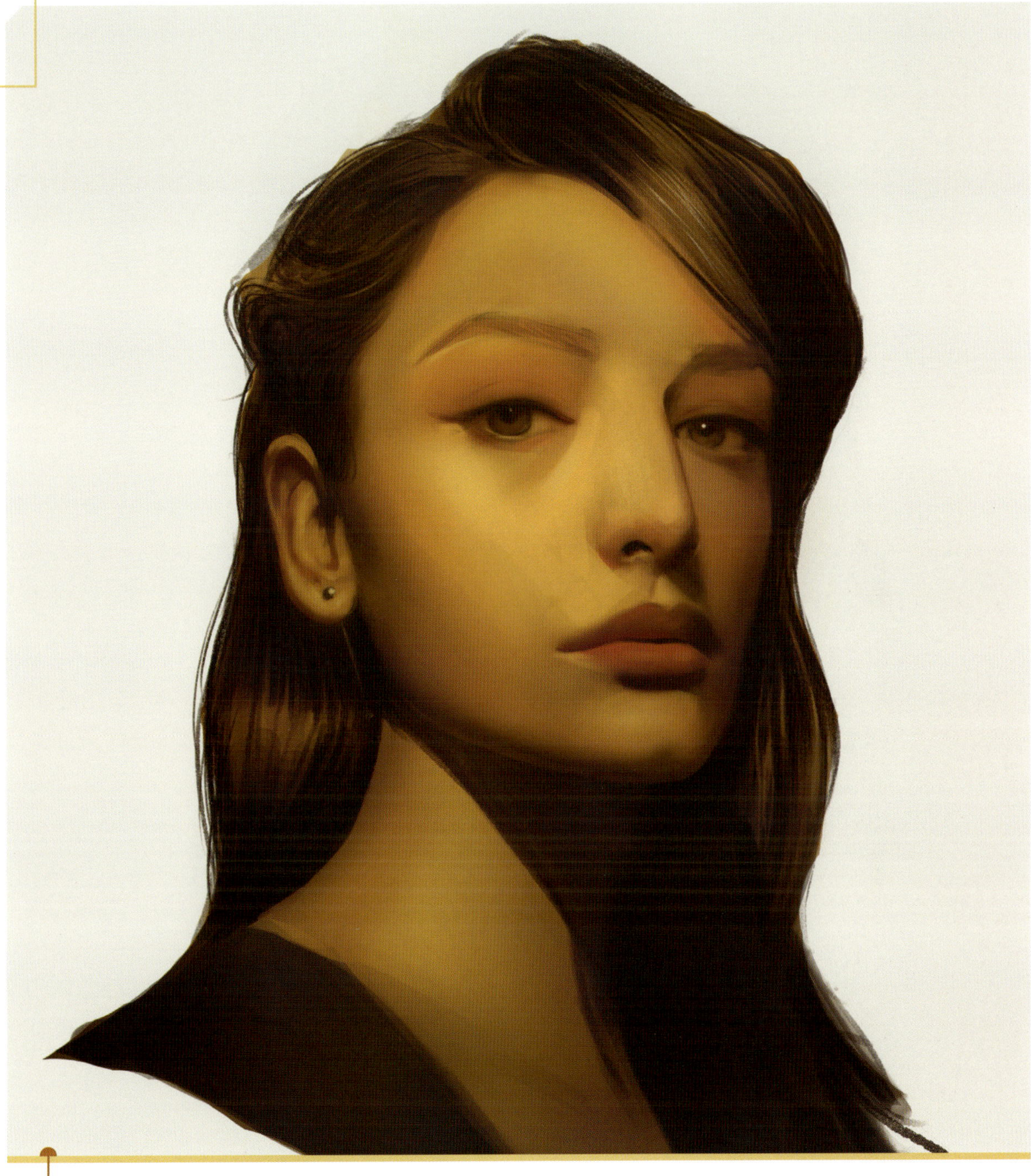

Paint highlights into the hair, introducing individual strands

Once you have built up the shapes of the hair, it's time to increase the highlights that will make the hair look like it has singular strands. Refer back to the reference photo to see where the highlights are, then use the round brush to create these bands of color. Reflecting the light source, think of the highlights as like bands on a ribbon; they should have both peaks and valleys. Take the time to identify these areas, then use the pencil brush to paint in thinner strands of highlighted hair. Paint the majority of these strands in the areas with the most detail or most light hitting them. Here, the largest highlight runs through her fringe that sits across her forehead. Take care to limit how many of these highlight strands you add, as too many will make the hair look overly cluttered. Remember to have "rest areas" with minimal detail. In this painting, the shadows act as rest areas, while the highlight areas are the points of highest detail.

30

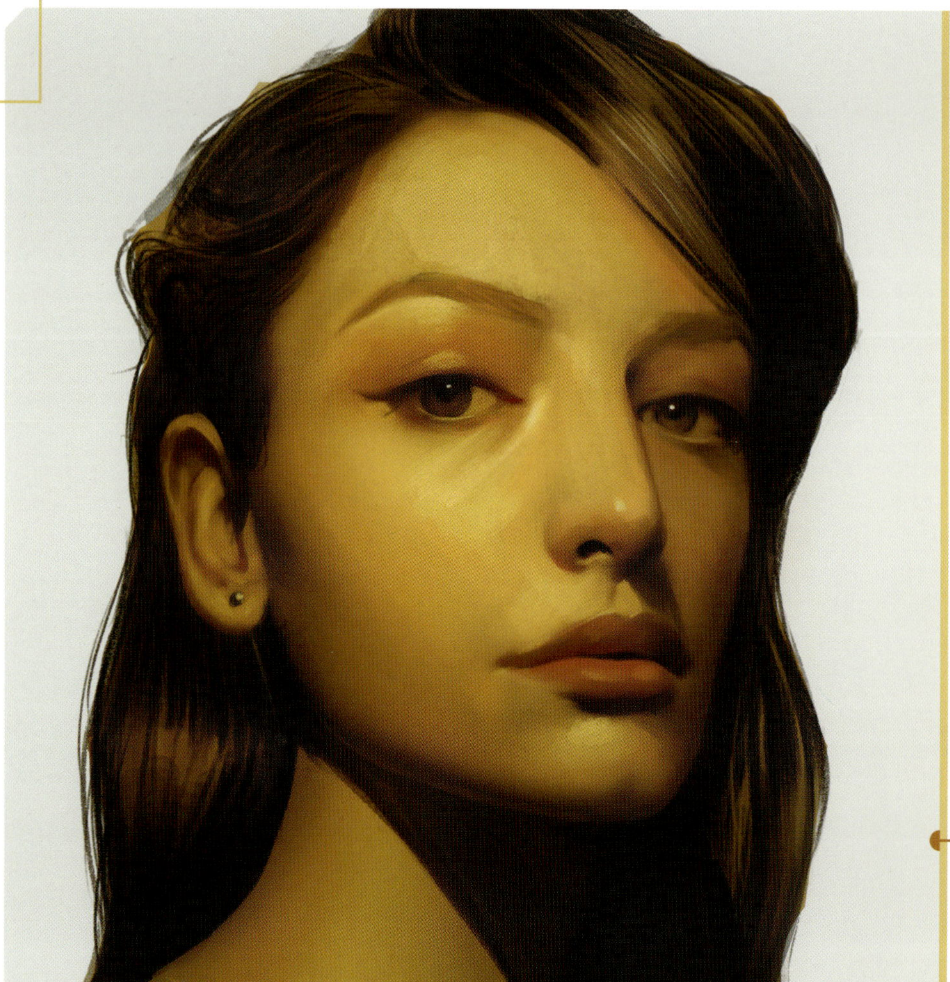

Paint highlights onto the face

There are several areas of highlight on the subject's face. These are the areas that face the light source directly, or are at an angle and partially face the light source. Using a round brush and the highlight color, paint a small brushstroke on the tip of the nose. Next, paint a highlight on the upper part of the nose, on a level with the eyes, then another near the tear duct. Moving on to the eyelids, paint a highlight on top to show the spherical bulge of the eyeball. Refer back to the reference photo and observe the patterns present in the highlights. Use the pencil brush to capture these, keeping them minimal and not too distracting. Moving toward the left eyebrow, use the round brush to paint a small highlight beneath the peak of the brow, followed by a highlight above the brows on the forehead. Next, paint small highlights just above the top lip, then on the lower lip also.

Artist tip

You will often find yourself overwhelmed when you see too much information at once. While simplification and rest areas are not fixed rules, it can help to simplify the details in areas of least importance, keeping the highest level of detail for the areas you wish the viewer to focus on. Don't think of the simplified areas as lazy or unfinished; they are crucial parts that help to guide the viewer's eye around the portrait, emphasizing the focal points you have put the most time and effort into.

31

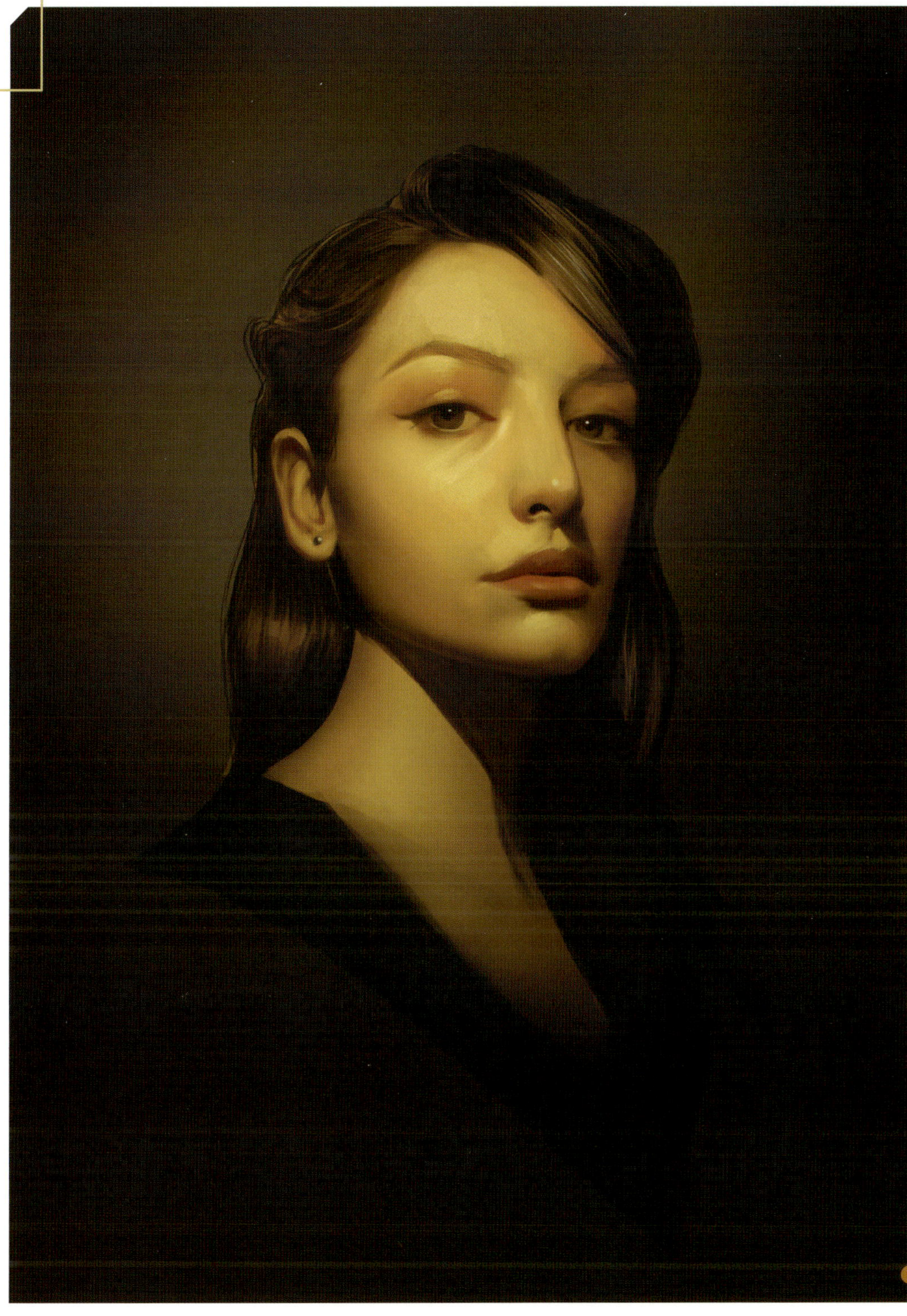

Enhance your portrait by adding a background

You can use a background, even a simple one, to your advantage. Consider the overall mood you wish to convey, as well as the colors already present in the portrait. Select a warm brown color that is a slightly higher value than the subject's hair, then use a soft airbrush, or similar tool, to begin painting a shape near to the left-hand side of the face. Fill in the space near the top of the face, before moving around to the right. Using the same brush, select a slightly darker color and paint down toward the lower right of the image, making a frame around the subject's face. Finish by filling the silhouette of the clothing with a dark color.

32

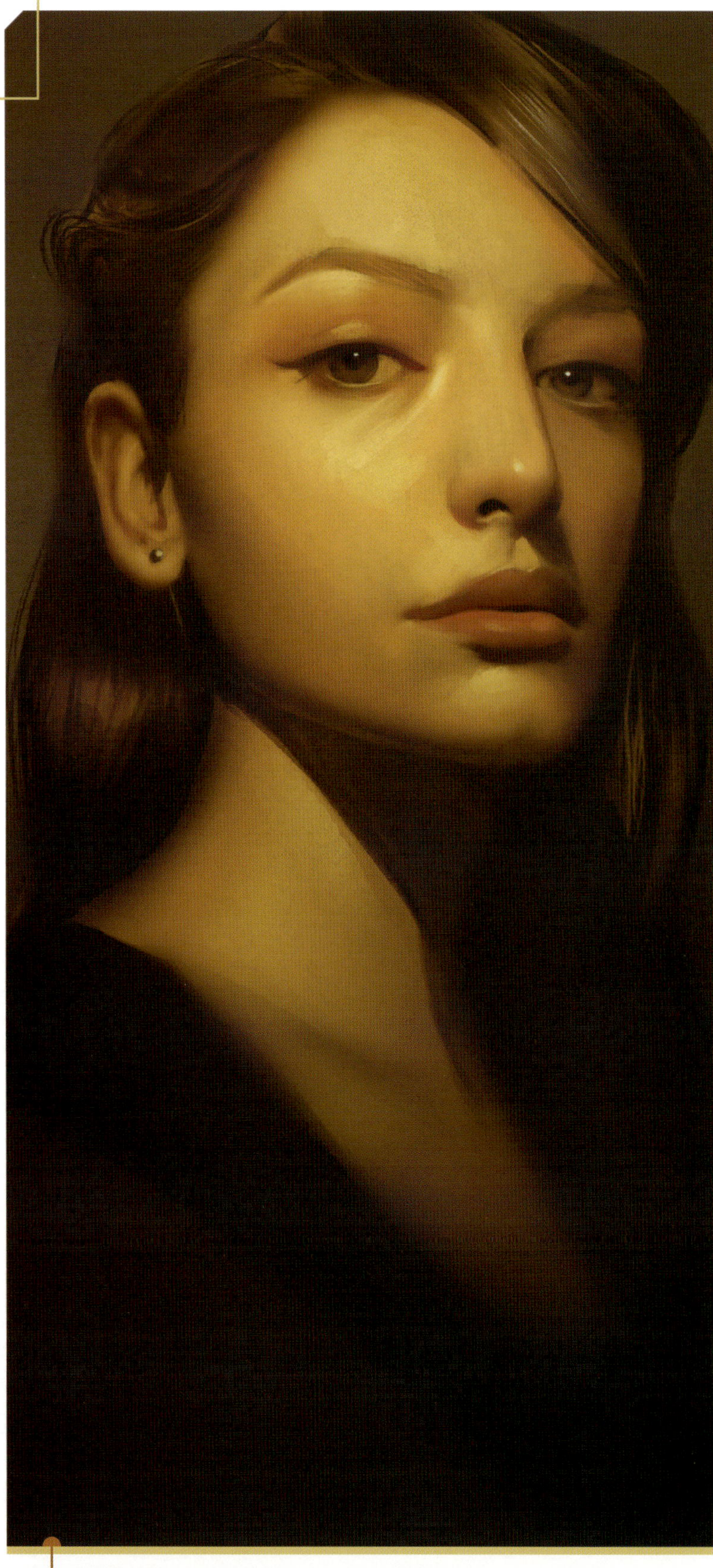

Smudge any hard edges to soften them, varying how the different forms are blended

There are areas of the portrait that have a hard edge, but don't need one, such as the lower edge of the subject's clothing. Smudge the hard edges to make them softer and less sharp. You can use the smudge tool if using digital software, or a similar tool or your fingers if using traditional media. Start with the sharp edge of the base of the clothing, before moving onto the sides of the neck and parts of the hair. There are no hard rules here; it's simply about guiding the eye to the areas with the highest amount of detail. Reduce the sharpness of any areas you don't want the viewer to look at. You can also blend any areas that you wish to appear softer, such as the nose and lips.

33

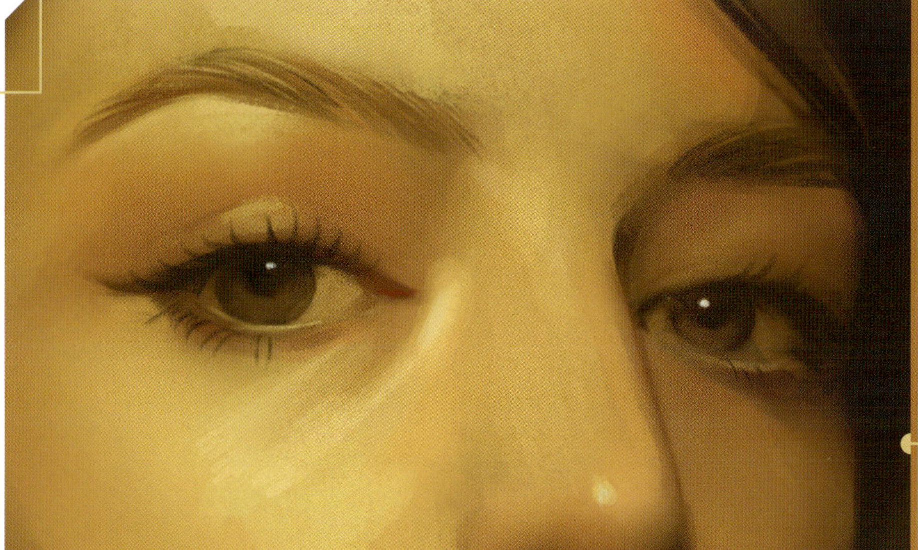

Paint in smaller details, including the fine hairs of the eyebrows and eyelashes

It's now time to make the finishing touches, starting with the finer details of the eyebrows. For the left eyebrow, use the pencil brush to paint small strands of hair that radiate from the middle of the brow, looking at the reference photo for guidance. Remember to paint the skin showing through the hair, as eyebrows are not opaque. Do the same for the right eyebrow but with a higher density of color, as this section of the reference photo is a lot darker in value. Moving on to the eyes, the lashes are a great way of framing the eyes. Use the pencil brush to create small strokes of hair, again radiating from the eye. Group these hairs together to avoid making them look like random, single strands. Look at the portrait through squinted eyes if you feel overwhelmed by all of the information, taking your time to gently paint the eyelashes into shape.

34

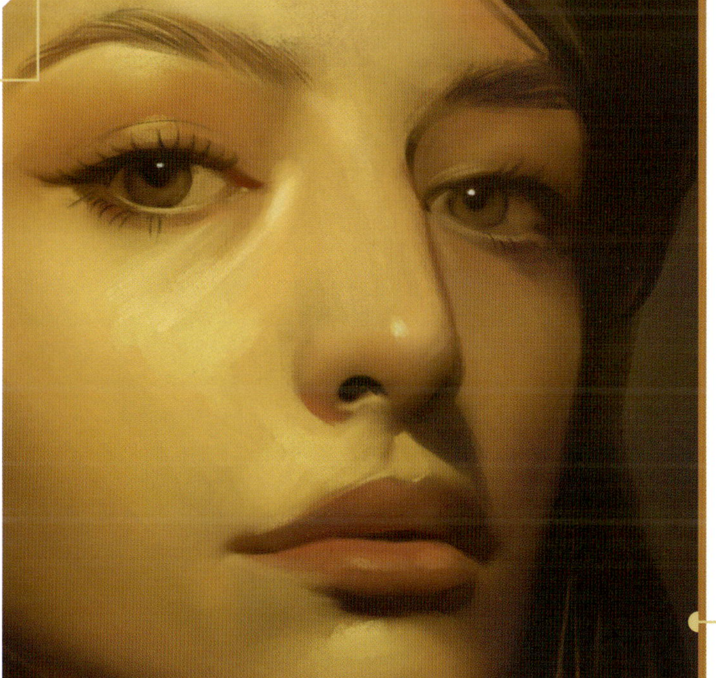

The eyes still need a little more detailing. Study the eyes in the reference photo, then use the round brush to recreate the small hints of color in each eye. Use the pencil brush to paint a highlight onto the bottom eyelid, as this is only a small highlight. Ensure the eyes contain the highest amount of detail, as they are a main focal point of the portrait. Next, study the nose and double-check that its size and overall height reflects that of the reference. It's also crucial to make sure the nose is sat at the correct angle. Observe the height of the two nostrils, ensuring they have the same orientation as the reference, then check to see if the tip of the nose faces the right direction.

Double-check the portrait and correct any mistakes

35

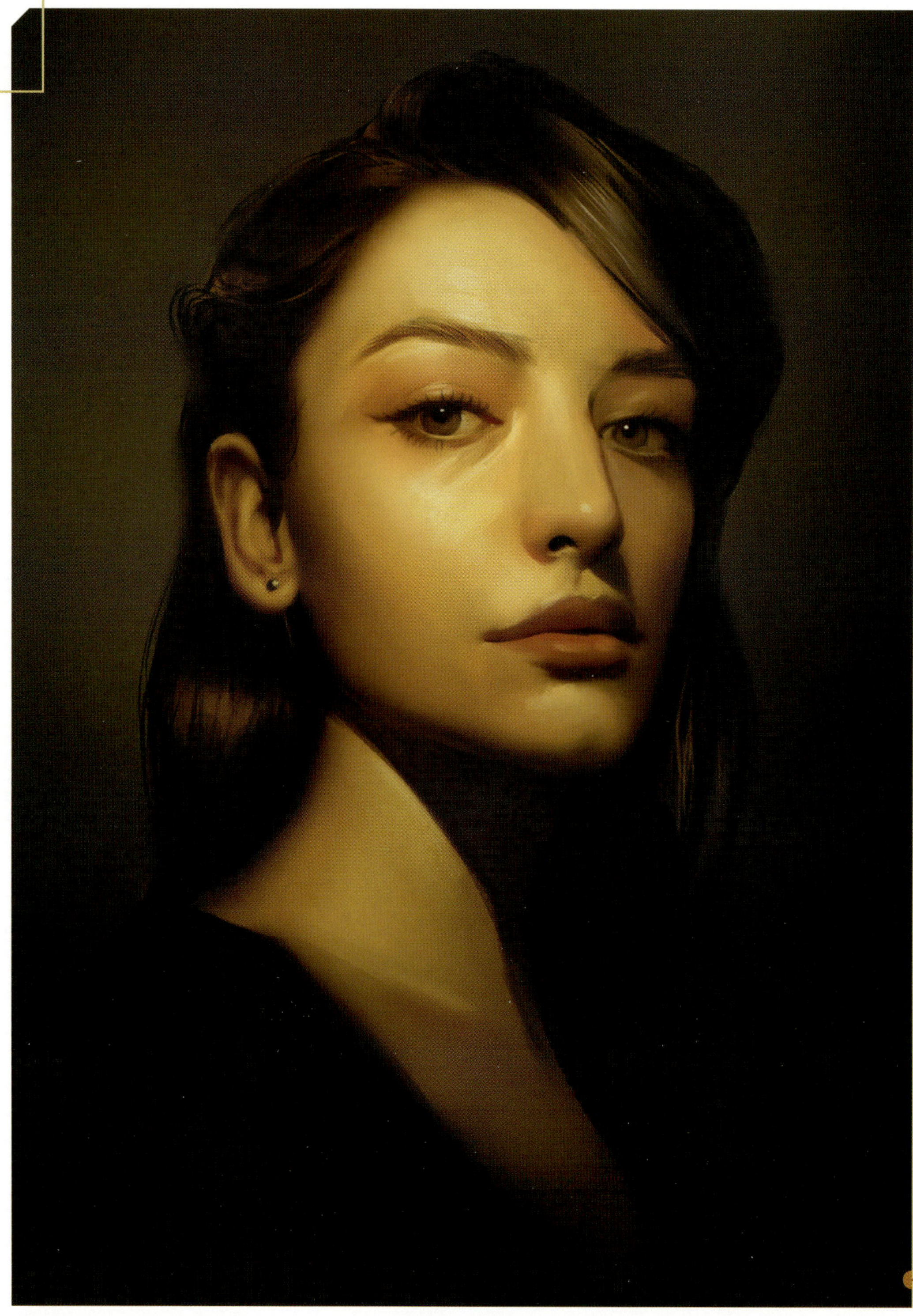

Add the final touches to the portrait

Using the soft airbrush and a light color similar to that of the highlights, lightly paint over areas in the light. This is to simulate the light scatter effect seen in real life, as well as to improve the coverage of the highlights. This is done as the last step, as you can now paint over every feature on the face. Paint a small amount of colder light to contrast with the warmer tone just added, then define the highlight on the neck area and give the shadow a harder edge to show it is a cast shadow. Next, return to the nose and add a little more softness to it. Finally, paint a few orange tones on the lower parts of the chin and shadow to convey the reflected light.

36

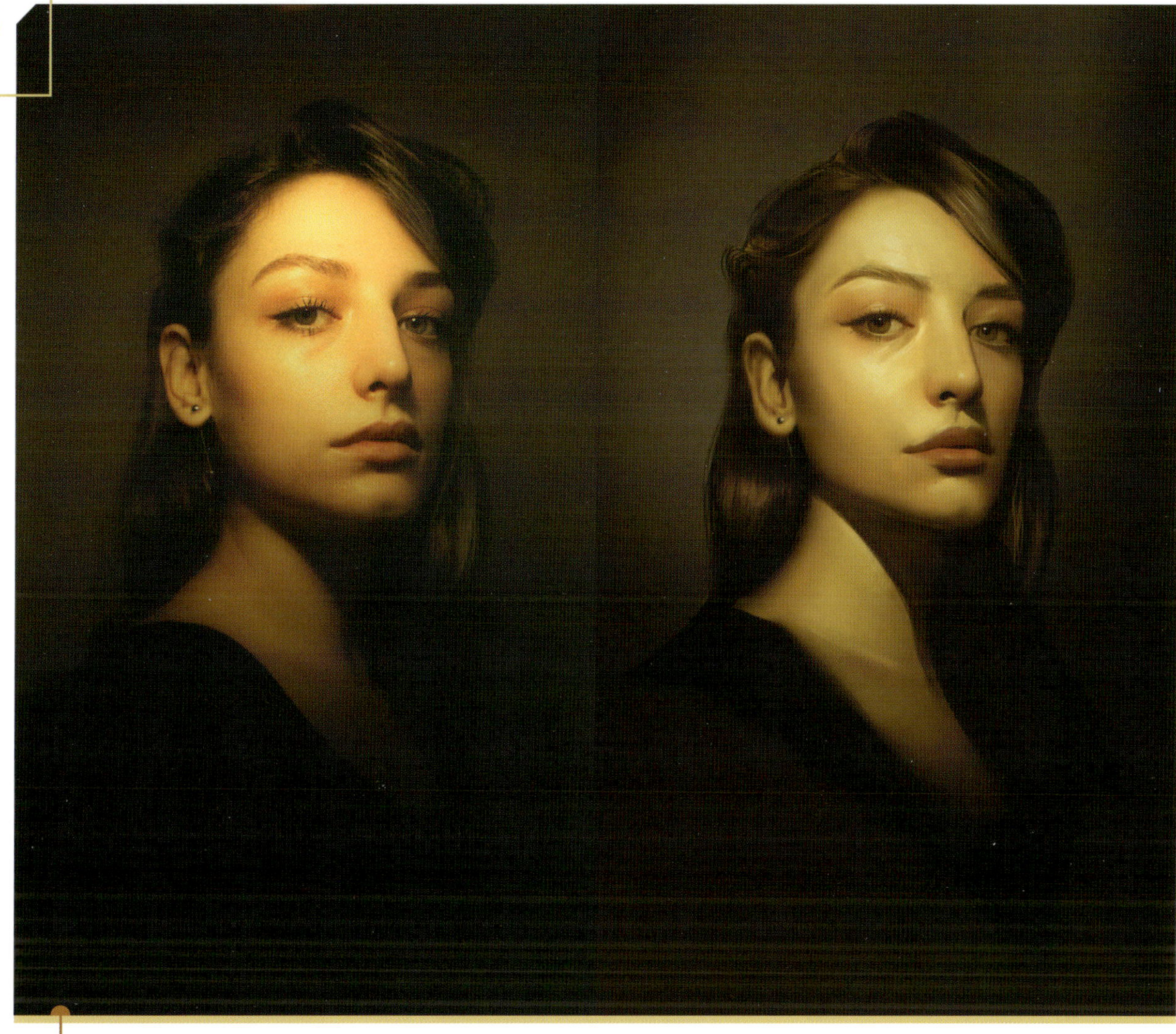

Compare your portrait to the reference photo, then fix any small details

Step back and view the portrait, asking yourself whether you have achieved the goals you set at the start of the process. Compare it to the reference photo and check if there is anything major that is hindering the likeness. A good way to check this is to place them side by side to observe the alignment and see what aligns with what. Sometimes they are not exact, but you can still see if the shapes are overlapping or not, as well as if the distances between features are accurate to the reference. Scan it with your eyes up close, then take a step back to look at it from afar. It's rare to view artwork zoomed in; viewing it from a distance is the best way to check if the overall image is working. Don't be afraid to go back a step and work on it some more. Nothing should be sacred and nothing is final until it is.

Conclusion

Your portrait is now finished! This is a great achievement and just the start of your portraiture journey. Becoming good at painting faces, or any skill, requires much dedication and practice. Even when you feel like the face you have painted looks off or nothing like the person you are painting, you can always try again. Sometimes you may need to start over, but perhaps it just needs a fresh set of eyes. Keep practicing and don't get discouraged.

This tutorial has demonstrated a simple process for painting a portrait from a reference photo. There are numerous other workflows, techniques, and methods for portrait painting out there, but that's the fun of art – there is always more to learn.

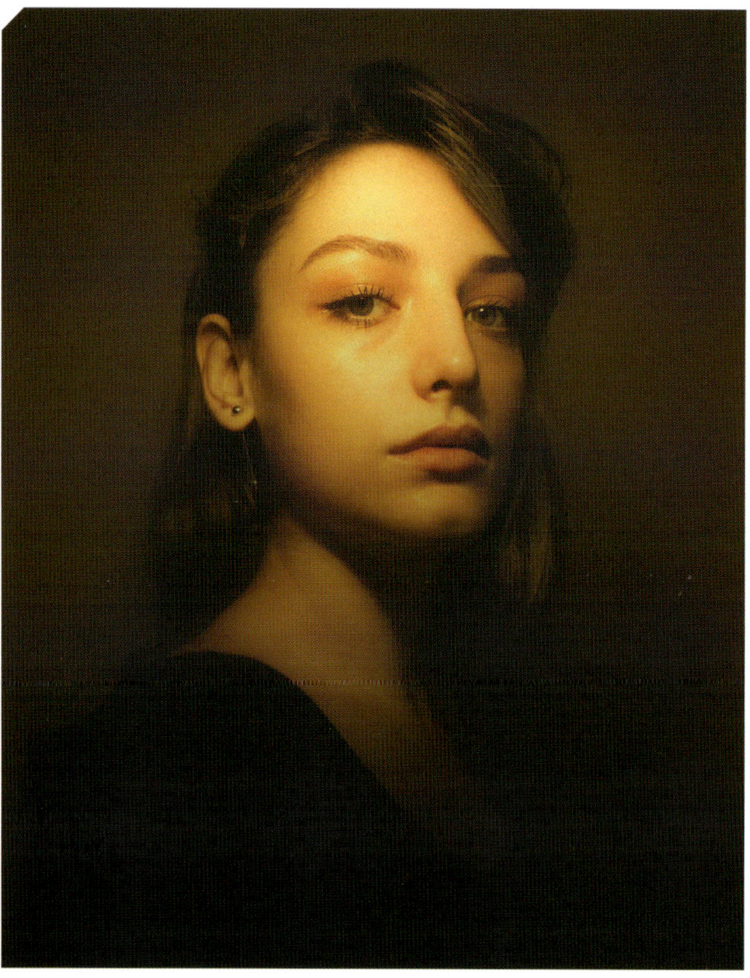

Photograph © Natalia Jaclin Kareta

Final image © Justine S. Florentino

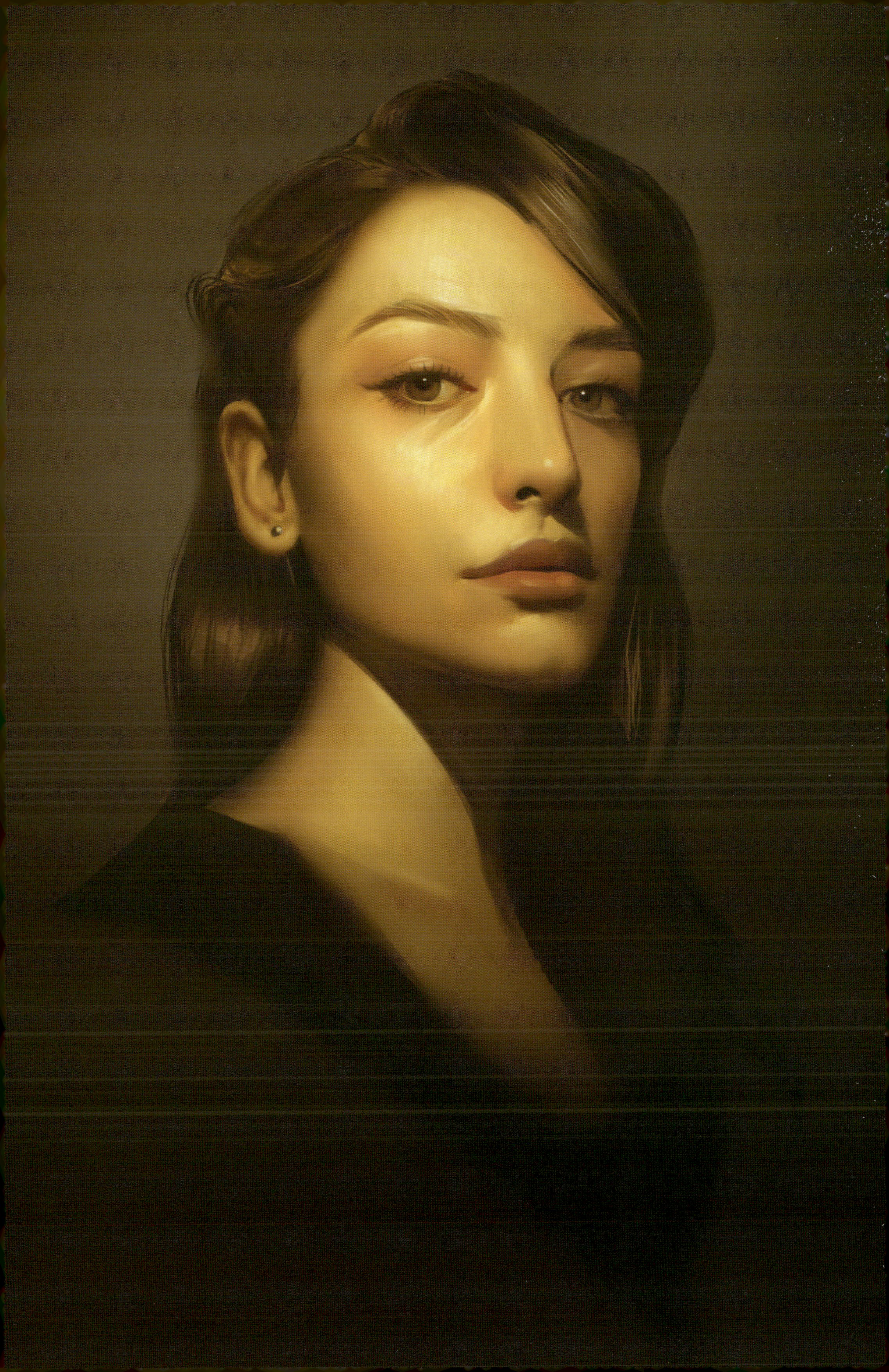

SARA TEPES

Introduction

This tutorial will walk you through how to paint a detailed, semi-realistic portrait. It has been created digitally in Adobe Photoshop, but you can use whatever digital software or traditional media you prefer. It will begin with how to use a reference photo to create a well-composed base sketch. Being able to create a clean sketch with accurate anatomy is a pivotal first step in setting the foundation for a well-structured portrait. After selecting a color palette to reflect your desired mood or motif, you will learn how to flesh out the details of the facial features and blend skin smoothly using minimal brushes. The tutorial will detail how to paint afro hair, achieving texture without drawing individual curls, before sharing expert tips and tricks for finalizing a portrait and taking it to the next level.

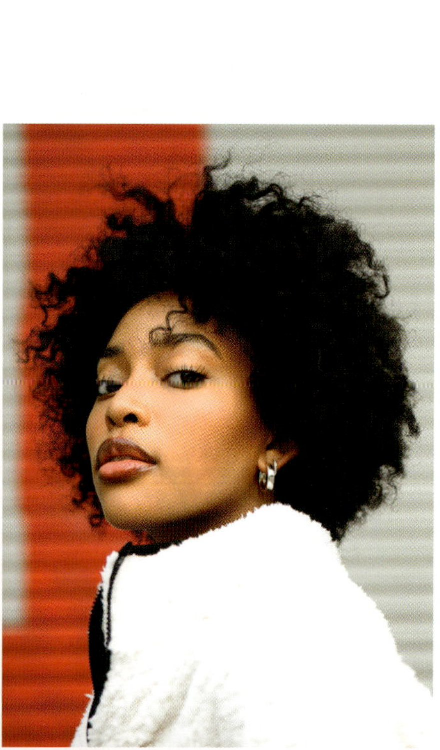

Photograph by Jeffery Erhunse on Unsplash

01

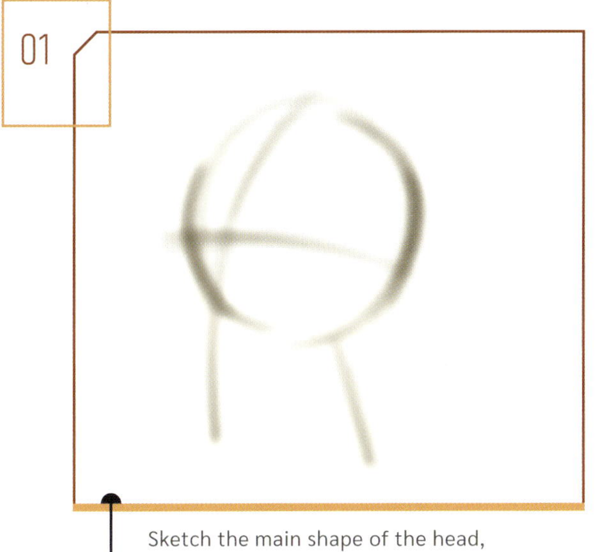

Sketch the main shape of the head, followed by lines to position the horizontal eyeline and central vertical line of the face

Decide whether you wish to paint from a live model or using a reference photograph. When selecting a photo, choose one that will push you to study the anatomy, angles, skin tones, textures, or lighting. Once you have your chosen image and have studied it closely, use a large, soft-edged brush, or similar tool, to sketch a loose circle where the main mass of the head will be. Observe the angle of your subject's face, then sketch an x-axis over the general area of the eyes, curved around the mass of the circle, and a y-axis over the middle of the face. Place both of these according to how the subject is angled. Draw a straight line down from the middle of the circle to show the general angle of the neck.

02

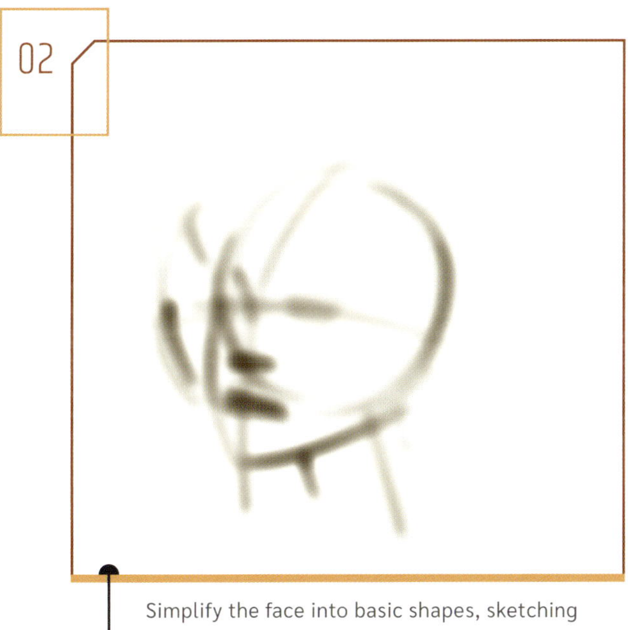

Simplify the face into basic shapes, sketching in the rough placement of the facial features

Define the basic shape of the face by placing a V where the chin will be. Sketch loose marks to indicate the general placement of the eyes, nose, lips, and neck. Study your reference closely and try to break the face down into simple shapes. Draw soft lines to suggest the general mass of the hair.

03

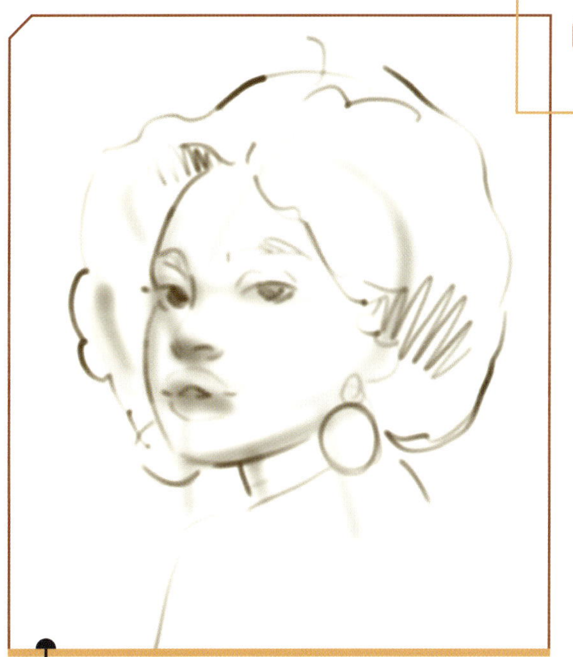

Sketch loose lines to solidify the general placement of the facial features

Using the rough sketch as a guide, begin to further flesh out the shapes. The goal of this step is to ensure you are confident with the basic composition of the portrait, as well as to solidify the general placement of the facial features. Use loose lines; don't be too rigid with your marks and allow yourself to erase or restart until you are satisfied with the sketch. It is better to take the time to set an accurate foundation now, than find it is at fault at a later stage.

04

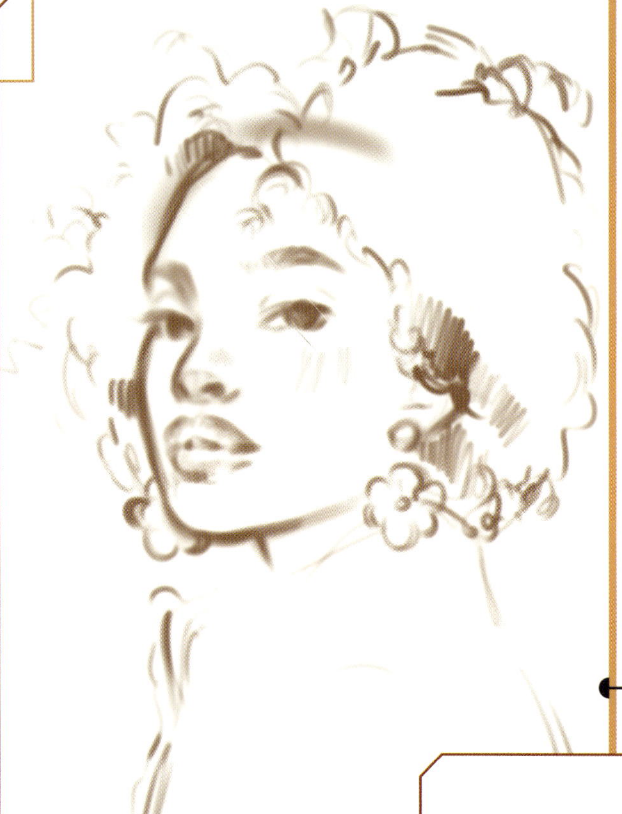

Now that you understand the general shape of your subject's face, sketch in defining details. Studying your subject's unique features will help you to capture their likeness. Focus on accurately depicting the anatomy by drawing out general shapes for the different forms and shaded areas. Use your brushstrokes to indicate light and shadow in your subject's face and hair.

Don't think about the details yet – focus on sketching correct anatomy and composition that will act as a base for the final image

05

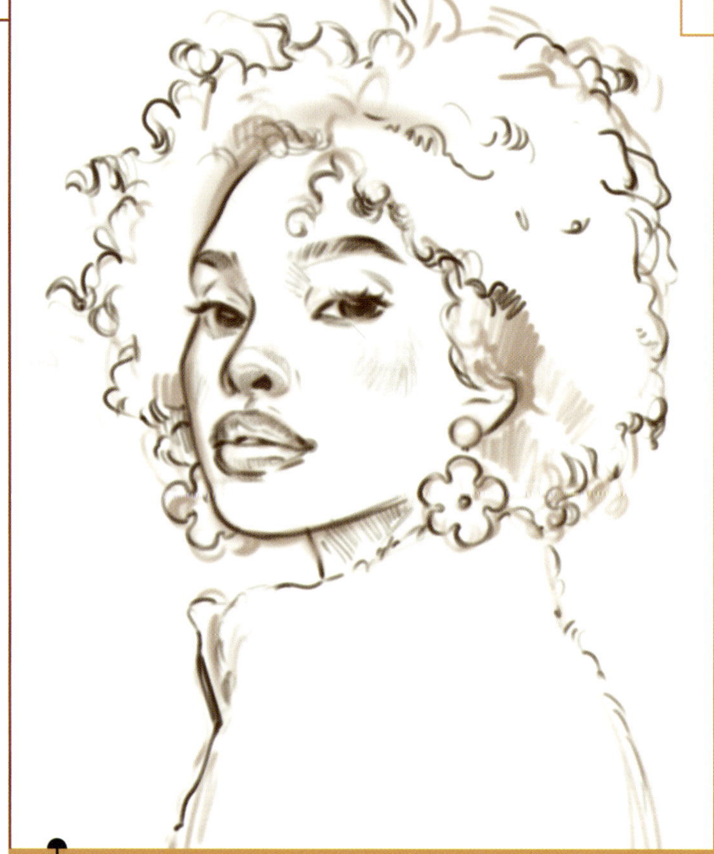

Begin to refine the sketch using a darker color and smaller, more precise brush. Using a soft-edged brush will help you to integrate and blend the sketch more smoothly into the painting. Ensure all of the features are correctly positioned, as it's much easier to fix mistakes in this early sketch stage than after you begin painting and laying down color.

Accent the shadow areas and rough details in the line work

06

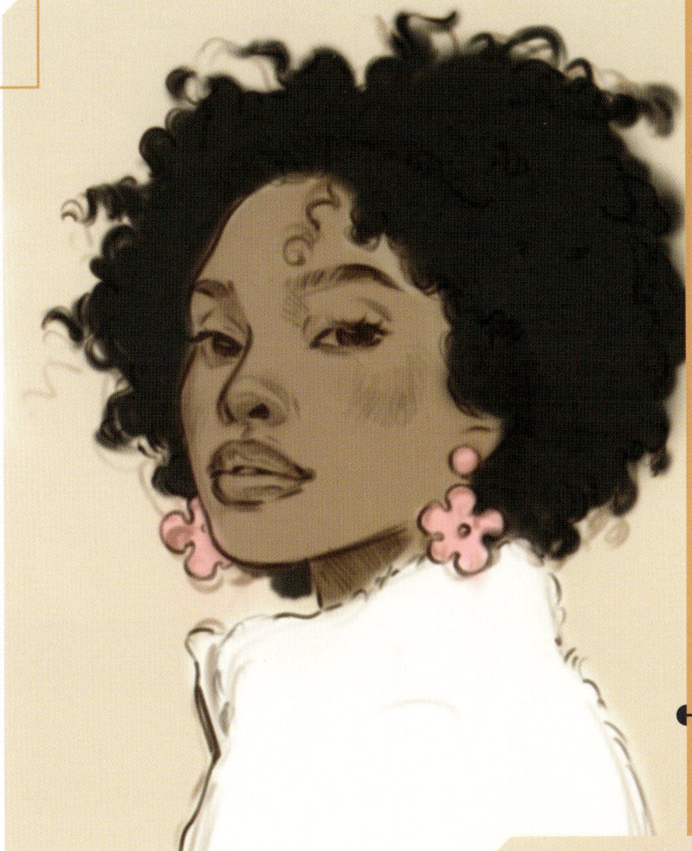

Start to paint the base colors. Consider what feeling you wish to evoke through the portrait, selecting an appropriate color palette that will convey this. Bright, soft tones will create a lighter, happier painting, while contrasting colors and harsh lighting will lead to a more dramatic final image. If you choose to use harsh true blacks or whites, this should be an intentional choice rather than your default palette. All colors are affected by the tone and intensity of the light that hits them. For example, while the subject's hair is black, opt for a dark slate gray for the base rather than true black. After studying the colors present in the reference photo, decide whether you wish to depict them accurately, or take intentional creative liberties.

Start to lay down the base colors, considering how this base palette will affect the overall mood and look of the portrait

07

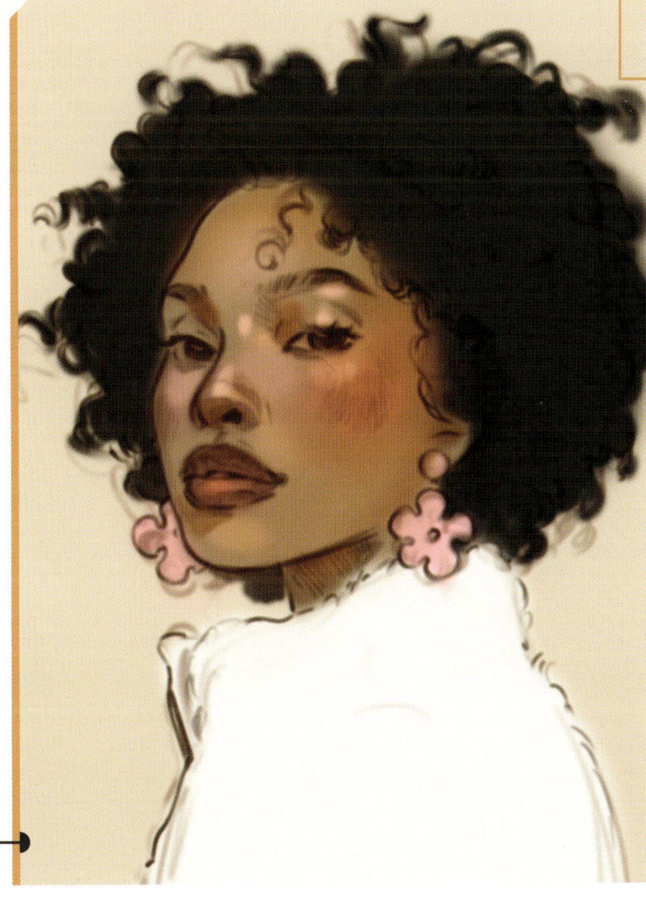

Observe the direction of the light source in your reference photo and how it falls across the subject's features. Paint initial shadows, highlights, and variations to the skin tones, such as blush and contour shades. Place every color where you want it to be in the final portrait; this will make it simpler to blend and refine the painting later in the process. Unify your painting by using the same colors throughout. Using matching tones in the shadows across different areas of the face will help to create a cohesive final image.

The tones in the earrings match the blush in the cheeks, producing a cohesive color palette

08

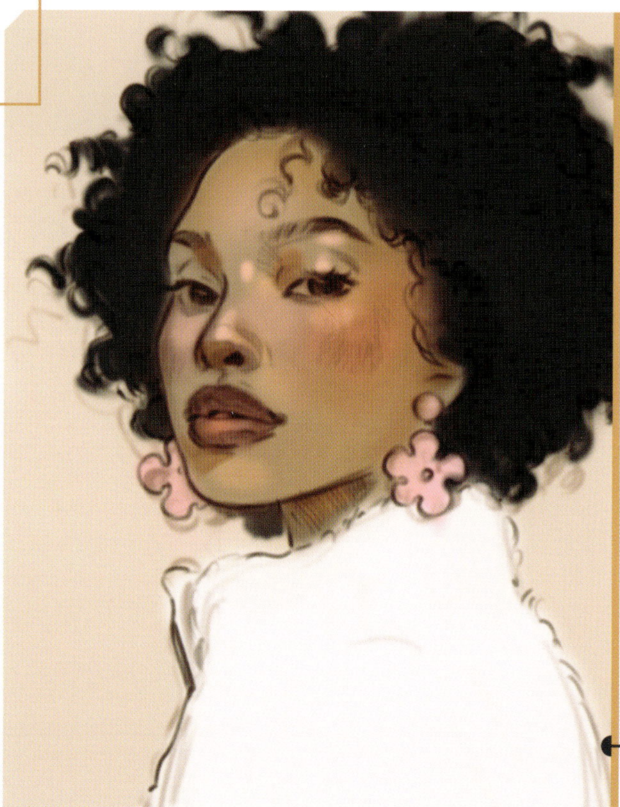

Experiment with the tones and hues until you are satisfied with the base colors. A good rule to keep in mind is that your base sketch and colors should almost be good enough to show off. It's crucial that the base is well-composed and that you have confidence in it before you begin to add details. Keep glancing between your reference photo and base image, looking out for mistakes. Fix problem areas immediately, rather them leaving them until later in the process when they're harder to correct.

Solidify the colors, fixing mistakes as you notice them

09

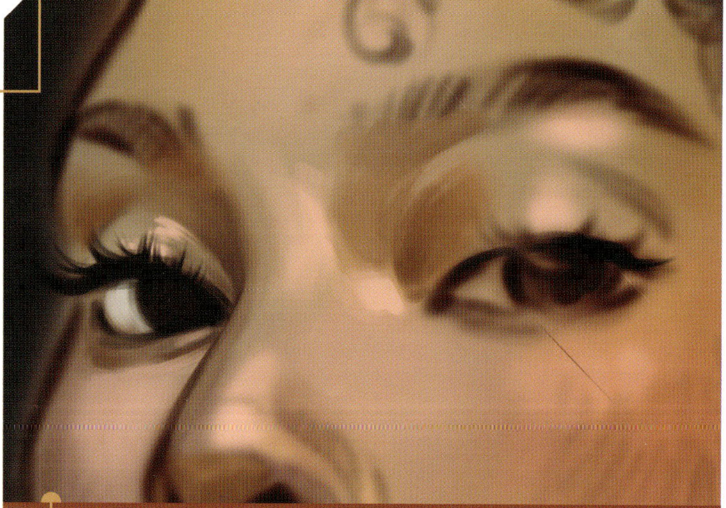

Detail the left eye and refine its form

Begin to paint in the details, going over your line work. If working digitally, select a round oil-type brush. The eyes hold much of the life and expression of the face, so start with them. Ensuring the eyes are symmetrical and positioned at the correct angle is crucial. Notice how the top and bottom eyelids fold around the circular sphere of the eyeball. Additionally, keep in mind that the skin around the eyes is much thinner than the rest of the face and more prone to wrinkling. Capturing these details will make for a more believable image.

Artist tip

Consider the different textures you want to create and how this can affect the mood of the portrait. This tutorial has been created digitally, using a soft airbrush for the line art and base colors, before switching to a round oil-type brush for the blending and details. Opt for similar brushes if you want to achieve a similar effect, or experiment with different brushes to create other types of moods and aesthetics.

10

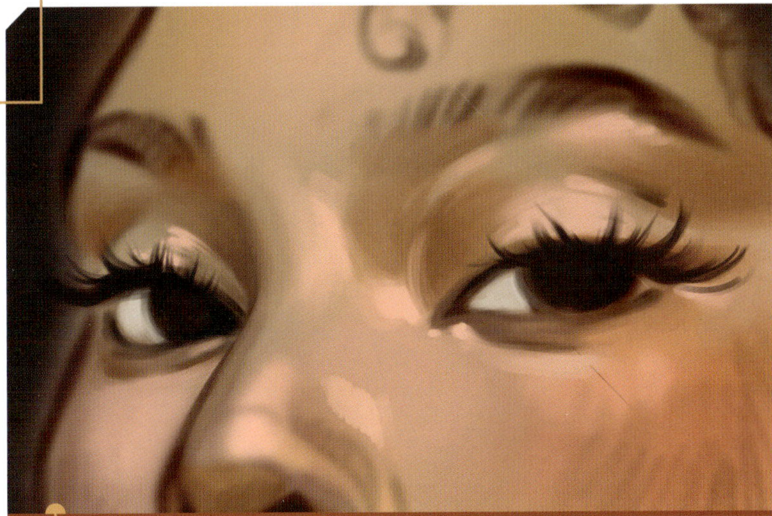

Utilize your reference photo when learning where to paint the shadows and highlights

An easy tip for painting the second eye is to reference the tones and shades used for the first eye. If you wish to create a more stylized look, paint large eyelashes onto both eyes. This can help to open the eyes and make them appear bigger, while giving the subject a feminine and dreamy aesthetic. Study your reference photo to see whether your subject has wrinkles, dark circles, or makeup surrounding their eyes. Consider their mood and energy. Wrinkles, under-eye bags, puffiness, or dramatic makeup can all help to tell your subject's story. As an artist, it's your job to incorporate these small yet important details into your portrait.

11

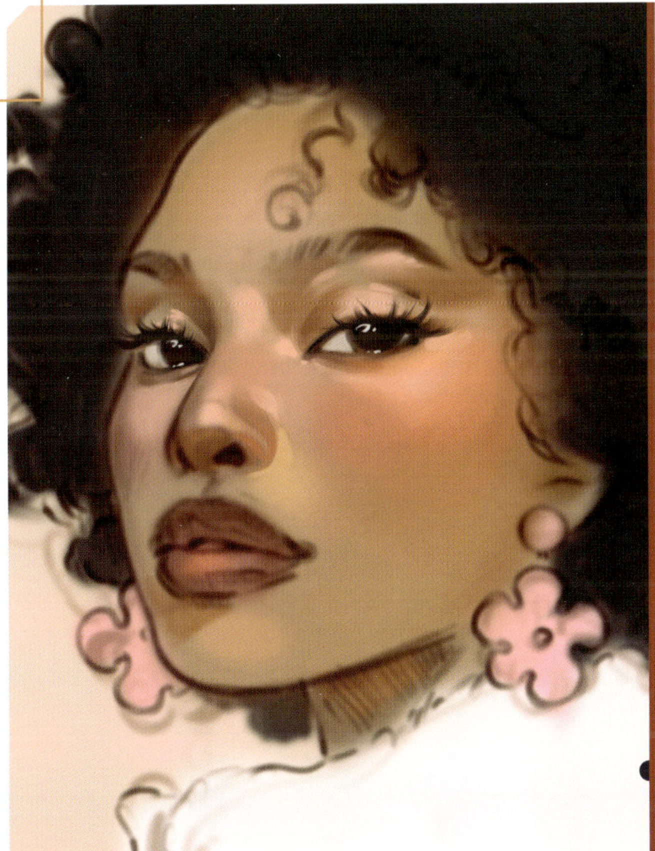

Study your reference photo closely and continue to paint the different tones into your subject's eyes, smoothing your brushstrokes with light pressure. Add any eye makeup they are wearing. Observe how the colors blend together on your subject's face and keep facial anatomy in mind. Blend the tones of the blush and cheek highlight into the eye area to create a smooth look.

Paint highlights onto the eyes to draw the viewer's focus to them

12

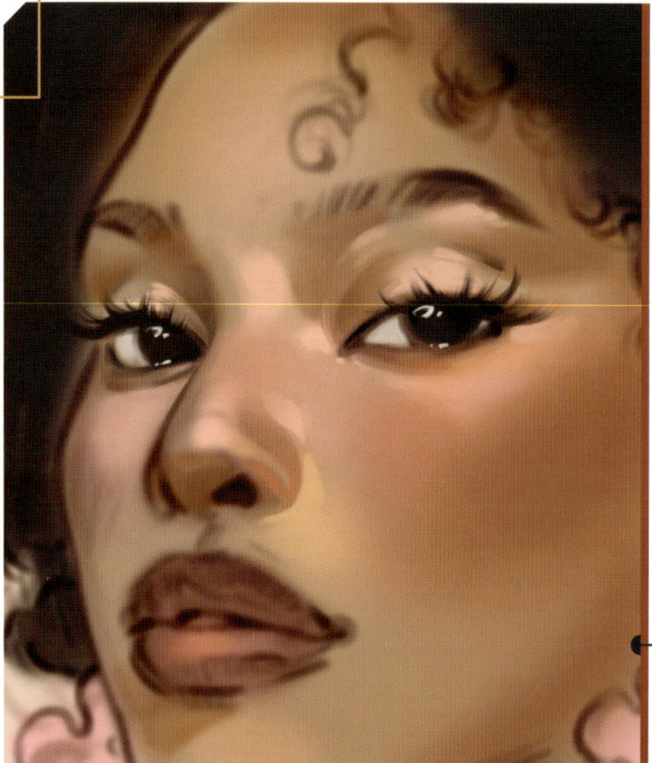

After you have finished detailing the eyes, start to shade around the perimeters of the face. Identify the light source in your reference photo and keep this in mind when placing the shadows and highlighted tones. Knowing the direction of the light, as well as the color of it, will help in correctly placing the shading. If the light is shining from above, as it is here, highlight the high points of the face, such as the cheekbones, brow bone, forehead, tip of the nose, and chin. Paint subtle contours to define the shape of the nostrils and the tip of the nose.

Add shading, working your way down from the eyes to the cheekbones and nose

13

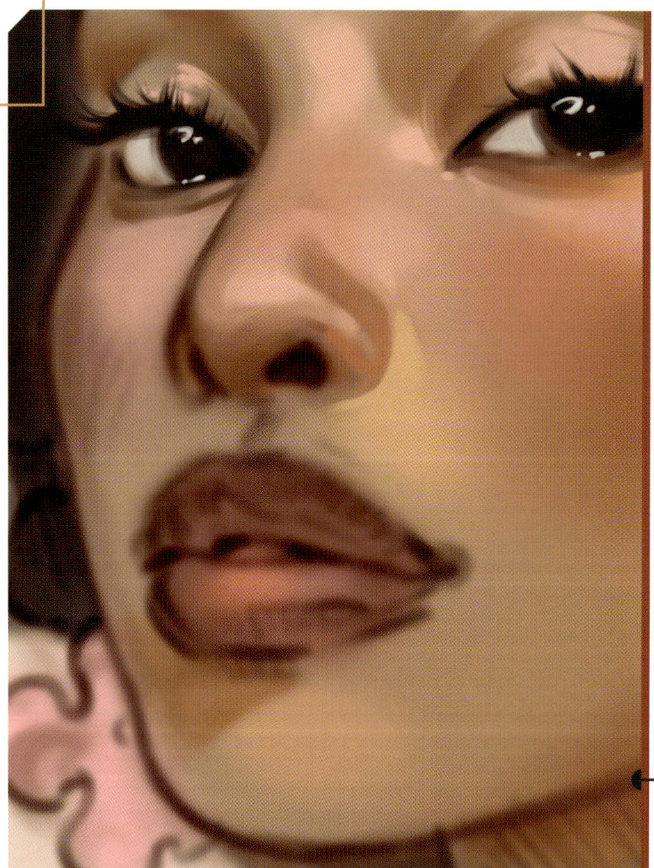

Noses come in all shapes and sizes; capturing each one accurately can be a hard skill to accomplish. Study your reference photo carefully and analyze the subtle highlights and shadows present on your subject's nose. Think of the shaded and brighter tones as general shapes to place, before blending the edges together. Slightly vary the tones of your highlights and lowlights as you paint; this will add interest and dimension to the portrait. Here a sandier highlight tone is added around the nostril and a pink tone is painted on the tip of the nose.

Use subtle tones to shape the nose, introducing shadows and highlights

14

Use a combination of hard marks to create hard edges, such as across the profile of the nose, and soft, light marks to paint subtle blending. Select a deep brown, instead of a black, for the darkest shadows across the skin. This will create dimension and the idea that the skin is translucent. If you feel unsure about anything, take a step back or zoom out to view the portrait as a whole and observe what is or isn't working. At this stage you should be color blocking rather than focusing on minute details.

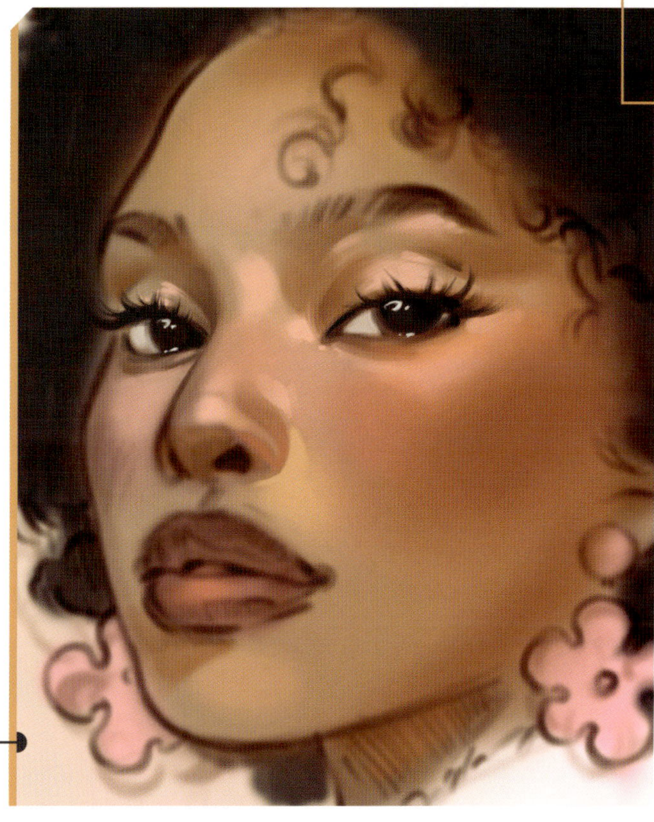

Add details and shadows across the face to create dimension

15

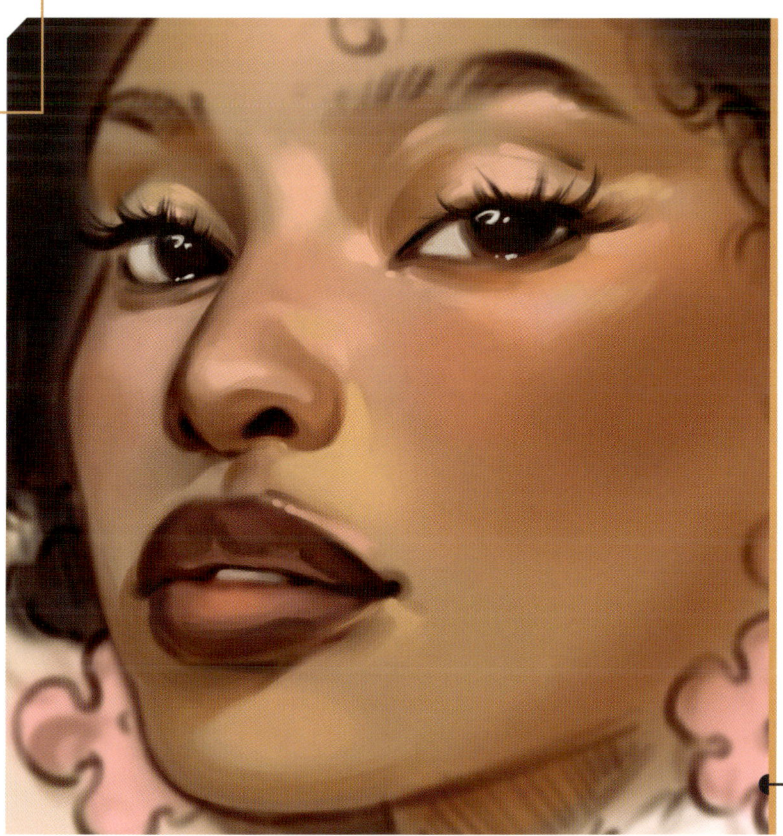

When painting the lips, remember that the fullness of the lips and their pigmentation are not dependent on each other. The edges of the lips will be raised and full, even if they're not highly pigmented. When adding color to the lips of subjects with a darker skin tone, you may wish to accentuate a dark outline and lighter center. Adding wrinkles and folds to the lips will add realism and texture, making your portrait more visually interesting. Deepen the shadows around the corners of the mouth to add the illusion of skin folding inward.

Study your subject's lips, experimenting with textures and colors for a stylized look

16

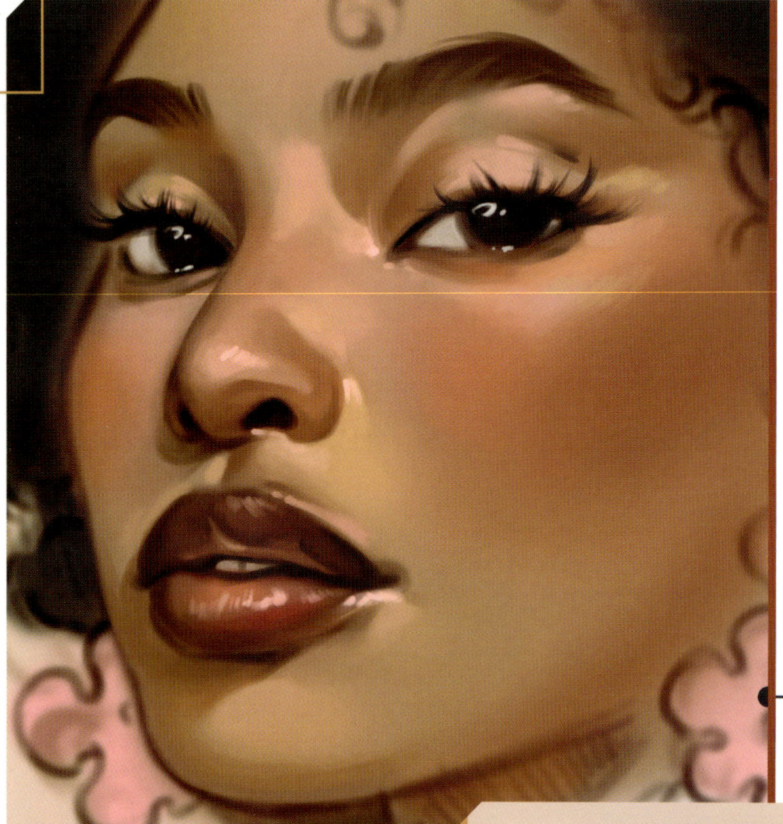

Study your reference photo to see if your subject's lips have a natural sheen or a high gloss, then alter the brightness and hardness of the highlights to reflect this. A softer, pink gloss has been added to the lips here to create a more natural look. Adding subtle shadows and highlights to areas like the inner and outer corners of the eyes, nostrils, bridge of the nose, and brow bone will lift the portrait, show your attention to detail, and improve your knowledge of anatomy. Fill in the eyebrows, creating a fuzzy, diffused look in the front hairs and a more precise tail.

Add highlights to the lips, nose, and eyes to unify the portrait

17

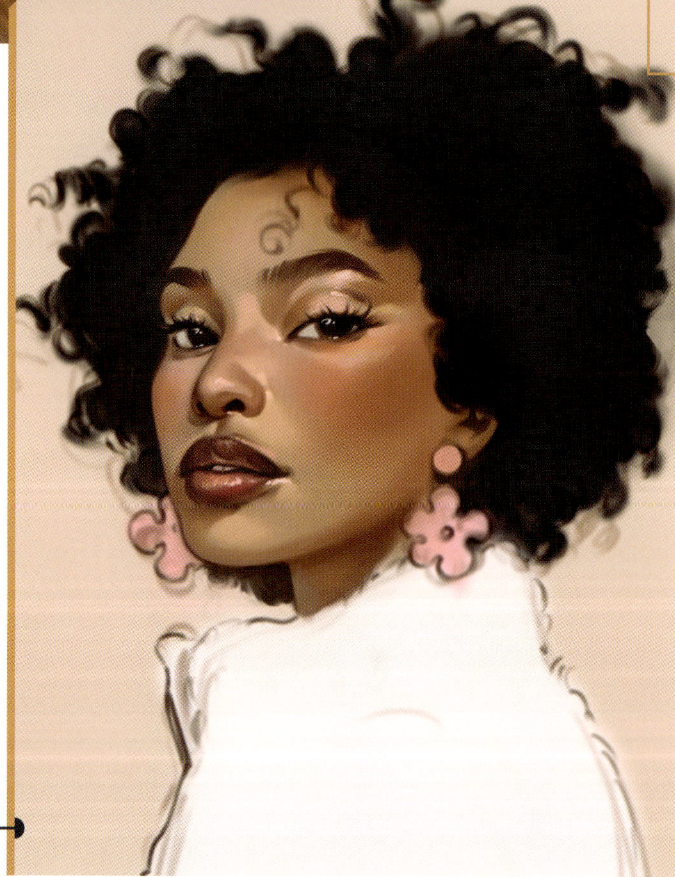

Begin to define and blend the edges of the face, chin, and neck, ears, and hairline. Choose colors from the shaded areas of the face already detailed to maintain a cohesive look. Use a variety of tones in the shadows on the neck, as there will be multiple light sources or objects bouncing light onto your subject. Next, use soft, circular motions to start painting the subject's curly hair.

Use colors already present in the portrait to define and blend the edges of the face and hairline

18

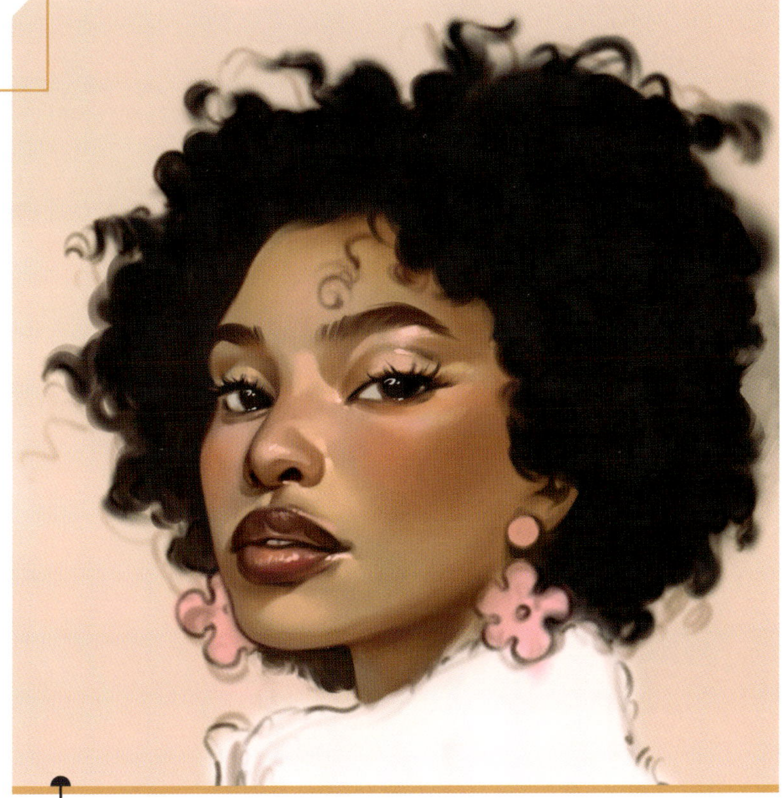

Add texture and dimension to the curls using a variety of dark indigo tones

When painting curly, afro hair, aim to make it as fluffy and cloud-like as possible. Use soft circular motions, building up the layers of paint. Avoid using true black, opting instead for dark indigo tones for the shadows and a muted purple for the highlights. You could use all black for the silhouette of the hair if increasing the stylization; however, if you wish to create dimension and texture, use a dark indigo in circular motions to paint cylindrical strands of hair spiraling outward from the scalp.

19

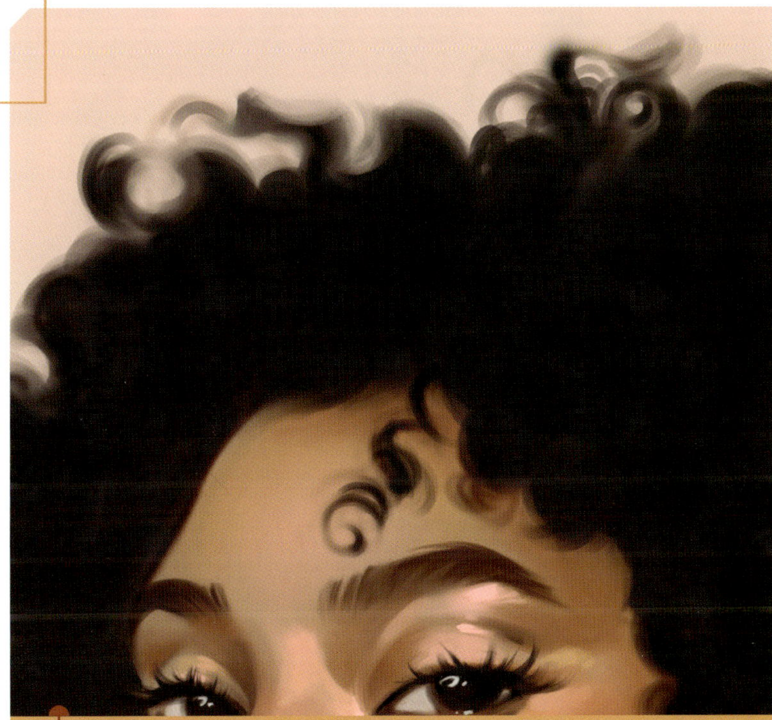

Paint a variety of shapes in the coils and kinks of the hair to add detail

Start to define the edges of the hair using a variety of sizes and pressures. As before, use circular motions to paint the curls and think of the hair as chunks and coils instead of individual strands. With a semi-realistic portrait like this one, you don't need to draw each individual strand of hair to indicate curls. Use soft pressure to create a diffused look for more out-of-focus strands, then harder pressure to define strands of hair at the front of the image, such as any that fall across the face.

20

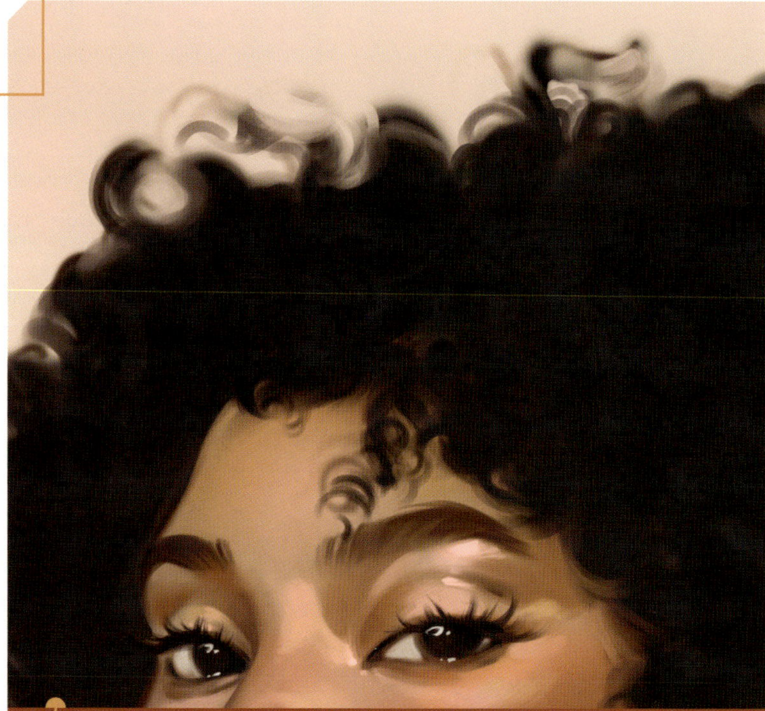

Continue to stack cylindrical coils until you have created the correct texture

Create dimension to the hair by alternating between using the shadow and highlight colors, stacking the cylindrical coils until you have achieved the desired texture. Continue to view the hair as solid shapes, rather than individual strands. Don't focus on the small separate strands yet – those will be added when painting the final touches. Pay attention to the type of curl of your subject's hair. Do they have tight ringlets or looser curls? Try to replicate this when painting.

21

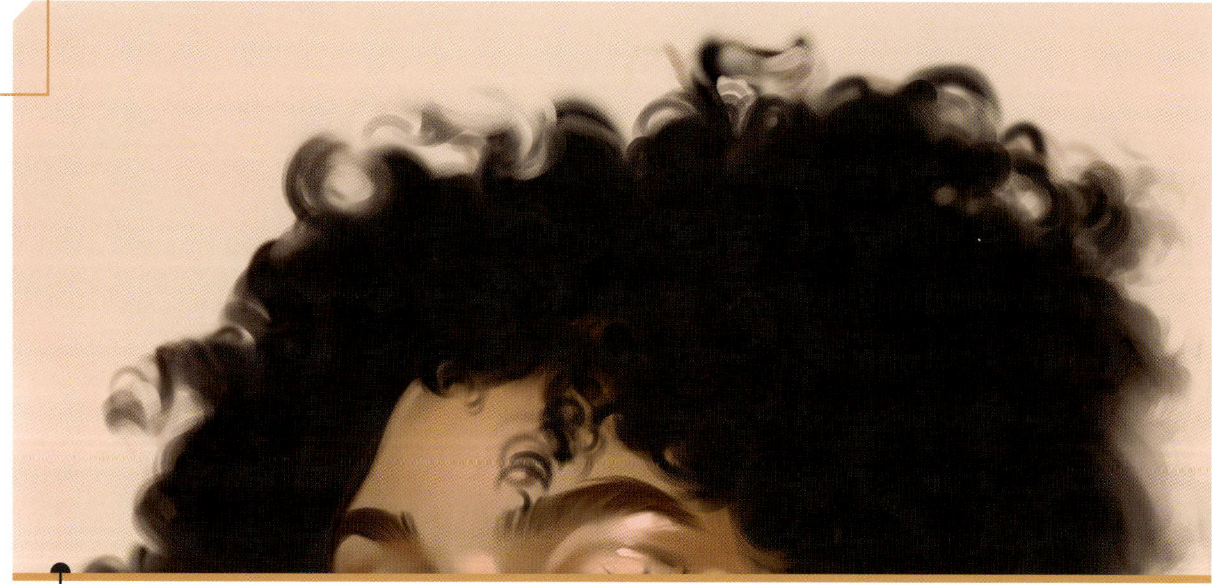

Diffuse the silhouette of the hair to create a fluffy, three-dimensional look

To make the hair appear as soft and fluffy as possible, diffuse some of the edges using soft pressure and circular motions. Painting curly hair is all about layering; steadily building up textures and repeating the same steps will create a natural and effortless look without spending hours tediously painting every strand of hair in a hyper-realistic manner. While you may grow bored of the repetitive process, be patient and stick with it to achieve voluminous, natural-looking hair.

22

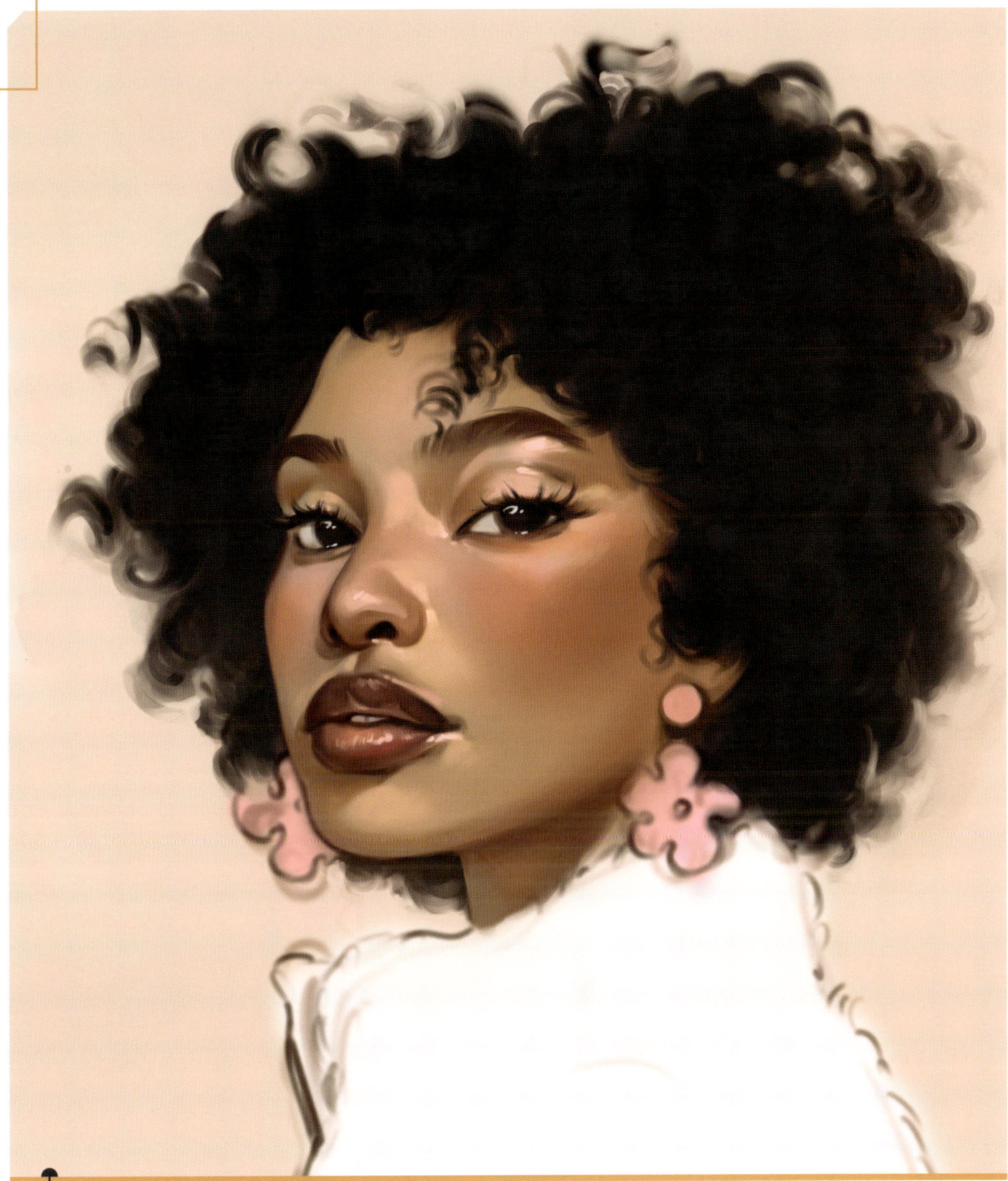

Detail the diffused silhouette to continue building the hair's texture

Begin to paint ringlets and details using similar tones to the ones used for the diffused sections of hair in step 18. The softer, faded colors will create subtlety and the illusion of depth instead of a rigid outline. Since an afro is spherical, there will be areas that are further away and therefore less detailed. Paint detailing to areas closer to the viewer to create a more realistic, three-dimensional look. Vary the size and pressure with which you make your marks to add a random pattern to the curls.

23

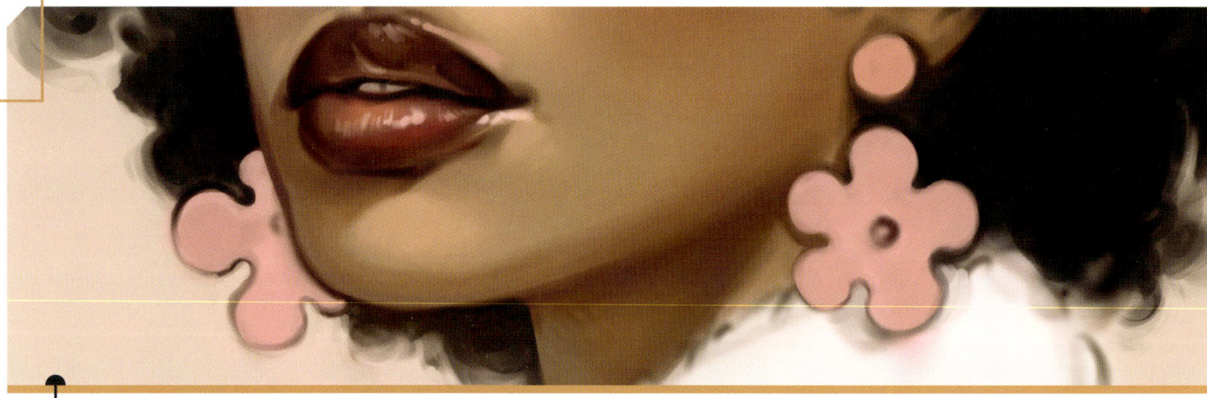

Color block the earrings, taking care to paint the neat, hard edges of the acrylic

Use strong pressure to paint defined edges around the silhouette of the earrings. Observe any jewelry your subject is wearing and identify what material it's made of. Take note of how the material reacts to light bouncing off of it and how it moves. The pink acrylic flower earrings painted here are different from the silver hoops the model wears in the reference photo. You may choose to change or add jewelry to stylize the portrait and create a certain aesthetic. The color-blocked acrylic earrings are used here to juxtapose the softness and depth of the model's afro, as well as to add visual interest to the portrait. Be aware of how composition can direct the viewer's gaze.

Artist tip

If you become restless and start to rush the process, step back from the portrait for a while. Setting distance between yourself and the painting process will allow you to come back to it with fresh eyes and an eagerness to continue working through any tedious details. Taking a break can also help you to assess if you need to correct the lighting, anatomy, or color choices before you solidify those features.

24

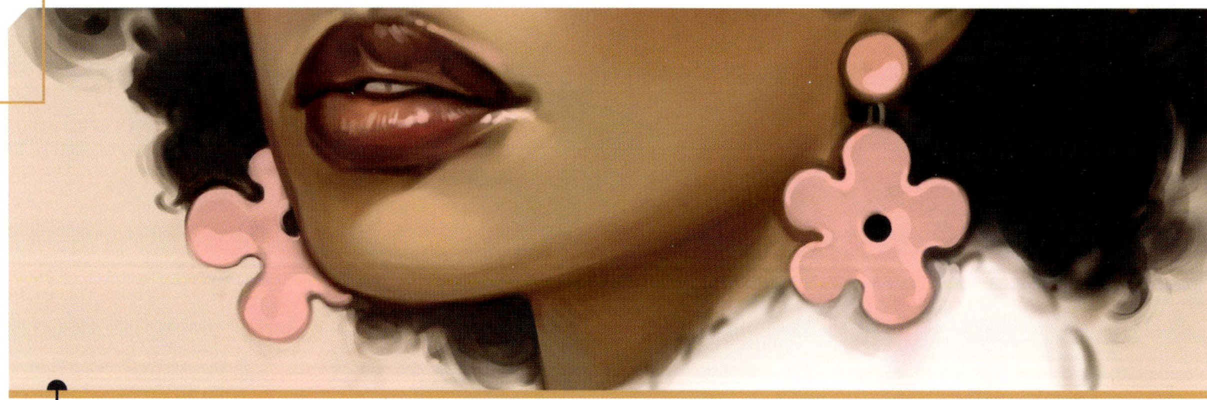

Add color-blocked highlights to the earrings and shadows behind them

Continue to define the edges of the earrings, adding shadows behind them on the ears and the coat. As the earrings are flat against the earlobes, the shadow there will be shorter and have a higher contrast than the shadow that falls across the coat collar, which will be more diffused. Since the earrings are flat and acrylic, the highlights should be blocky rather than soft and dimensional as they are on the face. Keeping textures in mind will create a balanced and cohesive final portrait.

29

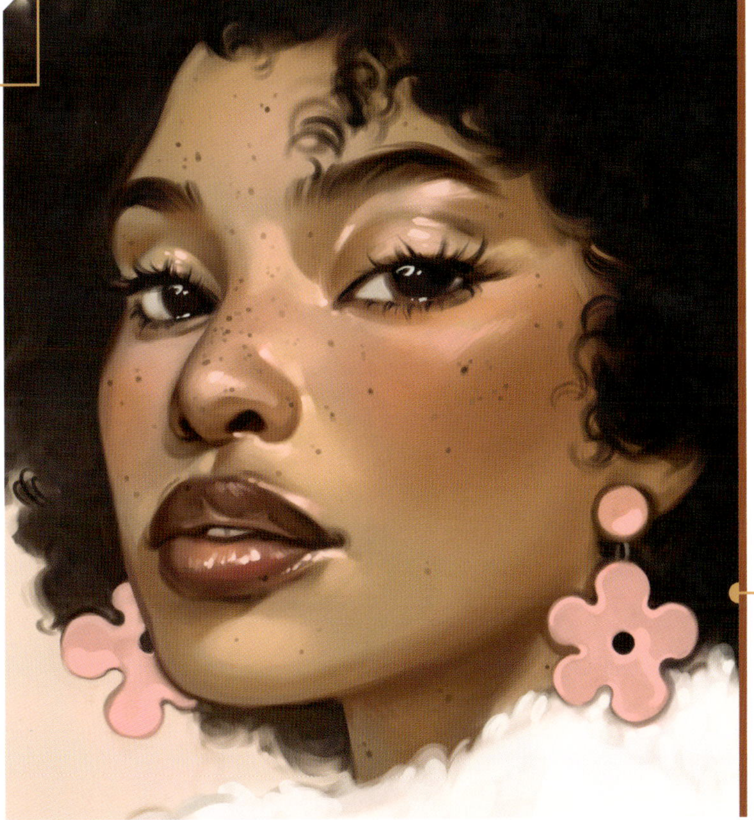

Freckles and beauty spots are a fun way to stylize a portrait, creating a cute, innocent, and feminine look. When painting freckles, vary the pressure of your brushstrokes to ensure some are dark and others light. Vary the size and placement of each freckle as well to create a sporadic, natural look. Avoid placing them evenly or all the same size, as this will look artificial. And don't limit freckles to only the cheeks and nose bridge; paint them across the forehead, chin, and neck too.

If you wish to stylize the portrait, paint freckles sporadically across the face

Artist tip

Experiment to find your own signature theme or style, then incorporate it into your portraits going forward. Knowing what you love and creating a signature portrait style can help to set you apart from other artists and make your artwork recognizable.

30

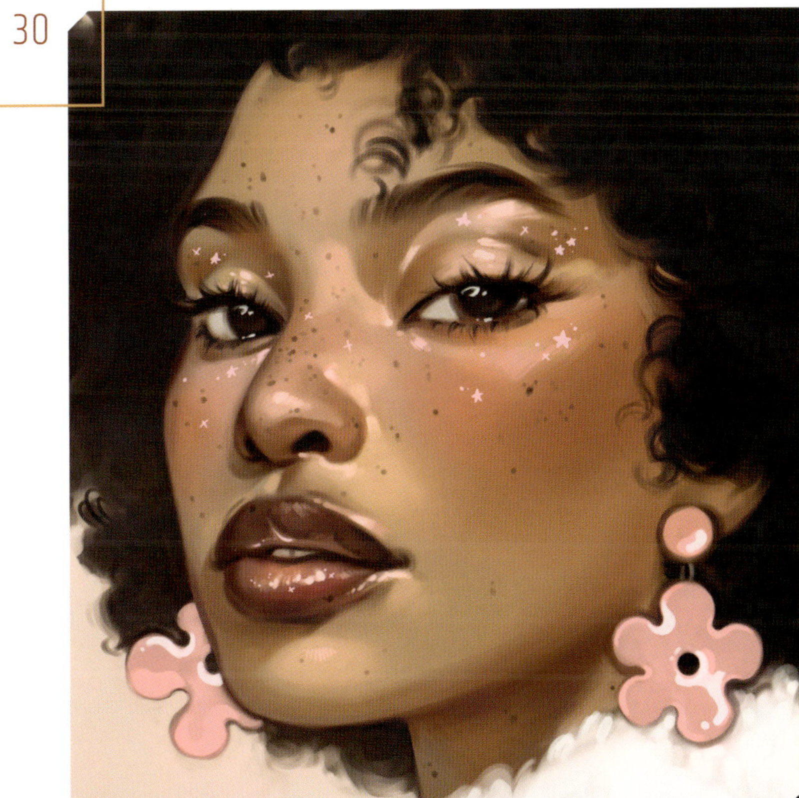

Note the direction of the light source, then paint more highlights onto the acrylic earrings to convey the glossy surface of the material. Next, add small stars and sparkles across the face to create a fantastical, dreamy effect. Stylized portraits allow you to introduce a fantasy element to an otherwise fairly ordinary subject matter to create a magical effect.

Add bright sparkles and stars across the face to create a magical aura

31

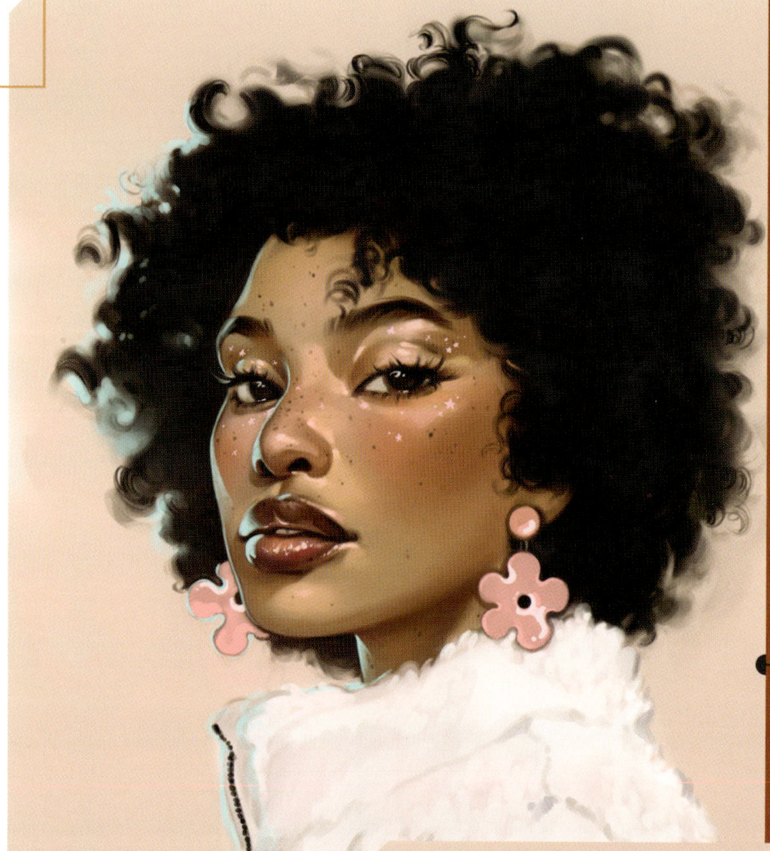

Rim lighting can help to take your portrait to the next level. A contrasting electric blue adds a pop to the overall image. Creating a stylized semi-realistic portrait allows you to take creative liberties not available with realism. Even though the rim lighting is not perfectly accurate, it still enhances the painting and adds a unique touch to the subject. Use precise lines across the edges of the face and softer, diffused strokes on her hair.

Add rim lighting to highlight your subject and give their facial features a three-dimensional quality

32

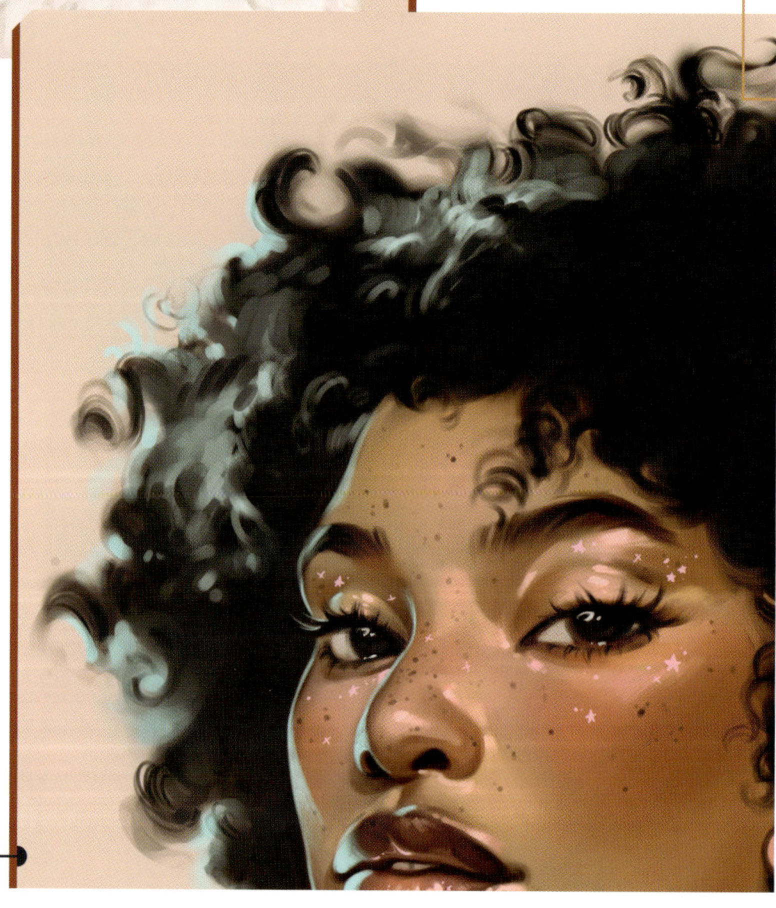

One of the best ways to add more depth to a form is to paint rim lighting across its mass. Further convey the shape of the hair by painting extra rim lighting around the side and front of the head. Build up the highlights using a variety of different brushstrokes, alternating between the blue and darker indigo to create layers and depth to subject's afro.

Create volume in the hair by painting rim light across the side and front of it

33

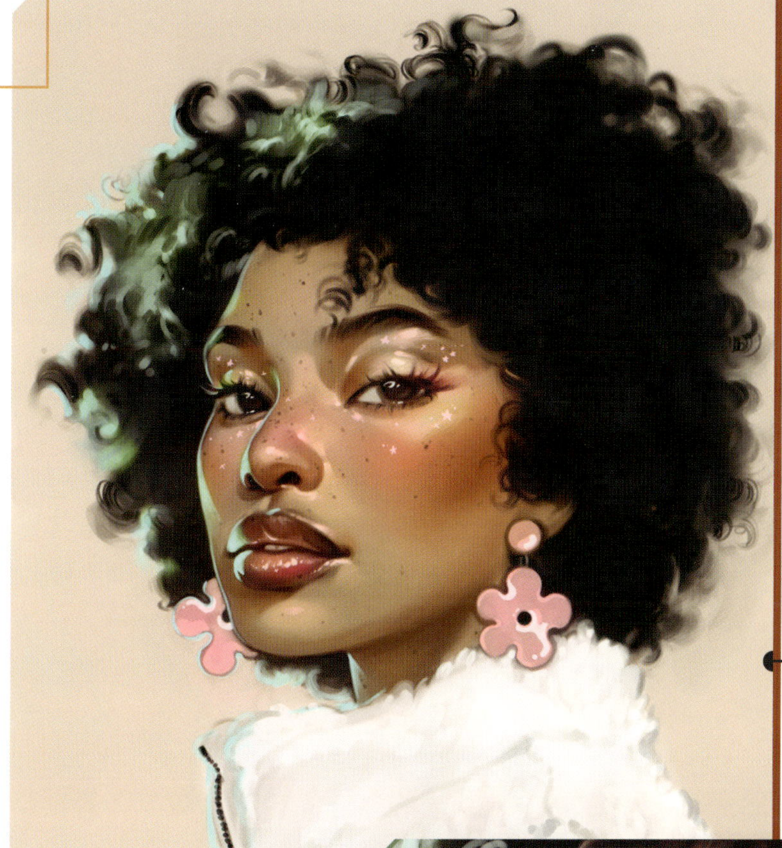

Step back from the painting and assess it. Observe if there are any areas you need to deepen, or colors that you wish to stand out more. Continue to deepen the shadows, contours, and curves around the subject's face to create extra dimension. Intensify the blush and highlight shades in the face, adding vibrancy to your colors. Adding thin washes of color to your portrait will create a rich, polished feel.

Paint thin washes of color to add more life and vibrancy to the image

34

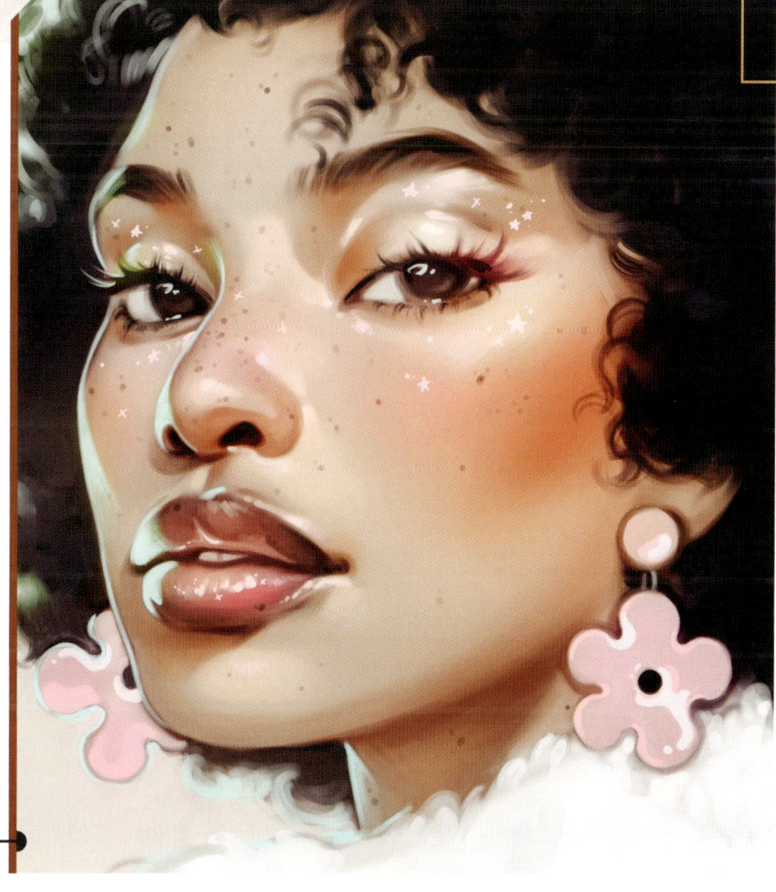

If using digital software, explore different color presets to add a filter to your painting. Finding one or two shades to add to the highlights and shadows will unify the portrait and make it more visually pleasing. These colors can drastically alter the mood of your piece; soft, warm tones will make your subject look friendly and inviting, while harsher greens and blues could create a harsher-looking image. Pink and purple hues have been used here to enhance the portrait, creating a feminine glow.

If painting digitally, use a color preset to alter the tones and mood of the portrait

35

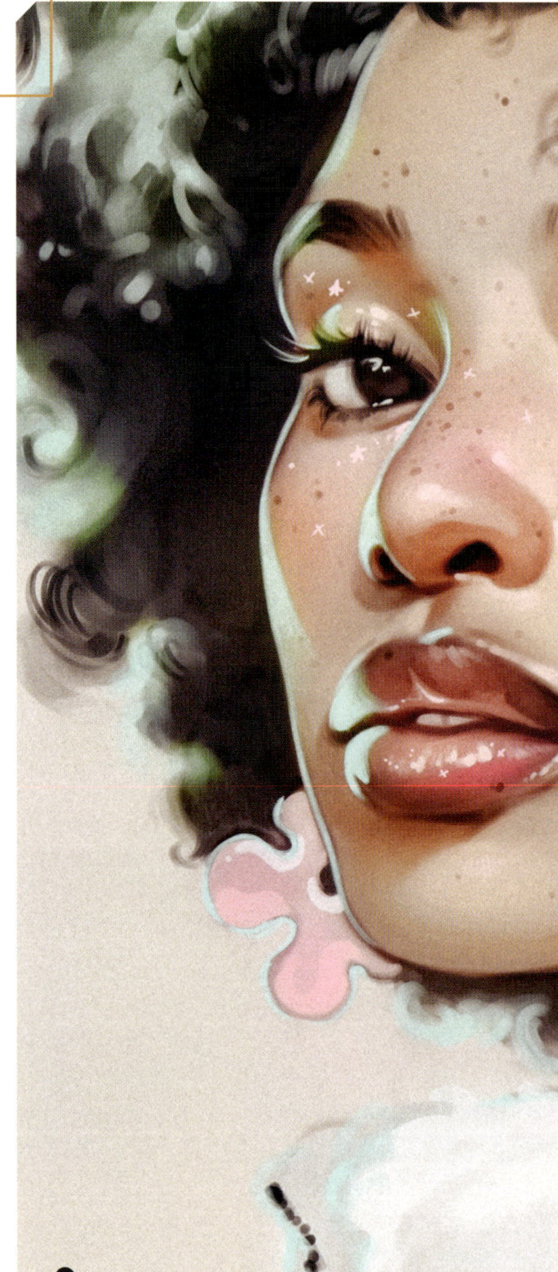

Adding grain to a digital painting is a good way to make it appear more organic

36

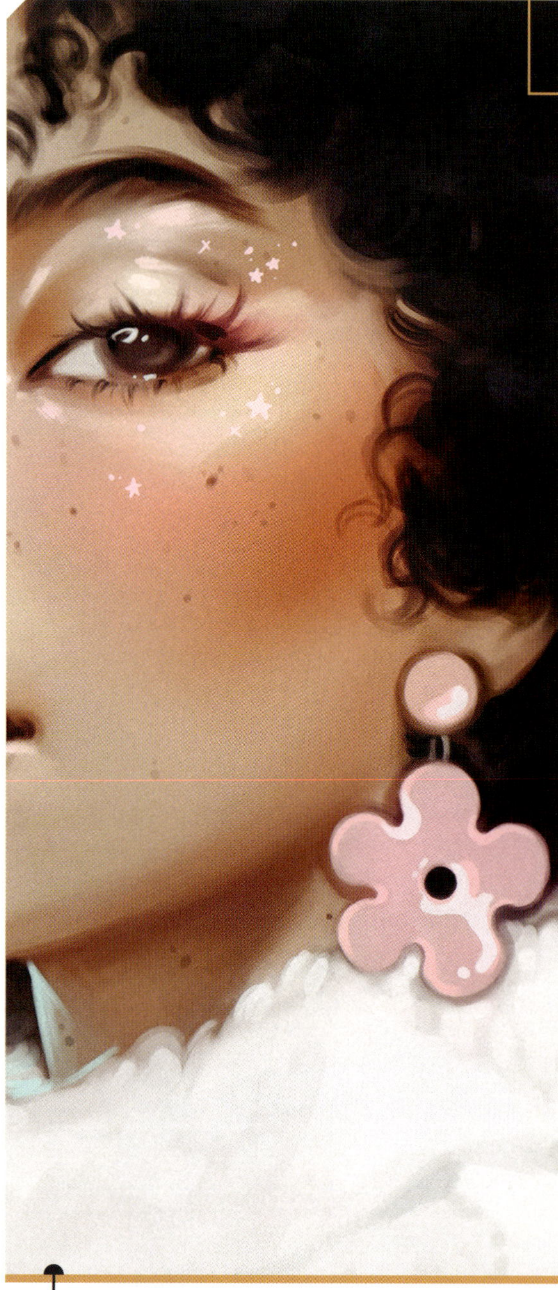

Sharpen the edges of the eyes, eyelashes, and lips to accentuate the details and create contrast

Decide on the type of finish you wish to achieve and how this can affect the overall mood of the portrait. Adding grain to a high resolution photograph can make it look less perfect and polished, giving it a more editorial appearance. The same method can be applied to digital painting. If painting digitally, experiment with adding a grain to your portrait, observing how it can make the image appear more organic and lifelike, rather than overly precise and digital.

Accentuate any defined details, including the eyes, eyelashes, lips, and any other sharp edges on the portrait. If painting digitally, this can be done using a Smart Sharper filter. Sharpening a painting will create contrast around lines or edges, intensifying the shapes and details. If using traditional media, you can achieve this same effect by using a small, sharp-edged brush and zooming in on details – such as the glossy highlights, eyelashes, or baby hairs – and sharpening the edges of those lines.

37

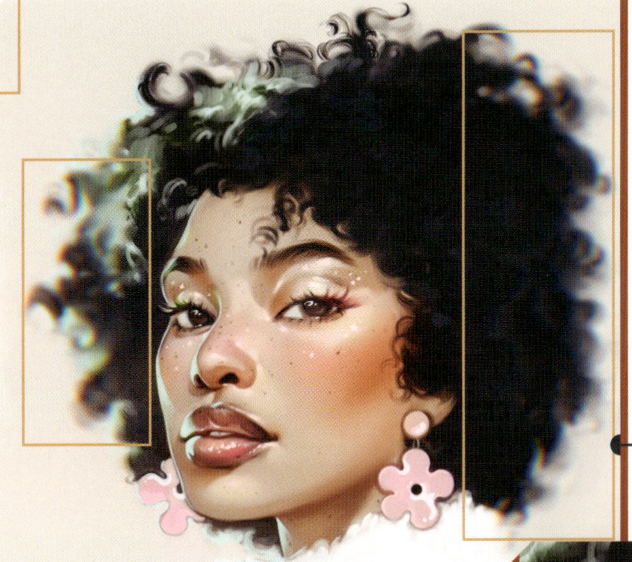

If working digitally, you can use a Prism filter and/or Gaussian Blur around the perimeter of the portrait to further the soft, dreamy look. This will also draw attention to the center of the painting, which is more in focus. Such filters and effects can help to bring your subject to life and should not obscure the detail and work you put into the edges earlier.

You can use a Prism filter and Gaussian Blur to enhance your portrait if using digital software

38

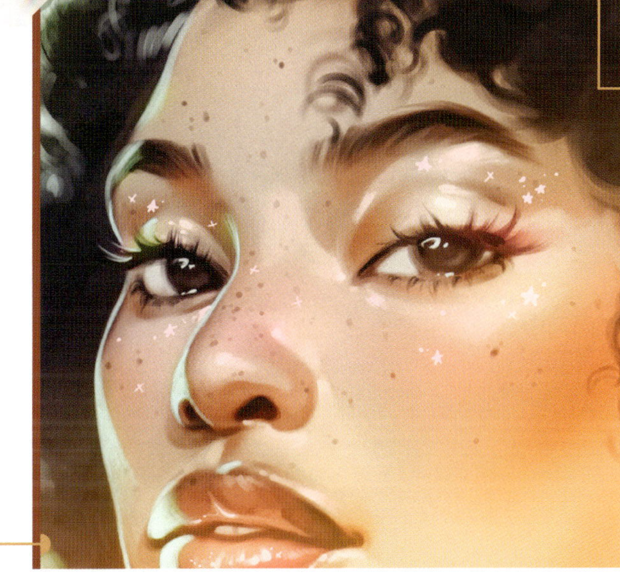

When painting with digital software, adding a flare can create an even more diffused final image. While flares may not work on every portrait, using them can help to draw the eye to the center of the image, or even make your painting look like a film photo. This combination of digital painting and photo editing will vary greatly between individual portraits and styles. Experiment with different flares and see what effects you can create to take your portrait to the next level.

If you wish to stylize the portrait, paint freckles sporadically across the face

39

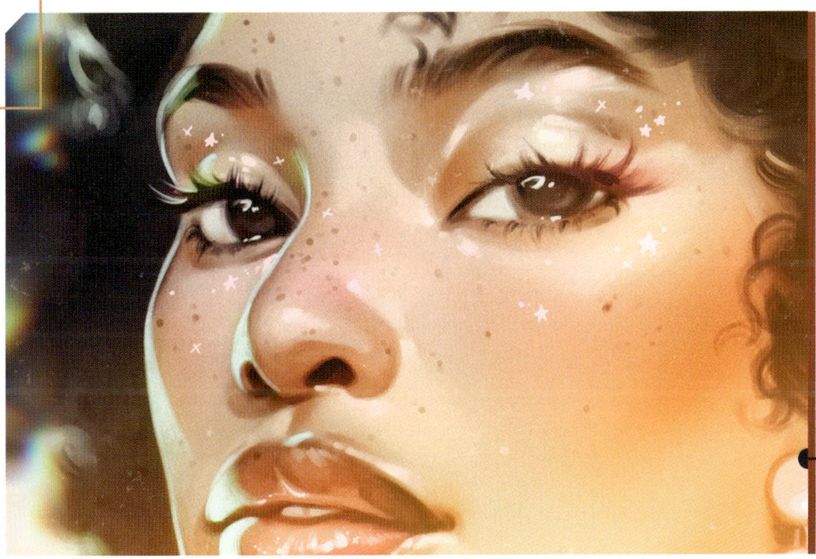

Adding dust and scratches will help to solidify the magical, 35mm film look of this stylized portrait. Paint the dust and scratches using a hard-edged brush, or scan in your own textures.

Adding dust and scratches completes this dreamy, stylized portrait

Conclusion

Following this tutorial will teach you how to create your own vibrant and magical stylized portrait. Utilizing soft and hard edges, a variety of colors, subtle tonal shifts, fine details, and realistic textures will set it apart as a portrait that has been carefully planned and executed. As you progress, experiment with different color palettes, angles, and incorporating your subject's environment. Always be on the lookout for inspiration as you seek to grow your portraiture skills.

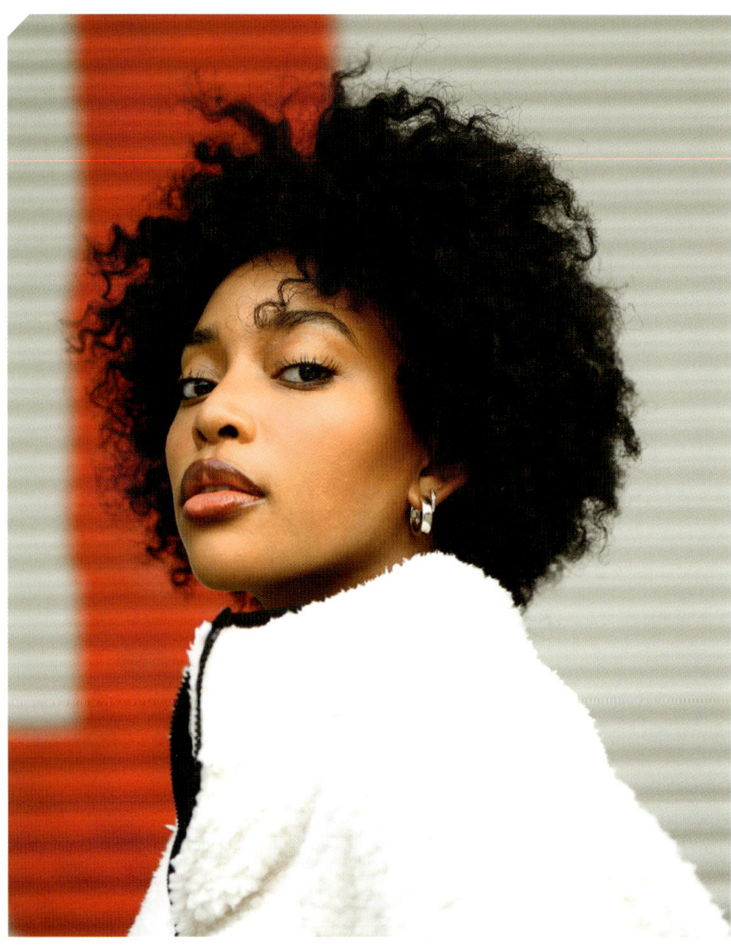

Photograph by Jeffery Erhunse on Unsplash

Final image © Sara Tepes

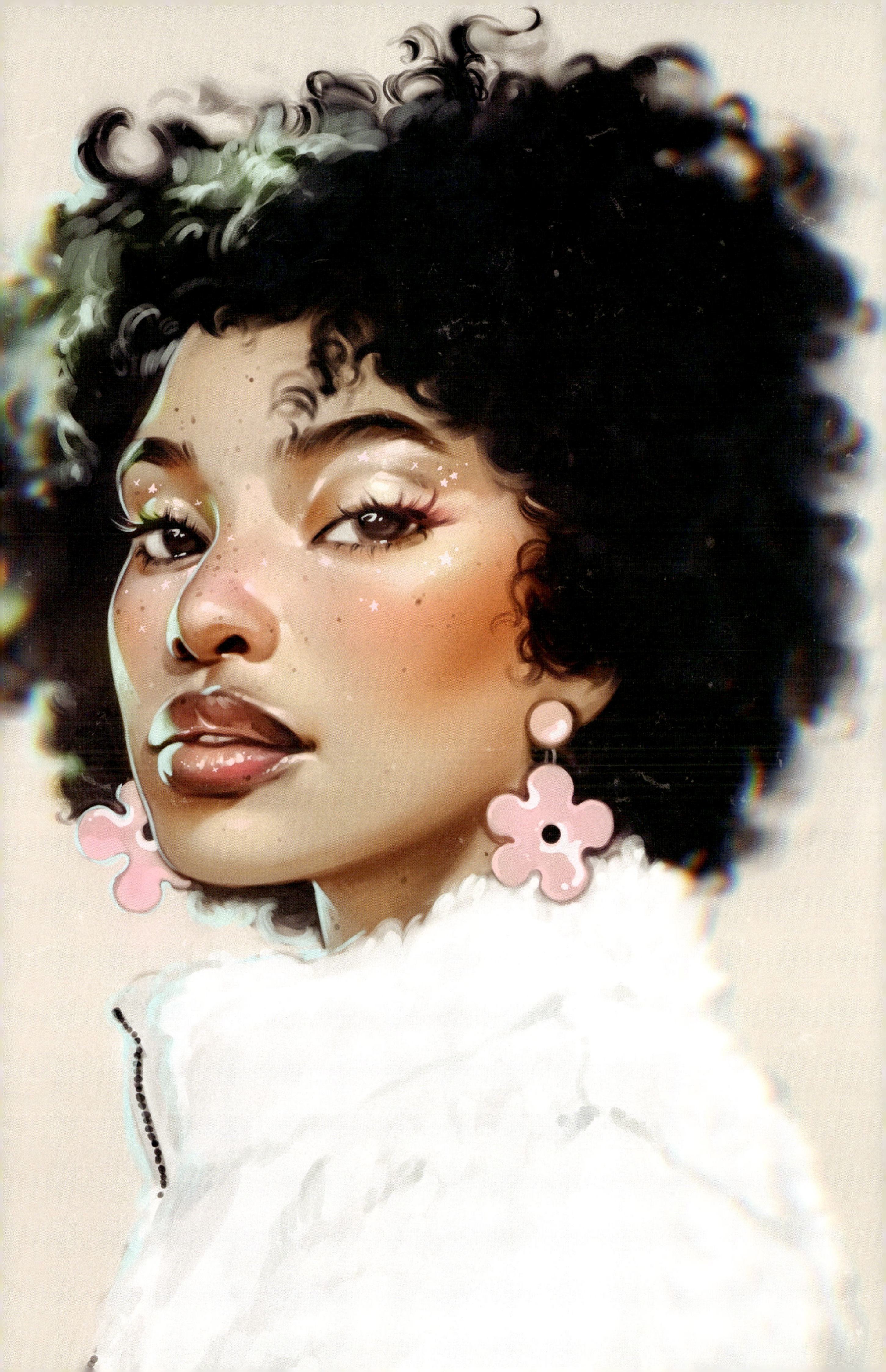

GENNADIY KIM

Introduction

There are infinite ways to create a stylized portrait; this tutorial will demonstrate just one of them. The step-by-step process will guide you through how to draw and paint a Southeast Asian older male subject, providing you with useful tips and tricks along the way. All of the techniques shown here are universal, so you can select any reference photo you like, or even work with a live model.

Following this tutorial you will learn how to create a powerful and striking image from start to finish. It will begin with building a strong composition, detailing how to draw and construct the head, before progressing on to building up the volume of the face, adding color, and painting in the details. This portrait has been created using Adobe Photoshop, but you can use any digital painting software with similar functionality.

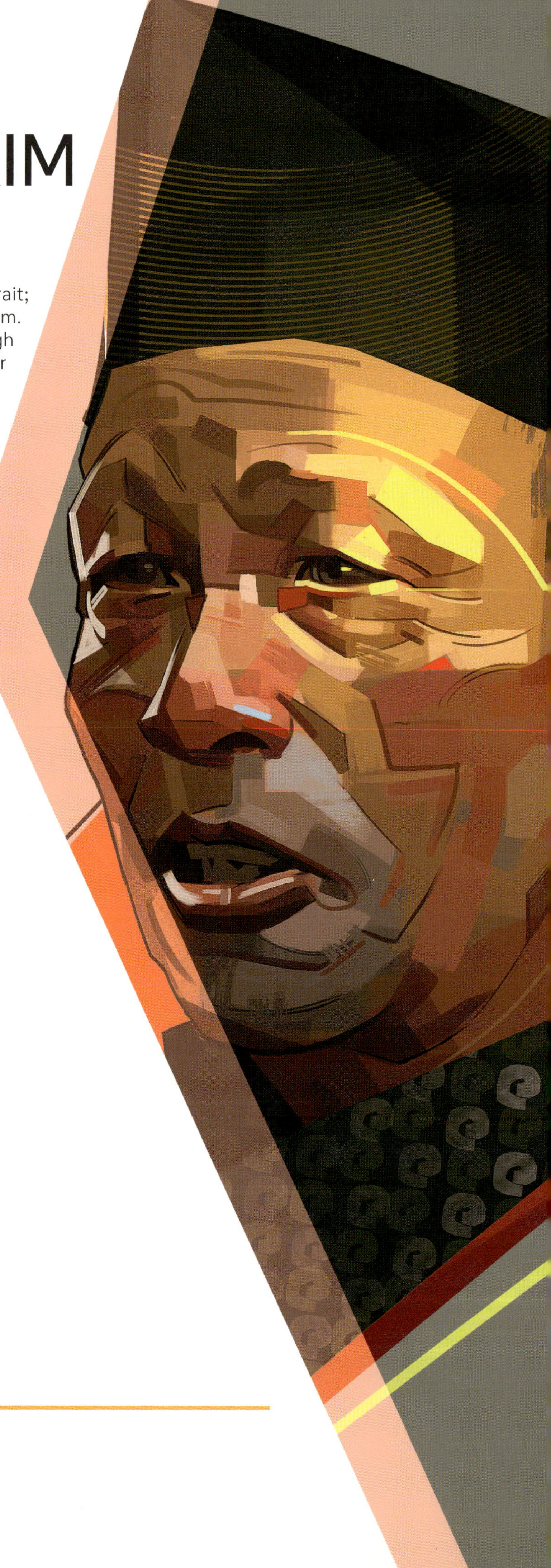

01

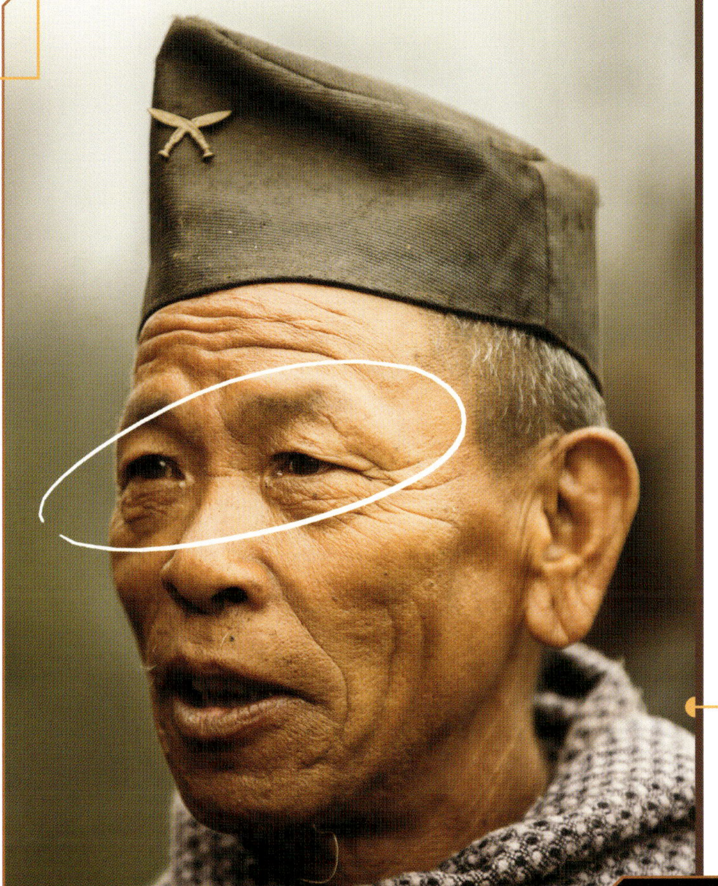

Start by selecting a photograph to use as reference. Pay attention to the lighting; the direction of the light needs to be clear. Another factor to keep in mind is the quality of the photo. Low resolution images can lead to confusion when it comes to the details. Once you have found an interesting, clear photo, work out what the most important feature in it is. Look for an expressive or striking feature; something that makes you want to paint this person.

Study the reference photo and determine its most important features

Photograph by Prijun Koirala on Unsplash

02

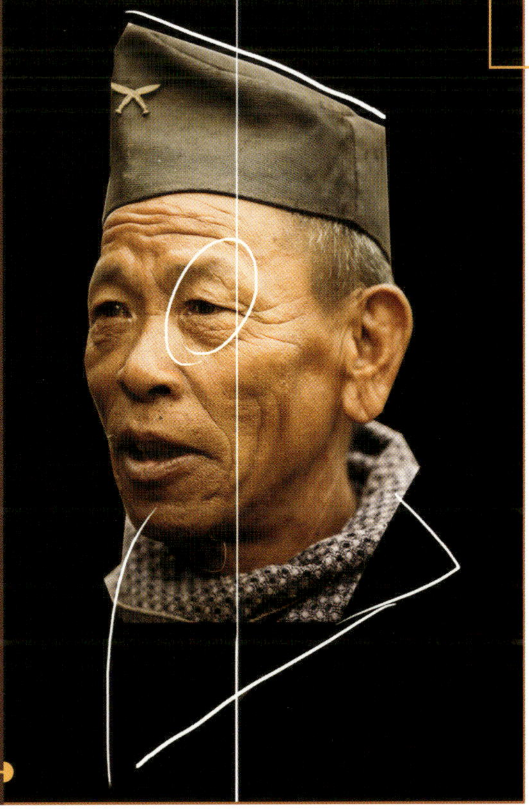

Establish the overall composition of the painting. Position a main focal point at roughly the centerline of the canvas. If needed, extend any existing elements, such as clothing or accessories. Think about how you wish to stylize the portrait and feel free to experiment with different ideas at this early stage. Once you have decided on your chosen idea, it's time to start drawing.

Plan the position of each element on the canvas, experimenting with different ideas

03

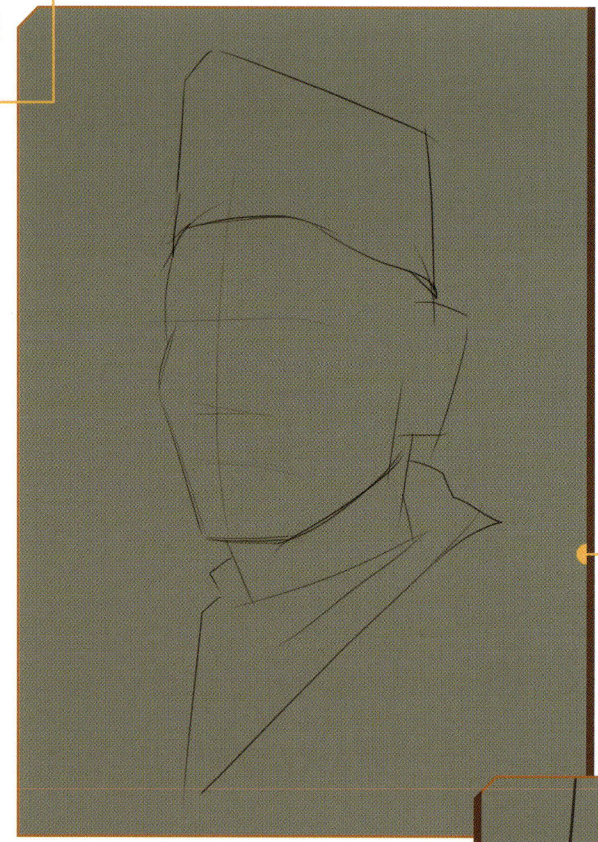

Outline the main silhouette. Keep it simple and don't go into detail yet. Look for the big shapes, angles, and curves in the reference photo. Next, draw a centerline across the face, then add lines to indicate the placement of the main facial features, such as the eyes, nose, and mouth. This stage won't make it into the final painting, so there's no need to make it look beautiful. It's important to be precise, however, as this construction drawing will act as the foundation for the finished portrait.

Outline the silhouette of the head and mark the position of the main features

04

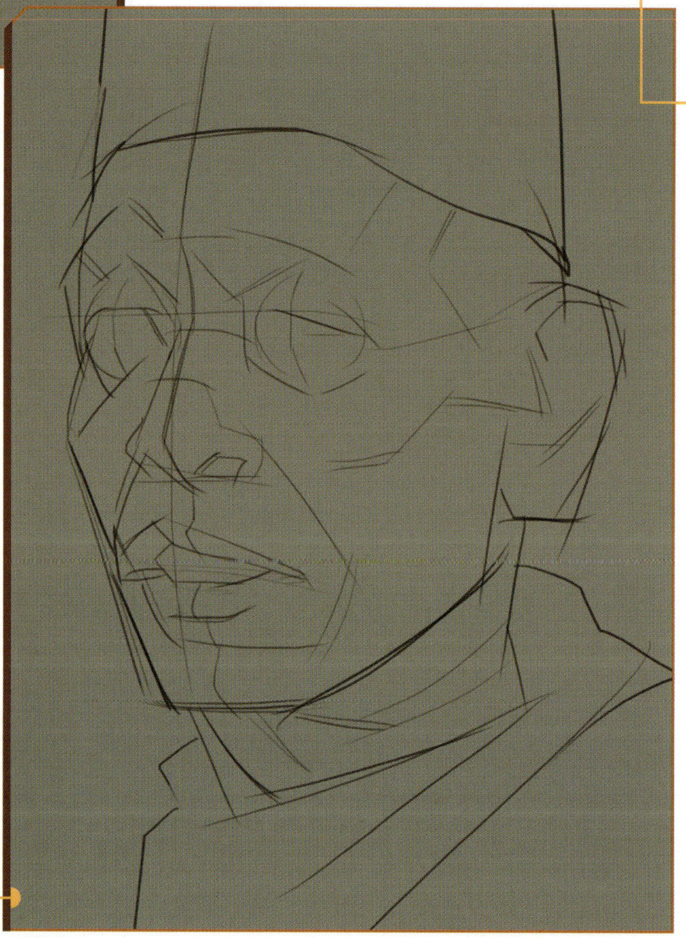

Add smaller details on top of that drawing, paying attention to the structure of a skull. Don't forget to draw lines to indicate the cheekbones, eye sockets, brows, and other details you can see in the reference photo. Correct the silhouette if needed. Next, sketch in more detailed shapes for the facial features. Draw a centerline across the nose, mouth, and each of the eyeballs. This will make it easier to understand the volume of each feature.

Add smaller shapes inside the silhouette and define the construction of the face

05

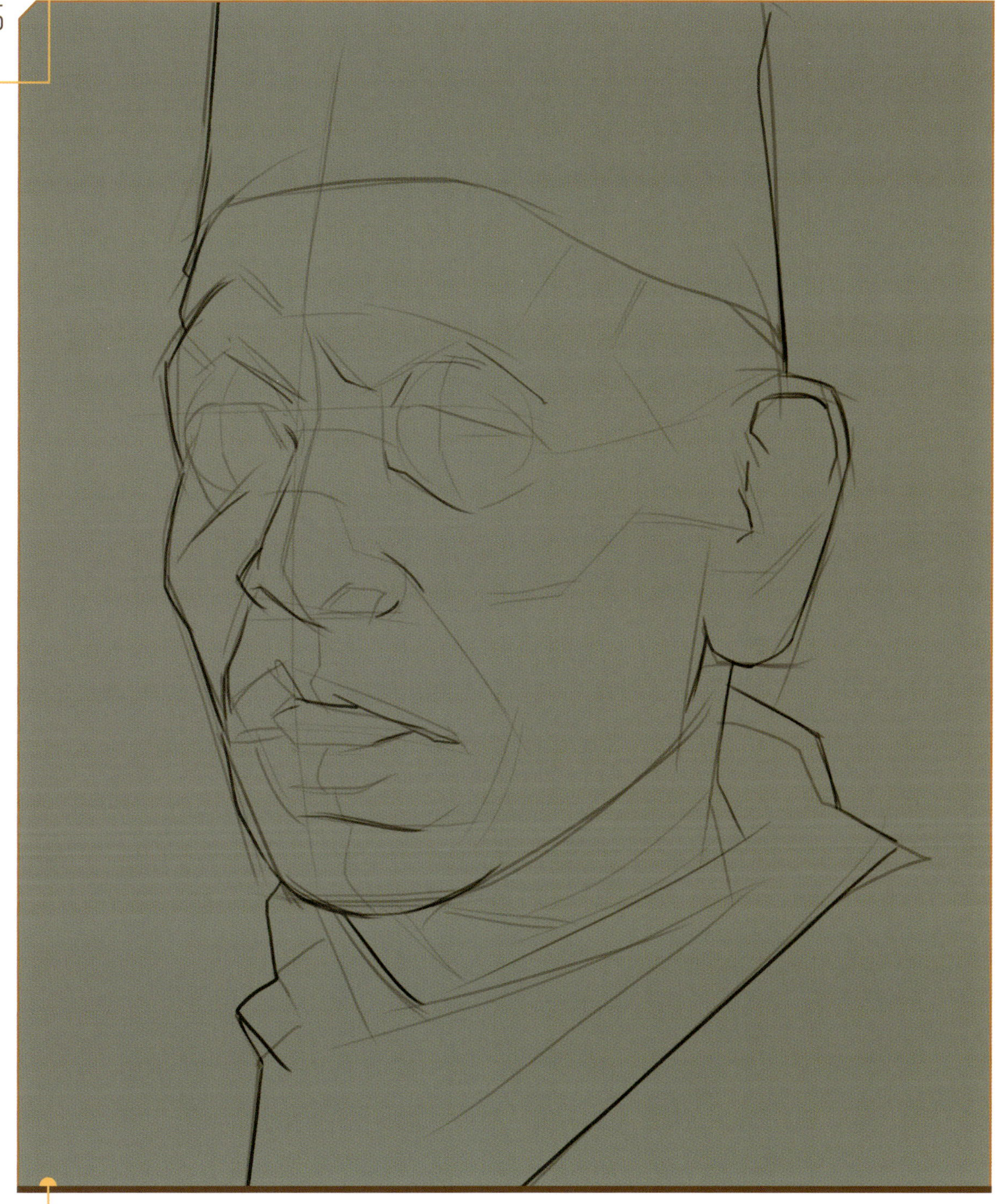

Ink a more accurate drawing by outlining the facial features

To create a more final drawing, outline the existing features while adding a little more detail to the face. Try to add more emphasis on the high contrast shapes you can see in the reference photo. Don't forget about the flow of your lines; the movement should not be interrupted. Every line needs to lead toward another.

06

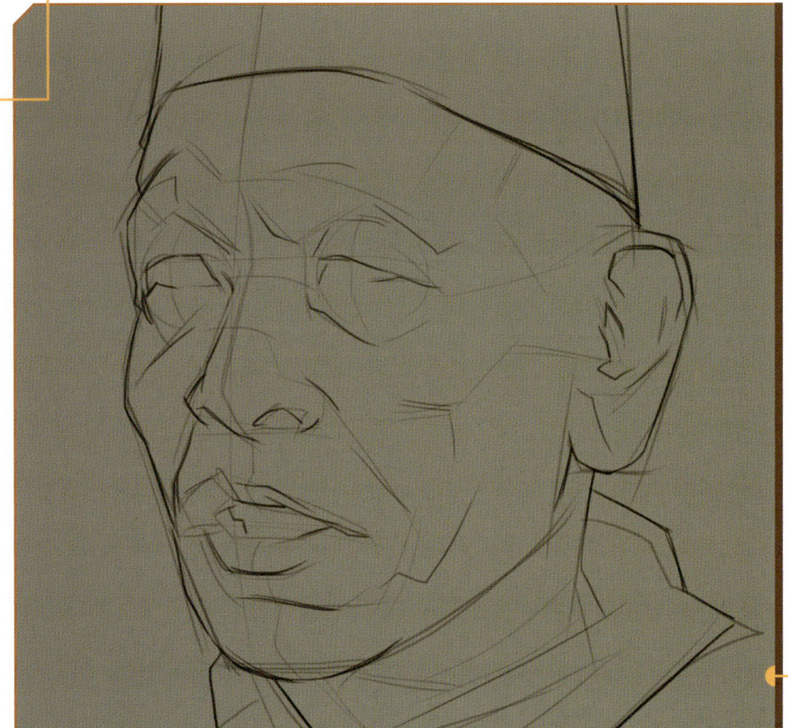

The next step is to add more detail to your drawing. Outline the different shapes present in big features, such as the eye sockets, nose, mouth, and ears. Draw lines representing the overall silhouette of the eyes, nostrils, and teeth. Outline the shape of the upper and lower lip. Correct the existing silhouette, if needed. As in the previous step, it's important to create a smooth, flowing movement through each feature. Use the guides established earlier, but don't be constrained by them.

Continue to add more detail to your drawing using the guidelines created earlier

07

Study your reference photo closely and compare it with your drawing. Correct any elements you notice don't look right, using an eraser if needed. For example, the left side of the silhouette in step 06 was too wide, so here it has been narrowed a little. If at any point in the process you feel the need to correct something, don't hesitate to do so. Don't become so attached to your work that you are reluctant to fix aspects of the drawing that appear incorrect.

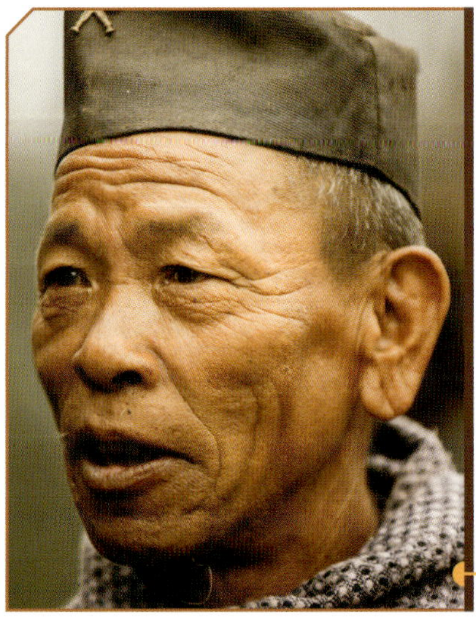

Examine the reference photo and correct any mistakes present in your drawing

08

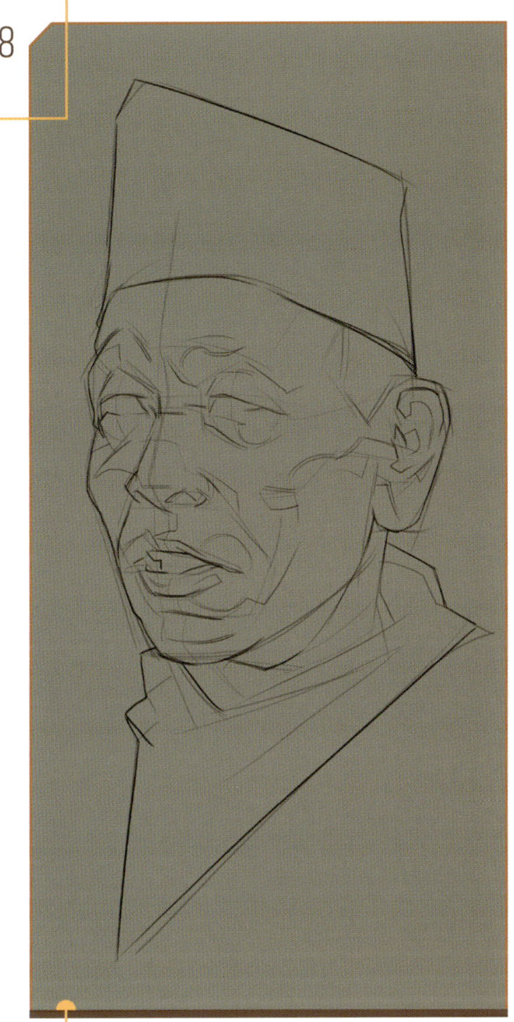

Plan out the value structure of the face and mark major shapes

Now it's time to outline the big value shapes. Try to keep it as simple as possible. For example, if you see a circular shape in your reference photograph, don't overcomplicate it; simply draw a circle or oval. Focus on the high contrast shapes and don't forget about the flow of these shapes. This step is important for future painting, but you don't need to draw it perfectly as these shapes will be used as guides for painting.

09

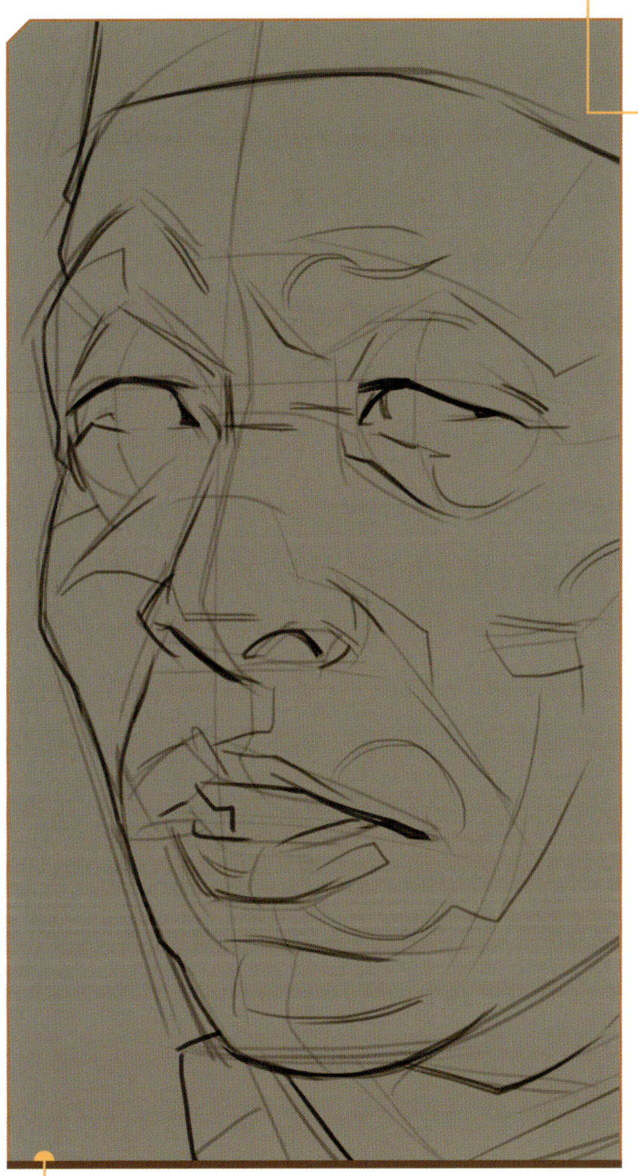

Add more emphasis on the main features of the face using thicker, darker lines

Remember the first steps of this tutorial? It's now time to use what you observed in the reference photo. Go over the details of the facial features one more time. Darker and thicker brushstrokes will create more contrast than thin, light lines. Carefully add them to the main feature; in this case, the eyes. Use these lines to separate features of the face, such as the nose. Make small marks to represent the eyeball in the eye socket.

10

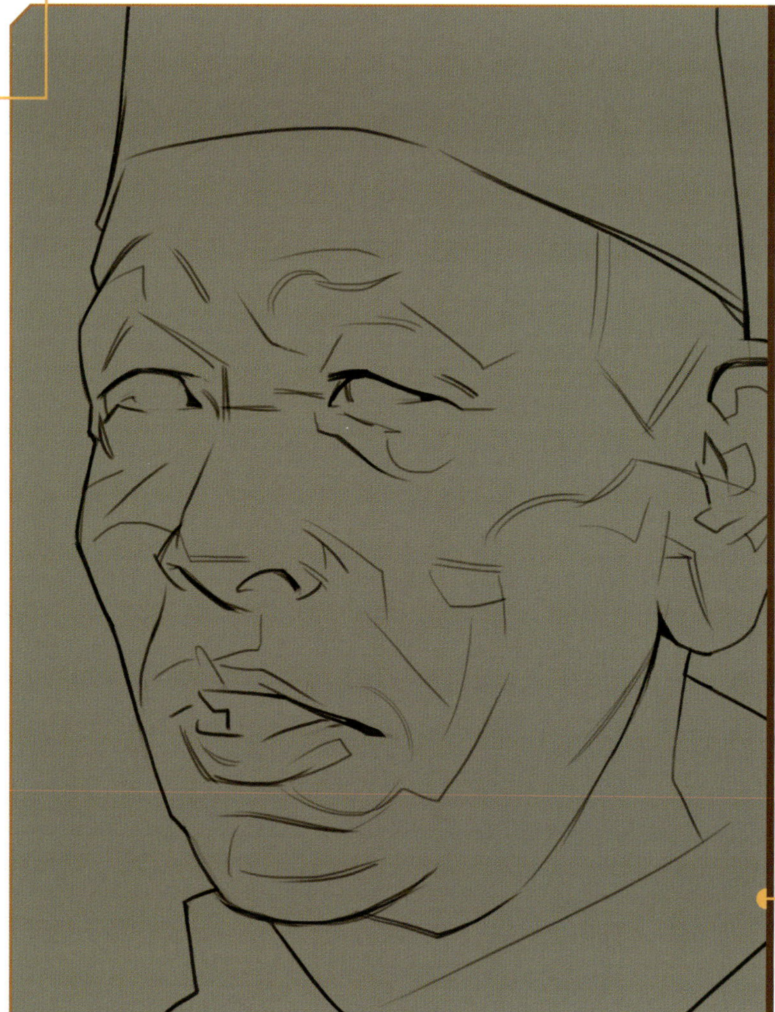

You are now almost finished with the drawing stage of the portrait, so it's time to clean up your lines. Before you do this, check if your drawing needs any corrections. Use an eraser to remove any unnecessary lines along with your construction drawing. Pay close attention to the silhouette of the head; it should be clean and enclosed. Without a construction drawing underneath, some parts may need some additional lines. For example, here a small line is added to indicate the jawbone.

Clean up your drawing using an eraser and correct any mistakes

Artist tip

Pay attention to the various types of line in your drawing. A line can be thick or thin, dark or light, curved or straight, indicative or suggestive. A combination of different types of line will create movement and variety in the portrait. Another factor to consider is the energy of your brushstrokes. Don't try to draw a perfect line on the first try. Instead, make decisive and confident marks on the canvas using various movements of your hand and arm.

11

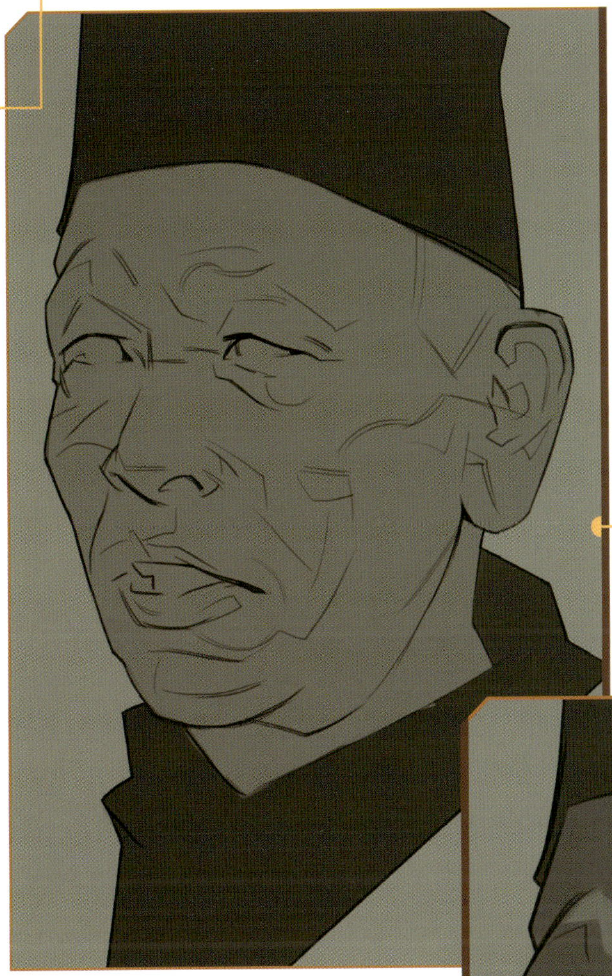

Fill each component of the portrait with a different shade of gray. Select a light gray tone to represent the skin color, and different tones to represent each accessory, such as the hat and clothing.

Establish a base tone for each object using gray colors

12

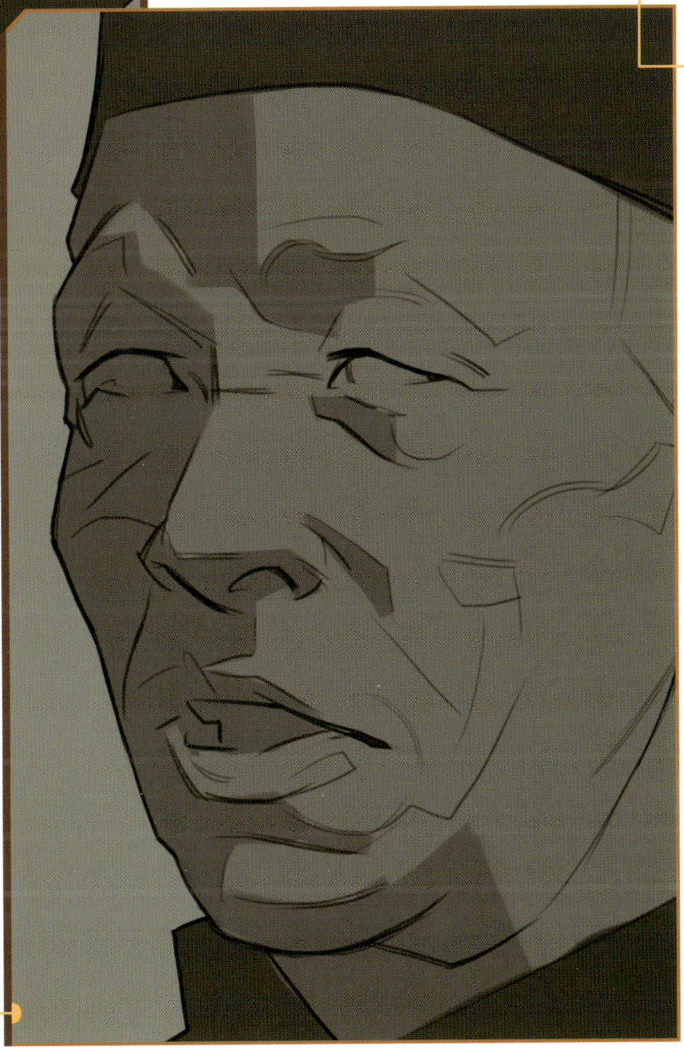

Select a color that is slightly darker than your selected skin color. Use this to paint the shapes of the areas that are in shadow using broad, confident brushstrokes. Refer back to your drawing and a reference photo to determine the placement of these shadows. If you see several shadow shapes near each other, combine them into one solid shape to keep it clean and simple. Create separate, smaller shapes around the focal point to help draw the attention of the viewer to the main features.

Paint in the major shadow shapes using a slightly darker color

13

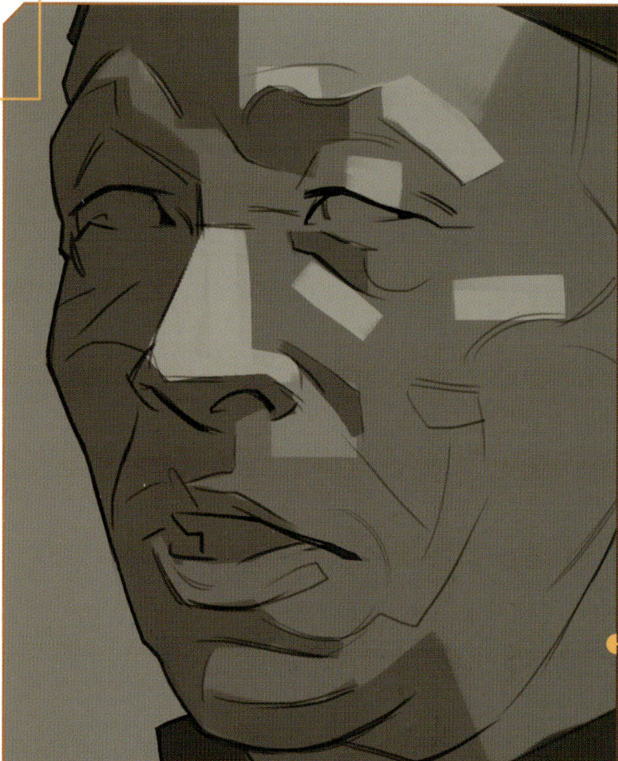

Choose a lighter gray color to represent parts of the face that are facing toward the light source. Position these light shapes next to the shadow shapes around the main area of focus to bring even more contrast to the focal point. Create a slight gradation by leaving the lower part of the face in the original gray skin color. Slightly darken any planes that face the light at an angle.

Add more volume to the face by painting lighter values

14

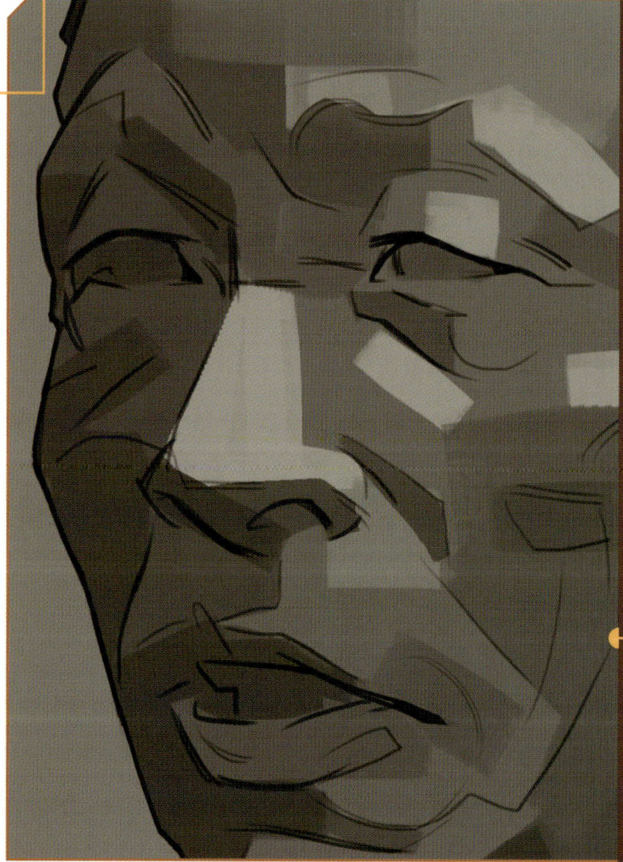

Carefully study the reference photo, then paint the areas of the face that are in between light and shadow. Use a shade of gray slightly darker than your base skin color. Next, select a color slightly darker than the shadows and paint over some parts of the shadows established in previous steps. Keep the contrast in the shadow shapes fairly low. And don't forget to add a very subtle shade of dark gray to the shadowed parts of the features positioned in the focal point.

Proceed to define volume by adding halftones and darkening the shadows

15

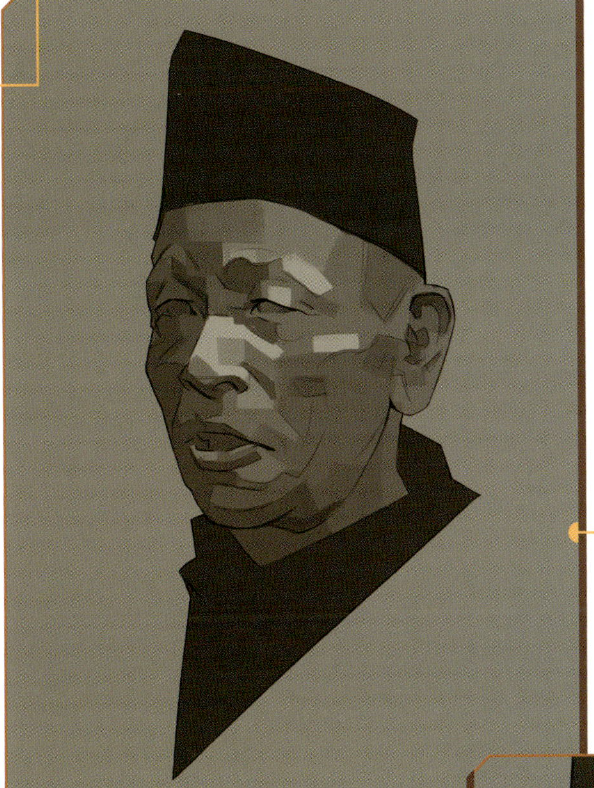

Add some more shapes that transition from one tone to the other. Refine all of the existing shapes by painting over them with slower, precise movements. Remember to keep the flow of the angles and shapes moving from one to another. Next, add more tonal gradation from top to bottom by slightly darkening the chin. Study your reference photo and pay attention to the different plane changes of the face. Correct any mistakes in values by painting over them with a darker or lighter tone.

Add more detail to the face and refine existing shapes

16

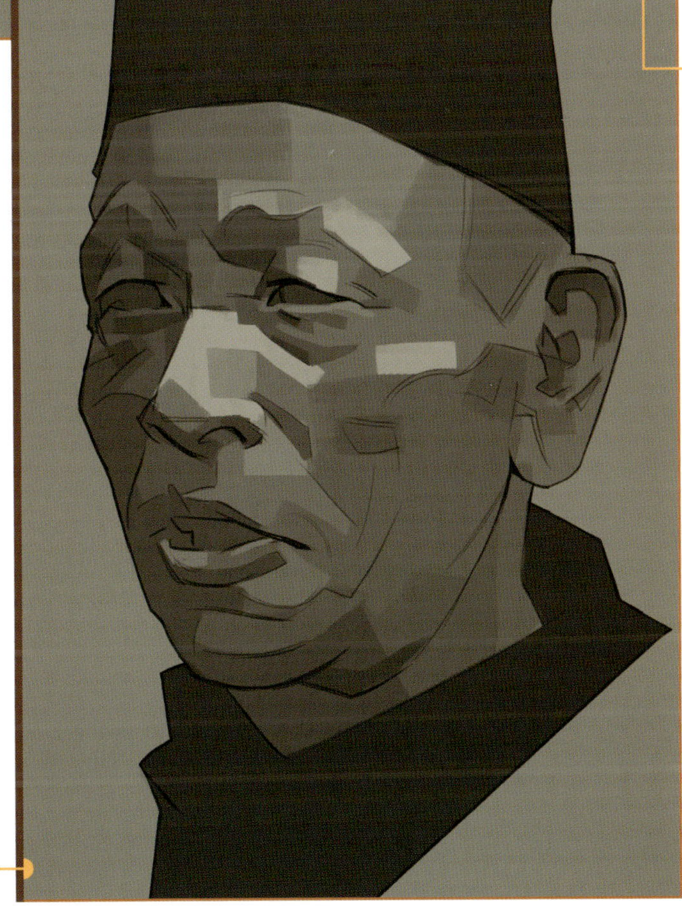

Add a little more detail to the facial features to define their volumes, starting with the eyes. Select a smaller brush and darken the parts of the eyes that are in shadow. Next, paint shapes around the eyelids to represent the spherical volume of the eyeballs. Add smaller details such as wrinkles and the part of the eyelid that faces the light source. Lastly, add darker tones on the brow ridges that face away from the light source.

Define the volume of the eyes and the area around them

17

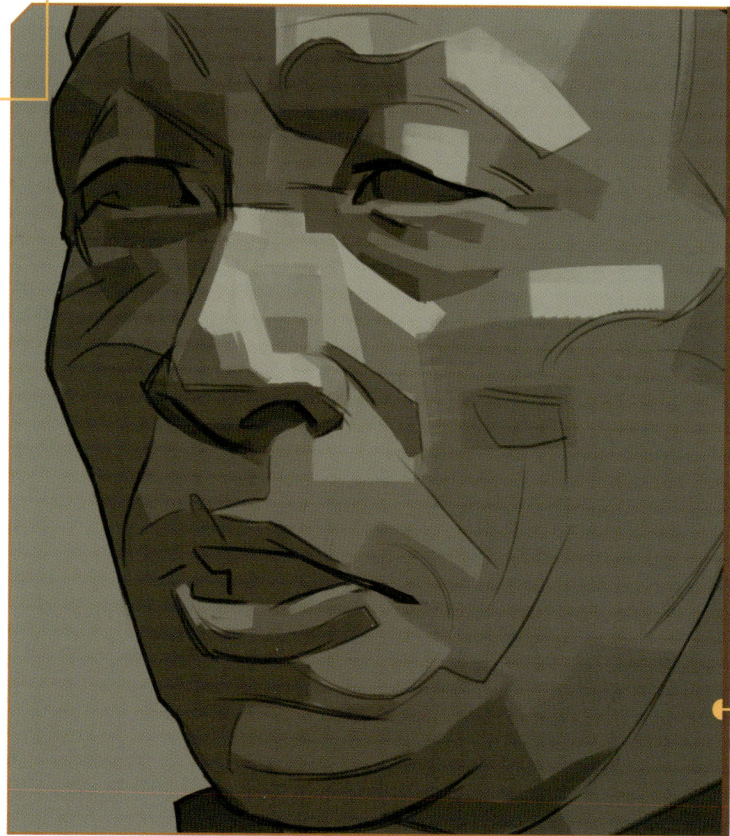

For the nose, add darker tones to the nostril area and around the wing that faces away from the light source. Next, create more volume on the bridge of the nose by painting a middle gray shape along the darker side of the bridge. Add more tonal variation in the areas around the nose to represent a smooth transition from cheeks to nose, then do the same for the tip of the nose.

Add more definition to the nose using smaller, detailed brushstrokes

18

Darken the upper lip and the part of the bottom lip that faces away from the light source. Add more tones around the mouth area to represent volumes created by the different muscles of the lower part of the face. Next, take some time to correct any parts of the drawing, if needed. For the teeth, don't be tempted to paint them white. Use middle values to achieve a more natural look instead. For example, here the teeth have a darker middle value.

Add volume to the face by painting in the mouth and teeth

19

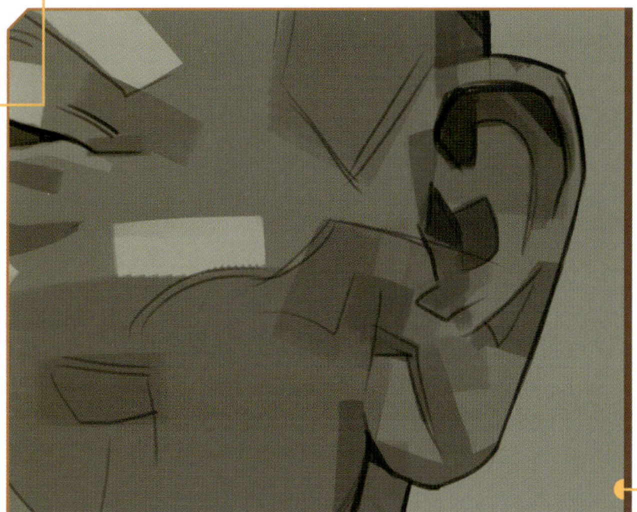

Moving on to the ears, observe the different plane changes present in the reference photo and paint a few simple shapes using slightly darker tones. You don't need to be too precise when painting ears, as they look fairly abstract by nature. Pay close attention to the area where the ear is attached to the head. Next, add transitional values along the line of the cheekbones. Lastly, darken the parts of the ear that go deeper into the head.

Define the various plane changes of the ear and the areas around it

20

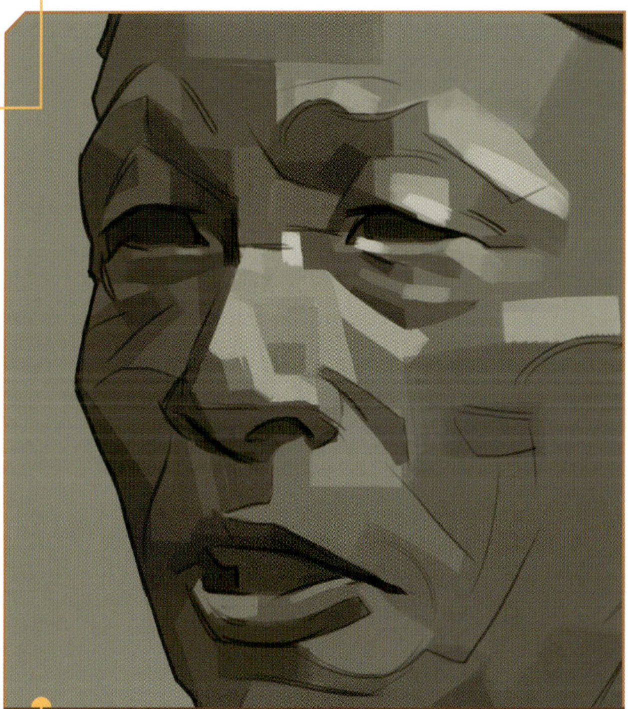

Draw contrast to the focal point by introducing darker tones and highlights

The value part of the tutorial is almost over, but before you move on to coloring the portrait, add some final details to your value painting. Introduce more contrast to the focal points by darkening parts blocked from the light by the geometry of the face and adding highlights. Carefully observe the reference image and correct any mistakes, as needed.

Artist tip

It's important to keep the design of your shapes fairly clean. You can construct complex shapes using various combinations of simpler shapes. To quickly check if a shape is too complicated, try to describe it with words. If you can describe it fairly easily, then it's fine. For example, a tall oval or a curved rectangle. But if you describe something like a six-pointed star with an obtuse trapezoid cut out of it, then it's likely too complicated.

21

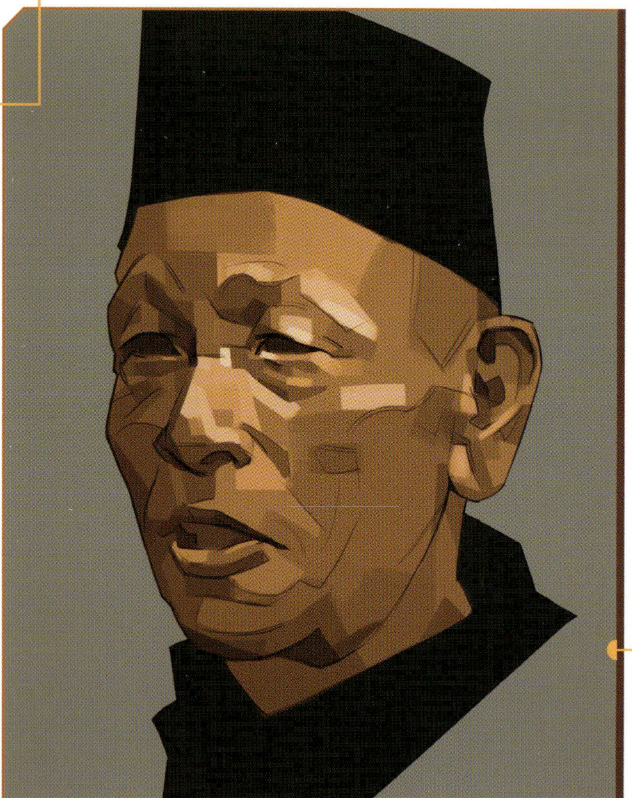

Next, select a middle value color that better represents each of the elements and apply it to the face, clothing, and hat in turn. You can do this digitally with a layer set to Overlay, or with a translucent medium such as watercolor or marker.

Establish base colors for each of the elements on the canvas

22

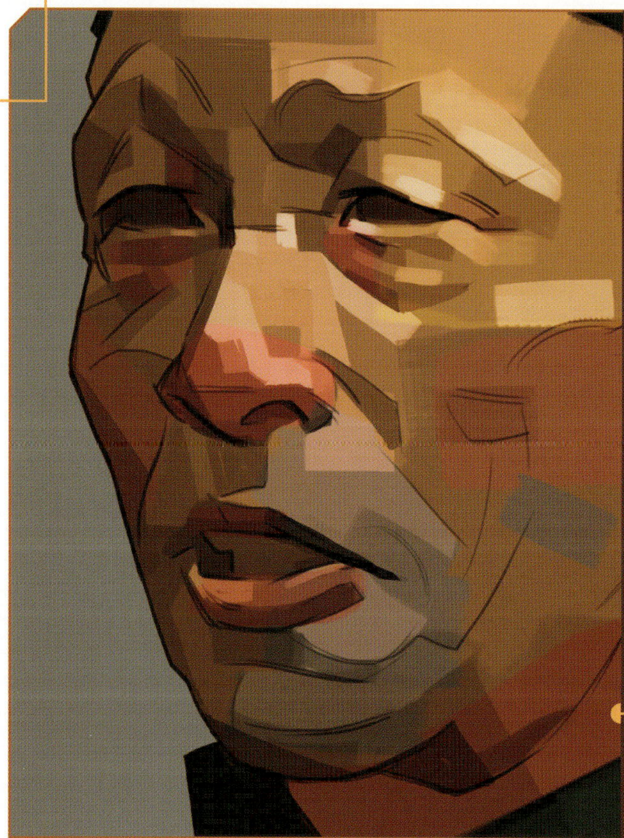

Begin to add variation to the skin color. Study the reference photo carefully and exaggerate what you see. Add a small amount of red to areas of the cheeks, nose, mouth, ears, and neck. Next, apply slightly desaturated variations of color to the lower part of the face. Add a slight yellow tint to the forehead area also. Lastly, paint low contrast shapes onto the clothing.

Create stylization and variety in color by slightly exaggerating what you see in the reference

23

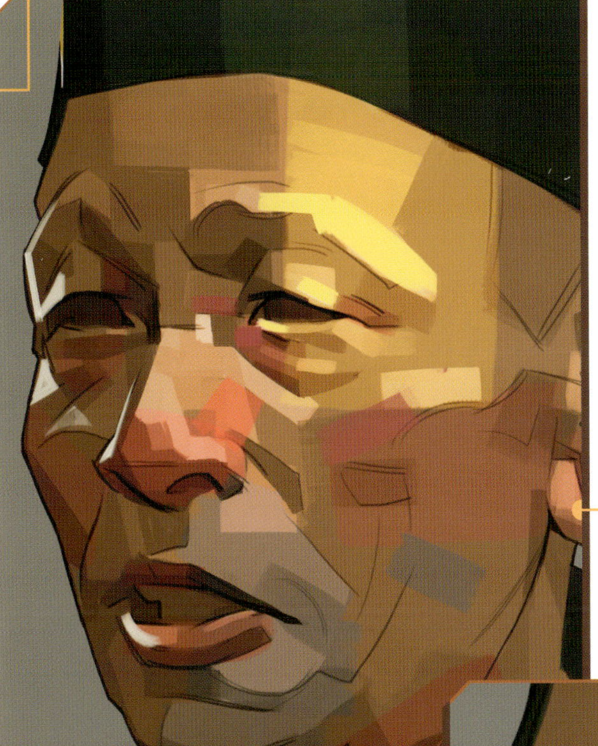

Start to add more exaggerated colors, painting a bright, warm yellow on top of the brow ridge. Extend red areas of the face by painting pink and muted purple spots along the flow of the movement. Next, choose a desaturated color and apply it to the side of the face in shadow. Study the reference photo to determine how the light will fall on the different volumes of the face.

Proceed to add more color variety, using the reference photo as a guide

24

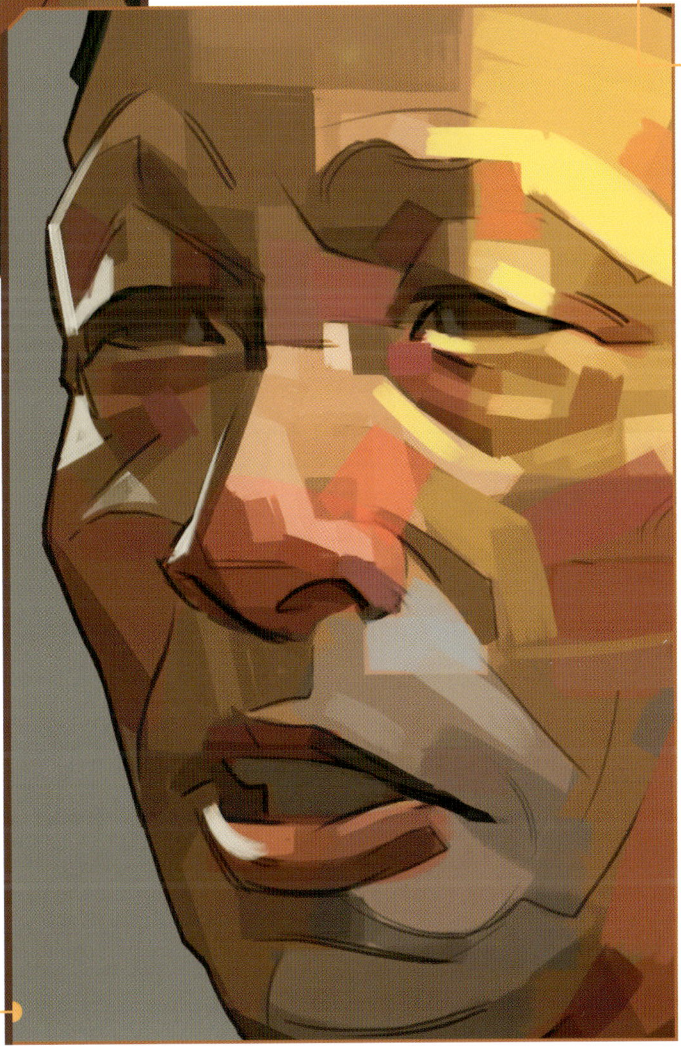

Now it's time to describe the established volumes in more detail. Start by applying brushstrokes between shapes, using a color that is darker than the lighter shape and lighter than the darker shape. This is essentially the same concept as painting values. Next, add some minor details, such as the white areas of the eyes. Keep in mind that the color of these areas is not white, but rather a desaturated brown.

Define the volumes of the face further by painting in a few more details

25

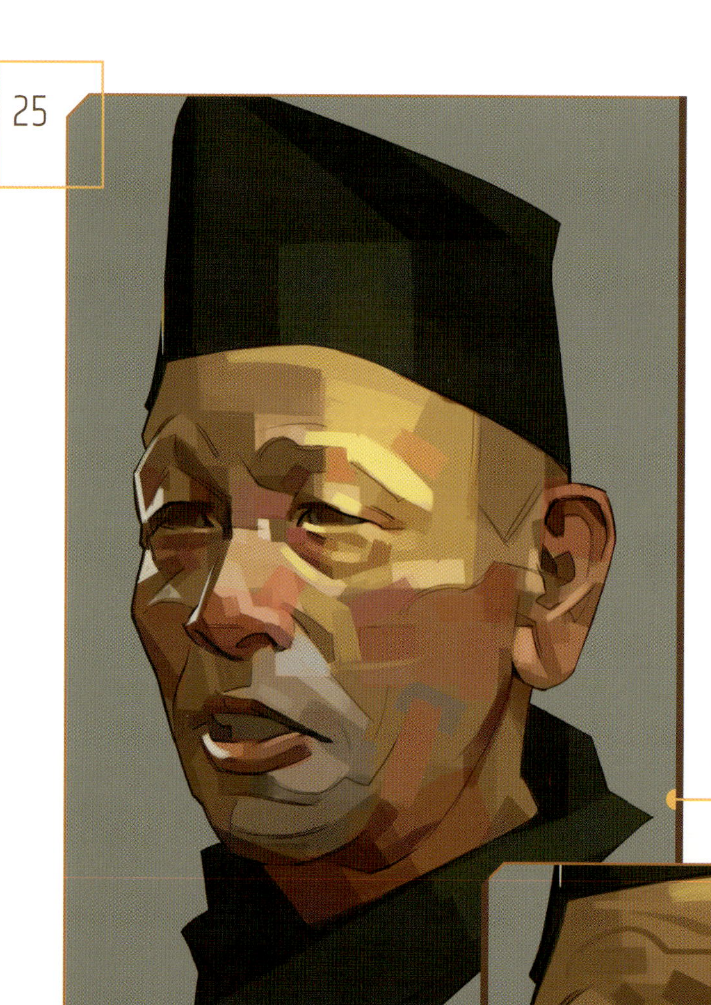

The next step is to make the colors a little more realistic. Comparing your painting to the reference photo, adjust and desaturate the colors so they are closer to the reference.

Create stylization and variety in color by slightly exaggerating what you see in the reference

26

Study the reference photo, paying attention to the details. Paint these smaller shapes onto the portrait. Correct any shapes that feel wrong, especially on or surrounding the eyes and mouth. Next, paint a few highlights onto the lips and observe how adding details in certain areas of the face can change the facial expression. Lastly, clean up any shapes and parts of the drawing that look messy.

Paint smaller details and correct any mistakes

27

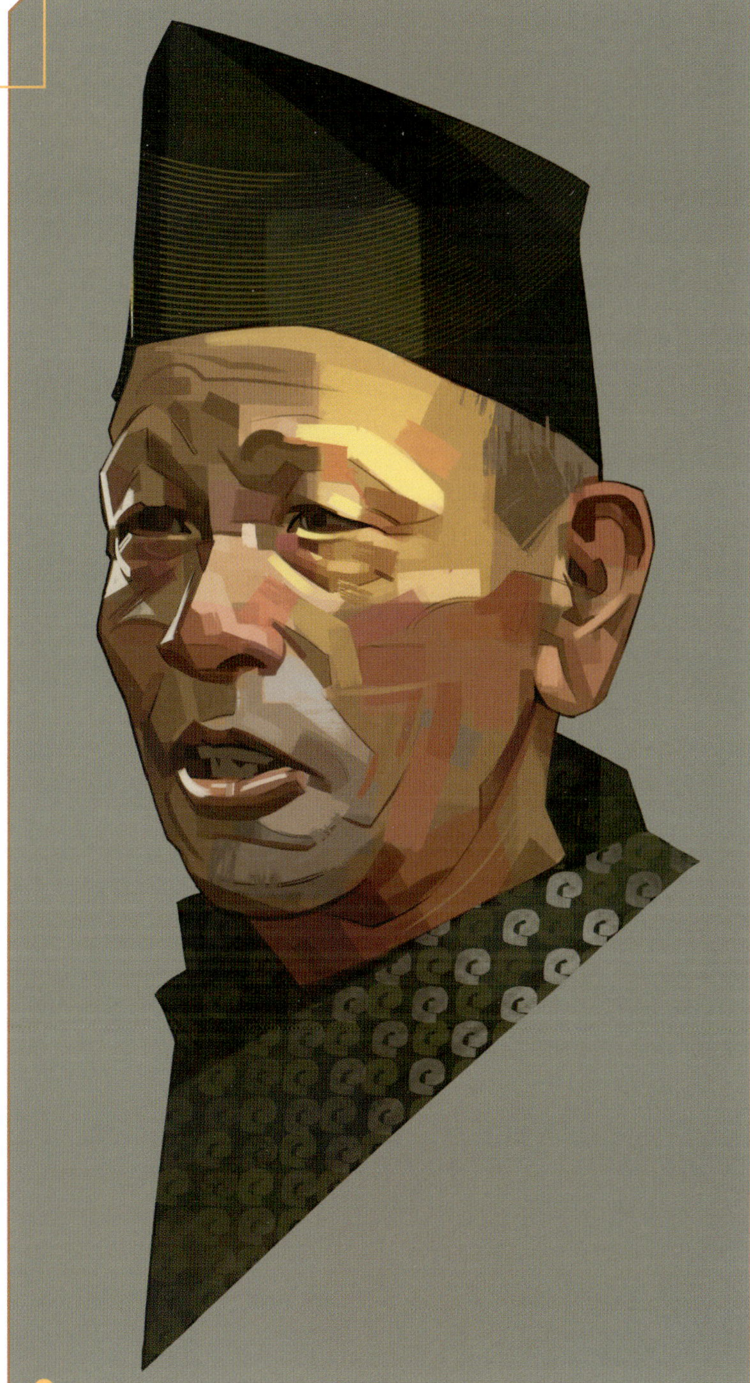

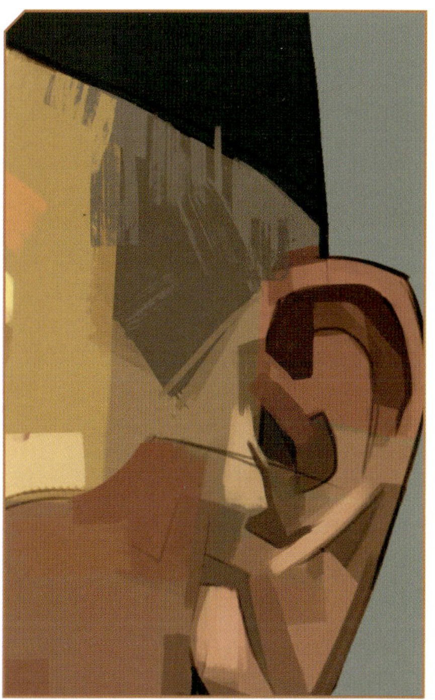

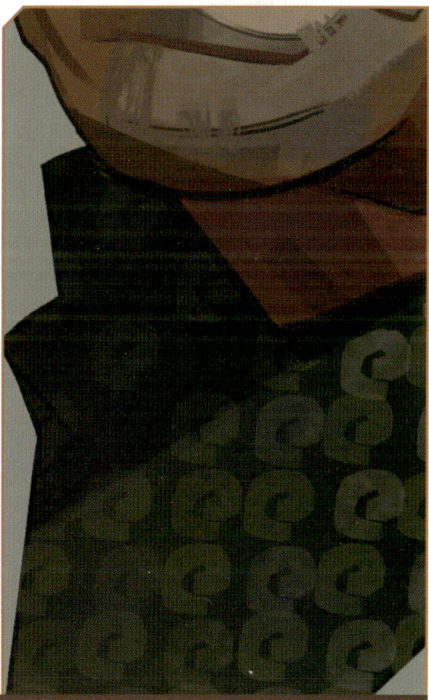

Add texture and patterns to the clothing and face

Use a textured brush to paint a little texture onto the noisy areas, such as the hair, wrinkled parts of the face, and beard. Use the colors that are already on the canvas for this. Next, add the texture or detail of the clothing. If working digitally, you can use the Transform tools to make the pattern fit the volumes of the object.

28

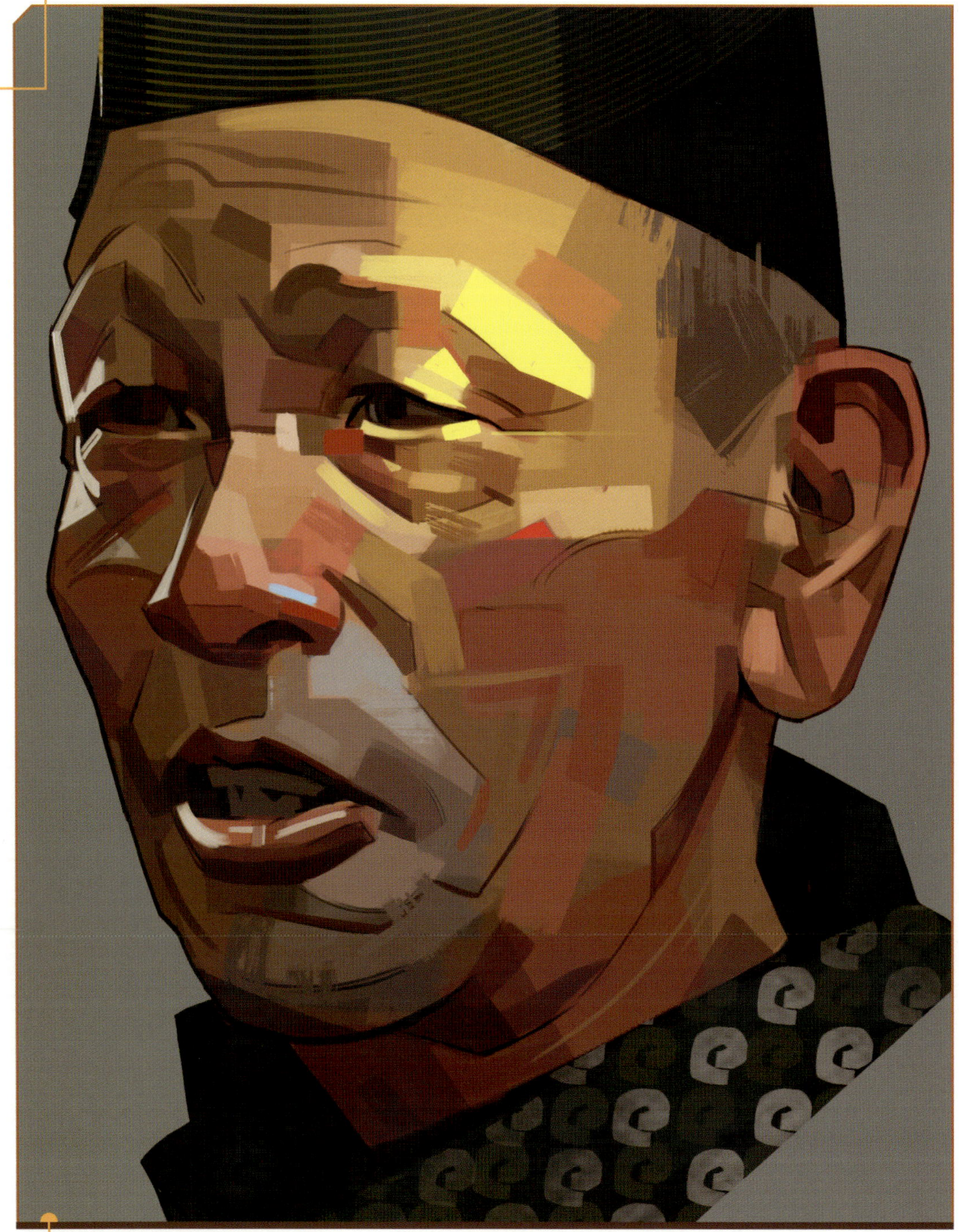

Introduce abstract spots of vibrant color to pull more emphasis to the focal point

Stylize the portrait by adding abstract spots of vibrant color, positioning them in a way that better guides the viewer's attention toward the focal point of the portrait. Use colors that are already present on the canvas, but increase their saturation. If you're using colors that are complementary to the whole piece, keep them fairly desaturated.

29

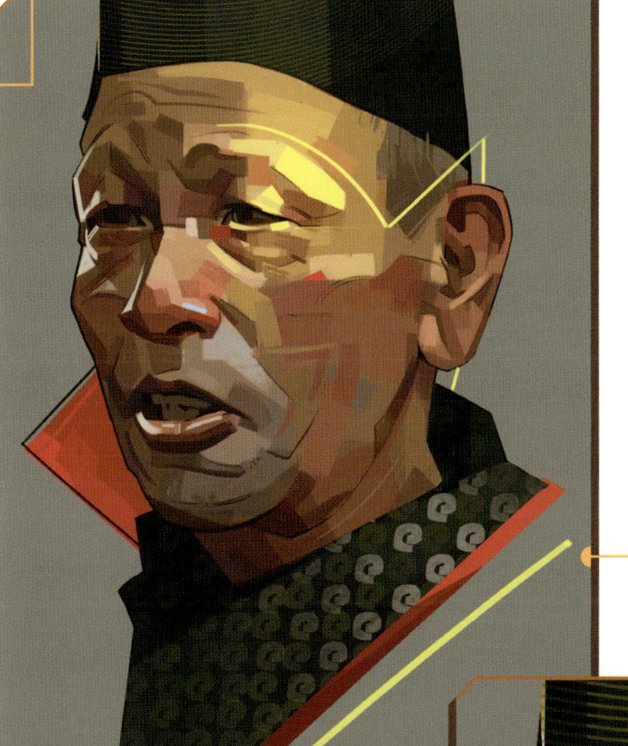

Consider what decorative elements you wish to add to your portrait. Use the colors introduced in the previous step to create a sense of cohesion between the abstract and figurative parts of the image. Be bold about your decisions, experimenting with different shapes, lines, and colors. Keep in mind the focal point of the painting and use these abstract elements to further strengthen the movement toward it. Remember to keep it as expressive as possible.

Reinforce your composition by adding abstract, decorative elements to your painting

30

Select a small brush and paint the final details of the face. Correct and clean up the existing shapes. Next, add highlights around the focal point, along with smaller wrinkles. When painting wrinkles, make them appear more three-dimensional by painting a lighter stroke next to the dark one. Outline shapes you want to emphasize, then add more detail to the main features of the portrait.

Paint in the finer details of the face using small, precise brushstrokes

31

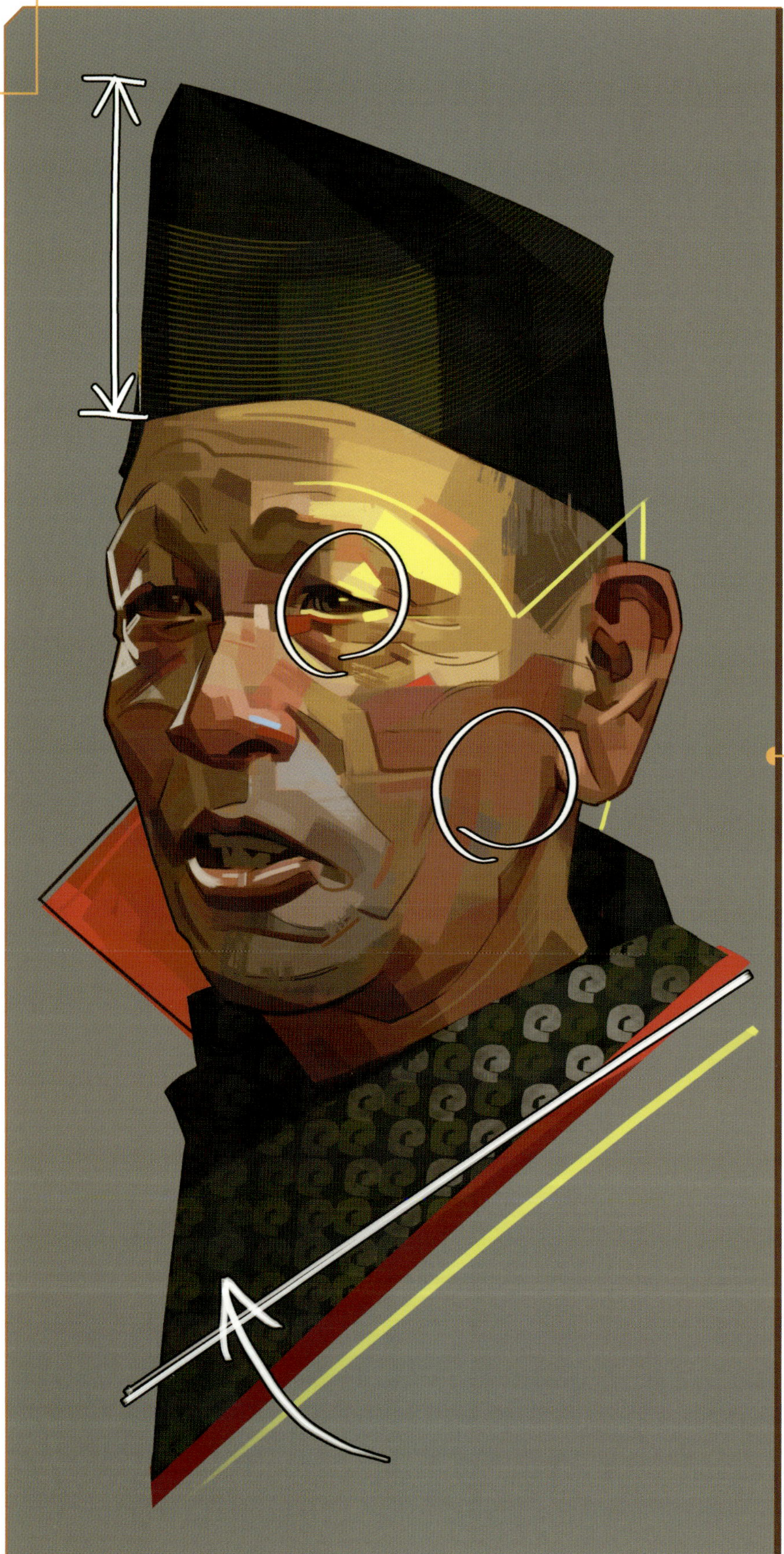

It's important to let your portrait rest for a while, so take a break and return to it a few hours later. This will give you a fresh view of your work and will help you to notice elements you wish to change or correct. This could include the incorrect placement of features, bad composition, or wrong proportions. The mistakes are circled here, showing what needs further work.

Taking a break from painting to return to it with fresh eyes will help you to spot mistakes

32

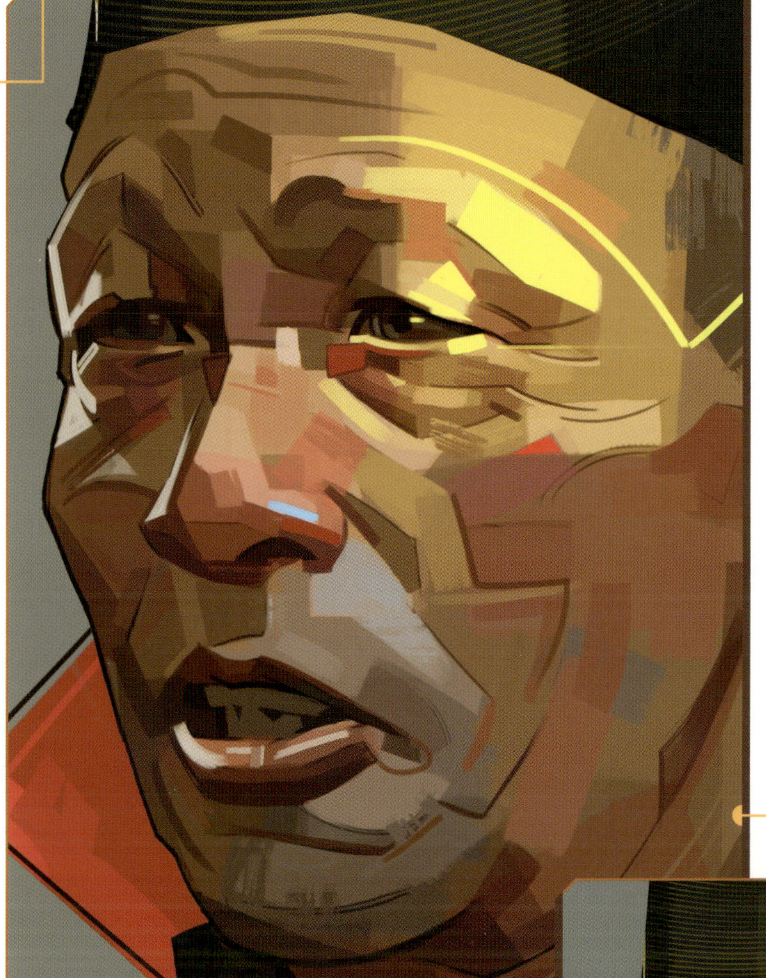

If you notice mistakes, don't hesitate to correct them right away. Pay close attention to the composition of your portrait, the flow of the silhouette, and all of the inner shapes. Compare it to your original idea and make adjustments as needed. If working digitally, you can make use of the different Transform tools to achieve the desired effect and experiment with different compositions, choosing the one you like the most. These changes are minor, but important nonetheless.

Make compositional adjustments and experiment with various Transform tools if using digital software

33

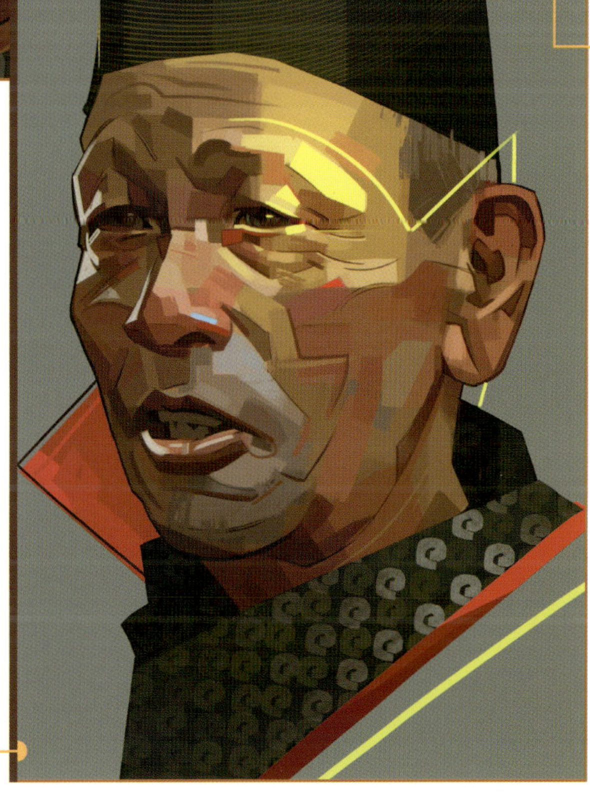

Regarding the other type of corrections, simply paint over the existing image to achieve the desired look. Study your reference photo and compare it to your painting. Look specifically for elements you want to incorporate into the final portrait. If working digitally and you wish to correct the facial expression, you can use the Transform tools or the Liquify tool. Once everything is in place, it's time for the final adjustments.

Observe your reference photo and make any final corrections to the portrait

Artist tip

One of the most important things when creating art is to enjoy the process. And one of the best ways to do this is to experiment with different ideas, techniques, and tools. Be daring; don't settle for a single way to paint the subject, but explore the various possibilities available. Rules are made to be broken, but do so with purpose. These decisions will help to form your unique vision of the world around you.

34

Draw more focus to the main area of the portrait by slightly increasing contrast between the focal point and other parts of the face. Using complementary hues such as orange for the light and blue for the shadows, very lightly increase the difference between the warm brow highlight and the shadowy blue stubble. Next, paint the second color over other parts of the face.

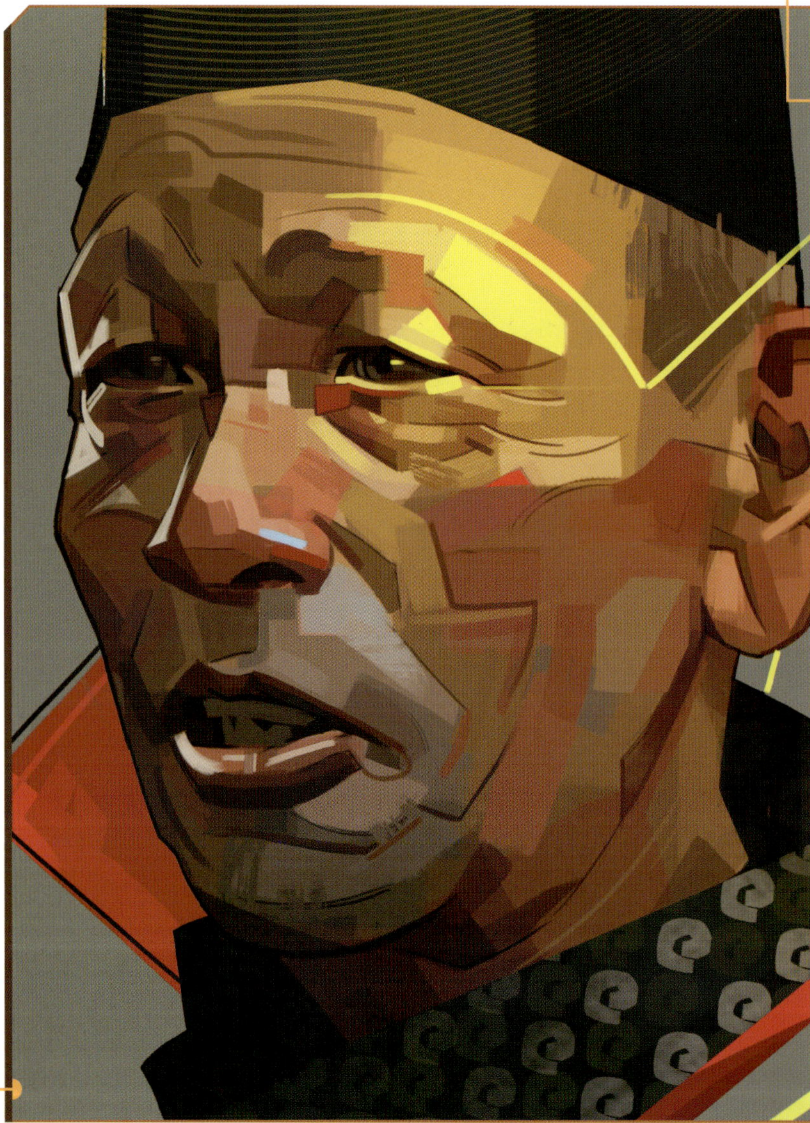

Add a subtle gradient to draw more emphasis on the focal point

35

Carry out final color corrections. If working digitally, you can use the various color adjustment tools available for this. Aim to create vibrant, pleasing colors without oversaturating the whole painting. If you have trouble working out how the final colors should look, refer to a painting by one of your favorite artists that uses similar colors. Carefully compare the colors they have used to the colors in your portrait, using their painting as inspiration for what colors you would like to achieve.

Make final adjustments to the colors to achieve the desired result

36

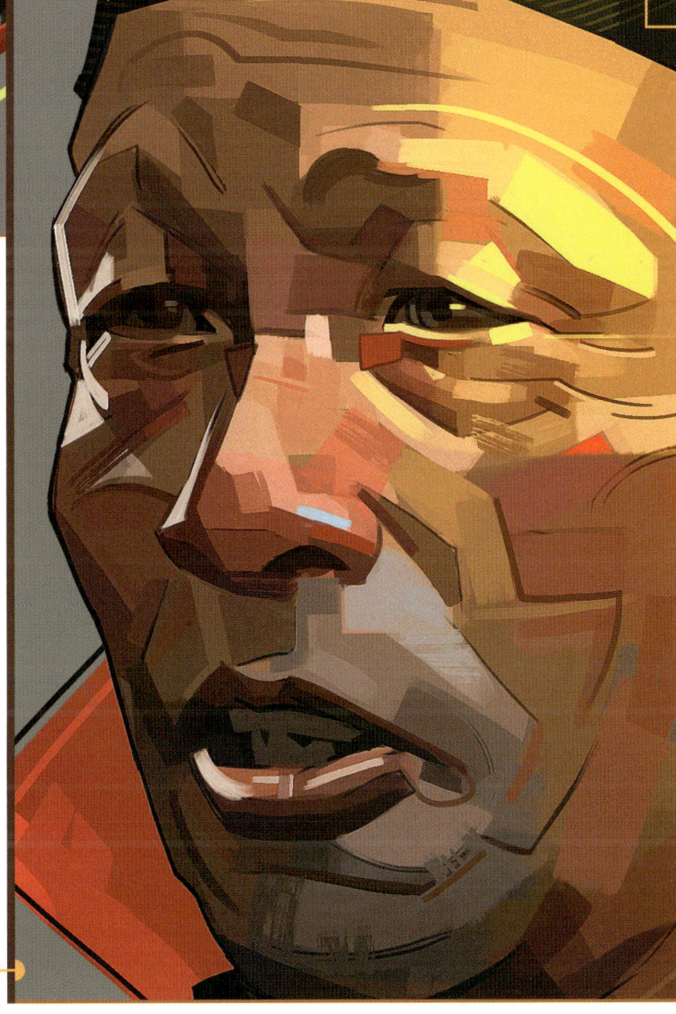

To finalize a digital portrait or add an extra pop to a scanned final painting, you may wish to make the image look slightly crisper using the Sharpen filter. You could also add a little texture using the Noise filter. While subtle noise can give a digital painting a more appealing look, don't overdo it. The effect should barely be noticeable, so set the amount to around 2–5%.

If working digitally, you can finalize your painting by adding sharpness and a little noise

Conclusion

Congratulations on completing this tutorial! The techniques used give the final painting a strong, vibrant, and graphical look. The simplified shapes of the face focus the attention on the most important features. And while the overall proportions of the head are fairly close to a reference photo, the colors are made more abstract by exaggerating certain aspects of reality. In the future, try rearranging or skipping some steps to achieve different results. Find a workflow that best fits your ideas, style, and way of working. And most importantly, enjoy the process!

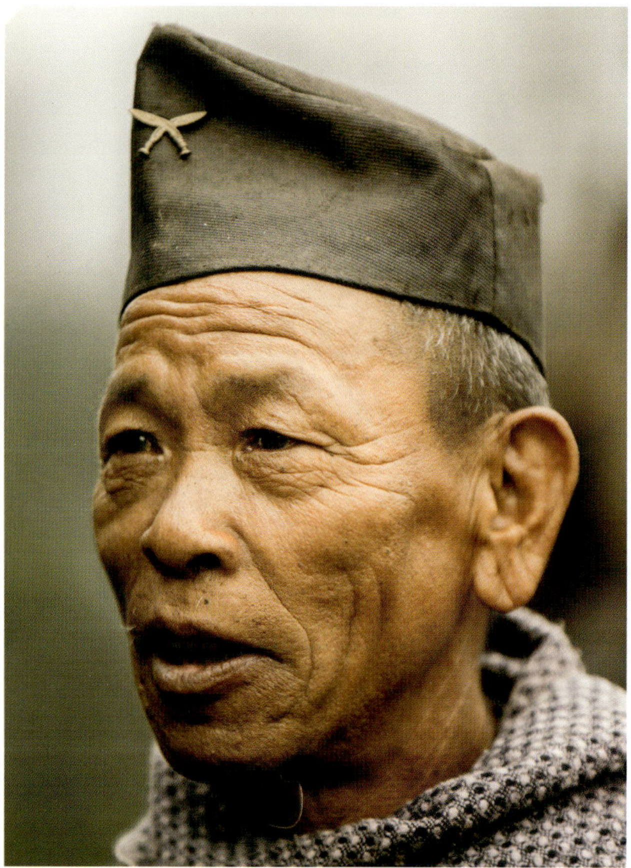

Photograph by Prijun Koirala on Unsplash

Final image © Gennadiy Kim

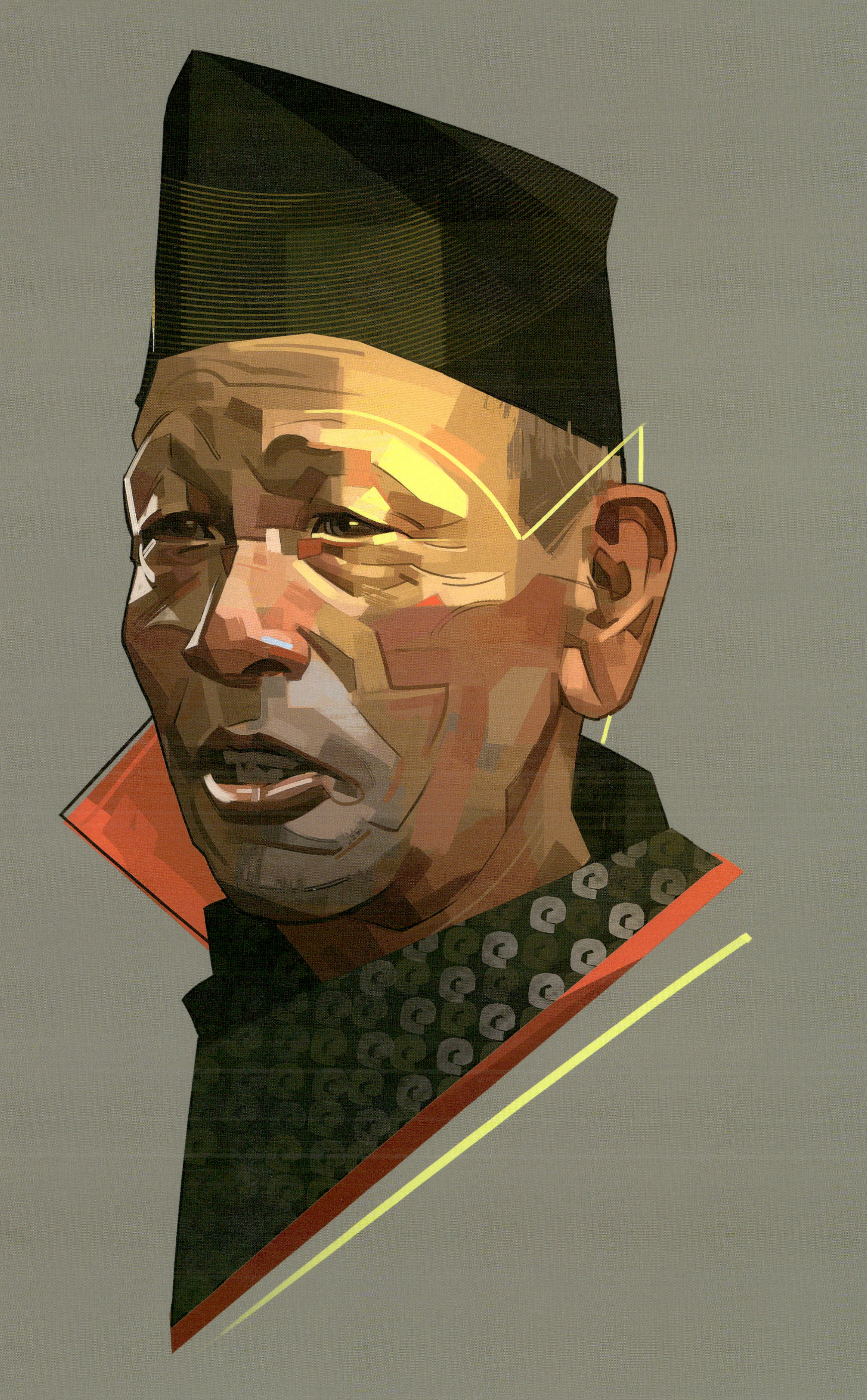

AVELINE STOKART

Introduction

This tutorial will walk you through the process of creating a stylized portrait based on a reference photo. It will focus on the importance of observing the model and capturing the mood or feeling the image evokes. Following along, you will learn how the different elements of the face work, allowing you to construct a portrait with greater understanding.

The goal is not to create a realistic portrait, but a stylized interpretation of what you see and feel. The tutorial will demonstrate how using simplification and exaggeration of shapes and details can achieve a stylized look, while still focusing on capturing the model's expression. Each stage will be detailed with step-by-step instructions that enable you to follow along easily. The stages of colorization will then be explained.

This stylized portrait has been created digitally, but feel free to experiment with different mediums to adapt the content and recreate it in your own style.

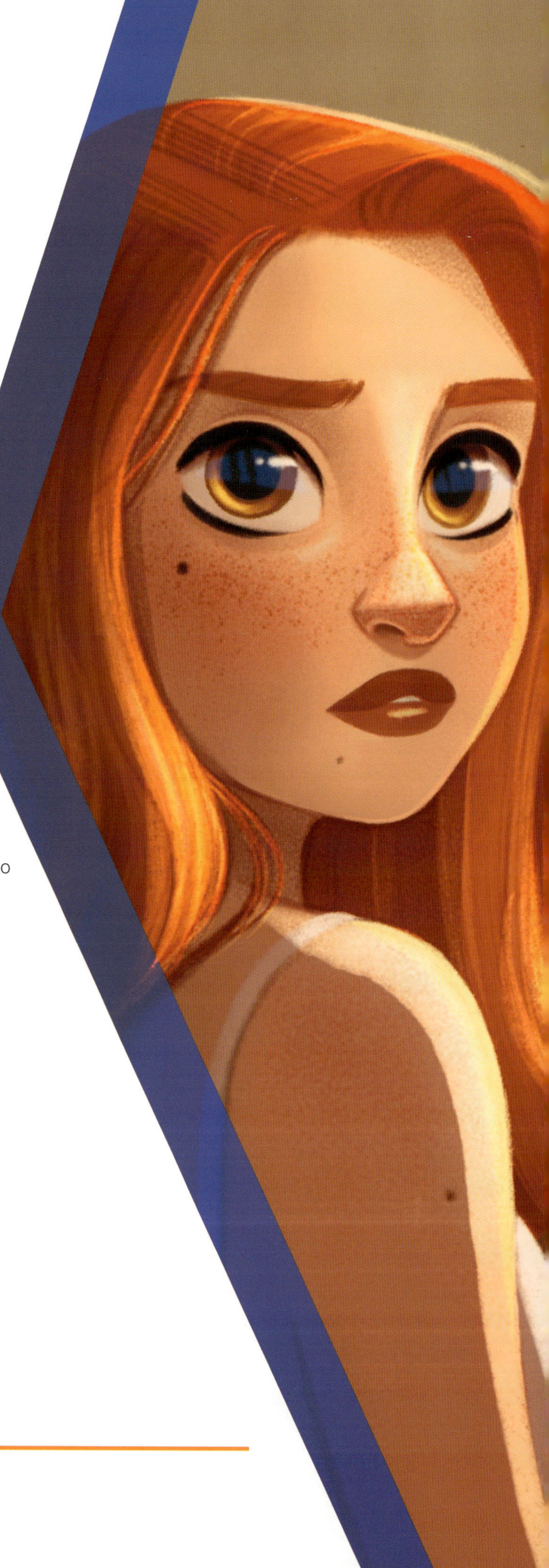

01

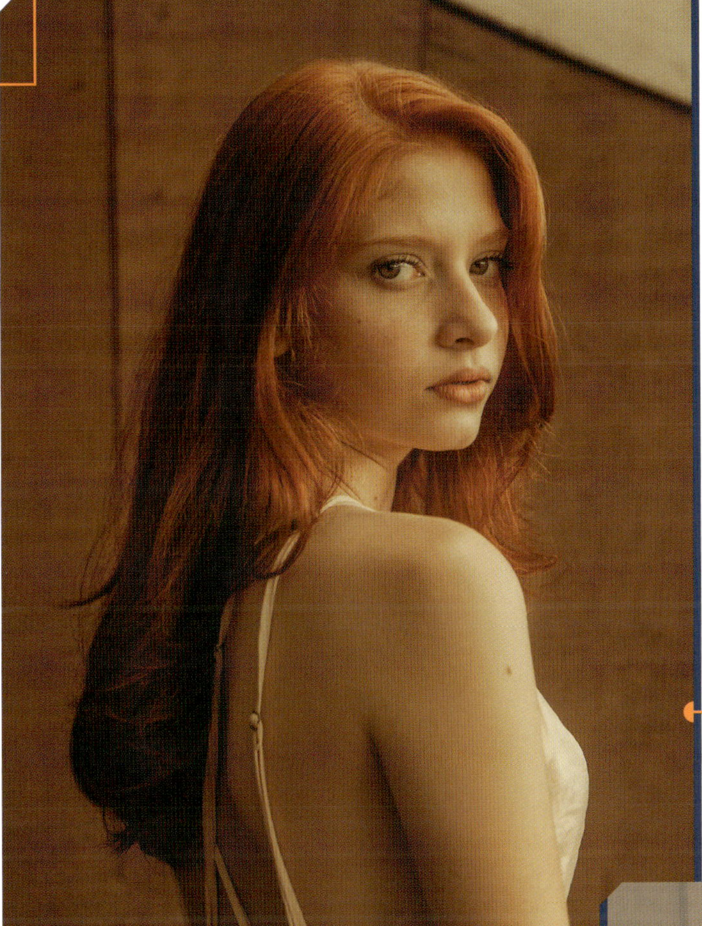

Start by choosing an inspiring reference photo to base your portrait on. If you are a beginner to portraiture, you may find it easier to start with a photo than to paint from reality. This could be a photo of a loved one, a photo of yourself, or an image found by browsing a license-free photo website. The important thing is that the person you are going to paint provokes an emotion in you. However, be sure to choose a reference photo that suits your level. If you are a beginner, avoid complex angles or an image with overly sophisticated lighting. Instead, choose a photo of a front-facing model, or a model in profile (side-view).

Reference photo; she has a pensive expression that pulls the viewer in, and the three-quarter angle will add visual interest

Photograph by Gabriel Silvério on Unsplash

02

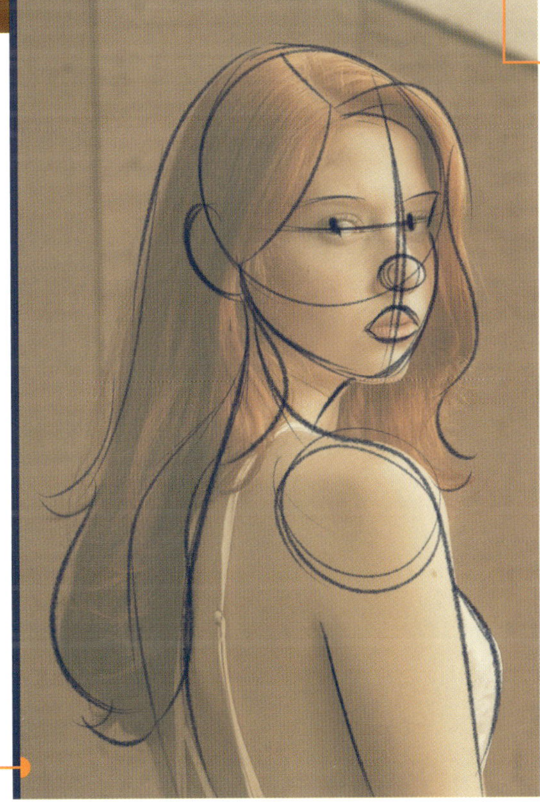

The next step is to trace onto the reference photo. This is not to trace outlines, but to figure out how the subject's face is constructed. Doing this will provide you with a greater understanding of the face you are about to draw and to unconsciously register it in your gestures. If using digital software, do this by creating a new layer on top of the image. If painting traditionally, you could lay tracing paper over your reference photo.

Start by drawing the construction lines: simple shapes that will serve as a guide as you begin to construct the face. Draw a sphere for the cranium, the vertical axis of the face to understand its orientation, and the horizontal axis to mark the positioning of the eyes. Sketch a circle for the nose and an oval for the mouth. You can also mark the spine and shoulder for bust positioning.

Draw basic constructions lines on a layer on top of the photo reference

03

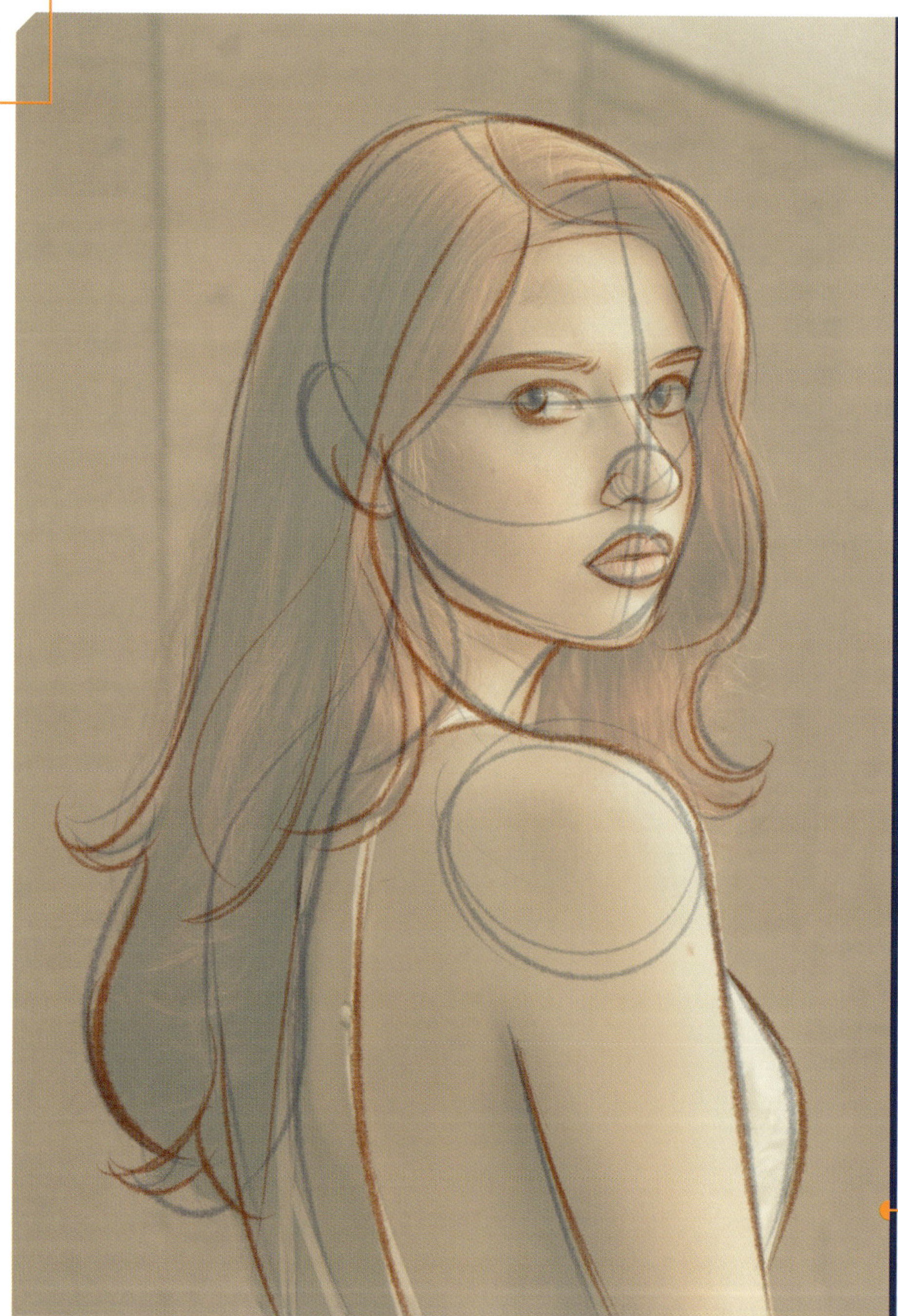

Sketch more detailed lines on top of the initial construction lines and photo reference

Draw additional lines to further detail the subject's features. Keep it simple; there is no need to be absolutely precise. Stay schematic and study the proportions of the face. Be aware of the space between the eyes, the direction of the irises, the size and shape of the nose, the size and shape of the mouth, the size of the forehead, and how the hair works around the face. Once complete, remove the photo reference below to view the basic sketch you have drawn.

04

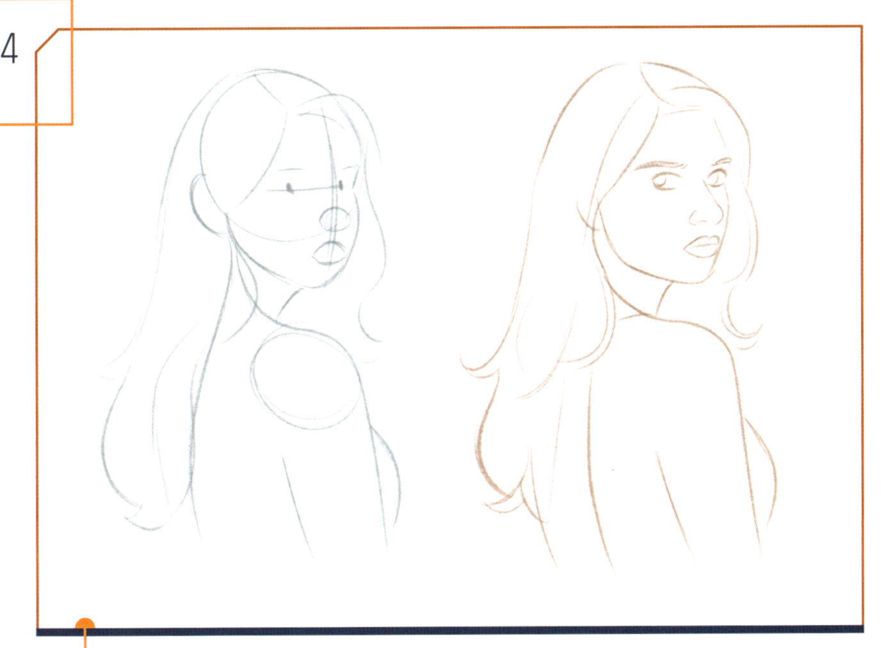

Use the construction lines and detail lines as a guide to draw a simple stylized sketch

Once you have mapped out the construction lines and simple features of your model, it's time to transcribe them. The goal is to create a stylized, or cartoon, portrait. To do this you will need to exaggerate as well as simplify certain elements of the subject's face. Stylization allows you to let go of reality, providing greater freedom and creativity in what you draw. Avoid getting too tied up in exact measurements; the construction lines drawn in the previous steps will serve as guidelines.

05

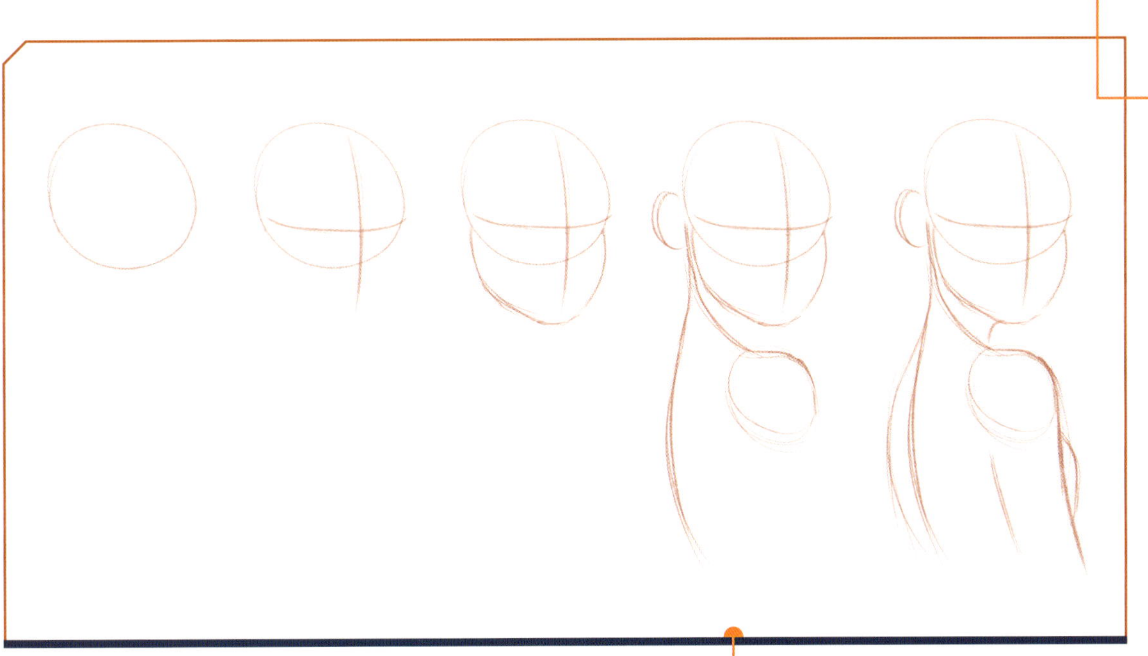

Step-by-step simple construction of the head, neck, and torso

On a new canvas, lightly retrace the construction lines (these will be invisible afterward). As the aim is to create a stylized portrait, feel free to draw the head slightly larger and the bust a little narrower than in your more realistic sketch from the previous step. Exaggerating the proportions in this way will create a more stylized look. You can also slightly alter the position of the subject's body. Tilt the head downward slightly and raise the shoulder a little. This will reinforce the pensive attitude the subject evokes, as if her intention were to hide her face behind her shoulder.

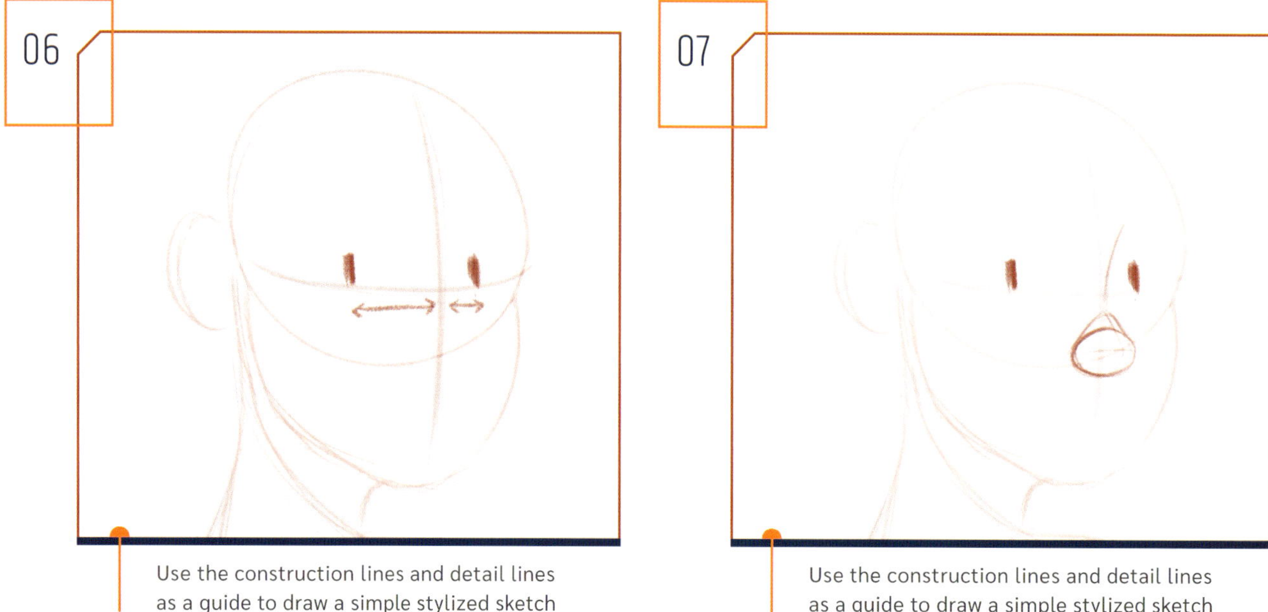

06

Use the construction lines and detail lines as a guide to draw a simple stylized sketch

When sketching the different elements, keep the angle of the face in mind. Here it is at three-quarter view, so the perspective will impact the placement of facial features. Refer to the vertical axis when sketching. Draw just two points for the eyes; this will be enough to serve as a guide. The eye closest to you is at a greater distance from the vertical axis, while the eye furthest away is at a shorter distance. Place the dots in a way that creates the impression that the model is looking at you.

07

Use the construction lines and detail lines as a guide to draw a simple stylized sketch

To place the nose, draw a sphere slightly to the right of the vertical axis. This sphere is a little offset to allow you to show where the tip of the nose is. Never place the nose in the middle of the axis; this will make it look like a flat potato. Every nose has its own volume, which makes it protrude from the rest of the face. The three-quarter perspective helps in showing this volume. Next, join the vertical axis using a triangle to signify the base of the nose.

08

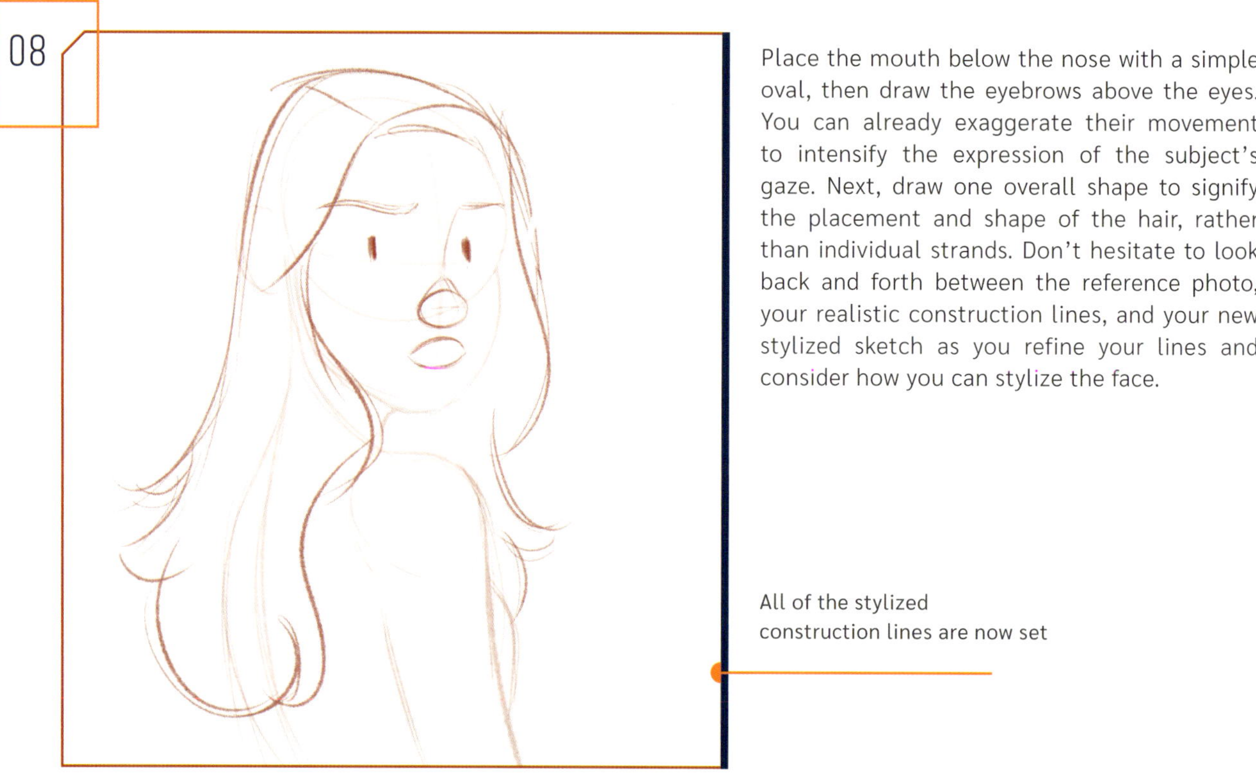

Place the mouth below the nose with a simple oval, then draw the eyebrows above the eyes. You can already exaggerate their movement to intensify the expression of the subject's gaze. Next, draw one overall shape to signify the placement and shape of the hair, rather than individual strands. Don't hesitate to look back and forth between the reference photo, your realistic construction lines, and your new stylized sketch as you refine your lines and consider how you can stylize the face.

All of the stylized construction lines are now set

Artist tip

Be observant and regularly look back and forth between the reference photo and your sketch. You don't need to do this obsessively, but enough to commit the characteristics of the model to memory. Take note of what mood or feeling the subject evokes. Here, her gaze conveys a touch of suspicion; she seems worried or preoccupied about something. Once you have observed the emotion that emerges from your subject, hold it in your mind. Let it guide your drawing and give the portrait intention.

09

Once the construction stage is finished, you can start to detail the different parts of the face. Let's start with the eyes. Before you begin, it's important to secure a basic understanding of how an eye is made up. Having this anatomical knowledge will help you to simplify the different elements accurately. To summarize, an eye is a sphere located in an eye socket, covered by two eyelids dotted with eyelashes that form a sort of oval. In the center of the sphere is the iris, and within that the pupil.

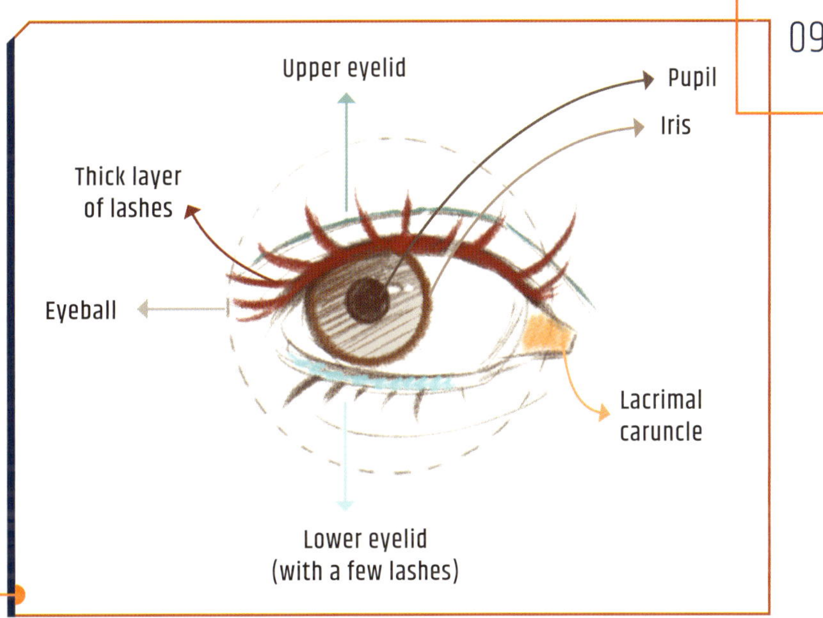

Simplified anatomy of the eye

10

The Zorro mask

The shape is recessed because of the eye socket

Use the mask method to place the eyes on the face. Start by drawing a Zorro-like mask. This will help guide the placement of features and allow you to better appreciate the volume in the space. Notice how the eye socket nearer to you is almost round, while the eye socket further away changes with perspective, creating an angle at the outer corner. This is because the orbit is recessed into the face, revealing the volume of the brow bone and cheekbone.

Apply the Zorro mask method in your construction of the eyes to help you understand the different volumes

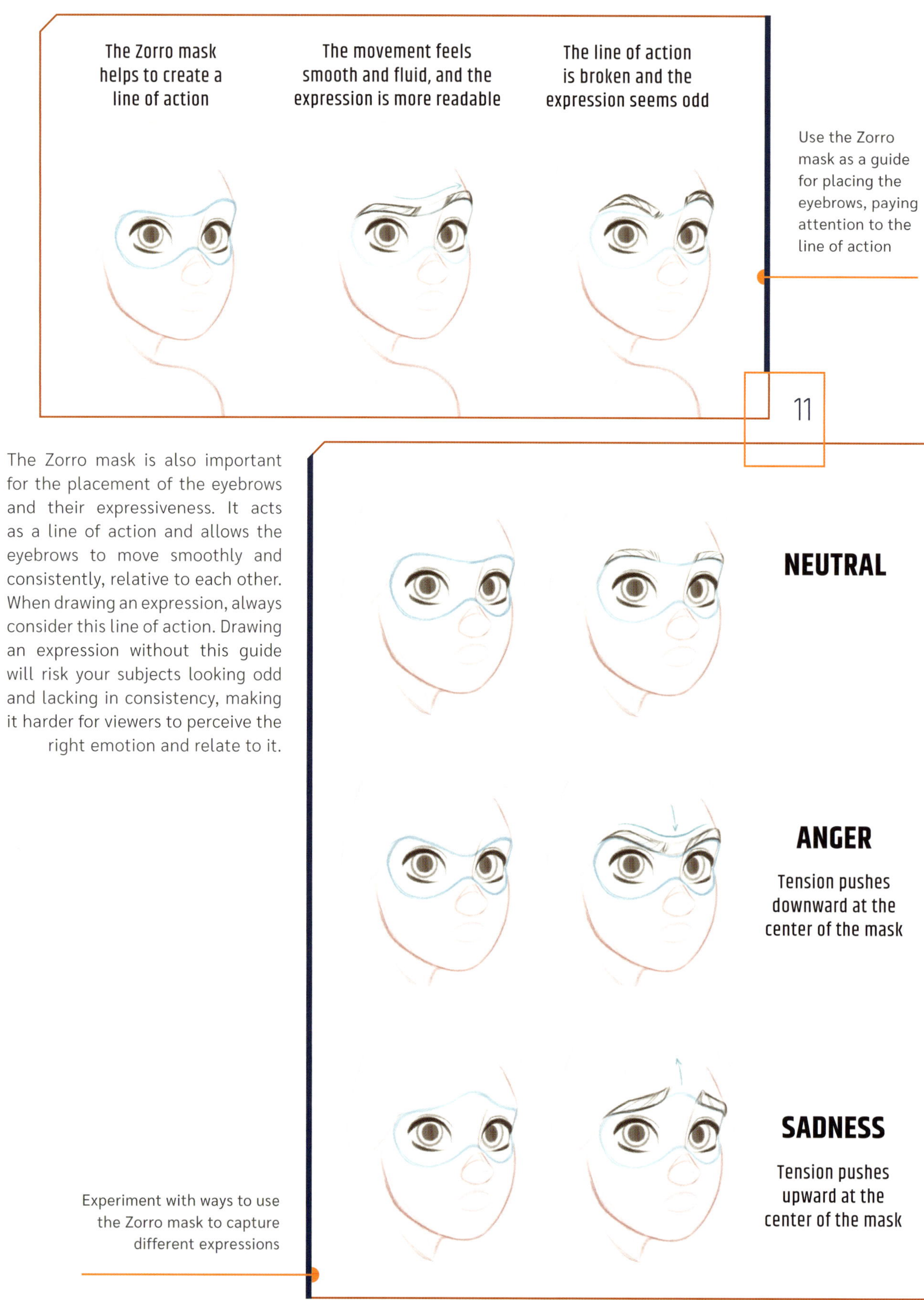

Use the Zorro mask as a guide for placing the eyebrows, paying attention to the line of action

The Zorro mask is also important for the placement of the eyebrows and their expressiveness. It acts as a line of action and allows the eyebrows to move smoothly and consistently, relative to each other. When drawing an expression, always consider this line of action. Drawing an expression without this guide will risk your subjects looking odd and lacking in consistency, making it harder for viewers to perceive the right emotion and relate to it.

Experiment with ways to use the Zorro mask to capture different expressions

12

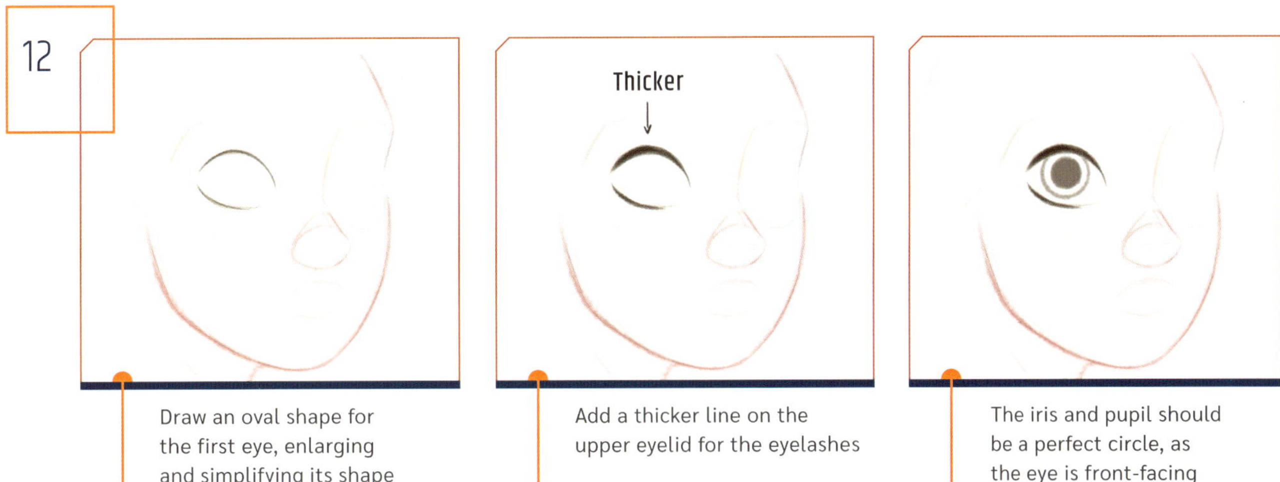

Draw an oval shape for the first eye, enlarging and simplifying its shape

Add a thicker line on the upper eyelid for the eyelashes

The iris and pupil should be a perfect circle, as the eye is front-facing

To stylize the eyes, enlarge their size and simplify their shape. Start by drawing a simple oval for the basic shape of an eye. Trace the upper arch of the eye, then the lower arch, keeping a slight angle toward the inner corner to create the impression of the lacrimal caruncle. Instead of drawing each eyelash separately, simplify them by drawing a denser, thicker line on the upper eyelid. When drawing the eye nearest to you, the outer corner should end with an almond-like shape. As this eye is almost front-facing, and because it is looking directly at the viewer, draw the iris and the pupil with a perfect circle.

13

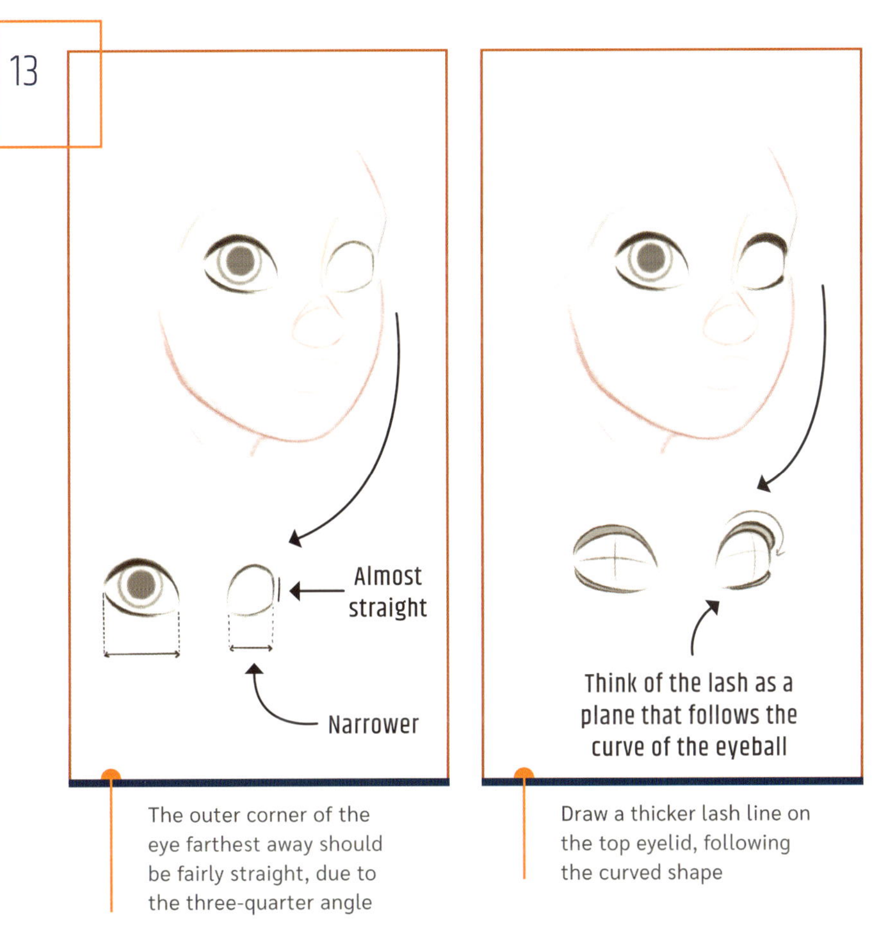

The outer corner of the eye farthest away should be fairly straight, due to the three-quarter angle

Draw a thicker lash line on the top eyelid, following the curved shape

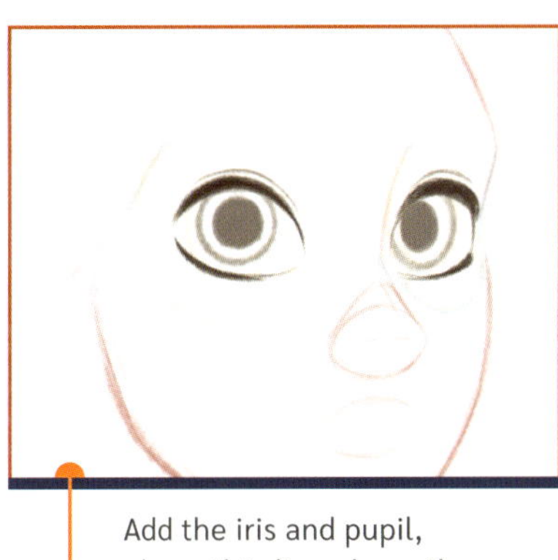

Add the iris and pupil, plus a thin line above the lash lid for the eyelids

Though the other eye, the one farther away, is not much smaller than the nearest eye, it looks narrower as if it has been squashed horizontally. Its outer corner should be mostly straight, because of the three-quarter perspective. Thicken the line of the upper lashes and let them protrude slightly from the outer edge, so it looks like it follows the curve of the eye. Next, draw the iris and the pupil using more of an oval shape this time to show the perspective. Finally, draw two thin lines above the lash lines to signify the thickness of the upper eyelids.

14

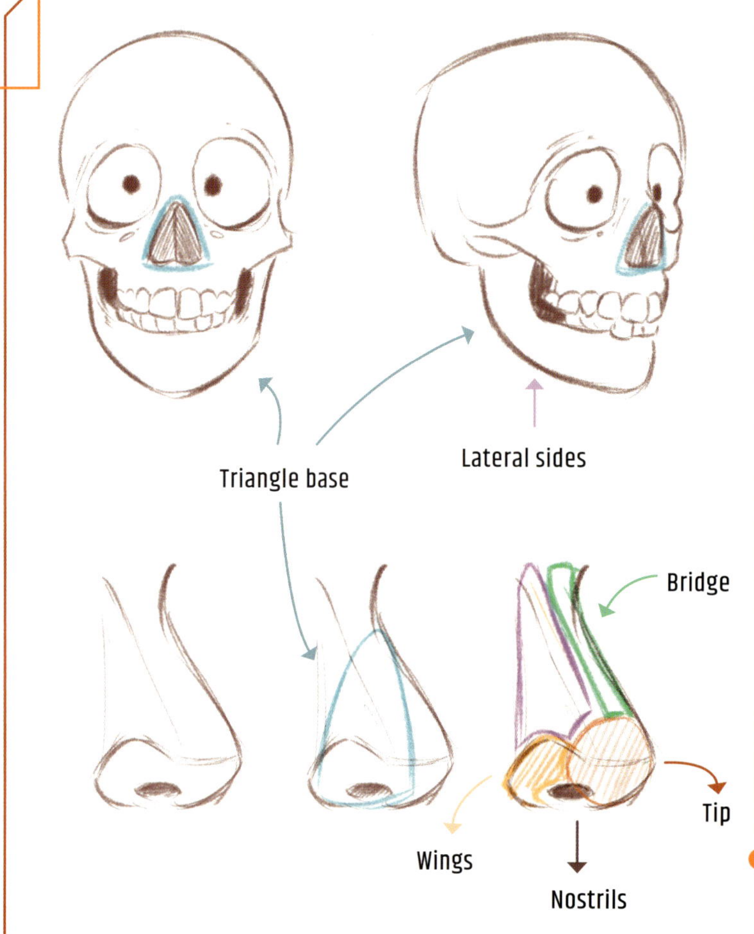

The nose is not a flat potato, but a three-dimensional feature that protrudes from the face and enables you to breathe. Begin by drawing a triangular base. If you were to look at a skull, you would see this respiratory cavity. The nose is built on top of this from cartilage and flesh. Construct a basic sketch of the nose using three planes and three spheres. Two planes form the lateral sides of the nose and a central plane will form the bridge of the nose. Then two spheres form the wings of the nose and a sphere will form the tip.

Start by drawing the triangular base of the nose, then build it up using planes and spheres

15

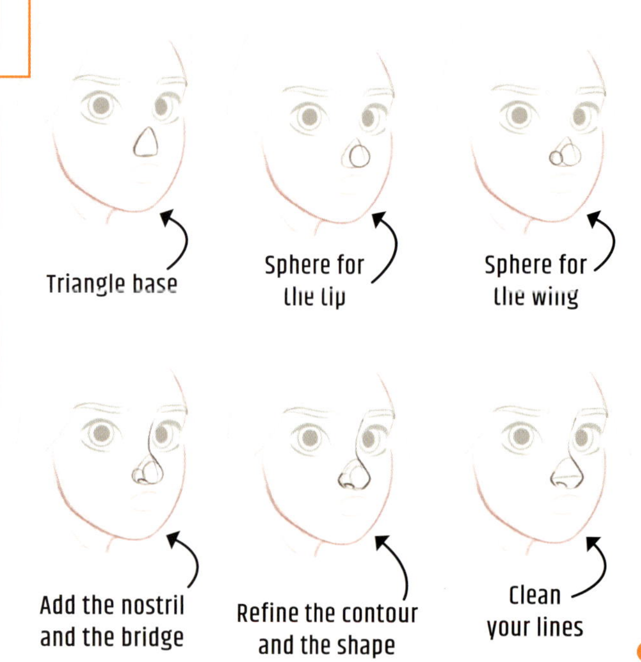

Experiment with the shape and proportion of the nose. This will depend on how you interpret the reference photo and how much you wish to stylize it. Here the nose is made smaller and lower to accentuate the stylized effect. To recreate this, draw a triangular base, followed by the sphere that will allow you to define the tip of the nose. To the left of this sphere, draw another smaller sphere to place the wing of the nose. At the intersection, draw a small arch for the nostril and connect the tip to the base with a line that will form the bridge of the nose. Next, lower the opacity of the lines you no longer need. Try to simplify the sketch as much as possible so you only keep the essential lines. Once you have cleaned up the sketch, add a straight line that runs from the tip of the nose to the nostril, to better show the lower plane of the nose.

Construct the nose using spheres and simple lines

The mouth is made up of two lips, which are soft muscle tissue that cover the teeth. The lips form two plump hems to better grip food, meeting in the corners. As with the other facial features, think of the lips in terms of volume. Begin to construct the mouth using three spheres: one sphere for the upper lip at the level of the Cupid's bow, plus two spheres for the lower lip. Next, mark dots to form the corners of the lips, then draw a curved line from corner to corner for the bottom lip, followed by the same for the upper lip. This should form an oval shape. Next, erase the center of the upper line and draw a downward arrow for the Cupid's bow. Finish by drawing a horizontal line to separate the two lips in the middle.

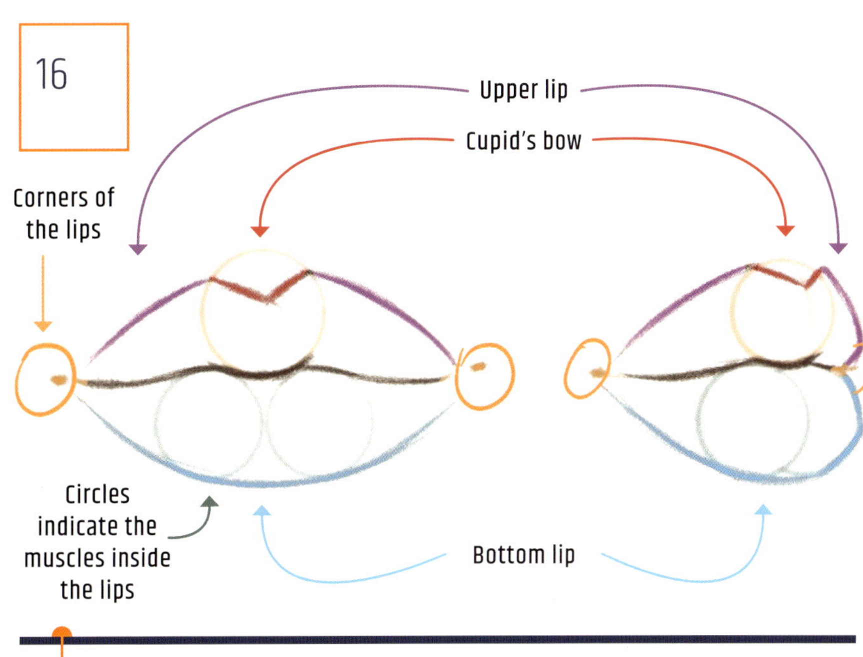

Start to construct the mouth using three spheres, followed by curved lines

17

Divide the oval with the axis

Draw three circles

Draw the Cupid's bow and the bottom lip

Link the strokes at the corners

Clean up the shape

Fill the shape

Erase a tiny triangle in the center

Stylizing the mouth is relatively simple. Redefine the oval you drew and locate the vertical axis. Divide the mouth in half horizontally, then create one sphere above and the other two below the center line. Draw the Cupid's bow with a straight line to keep it simple, then draw a line below for the lower lip. Finally, connect the lines to the corners. Once your shape is defined, fill it with color. To give the impression that her mouth is slightly open, erase a small triangle toward the center of the mouth. This will look like her teeth. In this instance, keep the mouth flat for simplicity.

Starting with ovals and spheres, begin to stylize and simplify the mouth

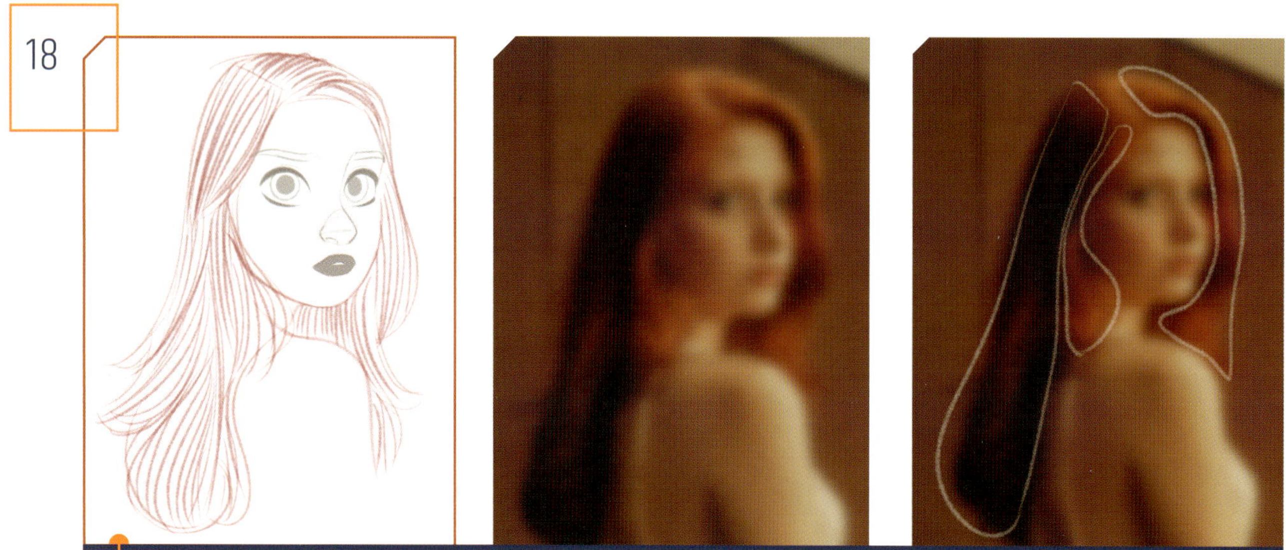

Don't draw hairs one by one, but squint your eyes to view the overall shape and better perceive the values

When sketching the hair, avoid getting lost in the details too early. You don't need to overcomplicate it by drawing every strand. Instead, you want to create the illusion of a mass of hair by thinking about the hair as a whole. Look at the reference photo while squinting your eyes to blur your perception and remove the details. Study the subject to better understand the values, volumes, and movement of her hair.

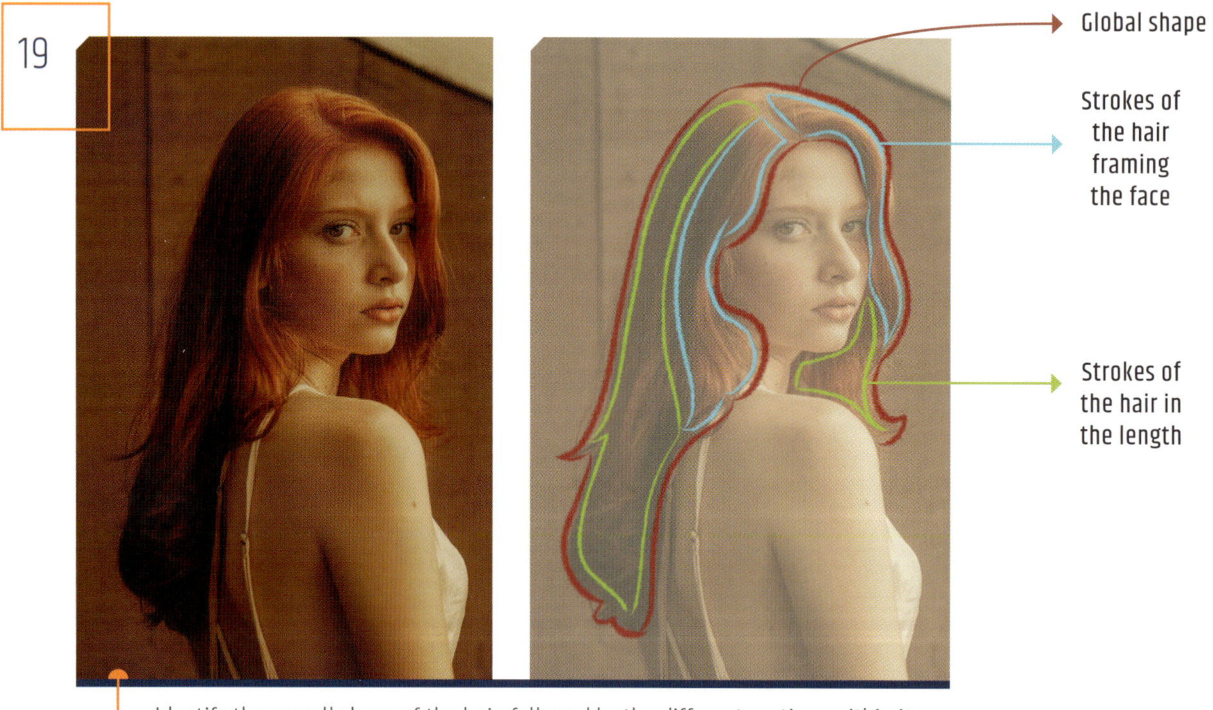

Identify the overall shape of the hair, followed by the different sections within it

Within the overall mass of hair, you can distinguish several groups: the volume of the hair toward the back, the left section at the front falling over her shoulder and down her back, the strand to the right of her face, and the lengths by her neck to the right. The aim is to locate and reconstruct these different masses on your drawing. You want to create the feeling of movement, while avoiding getting lost in the details.

20

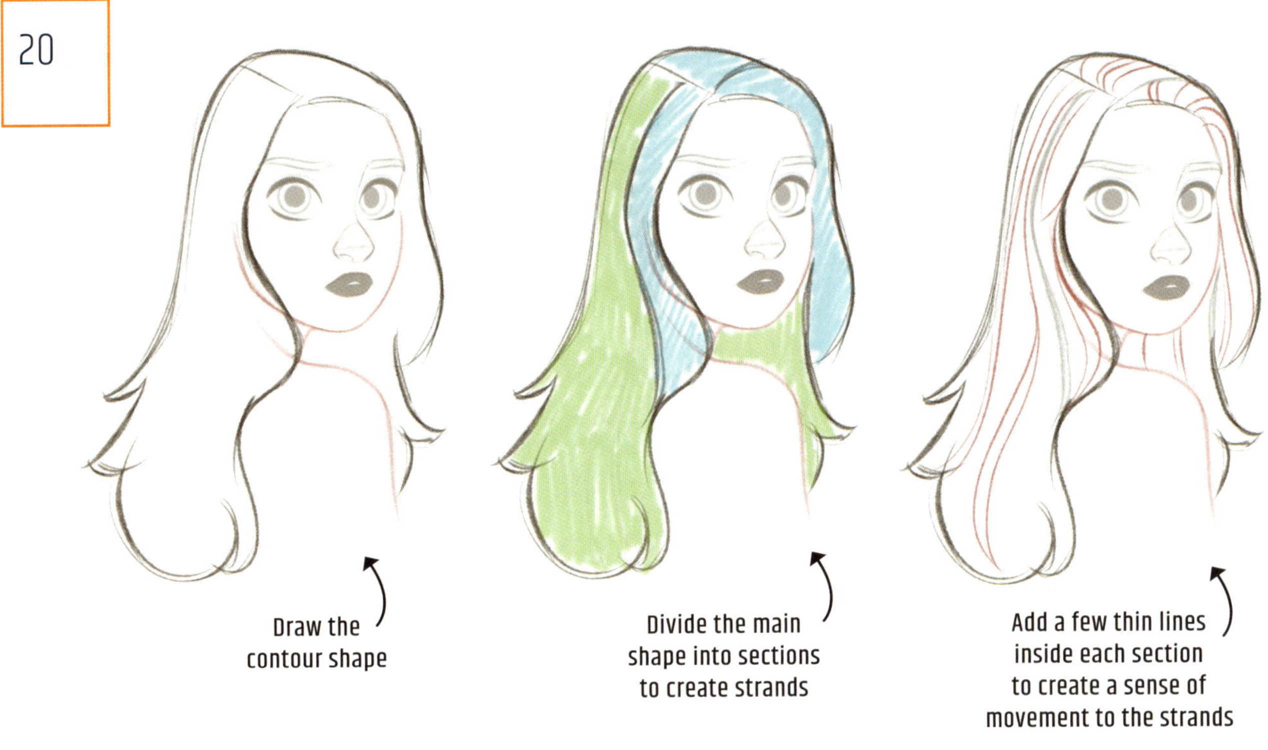

Group the different sections of hair, then add thinner lines to add minimal detail to the strands

Start by redrawing the main contour of the hair. Feel free to experiment with the shape a little to add an element of stylization, exaggerating or simplifying certain curves. Here, the overall shape is kept relatively flat and simple, as this matches the character's closed and pensive attitude. Divide the main shape into different sections to create the main strands of hair. Add a few thin lines to detail the strands and give them a feeling of movement. Keep in mind the contour curves to direct the movement and vary the directions slightly. Don't overdo it; avoid overwhelming each strand with too much detail. Take care to position them randomly to prevent an evenness that looks unnatural and fake.

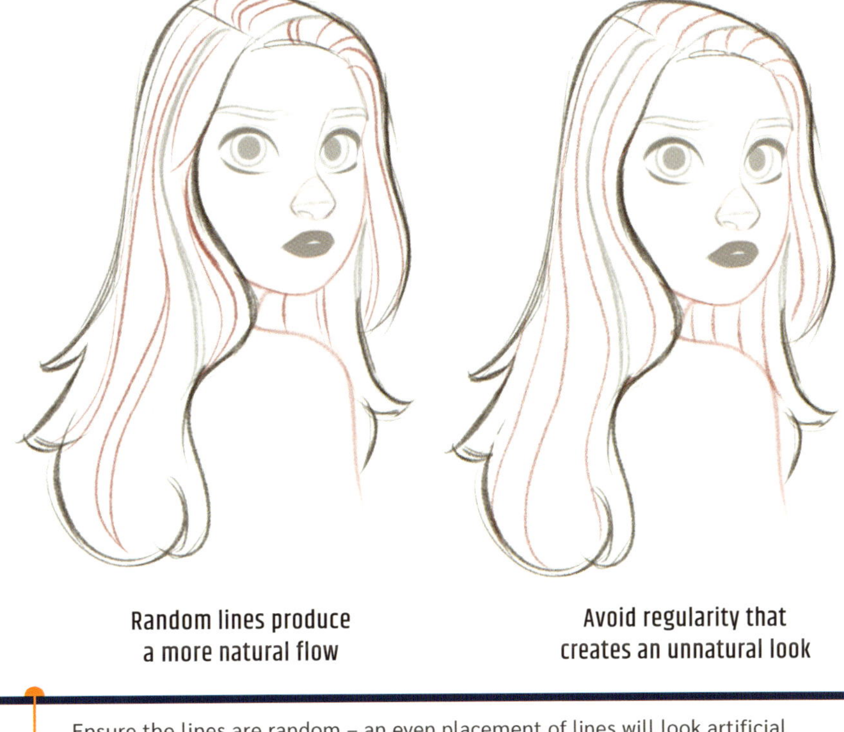

Ensure the lines are random – an even placement of lines will look artificial

Artist tip

Throughout this process, you are likely to be bent over your desk in concentration, nose pressed to your paper or device. Now is a good time to take a break. It may sound trivial, but it's important to take time to stretch, relax your fingers and wrists, and massage your neck. Get up and go outside to stretch your legs and breathe in some fresh air. What you're doing at the same time is taking a step back. Taking a break from the artwork for a few minutes (or even a few days) will allow you to return to it with fresh eyes. This will help you to spot details that need to be adjusted or refined that you might not have noticed before.

21

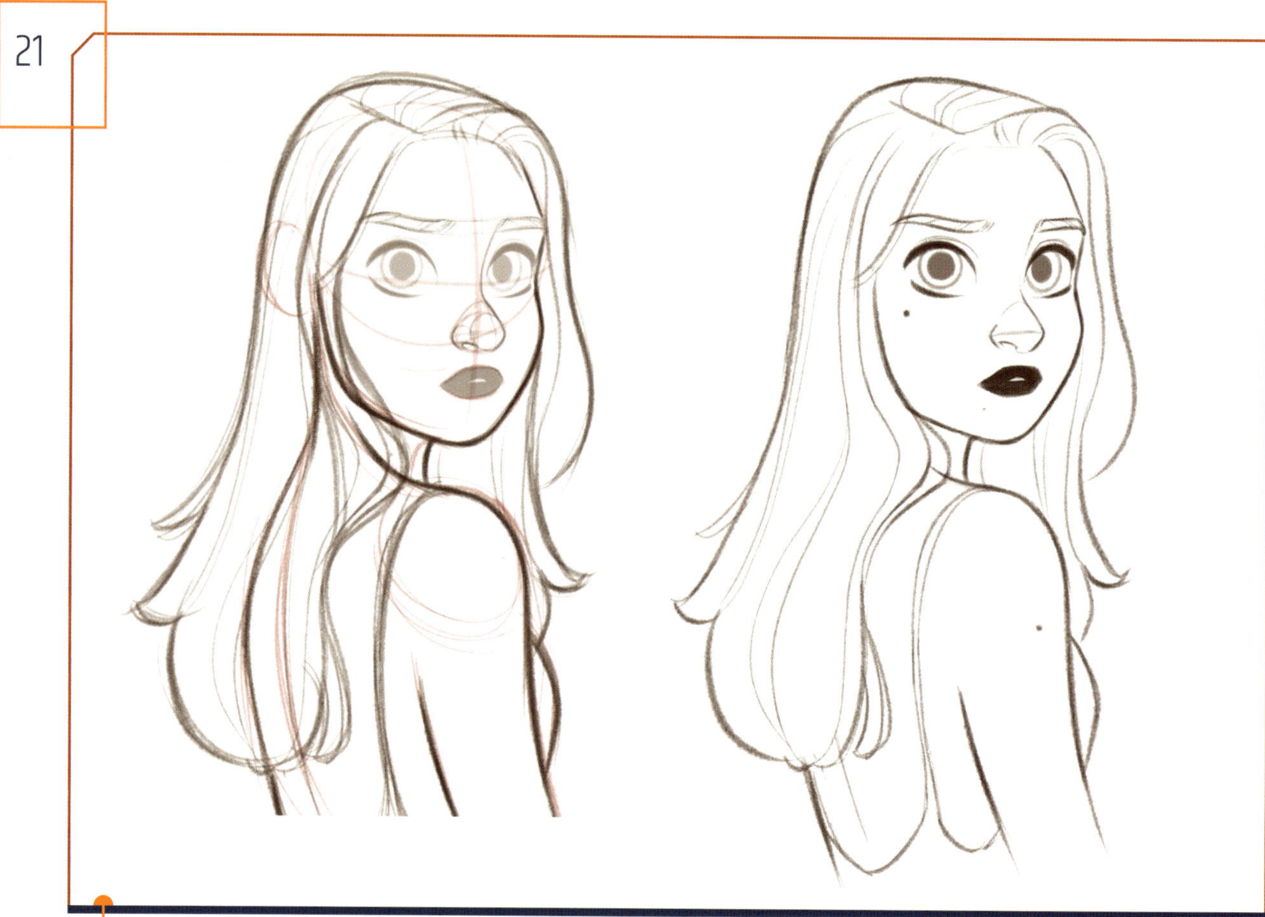

Turn your messy sketch into a new clean drawing

At this stage, your drawing is probably a little messy and littered with construction lines. If you are using digital software, you can create a new layer on top of your sketch and lower the opacity of the sketch. If working on paper, use a light table or a window and place a blank sheet over your drawing. Draw neater line art on top of the sketch, cleaning up your drawing by erasing the construction lines afterward. You can still modify the features during this step. Now is the time to make final decisions, so take some time to refine the shape of the eyes, nose, mouth, chin, and other shapes. You can also use this step to add details, such as moles and clothing.

22

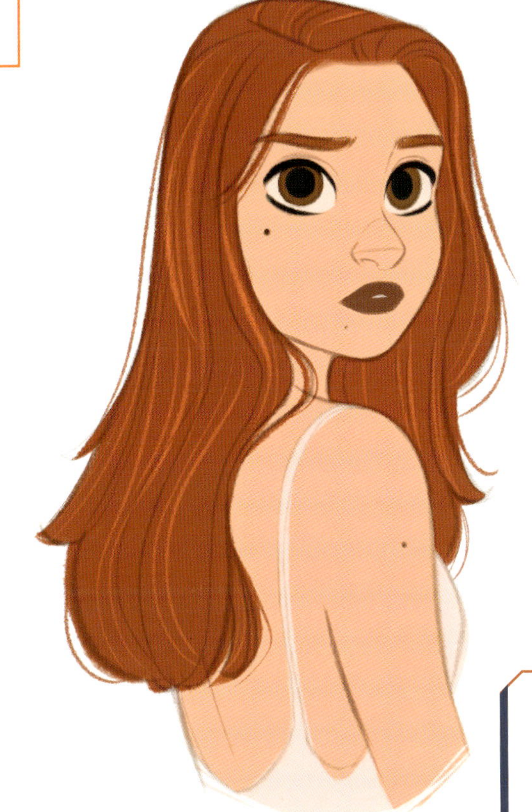

The next step is to add color. To do this digitally, decrease the opacity of your sketch and create a new layer below it. If using traditional media, you can simply paint straight on top of your line art. Study your reference photo, then fill each main shape in turn with a color that matches it. A fleshy pink is used for the skin, deep orange for the hair and eyebrows, amber-brown for the eyes, and burgundy for the lips.

Paint your drawing with flat colors that match the reference

23

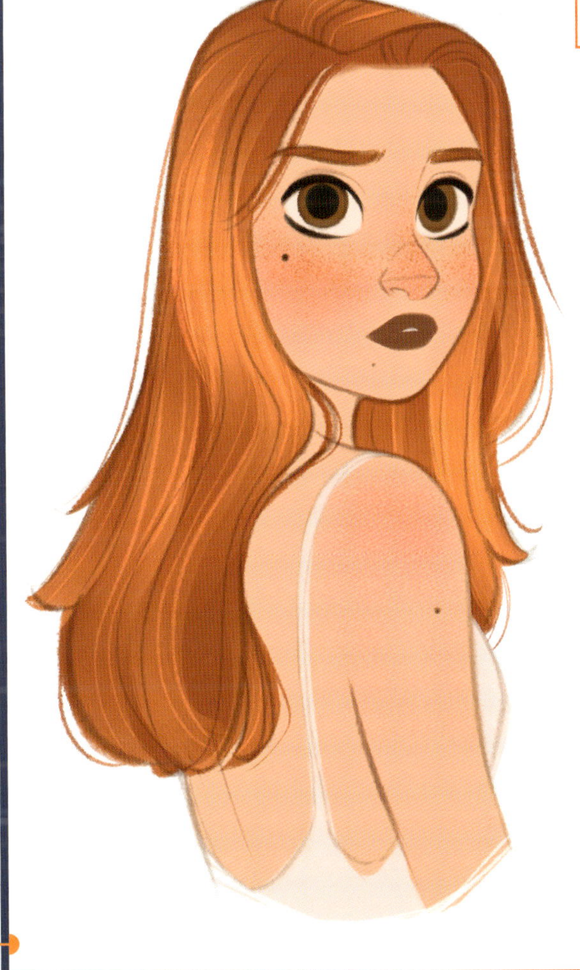

Feel free to experiment with different colors and to add different shades and tones in the hair to create a more natural look. Using both big and subtle brushstrokes, paint touches of red on the cheeks to bring more warmth and life to her face. You can also add a slight blush on the nose and shoulders. Use a light brown to paint details like freckles, as shown on the model.

Add nuances and details to the flat colors, bringing your portrait to life

24

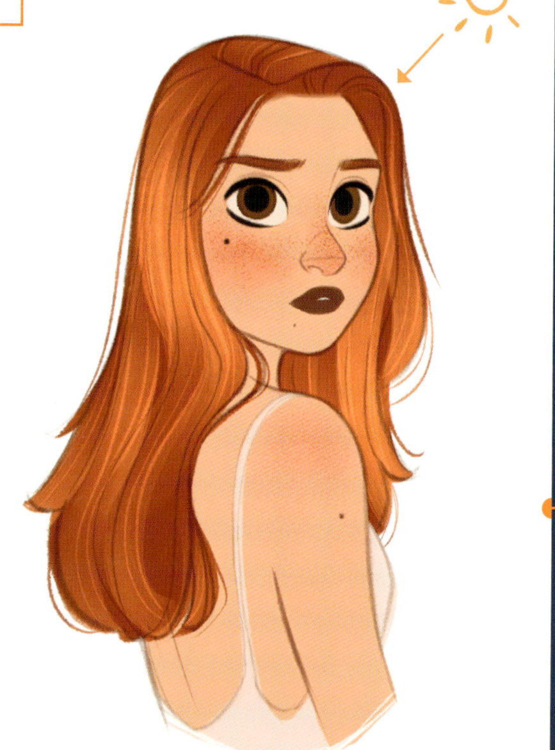

You could finish at this flat color stage if you are happy with a 2D cartoon style, but it will significantly enhance the portrait to progress it a little further. As covered earlier, the face is made up of volumes. The next stage is to use shadows, and therefore light, to indicate these volumes. Work out which direction the light is shining from. This is the top right in the reference photo. Drawing a small arrow in the corner of your painting can act as a useful reminder.

Sketch a small sun and arrow to indicate the direction of the light to ensure you don't forget

25

When placing your shadows, think about each obstacle that could prevent the light from falling onto your subject. Shining from above, the light first meets the strand of hair above her forehead, casting a shadow there. Lower down, the brow bone protrudes to protect the deeper eye sockets, so the underside of the brow is in shadow. The lower nose that protrudes from the face casts a shadow below it. Finally, her chin will also block the light, creating a shadow on her neck and the section of hair to the right of her neck. Use a darker flesh color to add the shadows on the skin and a darker amber-brown on the hair in shadow.

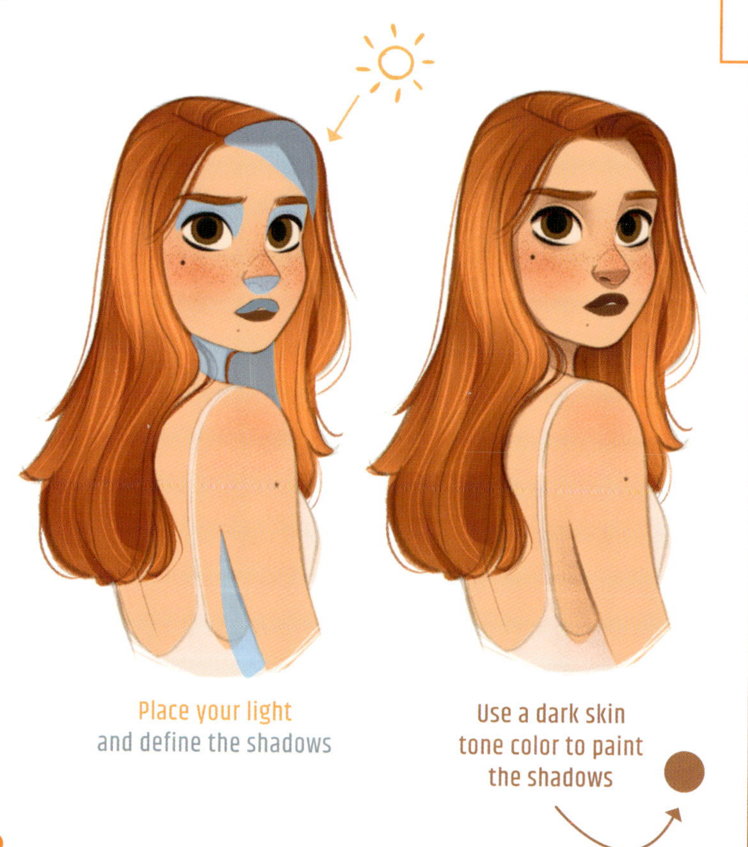

Identify the shadow areas in blue, then paint them on using a dark brownish skin tone

26

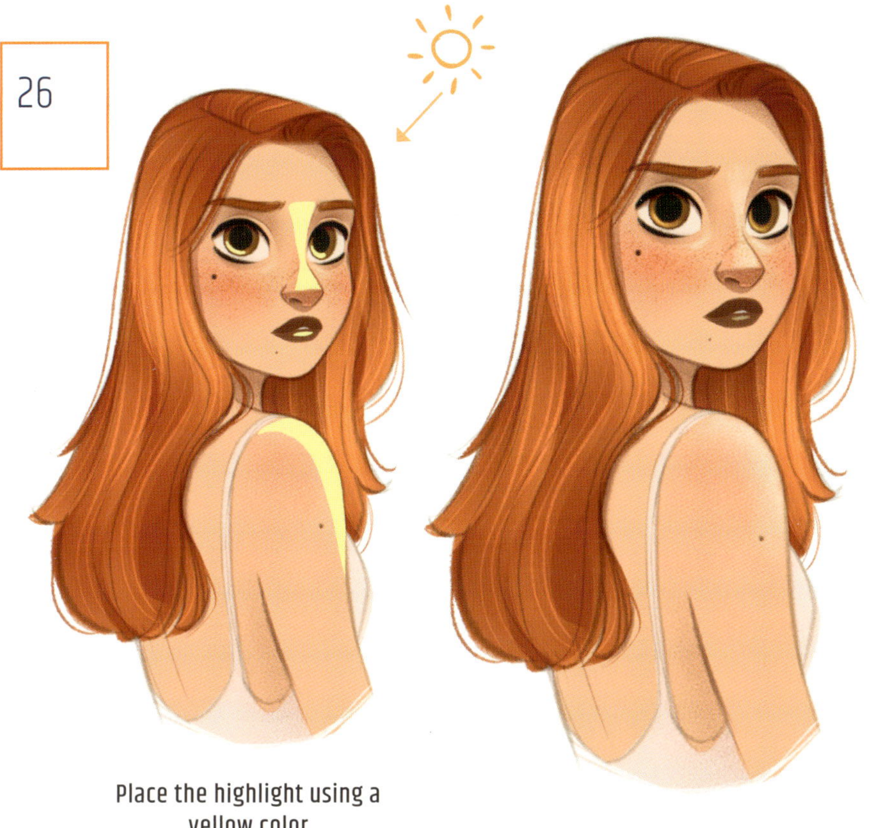

Introduce highlights to create more contrast and volume in your portrait. The opposite of shadows, highlight areas are those that face the light more directly. Paint a lighter yellowish flesh color on the nose to highlight the upper plane of the bridge of the nose. The shoulder is also fairly exposed to the light, so add a lighter area at its highest point. Paint a highlight on the lower lip to create a glossier look, and finally, illuminate the bottom of the iris with a subtle highlight.

Identify the highlight areas in yellow, then paint them on using a pale yellow flesh color

27

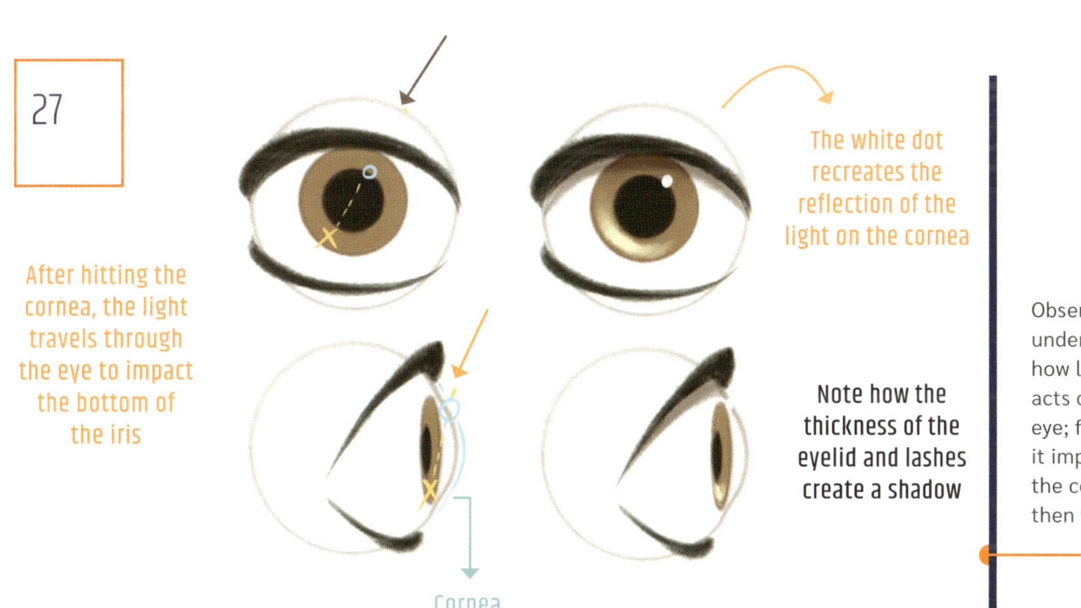

Observe and understand how light acts on an eye; first it impacts the cornea, then the iris

You may be wondering why you have added a highlight to the lower part of the iris. If it coincides with the direction of the light, should the highlight not be on the top half? The reason for this is as follows: the eye is a sphere, with an iris and a pupil, but covering all of this is the cornea. It is the cornea that is curved, while the iris is a flat surface and the pupil is a hole in the center. Under the light, the rays hit the cornea (which reflects a small, very bright point) then travel through it to hit the bottom of the iris. This is important to understand when painting a credible glow to eyes in a portrait, no matter the direction of the light.

Artist tip

Trust yourself, and above all, don't be afraid to mess up your portrait. Failure is a key, if not the most important, part of the process! Don't try to recreate the reference photo perfectly. The goal here is not perfection, but interpretation. Play with simplification and exaggeration to find your own style and graphic solutions. The only thing to keep in mind is the logic of understanding; how far can you push the stylization, while ensuring the image is still readable? Also, consider your own personal aesthetic criteria; what details would you like to keep, purely because you think they're pretty? Enjoy experimenting with what stylized portraits you can create.

28

The subject appears too bright compared to the dark background

An optional step that can enhance your portrait even further is to set your subject in an environment. Studying the reference photo, roughly recreate the background using beige and a rusty brown color. Alternatively, you could simply use one solid color – just make sure it has the same brightness as the reference, which in this case is quite dark. You will notice that the subject doesn't appear to belong in the scene and looks a little stuck on. This is because in terms of value, or light, the subject is far too bright compared to the background. Studying the reference photo, you can see how the light creates a much more pronounced contrast. The subject's back is in shadow, while her face is exposed to the light.

29

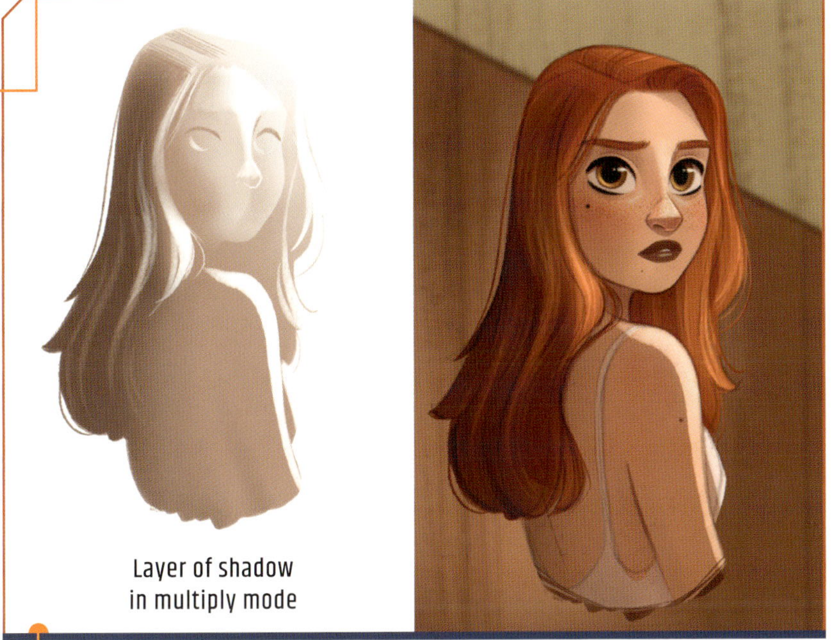

Darken the subject slightly by painting in the shadows using a rusty color

Decrease the subject's brightness to make it appear more like she belongs in the environment. You can do this digitally by selecting a rusty color (similar to the background), creating a new layer above your colors, then setting it to Multiply blend mode. Next, use the rusty color to softly paint the areas that are in shadow. If working traditionally, simply paint in the shadows using the rusty color. Keep in mind that the light is coming from the top right, so avoid darkening the exposed areas such as the shoulder, chest, and upper part of the head. This will create the impression that the subject is lit up.

30

Add the finishing touches by using a yellow color to paint highlights onto the exposed areas. Paint straight on top of your painting if using traditional media, or if using digital software, create a new layer above your colors and shadows, then set it to Overlay blend mode. Use the yellow light color to paint the highlighted areas that you let remain in the previous step, then decrease the intensity of the layer. Next, create a layer on top of everything and set it to Overlay as well. Use the same yellow color to add soft highlights to the hair, shoulder, and the strands of hair at the right of her face to accentuate the contrast and add volume. Finish by adding any last details.

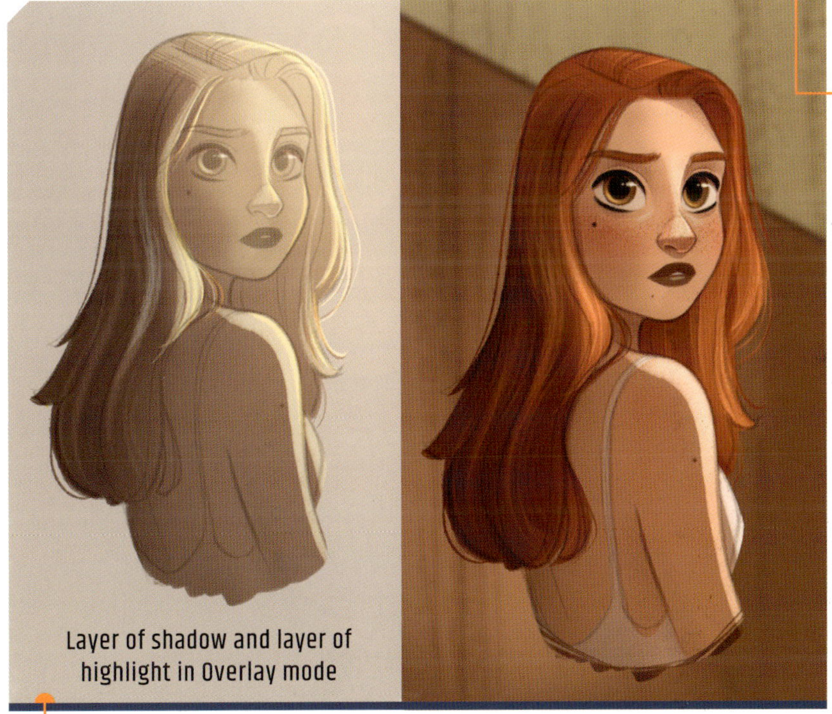

Paint highlights in the exposed areas to add volume and light

Conclusion

Congratulations on completing this tutorial! You now know how to observe a subject considering the volumes, and have a greater understanding of the anatomy of the face. Using simple global shapes, you have learned how to break down the different elements of the face to construct and reproduce a portrait. To take the stylization a step further, experiment with the proportions of the face, either by exaggerating the subject's actual proportions, like a caricature, or by exploring other designs and shapes to see what they express.

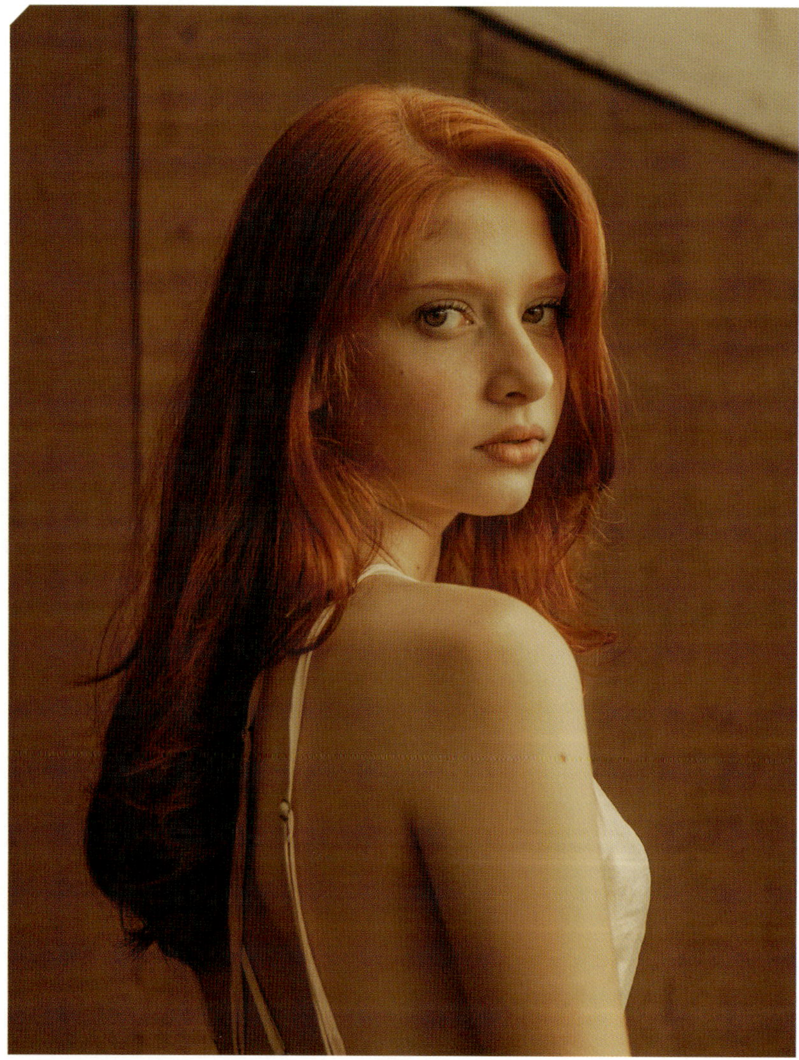

Photograph by Gabriel Silvério on Unsplash

Final image © Aveline Stokart

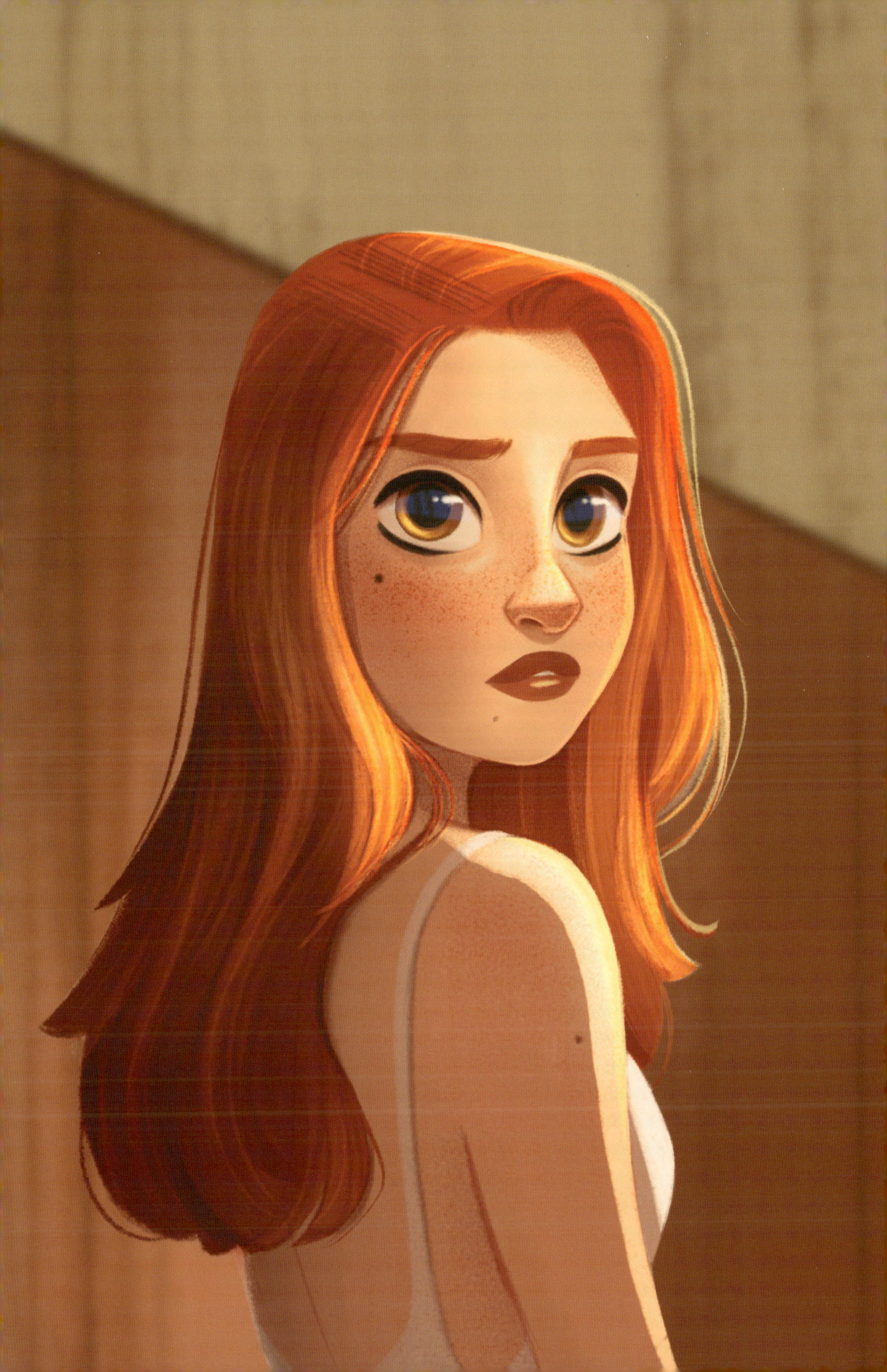

PORTRAIT GALLERY

- LAURA H. RUBIN
- TRAN NGUYEN
- GENNADIY KIM
- MARIA DIMOVA
- JUSTINE S. FLORENTINO
- AVELINE STOKART
- NICK RUNGE
- VALENTINA REMENAR
- ASTRI LOHNE
- SARA TEPES

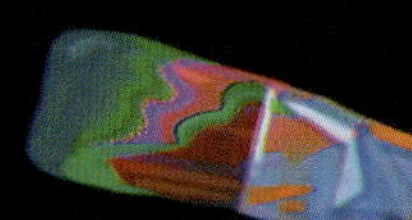

Artwork © Valentina Remenar

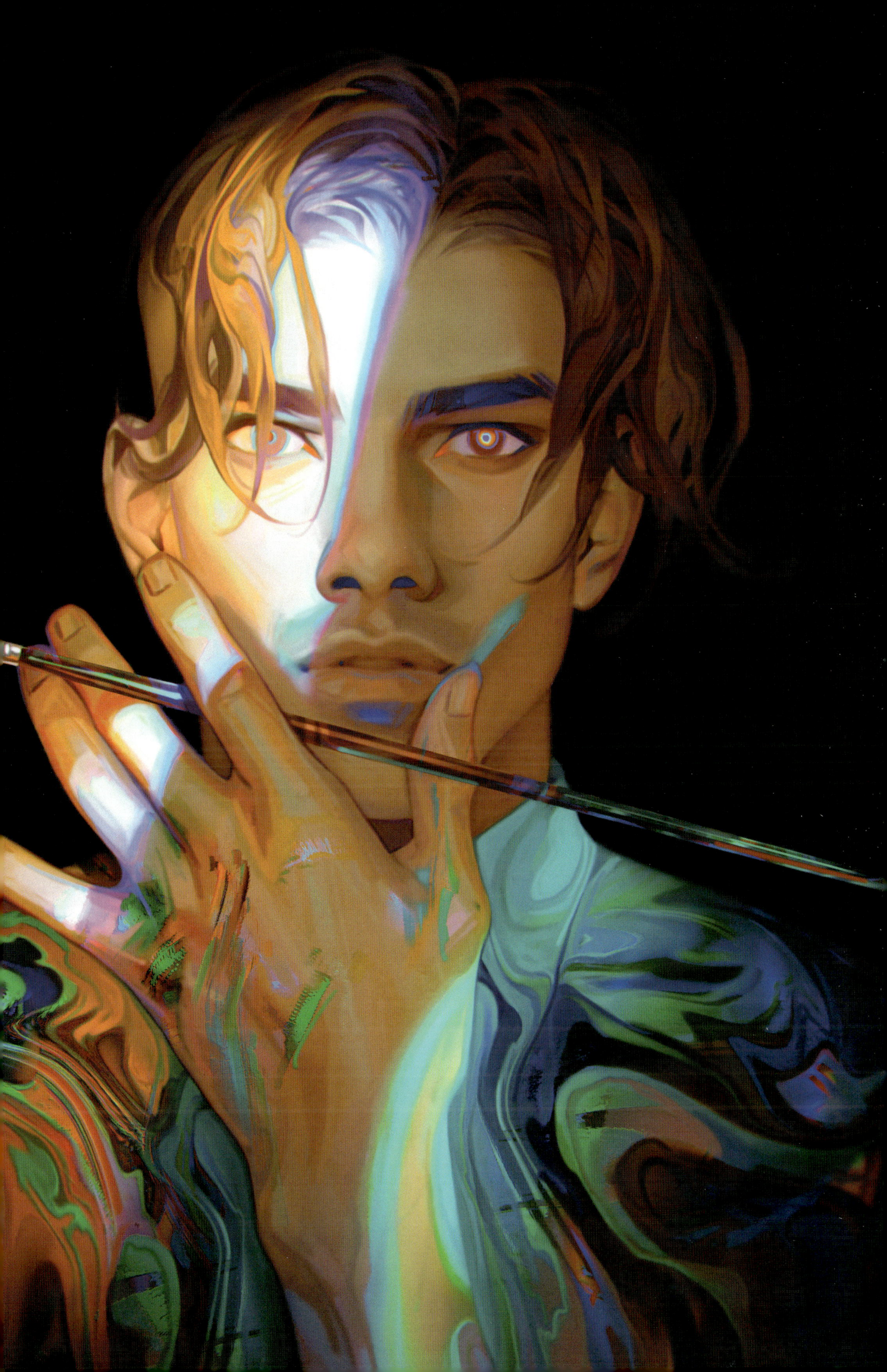

Gallery of Laura H. Rubin

Artwork © Laura H. Rubin

This page
Top right: Burtonesque
Bottom left: Nocturne
Bottom right: Morrows Thoughts

Opposite page
Top left: Carnivore
Top right: Alone In The Crowd
Bottom: Justice (left: early designs)

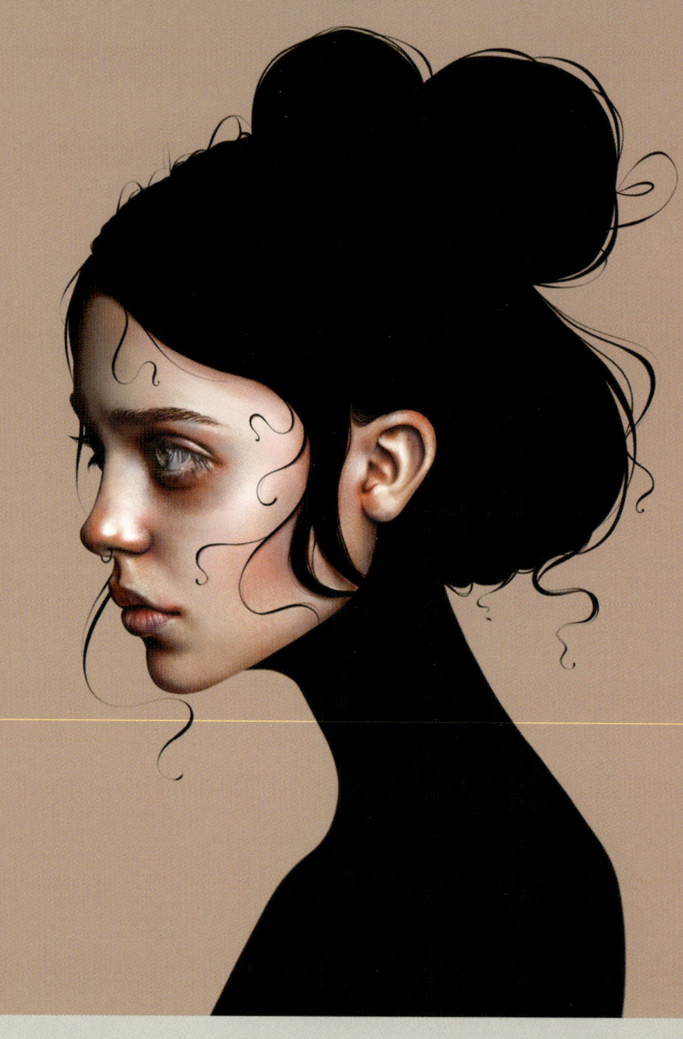

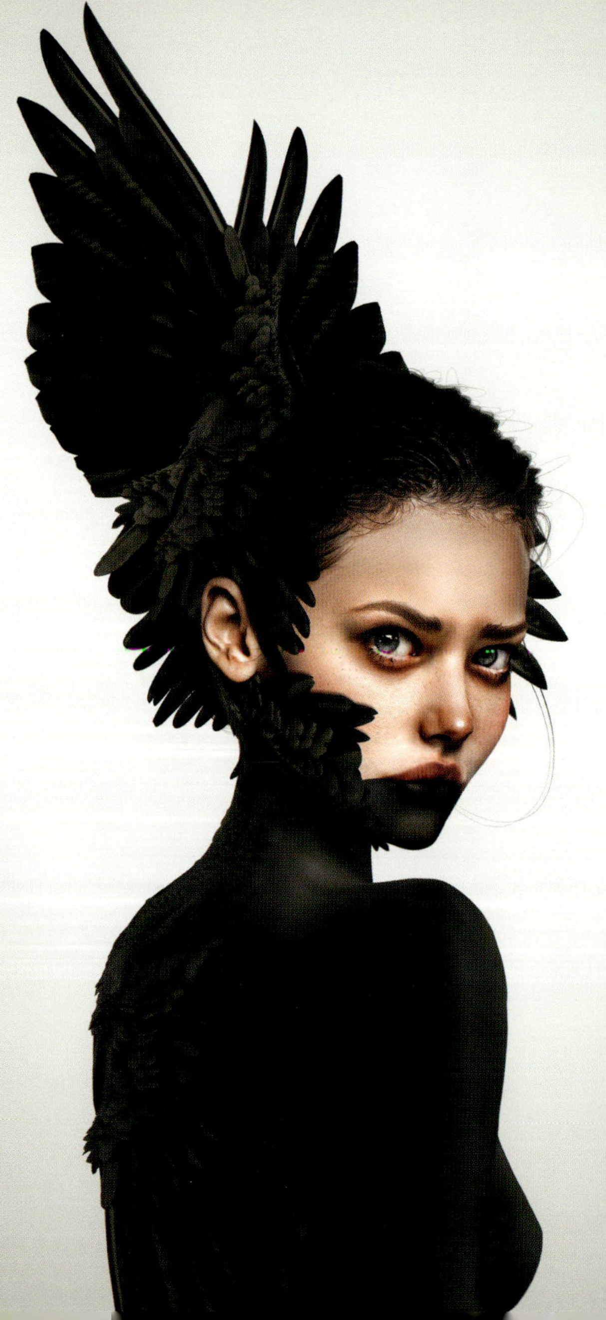

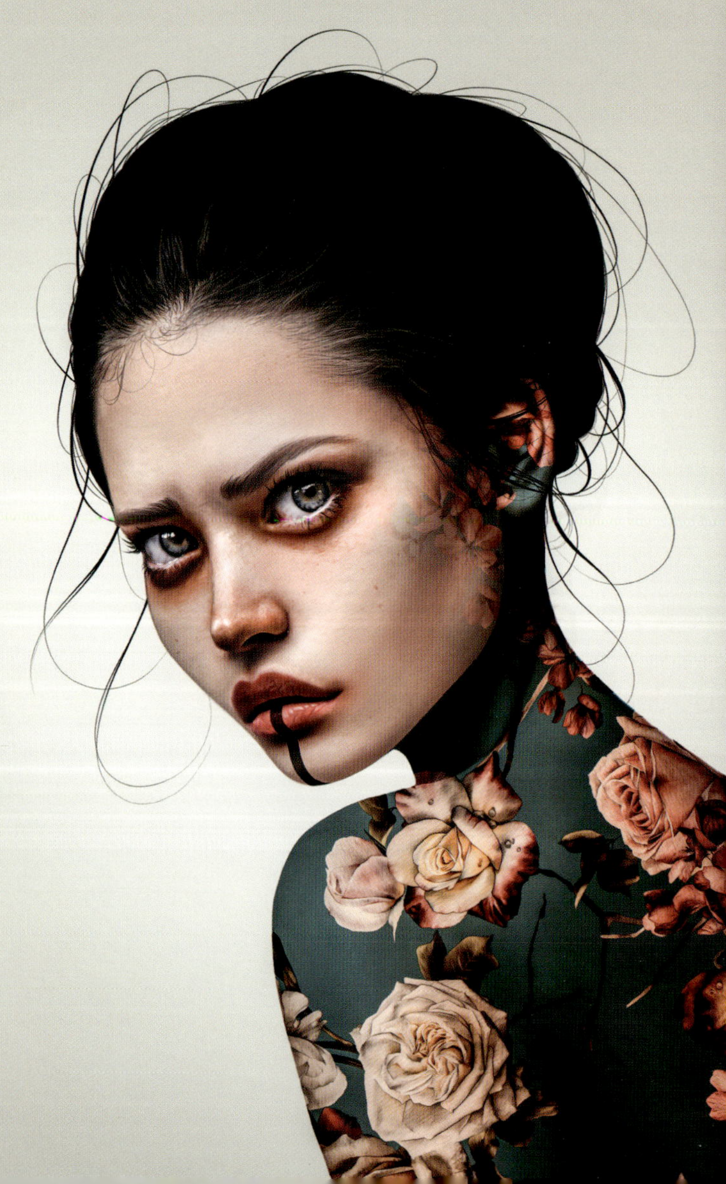

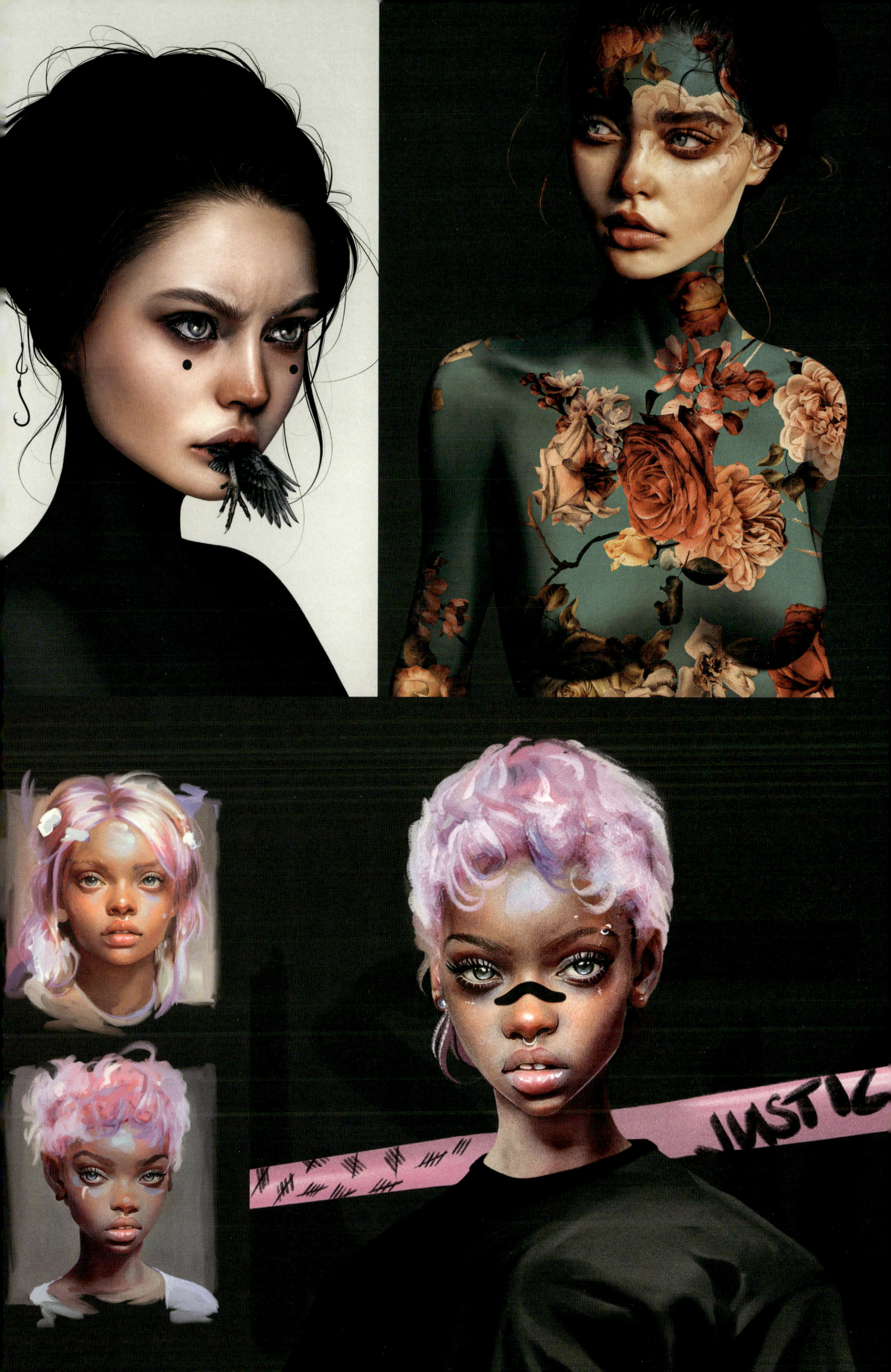

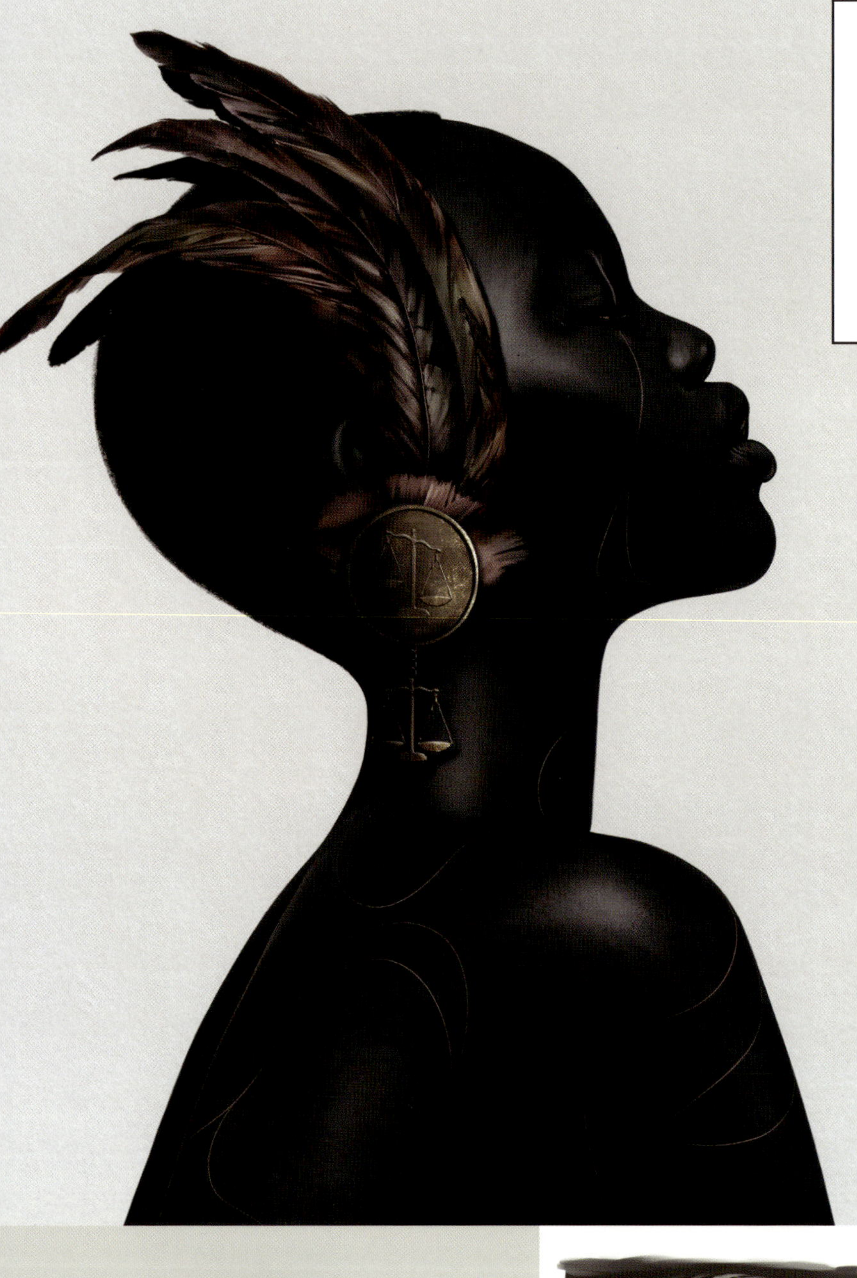

This page
Top left: Libra
Top right: Leo
Bottom left: Time For Change
Bottom right: Ria (middle: early designs)

Opposite page
Viored

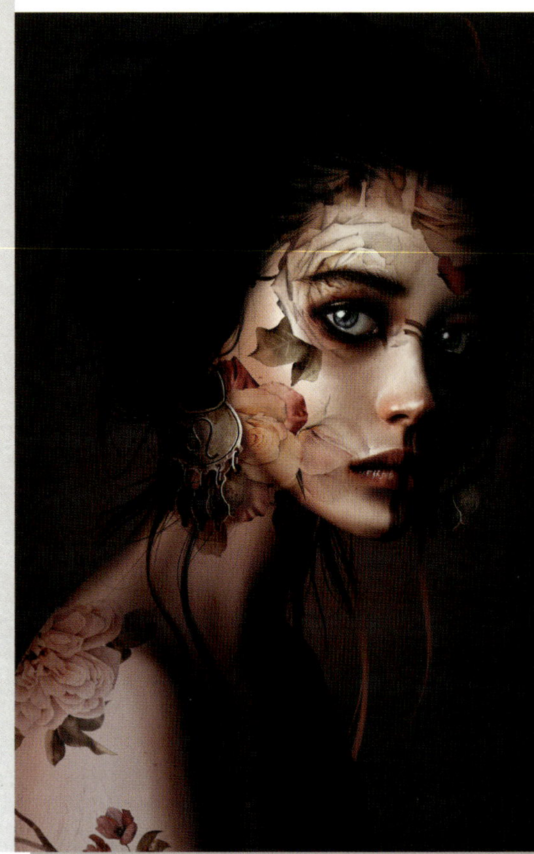

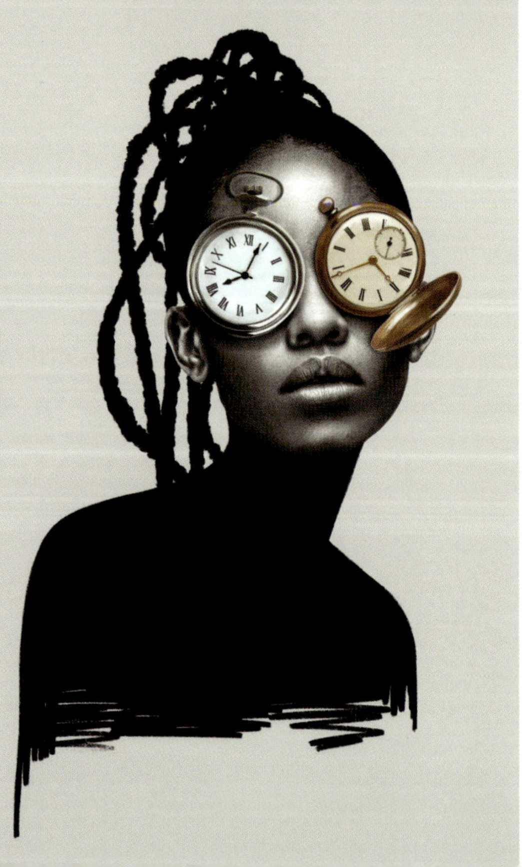

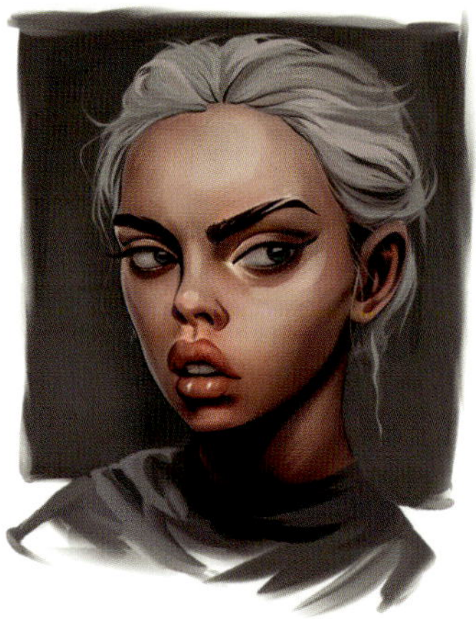

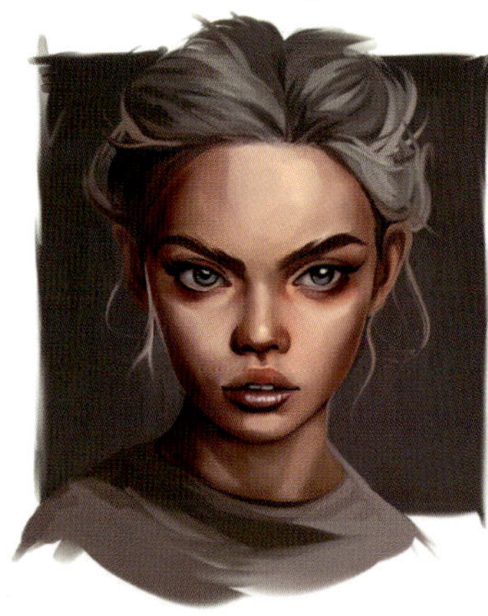

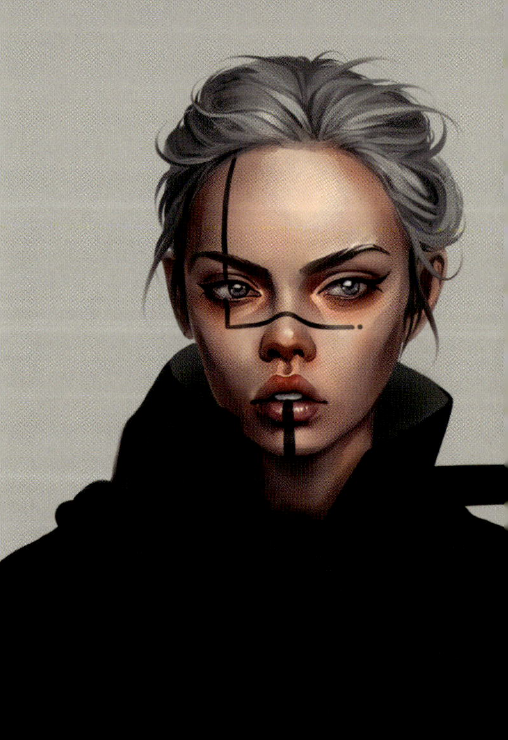

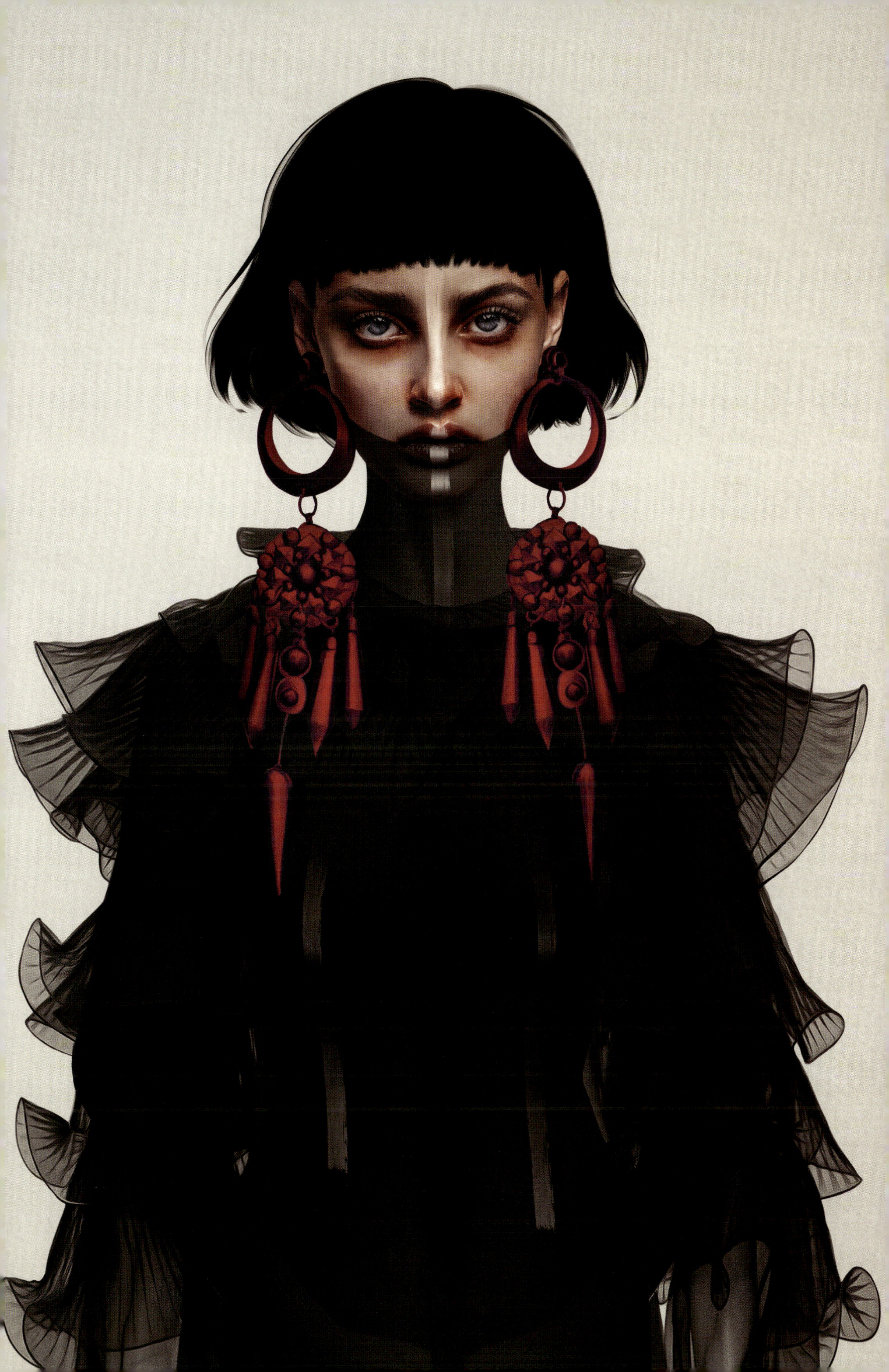

Gallery of Tran Nguyen

Artwork © Tran Nguyen

This page
Top right: Study 51
Bottom left: Study 44
Bottom right: Study 39

Opposite page
Study 25

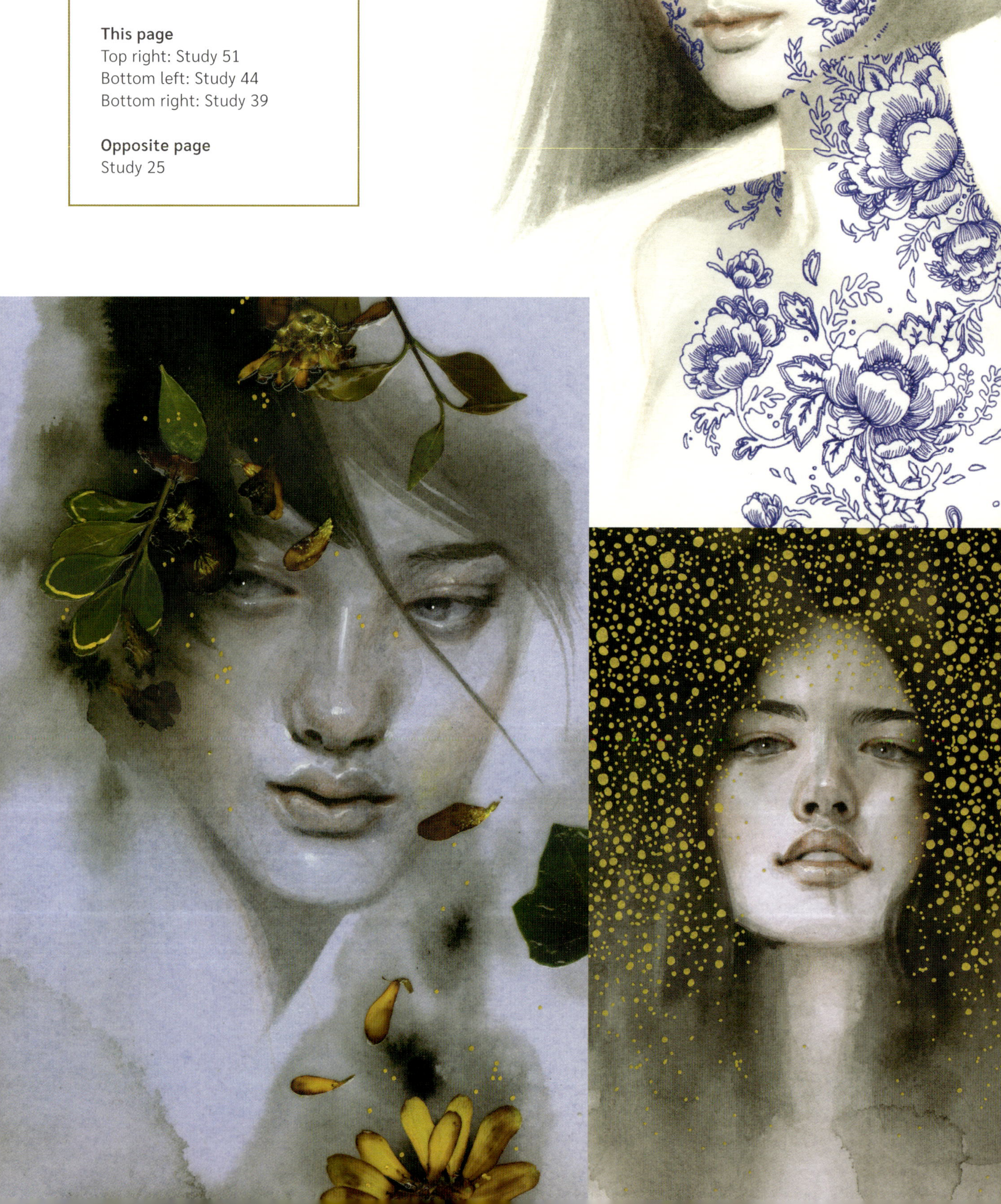

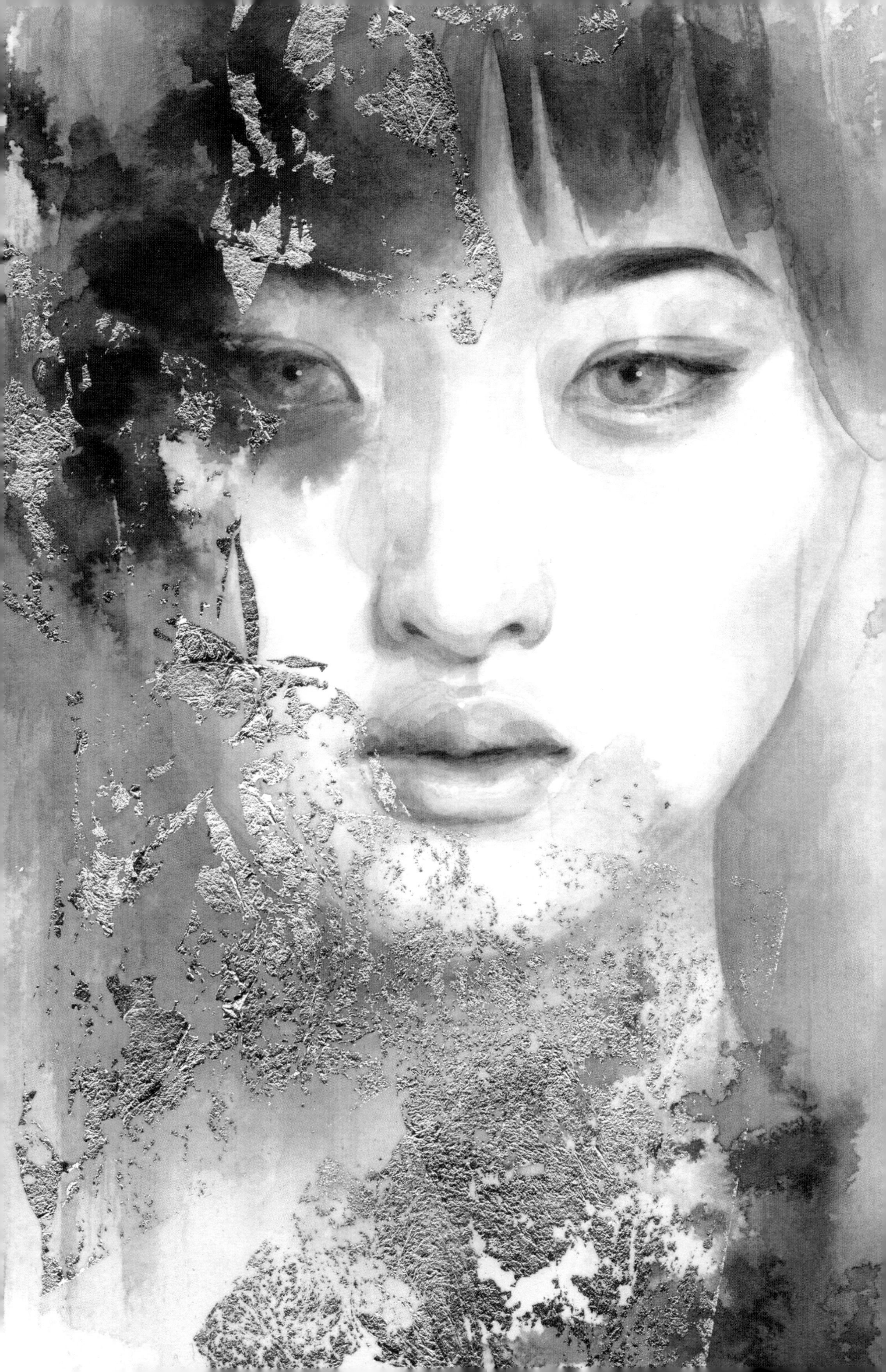

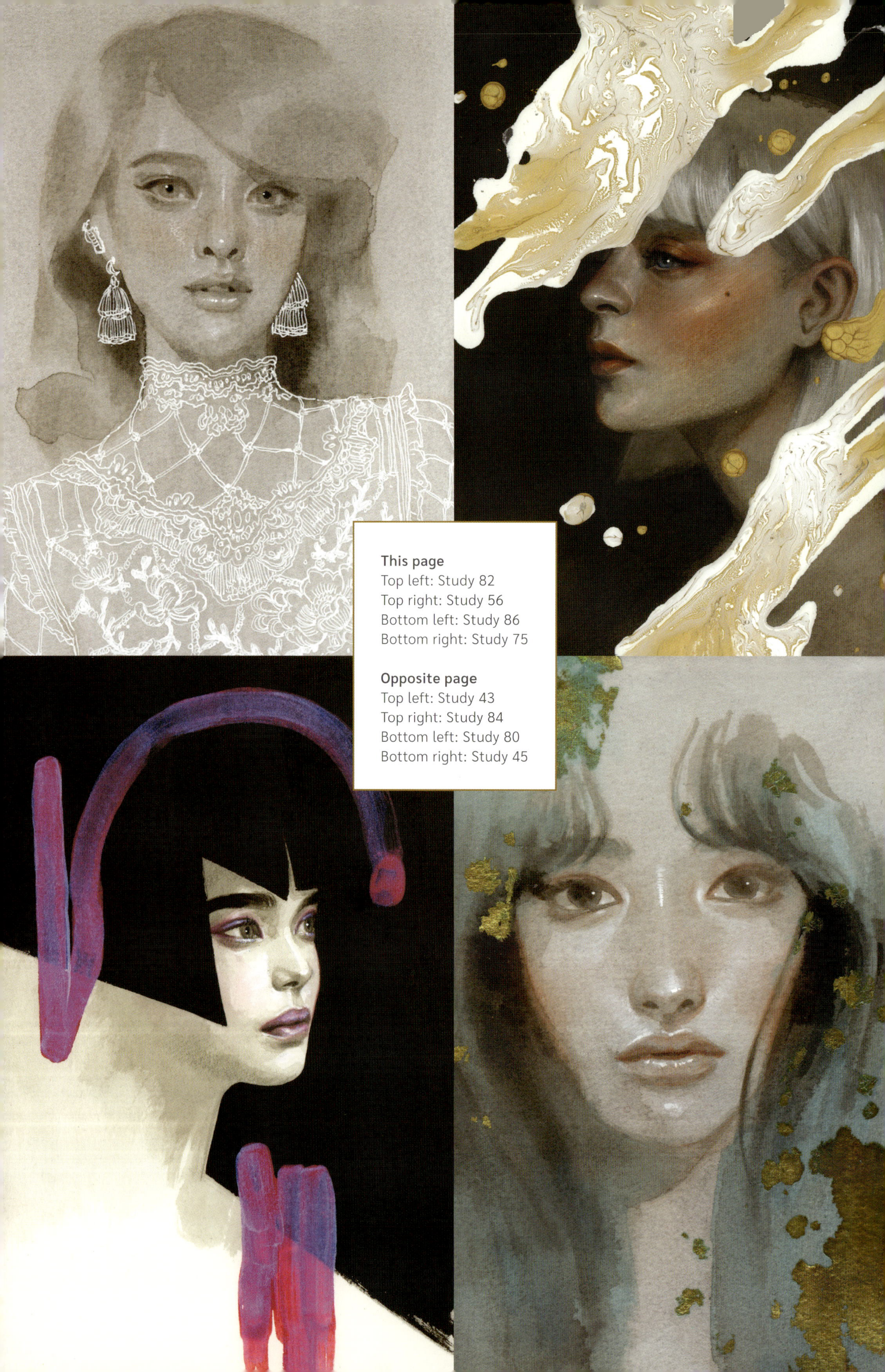

This page
Top left: Study 82
Top right: Study 56
Bottom left: Study 86
Bottom right: Study 75

Opposite page
Top left: Study 43
Top right: Study 84
Bottom left: Study 80
Bottom right: Study 45

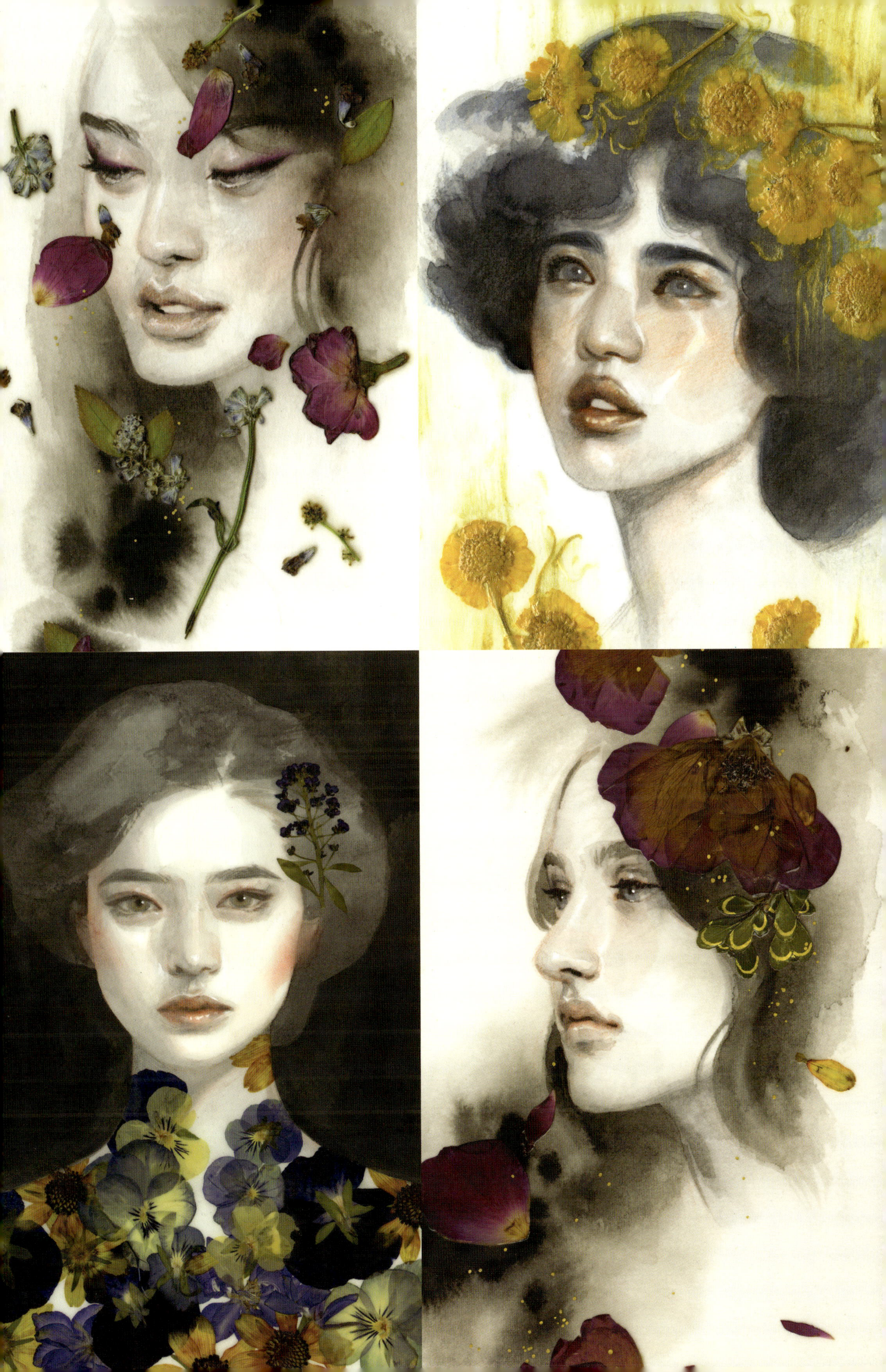

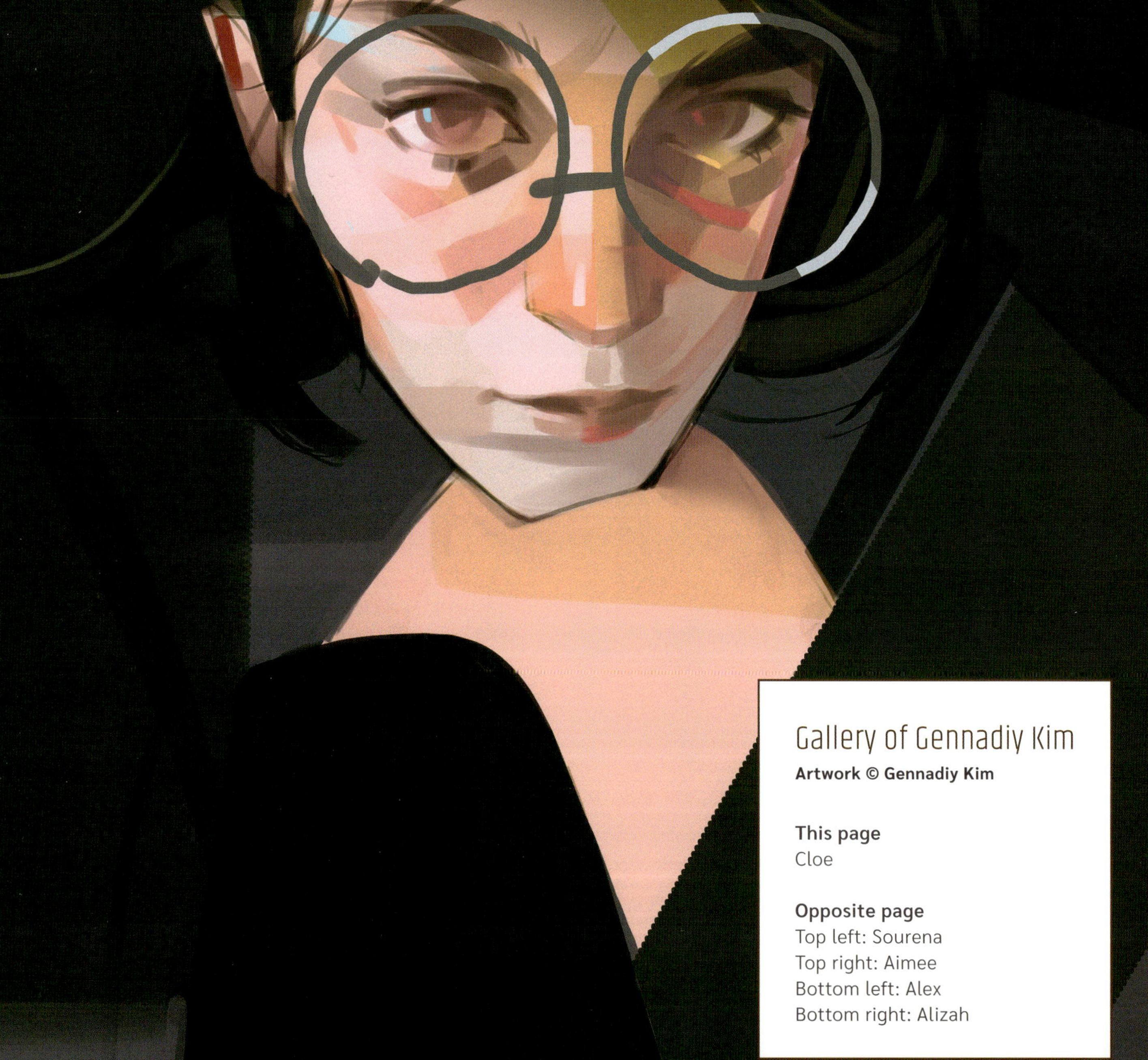

Gallery of Gennadiy Kim

This page
Cloe

Opposite page
Top left: Sourena
Top right: Aimee
Bottom left: Alex
Bottom right: Alizah

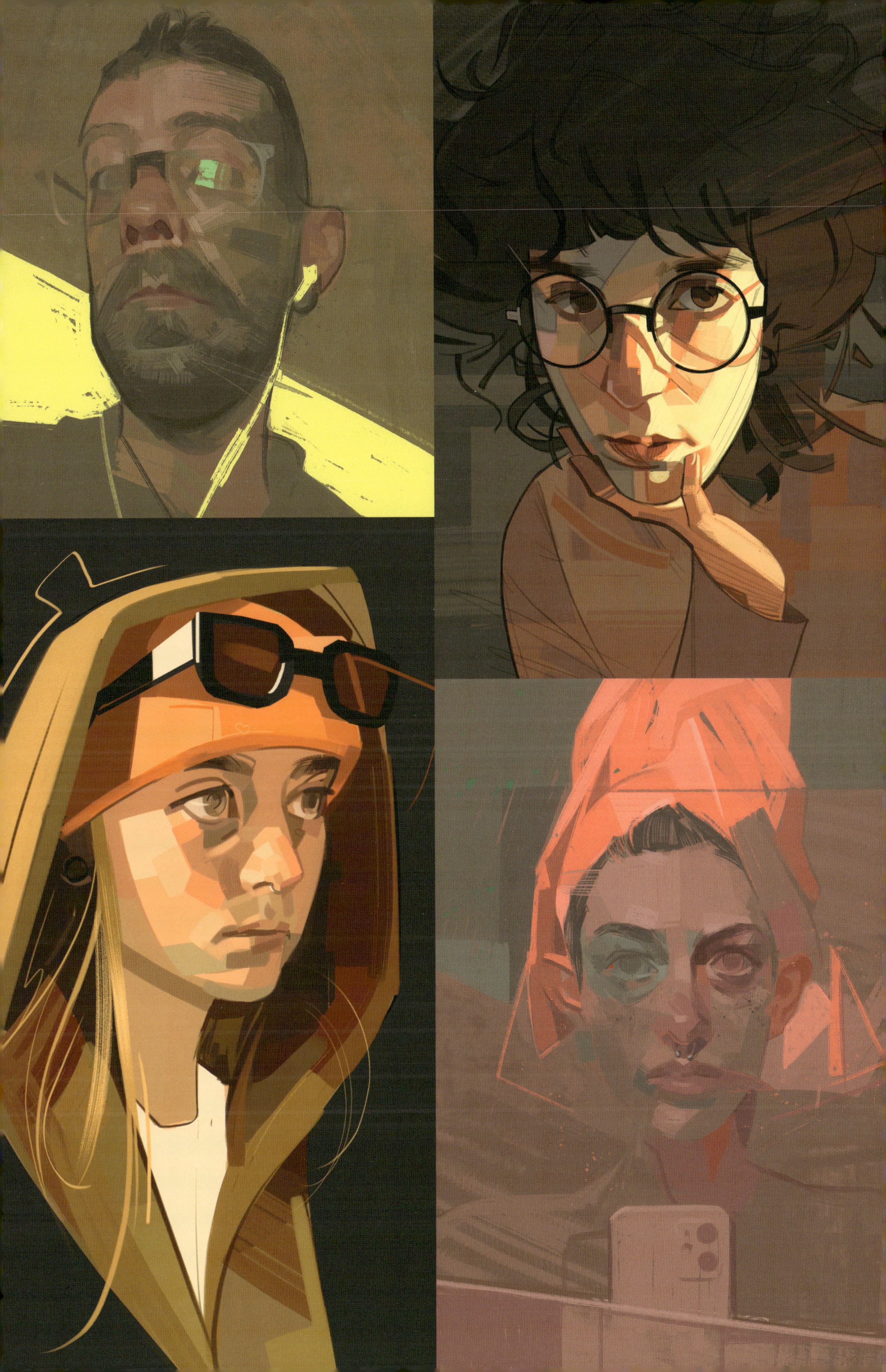

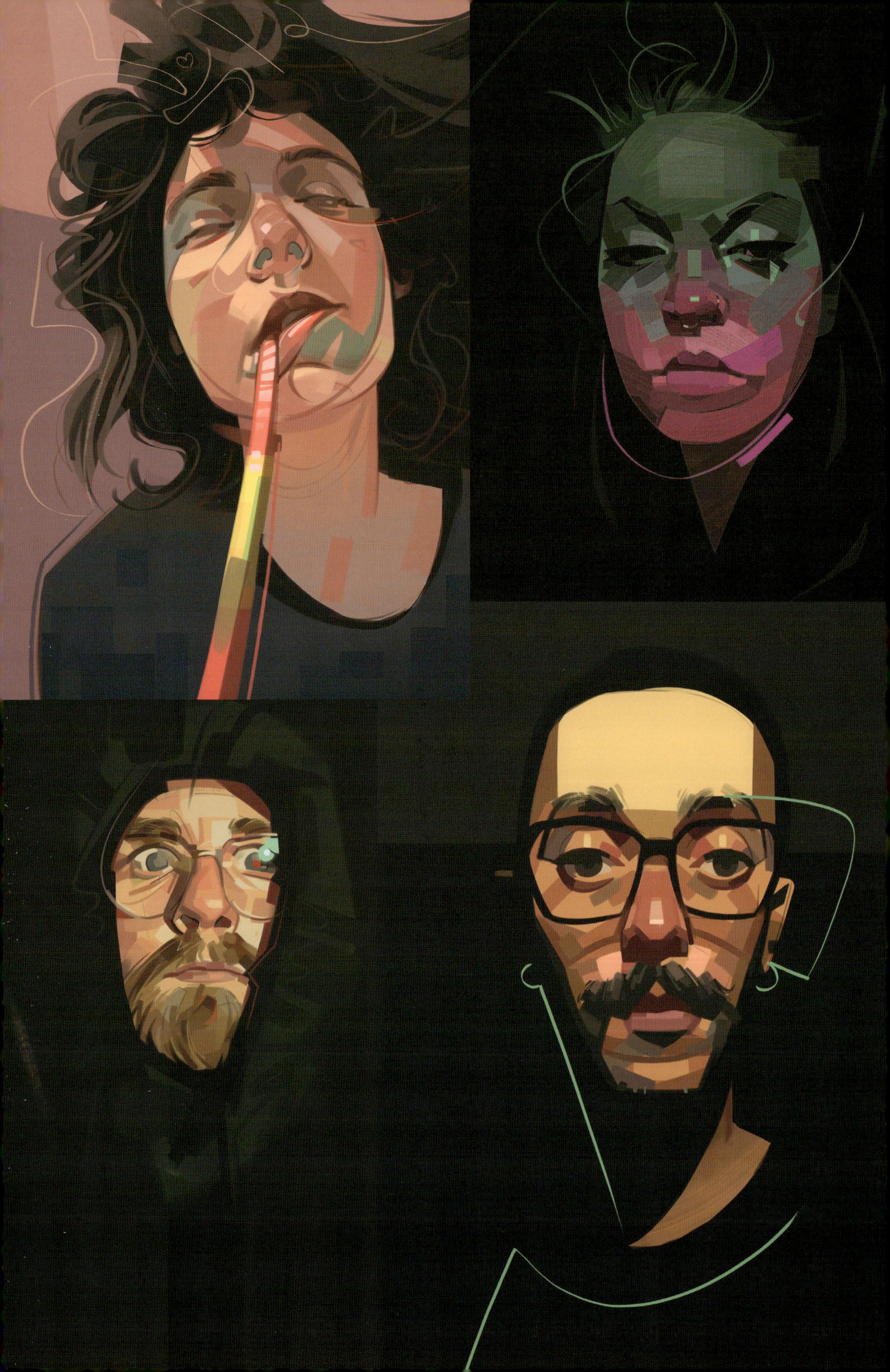

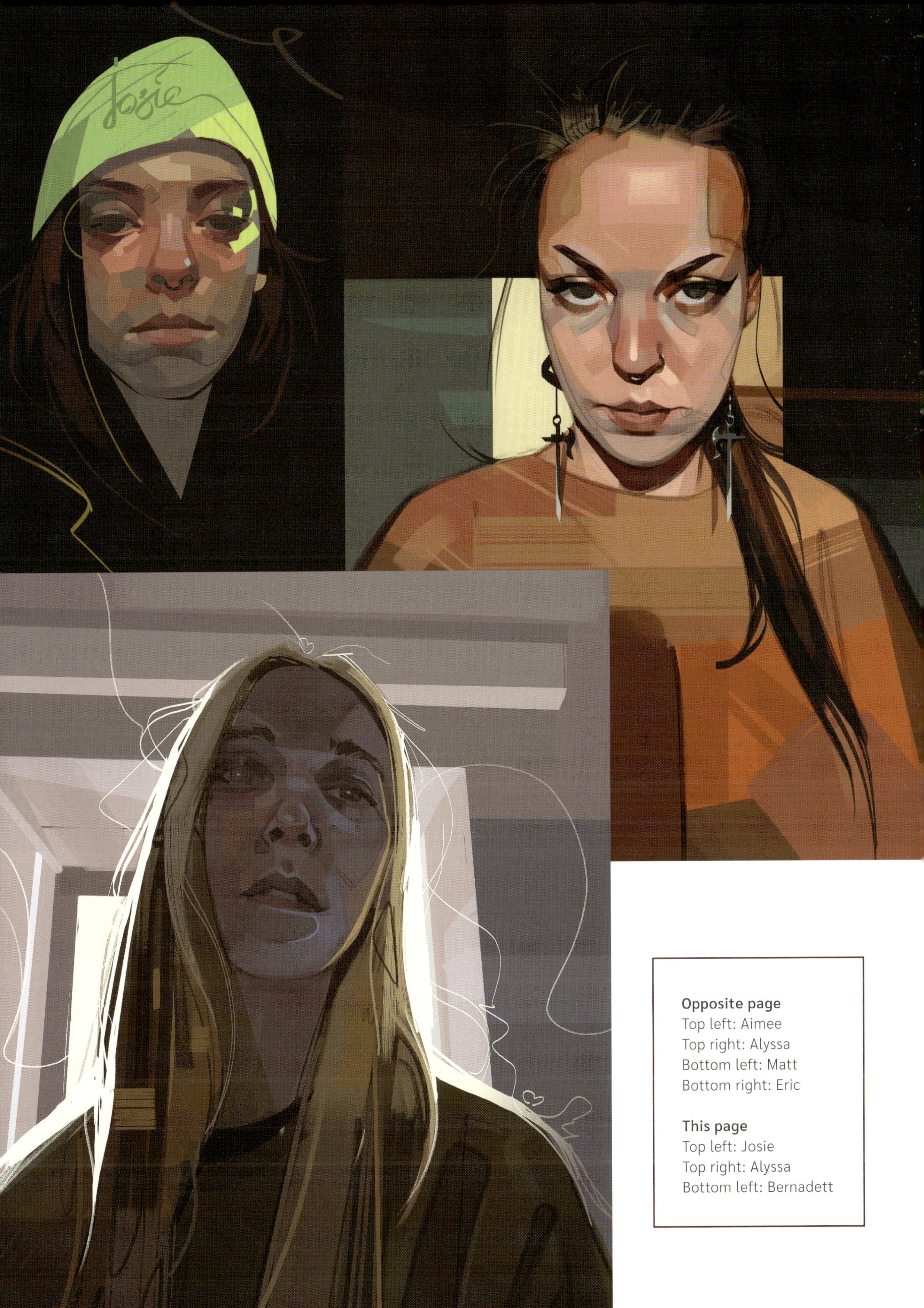

Opposite page
Top left: Aimee
Top right: Alyssa
Bottom left: Matt
Bottom right: Eric

This page
Top left: Josie
Top right: Alyssa
Bottom left: Bernadett

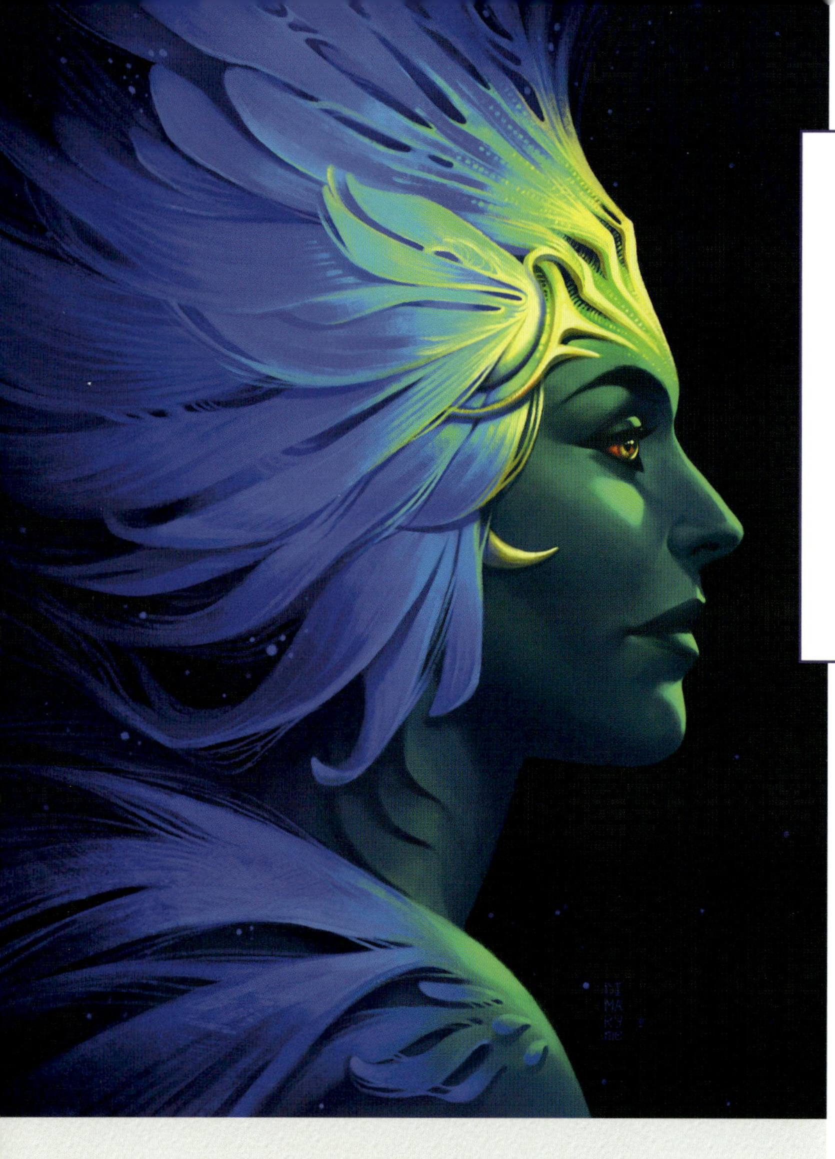

Gallery of Maria Dimova

Artwork © Maria Dimova

This page
Top left: Sea Queen, 2020
Middle right: Purple Witch, 2018
Bottom left: Fleur, 2021
Bottom right: Blue Bellflowers, 2020

Opposite page
Top left: Lake Maiden, 2021
Top right: Fox Witch, 2020
Bottom: Flora, 2021

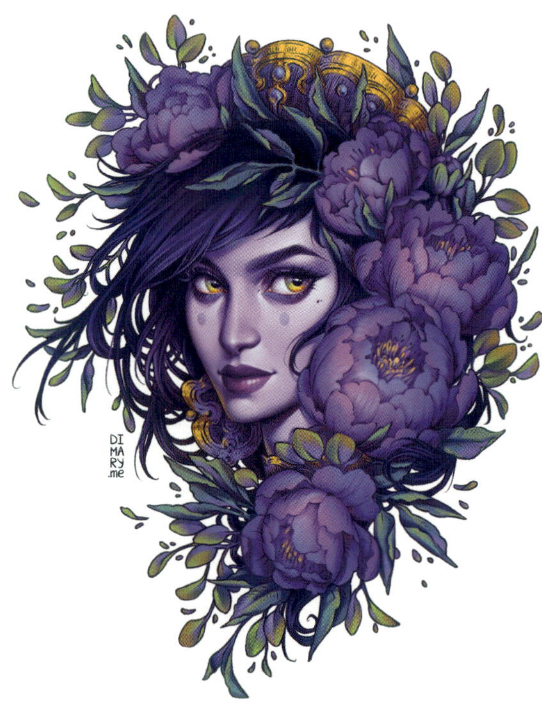

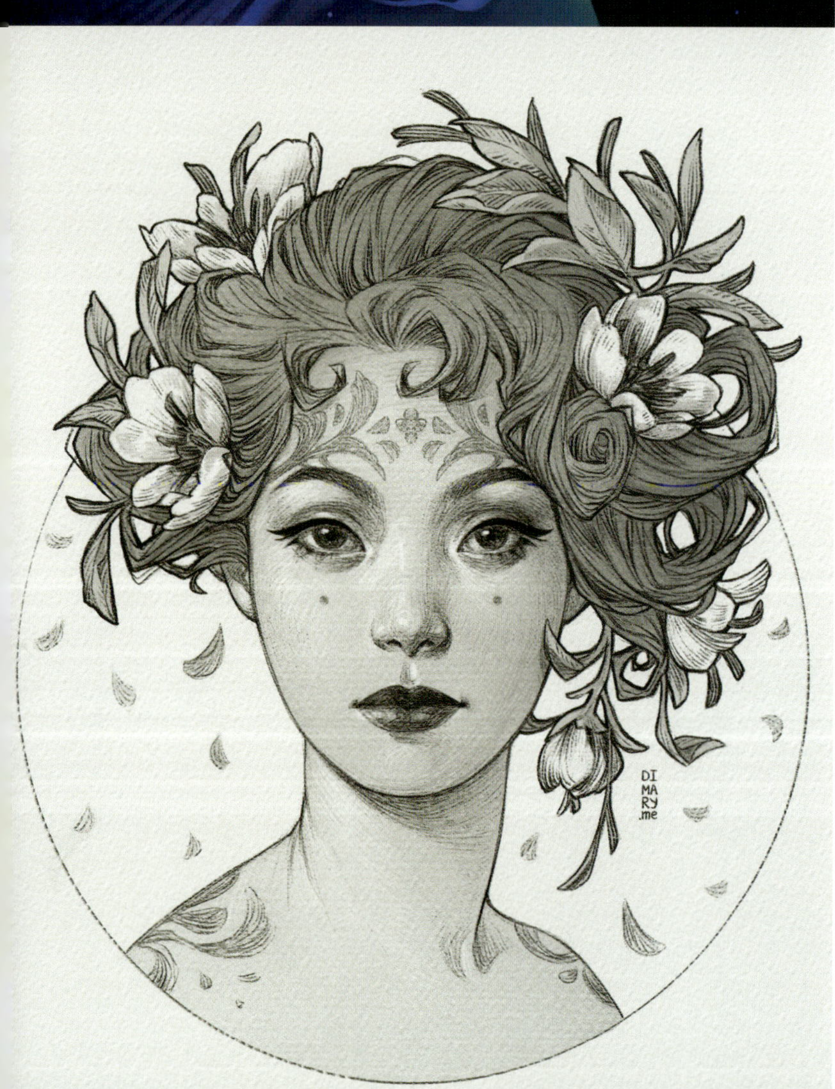

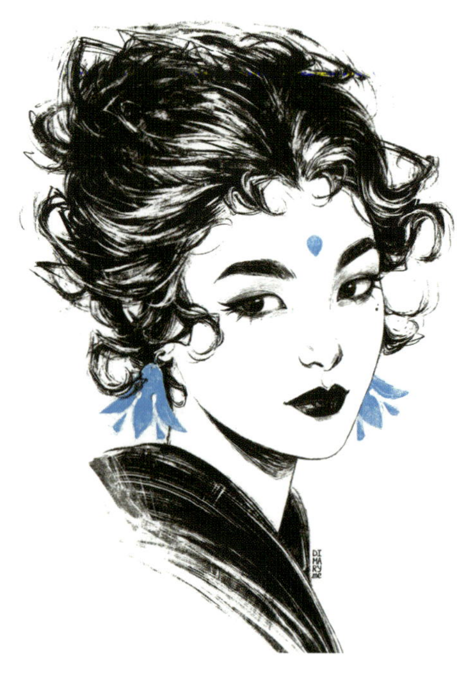

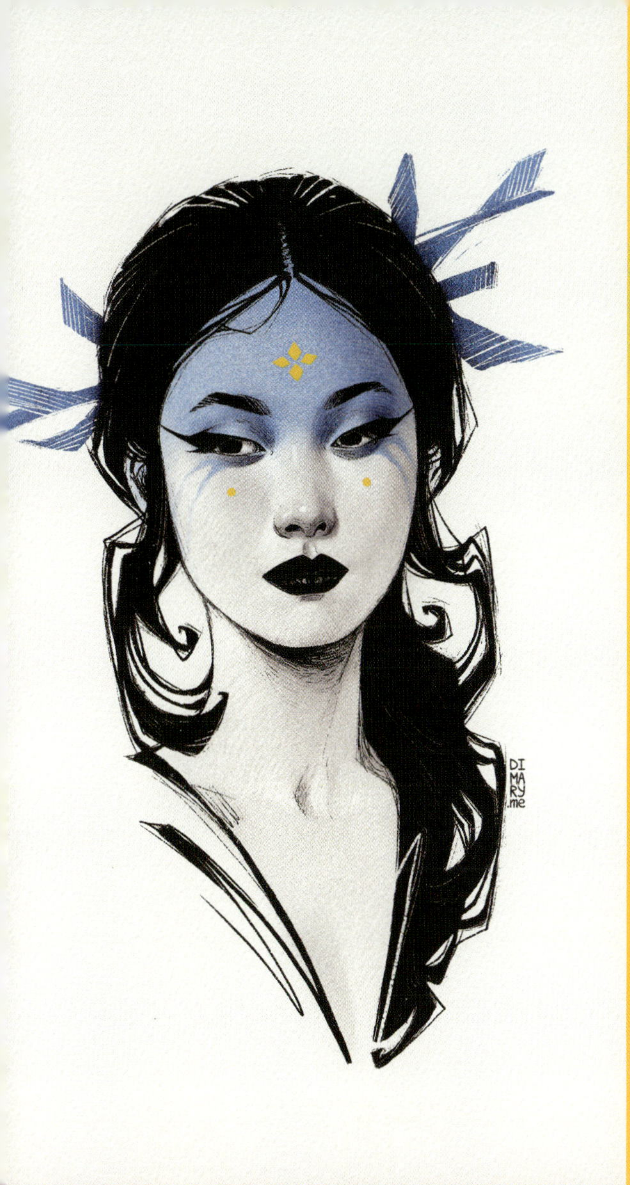

DIMARY.me

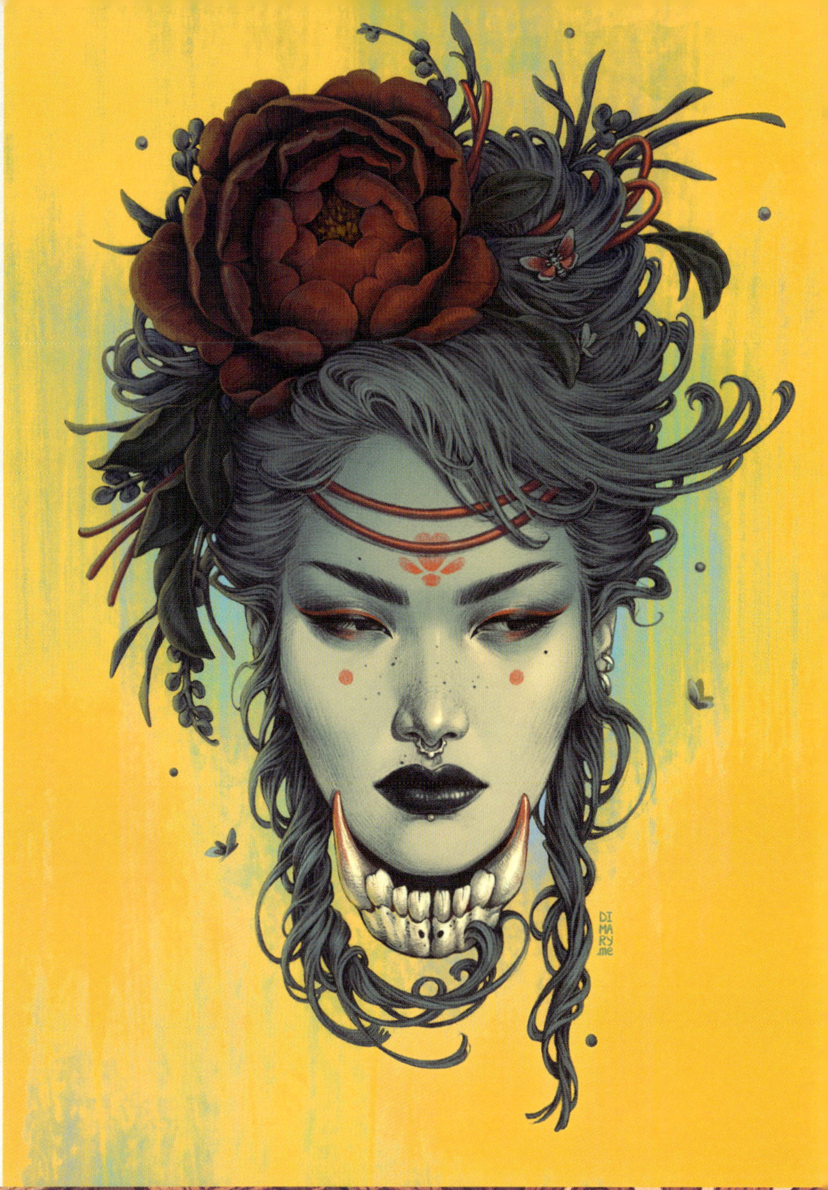

DIMARY.me

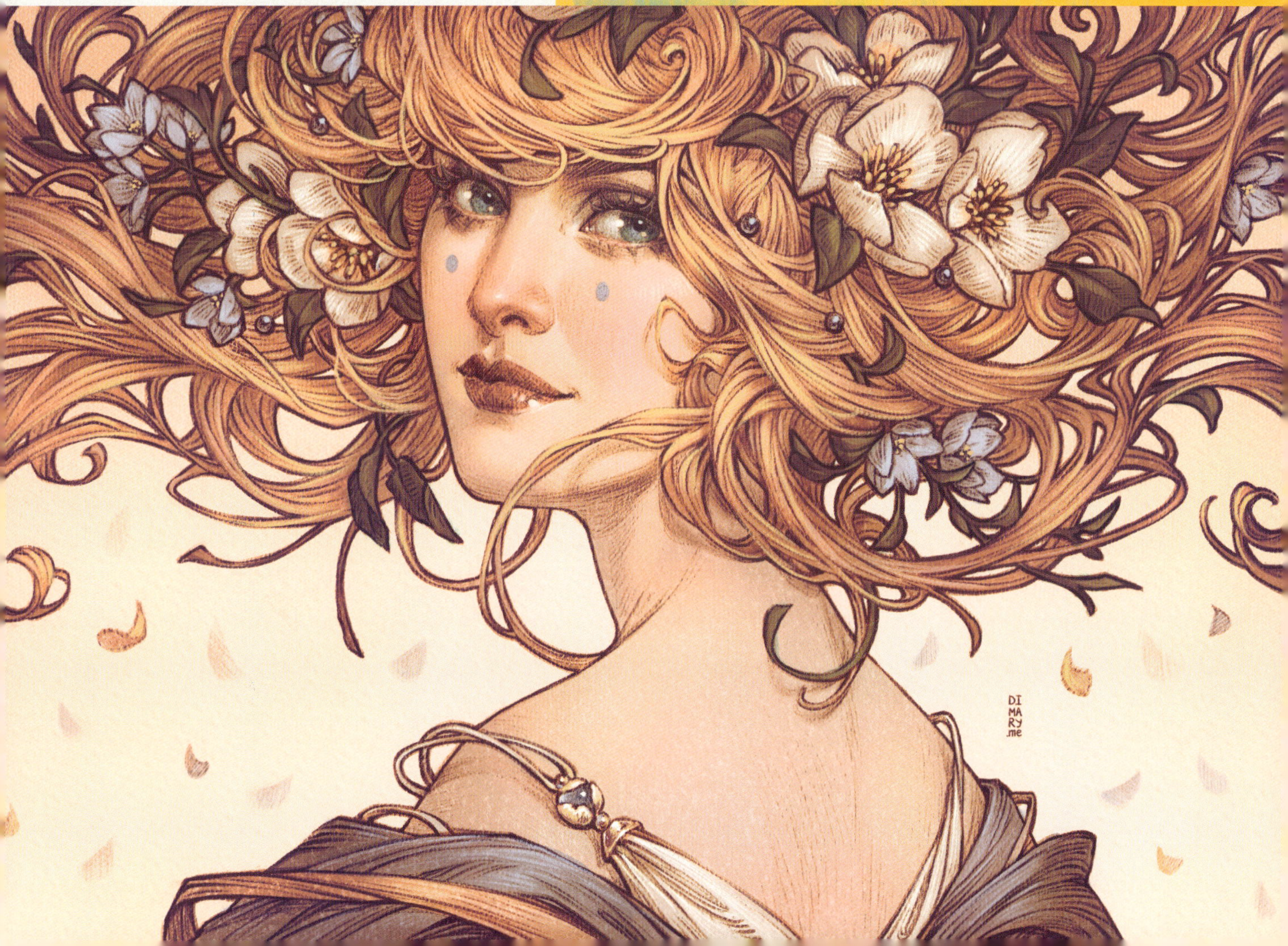

DIMARY.me

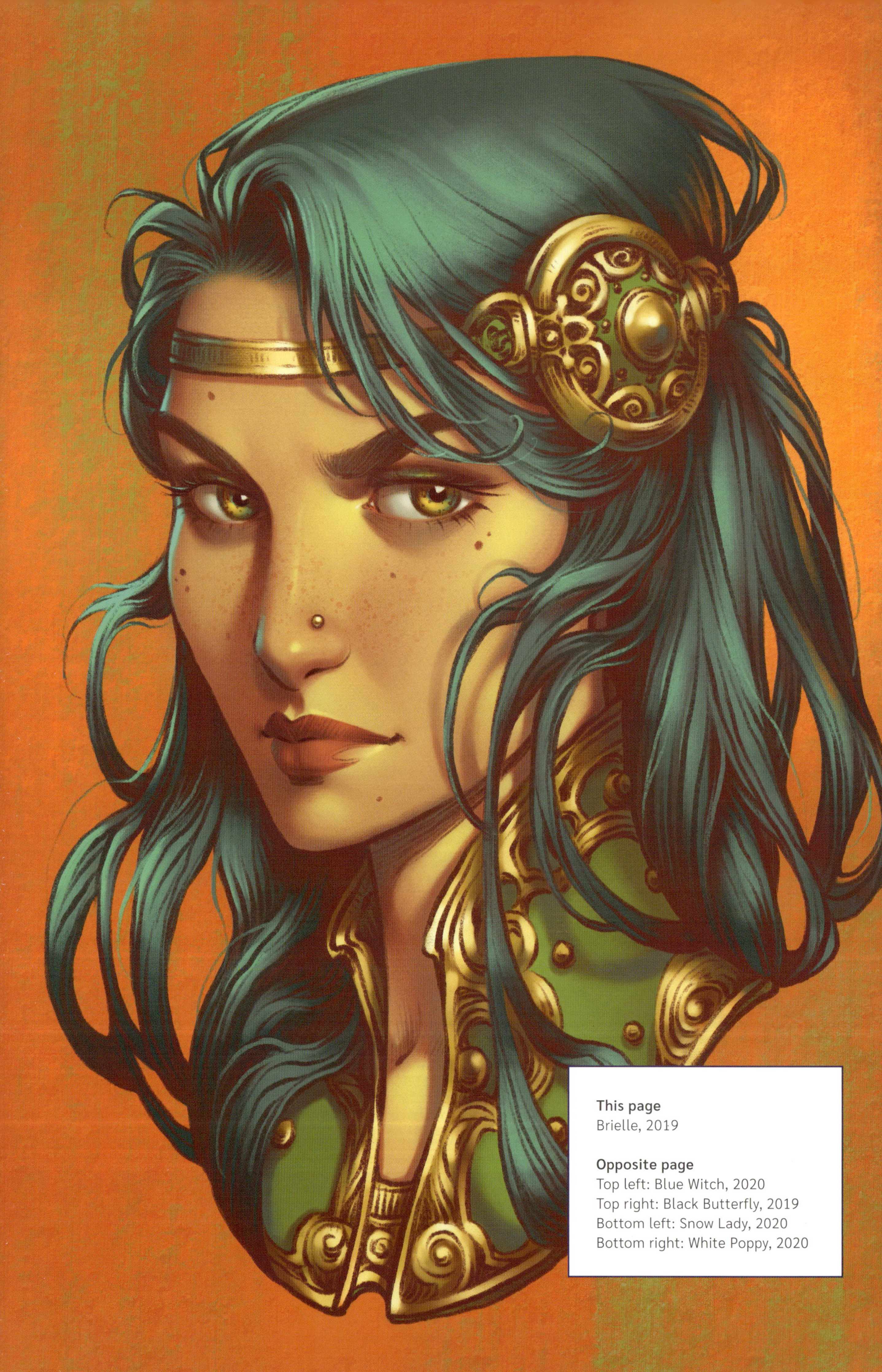

This page
Brielle, 2019

Opposite page
Top left: Blue Witch, 2020
Top right: Black Butterfly, 2019
Bottom left: Snow Lady, 2020
Bottom right: White Poppy, 2020

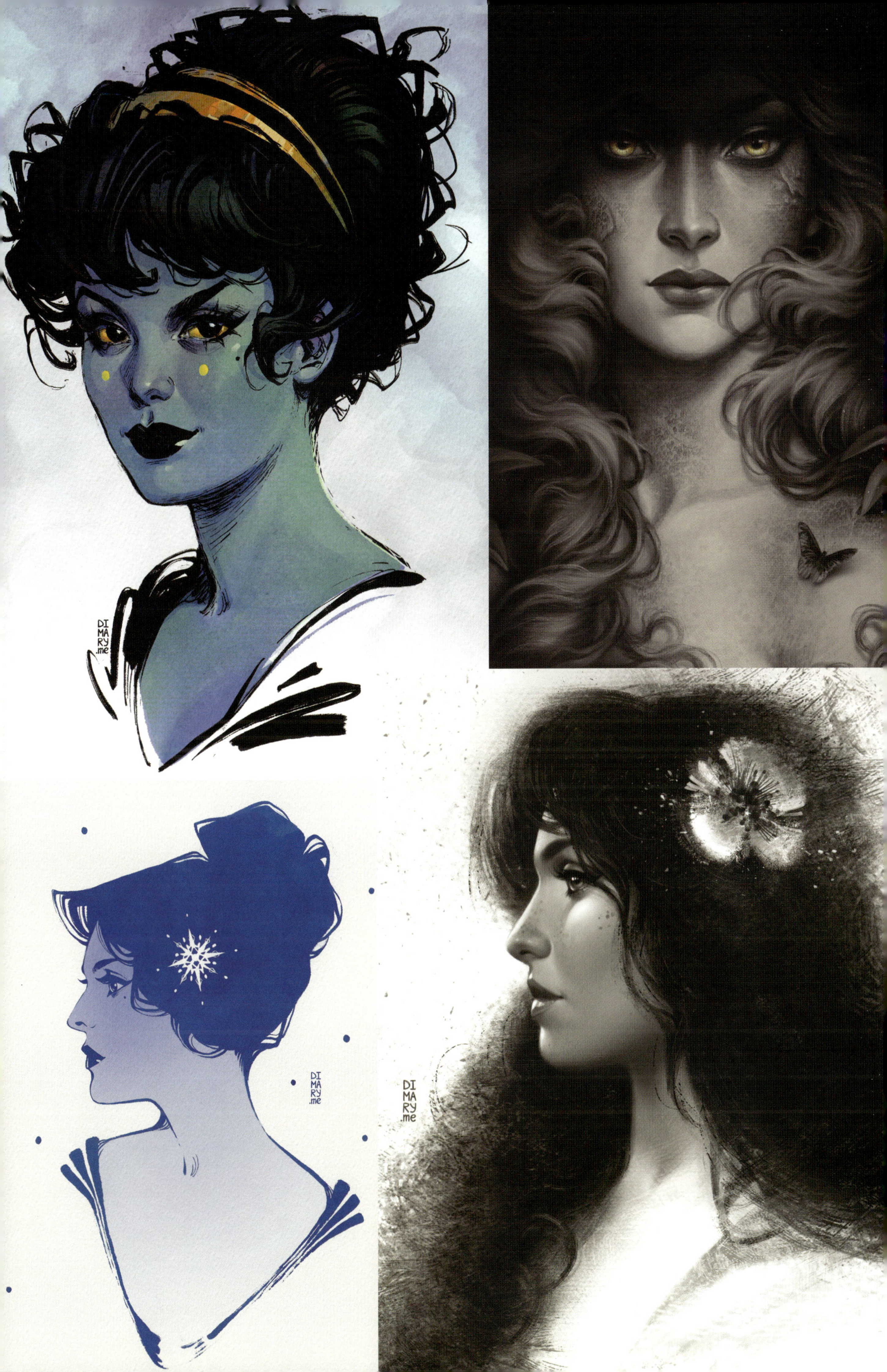
DI
MA
RY
.me
DI
MA
RY
.me
DI
MA
RY
.me

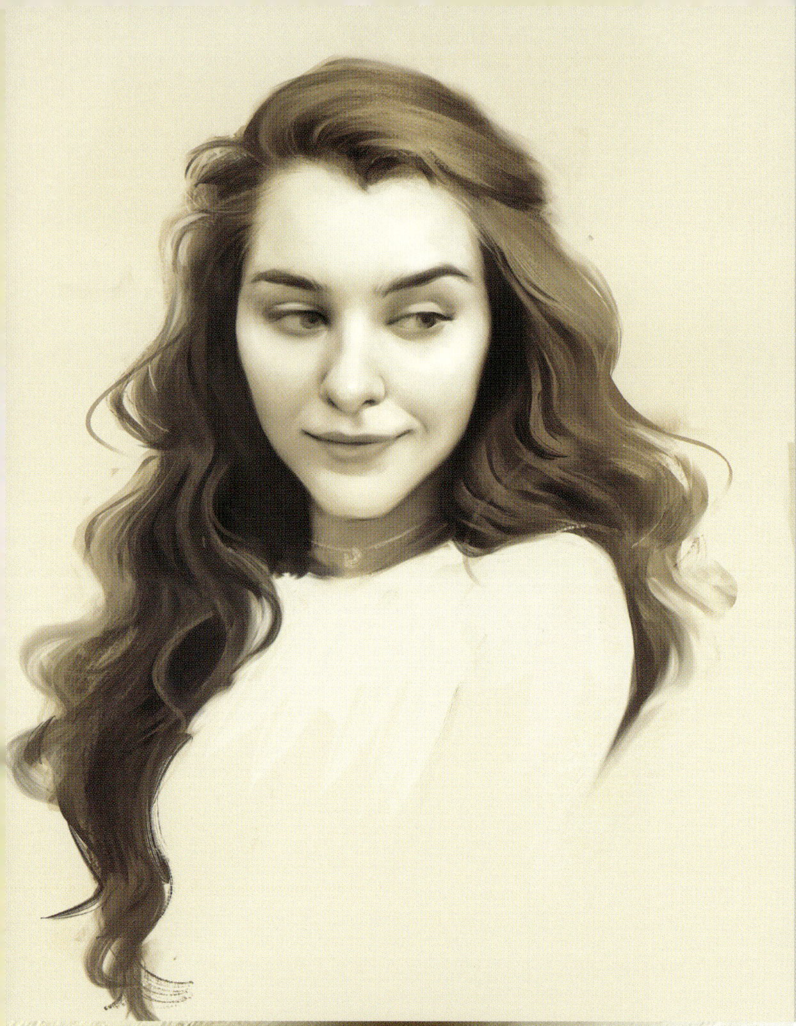

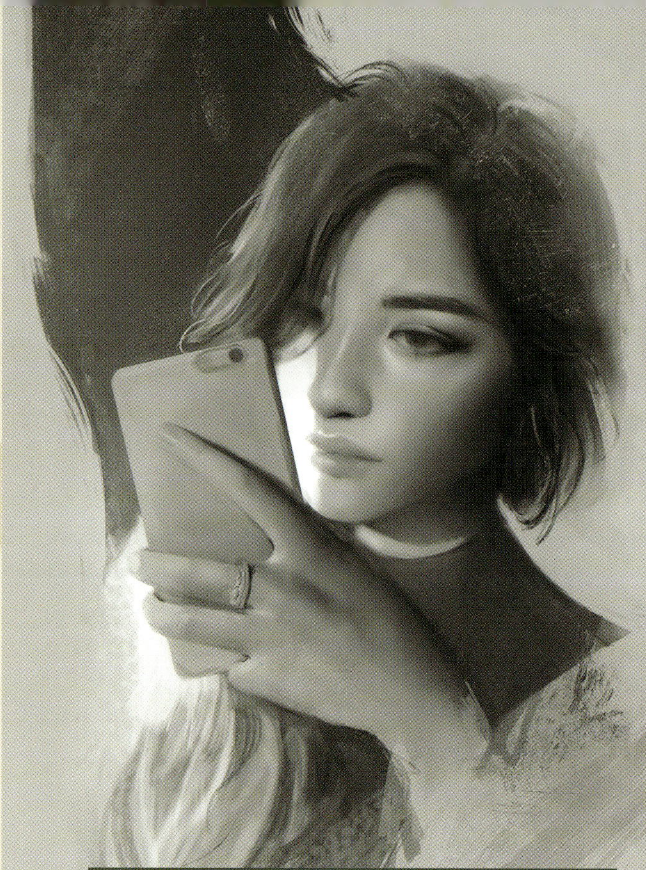

Gallery of Justine S. Florentino

This page
Top left: Val
Top right: Sketch
Bottom left: Maria
Bottom right: Feather

Opposite page
Stare

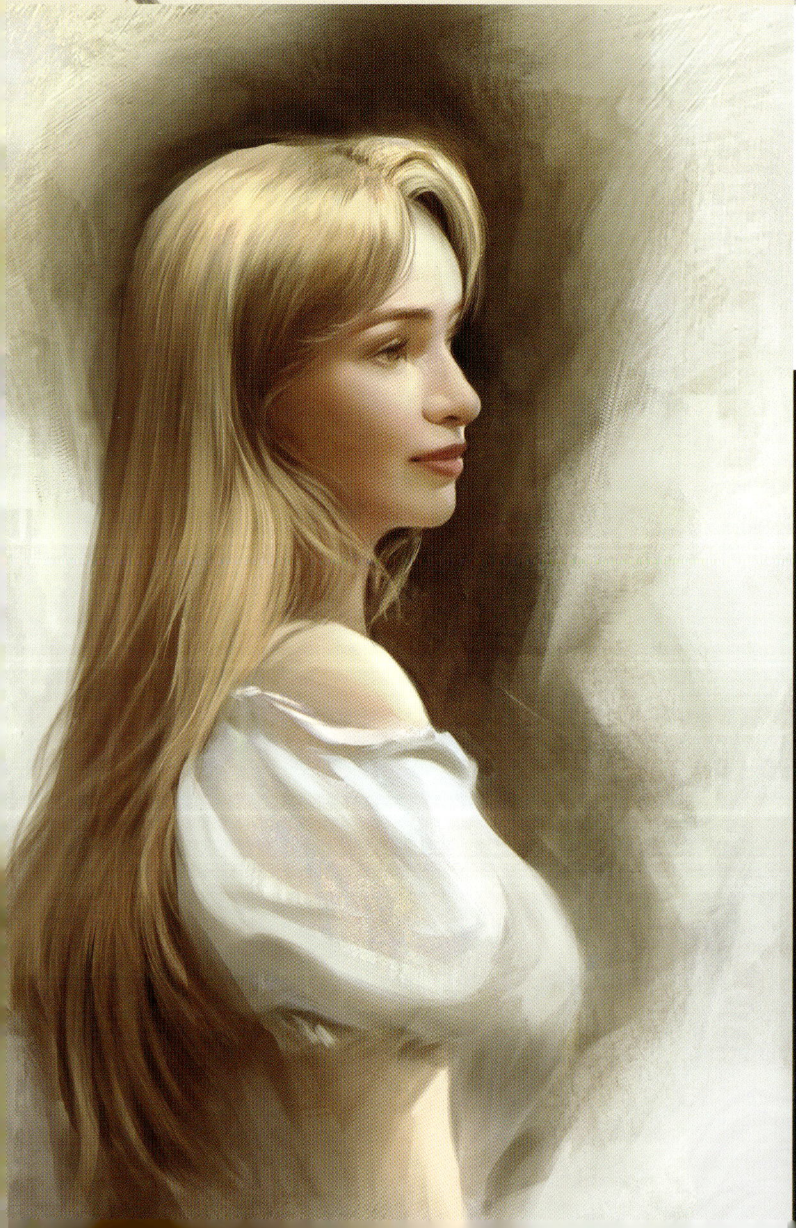

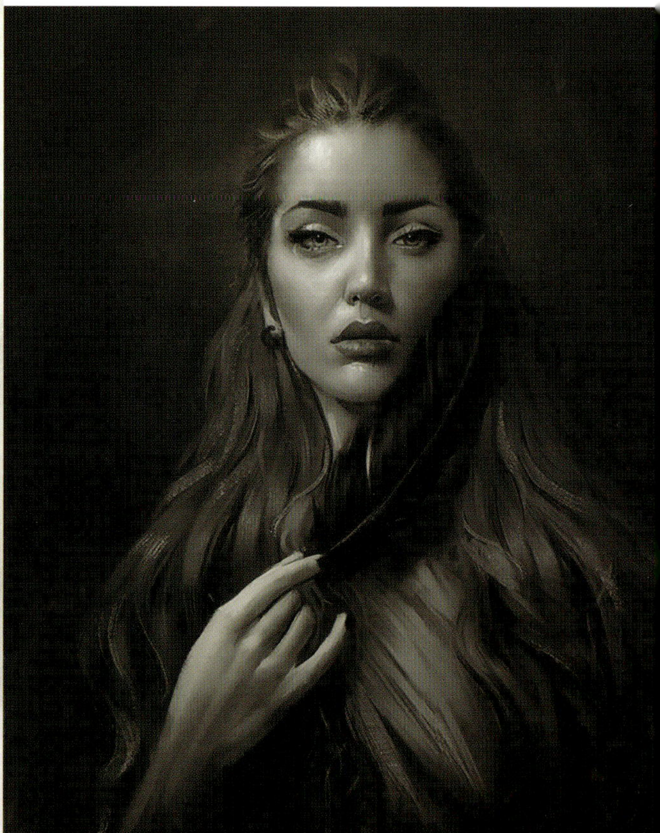

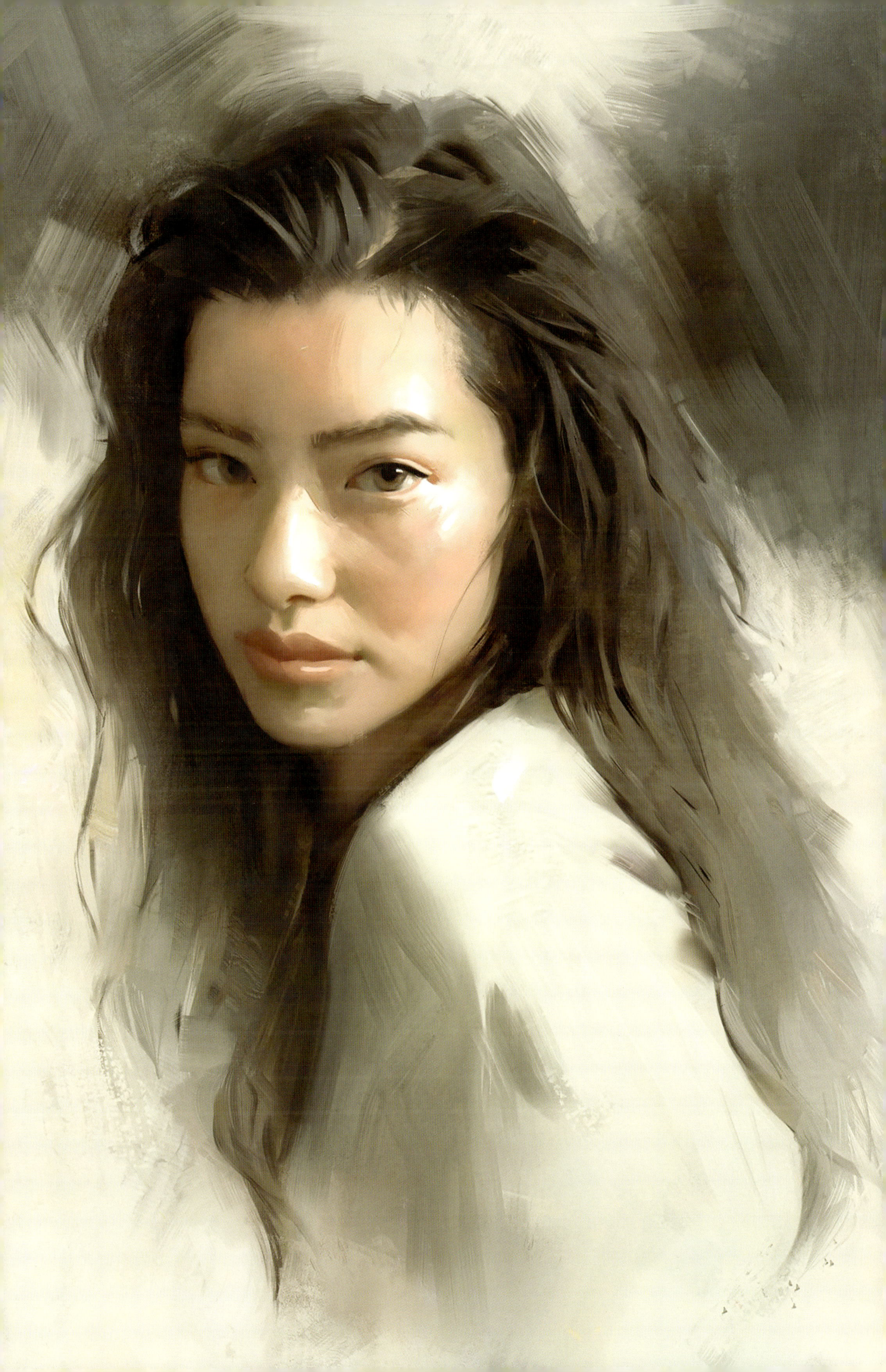

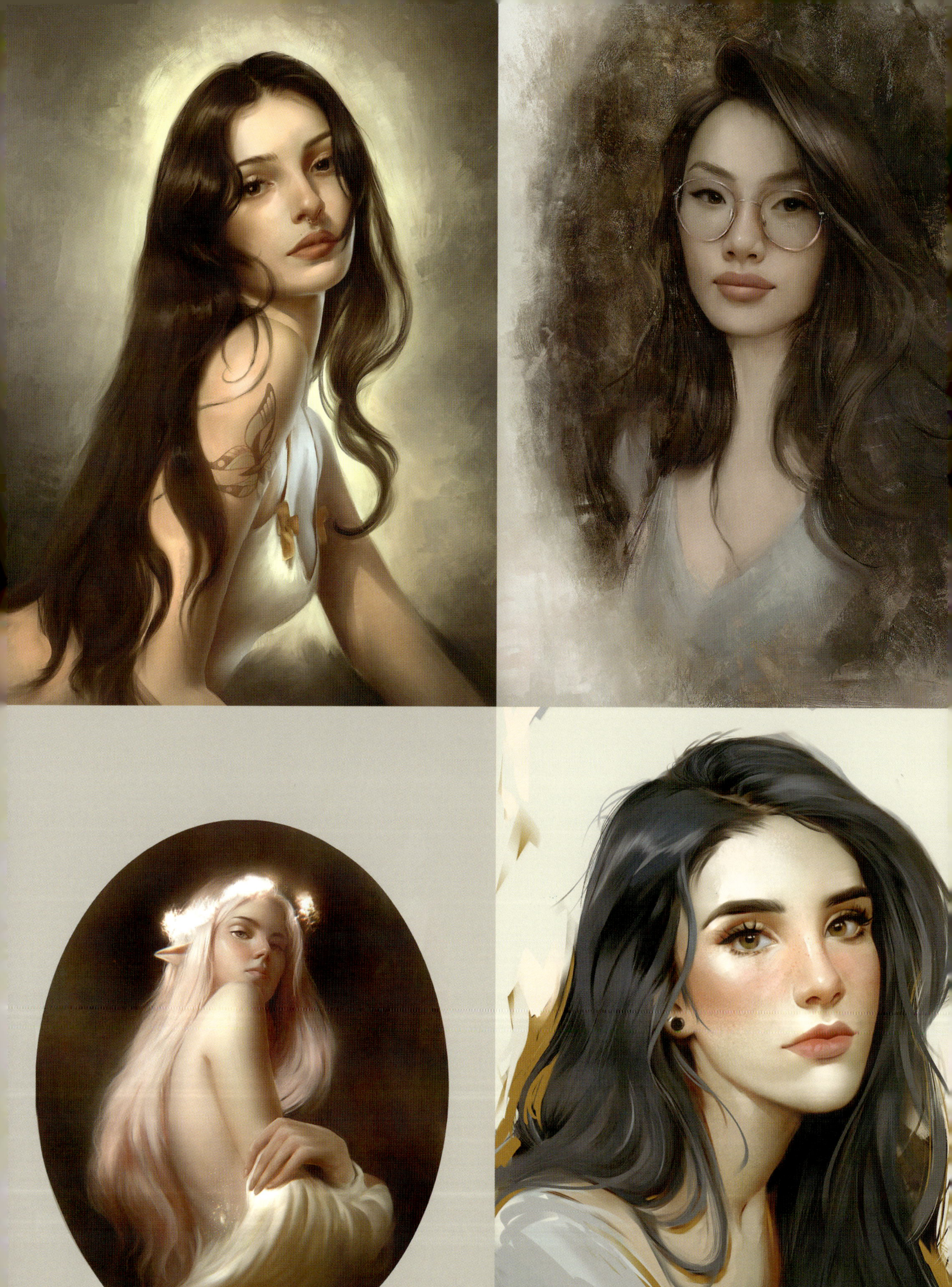

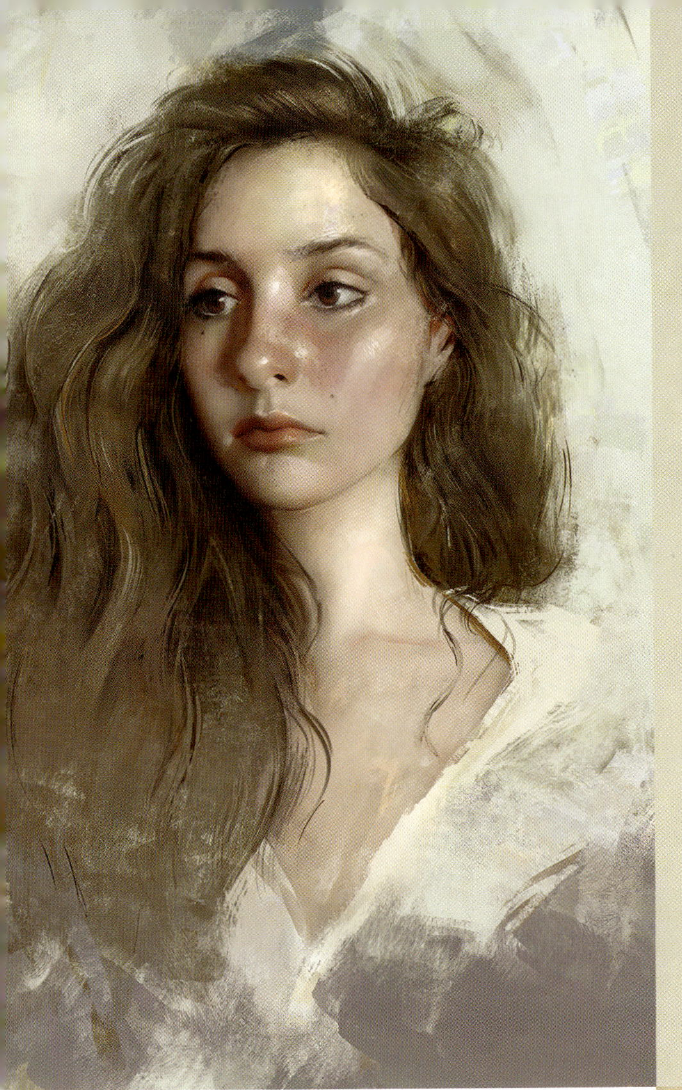

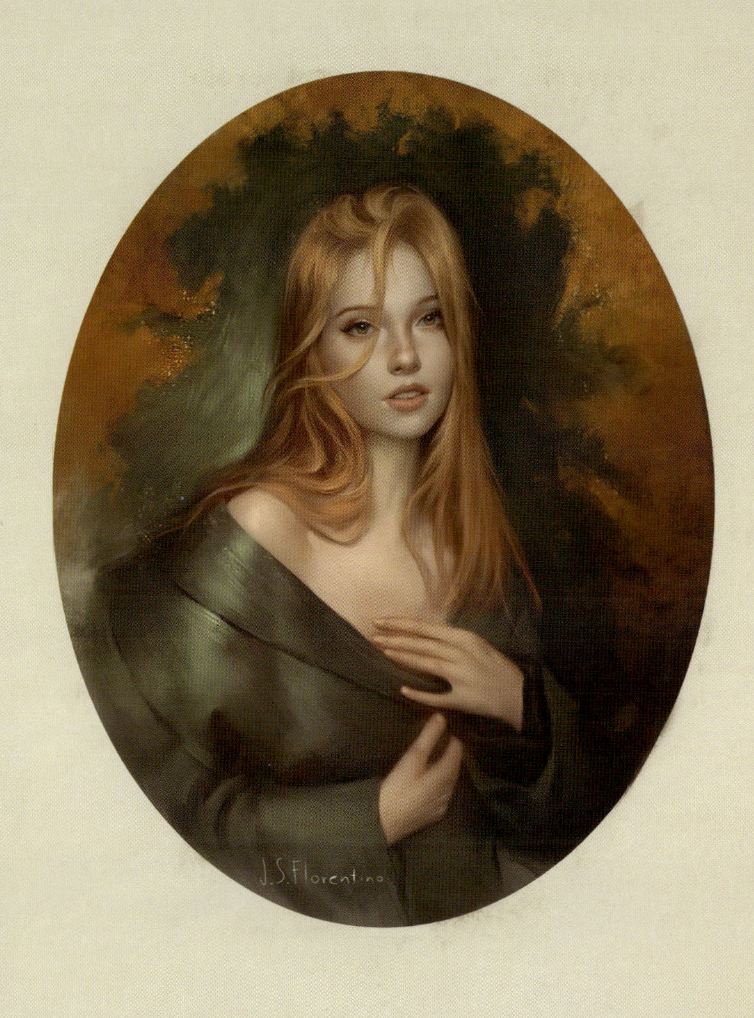

Opposite page
Top left: Ramona
Top right: Betty
Bottom left: Elf
Bottom right: Gab

This page
Top left: Nat
Top right: Kat
Bottom right: Jane

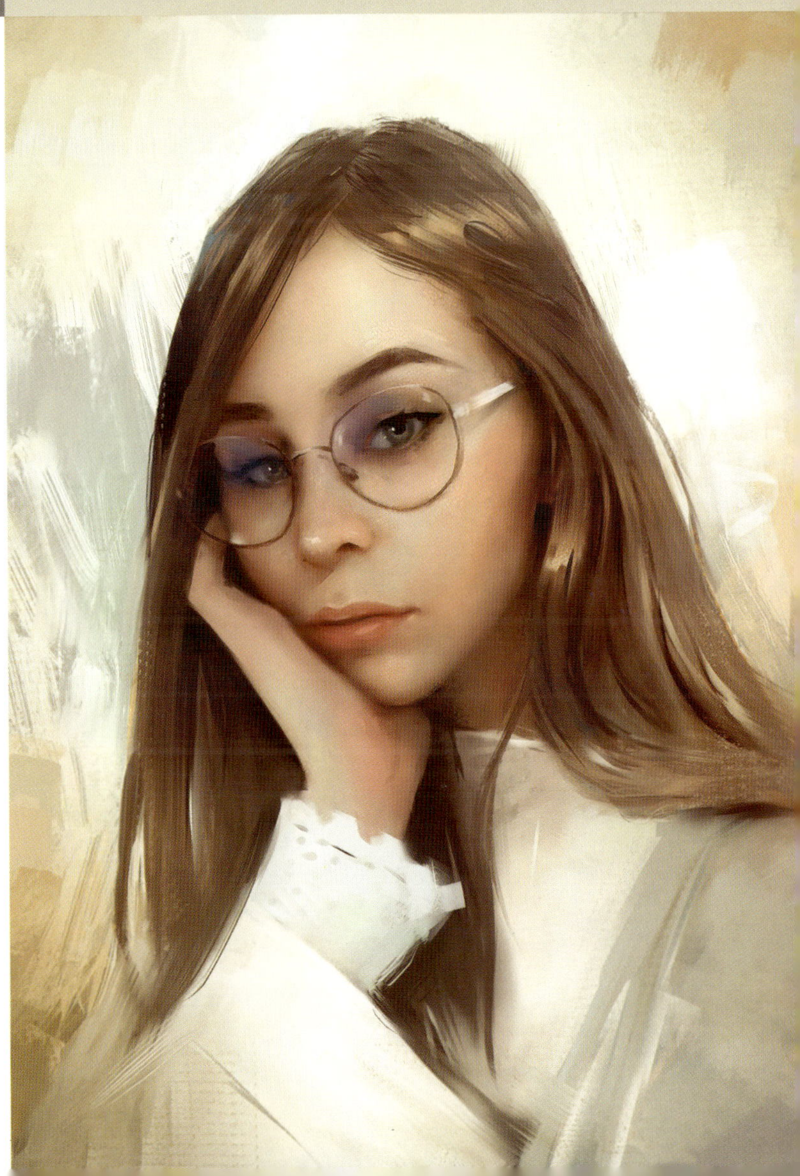

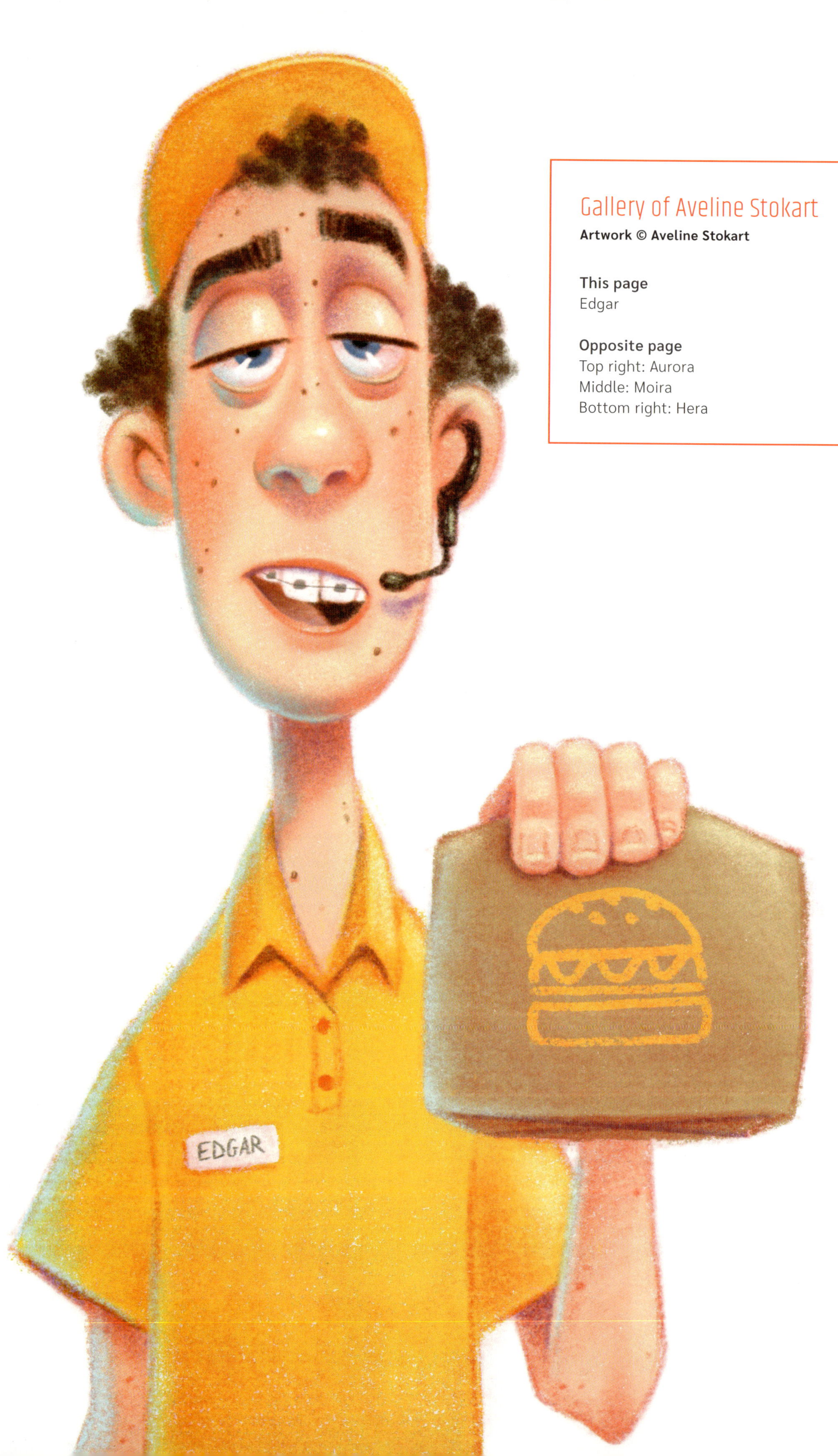

Gallery of Aveline Stokart

This page
Edgar

Opposite page
Top right: Aurora
Middle: Moira
Bottom right: Hera

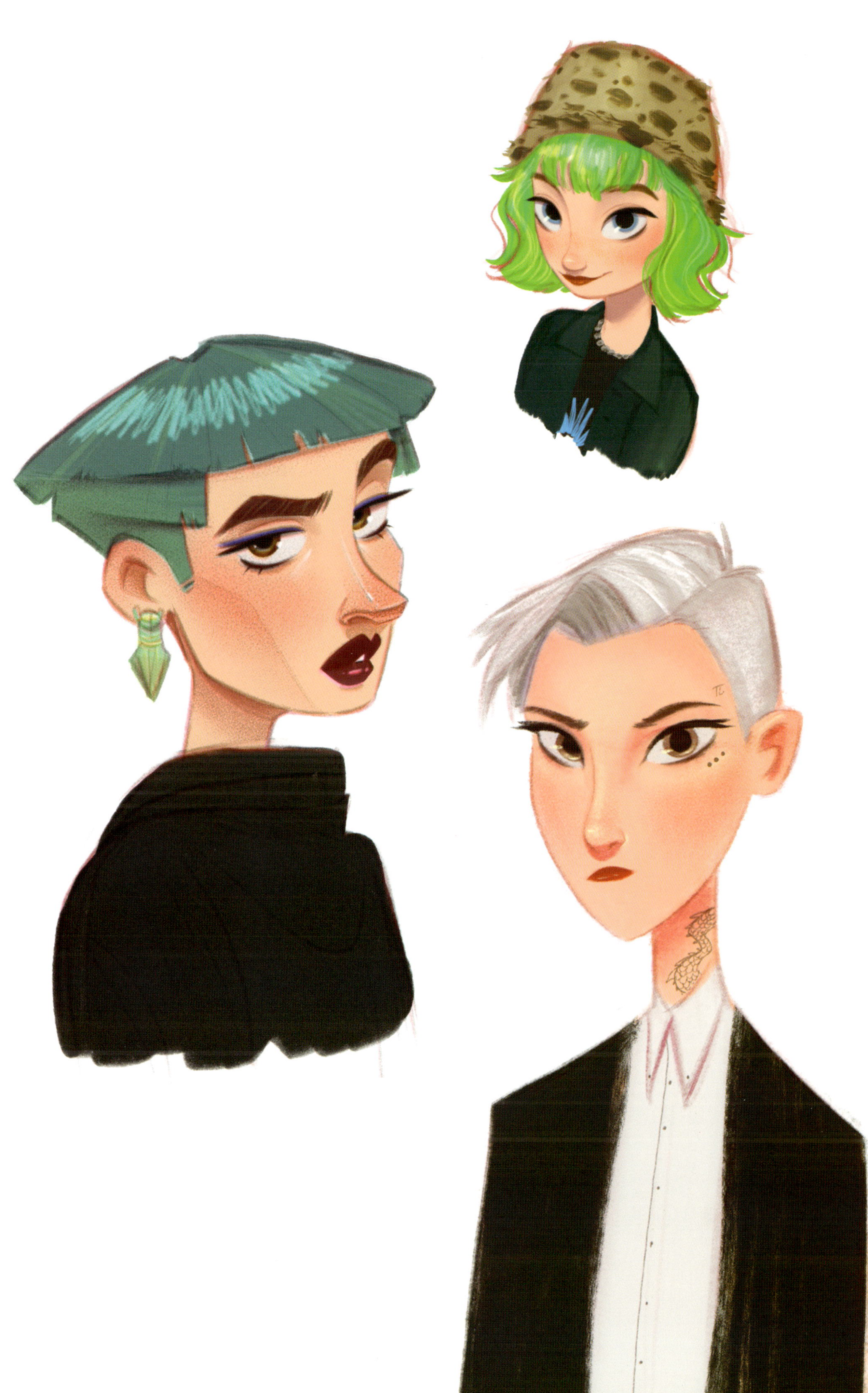

This page
Top right: Chloe
Bottom left: Alicia
Bottom right: Roger

Opposite page
Top left: Rosie
Top right: Hitman
Bottom: See You In Hell

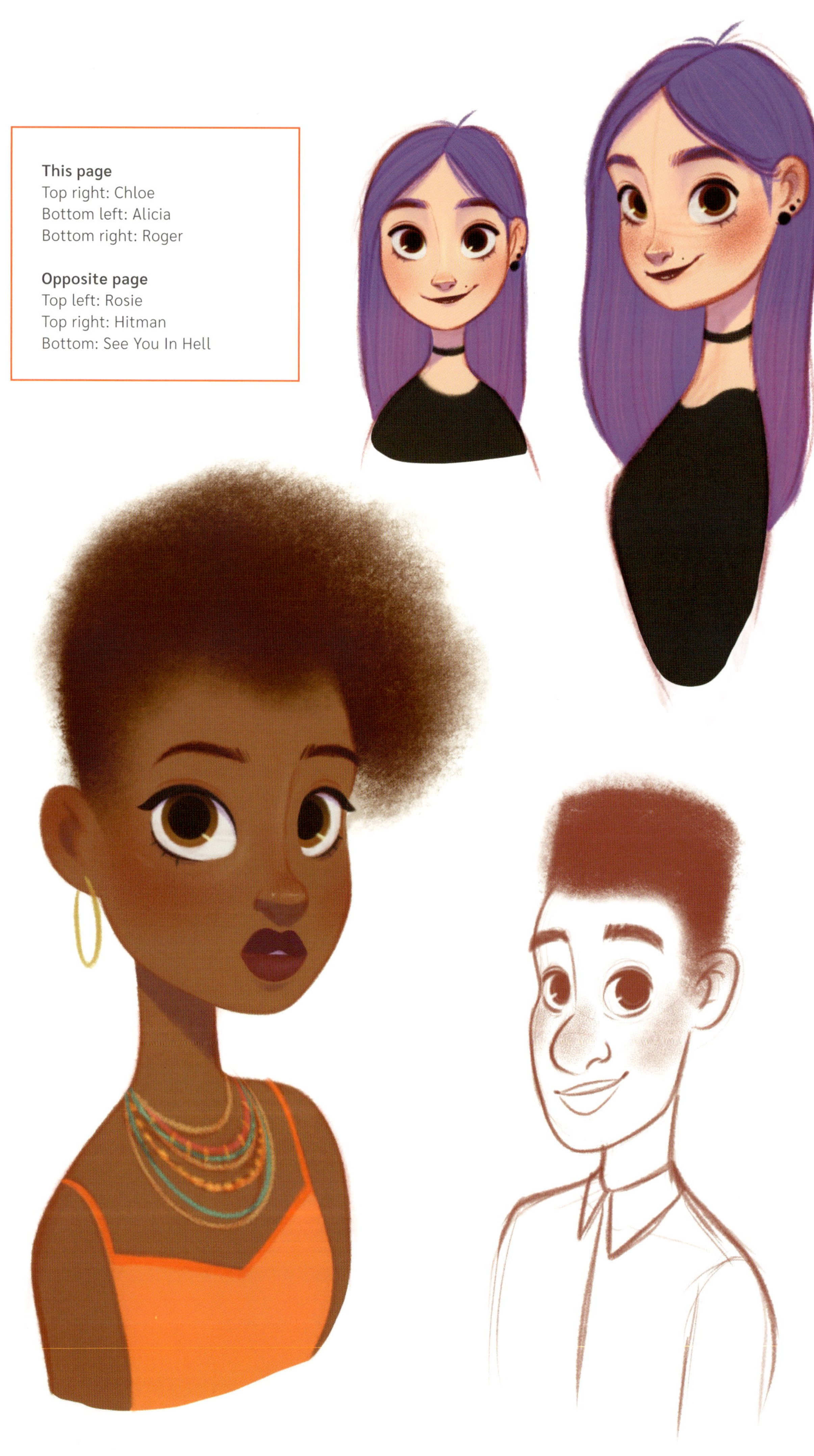

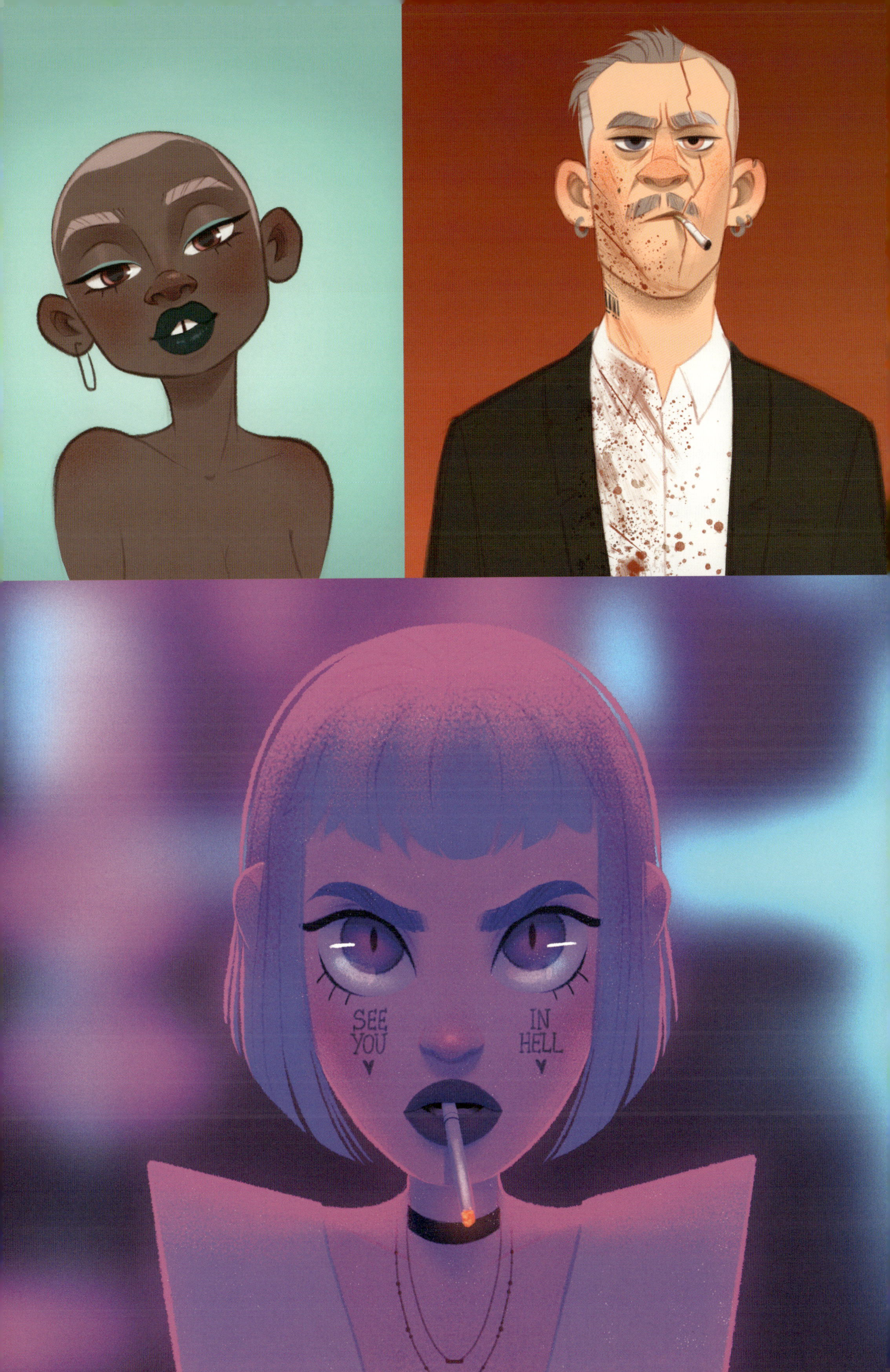
SEE YOU
IN HELL

Gallery of Nick Runge

Artwork © Nick Runge

This page
Top right: Untitled 3 (watercolor)
Middle left: Man with Glasses (watercolor)
Bottom left: Kat (watercolor)
Bottom right: Morning Stillness (watercolor)

Opposite page
Mother and Child (watercolor)

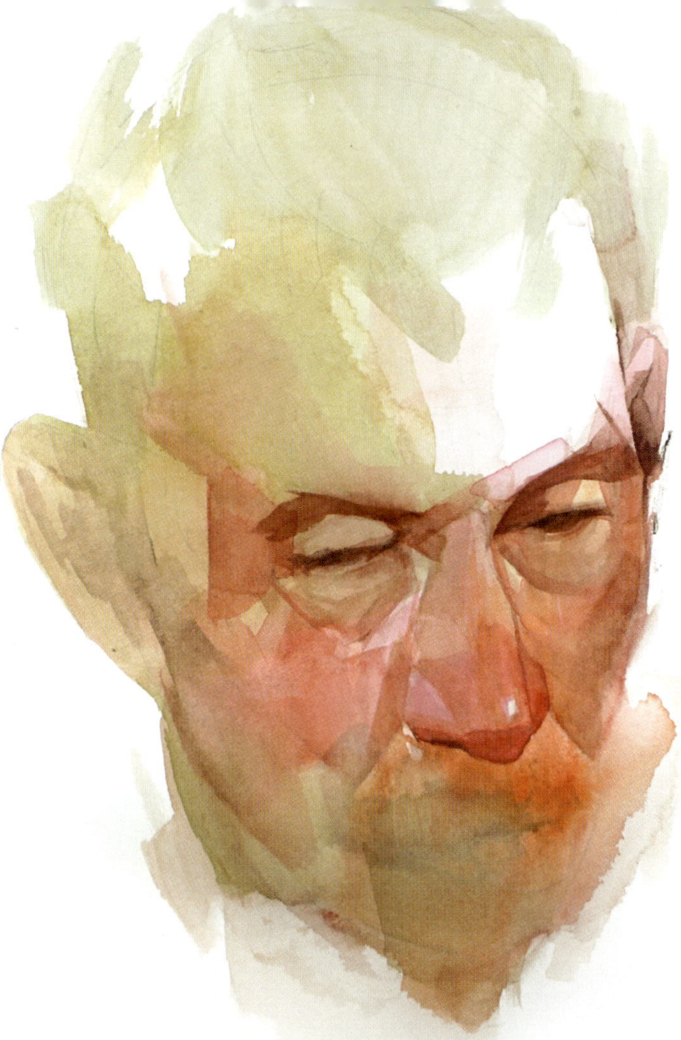

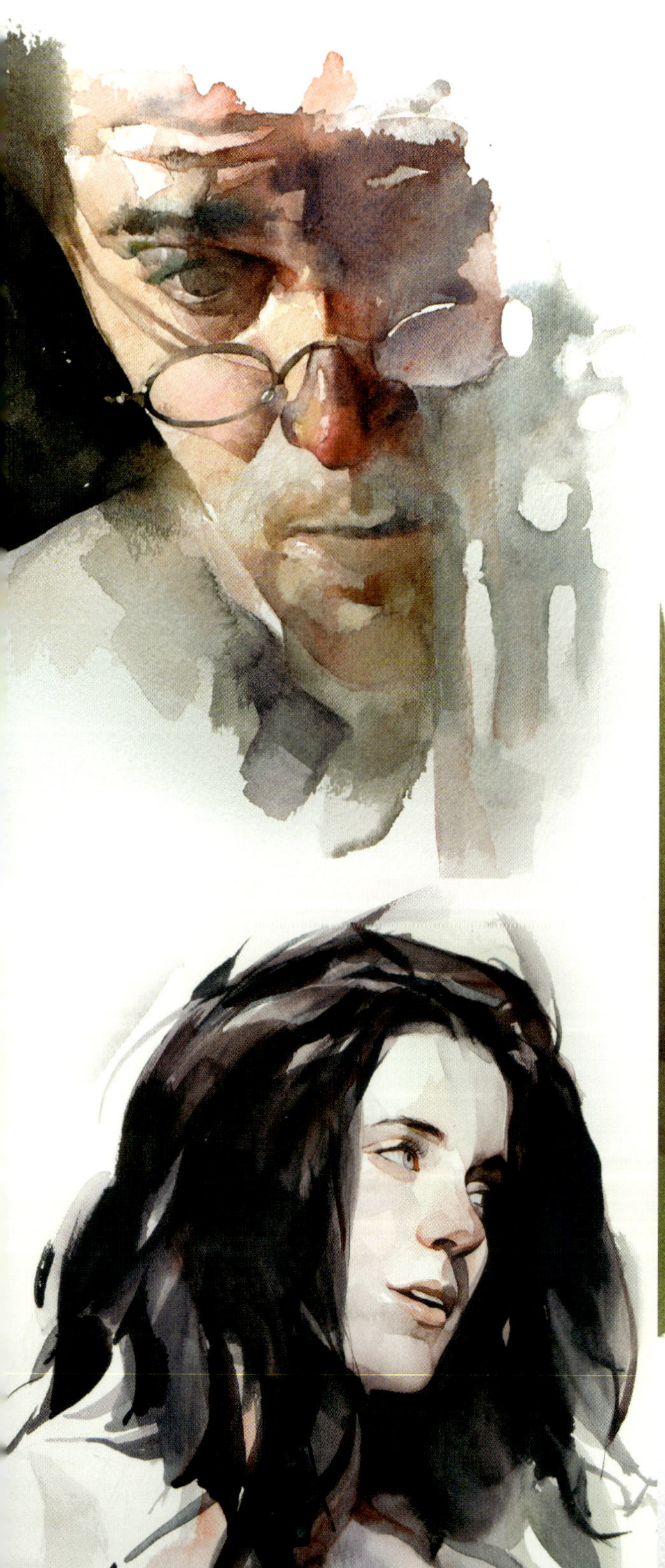

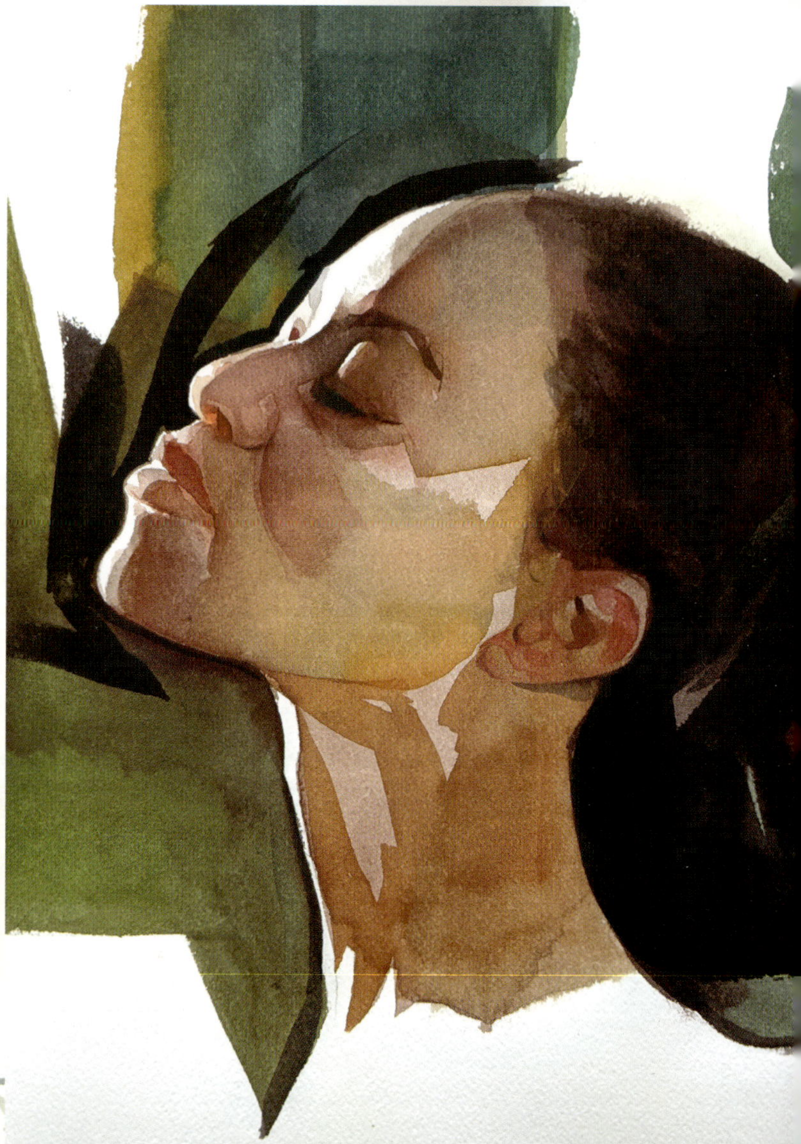

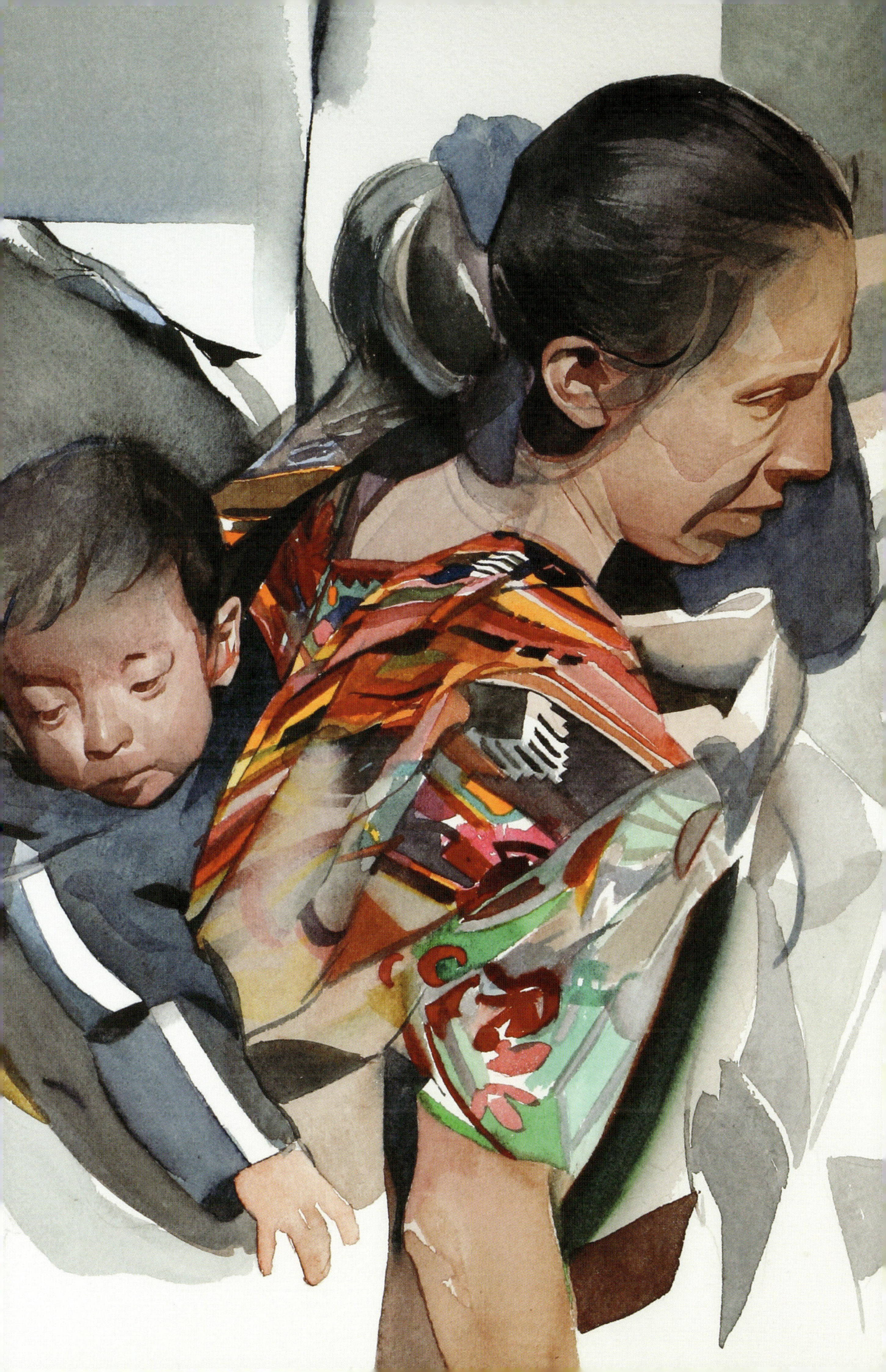

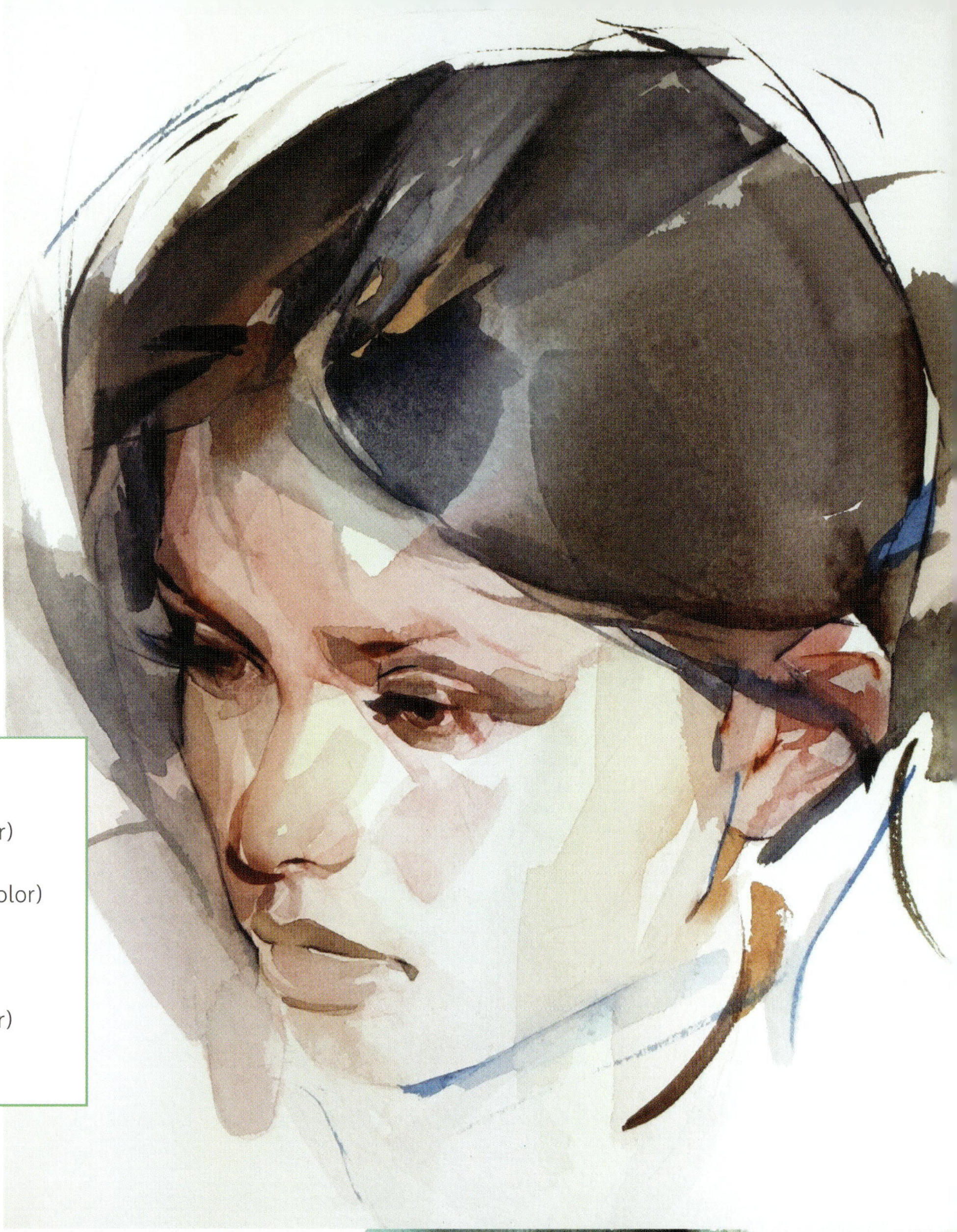

This page
Top right: Think Back (watercolor)
Bottom left: Music (watercolor)
Bottom right: Untitled 1 (watercolor)

Opposite page
Top left: Untitled 2 (watercolor)
Top right: Wilderness (watercolor)
Bottom: Echo (oil paint)

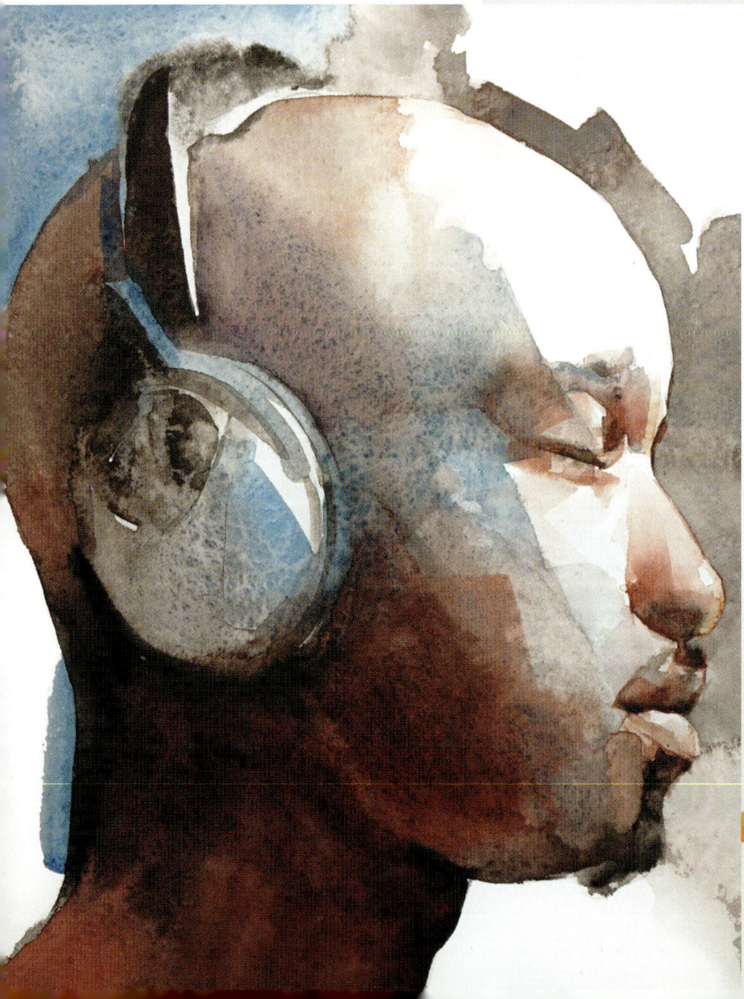

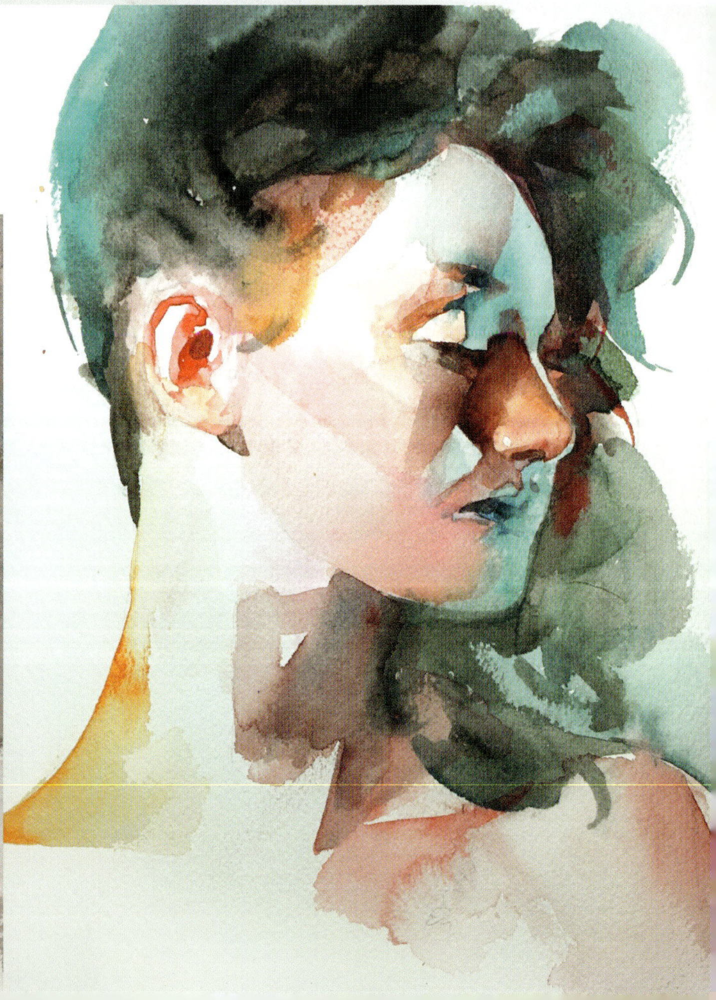

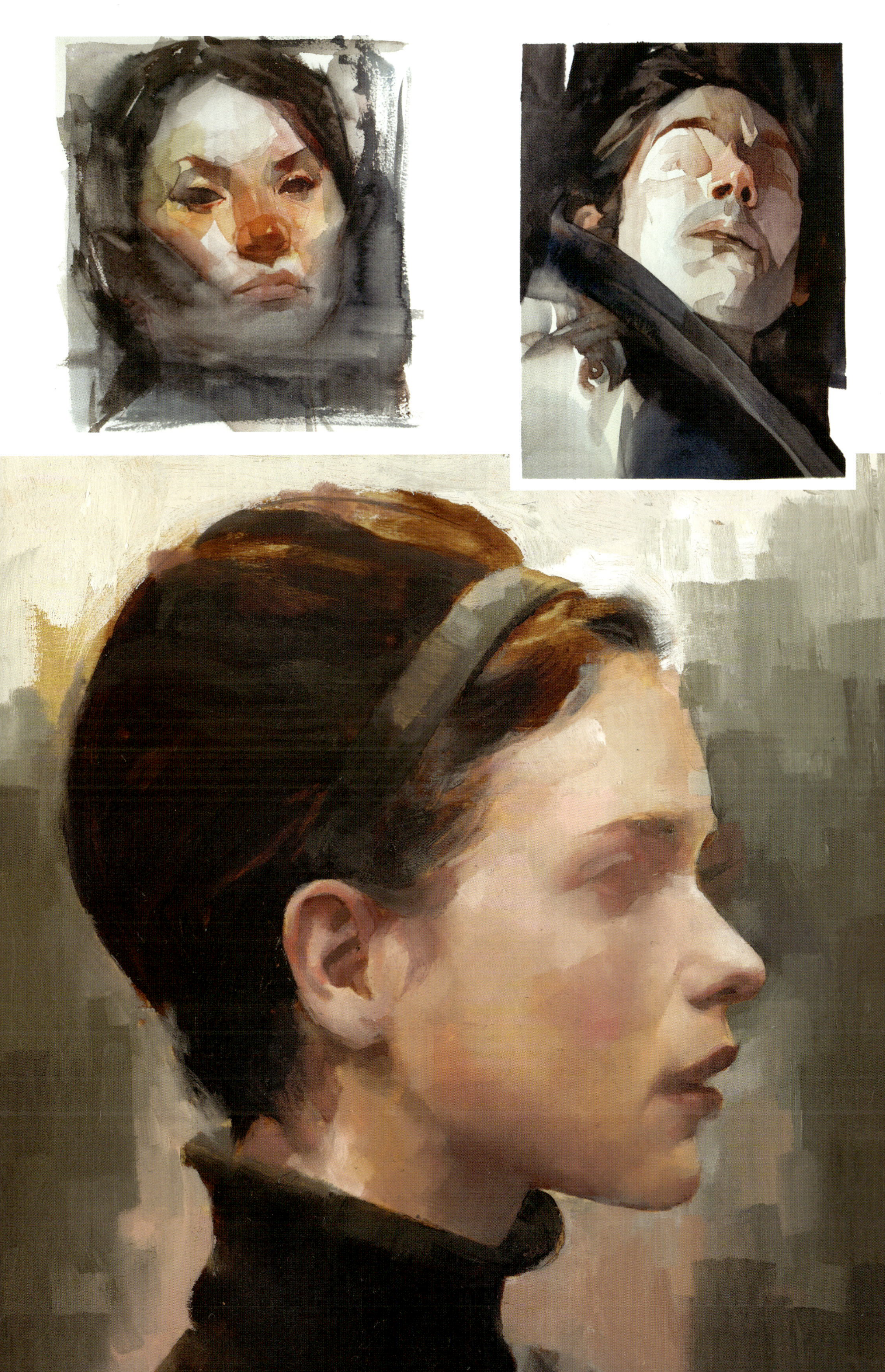

Gallery of Valentina Remenar

Artwork © Valentina Remenar

This page
Top right: Caution
Bottom: Key to Opportunity

Opposite page
Top left: Honey
Top right: State of My Head
Bottom: Poppy

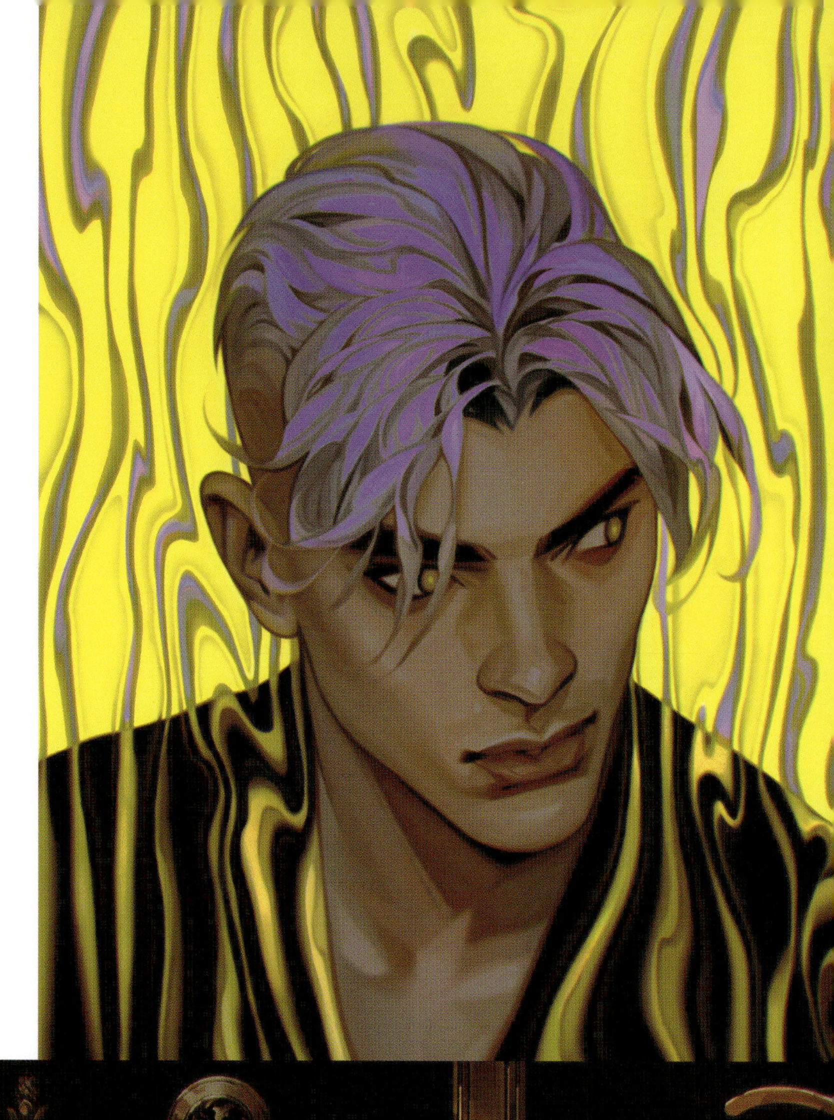

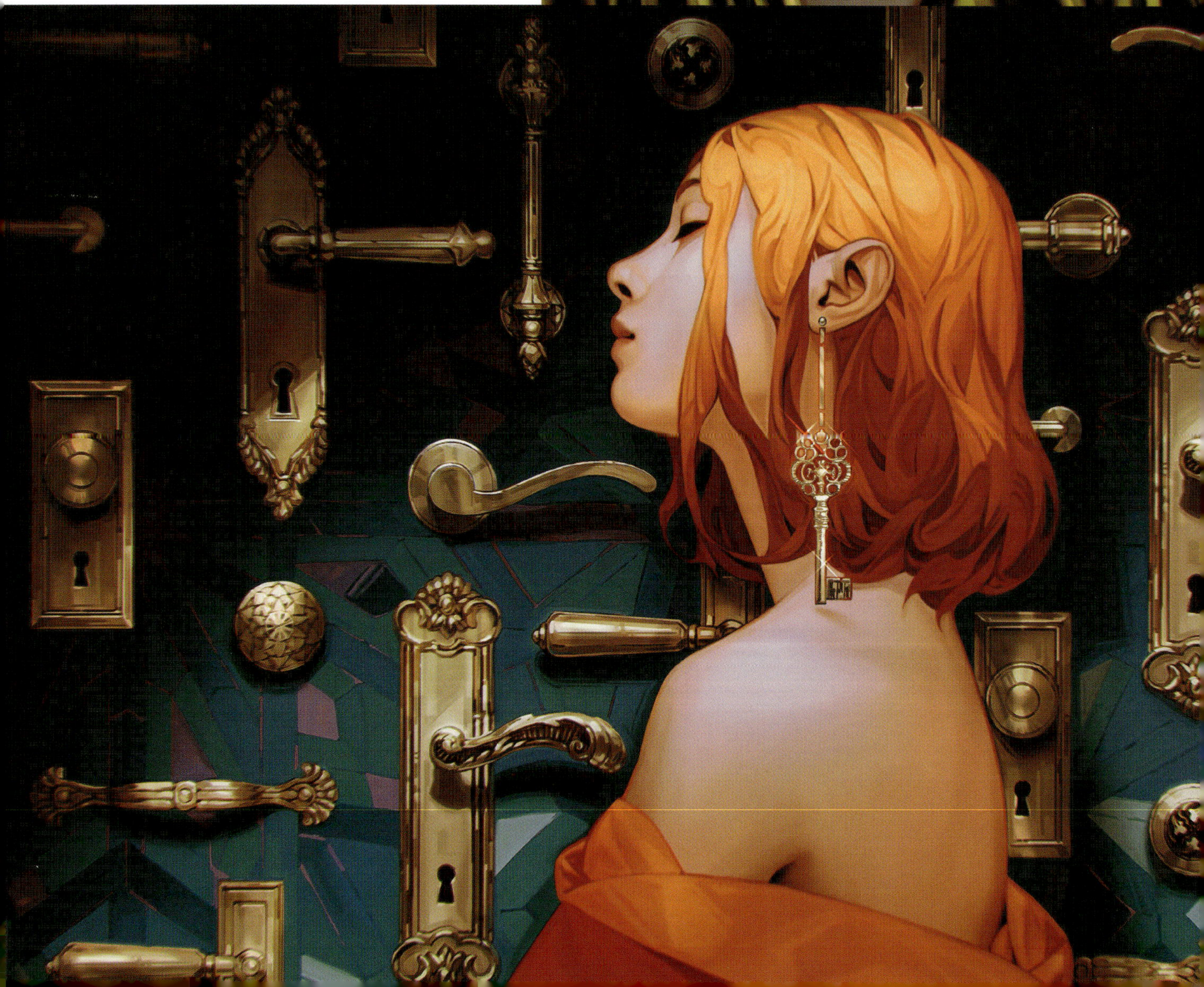

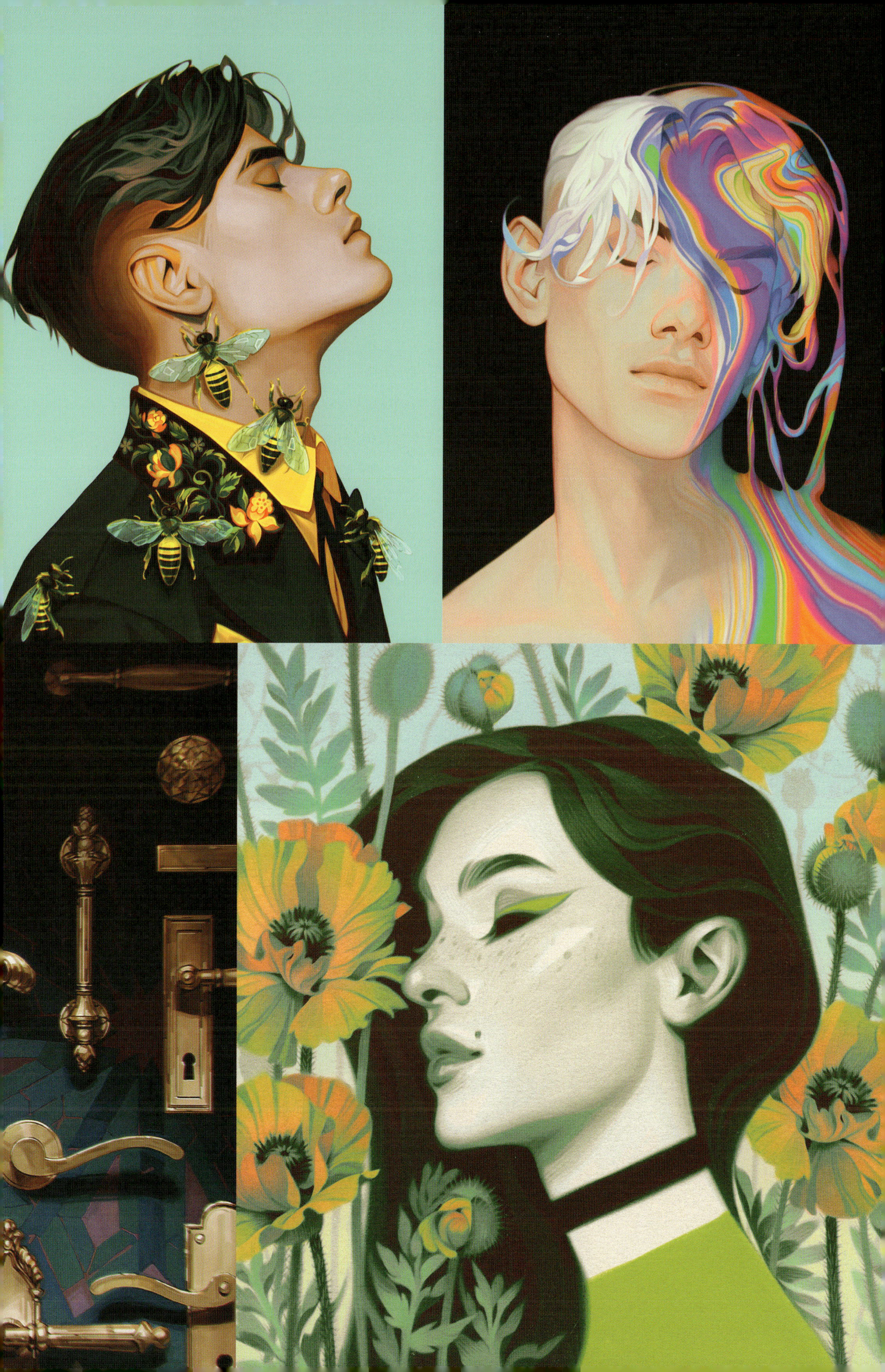

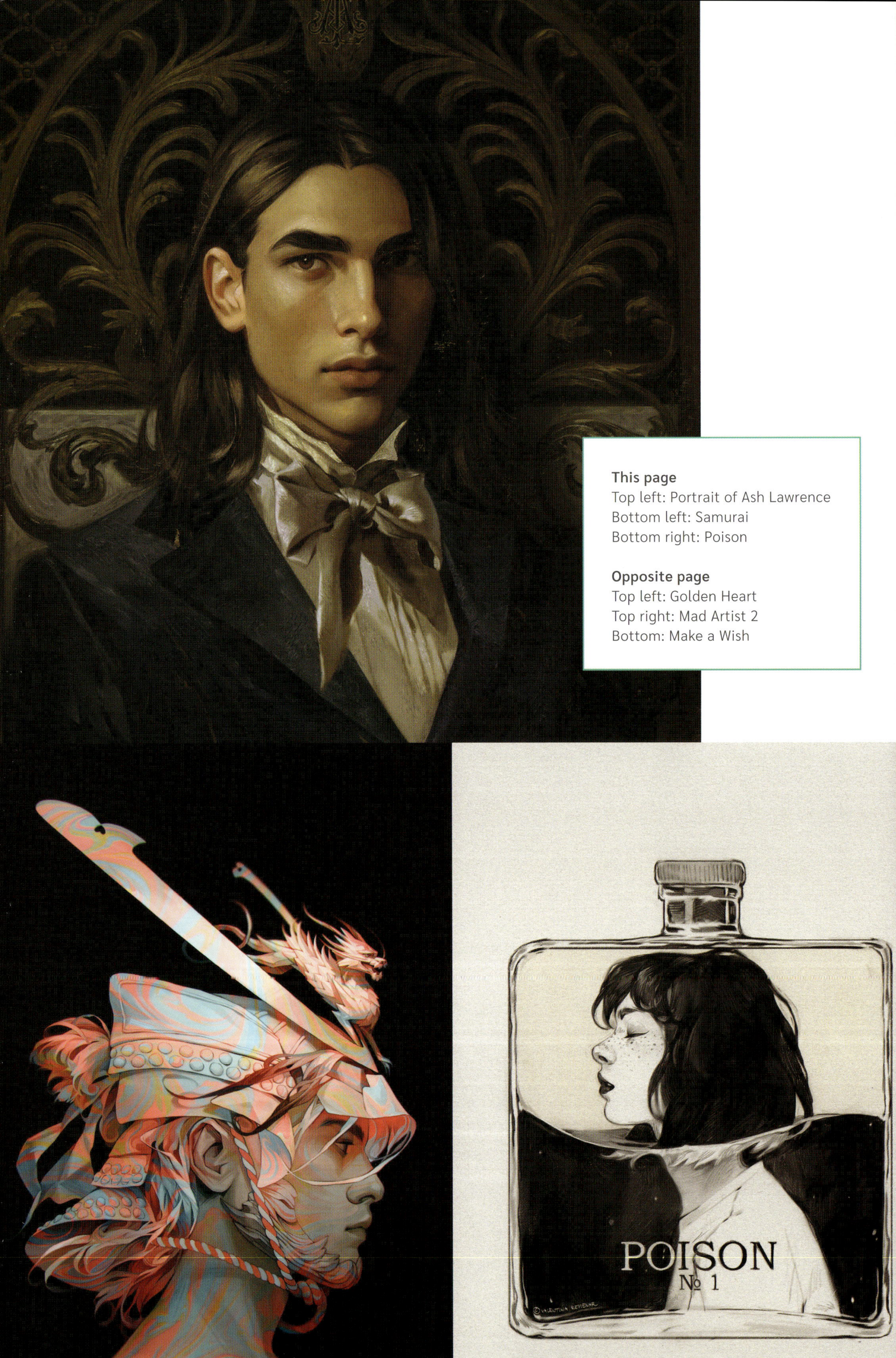

This page
Top left: Portrait of Ash Lawrence
Bottom left: Samurai
Bottom right: Poison

Opposite page
Top left: Golden Heart
Top right: Mad Artist 2
Bottom: Make a Wish

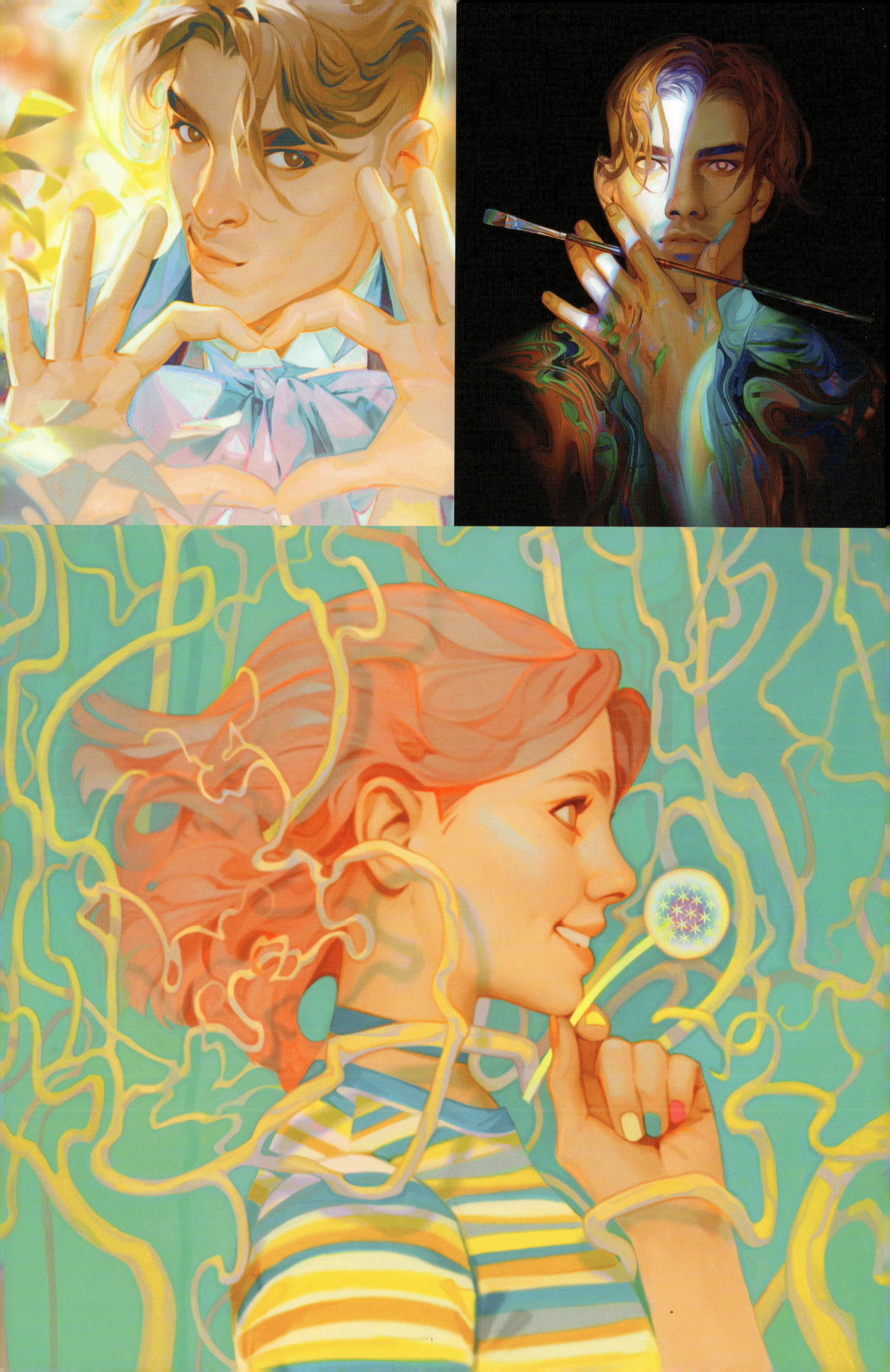

Gallery of Astri Lohne

Artwork © Astri Lohne

This page

Top right: Kei

Bottom left: Dying Light

Bottom right: Portrait of Gerard

Opposite page

Portrait Study

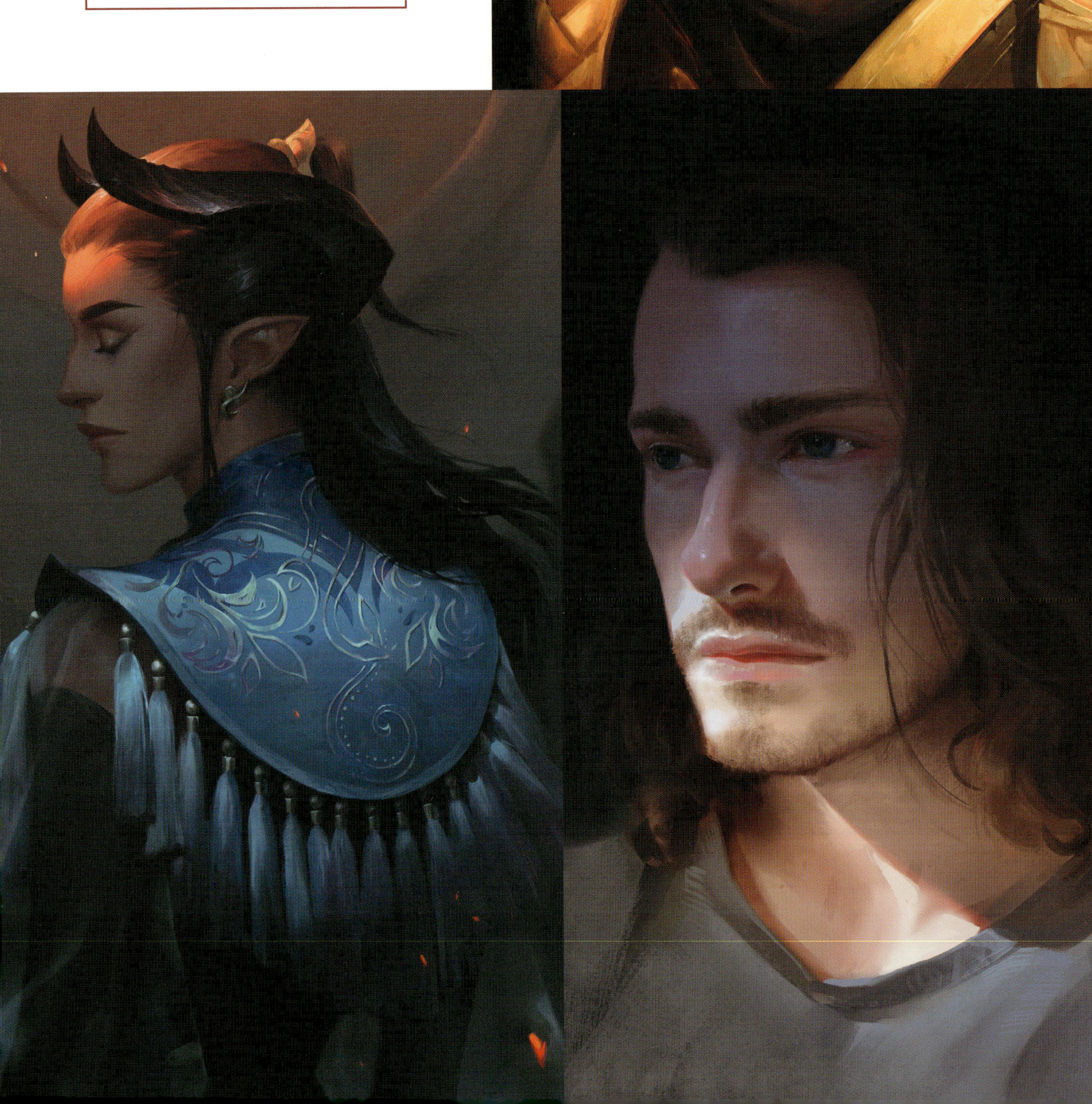

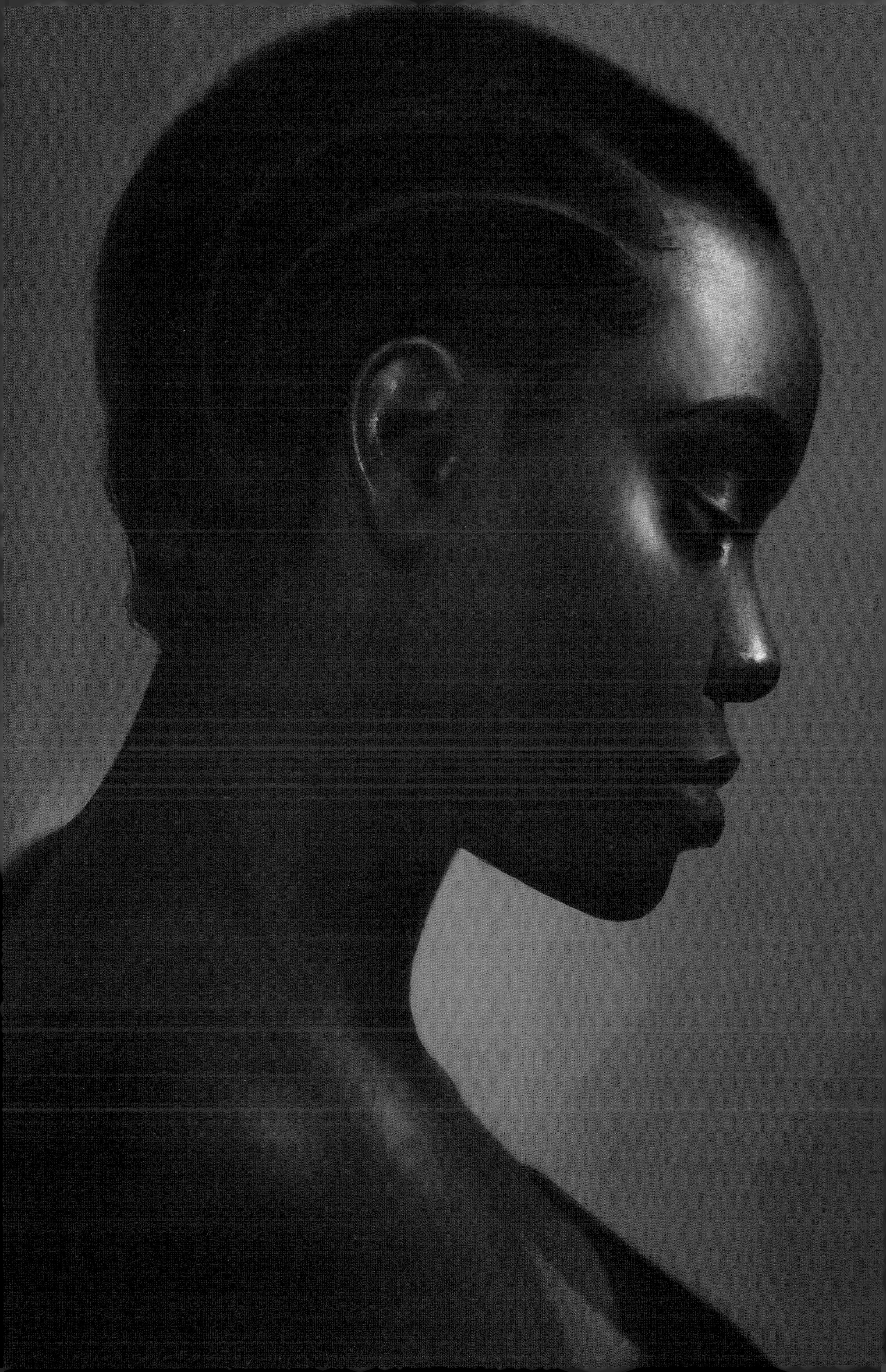

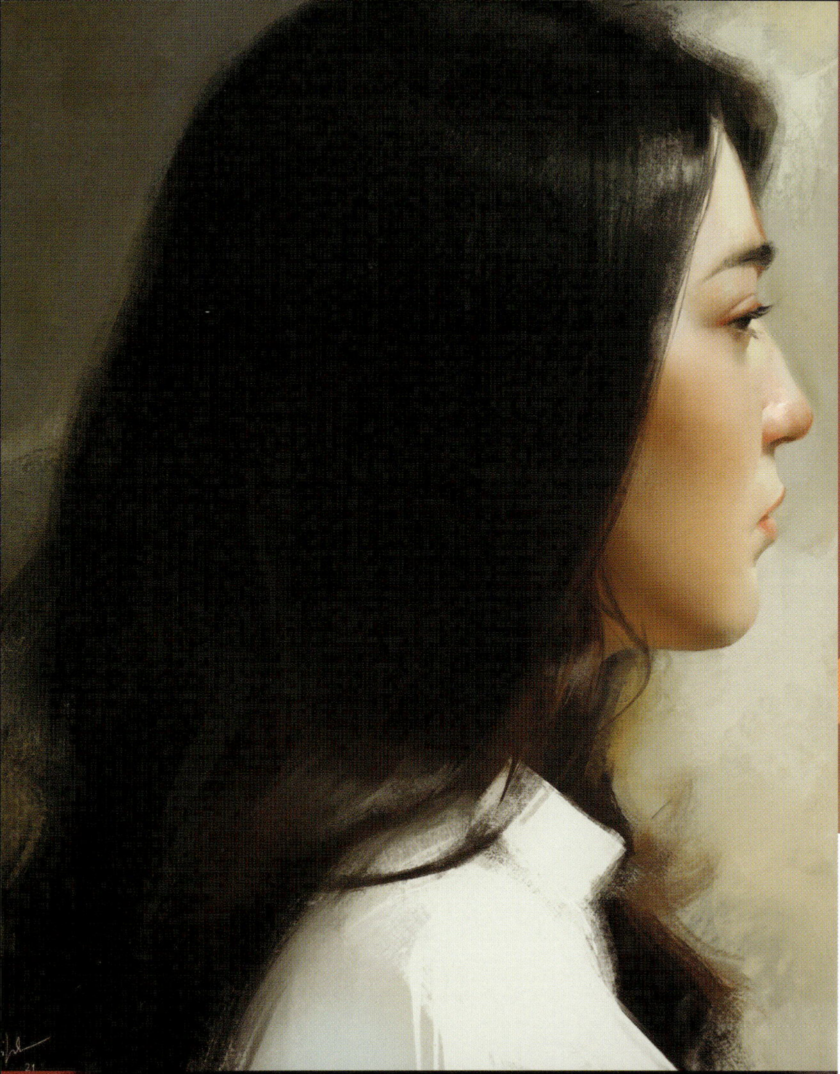

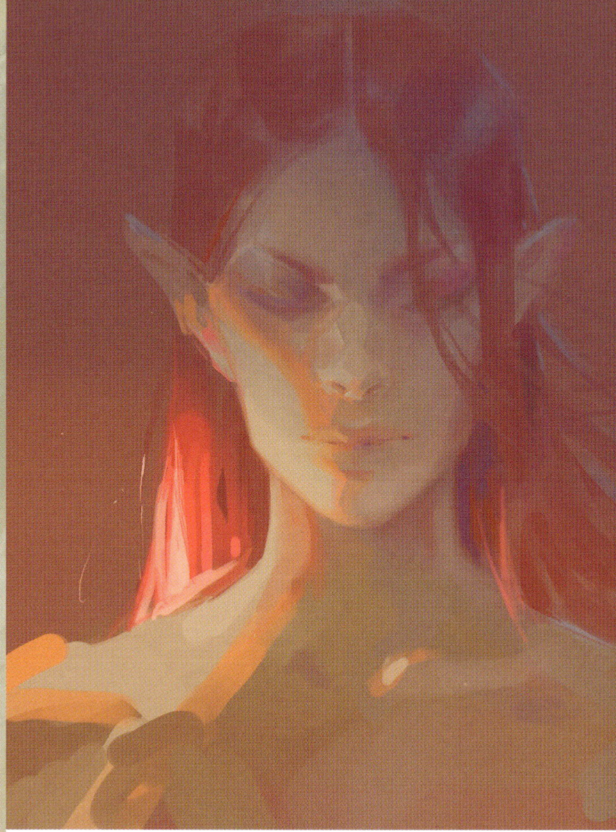

This page
Top left: Portrait Study
Top right: Sketch
Bottom left: Portrait Study
Bottom right: Inside

Opposite page
Top left: Sonya
Top right: Self Portrait
Bottom: Portrait Study

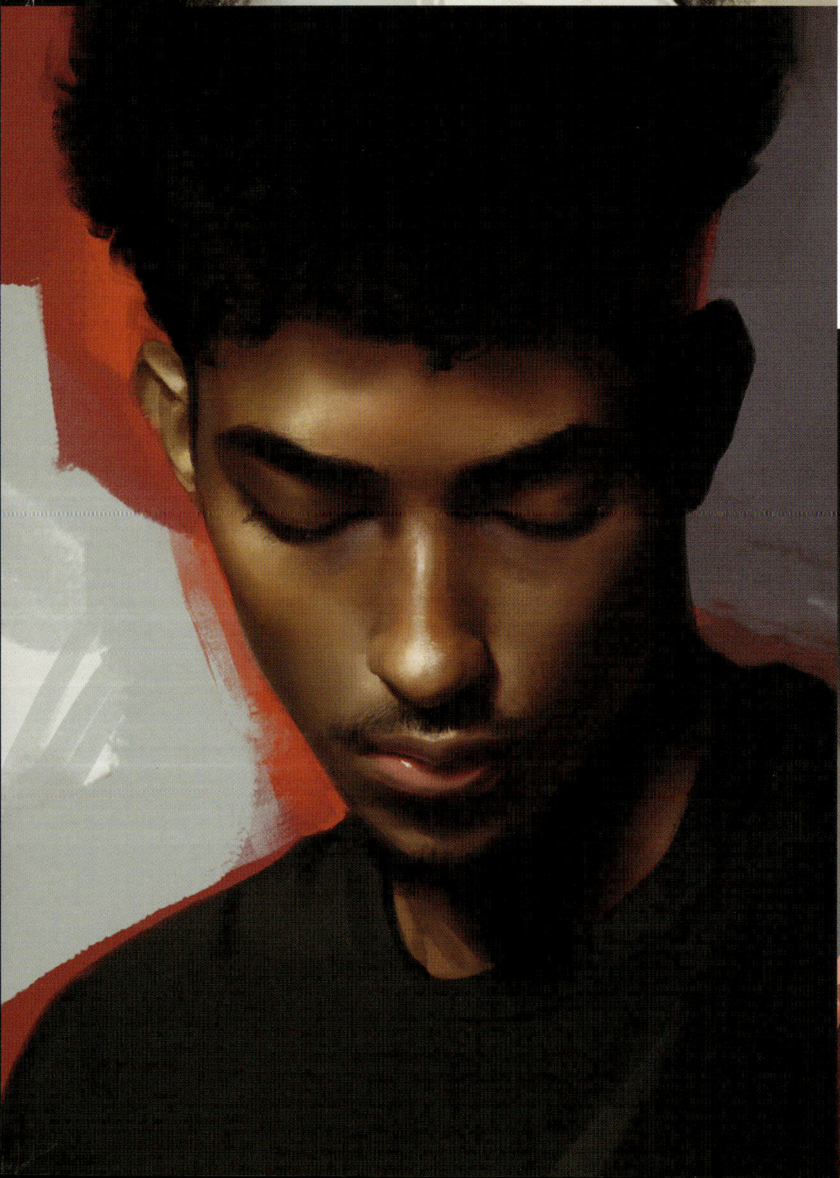

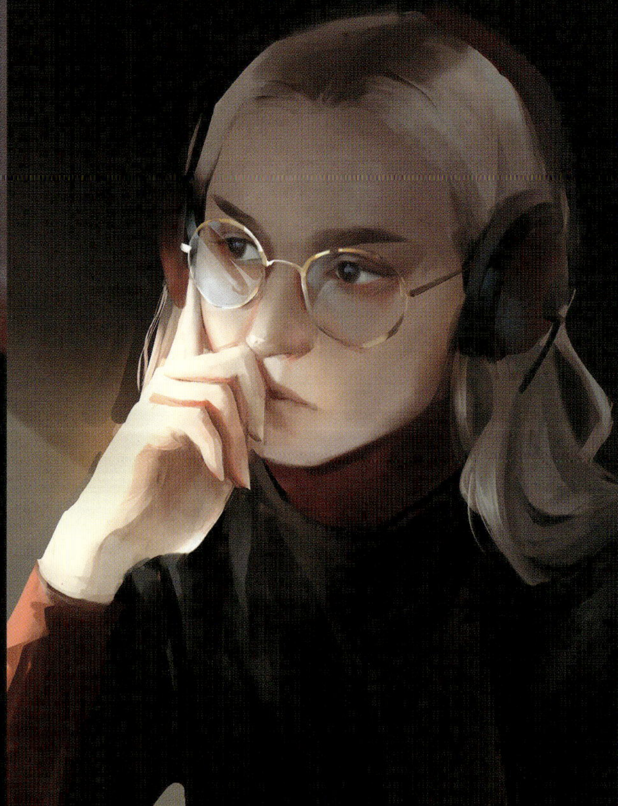

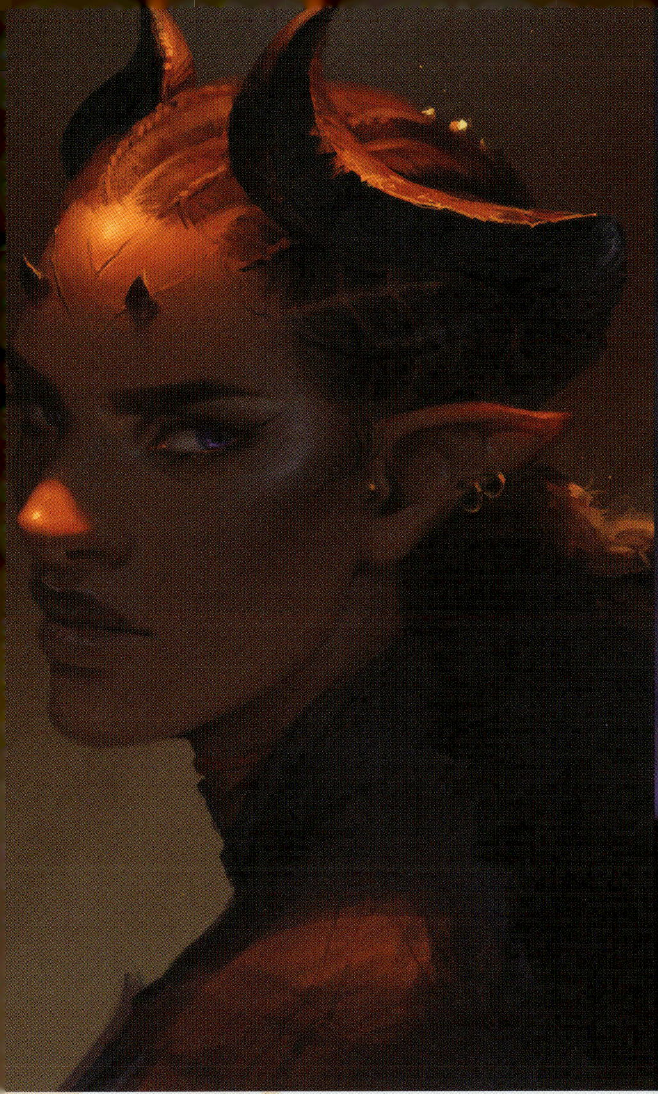

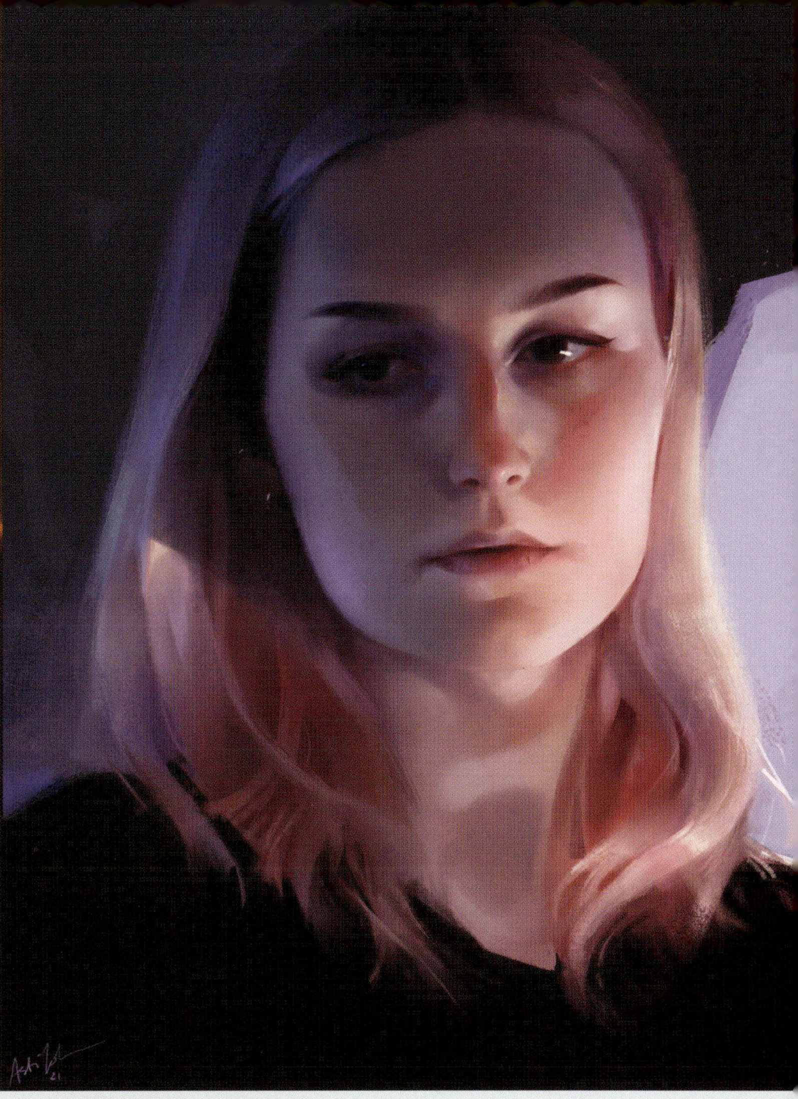

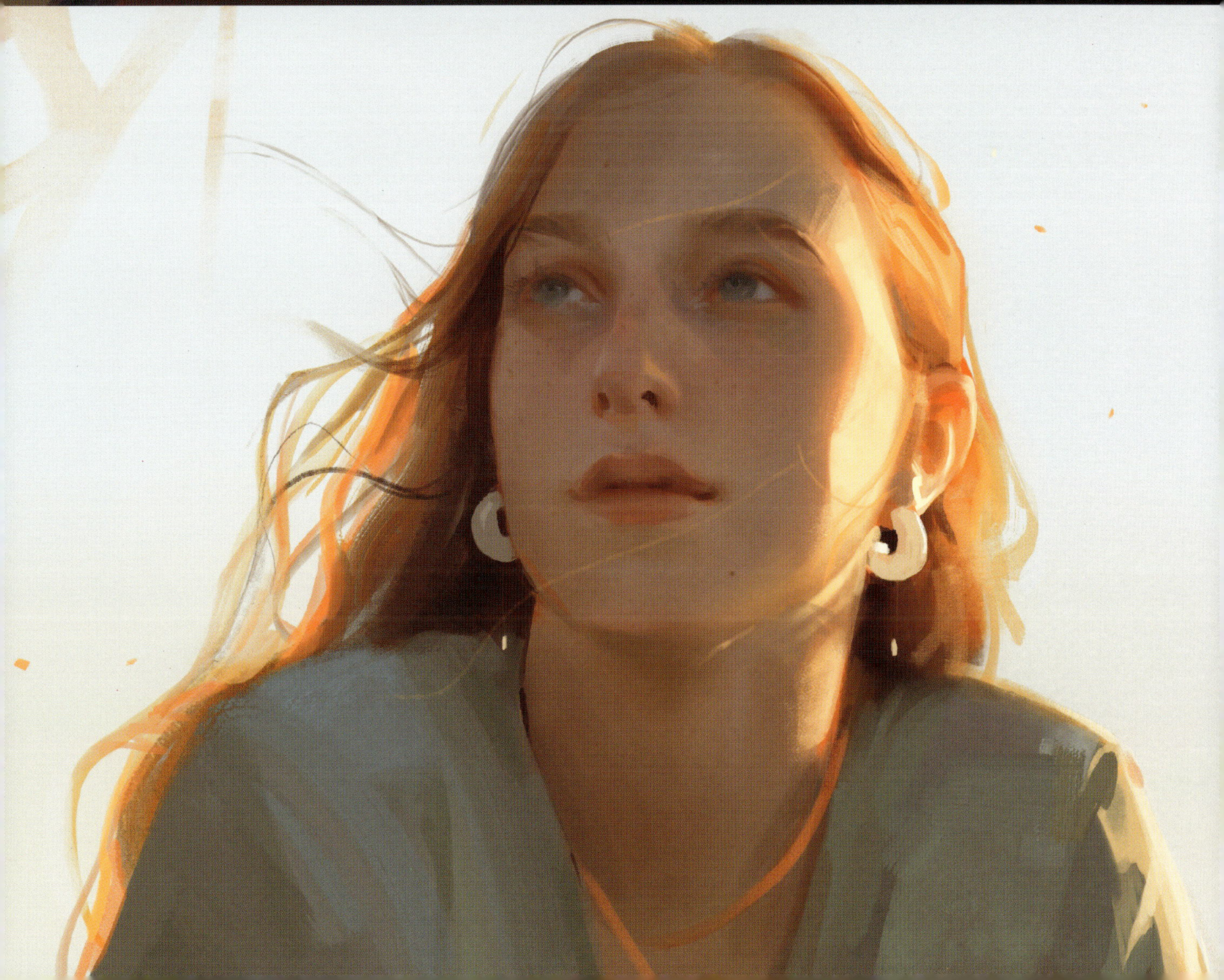

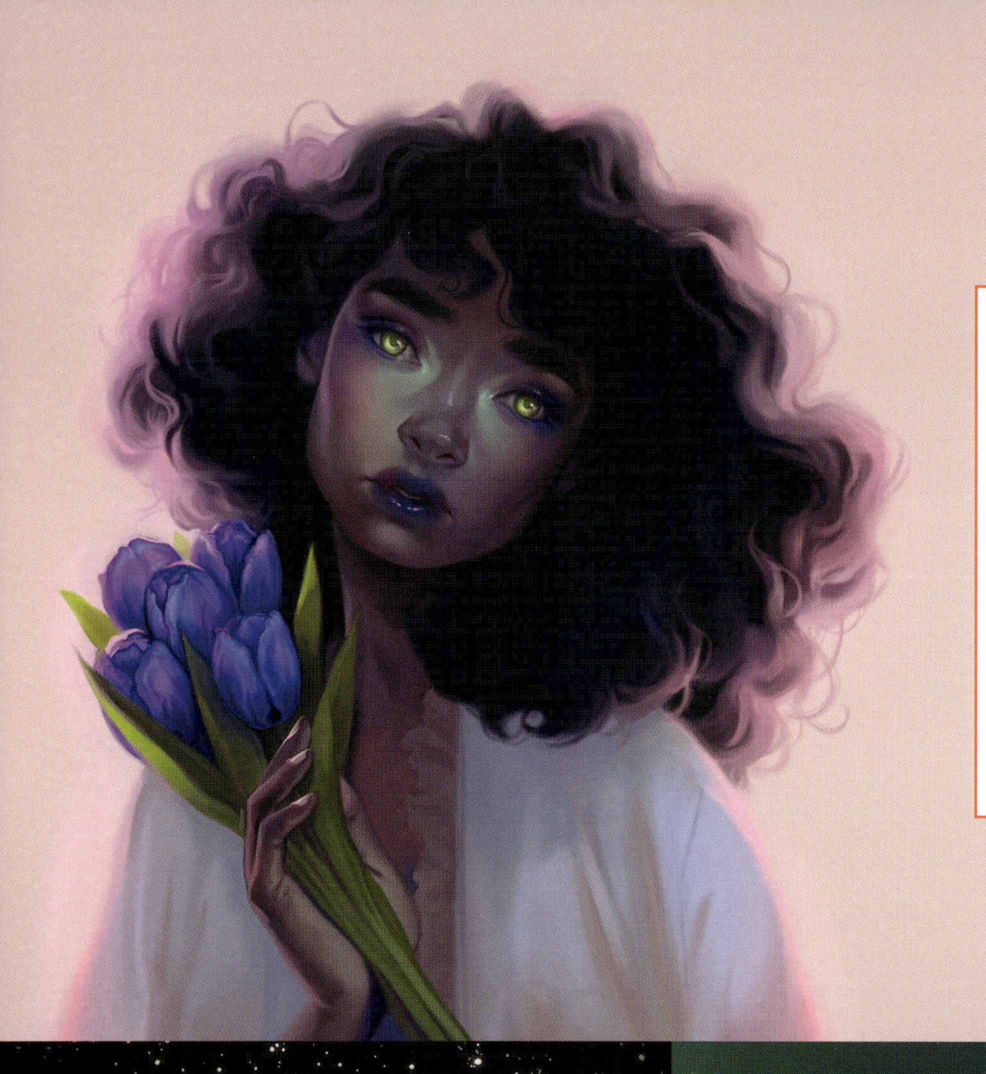

Gallery of Sara Tepes

Artwork © Sara Tepes

This page
Top left: Tulips
Bottom left: Nightwalker
Bottom right: Lemons

Opposite page
Top left: Yellow
Top right: Blue
Bottom left: Olive
Bottom right: Midnight

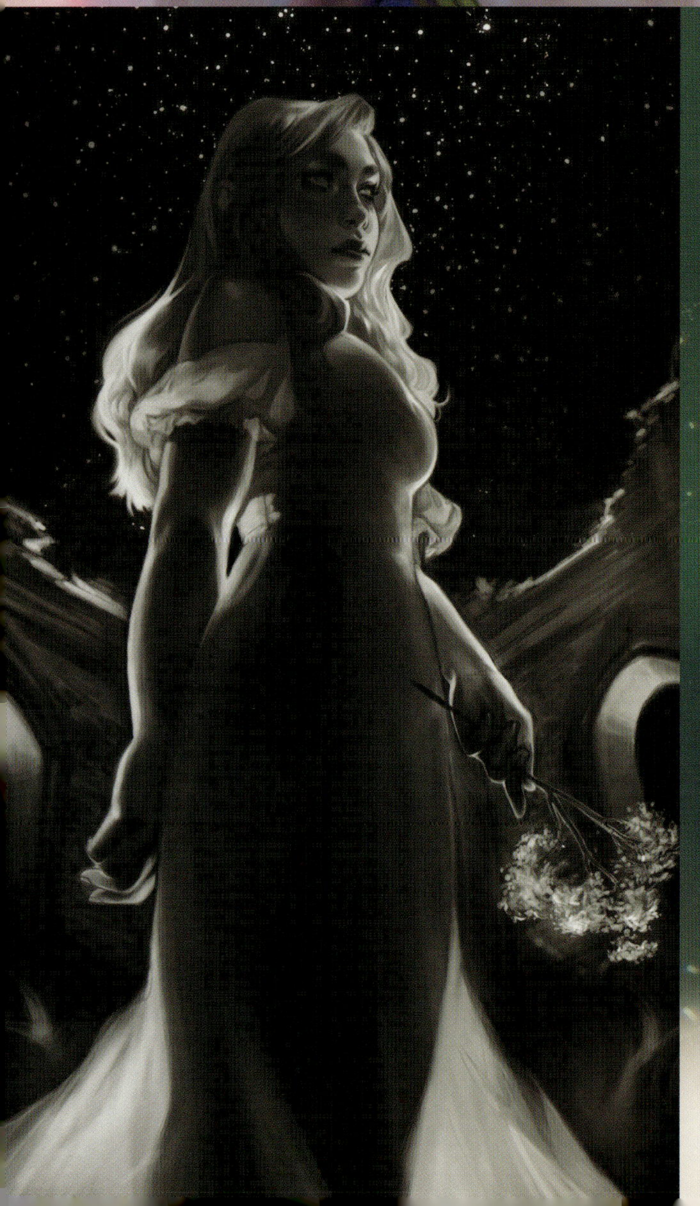

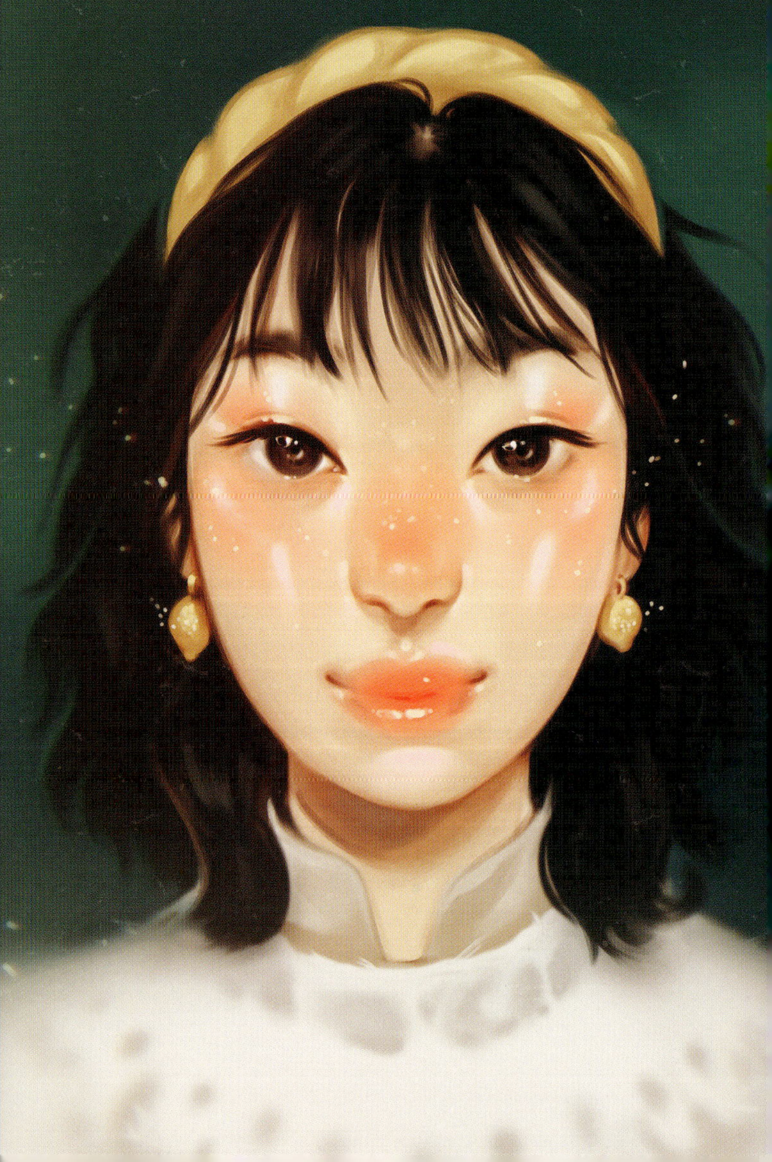

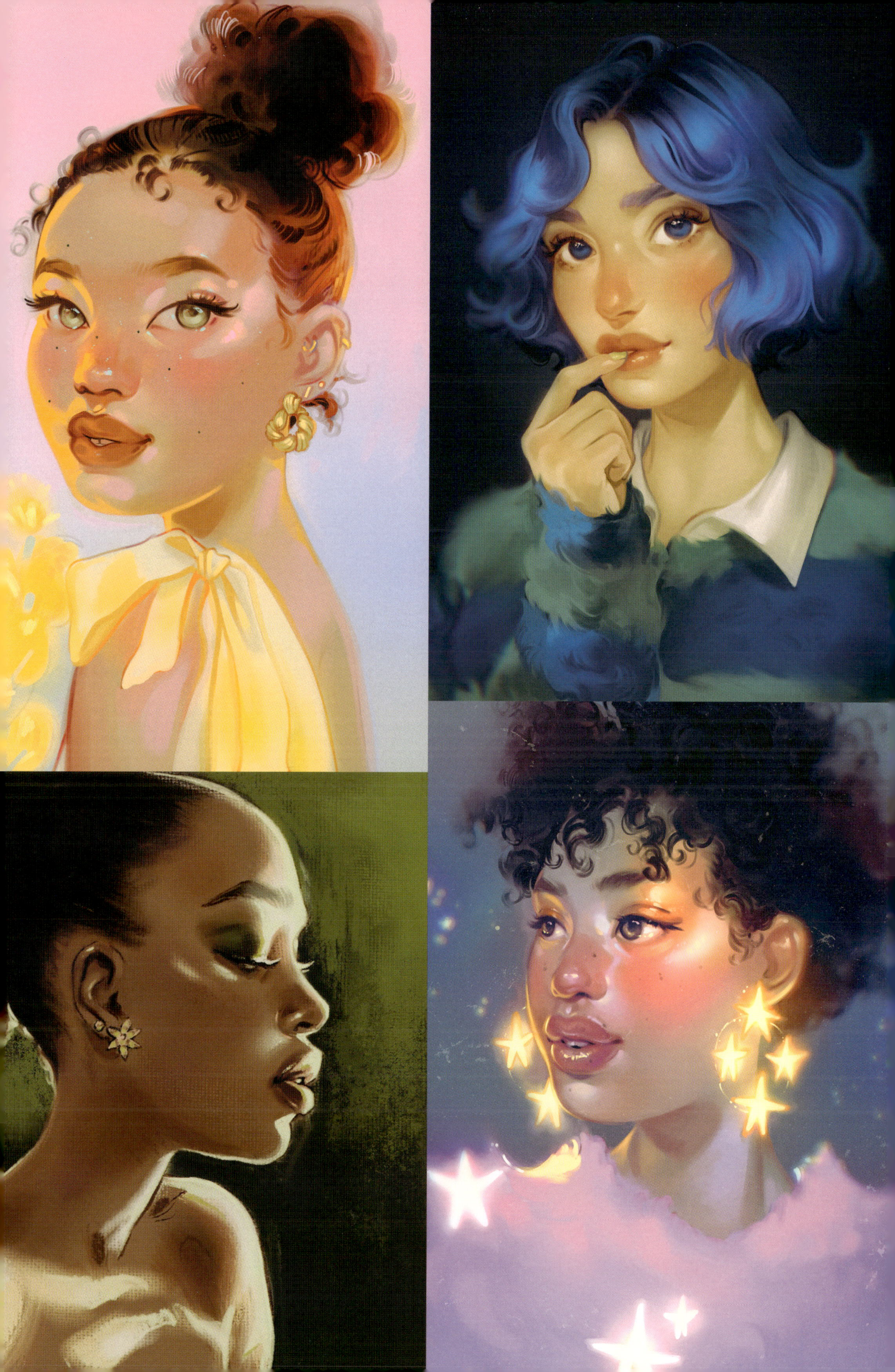

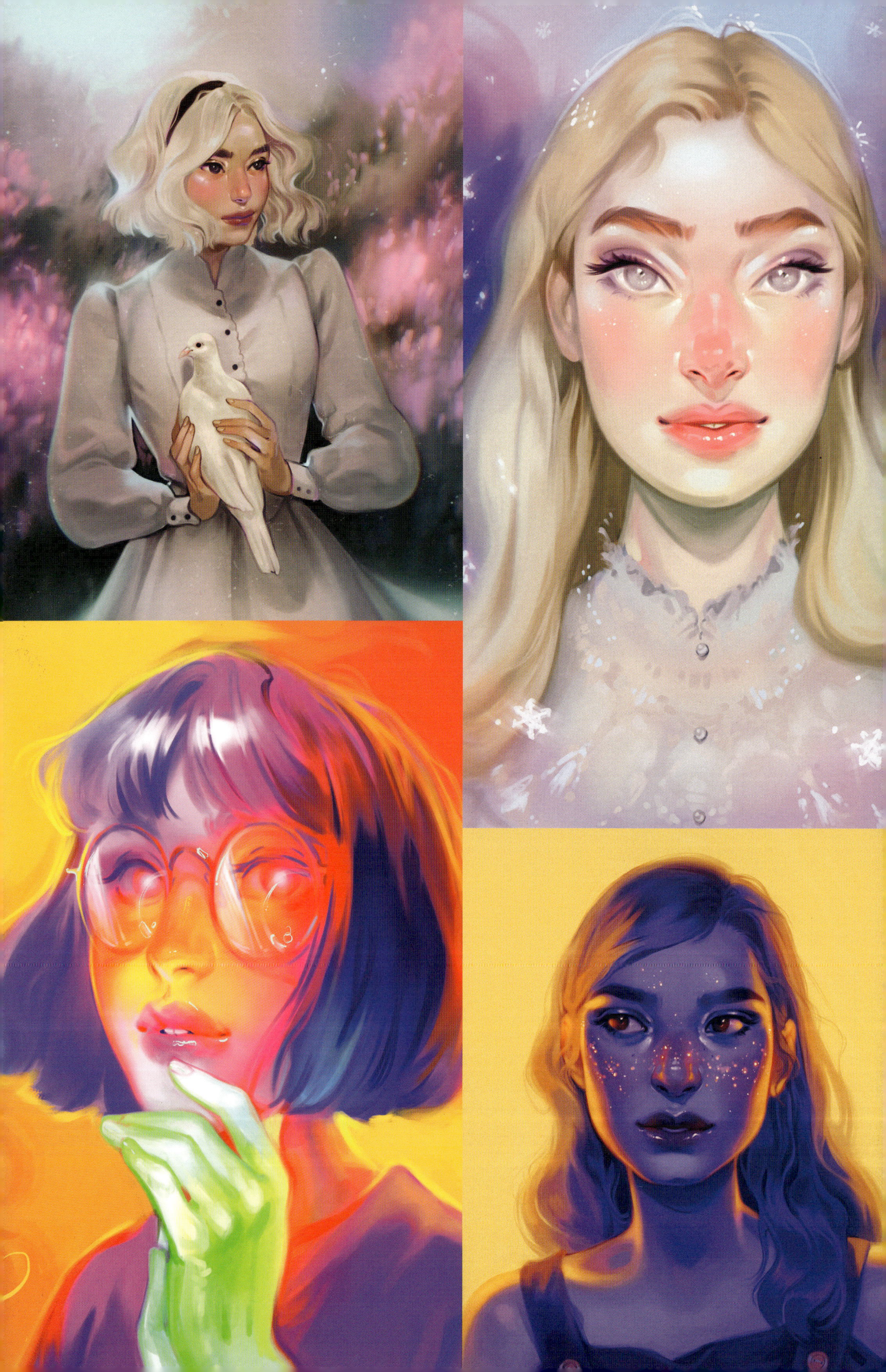

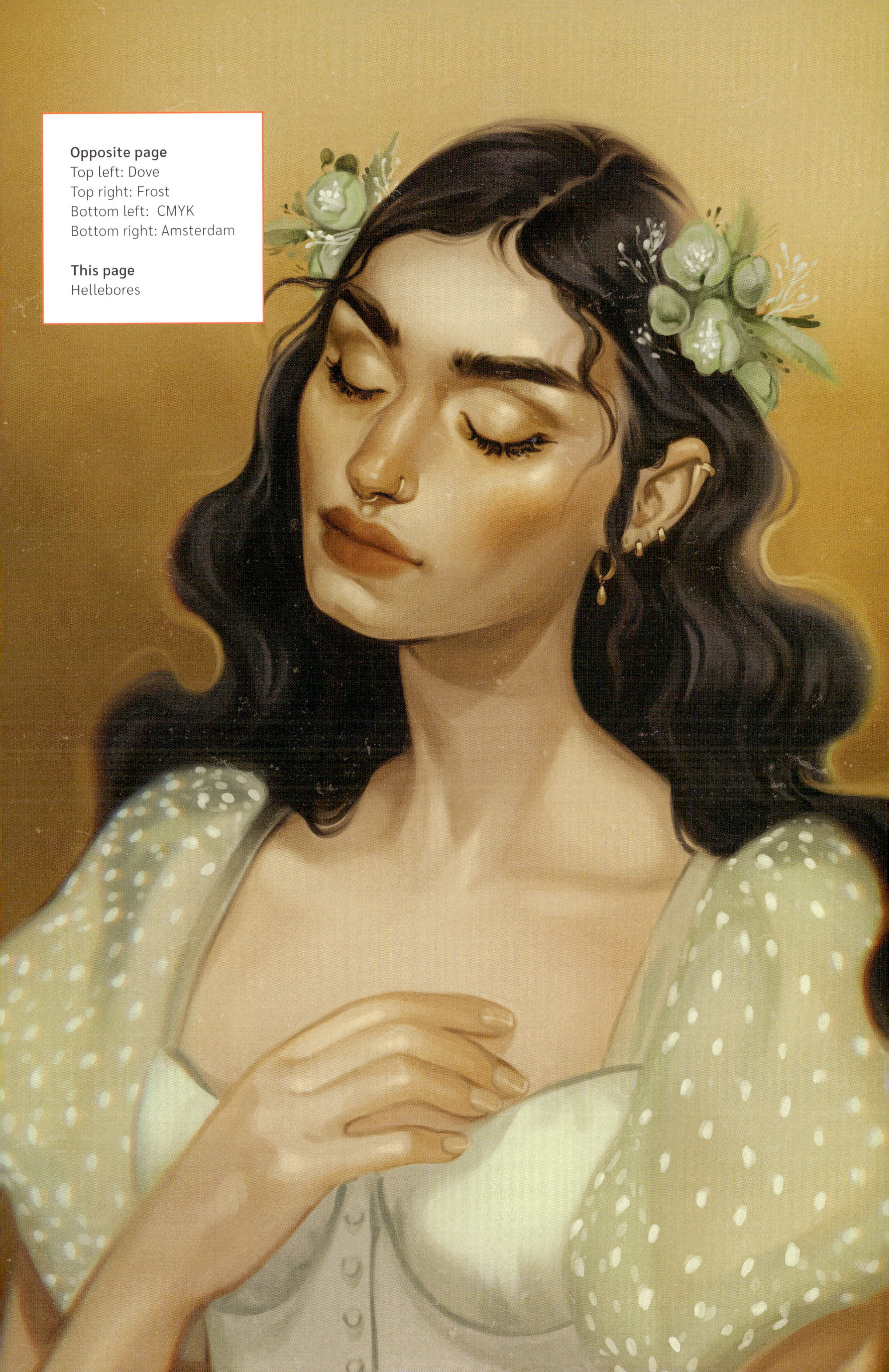

Opposite page
Top left: Dove
Top right: Frost
Bottom left: CMYK
Bottom right: Amsterdam

This page
Hellebores

GLOSSARY

Architectonic
A conceptual way of drawing that translates curved and naturalistic forms into architecture through the use of straight lines, blocky forms, and lines of symmetry.

Blocking in
An early stage in the drawing process where lines are kept simple and blocky in order to capture the simple essence of a more complex form. Typically only straight lines are used.

Box proportion
A ratio or proportion as it relates to a square or rectangular frame. For example, 8 x 10, 11 x 14, or 1 to 1½.

Broken edge
A broken edge is formed when two tones meet and intermingle in a staccato or broken way. There is no clear edge, but parts of each of the tones overlap and create a slight texture.

Color diversity
Diverse colors that have no unifying factor. The ultimate expression of this is the rainbow, which is made up of unique colors at full individual strength.

Color diversity with value unity
Within a given zone, such as a shadow, there can be many different hue and saturation shifts, but value does not really change. This allows you to create a color texture without interrupting the form.

Color key
The most important and reoccurring tones in a painting that summarize the major color values needed to describe the scene.

Color palette
A palette of main colors available for use in your painting, before mixing. This may be limited when using traditional media, while digital software provides greater possibilities.

Color unity
Multiple colors unified by a common singular color that is mixed into each of them. Colors can have more or less unity depending on the amount of this common singular color used.

Color unity with diversity
The ambiguous territory that lies between the two extremes, which is often the intended target. For example, a sunset will typically have a unifying atmospheric color, while also containing most of the colors of the rainbow. Therefore, it has color unity with diversity.

Color values
Color and value are often viewed as two separate entities, yet they are intrinsically linked. The term color values is used to describe the importance of seeing both well at the same time.

Color zones
Areas or shapes in an image that favor a certain color value.

Comparative measurement
A system of proportion that typically uses a scaling method and employs a standard of measurement.

Complementary
Colors that sit opposite each other on the color wheel that, when placed side-by-side, create the strongest contrast for those two colors. They cancel each other out (lose saturation) when mixed together, producing a gray.

Composition
The spatial property resulting from the arrangement of parts in relation to one another and the whole.

Concept mood board
A digital or physical platform or board, containing multiple images that convey and inspire a mood or concept. It can help to capture the vision for one or multiple works of art.

Conceptual portraiture
Portraiture that is driven by an idea or concept, as well as by the reference material. Most portraiture sits in between the extremes of conceptual and perceptual.

Construction lines
Lines used for sketching out a drawing that are usually erased and not seen in the final drawing. Examples include a line of symmetry, rhythm angles, and plumb lines.

Continents
A term used in portraiture to describe the main shapes that define an image. There are not usually more than three to five per image.

Contrast
The difference between dark and light colors, sharp and soft edges, or textured and smooth surfaces.

Creation cycle
The cyclical working rhythm for drawing a head: 1. Line drawing, 2. Color values, 3. Edges and brushstrokes.

Desaturated
Color that has been dulled down and moved toward neutral.

Digital media
Any artwork created exclusively through the use of digital devices and software.

Ebauché
A nineteenth-century underpainting technique that uses oil paint like watercolor (transparently, not opaquely). There is typically a preliminary drawing that is sealed, over which the ebauché layer is applied. The ebauché technique goes for the correct color immediately. Transparency is usually achieved with mineral spirits, letting the drawing shine through. The final painting layer is applied over the ebauché.

Facial armature
The structural landmarks of the face that connect with each other through the use of triangulation. Facial armature provides the rough alignment and layout of the face.

Facial grid
The symmetrical lines that mostly run across the face horizontally, but also include a vertical line that bisects the face. This grid allows you to set the features along these lines to create structural symmetry in the face.

Fall-off/pulling
The effect that happens when a brushstroke gently lifts away from the surface it's touching. If properly handled, this can be used to create a gradation or to turn form.

Focal point
The feature, in an artwork, that is the most interesting, important, or the most strongly emphasized.

Form
In the real world, this is a three-dimensional object. In drawing and painting, it often represents the qualities that help create the illusion of three-dimensions on a flat surface. It usually refers to the representation of the shading that turns the object from the light to the shadow.

Frame of reference
Using the frame proportion of your reference material to inform the size of your canvas. For example, if your reference photo is 8 x 10, it would be advisable to choose a canvas size that is 8 x 10, 16 x 20, or 24 x 30, which are all in proportion to the original reference. This allows you to translate the shapes of the original reference photo without any proportional distortion or confusion with measurements.

Gradation
The slow progression of change over a surface, such as lighter to darker, darker to lighter, or one color to another.

Grid method
This can be applied if your reference material and canvas are the same proportion. It involves drawing a grid over your reference photo and canvas, so you know which feature goes in which square when drawing out your subject. A simple grid can be made by drawing a center line horizontally and vertically, creating quadrants. A more complex grid would entail dividing the reference image and canvas into numerous corresponding squares.

Glaze
A dark color used transparently over a lighter color. It has a warming effect in traditional paint media.

Hard edge
A hard edge is formed when two tones touch but there is no blurring between them. Sometimes a hard edge can appear soft if the two tones are very close to each other in value, however the edge will still be classed as hard if there is no blurring between the two tones.

Hard light
A strong, focused spotlight that shines on a subject, creating areas of strong light and shadow. The opposite would be an overcast day with no strong shadows.

Highlights
The lightest areas of a painting that receive the greatest amount of illumination.

Hue
This refers to the actual color. The six primary hues are red, orange, yellow, green, blue, and violet. Hue is purely a color decision. Hue can also describe combinations of these six primary hues, such as red-orange, and is the broad category used to describe individual colors. Colorless white, black, and gray do not have a hue, but are considered values.

Likeness
The elusive quality that marries the proportions, character of the features, and spirit of the person that makes a portrait easily recognizable as the subject.

Line drawing
A drawing made up of lines, with no shading.

Lost edge
A lost edge is formed when there is no recognizable edge to the transitioning of one tone to another. This may also be referred to as a gradient or gradation.

Low resolution
The degree of definition in an image; how much detail you can see in a given amount of space.

Mood
The overall effect of artistic and compositional choices. Cropping, color palette, value key, and mark-making can all affect the mood of a painting.

Mother color (local color)
While some would refer to this as the local color of the object, it is referred to as the mother color in this book because other colors are born out of it. This mother color, especially in the representation of skin, is often the color used to describe the subject's skin if you only had one choice, such as a custom band-aid color for that individual. It's not the lightest or the darkest color, but is often found in the midtones.

Motif
A visual theme or idea by which a painting is directed.

Occlusion shadows
The deepest, darkest part of the shadow, which is usually a crevice of some sort. It is not usually a large area of shadow, but rather a small area that provides a dark accent for the shadow.

Perceptual portraiture
Portraiture that is focused on capturing exactly what is in front of you. Most portraiture sits in between the extremes of conceptual and perceptual.

Plane
Planes can be simple or complex. They can be used to visually describe forms as having flat facets, like a cut diamond. These facets are an extrapolation of more complicated fluid forms; however, they are helpful in seeing how light and color interact in a clear way.

Perspective
The art of drawing solid objects on a two-dimensional surface to create an accurate impression of their height, width, depth, and position in relation to each other when viewed from a particular point.

Plumb line
A vertical plumb line is created when a weight is attached to a string and left to dangle, creating a perfectly vertical line in relation to where you stand on the earth. Horizontal plumb lines are lines drawn or taped with string that are perfectly parallel to the canvas edge. Both can aid the artist in the placement of their image.

Portrait
A painting or drawing that depicts more than just a nondescript head. It attempts to reveal some characteristic, likeness, and essence of the subject.

Pounce/pouncing
Tapping or tamping down a material, such as paint or charcoal, with a brush or other tool.

Proportion
A ratio or relationship that compares a fraction of something to the whole. This can be understood by looking at a 16 x 20 frame, which has a 4:5 proportion.

Reference photograph
A photograph that is used as source material when creating artwork.

Rhythm angles
Construction lines that connect seemingly unrelated parts of the body or face on one side to the other. The angle the line creates helps with aligning those two points more accurately, rather than just copying a contour line on either side, which can often lead to inaccuracies.

Saturation
Saturation, or chroma, defines intensity of color.

Scumble
A light color used transparently over a darker color. When used with traditional media, it has a cooling effect.

Shadow
The area on a form that is not struck by the primary light source. Shadows can be light or dark and can have many changes, but they are generally considered areas that are not in the light.

Shape
While in the real world this is a two-dimensional object, in drawing and painting it often represents a drawing concept that helps to simplify three-dimensional objects into manageable flat tones. This simplification allows you to recognize and be more objective when accurately drawing these shapes without the added complication of form, texture, and color.

Shape drawing
An abstract way of drawing in which an artist ignores details and nameable features in favor of depicting the accuracy of the main shapes in the image.

Sight-size method
A method of drawing in which the subject is always on a one-to-one ratio with the drawing; they are the exact same size. This can apply to working from life, or working from a photograph. When working from life, you draw your subject the exact same size that you see them. There is no scaling up or down, or changing the visual relationship of that one-to-one ratio. The smallest inaccuracies become apparent when you remove the extra work of scaling up and down.

Span proportion

A ratio as it relates to a span or distance that has been subdivided. For example, if you measure a mile and put a marker at a quarter mile (A), the rest of that span is three-quarters of a mile (B). A fits into B three times, meaning the span proportion is 1:3.

Spirit of the center

A gentle curved line, starting at the anatomical center of the forehead where it meets the hairline, curving slowly all the way down until it strikes through the center of the chin. This is not an exact measurement, but rather a general guide for symmetry.

Soft edge

A soft edge is formed when two tones touch each other and have a slight blurring or softening effect where they meet.

Softening/pulling

Softening is a term used a lot in painting; however, when paired with pulling, it means softening with a purpose, or directional softening. When you soften, you should be moving a tone toward a given place, not just blurring tones.

Soft light

A frosted, distant, ambient light shining on a subject, such as the light of an overcast day. The opposite would be a spotlight in a dark room.

Structural symmetry

The idea that on the three-dimensional head you will find a landmark, such as the cheekbone, and look for its symmetrical correspondence on the other side of the head, the other cheekbone, making sure they line up in a symmetrical way.

Texture

The rougher or layered tactile quality of a surface.

Tone

While often used synonymously with color and value, it is the darker shades of a color. A tint would be the lighter shades of a color.

Traditional media

Media that has been used to create artwork for centuries, including oil paint, charcoal, acrylic paint, gouache, watercolor, and graphite.

Triangulation

A drawing concept in which three or more points are sketched in, then gradually made more accurate through the correct judgment of the angles between them. This often realigns the points that were originally sketched in, creating a relational proportion between them that locks them into correct harmony.

Value

The relative lightness or darkness of a color or tone.

Velatura

A light color used transparently over a darker color. This has a cooling effect in traditional media.

Vignette

An image that has been softened, lightened, or darkened at the edges in order to enhance the central focus.

Volume

Forcing the 3D aspects of a subject to create a sense of depth on a 2D drawing surface. This can involve using lines in an elliptical way, like an engraver would use to show the form of a face on a dollar bill. Or it could mean sculpting the form to create more dimension by deepening shadows and using various techniques to create the feeling of three dimensions.

Working rhythm

A technique of art-making that has repeatable elements in order to find consistency and flow in one's approach.

Wigmaker's block

A concept by artist John Singer Sargent as the general starting point for painting a head. It begins with painting the "wigmaker's block" of the subject, which is a blurry version of the head. The colors, the placements, and proportion are there, but soft. Nothing is specific or locked in, keeping it flexible.

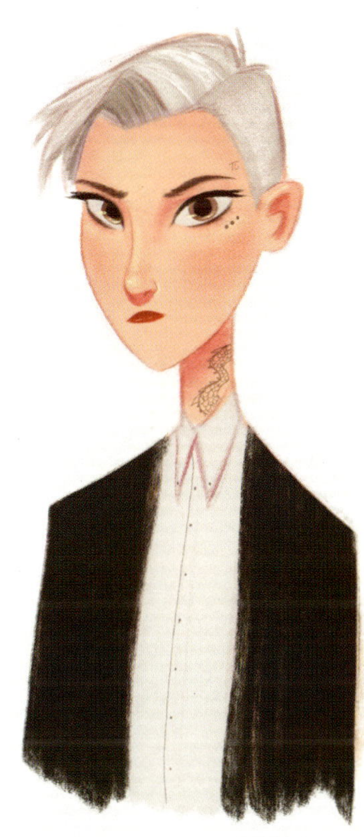

Artwork © Aveline Stokart

CONTRIBUTORS

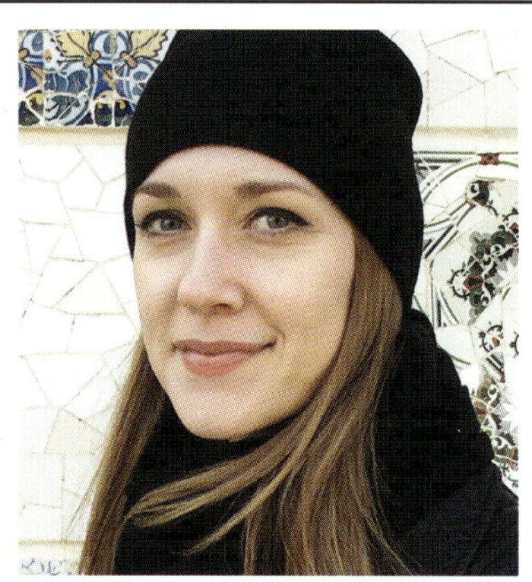

Maria Dimova

Illustrator
dimary.me

Maria's artwork is motivated by feminine beauty. She likes to decorate her portraits with ornaments and fantasy design.

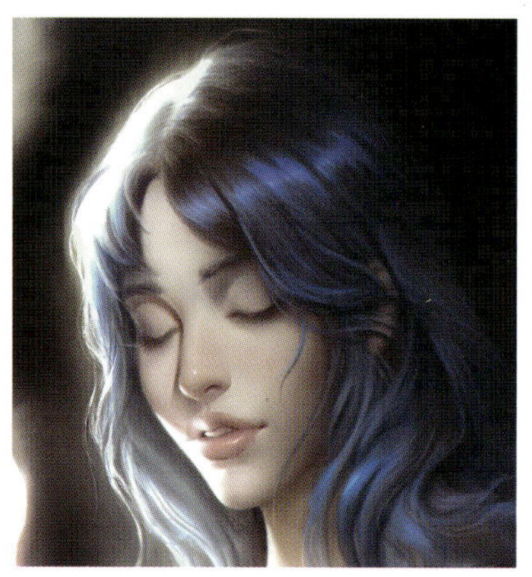

Justine S. Florentino

Freelance artist
instagram.com/justine.florentino

Based in the Philippines, Justine has been freelancing and teaching herself art for six years. She enjoys painting portraits of people, character artwork, and comic book covers.

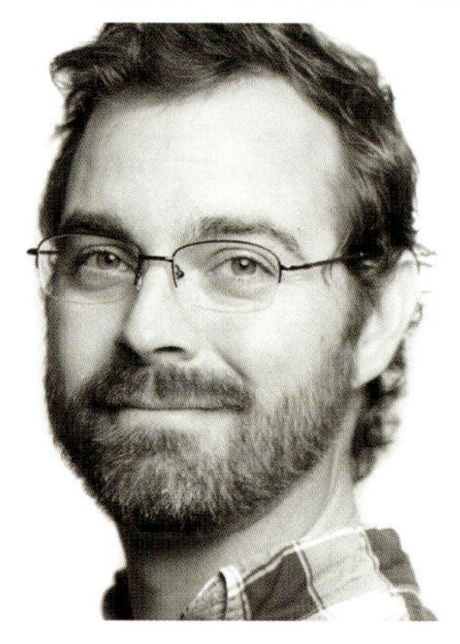

Steve Forster

Director
steveforster.net

Steve is Director of the Long Island Academy of Fine Art, and teaches painting at the New York Academy of Art. His paintings have been exhibited in solo and group shows nationally and internationally.

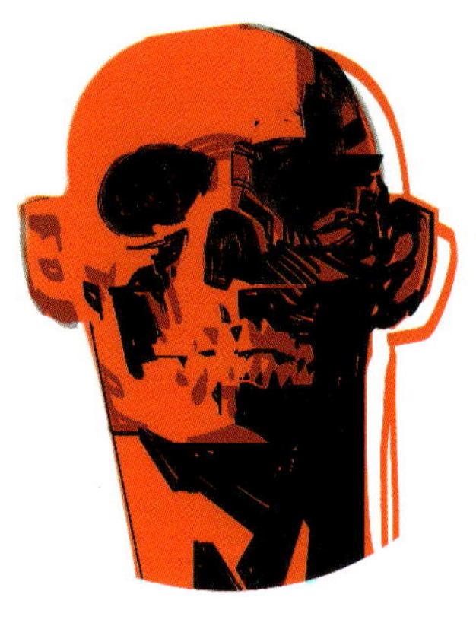

Gennadiy Kim

Freelance digital artist
instagram.com/gavn_art

Gennadiy is a self-taught artist based in Moscow who loves creating portraits.

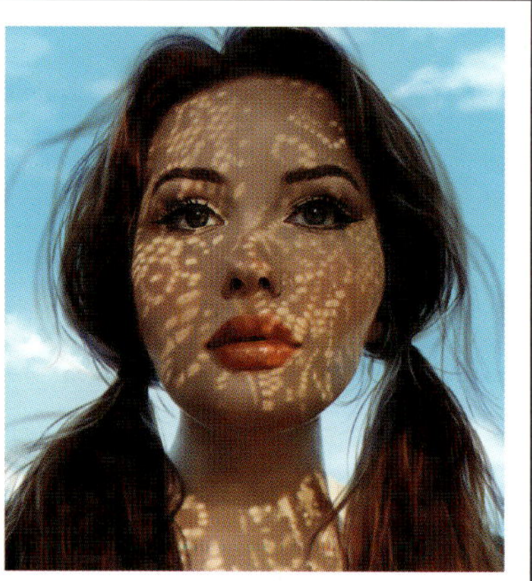

Robyn Leora Lowe

Freelance illustrator
instagram.com/robynleora

Based in Tennessee, Robyn has worked in the entertainment and gaming industries. Her biggest passion is combining the real and imagined to create striking, vibrant portraits.

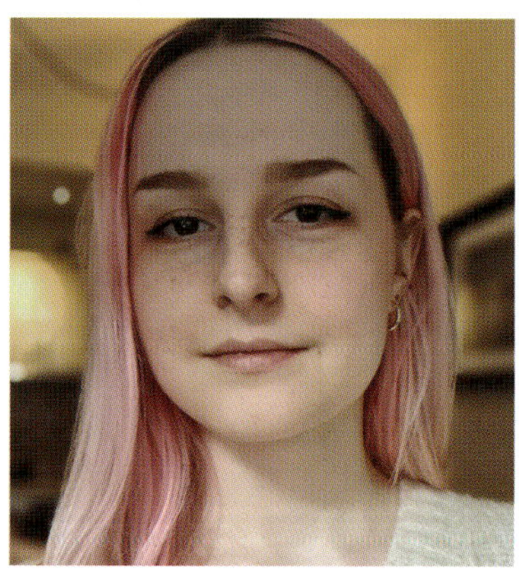

Astri Lohne

Illustrator & concept artist
artstation.com/sjursen

Astri is a Norwegian artist who splits her time between working in the game industry, teaching online, and being hyper-caffeinated through a never-ending slew of personal projects.

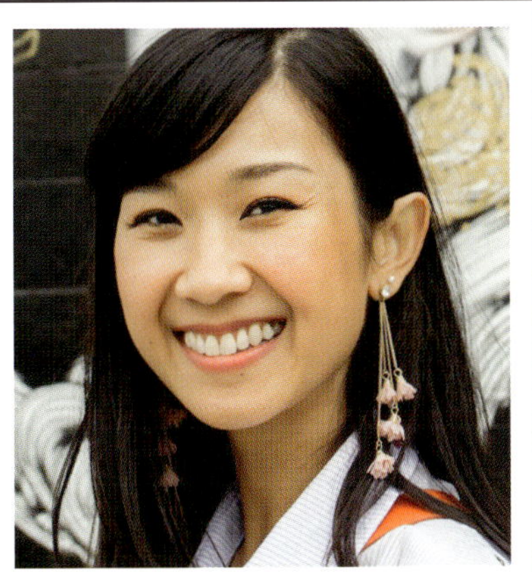

Tran Nguyen

Freelance artist
mynameistran.com

Tran is an award-winning illustrator, fine artist, and muralist. Using acrylic and colored pencil on paper, she has created art for clients including Hasbro, Netflix, and Tiger Beer.

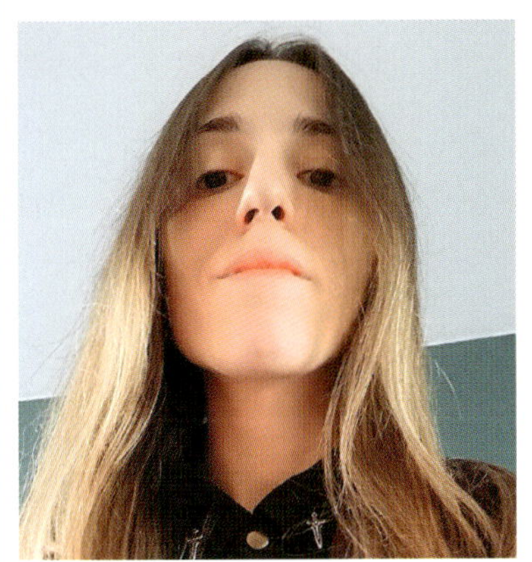

Valentina Remenar

Illustrator and concept artist
valentinaremenar.com

Valentina is a digital illustrator who enjoys painting her own characters, worlds, and concepts in her free time. She has created work for Wizards of the Coast, Penguin Random House, Marvel, and more.

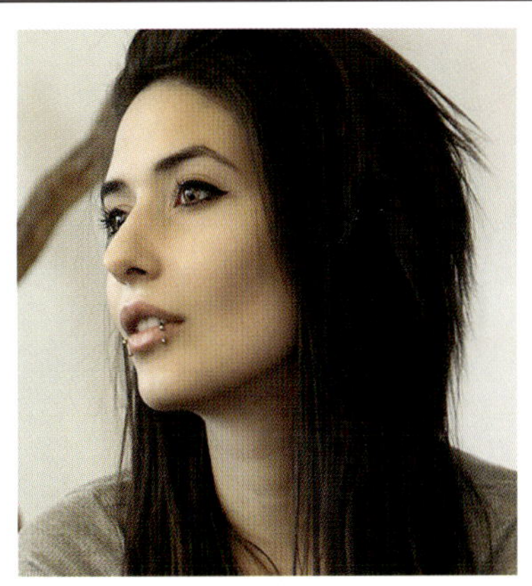

Laura H. Rubin

Digital artist
laurahrubin.com

Laura is an award-winning digital artist with a predilection for simple aesthetics. She has written multiple art and study books, and fascinates the art scene with her emotional portrait drawings.

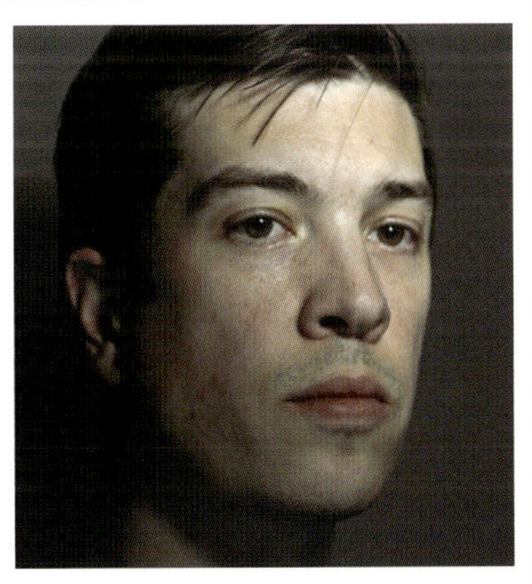

Nick Runge

Painter
nickrungeart.com

As a painter, Nick works with a simplified approach to his brushwork, giving an illusion of realism while breaking the form down enough to have a close balance with abstraction.

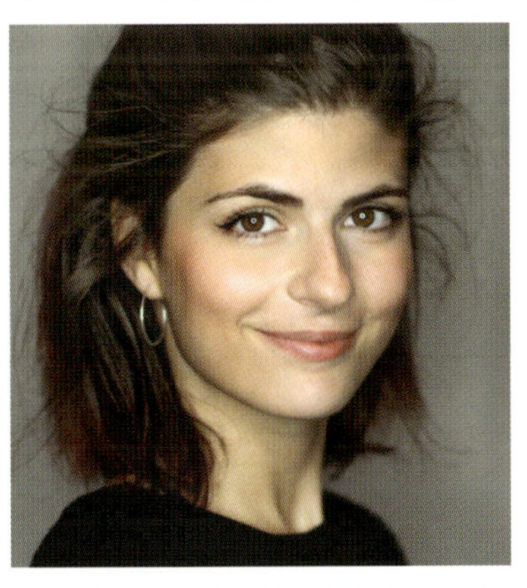

Aveline Stokart

Comic artist & character designer
instagram.com/aveline_stokart

Aveline is a Belgian artist who studied 3D animation before continuing with her self-taught learning. She currently works freelance for various clients in the fields of publishing and animation.

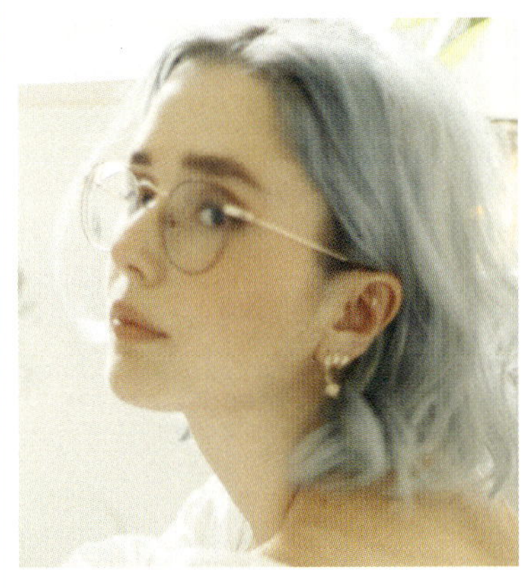

Sara Tepes

Freelance illustrator
sarucatepes.com

Sara is a freelance illustrator with a focus in art education on YouTube, Patreon, and Instagram.

3dtotal Publishing

3dtotal Publishing is a trailblazing, creative publisher specializing in inspirational and educational resources for artists.

Our titles feature top industry professionals from around the globe who share their experience in skillfully written step-by-step tutorials and fascinating, detailed guides. Illustrated throughout with stunning artwork, these best-selling publications offer creative insight, expert advice, and essential motivation. Fans of digital art will enjoy our comprehensive volumes covering Adobe Photoshop, Procreate, and Blender, as well as our superb titles based around character design, including Fundamentals of Character Design and Creating Characters for the Entertainment Industry. The dedicated, high-quality blend of instruction and inspiration also extends to traditional art. Titles covering a range of techniques, genres, and abilities allow your creativity to flourish while building essential skills.

Well-established within the industry, we now offer over 100 titles and counting, many of which have been translated into multiple languages around the world. With something for every artist, we are proud to say that our books offer the 3dtotal package:

LEARN • CREATE • SHARE

Visit us at 3dtotalpublishing.com

3dtotal Publishing is part of 3dtotal.com, a leading website for CG artists founded by Tom Greenway in 1999.